Democracy and the
Rule of Law

Democracy and the Rule of Law

Norman Dorsen
New York University School of Law

Prosser Gifford
Library of Congress

CQ PRESS

A Division of Congressional Quarterly Inc.
Washington, D.C.

CQ Press
A Division of Congressional Quarterly Inc.
1414 22nd Street, N.W.
Washington, D.C. 20037

(202) 822-1475; (800) 638-1710

www.cqpress.com

Cover design: Brian Barth

Printed and bound in the United States of America

05 04 03 02 01   5 4 3 2 1

♾ The paper used in this publication meets the minimum requirements of the American National Standard for Information Sciences—Permanence of Paper for Printed Library Materials, ANSI Z39.48-1992.

Library of Congress Cataloging-in-Publication Data
Democracy and the rule of law / edited by Norman Dorsen, Prosser Gifford; preface by James H. Billington and John E. Sexton.
    p.   cm.
  Includes bibliographical references and index.
  ISBN 1-56802-599-8 (pbk. : alk. paper)
  1. Rule of law. 2. Democracy. I. Dorsen, Norman. II. Gifford, Prosser.

K3171 .D455 2001
340′.11—dc21

2001032328

Contents

Introductory Remarks

Session 1: Transnational Justice and National Sovereignty

Session 2: Roles of Women: Norms and Culture

Session 3: Multiethnic and Multiracial States

Foreword

This volume contains essays drawn from a conference held in March 2000 that began in the Great Hall of the Library of Congress, with representation at the highest level from Congress and the Supreme Court, and concluded in the ceremonial rooms of the New York University School of Law. Our two institutions were partners in the enterprise, and we are pleased that it drew outstanding participants from many countries and all continents.

The year 2000 was the bicentennial of the Library of Congress. The first library established by Congress when it moved in 1800 from Philadelphia to an unfinished Capitol in Washington was a collection of law books. Thomas Jefferson's personal library reconstituted the Library of Congress after British troops burned the original library in 1814. Jefferson believed passionately in an informed citizenry, and the library he sold to Congress in 1815 covered a wide range of subjects in many languages.

The founding of a Law Library of Congress in July 1832 established the first special collection within the Library of Congress—assuring the continual centrality of legal materials to the library's collections. The Library of Congress has subsequently grown to house the world's largest and most linguistically comprehensive collection of the legislation and judicial rulings of other countries.

When the library decided to examine as one component of its bicentennial the complex relationships between democracy and the rule of law, it knew that the conference had to be international and that it needed as a partner a law school dedicated to the exploration of comparative and international themes in the law. The Global Law School Program of the New York University School of Law was the logical partner because of the quality and range of international jurists and academics it attracted to New York. In addition, having one part of the conference at the Washington Square campus of the New York University Law School, in the city of the United Nations and many international legal and financial institutions, made a natural complement to the Washington branch of the conference.

The papers in this volume have much to teach us as a rapidly changing world moves into a new century and a new millennium. We are proud to present them to readers throughout the world.

James H. Billington
Librarian of Congress

John Sexton
Dean, New York University School of Law

Preface

The seminar whose contents are contained in this volume, *Democracy and the Rule of Law*, gives ample evidence of Rudolph von Jhering's thesis that "the life of the law is a struggle, a struggle of nations, of the state power, of classes, of individuals" and that "every legal right—the legal rights of a whole nation as well as those of individuals—supposes a continual readiness to assert it and defend it."[1] Unlike other disciplines, law is called upon to struggle constantly to exist, to overcome impediments, and to find the "right way."

Von Jhering penned his words shortly after the close of the devastating American Civil War, a time when indigenous peoples were losing their homelands and retreating before the inexorable migration of determined occupiers both in the United States and in other areas of the world; before women and minorities in most nations obtained the right to vote or hold political offices; and before the Spanish-American War, the South African (Boer) War, the Russo-Japanese War, the revolutions in Russia and elsewhere, and, of course, before the terrible upheavals of the world wars of the twentieth century, to mention but a few conflicts. The authors whose work is represented in this volume are outstanding in their ability to identify often uncomfortable truths and have the breadth of vision to analyze challenges to justice and in many instances to offer a critical assessment of various means of ameliorating the complex legal-social and legal-economic quandaries of today.

The year 2000 appeared to many as a logical point in time for us to pause and assess both how far the law has brought us and what the law might yet accomplish in pursuit of justice. The Law Library of Congress is proud to have served as host, together with the New York University School of Law, for the far-ranging symposium in which the extraordinary presentations, printed here as a collection of essays, were first delivered. Law professionals in the field and on the Law Library staff applauded Librarian of Congress James H. Billington for his initiative and vision in selecting law as the subject for this historic symposium, part of the Library of Congress Bicentennial.

It was clear throughout the seminar that few issues today are truly local, and one can see from the contents of this volume that there was a consensus regarding the major challenges confronting society at the turn of the century. The experts culled from around the world had a common purpose—to voice concerns that affect them deeply and that must be recognized by serious students of governance everywhere. Although there appear to be great improvements in legal structure, as evidenced by the existence of transnational courts and international tribunals, achieving justice continues to be elusive. Imbalances and inequities always exist, and the pressing lessons one may learn from reading these pages should be a clear indication of what von Jhering was speaking of—if not in our own community or worldview, then in that of our neighbors. Finding the "right way," the search for justice as each group sees it, is a constant struggle for individuals as well as for states, but democracy appears to be a shared objective in that struggle. In von Jhering's assessment, "[t]he power of a people is synonymous with the strength of their feeling of legal right," that is, their respect for law at all levels.

A not insignificant aspect of this seminar for the Law Library of Congress has been the increased recognition given to the need for legal information exchanges worldwide. Over its nearly 170-year history, as the Law Library has performed a dual mission of serving the U.S. Congress and the American people, its foreign legal specialists and analysts have carried out research on all of the major topics dealt with in this seminar and have seen firsthand the value of such information sharing. The Law Library has been a constant advocate of expediting legal information exchanges with the aid of advances in information technology, as attested to by its Global Legal Information Network, begun as a parliament-to-parliament cooperative. It is hoped that support for such technological advances will also increase in order to further facilitate cooperation, perhaps in the form of worldwide "town meetings" via satellite to discuss in more depth some of the subjects explored here.

This volume will constitute an important historic resource of the critical legal issues of our day because of the expertise of its authors, the number of legal disciplines it covers, and the diversity of the perspectives it affords the reader. More important, this work may serve as a guidepost outlining the direction of our struggles toward social justice in today's world, at this point in our history—a guidepost written in a style that is direct and with authoritative analyses that are unflinching in the urgency of their message.

Rubens Medina
Law Librarian of Congress
Washington, D.C.
October 2000

Acknowledgments

To organize a major international conference that takes place over a week's time with two venues, first in Washington, D.C., and then in New York City, requires the dedicated assistance of many people. The planning and logistical efforts, the printing, publicity, and web-casting arrangements, the research and briefing requirements—all these activities and many others involved people behind the scenes, not obvious to conference participants but indispensable for a successful week of deliberating, listening, reflecting. We mention here those of whom we are aware, hoping that we have not inadvertently omitted someone in what was a remarkable team effort.

First, we thank our donors whose financial generosity made the whole conference possible. Both the Library of Congress and the New York University School of Law contributed substantially from their own private funds, for which we acknowledge especially the support and enthusiasm of James H. Billington, librarian of Congress, and John Sexton, dean of the New York University School of Law. In addition, the conference was funded in part through the generosity of Anthony and Beatrice Welters, Dwight Opperman, the William and Flora Hewlett Foundation, William S. Hein & Co., Court Record Services, Inc., and the Friends of the Law Library of the Library of Congress (in association with gifts from the Fannie Mae Foundation, O'Melveny & Myers LLP, the West Group, and LEXIS-NEXIS). Rubens Medina, the law librarian of Congress, offered sustained assistance in the search for funds.

Second, we thank the following people from the New York University School of Law: Jim Boyce, Frank Conti, Joan Dim, Jim Diotte, Matt Edwards, Dan Evans, Toni Fine, Carol Gardner, Zarah Guzman, Iqbal Ishar, Ken Kidd, Debra LaMorte, David LaVoie, Debra Martin, David Niedenthal, Shanell Pacheco, Evelyn Palmquist, Mike Papas, Ena Prince, Robin Schanzenbach, Bruce White, Joanne Wilhelm, and Danielle Yglesias.

Third, we thank the following people from the Library of Congress: Stanley Bandong, Marie Louise Bernal, Jill Brett, Irene Chambers, Rose Marie Clemendot, Luis deCastro, Donald DeGlopper, Craig D'Ooge, Gail Feinberg, Sandra Ferrell, Rubylene Gaskins, Natalie Gawdiak, Jacinda Gill, Janice Hyde, Jo Ann Jenkins, JoAnne Kitching, Nick Kozura, Allan McConnell Jr., Kim Moden, Amir Pasic, Barbara Sakamoto, Theresa Sartori, Teri Sierra, Robert Sokel, Roberta Stevens, Mark Strattner, Les Vogel, and Margaret Whitlock.

In addition, numerous volunteers helped to guide, direct, and provide materials for members of the audience. We hope that everyone involved derived some satisfaction from the events themselves and will find in this volume observations and reflections of continuing value.

Norman Dorsen
Stokes Professor of Law
Chair, Global Law School Program
New York University School of Law

Prosser Gifford
Director of Scholarly Programs
Library of Congress

Editors' Introduction

The year 2000 marked the bicentennial of the Library of Congress. Created initially as a small collection of law books purchased for Congress when it moved from Philadelphia in 1800 to Washington's newly constructed Capitol, the Library of Congress and its Law Library are coeval. Thus, in the varied celebrations to mark the library's bicentennial, the law and the Law Library merited a significant place.

Because the Library of Congress's Law Library has grown during two hundred years into the largest collection in the United States of the laws of other countries (in the vernacular and often, as well, in English translation), the celebration had to be international in scope and character. When we at the library sought an academic cosponsor who would be willing to share the conceptual and logistical planning, the enlisting of participants, and the fundraising for a major conference, we quickly found our way in 1997 to the New York University School of Law and its Global Law School Program. Both John Sexton, dean of the law school, and Professor Norman Dorsen, the organizer and informing spirit of the global program, were willing to take on the challenge. Early exploratory conversations grew over time into a real partnership.

From NYU's standpoint, the projected conference was consonant with the goals of the Global Law School Program, which was launched in 1994 with the objective of transforming legal education in the United States to take account of the remarkable changes occurring worldwide in communications, transportation, and financial and legal markets. Among the program's many initiatives are the approximately twenty-five courses and seminars taught each year to NYU law students by prominent faculty members drawn from outside the United States, the presence in NYU classes of about 350 foreign students from fifty countries, and the introduction of a wide range of new subjects with global implications throughout the curriculum. In addition, the program has established a large number of student fellowships and internships in other countries, new projects and centers with international ramifications in almost every area of legal study, and a steady agenda of international meetings and seminars featuring distinguished participants from every part of the world. Given the high aspirations of the Library of Congress for its bicentennial conference, and the range of topics to be discussed at an international level, NYU School of Law was enthusiastic about joining the library in this venture, and it was not disappointed.

The conceptual planning fell to two of us—Norman Dorsen for the NYU School of Law and Prosser Gifford for the Library of Congress. We enlisted an informal advisory committee and began to discuss with its members those issues that we believed would remain crucial topics for the development of the law in the next century. In addition to being international, our conference would be public—that is, the audience would not be limited to lawyers. At the conference itself, through its cybercast broadcast, and in print, we sought a wider public for our efforts. We believed also that the time had come for courts in the United States to take greater cognizance of the treatment of similar issues by courts in other countries, so we decided to structure our discussions to be deliberately cross-cultural and comparative. Of the three people invited to prepare papers on each topic, only one would be an American.

1

What were to be the topics? We wanted to tackle large issues that were widely shared, those that many societies would have to address. We thought first of those issues that were a direct result of "globalization," of the reach of economic and legal activity across national borders. Questions of transnational justice—the development of new transnational courts and the internationalization of legal remedies, for instance, in Europe—would be one focus. A second would be corporate power and national sovereignty—how do different jurisdictions handle multinational corporations in relation to domestic laws?

Another class of legal issues was generic—issues present in every society, although often treated differently—and increasingly subject to international standards. We felt we should address three: the violation of basic human rights, the roles permitted or enabled for women, and the conflicts over environmental resources. The treatment of these questions had begun to escape national boundaries so that precedents in one country became important arguments in other countries. We believed that all three would continue to evolve as controversial areas of the law in the twenty-first century.

Another set of concerns related more directly to democracy and its functioning. Can legal rules and practices advance democracy in multiethnic and multiracial states? At what point is law overwhelmed by politics? Second, what are the relationships among religion, culture, democracy, and the rule of law? Is the American experience exceptional, as many American scholars contend, or are there some general guidelines that hold even in difficult situations of conflict over fundamental values?

Finally, there were two questions about which we wanted discussion among panelists, so the panels were organized in such a way as to encourage interchange. The first raised the relationship among the concepts of democracy, legitimacy, and the rule of law. Did they necessarily or inextricably go together? Was it possible to have legitimacy without either democracy or the rule of law? Was it possible to have a rule of law without either legitimacy or democracy? Was it possible to have democracy without either legitimacy or the rule of law?

The second question concerned the usefulness of law and legal methods in "holding the past to account." How could or should states deal with horrendous, murderous aspects of its past when many of its citizens were complicit bystanders if not active participants? Did legal trials help or hinder justice and healing? What is the relationship between justice and reconciliation? What best serves to keep memory alive so that the past will not be repeated?

2

Having decided conditionally on the topics we wished to treat, we faced two crucial tasks: inviting the best participants and framing the conference as a whole. We decided that for each session we needed a moderator to chair the session and a commentator to consider relationships among the papers and to open points for discussion. In almost all cases, the remarks of the moderators and the commentators have been included in this volume.

Giving a coherent structure and providing a serious framework for the conference as a whole suggested, on both substantive and symbolic grounds, the desirability of involvement of members of the U.S. Supreme Court. We were fortunate to have Chief Justice Rehnquist deliver a welcoming address to the participants at the beginning of the conference, to have Justice O'Connor write a paper for the session on transnational justice, to have Justices Ginsburg and Kennedy participate in conference discussions, and to have Justice Breyer speak at the dinner at the New York University School of Law. The participation of the justices signaled that the issues with which the conference dealt were being seriously considered at the highest levels in the United States. An awareness of the thought and practice in other national jurisdictions and in international fora should be sought and studied. This theme was underlined by Senator Hatch, chairman of the Senate Judiciary Committee, and by Justice Grimm, recently retired from distinguished service on the German Constitutional Court. The theme thus provided an overall framework for the conference.

We were gratified in being able to secure the contributions of a wide range of participants. Few of those asked declined, and those few had other commitments or family concerns that took priority. In one terrible instance, all too pertinent to multiethnic politics about which he was to speak, a participant from Sri Lanka was assassinated a few weeks before the conference. Brief biographies of all the participants are given at the end of this volume, yet highly selective factual statements capture neither the depth of experience nor the openness of personality that participants displayed. Many had not previously met one another, and they took genuine pleasure in sharing ideas, stories, and legal approaches. The transnational theme was not only conceptual; it was also embodied in the conference itself.

3

As editors, we decided to retain in the volume the same structure and order of subjects as those we followed in the conference, except we have grouped the two panel discussions in a separate section at the center of the book. There is no ineluctable logic to the order of the subjects. The final two sessions, which took place at the New York University School of Law, were located in New York because we thought that international corporate and financial transactions would be of particular interest to the New York legal community and that human rights would be particularly relevant to some of the United Nations debates.

We have written brief headnotes for each section of the book, pointing to some of the issues raised in the papers and suggesting relationships among them. Each author has supplied appropriate notes and a bibliography that contains suggestions for further reading as well as the works cited in the notes. These appear at the end of the book for convenient reference. Contemporary events or judicial decisions mentioned in the essays refer to the situation as of March 2000, when the conference took place. We have not asked authors to take account of subsequent developments.

A question addressed implicitly by several conference participants is, what are the limits of the law? How tractable are ethnic or religious clashes, for instance, to legal solution? Eleven of our participants are not lawyers, and several of them suggested the limited efficacy of the law in the resolution of fundamental disputes. The issue was discussed most explicitly in the two sessions containing the fewest lawyers—that on political status and democracy in multiethnic and multiracial states and that on "holding the past to account." This suggests the value of having social scientists, historians, and philosophers comment on legal issues. They, in turn, suggested that some essential preconditions must exist before legal solutions can be brought into play.

Constitutions, the rights of minorities, and basic human rights cannot be maintained against people using military means to assert nonnegotiable demands for ethnic or religious purity. Asserted ideological primacy that exempts groups from the obligations of implied social contracts and humane reciprocity renders the rule of law meaningless. Civil barbarities, such as occurred in Kosovo, Sierra Leone, Sri Lanka, East Timor, Sudan, and several countries in South America, unfortunately require the use of outside pressure or even military force to recreate conditions sufficiently stable to permit the rule of law to be meaningfully applied.

Such situations and others have helped to stimulate worldwide interest in the safeguarding of human rights. Leading nongovernmental organizations, notably Amnesty International and Human Rights Watch, have brought violations to public attention and pressed for effective remedies. The international community has responded fitfully, but new institutional efforts, such as the South African Truth and Reconciliation Commission and a clutch of international criminal courts, have raised hopes that some of the worst horrors of recent decades will be avoided in the future.

In addition, there is a growing realization that a functioning, independent judicial system is a key element in the maintenance of civil society and the possibility of nonmilitary settlement of disputes. Realizing how crucial is a coherent safety valve for dispute resolution, the World Bank is now convening conferences on the role of the judiciary in economic development. The preconditions that make the rule of law possible, although not directly the subject of any of our sessions, underlie many of the issues treated in this volume.

4

The linkages among the component parts of this volume are provided by frequent reference, explicit and implicit, to the theme of internationalization. New courts with transnational jurisdiction have been and are being created; business activities of all sorts, from physical to virtual, are crossing national boundaries regularly, raising questions, inter alia, about air space, the enforcement of contracts, intellectual property rights, environmental pollution, and free speech. Basic human rights, relationships within the family, conflicts between secular and religious law, minority rights within a plural society—are all increasingly transnational. Isolated, parochial, aggressively national, or subnational points of view increasingly will be challenged by forces within and without.

The technology that is creating regular international transactions is also creating the need for new legal skills, new legal perspectives, and new sensitivities to the cultural context of law, as well as a more sophisticated awareness that similar results may be reached by the application of different norms in different societies. Existing structures will be adapted, modified, amplified; principles may evolve into international standards. Hard and imaginative work will be necessary if these goals are to be achieved. In particular, the many educational institutions of modern life—the media and the political process in addition to the academic establishment—must rise to the challenges that the new global realities present. If our conference and this volume contribute to a shared realization of these new needs, we will have established a useful point of departure for the new century.

Norman Dorsen
Prosser Gifford

Democracy and the
Rule of Law

Introductory Remarks

Opening Remarks

William H. Rehnquist

It is a pleasure to welcome all of you to this conference on "Democracy and the Rule of Law in a Changing World Order." I know that the organizers of the conference are pleased that so many distinguished jurists from around the world are here to participate, and I am pleased that you will be able to visit the Supreme Court tomorrow evening for dinner.

I extend a particular welcome to those of you who have come great distances to be here. Many of you come from societies where aspects of the rule of law are controversial and disputed. You will bring unique perspective to the topics discussed during the conference, and the conference programs will be enriched by your participation.

International conferences of this nature provide great opportunities for participants to exchange ideas and experiences across national borders and have become a subject of great interest to American judges and lawyers. As national boundaries grow less significant in this age of instant communications and easy international travel, it is all the more important that the legal communities of different nations exchange views and understand one another. Moreover, there has been an increasing recognition of the benefits of courts of one nation looking to the laws, decisions, and experiences of courts in other countries. I am seeing this in the field of constitutional law, and I believe that as more constitutional courts develop around the world we will see the courts of the United States looking more to the decisions of other nations' constitutional courts to aid in their own deliberative processes.

One of the fundamental legal tenets of the rule of law in the United States has been the idea of an independent judiciary exercising judicial review. Indeed, an independent judiciary exercising judicial review was one of the two original contributions to the art of government created by the U.S. Constitution over two hundred years ago. The second original contribution, a popularly elected president, has not been widely copied. Most democratic countries have preferred the parliamentary system and have rejected the presidential form of government.

But the idea of a constitutional court exercising judicial review *has* gained currency, particularly since the end of the Second World War. While the Supreme Court of the United States once stood alone, there are now many constitutional courts around the world. Within the past half century, numerous other nations have adopted written constitutions or Basic Laws and entrusted their courts with the power of judicial review. Germany, Italy, France, Hungary, Spain, Japan, India, South Africa, and Canada among other countries have all given some or all of their courts the power of judicial review. The provisions of the constitutions vary, the structure of the court systems may differ, but the underlying idea is the same.

Even in countries that do not have a written constitution, and therefore have no judicial review in the American sense of that phrase—such as the United Kingdom—or in those countries that have a written constitution that in theory grants judicial review but in which that power is unexercised—such as Sweden—there is considerable discussion about the desirability of granting this authority to the courts. The European Court of Justice of the European Union, which sits in Luxembourg City, now has the power of judicial review for those countries adhering to the Treaty of Rome. And the European Human Rights Court sitting in Strasbourg also provides a form of international judicial review. Thus more and more courts around the world are exercising the power of judicial review.

Yet for the first century and one-half after the adoption of our Constitution, we were pretty much alone in having an independent judiciary with the power of judicial review. During that time, our Supreme Court developed a body of law on its own, partly because there were no other legal systems that operated in the same way. In this respect, we became quite self-contained. We didn't have the advantage, as other emerging democracies have had and will have, of looking to a developed body of law interpreting constitutional rights and liberties and being able to modify it to meet our own needs. Now we are witnessing in the United States the advent of looking to the precedents and decisions of other nations for additional guidance on the future course of the law. And now American judges and lawyers attend these conferences with the idea that we have something to learn, as well as something to contribute. Even after such cross-fertilization, one nation may still differ from another on some important principle. But this does not mean that the exchange of ideas will have served no purpose.

As to learning from the American experience, there has been a great deal of interest in the U.S. court system on the part of judicial officials from emerging democracies. In 1999 alone, more than 475 representatives of over ninety-five foreign judiciary systems formally visited the Supreme Court of the United States seeking information about our system of justice. Of course, several other American judicial entities also play an important role in educating the many visiting jurists in the United States and in providing technical assistance to judicial systems worldwide, including the Federal Judicial Center, the Administrative Office of the U.S. Courts, and the International Judicial Relations Committee of the Judicial Conference. We encourage your visits.

Welcome, once again, to this week's conference. It should provide a stimulating series of sessions for you to address a variety of issues involving democracy and the rule of law. I applaud both the organizers and the participants in the conference and your combined efforts to improve our systems of law and justice around the world. Thank you for inviting me to address you.

Promoting the Rule of Law
in the Post–Cold War Era

Orrin G. Hatch

Thank you, Mr. Chief Justice, Dr. Billington, and distinguished guests. I am honored and delighted to be able to address such a prestigious group of international jurists and scholars tonight.

I commend the New York University School of Law and the Library of Congress for organizing this week's conference, one of a number of symposia put out during the bicentennial of the Library.

I have to tell you, even though I am in my twenty-fourth year in the United States Senate, I am still in awe that we in Congress have at our disposal one of the most prestigious scholarly institutions in the world, the Library of Congress. For someone who grew up as a poor Mormon kid—who worked as a janitor in order to pay for law school—I still find it magnificent and humbling that a scholar of Jim Billington's stature writes memos . . . *for me!* And, in fact, I have benefited many times by the counsel provided for me, on Russia and other topics, by my friend Jim Billington.

He's such a good friend that he did not hesitate to tell me, when he called me a few days ago, that I was his *second* fallback speaker for tonight, following the cancellation due to scheduling problems of Polish foreign minister Bronislaw Geremek.

He originally tried to get someone who has taken on what may be Washington's biggest challenge, someone who has recently come to rescue a previously disciplined and successful organization from the anarchy that has led it into successive failures. But, unfortunately, Michael Jordan couldn't be here tonight either.

As a member of the Senate for nearly twenty-four years, I have been involved in many foreign policy debates. I came to Washington in 1977, the post-Vietnam years.

As I began my Senate career, we were considering foreign policy issues such as U.S. policy toward China, the Iran hostage crisis, and problems with OPEC. Today, we are discussing foreign policy questions related to our policy toward China, the situation in Iran, and problems with OPEC.

Tonight, I am honored to have been asked to make some comments on the challenges of promoting the rule of law to support democracy around the world. This is not a topic unknown to some of us in the U.S. Congress—as we have appropriated over $1 billion since 1993 in support of programs to advance the rule of law.

In fact, I also have something significant in common with the Polish foreign minister. Minister Geremek was one of the intellectual leaders of the Solidarity movement, the underground movement in communist Poland that today provides democratic Poland with many of its political and civic leaders. Solidarity, as we all know, was one of the principal movements that catalyzed the collapse of Soviet control over Central Europe.

In the early 1980s, when I was chairman of the Senate Labor and Human Resources Committee and an active supporter of Ronald Reagan's assertive challenges to Soviet global strategy, I was befriended by a Brooklyn Jew named Irving Brown.

As the head of international affairs office of the AFL-CIO, Irving was already a legend as one of this country's leading trade union leaders in the fight against communism in post–cold war Europe. His career spanned from organizing resistance to the communists on the docks of Italy following the end of World War II to his last major campaign organizing international labor support for Solidarity in the 1980s.

A crusty, worldly intellectual, known to some as the "pumpernickel scholar," Irving was a mentor to me. He introduced me to another great organization supporting democracy, the International Labor Organization, and he enlisted my support in raising funds for equipment for the fledgling Solidarity. Irving Brown demonstrated proof that the individual spirit cannot be defeated by the totalitarian state. His legacy to me is that pragmatic idealism is not a contradiction in terms but a force that can change history.

That experience led me to become an original sponsor of the National Endowment for Democracy (NED), which the United States founded in 1982. The NED is dedicated to the principle that legitimate rule of law rests on individual liberty that can only be achieved through democratic government. At that time, the establishment of democracy in totalitarian and authoritarian nations was the goal. It sometimes appeared that it would be a long struggle.

Yet, here we are today, nearly a decade after the collapse of Soviet communism. As many have noted, while the advance of individual freedom in the world has been markedly achieved, the world is still a dangerous place.

Indeed, as the United States has struggled to find a new set of concepts for foreign policy in the post–cold war era, some have even remarked that the challenges were easier in the bipolar world, and others have urged that we turn inward. From some corners, support for promoting the rule of law has flagged. I reject all of these notions.

It is true that the collapse of the bipolar order has reinvigorated traditional great power conflicts, real and latent. It is also true that the end of bipolar competition has unmoored a number of fragile nations that have fallen into the category of "rogue states," as some would call them, or gangster states, as I refer to them.

The United States and its allies will have to continue to face these challenges with traditional tools of foreign policy: a strategic and hardheaded diplomacy is still needed that strengthens alliances, leverages our economic might, and, when needed, is prepared to use military force to protect clearly defined interests.

But I disagree with those who question the value of continuing to support rule of law programs. Some of that skepticism is the result of understandable disappointment over the Russian case.

Here a democratic Duma has brought to power retreaded communists and angry ultranationalists who have failed to stop Russia's decline toward gangsterism and corruption, and many of whom overtly favor challenging the sovereignty of nations in the region and U.S. foreign policy around the world.

It is dismaying that, on the federal level at least, the current Russian democracy has resulted in kakistocracy—government led by the worst.

In China, while we have seen some radical social changes, it is today by no means clear that the Beijing regime ever intends to replace traditional Chinese autocratic rule *by* law with consensual rule *of* law. To do so would reject not just half a century of communist rule, but also millennia of legal tradition that subjugates law to rulers. Obviously, this is the antithesis of the system the West has been developing since the Magna Carta.

Despite these challenges, it is decidedly not true, in my opinion, that promoting the rule of law as a tool of U.S. foreign policy is any less important in the post–cold war than it was during the half-century we fought against totalitarianism.

Instead, we must recognize that the profound geopolitical changes that have occurred since 1989 have caused us to change our thinking about many aspects of our foreign policy, a reconceptualization that is ongoing and that includes our approach to rule of law promotion.

During the cold war, the focus of our democracy-building was on subverting the totalitarian state by promoting democracy. Today, we are faced with a more complex task of shaping the institutions that will advance, preserve, and deepen the democratic state. Then, we were committed to the principle of individual freedom. Today, when more of the planet's population has political freedom than any time in history, we must dedicate ourselves to the practice of building institutions.

We must commit to this in recognition of a simple, demanding reality: If the rule of law does not entrench democracy, states that fall to authoritarianism, fascism, or communism will not advance global peace. Promoting the rule of law is the only mechanism that can secure the global democratic movement that will strengthen peace.

To those who doubt that we can shape the proper approach for rule of law promotion, I say we certainly have the intellectual capacity—in this room alone!—to meet that challenge. Furthermore, I say we have plenty of lessons to learn from already, from our own experiences and from around the world.

If we marshal our experiences with political will—and you're sitting before someone who helps successfully defend the appropriation for the National Endowment for Democracy every single year—we can succeed.

Of course, it helps when we are met with political will in recipient nations. President Jiang Zemin of the People's Republic of China still publicly reveres Mao Tsetung, the apotheosis of rule by leader, not rule by law.

But the Chinese leadership also knows that the unquestioning support of the masses is a thing of the past and that weakening acceptance erodes their legal tradition. The Chinese recognize, for example, that sustained economic development will require more legal codes that are transparent, equitable, efficient, and free of arbitrary manipulation. Further, the Chinese are aware that the Asian region is rapidly moving into the camp of democracies supported by the rule of law.

The situation is so much more promising in Indonesia, the fourth most populous nation and the nation with the largest Muslim population in the world. With last year's election of President Abdurrahman Wahid, it is now the third largest democracy in the world.

President Wahid is a modern Muslim scholar who studies and admires de Tocqueville. A proponent of democracy his entire life, he is inviting the democratic nations of the world to build the permanent institutions of democracy in his country.

We need to seize upon this opportunity and demonstrate, as I believe we can, that by building the institutions of democracy in Indonesia we can help that country address its economic and separatist challenges. I am glad that the Clinton administration has committed itself this year to expanding rule of law programs in Indonesia.

We need to share—not dictate—our expertise on all the components of the rule of law: On constitutional government and the mechanisms of separated powers; on independent, professional judiciaries; on the development of fair, transparent law that is accessible, efficient, equally applied, and subject to change by established democratic processes; on the role of civilian law enforcement to advance civil rights and combat criminality; on the protection of commercial obligations; and, of course, the preservation of human rights.

I have studied a bit of what the scholars and practitioners promoting the rule of law have done and written, and I think we need to keep in mind some practical principles in devising rule of law programs. These have to do with three of the basic aspects of rule of law programs.

First, we need to expand exchange programs whereby our experts train willing cadres in different countries about the principles and practices of legal regimes. For example, the Library of Congress used some of its experts from the Congressional Research Service to establish parliamentary assistance programs in Central and Eastern Europe, as well as in Russia, in the early 1990s. Without diluting their role here in Washington, such programs would be beneficial in other nations with nascent parliaments, and we should seek to reestablish these efforts.

But while conferences and seminars are valuable, I think we need to recognize the importance of immersion programs in making exchanges worthwhile. Only by exposing qualified individuals to extended, in-depth legal course work can you begin to develop personal expertise that is necessary for countries striving to advance rule of law practices.

I stress that the creation of cadres of legal experts is an essential aspect to modernizing law in China. Chinese legal tradition—going back to the third century B.C. writings of the Chinese philosopher Hsun Tsu—has always subjugated the importance of law to the idea of the enlightened leader and his bureaucracy. Creating expertise based on in-depth knowledge is one way to counter that legal tradition.

Second, in our efforts to promote specific constitutional reforms, we must be wary of not imposing doctrine void of local content. As Burke noted, it is tyrannical to impose the values and precepts of alien norms and mores upon a nation. One must build upon existing cultural traditions. When asked what he would do if he were made King of the Jews, Napoleon Bonaparte exclaimed that before imposing any reforms of modernization, he would rebuild the Temple.

In the West, since Montesquieu, we have thus understood that the importance of constitutions and the concomitant parsing of the powers of government is to preserve the liberty of the individual from the corruption of power.

Nevertheless, we must remember that in society law does not function in a vacuum. In advancing specific constitutional devices and laws, we need to be sensitive to the anthropological bases of indigenous rulemaking.

The rule of law must relate to the social logic and practices where it is to take root. As a historical analogy, the creation of the U.S. Uniform Commercial Code was based on studying the prior commercial activities in this country. Legal codes must embody a consensus that gives play to local rules.

Third, as we support programs developing the legal institutions necessary for the rule of law, such as courts and law enforcement agencies, we must have the foresight to commit to the time and resources necessary to achieve these ends. One training seminar will not establish a functioning judiciary.

We need to have sustained, on-the-ground programs. For example, the Asia Foundation is America's preeminent nongovernmental organization in this field. With support from Congress, it has established on-the-ground programs necessary to nurture rule of law institutions throughout Asia.

An important and related aspect necessary to consider in institution building is the idea of creating islands of excellency. It will not be possible, for example, to modernize the entire Indonesian court system. What needs to be done instead is to focus on discrete courts within that system, to create islands of professionalism that will serve as magnets for emulation. Otherwise, the best of efforts risk dilution.

I recognize that it is easier to speak in concepts than it is to implement actual programs. I mentioned earlier that Congress has appropriated over $1 billion for international rule of law programs. Since 1993, over thirty-five departments and agencies in our government have run rule of law programs.

Unfortunately, according to the results of a Government Accounting Office report a number of us requested last year, the sad fact is that, to this day, the U.S. government does not have a coordinated effort on this important issue. As recently as 1998, the State Department could not even effectively inventory our efforts on the rule of law!

Now, at least, there is the awareness about the need to coordinate executive efforts in promoting the rule of law. Perhaps this is a result of the increased scrutiny some of us in Congress have exercised. If that is the case, then I think Congress is providing a useful function in advancing these programs.

Above all, we must resist the urge to withdraw our global commitment to advancing the rule of law. Every effort has a learning curve. Furthermore, we need to be open enough to look elsewhere for lessons to be learned.

Central and Eastern Europe have shown pronounced progress toward constitutionalism. Other parts of the world also provide success stories.

In Palermo, Sicily, my friend Mayor Leolucca Orlando has used law enforcement and the underappreciated role of civic education to free that city from generations of control by organized crime.

Another example is provided by Hong Kong, where twenty years ago the International Commission Against Corruption was formed, and that city established one of the most transparent legal administrations in the world.

These are a few examples, ladies and gentlemen, that show that where there is political will, difficult problems can be solved.

Finally, we must remember that the rule of law has not been perfected. I often remind people that our Declaration of Independence states that we have the inalienable right of "life, liberty and the *pursuit* of happiness," which is entirely different from a right to happy outcomes. The rule of law remains a goal, and as we promote the rule of law abroad, we must keep this distinction modestly.

The conference you are holding this week will address some of the key components of the ongoing discussion on how to best advance the rule of law throughout the world. Based on the topics, papers, and presenters I see on the agenda, I am confident it will advance the issue in a way that will directly affect the way we policymakers continue to refocus our support for rule of law programs.

Remember: We are not talking about abstractions here but the implementation of pragmatic idealism. The conclusions you draw will serve the practitioners trying, with our support, to build the institutions that will, in turn, advance no less than global peace. Tonight I offer you my enthusiastic encouragement, and I look forward to the results of your work.

Thank you.

Address

Dieter Grimm

I.

It was thirty-five years ago that I first entered the building in which we were so generously received tonight—earlier than I got to see the highest court of my own country. I had arrived in the United States with some idea of the role the Supreme Court played in American politics and American law. But ultimately it was Paul Freund in the constitutional law class of 1964–65 at Harvard Law School who made me familiar with the true importance of the Supreme Court, the landmark decisions and the personalities of former and present justices. Thus, when I first visited the Supreme Court I knew who was sitting on the bench and could attribute opinions to persons, whereas I would certainly have had difficulties in naming even some members of the German Constitutional Court. The reason is that decisions of the German court are anonymous documents. Individual opinions did not exist at that time. They began to be permitted as late as 1970 and were not extended beyond the Constitutional Court.

I still remember my surprise that the building with its classical architecture dated only from the 1930s and that previously the Supreme Court had been sitting under one roof with Congress, while Germany symbolized the independence of the judiciary from the other branches of government not only by separate buildings but by locating the highest court in a city far from the capital. The robes with their modest black and plain design contrasted with the building as I found. In order to understand why this struck me one must know that the German justices, while sitting in a functional building with an almost austere courtroom, wear not just wigs but scarlet robes, copied from a Florentine pattern of the eighteenth century, which are so difficult to put on that one cannot manage without assistance.

II.

In 1965, the year of my first visit to the U.S. Supreme Court, I could not foresee that I would one day wear this fancy robe myself. But I remember that when I returned to this building in the capacity of a justice of my own country I had the clear feeling that I returned to the cradle of constitutional adjudication, which is, in my view, one of the greatest achievements in the history of political institutions and the most important contribution of America to political civilization. I have no difficulty in admitting that states can be based on the principle of democracy and the rule of law without entrusting a court with the power to review and annul government acts. But history teaches that, in general, democracy and the rule of law have a better chance of being respected by the rulers when these are submitted to a certain judicial control.

I am, of course, aware of the democratic problem that constitutional adjudication presents. But I am also convinced that the danger for democracy and the rule of law is in most parts of the world greater without than with constitutional adjudication. Under such circumstances, the constitution finds itself reduced to establishing government institutions and to organizing their procedures. But for the day-to-day political decisions, the constitution is not decisive, and in cases of conflict about what constitutional law requires the opinion of the majority always prevails. It is therefore not surprising that countries that had experiences with government similar to those of the American colonists with the British Parliament, and even more so countries that had freed themselves from dictatorship, felt it necessary to safeguard democratic order and the rule of law by establishing constitutional courts. Thus, the second half of the twentieth century has brought forth the victory of the idea of judicial review, and for the United States it must be a deep satisfaction that its Supreme Court was apparently so convincing an example of constitutional adjudication that it has frequently been copied.

III.

Particularly in the years after the fall of Communism and of suppressive governments in other parts of the world, delegation after delegation came to visit the United States Supreme Court and also the Federal Constitutional Court of Germany to inform themselves about the functioning of constitutional adjudication. In the period of formation, questions of status and organization were frequently of greater interest to these delegations than questions of content and methodology. I remember how disappointed the members of the Russian Constitutional Court were when, after their arrival in Karlsruhe (the residence of the German Court), they were not led to the impressive castle of the former prince of Baden with its majestic tower but to the modern building next door. They had seen pictures of the site and were convinced that the Constitutional Court resided in the castle. Relying on that conviction, they had asked Yeltsin for a building with a tower in Moscow, arguing that the German Constitutional Court was located in a building with a tower. There was also some disappointment for a number of delegations when we did not support their opinion that a Supreme Court justice should earn at least as much as the president of the republic; they feared they would not be respected by the rulers if ranking lower on the government payroll.

However, I do not want to create the impression that this problem was representative of the type of questions the visitors were interested in. Yet there is one question that was asked by every delegation: How can one achieve that politicians in general and majorities in particular obey the orders of the Constitutional Court even when they clearly collide with their own intentions? This, of course, is the crucial question of constitutionalism and judicial review, and there is much historical evidence that the mere existence of a constitutional court is not a sufficient guarantee for the enforcement of the constitution. Some of my colleagues tried to answer this question by referring to a provision in the statute providing that decisions of the Constitutional Court have binding force for any public power. But this apparently was not the expected answer, for law cannot guarantee its own respect. The answer lies outside the realm of law. It lies in its social and cultural context. Respect for the constitution must be so deeply rooted in society that politicians are not tempted to openly disregard its requirements or that it would become too costly for them to do so because of the popular reaction.

This answer left many visitors with a deep concern because they knew that the extralegal conditions of successful constitutional democracy were not given in their countries and could not be developed in a short time. The situation explains some of the difficulties of newly established constitutional courts in finding their way between activism and passivity. The Hungarian Constitutional Court, for instance, at times declared about one-third of the laws challenged before it unconstitutional, and when asked by politicians how this could be the case, answered that this was simply the Western standard, which is of course far from reality. On the other hand, there are courts whose first question is how a decision will be received by government and for whom avoiding a conflict is more important than enforcing the constitution.

IV.

Compared with the situation and perspective of some newly established constitutional courts, the German experience with constitutional adjudication was a particularly lucky one. Since the dark years between 1933 and 1945, Germany has become a stable democracy where, for the first time in its history, the constitution matters—not least of all due to the activity of the Constitutional Court. The divided Germany found its identity to a large extent in the Basic Law, and the notion of "constitutional patriotism" that unified right and left was an expression of this situation. In the unified Germany, the East German population is certainly less familiar with the constitution, but that has not affected the high degree of effectiveness of the Basic Law. The German Constitutional Court may be more active than the U.S. Supreme Court, for instance, in reviewing measures of foreign policy and particularly in deriving from the bill of rights not only limitations of government but also duties to protect liberties threatened by societal forces. Nevertheless, acceptance by the population and compliance by politicians is very high. Thus, Germany is an example of a successful transformation from dictatorship to democracy and the rule of law, and I think that it was precisely this success that made the German model particularly attractive for countries that had experienced dictatorship themselves and were determined to effectively ban it by means of constitutional law and constitutional adjudication.

The most important contribution constitutional courts can make to the success of constitutionalism is that, in spite of the political influence on the selection of judges, they act at a distance from party politics and make plausible that they derive their decisions not from political considerations but from the text and the meaning of the constitution. When I recollect the twelve years of my term on the German Constitutional Court, the most satisfying aspect of my experience was that the court is the rare example of a body that renders decisions of the highest political impact and nevertheless does not know factions that always vote together nor previous agreements among certain judges or bargaining processes. I always met an open discussion where everyone has to be taken seriously because everyone has an equal vote, where tricks do not pay off because of the need to cooperate in the same group for a rather long period of time, and where arguments count because the result has to be justified by reasons. I thereby do not deny the existence of limits of understanding or of willingness to continue the discussion, but I want to say that this discussion was always guided by legal reasoning and not by political affiliations.

The aim of discussion in my court has always been to find a solution acceptable to all members. Compromises, therefore, are not disapproved of, but not sought at any rate. However, the discussion may be long, long on the merits and long on the formulation of the opinion that is also discussed among all members of the court in a second round. In the second abortion case before the German Court the process of decision making and formulating the opinion took as long as nine months. Under

these circumstances, other cases age. We once had to decide the quality of a horse named "Sir X," which at the time of the decision was no longer living, nor its owner nor the lawyer who had written the first brief. This is certainly a difference from the Supreme Court where, if I am informed correctly, not only the oral argument is short but also the discussion after oral argument. The different opinions are registered, and reasoning follows the decision in the various separate opinions, whereas in Germany separate opinions are rare. I myself filed only two separate opinions in twelve years, which does not mean that in all other cases I belonged to the majority. I remember at least one case where the separate opinion impressed the majority so much that the deliberation was resumed and the result changed.

When I compare the discourse in court with academic discourse, the latter may be more sophisticated, more learned, more elegant. Still, it seems to me inferior to the judicial discourse. The necessity of reaching a common solution that cannot be avoided by simply walking away or abstaining from the vote, which is not just one opinion among others but acquires binding force for society and for which, in turn, one is accountable, gives court discussions a degree of reliability and responsibility that I have not found to the same extent in the academic world.

VI.

I shall end these short reflections by asking what the role of constitutional courts will be in a changing world order. The key word of this order is of course globalization. This means in particular that the radius and consequences of economic actions are wider than the radius of state actions. More and more problems exist that cannot be effectively solved in the national frame but require international solutions. This means that at the same time when constitutionalism and constitutional adjudication have gained worldwide recognition, their scope narrows. In order to illustrate what I mean I will mention a case, among the hardest ones I had to decide.

The case was about navigation. There is a general rule that on German ships German law applies. This means also that the high standard of fundamental rights protection—such as social security—applies although most of the sailors are from less developed foreign countries. The consequence was that it became too costly for German shipowners to run their ships under the German flag. Their reaction was to flag out, as it is called, and to run their ships under the flags of a foreign country with much lower legal standards. The German government wanted to stop this trend and modified the law so that, in short, German law still applies on German ships, but no longer fully. The amendment was challenged before the Constitutional Court, mainly on grounds of a violation of the principle of equality. The case put us in a dilemma: Should we have decided to keep the high standard of fundamental rights protection, there would no longer have been a field of application for it on the oceans. If we wanted to preserve a field of application for the German fundamental rights standard, we were obliged to lower it.

Cases like this will increase; they will be the type of cases with which courts have to deal in a globalized economy. Many of them can be solved only on a world level and in a world order. We want this order to be a democratic one that follows the rule of law. But the difficulties of establishing democracy on a supranational level are clear. Therefore, the time of the nation-state is not completely over. Correspondingly, national constitutional courts will retain an important role. But they will have to fulfill it more and more in an international framework so that knowledge of foreign courts' jurisprudence can be of tremendous help. Yet foreign sources are rarely used by national courts—partly because of lack of information, partly because of self-centeredness. Certainly the German Constitutional Court does not sufficiently use foreign authority, and the same is true for the U.S. Supreme Court. Younger courts, for evident reasons, often do better, and a particularly admirable effort has been made by the South African Constitutional Court. But most courts do not have the means, even when they are willing, to let themselves be guided or informed by the jurisprudence of foreign countries. Therefore, the time has come for organizing mutual information on constitutional jurisprudence. A collection of arguments and solutions for similar problems is imminent. Would it not be worthwhile for the country with the longest tradition in constitutional adjudication to take the lead? And could it not be done with the informational resources of the institution whose two hundredth anniversary we celebrate today—the Library of Congress?

Address

Stephen G. Breyer

This conference ratifies a modern revolution in the law—a revolution that we call "globalization." I recognize that *legal* revolutions do not necessarily stir the soul. Still, branches of the law, like those of science, sometimes undergo great and sudden change. They have their great formative periods, periods that see the development of major guiding principles, after which scholars, judges, and practitioners come to accept those principles as beyond challenge and apply them to the cases at hand. Think of the Marshall court and Constitutional structure; the Warren court and the protection of fundamental human liberty; labor law in the 1930s and again in the 1960s; civil procedure after the Federal Rules. Think of this conference and "globalization."

The law that we call "global" has already changed dramatically. Today the interaction of national and transnational law, along with the development of new transnational legal institutions, exerts influence upon almost every legal subject. Professors, practitioners, and increasingly judges regularly consider how foreign systems of law treat similar problems. We no longer have to convince others *that* we may gain important benefits from global economic and social interaction, benefits related to prosperity, human liberty, or the environment. Rather, we now undertake the more difficult job of determining precisely *how* to shape the law to bring these benefits about.

Answering "how" questions is complicated. They often call for detailed, complex subject matter or institution-specific responses. Answers depend not simply upon legal theory but also upon empirical facts, practical experience, and an understanding of how related nonjudicial institutions help to shape the law. I want to illustrate the point by raising four issues that focus upon the role of judges in a "globalized" legal sys-

tem. I take them from recent discussions I have had with judges and academics. Those discussions help to underscore the magnitude of the current revolution, its complexity, and the importance of the kind of study that your own agenda reveals.

The first issue concerns the need for interchange of substantive legal views, not simply among academics and practitioners but also among judges from the courts of different nations. Judges who enforce the law as well as those who write it increasingly turn to the experience of other nations when deciding difficult open questions of substantive law, particularly human rights law, but potentially environmental law or commercial law as well. This is fairly obvious outside the United States in respect to many constitutional questions, for example, in Canada, Europe, India, South Africa, and other jurisdictions where courts now routinely refer to judicial opinions from foreign nations. It is less obvious in the United States itself, for our courts less frequently refer to judicial opinions from abroad. And that is where the problem lies.

Our law is not closed to foreign judicial experience, at least if that experience is used to illustrate different possible judicial solutions to similar problems. But two years ago a professor at an NYU meeting asked me to "provide one concrete example of a comparison that has actually proved useful in your work at the Court." And I hesitated slightly in my reply. I eventually referred to the Conseil d'État's opinion about the right of Muslim girls to wear a veil or *chador* in class at a secular state school. I could provide other examples, including opinions by Canadian and European courts on such subjects as capital punishment execution delays and campaign finance laws.

Nonetheless, the professor had a point. There is a special American, "chicken-and-egg" problem: My own

Court is not very likely to look at cases that are not cited to us; the lawyers who practice before us rarely refer to material that is not strictly American; that fact reflects their own legal training—and the absence of references to foreign court decisions in American judicial opinions. The professor's challenge can ultimately be met only if members of the bar and the academy themselves become familiar with foreign material relevant to particular legal disciplines and facilitate the judicial use of that material. This conference, and others like it, may help.

I do not mean to suggest that judicial use is the only important (or the most important) use of comparative material. Insofar as "globalization" requires a more uniform law of, say commercial transactions or intellectual property, other institutions, for example, the international equivalent of Uniform State Law Commissioners, may suggest new law and legislatures may provide it.

Still, I find more than symbolic importance in the fact that during recent visits to new law school classrooms, I have seen installed audio and visual technology that will permit American and French, German, or Indian professors to "team teach" classes held simultaneously in different nations. Those technical changes, in part by facilitating comparisons, will inevitably bring about change in the law. Those changes will affect courtrooms as well as classrooms. And judges will have a role to play, particularly in areas where law, like much human rights law, is made in significant part by judges.

The second issue concerns the growth of new governmental structures, including many structures that might be called loosely "federalist" in shape. In Europe we see these structures both in the European Union and its member states and within individual nations, as, for example, in Britain, which currently is working out new legal relationships between a national Parliament and a "devolved" Scotland and Wales.

The issue of which decisions are best handled by distant decision makers and which are best left to local bodies concerns judges because their view of how a "federal-type" structure should work inevitably influences the system's shape. The issue is potentially global in its scope because the human problem to which "federalist" structures respond is near universal and of increasing importance. On the one hand, certain modern economic, social, and technological circumstances demand more technical, more central, and more distant decision making. Toxic waste dumped into the Danube in Romania will affect fish that swim in Hungary or the Ukraine and citizens of the several nations that eat them.

On the other hand, the public often objects to the placing of too much authority in the hands of a too distant central decision maker. A family that lives in Palermo, Italy, and a family that lives in Peoria, Illinois, may feel the same way about decision making at a distance, whether those decisions emanate from Brussels or from Washington, D.C. Distance makes it more difficult for a central administrator to understand local circumstances and the need for exceptions to general regulation. And the more distant the decision making, the more difficult it is for the local resident to participate in that decision. Yet the right of an individual to participate in the making of a decision that will affect him or her, a right that used to be considered part of the "liberty of the ancients," itself remains an important aspect of modern human liberty.

How will the law, say the law of the European Union, reconcile those competing needs? Will it divide legal topics by subject matter or develop procedural rules that encourage long-distance citizen participation? It has already started to create presumptions, such as "subsidiarity," which some believe potentially enforceable in court.

The experience in Europe and elsewhere in respect to the "federalist" problem has general relevance, including in the United States where our own well-established federal system, while fixed, is not immutable and remains subject to judicial interpretation. At a minimum, experience elsewhere helps American judges to understand the likely consequences of the interpretive paths not here taken.

Third, increased "globalization" may again force us to consider the familiar jurisprudential difficulty of the judge's democratic legitimacy. As others have pointed out, that legitimacy is a matter of lesser concern as long as international guarantees of human rights are only paper rights that are never enforced in practice. Nor does it pose much of a problem if enforceable rights exist only in extreme instances. Long before the twentieth century, the law permitted every nation to punish a pirate wherever caught and irrespective of the pirate's nationality, and few people cared which nation's judges did the punishing.

As international human rights norms of broad substantive content become enforceable in less extreme circumstances, however, the more it matters just who will enforce that law and how. Should ordinary magistrates in every nation, for example, have the legal power to enforce universal human rights norms? Should there be a special international court? Does it matter that ordinary magistrates in one nation are neither elected by the voters of another nation nor subject to confirmation by that nation's elected officials? The United States, after all, has created elaborate procedures designed to maintain some democratic check upon the decisions of its necessarily independent judges. And our judiciary, in turn, has created elaborate systems of Constitutional interpretation designed in significant part to respect the determinations of democratically elected legislatures. All this is a matter of current debate.

But this debate is not the only debate to which the "democratic element" is relevant. How are judges of a multinational court to take account of that element when they interpret broadly phrased legal documents protective of human rights? There is a rapidly growing number of adjudicative bodies that issue authoritative decisions binding the citizens of several nations. Consider a few that have achieved increased prominence fairly recently: the European Court of Justice; the European Court of Human Rights; the African Court of Human and Peoples Rights; the Inter-American Human Rights Court; an International Criminal Court; the ad hoc criminal tribunal for the former Yugoslavia; the ad hoc criminal tribunal for Rwanda; the World Trade Organization; the International Tribunal for the Law of the Sea; the UN Compensation Commission; the World Bank Inspection Panel; its Asian and Inter-American Development Bank counterparts; NAFTA; and the Andean and Mercosur systems, and other regional economic tribunals as well. In a world where trade, investment, environmental protection, the protection of basic liberties, and the democratic control of decision makers all matter, what is the proper relationship of these bodies to national courts and to each other?

Finally, the increased "global" importance of a rule of law has focused attention upon the need for fair application of that law and upon judicial independence—independence necessary to secure honest, effective judicial decision making. Increasingly, nations agree that a judicial process in which judges decide cases honestly, within a reasonable time, and without itself imposing unreasonable costs, is critically important—both because such a system helps guarantee fundamental human rights in practice and because it helps establish the economic security necessary for prosperity. But to maintain or to create such a system is difficult.

How much "independence" do we want? In many civil law systems an official called a "judge" or "judicial magistrate" performs investigating and prosecuting functions that Americans would place in the hands of a separate, nonjudicial official—a prosecutor. Should that prosecutor be separate from the judiciary? If so, is it necessary to import other elements of an American-style adversary system? Does complete "independence" for such a prosecutor itself threaten abuse? What is the proper relation between prosecutor and press?

We all abhor undue influence, what the Russians used to call "telephone justice" (the party boss would decide the case by telephone), and we prize honesty, believing it an absolute and necessary precondition. We know too that a judicial system must work with reasonable speed and at reasonable cost if it is to retain the public's confidence. To achieve these objectives requires more than just desire. It requires practical judgments about system details—about how to create governmental institutions that will guarantee the integrity of the judicial system and help it to function fairly and effectively. We know that a free press can help; so too does an independent bar and adequate judicial resources. What else?

The job before us—as nations increasingly emphasize the rule of law and the role of the judge—is to try to transfer knowledge from one nation to another so that, despite cultural, historical, or institutional barriers, we can create fairer, more effective judicial systems, including safeguards of institutional integrity where they now are lacking.

I shall stop without proposing solutions to the problems I have raised. I intend only to point out that these judge-related issues are important and topical for those immersed in "globalization." They have come to my attention recently, as I have listened, for example, to German and French constitutional judges discuss numerous substantive legal issues that our Court too considers in its daily work; to British and Europeans judges debating the judge's role in a newly "federalist" system; to judges from some of the newer international courts with criminal jurisdiction debate jurisdictional issues with European and American law professors; and to South American lawyers and judges as they struggle with problems of the prosecutor's independence and judicial integrity.

The issues I raise comprise only one part of the agenda of global matters that seek your attention, and that fact itself is perhaps the most important point about this conference. It indicates that there is more than a generation's worth of fundamental legal and institutional work to be done. It is important that you are undertaking that work. I encourage you to continue. And I encourage in particular the younger among you, including the students who are here.

After all, what could be more exciting for an academic, practitioner, or judge than the "global" legal enterprise that is now upon us? Wordsworth's words, written about the French Revolution, will, I hope, still ring true:

Bliss was it in that dawn to be alive/
But to be young was very heaven.

The Hague Tribunal, The Hague, Netherlands. *Source:* © Van Cappellen/Reporters/SABA, 1996.

Session I

Transnational Justice and National Sovereignty

Editors' Note

Transnational justice is at the core of a world where the rule of law would have meaning across many jurisdictions. Rules of law that can be regarded as legitimate and enforceable in many courts are now asserted, irrespective of venue or citizenship, when actions are so repugnant to human rights that they are almost universally condemned. There are many other issues. When will international law, or treaties ratified by many nations, take precedence over contrary domestic law? Will courts in one national jurisdiction take account of the decisions of other national courts or the legislation of other national legislatures? How likely is it that an action with transnational consequences will be treated in a similar fashion in the courts of the several nations affected? In a world increasingly characterized by global movements of people, ideas, money, goods, services, crime, disease, and pollution, the effectiveness of legal norms across jurisdictions is a question raised in the highest courts of many countries.

Professor Philip Allott issues a powerful call for a reimagining of human potentiality, particularly through a return to the great philosophical traditions of a positive search for the attainability of human ideals. Only thus are we likely to create conditions where the rule of law can be truly effective, responsive to the best norms and values that make possible civilized collective life, and hence the law. Justice Sandra Day O'Connor explores the idea of accountability for criminal actions, through both international tribunals and through national institutions—both political and juridical. Acknowledging that there is sometimes tension between international obligations and countervailing interests of national sovereignty, she discusses a variety of instances and approaches that can take account of criminal behavior without either remembering too much (so as to dwell on retribution) or forgetting too much (so as to risk repetition).

Professor Bruno Simma explicates the wide range of international adjudication and arbitration mechanisms now available for various kinds of disputes among nations. He comments that one effect of globalization is to dissolve national boundaries into spheres of specialized jurisdictions for trade, maritime events, criminal actions, intra-European disputes, and so forth. The other major theme of his paper is to trace the role of the United States in the creation of international law and international courts, lamenting the fact that at present the United States seems reluctant to make use even of those instrumentalities that it helped to create.

Ambassador Hisashi Owada comments that at the moment there is no solution to the dichotomy between "the existing normative system based on national competencies and the emerging socioeconomic reality of interdependence on a global scale." He hopes that more active involvement and participation in international adjudication by many nations may help to harmonize justice to individuals and the sovereign interests of states.

As moderator, Professor Anne-Marie Slaughter comments upon the relationship between democracy and the rule of law, calling attention to the need to outgrow the American parochial tendency to think that the relationship flourishes only here.

Law and the Re-Making of Humanity

Philip Allott

A two hundredth birthday. A new century. A new millennium. A time to look back—and a time to look forward. The future already exists as a potentiality within the present, just as the present is an actualized potentiality of the past. In the words of Schiller's Wallenstein: ". . . in today tomorrow is already on the move."[1] This is true of the future of the natural world and the future of the human world. But, in the case of the human world, there is an amazing difference: We make the human world; we choose the human future. We can choose to actualize *this* potentiality rather than *that* potentiality. The past offers us a range of possibilities, and we, individually and collectively, must make our choice among those possibilities.

The Challenge

The Mind's Freedom

We have a freedom of the mind that is like the freedom of the will. Using our freedom of the mind (reason, imagination, and feeling), we make a human reality that is a presence of *mind* within a world that we suppose to be a world of *nonmind,* which we call the physical world. We make our mental habitat as we re-make our physical habitat—unceasingly, inevitably.

We are morally responsible for what we think as much as for what we do. We cannot avoid the responsibility of choosing what we shall become, the burden of our self-creating freedom. Martin Heidegger said that human beings do not possess freedom; freedom possesses (*besitzt*) them.[2] Nor can we escape our self-made past—the potentialities that we have made possible and the potentialities that we have destroyed. Samuel Beckett said: "There is no escape from yesterday because yesterday has deformed us, or been de-

formed by us. . . . [W]e are rather in the position of Tantalus, with this difference, that we allow ourselves to be tantalised."[3]

The present paper is intended to set out a particular view of the present state of human reality and a particular view of human potentiality at this moment when we are unusually self-conscious of our past and our future, when we are unusually self-conscious of the burden of responsibility that rests on us—the burden of our responsibility for the human past that we have made and the burden of our responsibility for the human future that we will choose.

We must uncover a future that could be our future, a future that is ours to choose, if we have the collective intelligence and the collective courage to choose it.

Law's Power

In the making of the human world, nothing has been more important than what we call *law.* Law is the intermediary between human power and human ideas. Law transforms our natural power into social power, transforms our self-interest into social interest, and transforms social interest into self-interest. These transformations are effected in the name of ideas, ideas generated within the human mind, in the private mind of human individuals, and in the public mind of human society.

Law defeats the passage of time by retaining choices made in a society's past in a form that can take effect in a society's future. The law that is retained from society's past takes effect in society's present; as the law is interpreted and applied in the light of actual circumstances it helps make society's future. The law carries the past through the present into the future. The law offers to society stability in the midst of ceaseless change and change-from-stability as new human circumstances demand new human choices. You may not be able to step into the same Heraclitan river twice, but you can and cannot live in the same society twice. Society changes unceasingly, but something remains. Society's steady state is also a state of change. And it is, above all, the law that resolves that infinitely fruitful dialectic between stability and change, which is the nature of human society. Law is a wonderful, and insufficiently appreciated, human invention.

The wonderful creative capacity of law is now available to humanity as a whole, as a potentiality, in the making of international society, the society of the whole human race, the society of all societies. And so we have now to consider an ultimate form of human potentiality and human choice—the role we might assign to law in making the human future, in remaking the human world, in remaking humanity.

Millennial Potentiality

What have we learned, if anything, during the last millennium of human existence, especially during these last two centuries—two centuries like no others in the story of human self-creating, two centuries during which the Library of Congress has been a true mirror of turbulent times—the climax of a millennium full of the glory and the terror of the human world, the sadness and the grandeur of human reality?

A thousand years ago everything in the human world was much the same as it is today, and yet everything was very different. A thousand years ago ancient civilizations were in decay and decline, in different ways and to different degrees. Successor civilizations, Islam and Christendom in particular, were full of a latent energy that was liable to express itself in destructive rivalry, a cold war with intermittent episodes of hot war. A thousand years ago we in Europe had wasted our inheritance from Greece and Rome, if not our inheritance from ancient Israel. The human world was full of other peoples who had not known that inheritance, peoples with their own histories, their own realities, their own potentialities, and their own intellectual and artistic cultures.

Who in the eleventh century could have imagined the potentiality of human reality, a potentiality that would be actualized over the succeeding centuries—a

potentiality, we must say, for both good and evil? That potentiality must have been present in the capacities of the human body and the human mind and in the seemingly random residues of the past that had survived centuries of disorder and neglect.

It is hard to believe that in the year 1000 we in Europe did not know of the idea of zero in mathematics; that we did not even have an agreed way of representing the numerals from 1 to 10; that in the year 1600 all but a few Europeans believed that the sun orbited the earth; that in the year 1700 Isaac Newton still believed that God had created the world in 4004 B.C.E.

And yet we now know that ten centuries ago, within an apparently unsatisfactory human reality, there was a latent and obscure potentiality that must have contained the mathematics, the natural sciences, the arts and crafts, the philosophy, the social organization, and the economic systems that have made a new human world in the course of these last ten centuries, a ten-century frenzy of human self-evolving, a transformation that is now altering all human reality everywhere.

There is no reason why the next century and the next millennium should be any less glorious, and every reason why they should be much less terrible than the most recent chapters in the strange story of the self-evolving of the human species.

Surpassing the Past

We may say that the one unmistakable lesson of the last millennium is that humanity can transform itself by its own efforts using the creative powers of the mind, and hence that the next century and the next millennium can, if we so choose, contain new transformations, a new kind of human existence.

And yet humanity is entering the twenty-first century under a banner that reads: *Forward to the nineteenth century!* We are on a familiar highway with signposts leading to destinations that would have been perfectly familiar to our great-grandparents. *Great-power hegemonism. Global capitalism. Interstate rivalry. Science-led progress.* It is as if the relentless pounding of twentieth-century life had exhausted our capacity, or else our will, to reinvent ourselves. We are entering the new century with a global political worldview, which

Metternich, Gladstone, or Bismarck would recognize, that still contains the potentiality of violent conflict of all kinds, not excluding world war. And we are entering the new century with a global social worldview, which Marx, Ruskin, and Tolstoy had already condemned, that still contains the potentiality of unending human suffering flowing from global social injustice.

Surely the unnecessary deaths and unspeakable suffering of countless millions of human beings in the twentieth century will have been for nothing if global human society remains, in idea and in law and in fact, essentially the society that we inherited from the nineteenth century. Surely two centuries of experience, for better and for worse, of amazing new potentialities of human self-creating within human societies will be for nothing if we do not explore and exploit new potentialities of human self-creating at the level of the society of all humanity.

Our general failure of will and imagination may simply reflect an exhaustion of the human spirit. We have lived too much and thought too much in the long twentieth century. But beyond moral fatigue there is another symptom—an aching sense of spiritual confusion. At the end of the millennium, at the beginning of a new century, we are in two minds about human potentiality. Humanity is more than ever amazed at its own creative capacity. And humanity is more than ever uncertain of its ability to use that capacity well. It is this spiritual tension, in the depths of human consciousness, that we must try to diagnose. And we can reach an optimistic conclusion, seeing ourselves as greatly empowered not only by the intensity of our experience of human-made reality but also by a new capacity for human self-consciousness, a form of self-knowledge that has, once again, fundamentally altered human potentiality.

We live at the imperceptible intersection between our private mind and the public minds of the societies to which we belong. It follows that the way we understand human society and the way we understand the human mind are two aspects of a single process of human self-knowing. It follows also that the task of remaking our idea of humanity contains two projects—reconceiving human society and reconceiving the human mind. Central to both New Enlightenment projects is the task of reforming our idea of law and of the role of law as humanity's most effective instrument of perma-

nent social self-transforming through the purposive actualizing of its ideas and ideals.

We have done it before. We can do it again. The human mind has made the old human world in which we are obliged to live. The human mind must make a new human world in which we would want to live.

The Health of Nations—Human Inhumanity

First, we must attempt the self-diagnosis of our chronic *fin de siècle* and *fin de millénaire* spiritual confusion. Looking back over the last two centuries, it is possible to observe three leading symptoms of our present morbidity. We may call them inhuman humanity, dehumanizing humanity, and rehumanizing humanity.

Humanity's inhumanity remains a scandal and a mystery, a timeless scandal and a timeless mystery. Why do human beings continue to behave in ways that would shame animals? For centuries theologians and philosophers sanitized the phenomenon, calling it "the problem of evil." We who have experienced the twentieth century should be exceptionally expert now in the theology, the philosophy, and the psychology of evil.

And we have had particularly intense experience of what are, perhaps, the two most troubling of all forms of evil.

On the one hand there is the evil done by those who believe that they are serving the public interest—killing and exploiting people, individually and by the million, in the name of what they believe to be good ideas—with their good idea of the public interest sometimes conveniently coinciding with their idea of their private interest. On the other hand there is a form of evil that we may call social-systematic evil—evil generated by social systems for which no one in particular is personally responsible.

These two forms of evil—evil in the public interest and social-systematic evil—pose an agonizing problem, a problem that has characterized so much of the twentieth century. It is a problem that casts much doubt on the well-meaning movement to internationalize or deterritorialize the criminal prosecution of national public officials whose evildoing is so often the doing of evil in a supposed public interest and/or as a by-product of the functioning of social systems.[4]

Karl Popper and others have argued passionately that our bitter experience in the twentieth century should make us hate all forms of ideology, that is to say, the social enforcement of ideas.[5] But this is surely a tragically wrong conclusion. Socialized humanity will always be dominated by socialized ideas. The only answer is to socialize better ideas. In the words of an eighteenth-century preacher in England, why should the devil have all the best tunes? A big part of our project must be to find better ideas and to socialize them, as soon as possible. The social evil caused by ideas is a sickness that must be treated by the homeopathy of other ideas.

In the twenty-first century, as part of our ambiguous millennial inheritance, we are dealing now also with a planetwide phenomenon, a pandemic of social evil that is more than merely an aggregation of the dysfunctioning of subordinate societies. The globalizing of social phenomena is also a globalizing of social morbidity. Human inhumanity will be, more and more, the collective self-wounding of the half-formed society of all humanity.

The Health of Nations— Dehumanizing Humanity

In our new-century self-consciousness, we are acutely conscious also of something more pervasive, more intangible than human inhumanity, than evil in the traditional sense, namely, the relentless *dehumanizing of humanity.* Human self-dehumanizing has taken two main forms— social and intellectual.

Michel Foucault said that "man is an invention of recent date. And one perhaps nearing its end."[6] The ancient Greeks and Saint Augustine, among many others, were well aware of the significance of the human individual long before the supposedly individualizing effects of post-Reformation religion and early capitalism, but it is true to say that the intensity of human socializing over the last two centuries has created the possibility that human beings are becoming nothing but social epiphenomena. That is to say, the primary human reality is now so powerfully social that individual human beings have less and less significance, except as elementary particles within social force fields.

This is now, above all, an effect of *capitalism,* as Herbert Marcuse and many others have shown.[7] Capitalism

has become a form of totalitarianism in which every human individual is an economic actor with a role to play in the division of labor. And we now see that the so-called division of labor is, in fact, an aggregating of labor, a totalitarian integrating of human effort, including the totalitarian integrating of human consciousness.[8] One people, one market, one mind. *Ein Volk, ein Markt, ein Geist.*

The social integration of consciousness is not merely a side effect of capitalism. On the contrary, it is of the essence of capitalism that human beings should internalize an appropriate economic worldview and, still more important, should internalize the social and personal values necessary for the efficient functioning of capitalism, aligning their life-determining desire with the desire of all other economic factors. But this process is intrinsic also to the successful functioning of *liberal democracy,* capitalism's necessary and superefficient coworker. Democracy unites the general will of society and the personal will of society's members using an armory of powerful structural ideas—self-government, consent, representation, participation—so that the vast volume of law and public administration required by capitalism can seem to be the product of one mind and one will. One people, one will, one mind. *Ein Volk, ein Wille, ein Geist.*

The necessary tendency of democracy-capitalism is to socialize the citizen by integrating systematically individual consciousness and social consciousness, the private mind of the human being and the public mind of society. The globalizing of democracy-capitalism is the universalizing of a form of absolute socialism.

No less troubling is the intellectual dehumanizing of humanity. For two and a half centuries we have been searching for some truths about ourselves in the so-called human sciences. We have been trying to find what humanity is like by trying to study humanity objectively, as if we were natural phenomena of the natural world. A library is a repository of dead books from which undying ideas rise up to take possession of living minds, forming that metaphysical Library of Babel so memorably described by Jorge Luis Borges[9] in which we are tempted to search for the catalogue of catalogues, the truth of all human truths, in history, anthropology, sociology, jurisprudence, biology, neurology, and all the other -ologies.

However, what we can discover in the Library of Babel is something else. After two centuries of what is sometimes called the Enlightenment project, we have found no certain truths about ourselves, not even any universally accepted hypotheses, like the provisional certainties of the natural sciences. On the contrary, a reasonable dialectical response to the human sciences might take the form of three great negations. There is no such thing as *human nature*. There is no such thing as a *natural human condition*. There is no such thing as *natural human progress*. All three are dangerous illusions.

The ideas of human nature, the human condition, and human progress are a form of naturalism or biologism. Human naturalism and human biologism are dangerous for two reasons. They seem to offer an excuse (*eine Entschuldigung*—a de-responsibilizing) for human behavior, human failure, and human evil on individual and social levels. And secondly, they disempower and depress the human spirit. They suggest that we are victims of our biological nature, that we cannot overcome our psychological nature (so-called human nature) or our social nature (the so-called human condition). They lead to fatalism, defeatism, nihilism, negativism, passivity, realism, pragmatism, and general despair. They suggest that war, injustice, exploitation, and all other forms of social evil are natural, like epidemics or earthquakes.

The idea of natural human progress is now an article of faith in the theology of capitalism. And it is embodied now in the theology of the natural sciences as a social phenomenon. Natural human progress, it is said, is and will be an inevitable product of capitalism and science. But whatever capitalism and science may achieve in the long term, they are compatible with terrible horrors and miseries in the meantime. Capitalism and science are means, not ends. Human progress depends on human choice, on our intelligent and courageous use of our capacity for self-transcending and self-surpassing.

But it is we as we are who do the things that we do. It is we human beings, our human minds, that make war, injustice, exploitation, corruption—not God or evolution or our genes or the market. The human sciences alienate humanity from itself because they tend to deny the essential and overwhelming subjectivity of human beings. We are *not* merely natural phenomena;

we create ourselves every moment of our lives through the amazing power of subjective consciousness, individual consciousness, and social consciousness.[10] The mind is a mirror in which we see ourselves as we seem to be.[11] Everything human is a mind-thing.[12] Every body politic is a mind politic. The relative failure of the Enlightenment project of human empiricism has had other important psychic side effects. It has suggested that if we cannot transcend the *human* world in thought, as we are able to transcend the *physical* world in thought, there is nothing left for us but to return to a state of primitive irrationality or to submit humanity finally to the natural sciences, finding a physical basis for everything human, even for human consciousness. And that seems to be what is happening now. At the end of the twentieth century, human self-consciousness seems to be subject to collective fantasy or triumphalist natural science. They are both forms of collective alienation, not unlike the worst forms of mythology, superstitious religion, and general ignorance one thousand and more years ago. Mass culture in its most debased forms, together with the fantasy-reality generated by capitalism and degenerate forms of religion, are now alienating human beings yet again in a new century and a new millennium.

But the world-transforming achievements of science and engineering are also having an alienating effect. The magic and the mysteries and the miracles of Faustian science, assisted by engineering, its ingenious familiar, are taking power over what we are and what we will be. Science is trying to tell us what it is to be human, what it is to be conscious. In biology, physiology, neurology, even in computer science, we are being told how and why we think what we think.

The Health of Nations— Rehumanizing Humanity

Within human dehumanizing it is possible to discover a paradoxical potentiality of human rehumanizing. At last, at the end of this amazing millennium, we can *see* what is happening to us; we can begin to *understand* what is happening to us. This new kind of self-knowledge is a possibility of a new Enlightenment, a new kind of enlightenment.

One striking effect of capitalism has been a very great increase in what Adam Smith called the wealth of nations, that is to say, the *material* wealth of our nations. The idea of the totalized wealth of a nation is a somewhat metaphysical statistical concept, as national wealth is distributed, and distributed very unequally, among the members of the nation. But there is no doubt that the material life-conditions of the mass of the people, particularly in countries with capitalist systems, have vastly improved, including the range of personal choices in peoples' day-to-day lives. We must say that this has been a sort of humanizing, or a rehumanizing, of people dehumanized by centuries of slavery and serfdom and exploitation and poverty and ignorance.

Vast numbers of what for all recorded time has been a proletarian class in society, exploited and excluded from the full benefit of societal membership, have found a way of living that in the past was only enjoyed by a small privileged social class. But vast numbers of human beings, a global proletariat, remain exploited and excluded from the full benefit of membership in the society of all humanity, deprived of possibilities of personal self-creating. A rehumanizing of humanity could at last be a self-perfecting of all humanity, not merely of an exceptionally privileged class or nation.

The millennial challenge, and the rehumanizing opportunity, is to maximize the wealth of nations in the widest possible definition of the word *wealth*. At long last we must make the benefits of human socializing for all human beings exceed its costs, actualizing the human potentialities that we have discovered within ourselves. To meet this challenge we must undertake to improve the quality of human consciousness, not only our consciousness as members of self-perfecting societies but also our personal consciousness as self-perfecting human beings. It is a challenge for every form of human society and, above all, for the international society of the whole human race, the society of all societies.

A Response

Self-Resisting Mind

A challenge that is both a threat (to humanity's humanity) and an opportunity (to rehumanize human-

ity) calls for a response of self-surpassing intelligence and courage.[13] A response that invokes the self-transforming power of law in the self-transforming of all humanity is a self-surpassing challenge of human self-ordering. A response that consists of reimagining our ideas and our ideals of human self-socializing (*society*) and human self-contemplating (*mind*) is the challenge of all philosophical challenges.

Philosophy is the socially organized self-contemplating of the human mind. At the beginning of the twenty-first century, we find ourselves in a strangely impoverished situation as self-contemplating human beings. The self-inflicted poverty of philosophy at the beginning of the new millennium is an effect of complex but ascertainable causes, a paradoxical disenlightening at the heart of the Enlightenment project. Alongside, and not unconnected with, the dehumanizing effect of the human sciences and the spiritual hegemony of the natural sciences, philosophy has disabled itself by using its own activity to question its own possibility. Through the power of thought we have been able to suggest to ourselves that thought is incapable of transcending the conditions of its production—the social condition, the psychological condition, the linguistic condition.

We may use the names of three particular people to stand for intellectual movements that go far beyond their own work. What they have in common is that at one and the same time they have been major figures in the fact of our dehumanizing, and yet they can also be major figures in the ideal of our rehumanizing.

After Karl Marx, we cannot any longer ignore the *social* vector in the construction of human consciousness. After Sigmund Freud, we cannot any longer ignore the *unconscious* vector in the making of human consciousness. After Ludwig Wittgenstein, we cannot any longer ignore the *symbolic* vector in the making of human consciousness. Ancient philosophers knew all these things, but that knowledge is now available to us all, far beyond the field of professional philosophy, including to those engaged in the work of human self-redeeming.

How can we say that the work of these three people has been part of our dehumanizing? Like Rousseau and Nietzsche and Weber, among many others, they all knew that their work was incomplete. This knowledge created great personal anguish in the minds of all three of them, a sense of failure. And, much worse from humanity's perspective, each of their half-complete systems, their intellectual half-revolutions, has had big real-world effects.

The idea of the *social* construction of consciousness could be abused to explain and justify the enslavement of society members by those who control society and the mind of society, that is, the political and economic ruling classes. The idea of the *unconscious* construction of consciousness could be used to explain and justify every kind of evil and destructive behavior and to make us feel powerless in the face of the products of our own consciousness. The idea of the *symbolic* construction of consciousness could lead us to believe that there could be no transcendental basis for truth or for value, that all human ideas are equally worthful and worthless because ideas are condemned to be expressed in nothing but arbitrary symbols, including the arbitrary symbols of language.

These deformed versions of half-formed ideas have had huge real-world effects in our societies, profoundly demoralizing and dehumanizing us as individuals and as societies, a major contributor to our profound spiritual confusion. But, at so great a cost, they may also be seen as offering us a very great potential benefit. They mean that we are now able to see more clearly than ever before how it is that we make the human world, how it is that we make human reality, and hence how it is that we may remake them. They allow us to know ourselves in a way we have never known ourselves before, demystifying our limitless creativity and our self-inflicted suffering. In beginning to uncover the roots of human evildoing, they may have begun to reveal a new potentiality of human good-doing. When we can begin to understand our spiritual confusion, not only its symptoms but also its causes, then can we begin to find its cure.

There is no need for humanity simply to abandon itself to primitive fantasy and superstition or to surrender to defeatism in the face of our inability to find natural laws of human behavior. We do not need to give up hope in the face of the apparently hopeless phenomenon of social evil. And we do not have simply to submit to the iron will of capitalism or to the imperious dictates of science and engineering. We can resist. Humanity can resist its own dehumanizing. We can transcend and surpass ourselves once again. We have the capacity to redeem the human mind, to rescue it, to remake it, so that the new human mind is the mind we *want* to have, so that the human reality made by our minds is the human reality we *want* to have, so that we can inhabit a human world, a human habitat, that we *want* to inhabit.

Self-Knowing Mind

Our (post-Marxist) understanding of the social vector of human consciousness helps us to understand better the flow of energy between the private mind of the individual human being and the public mind of society. Society, like everything else in the human world, is manufactured in the minds of individual human beings but becomes a presence in the collective consciousness of society. As such, it returns as a decisive presence in the self-identifying and self-constituting of society members. It follows that there is no reason in principle, whatever may be the tendency of historical practice, why the consciousness of individual human beings should not transcend and take power over the self-constituting of society. There is no reason why the self-knowing and self-surpassing power of human consciousness should not reassert its authority over the power of society, even at the level of the society of all humanity.

Our (post-Freudian) understanding of the unconscious vector of human consciousness helps us to understand better both the internal limits on the freedom of the human mind and its apparently boundless creative energy. We surprise ourselves in what we think and in what we feel, and hence in what we do and what others do to us. In Pascal's hallowed formula, the heart has its reasons of which reason knows nothing.[14] In addition to the imperious phylogenic instincts that we attribute to our physiology, our minds contain ontogenic causes that are aspects not of the brain but of the mind. But unconscious consciousness is only one layer of the deep structure of our minds. The species-characteristic of the self-ordering rationality of the mind is as great and as strange and as powerful a wonder as its self-surprising anomie. And it is a wonder shared by the rational mind of all human beings and the public mind of the society of all humanity.

Our (post-Wittgensteinian) understanding of the symbolic vector of human consciousness helps us to understand better both the inherent limits and hazards of our capacity to communicate within ourselves and with others and also our apparently boundless capacity to construct a form of reality that is neither merely a photograph nor merely a dream, the second reality in which we live and die as thinking animals. In becoming conscious of language as a nontransparent, nonneutral, reflexive medium, we are able also to see better the role that truth and value play as ultimate structural axes in the making of human reality. The views of Richard Rorty and of many others notwithstanding, truth and value are neither delusions nor merely metaphors but existential ideas and ideals. Within the human mind-world, including the mind-world of the society of all humanity, they are what space and time are for the mind's idea of the physical world, that is, the necessary conceptual conditions of knowing and acting.[15]

It is for this reason that the two New Enlightenment projects are inseparable. The public mind of society and the private mind of the human individual are extensions of each other. Social evil arises at the intersection of the two, where the freedom of the mind and the freedom of the will of human individuals meets the freedom of the public mind and the freedom of the general will of society, and where the three vectors of human consciousness are integrated. It is at the same intersection that our new purposive pursuit of social good and of a better form of human society must originate. Transnational justice is not possible except as an ideal of a self-conscious society of all humanity.

The Misconceiving of Democracy

A school of thought that has come to be associated with the name of Immanuel Kant (1724–1804) sees the only reasonable prospect of a peaceful and progressive international society in a natural confederalizing tendency among "states" (that is, societies that are under the management of "governments") that have transformed themselves internally into constitutional republics. Constitutionalism would be universalized through the constitutionalizing of particular state-societies.[16]

It might be thought that our post-Kantian experience over the last two centuries had cast terminal doubt on such an idea, but Kant's modest but optimistic prophecy

has been revived in recent years in three forms of assertion: (1) that constitutionally reformed states have a natural tendency to recognize each other as members of an international society of states; (2) that there is a low-to-zero probability that "democratic" states will go to war with each other; (3) that democratic societies are in some sense fulfilled in their social development, thus removing a perennial cause of international conflict (an "end of history" view). At a more general level and in a less precise form, the Kantian view underlies the post-1989 triumphalism of the advocates of democracy-capitalism and the apologists of globalization.

Such naive or self-interested evangelism overlooks or underestimates four things.

1. The imperfection of democracy, especially as allied with capitalism, is not confined to the psychic totalitarianism that has been considered above. There are diseases of advanced democracy-capitalism of which we have much painful experience and that were foreseen by its early observers (including Jefferson, Mill, and de Tocqueville): the tyranny of the majority, the tyranny of minorities (factions and special interests), the corruption of politics (by money and crude populism), the devaluation of its own high values (liberty as a residue left by social regulation, equality as institutionalized inequality, fraternity as institutionalized selfishness), the devaluation of cultural values (antielitism, anti-intellectualism, antiexceptionalism), the devaluation of spiritual values (the triumph of materialism, the commodification of ideas, cultural products, and education), the depersonalizing of the human person. If the present condition of democratic-capitalist societies is the end of the history of human self-evolving, it is a tragic, if not farcical, end to the long experiment of human biological evolution. Democracy-capitalism is not a single or simple phenomenon. Democratic institutions are organic in character. They take on the characteristics of the ground in which they are planted. They take effect in a given society in a way that is specific to that society, a unique product of the physical characteristics, the history, the

psychic ethos of that society, and its relationship to other societies. Like sects within religions, different democratic-capitalist orthodoxies may well see their supposed fellow travellers as their most formidable adversaries.

2. Like religious evangelism, the negligent imposition of institutional elements of democracy-capitalism on societies whose specific situation is thereby violated can lead to a gross form of social evil that will dominate the twenty-first century as it dominated the last decades of the twentieth century, namely *fraudulent democracy*. In such societies, recent experience suggests that democracy-capitalism readily transforms itself into *plutocracy*, a form of internal colonialism in which the common interest of society is equated with the self-interest of an arrogant, greedy, and criminal ruling clan, associated by birth or marriage or dependency, in which the common wealth of society is simply stolen by the plutocratic oligarchy, a society in which a class of selfish *nouveaux riches* sustains the system with obsequious cynicism and over which some of the superficialities of democracy spread a veneer of worthless legitimacy. There are, and will continue to be, many such societies around the world.

3. There are also countless subordinate human societies other than those managed by "governments," in particular industrial and commercial corporations with worldwide interests.

4. The problem of socializing the competitive but mutually dependent coexistence of human societies of all kinds far exceeds the capacity of the piecemeal aggregating of the self-interest of all such societies or the potentiality of a dream-world of self-ordering "democracies."

Law and Freedom

The misconceiving of democracy makes necessary its reconceiving. Especially over the last two centuries, we have learned that the transformatory effect of democracy is not merely a matter of institutions or of a particular distribution of social power. The central ideal of democracy is better expressed as *nomocracy*, the rule of *nomos* (the law), rather than merely the rule of those who claim to represent the people (*demos*).

The two daring core paradoxes of the democratic ideal—freedom under law and self-government—rest upon the strange fact that law, which is the archetypal means of social constraint, is also our most reliable means of social liberation. Law, in the very act of distributing social power in the form of legal power, also sets the legal limits of social power. Law, with its own inherent substantive and procedural values, is also the enacting of society's high values, including its very high values of justice and social justice, whose function is to control the substantive and procedural content of law.

The hallowed ideal characteristics of democracy are all better seen as ingenious methods for using law to restrain law. *Constitutionalism* is law about law, law above law, law before law. *Separation of powers* is a division of legal labor, the interdependence of legal power. *Fundamental rights* are legal limits on the power of law in the name of society's highest values. *Representation* is the legal repersonifying of the holders of public realm powers, that is, legal powers to be exercised in the public interest. *Accountability* is the extrajudicial control of the public interest aspect of public realm legal powers, with elections as a form of legally imposed social judgment. The *rule of law* is the judicial control of the legal terms and conditions of all public realm powers. The *open society* is the legally imposed social inclusion of all citizens by means of legally organized education and legally protected social communication and other forms of social participation. (If we regard democracy and capitalism as inseparable social phenomena, with *economic freedom* as an eighth ideal characteristic of democracy-capitalism, then it is a wholly artificial freedom that is the integrated product of every kind of law—international, constitutional, public, civil, criminal.)[17]

Since 1945, a vast international public realm has been formed, as if by stealth, through the piecemeal cooperation of governments, determining the lives of all human beings everywhere. This largely unaccountable concentration of social power coexists with the largely unaccountable social power of industrial and commercial corporations with worldwide interests, both of them subject only to the intermittent influence of so-called nongovernmental organizations whose representative authority may be as dubious as that of many governments. The need is apparent and urgent for a presence of the nomocratic ideal at the level of international society, acting as a sanctioning and enforcing instrument of universal ideals of justice and social justice. But the full paradoxical power of law can only operate at the level of all humanity within an international society whose high values it enacts, including the values of justice and social justice.

The Eunomian Project

There cannot be law without society or society without law. There cannot be good law except in a good society. As a third thing, produced by and producing society's ideas, produced by and producing the everyday exercise of social power, law cannot be separated from the self-constituting of a given society.

The polemical and practical purpose of the project of reconceiving human society is to show that international society—the society of all humanity and all societies—need not be the crazy and archaic intergovernmental unsociety that has characterized international relations throughout this millennium, the archaism that has led in this century to more than one hundred million unnecessary deaths and to unspeakable human suffering caused by holders of public power, and unspeakable human suffering caused by the disgraceful inequality of social and economic development throughout the world, a structural injustice that is being perpetuated by the archaic and inhuman international system. In such an unsociety, international law was liable to be seen as little more than "a science which teaches princes to what extent they may violate justice without injuring (*sans choquer*) their own interests." [18]

As the emerging international society of the new century comes to be understood as a society, by human beings in general and by holders of public realm social power in particular, international law will at last be enabled to act at the global level as an effective agent of human self-empowering and self-perfecting through the distribution of social power in the common interest of society and in accordance with society's high values. [19] International society will be seen as a society of all human beings and all subordinate societies, not merely a coagulation of government-managed societies known as "states." And the common interest of society, which it is law's task to enact and then to disaggregate into the legal relations that determine the willing and acting of actual human beings and actual human societies, will be the common interest of all humanity, the common interest of the human species as one species among many in a habitat shared by all. [20]

The Eutopian Project

Prior to law is politics, the struggle to determine society's values and purposes and the struggle to take control over the making and the implementation of the law that actualizes its values and purposes. It follows that humanity will not socialize itself effectively under law until international society has its own form of politics and its own means of determining its own values and purposes.

The New Enlightenment project of reconceiving the human mind thus includes the task of reconceiving the way in which we form our ideas, our values, and our purposes. We must overcome our self-imposed poverty of philosophy and resume the great tradition of self-transcending philosophy that ended with strange abruptness sometime in the late nineteenth century, like a majestic highway suddenly coming to an end for no evident reason in the middle of nowhere. We live in the human reality made by the perennial philosophical tradition, which gave us the social and mental structures that we take for granted, but we have perversely deprived ourselves of the possibility of renewing and surpassing that tradition.

We need a new intellectual discipline—*international philosophy*—in which minds from all traditions and cultures across the world can contribute to a reunderstanding of what it is to be a thinking being. What am I? asked René Descartes—a thinking thing. A thing, yes. But a thing that thinks. And a thing that thinks about its thinking. [21] The capacity of human consciousness that makes possible our collective self-reconceiving is philosophy—the mind thinking about itself, the mind creating itself as it thinks about itself, reflexive thought, the self-consciousness of human reality. Philosophy is to humanism what mathematics is to scientism, if by humanism we mean the study of humanity as a set of mental phenomena, and by scientism we mean the study of the universe, including humanity, as a set of physical (putatively non-mind) phenomena. Philosophy and mathematics, respectively, are the conditions of the possibility of humanism and scientism.

The natural sciences cannot be instruments of human self-redeeming. They may tell us what we are; they cannot tell us what we might choose to be. No doubt physiology, genetics, and microbiology will explain the working of the human brain and the nervous system. The views of Daniel Dennett and of many others notwithstanding, the natural sciences will never explain the working of human consciousness. The capacity of the mind infinitely exceeds the capacity of the brain.[22]

We know that our bodies are conditioned and determined by the physical processes of the material world. And yet we cannot escape the anguish and the excitement of deciding, from moment to moment, what to *do* next. We know that our minds are conditioned and determined by the physical processes of the brain and the nervous system. And yet we cannot escape the anguish and the excitement of deciding, from moment to moment, what to *think* next.

As a first great task for international philosophy, we must find ways to explain to ourselves and to begin to overcome our spiritual confusion and our self-inflicted unhappiness. Why are we not more happy when we have the wonderful power to make our own world and to make our own reality? We will find ways to explain to ourselves and to begin to overcome evil in all its forms, including, above all, social evil.

Why do we persist in choosing to do evil, individually and as societies, when we have the wonderful power to choose to do good? To understand this we have to find a way of understanding the close correlation between the self-constituting of the private mind—our personality—and the self-constituting of the public mind—the constitution of a society. The self-constituting of the personality of a human being and the self-constituting of a human society are similar and connected processes. And

that is, of course, because the private mind of the human being and the public mind of society are extensions of each other.

The second great task and challenge for international philosophy in the next century is to think the ideal of the human future. The idea of the ideal has been the wonderful instrument of human self-evolving and self-perfecting. We can imagine and constantly reimagine the ideal as a dialectical negation of the actual, which nevertheless affirms a potentiality of the actual. The ideal is the perfectibility of the actual. And we can constantly concretize the ideal in ideas that have the form of truth and value. And, in that form, the ideal can become the controlling principle of our action, our personal and social action, giving us the self-transcending power to overcome both social totalitarianism and social evil at every level of social organization from the village to the international society of all humanity. The ideal can determine the way in which we understand our potentiality for self-perfecting. It can then condition our choice among our potentialities, the potentialities that we choose to actualize, as individuals and as societies. The ideal is the secret of human self-perfecting.[23]

A Revolution in the Mind

In dialectical opposition to a human reality dominated by war, social injustice, the corruption of public power, alienation, and money, we must establish a human reality dominated by the ideal, that is, by our intimate participation in the natural world, by our instinctive love of justice, truth, beauty, and goodness; a human reality dominated by the wonder and enthusiasm and joy that are so natural to us and by a species quality that we might call *grace*—the psychic antientropic binding force that holds together the personality of a happy human being and the constitution of a good society. Grace is the gravity of the better worlds that the human mind creates.

In Samuel Beckett's *Waiting for Godot,* a mysterious Boy comes with an equivocal message. "Mr. Godot told me to tell you he won't come this evening but surely tomorrow." The play ends with Vladimir saying: "Shall we go?" Estragon replies: "Yes, let's go." And then there is the final stage direction: *They do not move.*[24]

To remake humanity, we must move. We cannot wait for Mr. Godot, whether Godot is the capitalist market, the globalizing of democracy, the wonder working of natural science and human science, or natural human progress. Somehow, in the new century and the new millennium, humanity has to find the courage to believe in its own self-transforming potentiality, its unlimited capacity for self-evolving and self-perfecting.

Humanity is its own recreator. This is the truth that our predecessors rediscovered during the course of this last millennium, which they rediscovered so intelligently and so courageously. Both New Enlightenment projects—new society and new mind—are a call to humanity to be intelligent and courageous once again, yet again, before it is too late. It is a call to revolution, a revolution not in the streets but in the mind.

Vindicating the Rule of Law:
Balancing Competing Demands for Justice

Sandra Day O'Connor

I.

The rule of law is fundamental to the existence of a free society. It secures our liberty and separates civilization from anarchy. As Montesquieu wrote in 1745, "Liberty is the right to do anything which the law permits, [for] if a citizen were able to do what the law forbids, he would no longer have liberty since all other citizens would have the same ability."[2] To maintain the rule of law, accountability for transgressions against the law is essential.

Consequently, the question arises as to what accountability means. Generally, in the domestic context, we think of accountability in terms of imposing criminal sanctions on those who violate the law. This idea is premised on the concept of the social contract: By consenting to be part of the state, the individual implicitly agrees that should she violate the rules of society by breaking the law, the state has the power to impose punishment.[3] In this context, the rule of law is vindicated, not only by punishing the wrongdoer, but also by confirming to society that such behavior will not be tolerated. One function of criminal punishment, and therefore of "accountability," is to "maintain . . . the cohesion of society" by reaffirming the bounds of acceptable human behavior.[4]

Similarly, the international community also has an interest in vindicating the norms of "international society" by prosecuting and punishing those who transgress basic standards of human behavior. Some transgressions, such as piracy, genocide,[5] and war crimes,[6] are so universally condemned that any nation-state can exercise its authority to prosecute and punish the offenders,[7] thus vindicating the rule of the law of nations.

As several scholars have pointed out, however, this relatively straightforward description of "accountability" becomes more complicated in certain contexts.[8] For example, the social contract model breaks down in states that are in transition from one regime to another, particularly where the transition is from an authoritarian state to a democratic state. In those circumstances, where the previous regime itself may have been responsible for committing serious crimes, the new state must balance the need to prosecute and punish those responsible against the need to nurture the fragile emerging democracy by forgoing punishment. "Accountability" for crimes in these situations may focus more on acknowledgement of wrongdoing and documenting the abuses rather than on punishing specific individuals. Particularly when those who committed the abuses are still on the scene or in some cases even sharing power with the new regime, the need to stabilize the democratic regime first in the short run may counsel against aggressive efforts to prosecute the perpetrators and perhaps risk a renewed cycle of retribution.[9]

The twentieth century witnessed mass violence and atrocity with depressing frequency. From the massacre of Armenians in 1915 and the Holocaust of World War II to the killing fields of Cambodia, Bosnia, and Rwanda, war crimes, state-sponsored torture, and even genocide have tested our ability to maintain the rule of law. Not surprisingly, many situations involving internal strife and collective violence culminate in a change of regime. And the collapse of totalitarian regimes is often accompanied by mass violence. More surprisingly, perhaps, in many such situations, "less oppressive, even democratic regimes [have] emerged, for example, in Argentina, Brazil, Poland, reunified Germany, and South Africa."[10] As Martha Minow points out, these states in particular face difficult questions about how best to address the abuses of a previous regime. To the extent that war crimes, mass atrocities, and genocide most seriously threaten the rule of law, the tension between vindicating international norms of human behavior through prosecution and punishment of the perpetrators, and the countervailing national sovereignty interest in forgoing punishment, is at its height when such crimes are involved.

These tensions are unlikely to ease in the near future. As we enter the millennium, the world is both coming together and coming apart. That is, we are faced with increasing globalization of communications, transportation, economies, and even of politics and law. In this context, there is an increasing trend toward using international institutions to pursue accountability through prosecution of certain crimes, for example, through the proposed International Criminal Court (ICC).[11] At the same time, we are faced with increasing fragmentation and transformation of many nation-states with the proliferation of newly independent states in Eastern Europe and the many emerging democracies in other parts of the world.[12] Finding the best way for these emerging democracies to achieve accountability for war crimes and even genocide perpetrated by the previous regime is an enormous challenge. There can be no "one-size fits all" solution to this problem.[13] But by examining the available options, as well as some of the experiences to date with the exercise of these options, we may be able to develop a framework to help decide how best to vindicate the rule of law in each situation.

II.

The International Approach: Prosecution and Punishment

Traditionally, the principles of territoriality and nationality governed a state's ability to exercise its authority to apply its law in a transnational context. That is, a state had jurisdiction to exercise its authority within its territory and with respect to its nationals abroad.[14] Some transgressions, however, so offend universal norms of human behavior that they are in effect crimes against the law of nations, and international law allows any state to prosecute the perpetrators regardless of where the crime occurred or the nationalities of the victim and offender. Historically, this doctrine of universal jurisdiction developed to combat piracy on the high seas; pirates were considered the "enemies of all people" for their "particularly heinous and wicked acts." [15]

The scope of universal jurisdiction expanded after World War II, following the International Military Tribunal's reliance on universal jurisdiction principles to define and punish war crimes and crimes against humanity.[16] For example, the 1948 Convention on the Prevention and Punishment of the Crime of Genocide defines genocide as acts committed with the "intent to destroy, in whole or in part, a national, ethnical, racial, or religious group,"[17] and it obligates state parties to prosecute those accused of genocide.[18] Several other United Nations conventions set forth additional offenses for which universal jurisdiction exists. The four Geneva Conventions of 1949, which apply during international armed conflict, define certain offenses as "grave breaches," including "willful killing, torture or inhumane treatment, including biological experiments" or "willfully causing great suffering or serious injury to body or health."[19] State parties are obligated under the Geneva Conventions to prosecute or extradite the offenders.[20] Other offenses for which state parties have an obligation to prosecute or extradite the offender include certain human rights violations, such as torture,[21] and certain acts of terrorism, such as hostage taking[22] and the hijacking and sabotage of aircraft.[23]

To respond to genocide or mass atrocity "with legal prosecutions is to embrace the rule of law." [24] At the end of World War II, Stalin, and initially the British foreign office, advocated summary execution of Nazi leaders.[25] The decision to pursue formal trials instead was an effort to achieve true justice—to affirm that human behavior could be judged based on preexisting standards, and that with due process the guilty could be singled out and held accountable for their crimes without resorting to vengeance.[26] As Justice Jackson noted in his opening statement at the Nuremberg trials,

[t]he wrongs we seek to condemn and punish have been so calculated, so malignant and so devastating, that civilization cannot tolerate their being ignored because it cannot survive their being repeated. That four great nations, flushed with victory and stung with injury stay the hand of vengeance and voluntarily submit their captive enemies to the judgment of the law is one of the most significant tributes that Power has ever paid to Reason.[27]

One legacy of Nuremberg is the United Nations's establishment of international criminal tribunals for the former Yugoslavia and for Rwanda. The scope of the atrocities committed in the former Yugoslavia since war began there in early 1992 is difficult to fathom. Women and girls were systematically raped; noncombatants were tortured, starved, and murdered. The death toll exceeds 200,000 civilians and soldiers.[28] Responding to these widespread violations of international law, the United Nations Security Council established a commission of experts to study the matter; the commission recommended the creation of an ad hoc international tribunal.[29] In February 1993, the Security Council declared that the violations of international law in the former Yugoslavia constituted a threat to international peace and security, and on May 25, 1993 the Security Council, acting under Chapter VII of the Charter of the United Nations, unanimously adopted the proposed statute creating the International Criminal Tribunal for the Former Yugoslavia.[30] The tribunal has jurisdiction over war crimes, genocide, and other crimes against humanity.[31]

The process for establishing the International Criminal Tribunal for Rwanda closely resembled that for Yugoslavia. Rwanda had been embroiled in civil conflict between rival ethnic groups for several years, and in April 1994 the country "plunged into . . . genocidal violence that left between 500,000 and 1,000,000 Rwandans dead."[32] Again, the United Nations Security Council established a commission of experts to study the situation. The report concluded that the Hutus had "committed planned and systematic genocide against

the Tutsi ethnic group."[33] Although both groups were found to have committed atrocities, the commission of experts was unable to establish whether the Tutsis had committed genocidal acts against the Hutus with the requisite genocidal intent.[34] Acting under Chapter VII of the Charter, the statute for the International Criminal Tribunal for Rwanda was adopted in November 1994.[35] Although the structure of the Rwanda tribunal was similar to that for Yugoslavia, its jurisdiction differed in important respects. The tribunal's jurisdiction extends to genocide, war crimes, and crimes against humanity. Unlike the Yugoslavia tribunal, however, which has jurisdiction only over crimes committed in international or internal armed conflict, the Rwanda statute does not explicitly require that the crimes be committed during wartime.[36] At the same time, jurisdiction only extends to those crimes committed within the territory of Rwanda or by Rwandan nationals in neighboring states during 1994.[37]

Although the very existence of the tribunals sends a powerful message that those who commit atrocities will be held accountable for their actions under the law, these tribunals have faced serious problems in turning that message into reality. The number of prosecutions has been limited, and in the former Yugoslavia most of the indicted are still at liberty.[38] Several factors may explain these difficulties. Unlike the Nuremberg and Tokyo trials, which took place following World War II in the context of total military victory, with Allied forces physically occupying Germany and Japan, the situation in the former Yugoslavia and Rwanda is much different. Simply apprehending indicted and suspected war criminals in the former Yugoslavia, some of whom remain in power, has proven to be an enormous challenge, and aggressive pursuit of these individuals risks upsetting the fragile peace.[39] The opposite problem is confronted in Rwanda—the new government of Rwanda, headed by a Tutsi, arrested and jailed over 100,000 Hutus and charged them with genocide and mass murder.[40]

Aside from these logistical difficulties, pursuing accountability for genocide and other mass crimes through formal legal process under the auspices of international institutions is subject to other criticisms. The two most serious are charges of politicization and selectivity.[41] Fairness and "scrupulous lawfulness" is essential if international tribunals are to uphold the rule of law.[42] But the very international consensus needed to establish the tribunal may involve political pressures and compromises that undermine such impartiality.[43]

A more fundamental criticism is that of selective prosecution. The idea of individual criminal responsibility is fundamental to our notions of the rule of law.[44] In the context of mass atrocities, the "emphasis on individual responsibility offers an avenue away from the cycles of blame that lead to revenge, recrimination, and ethnic and national conflicts."[45] And the notion that individuals can bear responsibility for mass atrocities also reflects the idea that individuals "owe duties to international norms that transcend national obligations."[46] At the same time, assigning individual responsibility for mass atrocities is difficult, and it is almost inevitable that many of those responsible will escape punishment. Not only does such selectivity diminish the sense that the offenders have been called to account for their actions, but it also diminishes the sense of fairness in the proceedings, undermining the very idea that the prosecution is upholding the rule of law.

Also, although the focus at the Nuremberg and Tokyo trials (as well as at the tribunals for Yugoslavia and Rwanda) was to identify the guilty and to hold them individually responsible for their actions, an important function of the trials is the *appearance* of justice being done. The symbolic value of seeing the offenders punished contributes to the sense that justice has been done—that the guilty have been held accountable. For example, Hermann Goering, sentenced to death by hanging at Nuremberg, committed suicide in his prison cell shortly before the sentence was to be carried out. After the other ten condemned Nazi leaders had been hanged, Goering's corpse was brought into the execution chamber to "carry out the sentence at least in symbol." [47]

A related goal of prosecution is simply to document the truth of what happened. As Justice Breyer noted in his address "Crimes Against Humanity," given to mark Yom Hashoah (the Day of Remembrance), one of the most important achievements of the Nuremberg trials was the creation of a vast evidentiary record, cataloging Nazi crimes "with such authenticity and in such detail that there can be no responsible denial of these crimes in the future and no tradition of martyrdom of the Nazi

leaders can arise among informed people."[48] In this sense, the trials were "as much historical as legal."[49] This suggests that punishing individual perpetrators for their individual crimes is not the sole function of accountability in these proceedings. In fact, it is doubtful that punishment alone is enough for these crimes. As Hannah Arendt noted, the Nazi crimes "explode the limits of the law; . . . [f]or these crimes, no punishment is severe enough." The "guilt oversteps and shatters all legal systems."[50] While it may be true that we cannot adequately punish these crimes, we can ensure that we do not forget such crimes, and holding a trial and imposing punishment contributes to that memory. Collective memory is part of accountability.

The importance of documenting such crimes for history indicates that there may be other avenues, aside from punishment, that may equally serve this function of accountability. And when a country is emerging from a totalitarian regime marked by criminal abuses, the national sovereignty interests in pursuing a peaceful transition to a democratic regime may trump that state's interest in holding the perpetrators accountable for their actions through criminal prosecutions. Accordingly, some states have pursued other paths to accountability, notably through truth and reconciliation committees.

National Sovereignty Approach

General grants of amnesty for war crimes or other atrocities are not uncommon as a means to secure a peaceful transfer of power. For example, the 1962 Evian Agreement ending the war between France and Algeria provided a blanket amnesty for war criminals on both sides.[51] Similarly, India and Bangladesh agreed to grant amnesty to Pakistani soldiers at the close of the Bangladesh war in 1971.[52] In recent years there has been an increasing trend toward granting amnesty through the use of truth and reconciliation commissions, particularly within those states transitioning from totalitarian to democratic regimes. Although "truth commissions" may vary widely from state to state, they generally share several characteristics. The commission often consists of a panel that investigates human rights abuses or crimes during a specific time period and produces a report on such crimes at the conclusion of its investigation.[53] General amnesties may be granted in conjunction with the commission's report, or amnesty may be granted individually only for those individuals who acknowledge their offenses.[54]

A grant of amnesty is susceptible to the charge that it is really a grant of impunity; a charge that diminishes our sense that justice is being served. In Brazil, for example, the armed forces granted themselves amnesty before ceding power in 1979.[55] In Argentina, a democratically elected government was established in 1983 with the election of Raul Alfonsin. Although the members of the outgoing military junta had granted themselves amnesty prior to stepping down, President Alfonsin refused to recognize the amnesty and instead established a commission to investigate the crimes of the previous regime, which included assassinations and forced disappearances.[56] Efforts to prosecute those identified in the commission's report were abandoned, however, in the wake of military rebellion against the civilian government, with Alfonsin's successor ultimately pardoning the military leaders.[57]

Amnesty does not necessarily undermine accountability, however. South Africa, drawing on the experience of countries such as Argentina, established a Truth and Reconciliation Commission that provides only conditional grants of amnesty.[58] The Preamble to the Reconciliation Act, which established the Truth and Reconciliation Commission, identifies its goals as "reconciliation, amnesty, reparation, and the search for truth."[59] The commission considers "gross violations of human rights," which include "the killing, abduction, torture or severe ill-treatment of any person."[60] These "gross violations of human rights" are limited to acts that were crimes under the apartheid legal system, and liability extends not only to acts committed by the apartheid regime, but also to acts committed by members of liberation movements such as the African National Congress.[61] Although the negotiated end to apartheid included the agreement that some form of amnesty would be available for the outgoing leaders in return for a peaceful transfer to a fully democratic society, blanket amnesties were not given.[62] Instead, conditional grants of amnesty are given to those who acknowledge their crimes by providing complete and truthful testimony regarding their

actions.[63] The commission investigates the testimony and decides whether to grant the application for amnesty. If amnesty is denied, prosecution can proceed.[64] Perpetrators whose crimes are deemed "disproportionately" heinous or not motivated by politics can also be denied amnesty.[65]

This process has several advantages. First, because the amnesties granted under this process are not designed to exculpate the state's own agents but instead to expose and acknowledge the crimes of a previous regime, the process promotes truth and accountability. Second, the focus on reconciliation and healing ensures that the process looks forward to strengthening the new democratic regime rather than looking backward toward retribution. Finally, the process signals a break with the past regime and can be used to build political legitimacy for the new regime.[66]

But just as there are limits to the effectiveness of punishments, there are limits to amnesty. The balance between vengeance and forgiveness is in many ways the balance between too much forgetting and too much remembering.[67] Blanket amnesties risk too soon forgetting the atrocities and thereby risking their repetition. Drawn out trials or truth commission investigations risk wallowing in the past and risking renewed cycles of violence and vengeance. As South Africa's justice minister noted, "we want to put the past behind us but we don't want to forget."[68] Despite the difficulties, the South African approach appears to effectively balance these two goals, encouraging public accountability without the destabilizing effects of a full-fledged trial.

III.

As described above, there are many practical problems, as well as legal and philosophical problems, with both the international approach and the national sovereignty approach to pursuing accountability for the crimes of a previous regime. Prosecution of the offenders, to the extent it holds the perpetrators individually responsible for their actions, would appear to best serve the traditional attributes of the rule of law—accountability, deterrence, and fairness. Forgoing punishment in return for acknowledgment of past crimes, therefore, would seem to be a poor way to vindicate the rule of law. But attempted prosecutions by emerging democratic states may undermine the rule of law in the long run if by prosecuting the offenders the fledgling democratic state loses its tenuous hold on power. As Voltaire said, "I was never ruined but twice: once when I lost a suit, and once when I won one."[69] Where the cost to an emerging democracy may be a slide back into totalitarianism or a renewed cycle of retribution and revenge, the cost of prosecution may outweigh the benefits.

How to balance these competing demands is a difficult question. As one scholar has noted, "[t]he instinct to balance justice, with its presumed prerequisite, truth and reconciliation, and its hoped for consequence, stability, . . . has haunted . . . many countries in the throes of transformation." [70] There is no right answer to which approach is the best way to secure the rule of law. Every situation will be different and will require the balancing of different factors.

There are some factors, however, that may help determine which approach is best in a given situation. First, acts of terrorism should be prosecuted, either by national courts or by international institutions under universal jurisdiction. Unlike the situation involving crimes committed by a previous regime or its agents, in which the successor regime has an interest in punishing the offenders but also has a countervailing interest in a peaceful transfer of power, there are no countervailing national sovereignty interests in "reconciliation" with terrorists.

Second, when atrocities or war crimes create large refugee flows across international borders, the effect on surrounding nations argues in favor of prosecution of the perpetrators, probably under international auspices. When armed conflict or other mass violence creates such refugee flows, the potential threat to international peace and security provides a legal basis for international action under Chapter VII of the Charter of the United Nations. This right to exercise legal authority is premised on the idea that the exercise of international authority is justified by the threat to the international community. And because the national sovereignty interests in reconciliation would not account for this international interest, the balance of the equities suggests that prosecution is the better approach.

On the other hand, where the above factors are not present and where prosecution would clearly undermine the peaceful transition to democracy, then the national sovereignty approach is appropriate. Although a blanket amnesty would not be appropriate because it could not achieve accountability in any meaningful sense, a conditional amnesty process similar to that used by South Africa may be appropriate. Acknowledgement of past crimes, combined with reconciliation, will likely result in a stronger democratic rule in the long run in such situations. Of course, in any given situation it will likely be difficult to determine whether, and to what extent, prosecution may undermine the peaceful transition to full democracy. One relevant criterion that may be helpful in determining whether to defer to national sovereignty interests, however, is whether the government in question respects popular will and the rule of law.

At a more general level, there are some parallels in other areas of the law that may shed some light on the factors that should be considered in evaluating this balance between international interests and countervailing national sovereignty interests. In our own system, under the political question doctrine, we recognize that in certain situations, often involving issues of international relations, prudential considerations may deny the judiciary its traditional role of conflict resolution. The rule of law is not threatened by deferring to the executive or legislative branch in these situations, rather, countervailing interests dictate that these questions be resolved by another branch. Similarly, the act of state doctrine, which can be characterized as an application of the political question doctrine to actions of foreign governments, reflects a recognition that under our constitutional system of government foreign policy is best left to the judgment of the political branches, without undue interference from the courts. This idea is not unlike the idea that the international community may choose to forgo prosecution of certain crimes under universal jurisdiction and instead defer to the domestic interests of the victim state in addressing the crimes of a previous regime.

Similarly, concepts of federalism can also provide analogies to this issue. Our "dual sovereignty" incorporates the idea that local control and accountability often vindicate political accountability better than central control. In this regard, the argument could be made that local states should have the flexibility to address transgressions of the law before the international community exercises universal jurisdiction. Of course, nation-states are not subordinate sovereigns as are states in the United States. When a nation-state fails or is incapable of addressing the crimes of a former or current regime, however, then the exercise of universal jurisdiction is more appropriate. Although the analogy to federalism is a loose one, the fundamental lessons of dialogue and mutual respect that we have learned from our federalist tradition could be put to good use in defining the relationship between national courts and the various international tribunals. As such, the idea of "the federalism of free nations" may best describe the proper relationship between domestic institutions and transnational tribunals.[71]

The interplay of international norms and national sovereignty interests raises other interesting and difficult issues. To this point we have been discussing how domestic interests may argue against prosecuting and punishing criminals in certain contexts even though international norms demand prosecution. In the context of the death penalty in the United States, we face the converse issue: National sovereignty interests in punishing certain types of murders are in tension with certain international norms disapproving of the death penalty.

Some members of the international community have criticized the United States for retaining the death penalty and, in particular, for its application to those under eighteen years of age on the ground that it is inconsistent with evolving international norms.[72] For example, the International Covenant on Civil and Political Rights (ICCPR) was adopted by the General Assembly on December 16, 1966.[73] Article 6(5) of the ICCPR provides that a "[s]entence of death shall not be imposed for crimes committed by persons below eighteen years of age and shall not be carried out on pregnant women."[74] Article 7 provides, *inter alia,* that "[n]o one shall be subjected to torture or to cruel, inhuman, or degrading treatment or punishment." Although the Senate ratified the ICCPR in 1992, it included a package of conditions in its resolution of ratification.[75] Those conditions included a declaration that the

ICCPR is not self-executing and a proposed reservation to Article 6(5), stating that the

> United States reserves the right, subject to its Constitutional constraints, to impose capital punishment on any person (other than a pregnant woman) duly convicted under existing or future laws permitting the imposition of capital punishment, including such punishment for crimes committed by persons below eighteen years of age.[76]

The United States also formulated a reservation to Article 7 of the ICCPR, stating that the

> United States considers itself bound by Article 7 to the extent that "cruel, inhuman, or degrading treatment or punishment" means the cruel and unusual treatment or punishment prohibited by the Fifth, Eighth, or Fourteenth Amendments to the Constitution.[77]

In *Stanford v. Kentucky,* a plurality of the United States Supreme Court concluded that imposing capital punishment on those who were sixteen or seventeen years of age at the time of the crime did not constitute "cruel and unusual punishment" within the meaning of the Eighth Amendment.[78] In determining whether such punishment was contrary to "evolving standards of decency that mark the progress of a maturing society,"[79] the plurality specifically rejected the idea that the Court would look to international norms or practices for insight into these "evolving standards of decency." Instead, the plurality "emphasize[d] that it is *American* conceptions of decency that are dispositive," noting that "[t]he practices of other nations . . . cannot serve to establish the first Eighth Amendment prerequisite, that the practice is accepted among our people."[80] Although in some circumstances international practices and norms may at least be relevant in evaluating evolving standards of decency,[81] the plurality's approach reflects the idea that in matters of domestic criminal law, the national sovereignty interests weigh more heavily in the balance than do international norms.

At the same time, in some of the oldest statements from the Court, we have observed that the laws of the

United States incorporate fundamental principles of the law of nations. In 1804, in *Murray v. The Charming Betsy*, Chief Justice Marshall stated that "an Act of Congress ought never to be construed to violate the law of nations if any other possible construction remains." [82] And in the famous case *The Paquette Habana*,[83] the Court stated that

> [i]nternational law is part of our law, and must be ascertained and administered by the courts of justice of appropriate jurisdiction. . . . For this purpose, where there is no treaty, and no controlling executive or legislative act or judicial decision, resort must be had to the customs and usages of civilized nations.

Our precedents demonstrate an attempt to strike a balance between the requirements of international law and respect for the judgment of the political branches in matters of foreign policy. It is obviously a delicate balance, and one that continues to be refined in the cases that require us to apply these doctrines.

IV.

"Where law ends, tyranny begins."[84] To preserve liberty, then, we must preserve the rule of law. To preserve the rule of law, we must hold those who violate it accountable. But holding these individuals "accountable" does not necessarily mean prosecution. There is tension between the international obligation to prosecute certain crimes and the countervailing interests of national sovereignty in choosing to pursue accountability through some combination of amnesty and public acknowledgment of the crimes. Neither approach will be appropriate for all situations; indeed, it is doubtful that there can be any adequate response to mass atrocities. But as T. S. Eliot cautioned, we cannot "try to escape from the darkness outside and within by dreaming of systems so perfect that no one will need to be good."[85] Instead, we must take the route that best vindicates the rule of law in each situation, pursuing justice while nurturing burgeoning democracies.

International Adjudication and U.S. Policy—Past, Present, and Future

Bruno Simma

Introduction: Sovereignty and International Adjudication

Never before in the history of international relations has international adjudication—understood as the legally binding settlement of international disputes by an impartial third party—been as intensive as today. International courts and tribunals are proliferating, and the caseload of some of these institutions appears to explode. The International Court of Justice (ICJ) currently has no less than twenty-four cases on its docket; the European Court of Human Rights is almost suffocated by the number of applications submitted to Strasbourg; the Court of the European Community in Luxembourg frequently renders decisions touching upon the very core of European Union (EU) member states' constitutional self-understanding; the International Criminal Tribunal for the Former Yugoslavia has dispelled earlier doubts about its relevance and effectiveness; the World Trade Organization (WTO) dispute settlement machinery is tackling trade controversies of the most profound nature. This list could be continued.

In a world of sovereign states, international adjudication is based on the consent of the state parties. If they cannot agree to entrust this role to a third party, it is left to the states themselves to "judge" the lawfulness of both their own behavior and that of others. Thus, auto-interpretation, and even auto-enforcement, is still the rule. Nevertheless states do agree, for specific subject matters and sometimes even in a more general way, to submit their disputes to legally binding settlement by third parties. As with any other decision of a dispute by a third party, such submission includes, of course, the risk to lose. What, then, makes sovereign states agree to third-party settlement and eventually implement decisions that are not to their advantage?

States will only refer a matter to third-party dispute settlement when they consider this to be in their interest. For instance, states may believe that they have the better legal arguments. Or, states may consider that a dispute is not worth the damage to their mutual relations in other respects or a resort to unfriendly or even violent means, with all the grave risks involved, including the uncertainty of the results that might by far exceed the uncertainty of the outcome of legal proceedings. Further, governments may believe that it will be easier for them to "sell" a negative outcome to their domestic audiences if it emanates from an outside body considered fair and legitimate. And, finally, as the Permanent Court of International Justice (PCIJ) emphasized in its very first judgment, "the right of entering into international engagements is an attribute of State sovereignty":[1] By instituting proceedings governed by international law or other rules recognized by all the parties involved, states do not renounce their sovereignty but rather exercise it. Also, in agreeing to third-party dispute settlement, states do not submit their freedom of action to an outside power but to a body composed of experts either selected by the parties or considered neutral. And this body will apply the very rules of international law that the states involved have agreed to or acquiesced in.

Of course, the specific characteristics of interstate relations imply specific methods of dispute settlement. For a long time, conciliation or arbitration were the only means available in this regard. As defined in Article 37 of the (I) Hague Convention for the Pacific Settlement of International Disputes of 1907,

> [i]nternational arbitration has for its object the settlement of disputes between States by judges of their own choice and on the basis of respect for law. Recourse to arbitration implies an engagement to submit in good faith to the award.

Standing courts developed in the course of the twentieth century only. They distinguish themselves from international arbitration by being organized and permanent, composed of judges elected according to the respective statute and not by the parties. They decide legal disputes between states on the basis of international law in force. But judicial bodies, such as the International Court of Justice or the International Tribunal for the Law of the Sea, also only possess jurisdiction with the consent of the parties, declared either generally or on an ad hoc basis. Of course, any abstract distinction between arbitral tribunals and courts remains subject to the specific rules of the institution concerned. Thus, before the International Court of Justice, parties to a dispute not having one of their nationals on the bench may each appoint a judge ad hoc (Article 31 of the statute); they may authorize the court to decide according to equity (*ex aequo et bono*) instead of international law (Article 38, paragraph 2 of the statute); or agree to bring their case before a chamber of the court, the members of which are determined by the court in consultation with the parties (Article 26, paragraph 2 of the statute; Article 17, paragraph 2 of the Rules of Court); thus introducing elements of arbitration into the court procedure. Or, a treaty may regulate arbitration in a way resembling court proceedings, as in the case of the panels and the Appellate Body of the WTO.

In order to assess the prospects of third-party adjudication at the dawn of the third millennium and the respective contribution of the United States, let me first review the history of international adjudication in three stages, at the turn of three centuries: First, at the foundational period both of the United States and of modern international arbitration, that is, at the end of the eighteenth century, second, at the time of the establishment of the first standing bodies for the adjudication of international disputes by the Hague Conferences of 1899 and 1907 and in the aftermath of the First and Second World Wars, and third, today, at the beginning of the new millennium, when the third-party settlement of international disputes appears to be thriving.

Such third-party adjudication of international disputes is an expression of both universal and American values—peace, justice, equality, and fairness. Therefore, it is not surprising that during most of its history the United States has been a faithful supporter, or even a pioneer, in the field of transnational justice realized by international adjudication. What is a cause for concern, however, is that this traditional support for international adjudication by the United States seems to be diminishing. Such a waning of support coincides with the emergence of the United States as the sole remaining superpower. However, it is precisely this status of the United States that renders its attitude toward the peaceful settlement of international disputes by legal means so decisive.

II. International Adjudication and United States Policy

Let me begin by tracing the history of modern international arbitration back to its origins two hundred years ago. At the end of the eighteenth century, third-party dispute settlement was in the very early stages. There existed some precedents, but states submitted their disputes to an outside body only very rarely. In addition, there were no, or very few, generally recognized rules on how dispute settlement by arbitral tribunals, commissions, or other ad hoc bodies was to proceed. There existed no standing body in this regard or a set of ready-made rules that states could use. In addition, the status of much of international law was unclear, and states had to rely more on custom than on written rules. Thus, the first task of parties to a dispute wanting to submit it to arbitration was the consensual establishment of such a body ad hoc and the drafting of the instrument prescribing its jurisdiction, competence, and the applicable rules of law.

The United States and International Adjudication Two Hundred Years Ago: The Jay Treaty and Its Aftermath

It is in the regard just described that the influence of the United States at the first two of the junctures dealt with here—the development of international adjudication at the turn of the centuries one hundred and two hundred years ago—has been so important. Indeed, the United States and modern international arbitration are more or less of the same age—and this is not merely incidental.

The origins of modern arbitration in the Jay Treaty

With the conclusion of the Jay Treaty in 1794, the young United States made a decisive step to rejuvenate an ancient practice. President George Washington himself had taken the initiative of resolving the differences, which had almost led to another war, with the former mother country through legal means. The first chief justice of the United States, John Jay, a former secretary of state, was the chief U.S. negotiator. The Jay Treaty, as the Treaty of Amity, Commerce and Navigation between Great Britain and the United States was to be called, was signed on November 19, 1794. Initiating a pattern that would become usual in the future, the U.S. Senate demanded some modifications of the treaty concerning West Indian trade. After Great Britain accepted this condition in an additional article, the instruments of ratification were exchanged on October 28, 1795, and the treaty became binding on both parties.

The Jay Treaty had a considerable influence on international law in several respects. In the present context, we are less concerned with its contribution to the practice of commercial agreements or to maritime law than with its provisions on binding settlement of disputes by arbitration. "Mixed Commissions" consisting of three or five members each—one or two named by the British Crown, one or two named by the president of the

United States with the advice and consent of the Senate, and one commissioner appointed by agreement of the others or by lot—were to decide, first, on the northeastern boundary of the United States with Canada (Article 5), second, on compensation claimed by British creditors for losses suffered during the American Revolution that they had been unable to recover due to restrictions in the law of some of the U.S. states, as well as compensation claimed by American citizens (Article 6), and, third, on claims by U.S. citizens for losses by reason of the illegal capture of their vessels during the Anglo-French War (Article 7). The claims of both American and British citizens were to be decided "according to Justice and Equity."

The decision on the northeastern boundary rendered on October 25, 1798,[2] was accepted by the parties. However, this could not prevent the outbreak of further disputes on the subject in the course of the nineteenth century. The commission dealing with the British claims was dissolved by U.S. secretary of state Pickering on February 2, 1799, after serious divisions between its members had occurred. By a convention concluded on January 8, 1802, Article 6 of the Jay Treaty was annulled. The convention determined that the United States was to pay a lump sum of £600,000 (at the time about U.S. $2,700,000) to cover the "confiscated debts." As to the third commission, it was able to fulfill its task only after the dispute concerning the second had been settled. It appears to have been more successful, awarding no less than $11,650,000 to U.S. citizens.

What were the motives for the United States to agree to such arbitration, even if the initial results were modest? The young republic established by a democratic revolution needed international recognition to deal with other states on an equal footing. It could not afford another war, and its trade depended on the recognition of its neutrality in the Anglo-French wars and the cessation of the seizure of American ships and cargoes by Great Britain. To submit to arbitration according to international rules based on the equality of the parties offered a great opportunity to be accepted and treated as equal. Another problem that could only be solved by international arbitration was the nonexecution by the states of the Union of the Treaty of Peace with Great Britain, which provided for the recovery of American debts by British subjects.[3] After the adoption of the new U.S. Constitution, which its Article VI, clause 2 had elevated treaties to the "supreme law of the land," this issue could be addressed with better chances of success. Lastly, the expanding United States more and more frequently incurred problems with its boundary to Canada, which could best be solved by arbitration.

In spite of its mixed record in the short term, the Jay Treaty is still considered a landmark in the development of modern international arbitration. All subsequent boundary disputes between the United States and the United Kingdom were decided by arbitration. In the words of a former president of the International Court of Justice, Sir Muhammad Zafrulla Khan, the Jay Treaty was

> the historical landmark from which the trend which was to lead to the establishment of a true international judicial system is usually dated.[4]

For the first time in history, the Jay Treaty established a procedure by which, even though both parties were involved in the establishment of an arbitral tribunal, an outcome was ensured by the appointment of an additional "neutral" member of the commissions. And it set a precedent to the effect that disputes could be decided by peaceful means and not by war, and yet that both parties could protect certain interests and those of their citizens.

The Alabama arbitration

In the decades that followed the United States was a party to some of the most important international arbitral awards. The most famous example, this time not involving a boundary dispute, is probably the *Alabama* arbitration, which in all likelihood prevented a war between the United States and Great Britain. After the Civil War, U.S.-British relations were extremely strained due to the indirect support that Britain had given to the Confederacy. In the words of John Bassett Moore:

> At no time since the year 1814 had the relations between the United States and Great Britain worn

so menacing an aspect as that which they assumed after the close of the civil war in the United States.[5]

One of the reasons for this tension was the alleged breach by Britain of the law of maritime neutrality in the American Civil War. The *Alabama* was a raider being built in Britain for the Confederacy. The British government had refused to intervene and prevent the ship from reaching a Confederate port as it was obliged by the law of neutrality, claiming that the representative of the Union had not provided sufficient proof for his allegations. When the London government finally decided to seize the ship, the *Alabama* had already left British waters. In the following years, the ship had a distinguished career interrupting the trade of the Union all over the oceans and sinking, burning, and ransoming close to seventy Union ships until it was finally sunk before the French coast off Cherbourg on June 19, 1864.

Concerning the U.S. claims to damages for the alleged British misconduct in the *Alabama* case and similar instances, the U.S. representative in London, Mr. Adams, declared the readiness of the United States to go to arbitration:

> I am directed to say there is no fair and equitable form of conventional arbitrament or reference to which they (the United States) will not be willing to submit.[6]

However, a first agreement to settle the conflict, the Johnson-Clarendon Convention, which provided for a mixed British-American commission, failed due to the refusal of the Senate to give its advice and consent to ratification.[7] This throws light on an important aspect of the American position vis-à-vis international adjudication: Since approval by the Senate is a necessary precondition for the conclusion of a treaty, no international court or arbitral tribunal can be established without the assent of democratically elected representatives and, thus, some measure of public support. On the other hand, at a time when foreign policy was still considered a prerogative of the executive in most countries, the rejection of a negotiated treaty or *compromis* on arbitration by the Senate was not easily understood abroad, even if, in the words of the instructions to the American representatives for the renegotiation of the Johnson-Clarendon Convention,

> the rejection of a treaty by the Senate of the United States implies no act of discourtesy to the government with which the treaty may have been negotiated.[8]

Finally, in the Treaty of Washington of May 8, 1871, the United States and Britain were able to agree on the establishment of an arbitral tribunal to settle the American claims. The treaty did not only provide for an arbitral tribunal but also determined the applicable law, particularly that relating to the duties of neutrals in maritime warfare.[9] Pursuant to Article VI of the treaty, the arbitral tribunal was to apply both those newly defined rules and the applicable principles of international law consistent with them.[10] This formula displays another element by which the parties ensure their control of the process and result of an arbitration: Not only do they choose the arbitrators, but they decide also on the procedure to be followed and the law to be applied. Thus, the parties may simply direct the arbitral tribunal to apply international law in force, but they may also decide to conclude a special agreement defining the legal principles to be applied. Sometimes, as in the *Alabama* arbitration, the state of international law on the matter may be in doubt. In that case, the parties may choose to first agree on the applicable legal principles and only leave the determination of the facts and the application to them of these principles to the arbitrators. Similarly, the *compromis* will determine the permissible claims and the extent of the jurisdiction. The tribunal will then be called upon to interpret it, but not to change it in any way.[11]

On September 14, 1872, with the Geneva church bells ringing, the tribunal decided that Great Britain had indeed failed the test of due diligence and awarded the United States a lump sum of $15,500,000 in gold.[12] The opening statement of the president of the tribunal, Count Sclopis, reads like an excellent job description of an arbitrator:

> [A]cting sometimes with the large perception of statesmen, sometimes with the scrutinizing eye of judges, and always with a profound sentiment of

equity and with absolute impartiality, thus to discharge its high duty of pacification as well as of justice to the two governments.[13]

And the American arbitrator, Mr. Adams, added:

> The arbitrators appear to me at least to have a duty to the parties before the tribunal to state their convictions of the exact truth without fear or favor.[14]

Indeed, what the award also showed was that the two arbitrators appointed by the parties had not always voted in favor of the propositions of their countries. The largest part of the award was adopted unanimously. On the other hand, the British arbitrator, Sir Alexander Cockburn, dissented from the most pertinent statement concerning the *Alabama* and refrained from signing the award.[15] But Britain, having more or less lost the case, paid the sum awarded to the United States in full.[16]

In addition to solving a crisis that could easily have led to another war, the *Alabama* award contributed considerably to the international law on the duties of neutrals and on international responsibility.[17] The International Court of Justice later cited it as proof of the general acceptance of the proposition that an arbitral tribunal has the right to decide on its own competence[18]—a rule of utmost importance in international arbitration.

Let me enumerate once more the common characteristics of arbitration as it had developed in the nineteenth century: Arbitral tribunals were constituted for a specific case only; their composition, the applicable law, and the procedure were to be determined by the parties. In most cases, however, arbitral tribunals were authorized to apply the pertinent rules of international law in force. The tribunal's award was to be final except if the tribunal overstepped its competence. In general, however, it is for the tribunal itself to determine the extent of its jurisdiction.

The United States and International Adjudication One Hundred Years Ago: The Hague Peace Conferences of 1899 and 1907 and Their Aftermath

Following the settlement of the *Alabama* dispute, arbitration as a means of resolving interstate disputes gained momentum. Arbitration clauses in international treaties both of the United States and of various European states became more and more frequent. Private international law associations, such as the Institut de Droit International and what was to become the International Law Association, drafted rules for arbitration. However, for all its success in the course of the nineteenth century, international arbitration still remained the exception rather than the rule in the settlement of international disputes. Constituting an arbitral tribunal anew in each new case, and providing it with all necessary provisions on applicable law and procedure, was a burdensome process.

The Hague Peace Conferences

The Hague Peace Conference of 1899 was convoked at the initiative of Russia and at the invitation of the Dutch government. It was to set up legal regimes on arms control and the law of armed conflict but also to draft rules on good offices, mediation, and voluntary arbitration. "[A]ll questions concerning the political relations of States," however, were to be excluded from the deliberations of the conference.[19]

The genesis of what was to become the Hague Convention for the Pacific Settlement of International Disputes was "not without drama."[20] The German delegation initially opposed any agreement on the subject. A joint mission of a German and a U.S. delegate to Berlin solved the impasse, under the condition that arbitration was not to become compulsory. Ultimately, the first Hague Convention of 1899 provided for three different mechanisms to be employed in the pacific settlement of disputes: good offices and mediation, a Commission of Inquiry, and, finally, the Permanent Court of International Arbitration.

Viewed realistically, this outcome was modest. First, the use of all these peaceful means was not compulsory, with the states' parties only pledging "to use their best efforts to ensure the pacific settlement of international differences."[21] As Article 16 of the 1899 Convention puts it:

In questions of a legal nature, and especially in the interpretation or application of International Conventions, arbitration is recognized by the Signatory

Powers as the most effective, and at the same time the most equitable, means of settling disputes which diplomacy has failed to settle.

Article 38 of the 1907 Convention for the Pacific Settlement of International Disputes—a revised version of the 1899 Convention—adds:

Consequently, it would be desirable that, in disputes about the above-mentioned questions, the contracting powers should, if the case arose, have recourse to arbitration, in so far as circumstances permit.

According to the rules of the convention, good offices and mediation do not include any third-party adjudication in the proper sense of the term.[22] A commission of inquiry may independently establish the facts of a case but not decide it in a manner binding on the parties.[23] Only arbitration would lead to a legally binding result.[24] As to the Permanent Court of Arbitration itself, it was neither permanent nor a court in the true sense of the term but consisted of little more than a list of arbitrators and a permanent secretariat. Nevertheless, the Hague Conference marked the beginning of the institutionalization of international adjudication.

It is not so much by virtue of what was *achieved* as rather by what was *begun* that the 1899 Hague Conference must be hailed as a pivotal event to international understanding and the ultimate source of The Hague's present claim as Judicial Capital of the World.[25]

The atmosphere of the time, in the heyday of state sovereignty, may best be illustrated by the provision in the 1899 and 1907 Hague Conventions that an offer of good offices or mediation "can never be regarded by one or the other of the parties in conflict as an unfriendly act."[26] If it were possible to regard the mere offer of nonbinding third-party involvement as an unfriendly intrusion, one may imagine how difficult it must have been to reach agreement on means settling disputes beyond an ad hoc agreement on every single step by the states involved. Nevertheless, the speedy ratification of the 1899 Hague Convention by all participating powers convincingly demonstrated a certain willingness to go ahead.

The second Hague Peace Conference of 1907, this time convened upon an initiative by the United States taken up by Russia and the Netherlands, introduced some modest improvements in the (1899) Convention for the Pacific Settlement of Disputes but again failed to provide for compulsory arbitration. Thirty-two states, among them the United States, were in favor of including it, but since the conference was to take its decisions according to the principle of unanimity, and Germany, Austria, and nine other states vigorously opposed compulsory arbitration, the project was abandoned. However, according to its Final Act, the conference was:

unanimous—

1. In admitting the principle of compulsory arbitration.
2. In declaring that certain disputes, in particular those relating to the interpretation and application of the provisions of international agreements, may be submitted to compulsory arbitration without any restriction.[27]

The project of a convention on the establishment of a truly permanent court of arbitral justice was recommended and annexed to the Final Act but not signed.

The U.S. position at the Hague Conferences

At the two Hague Conferences of 1899 and 1907, the establishment of a permanent international tribunal was one of the central concerns of the United States delegation. In the instructions to the American delegates to the first conference, the relevant passage reads:

The duty of sovereign states to promote international justice by all wise and effective means is only secondary to the fundamental necessity of preserving their own existence. . . . Nothing can secure for human government and for the authority of law which it represents so deep a respect and so firm a loyalty as the spectacle of sovereign and independent states, whose duty it is to prescribe the rule of justice

and impose penalties upon the lawless, bowing with reverence before the august supremacy of those principles of right which give to law its eternal foundation. . . . The long-continued and widespread interest among the people of the United States in the establishment of an international court . . . gives assurance that the proposal of a definite plan of procedure by this Government for the accomplishment of this end would express the desires and aspirations of this nation. The delegates are, therefore, enjoined to propose, at an opportune moment, the plan for an international tribunal . . . .[28]

Consequently, the United States introduced a project for a permanent international tribunal.[29] However, the American proposal did not foresee compulsory jurisdiction either. Due to German intervention, the final product of the conference left it to the discretion of the member states to decide when arbitration was actually to be employed but took the U.S. proposal into account by providing at least for a permanent secretariat.

Again, based on several U.S. proposals, the Final Act of the 1907 Conference recommended recourse to compulsory arbitration of disputes:

subject, however, to the condition that they do not involve either the vital interests or independence or honour of any of the said parties.

The United States abstained, however, from voting on the report of the commission dealing with the proposal because the U.S. delegation was disappointed about the failure of the convention to provide for compulsory arbitration:

and not because we are not in favor of the principle of obligatory arbitration, for that is what we have striven for from the beginning.[30]

As another U.S. delegate later observed in an article in the *American Journal of International Law:*

It is proper to say that the project was essentially an American project, although presented conjointly by

Germany and Great Britain, and the establishment of the court in the near future will be an American triumph.[31]

Due to the outbreak of World War I, a third Hague Peace Conference envisaged in the Final Act was never convened.

In spite of the shortcomings of the Hague Conferences, the reactions to their outcome were quite enthusiastic. In the words of the American secretary of state Elihu Root,

> the work of the Second Hague Conference . . . presents the greatest advance ever made at any single time toward the reasonable and peaceful regulation of international conduct, unless it be the advance made at The Hague Conference of 1899. . . . The achievements of the Conferences justify the belief that the world has entered upon an orderly process through which, step by step, . . . there may be continual progress toward making the practice of civilized nations conform to their peaceful professions.[32]

Nevertheless, the U.S. attitude was not free of contradiction. In spite of U.S. readiness to participate in a convention on the binding settlement of certain disputes, an American reservation maintaining the Monroe Doctrine[33] was a negative signpost for the project. Then, as today, no state was ready to submit its essential, vital interests to international third-party decisions.

Parliamentary control of international adjudication

At the beginning of the twentieth century the United States has already encountered certain difficulties in our area arising from the consequences in the foreign policy field of its specific form of democratic government. At a time when in Europe foreign policy was still considered a prerogative of the executive, the U.S. Senate was to give its advice and consent to every *compromis* (special agreement) submitting U.S. interests to third-party adjudication.

The Senate approved the ratification of various general treaties of arbitration with an amendment requir-

ing a separate treaty, again subject to its approval, for the establishment of a *compromis* in each specific case. Further, these treaties excluded, just like the U.S. proposal at the 1907 Hague Conference, matters affecting "the vital interests, the independence, or the honor of the two Contracting States."[34] In the words of Michael Dunne:

> The specific point to notice is the long history of the Senate requiring its own consent to diplomatic arbitrations and international judicial proceedings. . . . Under Presidents McKinley, Roosevelt, Taft, and Wilson any number of treaties were negotiated with foreign governments, only for the final text to carry a provision, proposed by the Executive or added by Senators, that a two-thirds vote would be needed to approve the exact terms of any particular proposal to arbitrate a dispute. . . . If indeed the United States had established a claim to being a world leader in the field of arbitration, the Senate had also shown a determination to retain its own prerogatives.[35]

Hence, a certain pattern becomes apparent in the American attitude to international adjudication: On the one hand there is undoubtedly a strong commitment toward the peaceful settlement of disputes by arbitration on the basis of international law; on the other, however, democratic control of these means by the legislature is considered necessary not only at the stage of the establishment of international bodies for the adjudication of disputes but also at the stage of the submission of specific cases to these institutions.

U.S. absence from international adjudication between the two world wars

A couple of decades later, after the First World War, the United States again came to the conclusion that one of the causes of this catastrophe had been the lack of international adjudication of disputes.

The first international body of a truly judicial character, the Permanent Court of International Justice (PCIJ), was based on American preparatory work, even if recent scholarship has rightly challenged the view that the PCIJ was exclusively of American design.[36] Part of the resentment by the United States against the Covenant of the League of Nations did not stem from hostility towards international adjudication but, on the opposite, from frustration regarding the League's political—as opposed to legal—approach to the settlement of disputes. In the words of Elihu Root, Theodore Roosevelt's secretary of state and winner of the Nobel Peace Prize in 1912 for his role in the establishment of the Permanent Court of Arbitration:

Nothing has been done to provide for the reestablishment and strengthening of a system of arbitration or judicial decision upon questions of legal right. Nothing has been done toward providing for the revision or development of international law. In these respects principles maintained by the United States without variation for half a century are still ignored, and we are left with a program which rests the hope of the whole world for future peace in a government of men, and not of laws, following the dictates of expediency, and not of right.[37]

The commission charged by the League of Nations Council to draft the statute of the future Permanent Court of International Justice did comprise an American expert, again Elihu Root, even though the U.S. Senate had earlier rejected the League's covenant. Whereas Root succeeded with a proposal concerning the election of judges, his attempt to have the PCIJ system embrace true compulsory jurisdiction failed. Ultimately, the jurisdiction of the PCIJ only comprised "all cases which the parties refer to it and all matters specially provided for in Treaties and Conventions in force" [38] (Article 36 of the Statute[39]). Acceptance of the jurisdiction of the PCIJ as compulsory ipso facto could be effected by a separate declaration left to the discretion of the parties—the so-called "Optional Clause" system that has been retained in the Statute of the International Court of Justice. An advisory capacity of the court at the request of the Council or the Assembly of the League was not included in the statute but was provided for by Article XIV of the League's covenant. This competence was an important reason for American abstinence from the court because it indicated to the opponents of the League the danger of indirect participation in the Geneva system. However,

the rejection by the Senate of the Covenant of the League of Nations on November 19, 1919, was in no way due to the covenant's provisions dealing with arbitration and the future Permanent Court of International Justice (Articles XIII and XIV). As to the statute of the court, the Senate voted on it as late as January 29, 1935. A previous U.S. ratification had not been accepted by the League because of five reservations entered together with it—one of them again preserving the Monroe Doctrine. With fifty-two ayes and thirty-six nays the approval of the statute fell seven votes short of the required two-thirds majority[40]—and this in spite of public opinion favoring American participation. The refusal by the Senate to consent to the ratification of the League's covenant as well as the Statute of the Permanent Court of International Justice certainly constituted one of the reasons for the ultimate failure of these institutions.

The rejection of the PCIJ statute had an element of tragedy in another way, too: At both Hague Conferences the United States had been an ardent supporter of a permanent international judicial body with a consensual basis of jurisdiction. At the very moment in which such an institution was finally established, the United States did not participate for fear of entanglement with the League through the back door. The American "coparents" of the court—most of them critics of the League such as Elihu Root, J. B. Scott, and the influential American judges at the court, John Bassett Moore and later Manley O. Hudson—were thus left out in the cold.[41] Perplexingly, some of the most fervent opponents of the League, such as Sen. William E. Borah of Idaho, supported the idea of an international court but only under the condition that it was to have compulsory jurisdiction. Thus, Senate Resolution 441 sponsored by Borah proposed:

that a judicial substitute for war should be created (or if existing in part, adapted and adjusted) in the form or nature of an international court, modeled on our Federal Supreme Court in its jurisdiction over controversies between our sovereign States, such court to possess affirmative jurisdiction to hear and decide all purely international controversies as defined by the code or arising under treaties, and to have the same power for the enforcement of its decrees as our Federal Supreme Court, namely, the respect of all enlightened nations for judgments resting upon open and fair investigations and impartial decisions and the compelling power of enlightened public opinion.[42]

Despite U.S. nonparticipation in its statute, the Permanent Court of International Justice displayed considerable American influence. For instance, due to the difficult relationship between great and small powers, one major stumbling block since the Hague Conferences had been the procedure for the election of the judges. A solution was finally found for the PCIJ in their joint appointment by the Council and the Assembly of the League, respectively the General Assembly and the Security Council of the United Nations. This construction was based on the American federal experience with the House and the Senate.[43] And even if the political process leading to the International Court of Justice a quarter of a century later was completely different from that of the League period—it was much more open to public scrutiny, and the administration worked closely with Congress to be assured of Senate approval of both the United Nations and the court—the result at the international level was surprisingly similar to the model of the Permanent Court of International Justice.

U.S. acceptance of the jurisdiction of the International Court of Justice and its limits

In 1945, U.S. participation in the United Nations and the International Court of Justice was never seriously in doubt; the vote in the Senate on both the UN Charter and the Statute of the International Court of Justice was seventy-six to two. Even the U.S. declaration of acceptance of compulsory jurisdiction received the approval of the Senate. However, the traditional reluctance of the Senate to accept international adjudication in any general and abstract way again came to the fore. The Connally amendment excluded from compulsory adjudication all disputes "with regard to matters which are essentially within the domestic jurisdiction of the United States of America as determined by the United States of America."[44] Even though the ICJ apparently accepted a similar "self-judging reservation" in the *Norwegian Loans* case without, however, expressly ruling on the admissibility of

such a reservation (violently opposed by two of its members),[45] the United States declined to use the Connally reservation in the *Nicaragua* case, thus staying in line with its insistence in another case that it:

> does not consider that reservation (b) [the Connally Amendment, B.S.] authorizes or empowers this Government . . . to make an arbitrary determination that a particular matter is domestic, when it is evidently one of international concern and has been so treated by the parties.[46]

Indeed, it is evident that the mining and blockade of ports in Nicaragua and the support for the contras were not of a domestic character.

Another reservation, the Vandenberg amendment, excluded from compulsory jurisdiction "disputes arising under a multilateral treaty, unless (1) all parties to the Treaty affected by the decision are also parties to the case before the Court, or (2) the United States of America specifically agrees to jurisdiction."[47] The precise meaning of this reservation was subject to extensive debate in the *Nicaragua* judgments of the court, which eventually confirmed the validity of the reservation but accepted jurisdiction on other grounds.[48]

Be that as it may, in 1945 the United States appeared finally to live up to its lofty goals. It had contributed to the establishment of a world judiciary for interstate disputes, which, even though it would still not have compulsory jurisdiction, at least offered an optional clause system permitting states to subscribe to such jurisdiction on the basis of reciprocity. However, at the same time, the United States reserved its freedom to withhold from international judicial settlement matters that it considered domestic, independently of the opinion of the court.

The United States and International Adjudication at the Dawn of the New Millennium

At the dawn of the new millennium, international adjudication again finds itself in a process of profound transformation. Whereas hopes for the development of the International Court of Justice into a kind of constitutional court of the international community might have faded away, new courts and tribunals with more limited scopes of jurisdiction proliferate, both at the universal and the regional level. Some of these bodies are accessible not only to states but also to individuals and companies. U.S. participation in these judicial institutions, however, is declining. In the following, let me first present my assessment of international adjudication as it presents itself at the turn of the millennium. Then, I will have a look at the U.S. position vis-à-vis these developments. Finally, I will make some remarks on the future of international adjudication and the role of the United States.

The International Judiciary Between Constitutionalization and Fragmentation

The World Court between new strength and decline

As I have already described in the introduction, on the surface the international judiciary is thriving. More and more tribunals render fast-growing numbers of decisions. Almost no area of international concern is left unaffected by international adjudication of some kind, if not globally at least regionally. But on the other hand, this very development threatens the unity of the international system of adjudication: Even though the caseload of the International Court of Justice is the heaviest ever, it remains doubtful whether the court has managed to establish itself as a true world court rather than a mere permanent arbitral tribunal of the kind already envisaged at the beginning of the twentieth century. Instead, special bodies for the adjudication of international disputes (in a wide sense) have emerged, most visibly in the areas of trade law—with the Dispute Settlement Understanding of the WTO—and international criminal law—with the Rwanda and Yugoslavia tribunals—but also in the law of the sea. Regional courts and tribunals gain more and more weight in areas such as human rights and economic law; the European and American Courts of Human Rights, the European Court of Justice, but also the NAFTA panels furnishing impressive examples. How can the unity of international law and international dispute settlement be preserved in the presence of so many judicial bodies with divergent jurisdictions, applying different subsets of international rules?

As to the World Court, its success in those cases in which it has exercised its jurisdiction with the consent of both parties can hardly be put into question—consider the various cases on delimitation of boundaries on land and at sea. At times, the court's approach to the question of whether consent to submit a case to it really exists appears to be rather robust.[49] In cases not referred to the court jointly by the parties but by unilateral application based on a general acceptance of ICJ jurisdiction, uncertain. In almost all of these cases the defendant will raise preliminary objections concerning jurisdiction and admissibility, to be dealt with in separate proceedings before the court may go ahead on the merits. Further, in cases in which the claimant invokes the jurisdiction of the court on the basis of the Optional Clause, a decision of the court in favor of its jurisdiction will frequently not be well received by the defendant. In two prominent cases, a decision of the court to that effect has led to both the nonappearance of the defendant and the withdrawal of acceptance of jurisdiction, namely in the *Nuclear Tests*[50] and *Nicaragua*[51] cases. Already before these incidents, Sir Humphrey Waldock had spoken of the "decline of the optional clause."[52] Even if this tendency seems to have slowed down more recently with new declarations of acceptance from Eastern European and African countries arriving, the Optional Clause system can hardly be considered a success. Only one of the permanent members of the Security Council, the United Kingdom, is currently subjected to this system, and most other powerful states have also decided to remain absent. In addition, many declarations that have been made are garnished with weighty reservations that the court has tended to accept even if they were obviously not made in good faith.[53] But there are also positive examples. In a recent case, the boundary litigation between Cameroon and Nigeria, Nigeria has continued to take part in court proceedings initiated on the basis of the Optional Clause even though most of its preliminary objections (no less than eight) to ICJ jurisdiction and admissibility had been refuted.[54]

An alternative basis of jurisdiction aside from special agreements, namely clauses conferring jurisdiction on the World Court with regard to the interpretation and application of a specific treaty, has been somewhat more successful; indeed, it seems currently to undergo a certain revival. Some of the most important cases now before the court are based on such compromissory clauses, such as the one contained in the Genocide Convention in cases between Bosnia-Herzegovina and the Federal Republic of Yugoslavia (FRY), Croatia and the FRY, as well as in the case that the FRY brought against some NATO countries that were taking part in the Kosovo intervention.[55] In the *Lockerbie* case, Libya has brought both Britain and the United States before the World Court on the basis of a provision of the 1971 Montreal Convention.[56] Of course, this basis of jurisdiction may encounter the same kind of problems as the Optional Clause, as exemplified in the *Tehran Hostages* case,[57] in which Iran, charged by the United States with violations of the Vienna Convention on Diplomatic Relations, chose to remain absent.

Another point gains more and more importance: Following the revival of the UN Security Council after the end of the cold war, some authors have diagnosed a certain "constitutionalization" of the international system. According to these views, the UN Charter is to be seen as the emerging constitution of the international community, and the Security Council is then perceived as an embryonic world executive. Such a view leads to the obvious question as to whether the International Court of Justice, "the principal judicial organ of the United Nations" (Article 92 of the Charter), could be transformed into a true world constitutional court with the task of not only resolving interstate disputes but also of controlling the exercise of the executive functions by the Security Council.

This is not the place for a discussion on the extent of the discretion of the Security Council to take binding decisions in cases where it determines "the existence of any threat to the peace, breach of the peace, or act of aggression" (Articles 39 and 25 of the Charter).[58] But as far as the International Court is concerned, what is apparent is that in its present status it will hardly be capable of taking on the role of a constitutional court in any comprehensive manner. If the World Court acts on the basis of treaty clauses, like in the *Lockerbie* case, the question of the validity of a Security Council resolution, if relevant, will only appear as a preliminary matter, which the court will tend to avoid.[59] As the *Lockerbie* case has shown, the appetite of the International Court to render a judgment along the lines of

Marbury v. Madison is rather limited, even if the court carefully avoided denying in express terms its competence to review the legality of Security Council measures as a preliminary matter. The only way in which the court can exercise a truly constitutional function is its advisory capacity (Article 96 of the Charter). But on that avenue it is up to the Security Council or the General Assembly to submit the relevant question to the court, which is unlikely to occur in cases concerning Security Council competencies under Chapter VII.

The suggestion to authorize the UN Secretary-General to request advisory opinions[60] also remained unsuccessful. On top of this, advisory opinions are, as their name already indicates, only advisory and thus not legally binding. This notwithstanding, following a strong NGO campaign, a majority of the General Assembly recently requested the World Court to pronounce on the legality of the threat or use of nuclear weapons. The court replied to the most controversial aspect of that question by seven votes to seven, and the president's casting vote, that

> in view of the current state of international law, and the elements of fact at its disposal, the Court cannot conclude definitively whether the threat or use of force would be lawful or unlawful in an extreme circumstance of self-defence, in which the very survival of a State would be at stake.[61]

This *non liquet* demonstrates the limits of a purely advisory jurisdiction, with no concrete case lying at the basis of a decision. Both sides to the debate—the nuclear weapon states and the states challenging the legality of those weapons—saw themselves as winners and declared the legality of the current practice of deterrence either as confirmed or as rejected. In my opinion, such confusion should be avoided by limiting the advisory function of the World Court to questions that can be answered at a more concrete level, such as in the recent opinions on the immunities of Special Rapporteurs of UN human rights bodies.[62]

In sum, the constitutional role of the World Court remains rather limited, and its genuine judicial function, the decision of disputes submitted to it unilaterally, is not working too well either. On the other hand, as an institution at the disposal of parties jointly requesting its involvement, the World Court is very successful. As the current president of the International Court of Justice, Gilbert Guillaume, once observed:

> With regard to the resolution of inter-State disputes, analysis reveals that, not unlike the Permanent Court, the international Court has dealt mostly with what might be termed 'middle-range disputes' relating to the existence, scope or limitation of the jurisdiction of States, in particular in respect of land boundaries or maritime delimitation. It should be noted that, in terms of both domestic policy and international relations, these cases are, for the most part, emotionally charged. Viewed in this light, the recourse to international justice appears to be a means of resolving a crisis and of reaching reasonable solutions, without imposing direct responsibility upon the governments involved.[63]

As to the procedures of the World Court, they need to be updated in view of the recent increase in the caseload. Lengthy proceedings hardly contribute to the effectiveness of international dispute settlement. Further, more openness of the court to the public will enhance its credibility and reputation not only among states but also in public opinion, which is often instrumental to its success. The International Court of Justice appears to live up to this challenge. In recent instances, provisional measures have been pronounced very quickly, even if sometimes not in a very detailed manner. The newly elected president of the court, Gilbert Guillaume, has recently made a remarkable overture to the public by holding the first press conference ever in the courtroom in The Hague. Guillaume, while defending the World Court against the charge of slowness, remarked:

> Even though the length of a case depends largely on States, we shall need to improve our methods of work and in particular to invite parties to reduce the huge amount of documentation they submit to the Court. We shall also need to ensure that hearings do not last longer than necessary. We shall need to spend less time on our own deliberations wherever

possible. . . . I can assure you . . . that I shall begin this action and pursue it with full determination.[64]

Finally, if states intend to use the World Court more frequently, they should also see to its appropriate funding and staffing. With a budget of $10,000,000 per annum and a staff of sixty-two persons, the court is inexpensive and lean indeed (compared, for instance, with the International Criminal Tribunal for the Former Yugoslavia that has a staff of nine hundred and ten times the budget of the ICJ).

The proliferation of international judicial institutions

As has been stated earlier, the International Court of Justice is not the only international judiciary institution any longer. On the global level, adjudicative bodies with limited jurisdiction abound; older institutions like the Permanent Court of Arbitration coexist with the World Court. All this provides states a veritable shopping list of institutions for the settlement of disputes from political settlement at the United Nations or some regional institution such as the OAS and the OSCE to issue-related courts and tribunals, such as the International Tribunal for the Law of the Sea or the dispute settlement system of the WTO, both international adjudicative institutions of a new type.

The United Nations Convention on the Law of the Sea (UNCLOS)[65] grants states considerable choice in the matter of binding adjudication. According to Article 287 of the Convention:

> When signing, ratifying or acceding to this Convention or at any time thereafter, a State shall be free to choose . . . one of the following means for the settlement of disputes concerning the interpretation or application of this Convention.

Such means for the settlement of disputes are the International Tribunal for the Law of the Sea, the International Court of Justice, or an arbitral tribunal. If a state party to UNCLOS does not make a declaration under Article 287, it shall be deemed to have accepted arbitration. However, until an arbitral tribunal is constituted, the Hamburg tribunal possesses jurisdiction according to Article 290, paragraphs 5 and 6, of the Convention to prescribe provisional measures binding on the parties. In addition, UNCLOS provides further means of peaceful settlement for specific subjects. It is still too early to tell whether such a comprehensive system is going to work. Some observers have criticized it as a "cafeteria approach" to compulsory dispute settlement.[66] So far, the Hamburg tribunal has decided three cases only, among them a single one on the merits—hardly worth the establishment of a special tribunal.

Whereas the International Tribunal for the Law of the Sea has a structure typical of the seventies, with its emphasis still on sovereignty and freedom of choice for states, the WTO dispute settlement system is firmly anchored in the atmosphere of the nineties. The Dispute Settlement Understanding (DSU)[67] establishes a uniform system for the entire body of WTO law, covering the areas of trade, services, and intellectual property rights (GATT, GATS, TRIPS). Its central feature is the consideration of cases by a panel of three or five independent experts (Article 8 of the DSU). According to Article 11 of the DSU, the panel shall make an objective assessment of the facts and the law and "make such other findings as will assist the DSB [Dispute Settlement Body] in making the recommendations or in giving the rulings provided for in the covered agreements." Thus, the procedure is not purely legal in nature. Just as in the case of arbitration, settlement of the dispute and not application of the law is the central task. The Dispute Settlement Body, which consists of all member states of the WTO, may in theory refuse to establish a panel or decline to adopt a panel report, but it could only do so by consensus, including the parties to the dispute. Thus, such a refusal will hardly ever happen. The DSU has also introduced an appellate review: It has created an Appellate Body, a standing institution consisting of seven independent experts (Article 17 paragraph 3), three of whom decide a given case. Appeals are "limited to issues of law covered in the panel report and legal interpretations developed by the panel" (Article 17 paragraph 3 of the DSU). In practice, therefore, the DSU provides for compulsory adjudication in accordance with legal criteria.

In the WTO dispute settlement system, the emphasis is not on choice of means or on the upholding of the law but on effective and quick settlement of disputes. In the words of Article 3 paragraph 4 of the DSU:

> Recommendations or rulings made by the DSB shall be aimed at achieving a satisfactory settlement of the matter in accordance with the rights and obligations under this Understanding and under the covered agreements.

Nevertheless, the binding and compulsory character of the procedure confirms the observation that under the DSU the GATT/WTO system has changed from a "power-oriented" to a "rule-oriented" approach.[68] Confirmation of this can be found in Article 3 paragraph 2 of the DSU, according to which the purpose of WTO dispute settlement system is

> to preserve the rights and obligations of Members under the covered agreements, and to clarify the existing provisions of those agreements in accordance with customary rules of interpretation of public international law.

In addition to the law of the sea and the WTO dispute settlement system, international judicial and quasi-judicial bodies also monitor the behavior of states vis-à-vis their own citizens, especially in the human rights field, ranging from global institutions such as the UN Commission on Human Rights and treaty bodies like the Human Rights Committee overseeing implementation of the International Covenant on Civil and Political Rights to regional human rights courts such as the Inter-American and the European Courts of Human Rights.

The recent adoption of the Rome Statute of the International Criminal Court (ICC)[69] marks a new step in the development of both international adjudication and the enforcement of human rights and humanitarian law. For the first time, the Rome Statute establishes a permanent independent judiciary at the international level possessing general jurisdiction for the criminal prosecution of the worst offenses against the law of nations, namely the crime of genocide, crimes against humanity, and war crimes, in the future possibly also the crime of aggression (Article 5 of the Statute). However, the ICC will not, as some might hope and others fear, constitute a global court of appeals against the decisions of national courts.

According to the principles of subsidiarity and complementarity enshrined in the Rome Statute, the ICC will only act when national institutions are "unwilling or unable genuinely to carry out the investigation or prosecution," in particular if the national "proceedings were or are being undertaken . . . for the purpose of shielding the person concerned from criminal responsibility for crimes within the jurisdiction of the Court . . . [or] conducted in a manner which, in the circumstances, is inconsistent with an intent to bring the person to justice" (Article 17, paragraphs 1 (a), 2 (a), (c); Article 20, paragraph 3 of the Rome Statute).

In her paper to the present symposium, Justice Sandra Day O'Connor has presented the alternative between international criminal justice and a national sovereignty approach in cases of transition to democracy. Justice O'Connor adopts a balancing approach entirely appropriate in many, if not most, cases. However, as she has also correctly observed, there must be limits to the permissibility and international acceptance of amnesties. I submit that the crimes listed in the Rome Statute constitute such a limit to a national sovereignty approach in international criminal law. It is simply unacceptable to envisage an amnesty for the horrendous Nazi crimes or the genocides committed in Cambodia or Rwanda. Experience has shown that compromising justice in such extreme cases will not lead to national reconciliation but rather to an eternal cycle of retribution during which any healing of society will be impossible. This does not mean that international criminal justice can, or should even try to, reach closure—the troubled history of my own country is testimony to the fact that some wounds never heal and, indeed, that learning the lessons of a horrendous past is the responsibility of the whole of society. Prosecution of the worst perpetrators is not sufficient for dealing with such collective responsibility. However, accepting responsibility to cope with one's past does presuppose the prosecution of the worst instances of individual guilt.

My panoply of international adjudication is far from complete. Today, international arbitration not only reaches out to interstate disputes but also to disputes between states and individuals or between individuals, according to internationally recognized standards, such as in the framework of the International Centre for the Settlement of Investment Disputes (ICSID) or the regimes of arbitration of the International Chamber of Commerce or according to the UNCITRAL rules. Regional procedures for the settlement of trade, economic, political, or human rights disputes are too numerous to be listed here. Finally, national means of dispute settlement can also be used in international law cases. The recent Pinochet case or the proceedings before U.S. courts on the question of compensation for slave labor in Nazi Germany constitute only the most prominent examples.

The resulting tableau of all these institutions and procedures may be described as follows: There is no single system of international adjudication but several. A constitutionalization of international dispute settlement has not yet taken place. On the contrary, states have at their disposal an impressive range of means for the adjudication and peaceful settlement of their disputes, and unifying tendencies prevailing in the first part of the twentieth century have been superseded by increasing specialization of international judicial bodies. The late German sociologist Niklas Luhmann has described globalization as a process in which territorial boundaries are increasingly substituted by the borderlines of different systems determined by their respective subject matter.[70] The current state of international adjudication confirms this assessment.

Obviously, this development carries the danger of a fragmentation of the international legal system. However, I submit that to suggest introducing a procedure according to which international tribunals or even national courts might submit questions of general international law to the International Court of Justice, following the example of the European Court of Justice concerning questions of European Community law in national proceedings (Article 234 of the EC treaty),[71] would be futile—not the least because proceedings before the International Court of Justice are so costly and lengthy.

U.S. Attitude to International Adjudication Today

While international adjudication is thriving, the only remaining superpower seems more and more hesitant to submit to it—with the notable exception of international trade disputes. For a nation that has made the rule of law a cornerstone of its understanding of a fair and viable political system, and which has supported international adjudication throughout much of its history, this is highly surprising and, from the perspective of the rest of the world, also disappointing.

What a difference ten years make! In 1976, at a point in time at which the World Court was in deep crisis and underused,[72] the U.S. Department of State suggested remedies as far-reaching as withdrawing the Connally reservation, permitting national courts recourse to the ICJ for advisory opinions, and allowing the United Nations to appear before the court.[73] Ten years later, after the controversial decision of the World Court to take on the merits of the *Nicaragua* case, the United States withdrew its acceptance of the compulsory jurisdiction of the court. As I already mentioned, the United States did not resort to the self-judging Connally reservation in this case. But it did invoke the Vandenberg reservation, claiming that Nicaragua's neighbors, and members of the UN, were going to be affected by a decision but were not parties to the proceeding. In its judgment on the merits, the World Court accepted this position and did not apply the UN and OAS charters as such.[74] But the court upheld its jurisdiction on the basis of customary law and the bilateral Treaty of Friendship, Amity, and Commerce concluded with Nicaragua.

The furor about this decision in parts of the U.S. establishment was understandable because of the broad construction by the World Court of U.S. and Nicaraguan consent to jurisdiction. But even the American judge Stephen Schwebel considered the United States in violation of international customary law by failing to make known the existence and location of mines laid by it.[75] Instead of staying away from the further proceedings, the United States should have defended those of its actions that it considered legal more vigorously before the court, but it should also have accepted its responsibility and brought its practices in conformity with its international obligations instead of complaining about procedural niceties in the face of grave—and certainly not wholly unjustified—charges of violations of international law. The withdrawal of U.S. acceptance of the compulsory jurisdiction of the World Court was all the more regrettable because it sent a signal to the international community that states can avoid their international responsibility by simply not appearing in court proceedings.

Nevertheless, the United States soon demonstrated its willingness not to ignore the World Court in the future by submitting a case to a chamber of the court in 1987 on the basis of a special agreement. This case concerned an alleged violation of the property rights of an Italian company owned by a U.S. firm, a matter which, of course, can hardly be compared with the political weight of the *Nicaragua* case.[76] In the nineties, the United States has appeared before the World Court several times as a defendant in cases in which the applicant invoked jurisdiction clauses contained in treaties to which the United States is a party, for instance, in the *Lockerbie* case brought by Libya. In the *Aerial Incidents* case brought by Iran under aviation agreements, which concerned the accidental shooting down of an Iranian civil aircraft, and in the *Breard* case concerning the execution of a Paraguayan citizen not informed of his right to consular assistance under the 1963 Vienna Convention, the United States settled the claims before the first hearing.[77] In the *Legality of Use of Force* case brought by the Federal Republic of Yugoslavia, inter alia under the Genocide Convention, the case against the United States was removed from the list for obvious lack of jurisdiction.[78] But the *Lockerbie* case brought by Libya,[79] the *Oil Platforms* case brought by Iran,[80] and the *LaGrand* case brought by Germany[81] are still pending.

From all this, the following policy towards the World Court is discernible: The United States will submit cases to the court, preferably to a chamber composed of "Western" judges known to adhere to a classical, consent-based doctrine of international law, when this conforms to its interests, as in the *ELSI* case with Italy. It will also fulfill its obligations under treaties in force. On the other hand, there seems to be no intention to renew the U.S. declaration of acceptance under the Optional Clause. And the U.S. Senate will either not accept new treaties providing for compulsory jurisdiction of the World Court in sensitive areas or prescribe reservations excluding such jurisdiction. For instance, in 1988 the United States finally ratified the 1948 Genocide Convention and in 1994 the 1984 UN Convention against Torture, but in both cases it entered reservations excluding the compulsory jurisdiction of the World Court.[82]

However, what is more troubling from the viewpoint of international law is the position of the United States on provisional measures indicated by the Hague court. In two recent cases involving the lack of consular notification prior to the trial and execution of nationals of other countries, the Paraguayan citizen Angelo Breard, executed in Virginia in 1998, and Walter LaGrand, executed in Arizona in March 1999, the U.S. Supreme Court refused to provisionally halt the execution of these foreigners in order to give due regard to provisional measures indicated by the International Court. In its orders on provisional measures, in both cases adopted unanimously, that is, with the concurring vote of the American judge Stephen Schwebel, the World Court had requested the United States to

take all measures at its disposal to ensure that Angel Francisco Breard [or Walter LaGrand, respectively] is not executed pending the final decision in these proceedings.[83]

The Supreme Court did not even consider the question of whether such an order of the World Court was to be regarded as binding. All it did was to declare, in the *Breard* case, its general readiness to

give respectful consideration to the interpretation of an international treaty rendered by an international court with jurisdiction to interpret such.[84]

Neither did the U.S. government use its constitutional leverage to demand compliance from the Virginia and Arizona authorities in these cases.

In his brief to the Supreme Court in the *Breard* case and in a statement to the Supreme Court in the *LaGrand* case, Solicitor General Seth B. Waxman argued for the U.S. government that "an order of the International Court of Justice indicating provisional measures is not binding and does not furnish a basis for judicial relief," to quote the latter statement. Two justices dissented and two justices concurred, basing their decision expressly on the statement of the executive.[85] Even if one did not regard such orders of the International Court as binding—which is difficult to maintain because what other sense should they make—the disrespect for the

proper functioning of the World Court on the part of both the executive and the judicial branches of the U.S. government is palpable. It is not only European writers that deplored the U.S. attitude in these cases but also the majority of American international lawyers.[86]

Such a problematic attitude toward international adjudication also extends to the more recent instruments of dispute settlement. Contrary to most of its allies, the United States has yet to subscribe to the United Nations Convention on the Law of the Sea and the binding dispute settlement procedures established by that instrument. The WTO dispute settlement system functions under the permanent threat of U.S. withdrawal, Section 125 of the Uruguay Round Agreements Act[87] providing for a review of U.S. participation in the WTO every five years. According to this provision, a joint resolution of both houses of Congress may terminate U.S. membership in the WTO following a report on WTO membership by the U.S. trade representative. In addition, the U.S. Congress has maintained that the famous Section 301 of the 1974 U.S. Trade Act[88] permitting unilateral U.S. measures to enforce its perceived rights remains in force in spite of its obligations under the Dispute Settlement Understanding.[89] Thus, in the only instance in which the United States has agreed to compulsory (quasi-) adjudication it chooses to continue to claim a right to act unilaterally whenever it pleases.

Finally, U.S. opposition against the Rome Statute of the International Criminal Court can only partly be explained by legitimate concerns for American troops abroad. There exists a general reluctance, to say the least, to allow any international institution to enforce international law against U.S. citizens—and, of course, the insistence on U.S. prerogatives as a permanent member of the Security Council. Let me emphasize that I understand this concern quite well—the first one, that is—coming from a country that is prevented by a constitutional prohibition to extradite its nationals to foreign states. But Germany is now ready to change its Basic Law to be able in the future to surrender its nationals to the ICC. In the case of the United States, which has a tradition of extraditing its own nationals to foreign countries, it would be even more natural to allow the surrender of U.S. nationals to an international institution with limited, precisely circumscribed, jurisdiction for the most egregious crimes only and which is going to provide every imaginable due process. Regarding the ad hoc tribunals for Yugoslavia and Rwanda, the United States has always maintained that these bodies do not create new law but confirm existing international law. It is therefore not very convincing to argue that in case of tribunals established by the Security Council, such as the two tribunals just mentioned, international law does permit the surrender of foreign nationals by the state in which they are arrested to these tribunals or another country, which thus is not the case with regard to the future International Criminal Court.

Conclusion

The Case for U.S. Participation in International Adjudication in the New Millennium

International adjudication is a means to foster world peace. As the U.S. representative in the Sixth (Legal) Committee of the United Nations General Assembly, Robert Rosenstock, observed twenty years ago:

> The Charter wisely listed the obligation to "settle disputes by peaceful means" ahead of the prohibition of the threat or use of force because disputes must be settled if we are to avoid violence. The two norms are part of an inseparable whole. . . . [A]cceptance of dispute settlement procedures involving impartial third parties for future disputes is essential if we are to eliminate force as a means to settle disputes.[90]

International adjudication derives its authority from the very sources that have made America a power based on the rule of law, which is, as Justice Sandra Day O'Con-

nor so aptly observed, fundamental to the existence of a free society and separates civilization from anarchy. Therefore, further—and more active—participation of the world's only remaining superpower in judicial settlement of international disputes is not only in the best interest of the international community but also in the best interest of the United States. In the words of Theodore Roosevelt's secretary of state, Elihu Root, one of the early champions of international adjudication,

> while it is highly important to have controversies between nations settled by arbitration rather than by war, and the growth of sentiment in favor of that peaceable method of settlement is one of the great advances in civilization to the credit of this generation; yet the true basis of peace among men is to be found in a just and considerate spirit among the people who rule our modern democracies, in their regard for the rights of other countries, and in their desire to be fair and kindly in the treatment of the subjects which give rise to international controversies.[91]

It is to be hoped that this traditional U.S. attitude toward the judicial settlement of disputes will prevail over the "national sovereignty approach" in the international arena in the next millennium. Whether this will result in a self-socializing of humanity as advocated by Professor Philip Allott I leave to your judgment. In a world moving closer together every day but still separated by diversity of cultures, religions, and ideologies, international adjudication on the basis of universally recognized rules of international law is possibly the best means to secure that in the next millennium the world is ruled by a "government of laws, and not of men."[92]

The Problem of Justice in a Changing World Order

A Comment

Hisashi Owada

Introduction

The title of this international symposium is "Democracy and the Rule of Law in a Changing World Order." The present session is assigned to look at this problem in the context of transnational justice and national sovereignty. This is a vast territory. Each of the three speakers has dealt with this problem from widely divergent angles. It will therefore be impossible for the present commentator to offer comments that cover all of the concrete points that the three speakers have taken up in their different fields. Instead, I shall try to offer my own views on the changes that have come about in the international system to affect the problem of world order and to touch upon only a few aspects of their impact upon the theme of the symposium that the three speakers have dealt with in their respective ways.

My starting point is a banal one. Let me say, nevertheless, that the present-day world is going through a period of great transformation. The whole structure of the modern international system, together with the traditional tools that we employ for managing the system, may have to be reexamined and reconstrued in the light of this new development. International law as we have known it, as a body of norms governing the international system established since the Peace of Westphalia, is no exception.

What I regard to be the most fundamental aspects of the changes that affect the present-day international sys-

tem are twofold. One is the rapidly growing reality of social interdependence of human activities within international society in an age of globalization. As a result, an increasing tension is created between this new reality of transnational human activities that defy national borders and the institutional framework of the traditional international system based on the principle of national distribution of competence to regulate such activities.

The other is the increasing awareness of people who have come to assert the primacy of human dignity as individuals in the process of democratization of governance throughout the world. As a result, the notion of the rule of law in the international system has acquired a growing relevance in relation to individuals representing pluralistic values in society, as compared with the traditional notion based on the principle of sovereign states constituting the international system as its essential constituent elements.

Against the background of these two new factors, it is increasingly apparent that the problem of world order has to be considered, taking into account the concept of public policy in a global context rather than in an international context. This is due to the fact that the growing process of globalization is moving toward making the world one society of humankind and that the increasing trend in democracy as a system of governing a society is moving the world toward the creation of a new system of global governance. Nevertheless, this is not a completed process as yet. The absence of a universal system of global governance to regulate the world public order on the basis of a global public policy makes it impossible to solve the dichotomy between the existing normative system based on national competencies and the emerging socioeconomic reality of interdependence on a global scale. This is a problem that we are struggling with during this transitional period in which the traditional system based on the Westphalian legal order will go through a major transformation.

It is my view that all the three presentations that we have heard, while they are widely divergent in their treatment of the subject matters, address the same problem of this dichotomy and argue in their respective ways how the issue of world public policy seen in its global context can be made relevant to the world order of the existing international system.

Thus, when Professor Philip Allot speaks about "the apparent and urgent need for a presence of the nomocratic ideal at the level of international society, acting as an enacting and enforcing instrument of universal ideals of justice and social justice," he seems to be pointing to this problem and expressing his own aspiration to overcome this problem, although it is my impression that he is not offering us concrete ways to get out of the present dilemma.

It is also my understanding that Justice Sandra O'Connor addresses the same problem when she emphasizes the importance of "how to balance conflicting demands for justice" at the national and international levels on the same issue. Her conclusion would seem to me to be somewhat eclectic, as she concludes that there is no right answer to which approach is the best way to secure the rule of law. This, however, is not only inevitable but also wise, given the transitional nature of the era that we are living through.

Professor Bruno Simma's presentation also refers to the same situation that arises in the field of international adjudication. In going through a thorough examination of the U.S. policy on the matter of international adjudication from the perspective of its historical evolution, Professor Simma focuses on the tension that exists between the public policy consideration of international society reflecting its community interest *qua* society and the public policy consideration of the United States reflecting its national interest as a sovereign member of this society. The prescription that he offers for dealing with this tension, however, would seem to be an essentially traditional, though realistic, one when he recommends an approach based on the notion of the enlightened self-interest of the sovereign state involved. Thus, according to his conclusion it should be recognized that "further—and more active—participation of the world's only remaining superpower in the judicial settlement of international disputes is not only in the best interest of the international community but also in the best interest of the United States."

Thus it is noteworthy to see that these three eminent scholars, although treating issues in different fields, focus on the same central problem that we face now. In view of this, it may be useful at this juncture to offer my own view on this same problem in an attempt to bring to the surface what I regard to be the major factors that are affecting the present international system under stress in a changing world order. My main theme is that the transformation that is going on within the international system, as manifested by the two developments that I described earlier, has produced a situation in which the concept of justice, as a key concept for the world order based on the rule of law, is going through challenges in three different dimensions. They are:

(a) a challenge to the contents of justice in the context of pluralistic values in society;

(b) a challenge to the scope of justice in the context of a tension between justice and stability in the international order; and

(c) a challenge to the nature of justice in the context of a dichotomy between interstate and global societies.

The Contents of Justice in the Context of Pluralistic Values

In any sufficiently organized society, law is the instrument that endows this organized body with a basic framework for order *qua* society. As the Romans put it, *ubi societas ibi ius*. However, for this order to prevail and serve as the societal framework for stability, it has to be based on a system of law that represents justice in that society. The complication arises when one realizes that justice, like fairness, is a concept that in its abstract form may represent an eternal and universal value in society but when translated into a practical form susceptible of application will have to acquire its concrete contents to represent the embodiment of a notion of justice as accepted by the society in question.

It follows that while the concept of justice must reflect what is inherent in society as its core value, the concrete contents of justice as manifested in a normative form may not be totally free from the idiosyncrasies of a particular society conditioned by time and space. Thus a concrete legal norm that is regarded as the embodiment of the sense of justice prevailing in a society may not always be accepted in a different society as a norm of the same universal value.

In my submission, it is precisely on this point that the recent developments taking place in the international system have come to present a new implication to the international legal order in an age of globalization. It is quite possible that different normative systems prevailing in two different domestic societies come into conflict with each other in this age of interaction between two societies through transnational socioeconomic activities.

Let me illustrate this problem by reference to one of the more complex legal problems that exist in the field of economic activities in any society, namely, the problem of unfair competition. Any society that is concerned with the problem of unfair competition in the conduct of economic activities will condemn unfair competition, almost by definition, as being contrary to its sense of social justice and its public order. However, when it comes to determining what concrete action constitutes such an act of unfair competition that should be made the subject of sanction by society in the form of normative rules, the question becomes much more complex. I suspect that there will be a fairly broad range of peripheral norms in this field to which some societies will take an extremely puritanical and rigorous position, while others will display a much greater degree of receptiveness, if not outright approval, at least to the extent that such activities in those societies are not punishable by law.

Another example that comes to my mind is the case of capital punishment in its relationship to human rights. Such issues and many others of a similar character would not be a serious problem to the international legal order if we lived in a compartmentalized world of the Westphalian international system. Each nation-state, as a sovereign in harmonious coexistence with other nation-states based on the principles of sovereign equality and nonintervention in domestic affairs, could persist in its own self-contained system that forms a completely closed circuit. Within that closed circuit of society, each sovereign government would insist that its sense of justice in society, as reflected in its legal order, should prevail. However, in the brave new world that we are now entering, where socioeconomic activities across the national border—rather than activities solely confined within the national border of one country—are the rule and not the exception, the question of how to determine and apply what constitutes justice and fairness in a concrete case becomes much more complex, particularly in the present transitional phase where we have not yet succeeded in reorganizing ourselves into an international community in its institutional aspect.

I suggest that this is exactly the state of affairs that Professor Allot condemns as "leading symptoms of our present morbidity."

The thesis put forward by Professor Allot that "international society—the society of all humanity and all societies—need not be the crazy and archaic intergovernmental unsociety that has characterized international relations throughout this millennium" certainly makes sense from a theoretical point of view. I also feel very much in sympathy with Professor Allot when he advocates that "the need is apparent and urgent for a pressure of nomocratic ideal at the level of international society, acting as an enacting and enforcing instrument of universal ideals of justice and social justice." However, to me the real question is how we can translate this prescription into reality in the next millennium, as Professor Allot advocates.

This requires a transformation of society in which we live from what we are (the world of *Sein*) to what we should be (the world of *Sollen*). While it is true that we cannot just "wait for Godot" and that we have to carry out "a revolution in the mind," it is my humble submission that such a "revolution in the mind" can only come about through the process of societal evolution in the international system that we are at present going through. Without being fatalistic, I must conclude that this will be easier said in theory than done in practice.

The Scope of Justice in the Context of Tension Between Justice and Stability

The function of law is to attain a harmonious integration of justice and stability in society. Under normal circumstances the two will go hand in hand together to the extent that the element of justice is expected to be inherent in the concept of law and order, which alone can ensure stability in society in a sustainable manner. Thus, in the context of international law the Charter of the United Nations, in Article 2, paragraph 3, provides as follows:

> All Members shall settle their international disputes by peaceful means in such a manner that international peace and security, and justice, are not endangered. (Underline supplied)

Nevertheless, at a moment of turbulence in any society, and in international society in particular, there can arise a situation in which this harmonious amalgam between justice and stability—or peace in the international context—is disturbed, with the result that the two essential elements of order come into mutual tension and conflict. This tension between justice and stability tends to surface in the form of a dichotomy, confronting the practitioner in the management of international relations with a painful choice. As is the case with domestic society, this dichotomy becomes particularly acute in a situation of social disturbance and conflict in international society.

I submit that this tension between justice and stability in the international legal order has now become even more acute and real in the face of a major societal evolution that we are going through in the international system. In this sense, the end of the cold war would signify the final demise of "the good old days" when things were simpler and more clear-cut in terms of values to be defended within the context of confrontation between the West and the East, which were vying for totally opposing value systems in various respects.

In contrast to these past years, the reality of the present-day world is much more complex, with the tension between upholding justice and safeguarding peace in a given situation becoming much more acute and harder to harmonize.

The controversies that have been raging surrounding the situation in the former Yugoslavia are a case in point. In Resolution 713 (1991) of the UN Security Council of September 25, 1991, the Security Council declared as follows:

> [It] decides, under Chapter VII of the Charter of the United Nations, that all States shall, *for the purposes of establishing peace and stability in Yugoslavia,* immediately implement a general and complete embargo on all deliveries of weapons and military equipment to Yugoslavia until the Council decides otherwise following consultation between the Secretary-General and the Government of Yugoslavia. (Underline supplied)

This arms embargo was applied, as is unequivocally stated in the resolution in question, "for the purpose of establishing peace and stability" in the region. However, a fierce opposition to this arms embargo came to be advanced by one of the warring parties, the government of the Republic of Bosnia and Herzegovina. The essence of this opposition was that the principle of justice involved in the concrete situation was being trampled in favor of a position to put priority on stability and peace at any cost. One most forceful advocate for the lifting of the arms embargo, representing the government of Bosnia and Herzegovina, stated in the General Assembly as follows:

> it is [the Muslim Bosnians'] inferiority in quality and quantity of weapons that has allowed this aggression [by Serbians] to be continued. . . . We [the Muslim Bosnians] do expect our right to self-defense to be honored and our desire to control our own fate to be respected, once and for all.

The question is not new. The whole mechanism of peaceful settlement of international disputes under Chapter VI of the Charter, in spite of the caveat in Article 2, paragraph 3 thereof, presupposes the existence of this tension, while hoping that a harmonious equilibrium between justice and peace will somehow be struck in the process of reaching peaceful settlement. The situation would essentially be the same with respect to the peacekeeping operations of the United Nations, at any rate to the extent that the operations are based on faithful adherence to the principle of impartiality, within the confines of Chapter VI of the Charter.

It is true that under this system of the UN Charter the situation envisaged under Chapter VII of the Charter is treated in an inherently different manner from that instituted under Chapter VI. The determination of the existence of a threat to the peace, breach of the peace, or act of aggression by the Security Council under Article 39 should be in its nature a determination that fundamental justice is endangered or infringed and that the collective decision of the Security Council as the executive organ of the international community in this regard is directed to make justice prevail. That the reality is not so simple, however, has been illustrated by the example of the former Yugoslavia that I have just quoted. Also, the recent controversy surrounding the situation in Kosovo is yet another evidence of this dichotomy.

The dichotomy is not an easy one to solve in practice. Obviously, there cannot be a complete solution to this state of affairs as long as the international community is not equipped with an organ endowed with an effective centralized power to execute a decision of the international community. Nevertheless, the point I wish to make is that given the evolving trend in the international community to prevent states from individually taking justice into their own hands, this dichotomy between justice and stability will be likely to grow unless this trend is matched and buttressed by an international effort to strengthen a collective mechanism to ensure a harmonious equilibrium between justice and stability in international society.

It seems to me that "the tension between international and domestic approaches to accountability" that Justice Sandra O'Connor speaks about in her presentation in essence is very much this same problem. I am in agreement with Justice O'Connor in the sense that this dichotomy between the pursuit of justice in terms of imposing criminal sanctions on those who violate the law and the pursuit of societal reconciliation as the essential basis for consolidation of democracy on fragile soil is a dilemma one has to face as an existential problem.

There is no question whatsoever that truly durable peace, whether domestic or international, can only be realized when it contains as its essential ingredient the realization of justice in some form. Peace that is not based on the consideration of justice is not going to be sustainable. In this sense, peace and justice go hand in hand together. On the other hand, blind pursuit of justice does not necessarily ensure the arrival of durable peace. Pursuit of justice can sometimes bring about an insurmountable obstacle to the process of national/societal reconciliation, which is essential to the solid foundation for democratic governance in society, especially when such pursuit is carried out in a spirit of vengeance and retribution.

"There is no right answer which approach is the best way to secure the rule of law" in this sense, as Justice O'Connor candidly admits. "Every situation will be different and will require the balancing of different factors."

The Nature of Justice in the Context of Dichotomy Between Interstate and Global Societies

The third area that I wish to touch upon from the viewpoint of the rule of law in international society is the growing dichotomy, if not divergence, between the concept of justice in human terms in the context of global society and the concept of justice in sovereign terms in the context of international society.

Justice in society is a concept that has its relevance in relation to the sociojuridical status of the constituent members of that society. Thus, when slaves were not regarded as legitimate component elements of society, the problem of social justice in relation to the slaves was not on the conscience of the people. By the same token, when the policy of apartheid was practiced in the Union of South Africa, the injustice being done to the colored population in South Africa was ignored by the officialdom of that country.

In the context of international society this would mean that the concept of justice could vary, depending upon whether one was thinking primarily of justice in relation to sovereign states as constituent members of this community or in relation to the individuals or groups of individuals as component elements of this community. In the traditional context of the Westphalian legal order, where sovereign states are the basic constituent units of international society, the realization of justice as the ultimate objective of the international legal order has always been conceived of primarily in relation to the sovereign states.

The problem is again one of divergence between the conception of an emerging global community with human beings as its essential components in the societal sense and the conception of the existing international community with sovereign states as its basic components. This divergence can, and often does, create a tension between the two to the extent that the values in society, including the aspect of justice involved, can be divergent depending upon whether one looks at the problem from the viewpoint of individual interests of its constituent sovereign states or from the viewpoint of common interests of the community consisting of individual human beings.

A typical case that demonstrates this dilemma is the one related to the principle of self-determination. Thus the Declaration on the Granting of Independence to Colonial Countries and Peoples, adopted by the General Assembly in 1960 (resolution 1524 (XV)), states as follows:

Any attempt aimed at the partial or total disruption of the national unity and the territorial integrity of a country is incompatible with the purposes and principles of the Charter of the United Nations.

This same viewpoint is repeated, word for word, in the Declaration on Principles of International Law Concerning Friendly Relations and Cooperation among States in Accordance with the Charter of the United Nations, adopted by the General Assembly in 1970 (Resolution 2625 (XXV)).

What these two declarations try to do is to find a balance in the dichotomy that exists between the principle of self-determination as the right of people and the principle of territorial integrity as the right of sovereign states. The declarations try to do this by attempting an intrin-

sic limitation on the sphere of application of the principle of self-determination to cases linked to the right of "a nation" to become a sovereign member of the community of nations. Whatever that concept of "a nation" may mean in this context, however, such an attempt is bound to fail as being superficial and tautological as long as the term "nation" cannot be clarified in relation to the people and in relation to the state respectively.

What is significant in comparison is the International Covenants on Human Rights—both the one on Civil and Political Rights and the other on Economic, Social and Cultural Rights—adopted by the General Assembly in 1966 (Resolution 2200 (XXI), which provide as follows in Article 1:

All peoples have the right of self-determination. By virtue of that right they freely determine their political status and freely pursue their economic, social and cultural development.

Here, one can clearly detect the tension in operation between the consideration of justice in human terms and that of justice in sovereign terms in the international legal order. Aware of this tension, the International Court of Justice, in its judgment of the Chamber in the case *Burkina Faso v. Mali,* observed:

At first sight this principle [of territorial integrity] conflicts outright with another one, the right of peoples to self-determination. In fact, however, the maintenance of the territorial *status quo* in Africa is often seen as the wisest course. The essential requirement of stability in order to survive, to develop and gradually to consolidate their independence in all fields has induced African States judiciously to commit to the respecting of colonial frontiers, and to take account of it in the interpretation of the principle of self-determination of peoples.

It is noteworthy that in this passage in the judgment the International Court of Justice put its finger on the tension that exists between the two factors and emphasized "the essential requirement of stability," referring to the decisive relevance of the element of stability in the legal order in this particular setting. The critical question under such circumstances is whether one should be thinking about this problem primarily in terms of the legitimate interest and justice of a sovereign state or in terms of the legitimate interest and justice of individuals to decide upon their own destiny, or both in harmony from the broader viewpoint of the community interest of the world.

If one looks at the situation, not from the viewpoint of justice in relation to an entity entitled to become a sovereign member of international society but from the viewpoint of justice in relation to individuals or people as members of global society, it will be seen that the conception of justice involved in the principle of self-determination could be a much broader one, extending to the case of the freedom of groups of individuals as communities to choose their own self-government. This naturally would not mean that a secessionist movement from an existing sovereign entity by a local community claiming independence is always justified. It would not mean either, at the same time, that the principle of self-determination is a principle that is applicable only to the process of decolonization and disintegration of a colonial empire and has therefore ceased to apply to the postdecolonization world of today.

In this situation of dichotomy at this transitional phase of the international system, a harmonious equilibrium would appear to be required between the conception of justice in society as seen from the viewpoint of sovereign states in the interstate setting and the conception of justice in society as seen from the viewpoint of individuals in the global setting. It is suggested that this would be possible only if good governance in the respective societies of each of the sovereign states is secured on the basis of the practice of democracy so that the legitimate aspirations of different groups of people in society are reflected in the process of democratic governance within the new framework of world public order.

It is precisely here that the great significance of the establishment of the International Criminal Court as adopted in Rome in 1998 is to be recognized. At the same time, as Professor Simma argues so forcefully in his paper, here lies also the paradox of the situation, as the United States is so painfully experiencing, that a tension is inevitable between the need to uphold the common interests of the global community by holding individuals accountable for certain heinous crimes in the new framework of world public order and the need to protect the national interests of sovereign states by subjecting the intervention of the international community to the ultimate consent of the state whose legitimate national interests are perceived to be at risk. The recent controversy surrounding the extradition of General Pinochet would seem to reveal an element of the same dichotomy.

The whole thrust of Professor Simma's paper, with which I also agree, focuses on one point: the proposition that "more active participation/submission of the United States to judicial settlement of international disputes," prevailing over "the national sovereignty approach" in the international arena, is not only in the best interest of the international community but also in the best interest of the United States.

It is my humble submission by way of a conclusion to this session that it is through such a process of harmonization that the concept of justice as defined in terms of interstate society on the one hand and the concept of justice as defined in terms of global society on the other hand should and indeed could be brought together as a harmonious unity to form the key concept to govern the world public order in this transitional period of societal transformation of the world.

Closing Remarks

Anne-Marie Slaughter

The Library of Congress sits between the two great parallel axes of the American Capitol, Independence and Constitution Avenues, each lined with the majestic public buildings of a proud republic. Their symbolism is deep; they are the foundational principles on which the republic stands. Yet, conceptually, they really should intersect. The independence of a people and the charter of their self-governance each flow into and feed the other; at their intersection is the rule of law. If a people are to be free from external control and govern themselves, they must set the rules they will live by and cherish them.

This conference explores exactly those connections: the nature of the rule of law, the construction of the rule of law, and the relationships between the rule of law and democracy. It is the American habit, at the very mention of the rule of law, to claim it as a distinctively American tradition. One of the purposes of this conference is to widen the typical American conversation, to encompass perspectives from around the world. From the perspective of many of those participants, this proud republic is somewhat too proud, and somewhat out of step with global efforts, to promote the rule of law.

That is ultimately our task. Writing in the *Wall Street Journal* in 1999, historian Paul Johnson argued that the project for the last millennium was the construction of a national rule of law in countries around the world. The project for this millennium, he claimed, will be the construction of a global rule of law.[1] But how to achieve it? How even to take the first steps?

The move from a nation under law to a world under law will require a world of nations under law. Philip Allott, in the proper millennial spirit, calls for a "new Enlightenment." But he also invokes the spirit and sub-stance of one of the great figures of the old Enlightenment. Kant foretold that world order would rest on a "federalism of free nations," in Justice O'Connor's formulation.[2] He envisioned perpetual peace among a community of liberal republics, each committed to some form of democracy and the rule of law. A world government, even under law enforced by a world court, would be a tyranny.

On this view, world order must come from the bottom up, from each society struggling, in Professor Allott's words, to "reimagine itself" and particularly to reimagine itself under law. For Kant, the ability to achieve individual and collective self-governance was the glory and paradox of humankind. That is only possible, as Allott reminds us, when law becomes "the enacting of society's highest values, including justice and social justice."

Professor Simma and Professor Owada continue these themes in their contributions. Professor Simma underscores the folly of trying to establish a global rule of law by making the International Court of Justice (ICJ) a global Supreme Court. He does not for a moment denigrate the ICJ's achievements, but reminds us that it is one court among many and that a global legal system will require a multitude of national and international tribunals. Professor Owada equally emphasizes the pluralism of values embedded in national legal systems and the importance of encompassing them within a global framework.

All these views, and indeed the invocation of Kant himself, a great German philosopher, also remind us of the point I raised at the outset of these remarks. The rule of law is not simply an American idea. It is not simply a reflection of American power, something the

United States wishes to impose on the rest of the world. It is in part the heritage of the Western enlightenment, but it is also a heritage to which all societies have contributed and continue to contribute.

Senator Hatch speaks of the Chinese concept of the rule *by* law rather than the rule of law. Yet the Chinese gave us the concept of the scholar official, the Mandarin, of law of a sophistication and detail that today we can barely imagine. Islamic law is similarly refined and elegantly elaborated over centuries; it balances the most complex questions of communal faith and individual obligation.

All cultures have contributed to our understanding of the rule of law; all cultures have something to contribute. Consider the poster for this conference, the bookmark from the Library of Congress. It celebrates legal texts from different cultures, texts embodying ideals of truth and value enshrined within a specific concept of culture and indeed of art.

The United States is entitled to celebrate its own values and history as part of this great human tradition. But as Justice Rehnquist reminds us, U.S. judges and lawyers increasingly understand that they have as much to learn as to teach. Justice O'Connor has been tireless in urging U.S. lawyers to learn and cite foreign and international law. Justice Ginsburg has written about the Indian and German approaches to affirmative action, urging her colleagues to learn from these different traditions as they grapple with our own. And Justice Kennedy has participated in many "summits" between the U.S. Supreme Court and its foreign counterparts.

Recently, in a sparring match with Justice Thomas over the value of foreign perspectives on American law, Justice Breyer wrote that although the views of the foreign authorities are not binding, the "[w]illingness to consider foreign judicial views in comparable cases is not surprising in a Nation that from its birth has given a 'decent respect' to the opinions of mankind."[3] He was paraphrasing, of course, the words of Thomas Jefferson, the second founder of the Library of Congress. In a true Jeffersonian spirit, these justices are leading a movement to jolt American lawyers and judges out of their traditional parochialism.

The work of these justices and a growing number of other American judges is part of the much larger phenomenon of judicial globalization. It is a conversation among national and international judges, all animated by at least a core of common ideas and ideals of the rule of law. Many of these judges address the relationship between the rule of law and democracy on a daily basis, case by case. The sum of their struggles, nation by nation, will be the foundation for a global rule of law.

Source: Library of Congress.

Session 2

....

Roles of Women:
Norms and Culture

Editors' Note

Democracy and the rule of law cannot be addressed without reference to the complex, ever changing, and emotionally charged issues relating to the status of women. Throughout history, females have rarely been accorded a semblance of equality with males, and there is now wide agreement that this discrimination has deprived humankind of the creative and productive energies of half its population while simultaneously inflicting cruel restraints and injustices on countless women and girls. The session's broad title was designed to elicit varied reflections on a range of topics.

We were not disappointed. Under the guidance of Justice Ruth Bader Ginsburg, herself a pathbreaking women's rights lawyer, the panelists considered such basic problems as education, employment, personal (including sexual) autonomy, and domestic violence. Speaking from their own experience in Brazil, Italy, the Muslim Middle East, and the United States, the panelists recognized the influence of race, religion, poverty, and class as they bear on the lives of individual women and the overall status of women in different societies. If there is an overall theme that can be discerned in the papers that follow, it is that great progress has been made in gender equality in recent decades and that women's control of their destiny has never been greater, but also that enormous inequities towards women persist throughout the world and much effort will have to be expended to overcome them.

Born Free and Equal in Dignity and Rights

Ellen Gracie Northfleet

1.

Some years ago, during one of my visits to this beautiful country, I traveled up to Maine. It was summertime and I drove by myself in a rented car. Having planned ahead and consulted the maps, I had plotted the way. Little card notes, which I could hold by the driving wheel, indicated all the significant reference points so that I could easily check my route. The radio was on, and as I crossed the country I would tune it to some local station according to my whims.

All of a sudden I realized that I was relishing what was probably the highest degree of freedom that a woman had ever enjoyed. To be able to travel alone, in a fully equipped car, through well tended roads, without having to ask permission of anyone and being well accepted and respected, finding lodging and good meals everywhere my budget would allow me to go, and even listening to the tunes that best pleased me, was in itself (beyond consideration of the purposes of my trip) a blessing. I felt very much grateful for all those who had pushed the progress of humanity to this point. I was quietly and consciously happy!

2.

Something so simple took a long time to happen. And as we enter the third millennium of history, in many parts of the globe the very common pleasures mentioned above are not accessible to most women. Freedom to come and go is hindered by all sorts of barriers. Some derive from external circumstances, as economic constraints, others from prohibitions and complete subjection to the will of others, be they parents, husbands, or children. Some spring from internal feelings of unworthiness that take the form of all sorts of fears. Some are explained by the lack of knowledge of one's own desires and preferences, for many women never received any encouragement to tap into their inner selves, since, from an early age, they spend most of their time trying to please somebody else and thus get astray from their own being.

3.

The *Human Rights Watch World Report 1999* denounces that in many countries statutory restrictions curtail women's freedom of movement, as is the case in Bangladesh where the government imposed a total ban on women traveling abroad to work. The reality is even worse in Afghanistan where women are not allowed to leave their homes unless accompanied by a male relative.[1] Even where legislation has evolved to formally extend equal rights to women, it may happen that local custom effectively prevents them from exercising these rights.[2] And where neither law nor tradition prohibits women from doing whatever they please, it may be that their horizons are restricted by internalized stereotypes that do not allow their own individuality to come to light.

What I mean is that no matter all the time and effort spent during the last decades of the past century, we haven't gone very far. Only few of us, as individuals, actually enjoy the benefits of the female revolution. The vast majority of our sisters still remain in the previous condition of functionally handicapped human beings. In my opinion it will take another century for women to reach the status of fully developed individuals, with the right (and a willingness to use that right) to fulfill, to their utmost extension, their potential and capabilities; to have and to pursue their individual goals and dreams.

Drawing from the several international conventions that affirm that "all human beings are born free and equal in dignity and rights," we should stress that the idea of a right to life doesn't mean solely not to be put to death, but, just as important, it means the right to the opportunity of living a meaningful life, where no part of self—no talent, no capacity, no ability—is thwarted or discouraged. The right to liberty doesn't mean just the absence of formal slavery but encompasses the right to choose the role in life that one would rather play, without being limited by the stereotypes that constantly present us with very few options. And as for the pursuit of happiness, most women are not happy at all. The surveys show us that (no wonder) they present higher rates of discontent, insecurity, and depression than men. Many, being obliged to live "empty" lives, just fill their time with routine activities where there is no room for creativity or fulfillment. All this means an intolerable waste of valuable human resources.

All the progress obtained through the action of the feminist movement, though very present in daily life, was somehow slowed down in the last two decades of the century. This was due in part to the infamous backlash that meant resistance to further advance. It was also result of a loss of enthusiasm among women for a movement that was, at a given moment, perceived as antimale, antifamily, antifeminine.[3] This caused a disbandment of feminist hosts in countries where the movement was well structured and hindered the formation of strong action groups in the rest of the world.

4.

The Portuguese anthropologist Boaventura de Souza Santos pointed out that the male advantage, which can be verified all over the world, is even more stressed among third world countries.[4] Where unemployment rates are high, women tend to be neglected and have to conform with lower wages and resort to the informal sector.[5] This situation makes them increase their working hours and engage their children in less skilled tasks.[6] Still, their families rely heavily on them for almost all the domestic chores, from water fetching and wood picking to cooking, sowing and mending, and caring for infants and sick members of the household.

On account of the segmentation of the labor market in the process of economic globalization, women have been submitted to an even higher degree of exploitation with international ventures shopping around the globe for the lowest possible wages. Individual countries engage in injurious competition on the basis of cheap labor and lax labor standards, a true "race to the bottom," vying for advantage in world trade and capital flows.[7] The erosion of basic worker rights demanded in some adjustment plans has affected more severely the feminine labor force. These same plans entail reduced expenditures on social services and consequently have an enormous social impact. This impact is even greater on women who have to make up for these losses on behalf of their children and the elderly in their families. The volatility of capital flows and the entailing economic disruption recently verified in several third world countries only accrues to that grim picture. Much labor-intensive work does not depend on the establishment of large industrial plants. Shoe and clothing production is, for the most part, executed at home with very simple equipment. This practice restores the labor process previous to the industrial revolution and has for women the consequence of maintaining and enforcing the paternalistic structure that still rules the family in these peripheral economies.

For his analysis the Portuguese author brings some conclusions of Esther Boserup's work, *Women's Roles in Economic Development,* first published in 1970, and he wonders whether this data might not be outdated. On the contrary. It is impressive that those conclusions are still valid as states the report of the meeting of the second committee (Economic and Financial) of the United Nations, held October 29, 1999. The representative of Guyana, Ms. Sheridan Ameer, speaking on behalf of the Group of 77 developing countries and China, stressed the acceleration of the feminization of poverty. For her,

the internationalization of production, reorganization of work and patterns of labor mobility in the globalized economy had mainly affected women. The Group was alarmed at the growing trends towards increased outsourcing by multinational corporations, usually to low-wage sites in developing countries, and the undue exploitation of women that resulted from that practice.

On the same occasion, Angela King, special adviser to the Secretary-General on gender issues and the advancement of women, made comments on the *1999 World Survey on the Role of Women in Development*. Increased economic volatility, job insecurity, and lower enjoyment of basic worker rights show that globalization has had strong gender employment effects. The survey found that

globalization did not relieve the gender-based discriminatory practices that characterized every stage of economic development. Nor did it tend to minimize gender inequalities. It might even, in some circumstances, exacerbate them.

Under family law, in many places women remain subject to male authority and guardianship, have their access to divorce severely restricted, even in cases of domestic violence, suffer from limitations in their exercise of guardianship over children, and are denied the right to inherit from their husbands. As to working conditions, they may be prevented from working outside the home, attending school, traveling, and, in extreme cases, even obtaining health care. In neighboring Mexico,[8] they may be denied their right to intimate privacy and be subject to on-the-job pregnancy discrimination, after pregnancy tests upon hiring. Discrimination takes an economic bias when it comes to participation in loan programs for populations displaced by war.[9] Women are provided with significantly smaller loan amounts and steered to gender-stereotyped, low-paying occupations.

Slavery still survives in the twenty-first century.

The United States government estimated that one to two million women and girls were being trafficked annually around the world for the purposes of forced labor, forced prostitution, servile domestic labor or involuntary marriage.[10]

Even when not actually displaced, women and young girls can be forced into prostitution by desper-

ately poor families, and sexual tourism flourishes in many third world countries, like Brazil, Cambodia, and Thailand.

The big picture shows us that women are, as always, mostly kept in a servile condition either at home or work, and the economic difficulties of developing countries only accrue to their distress. There is for sure an interrelatedness of economic development and discrimination. This is why nowadays the right to development is an integral part of the women's rights agenda. It also shows that the movement has broadened its perspective from a domestic or individual focus into a more comprehensive one.[11]

5.

Developed countries present different forms of the feminization of poverty. It shows in the increasing numbers of teenage pregnancies and the toll that such precocious responsibilities take on young women's perspectives of education and career building. It also shows in the large number of households that have the mother as the only breadwinner. The capitalist economy encouraged the two-wage-earner family. Women were made to believe that there was a gain in status from paid work outside the home. But the unpaid jobs are still there and the unpaid work must still be done. Women managed to "fit in" this new arrangement of society, rapidly surmounting their shortcomings in education and skills but, in the process, accepting an overburden of their traditional, less recognized tasks that have only in part been shared with their male partners, where there is one. When families part it gets even worse. No matter how strict legislation passed is, a large number of divorced men still flee from their responsibilities toward their children leaving them to the sole support of their ex-wives.[12]

The report of the UN Secretary-General, *1999 World Survey on the Role of Women in Development: Globalization, Gender and Work,* points out that

in many middle- and upper-middle-income countries, labor demand has been shifting towards relatively high skill manufacturing; while employment growth in traditionally low skill sectors, such as textiles and apparel, where women workers predominate, has been declining.

This statement reveals clearly that while this shift in employment took place (since perhaps as early as the late 1980s) no serious and comprehensive efforts have been undertaken to increase educational and training opportunities in nontraditional subjects for women so that they could fairly compete for the new, high-skill jobs. The result is that, generally speaking, the great majority of women are, more and more, contending among themselves just to keep their low-pay, dead-end jobs.

But poverty means more than a lack of minimum income. It also means a life filled with uncertainty, vulnerability, powerlessness, physical isolation, and social exclusion.[13] It can also mean diminished quality of life for the perpetually hurried working mother:[14] diminished creativity and opportunities for exploring hobbies and interests, and diminished time for social change. Having no time to be heard in the public sector, women can do little for social improvements and have little influence on the political arena.

Even where awareness of the problem is consistent and human rights and women's rights activism is outstanding, as is the case in the United States, violence against women prevails in the forms of battering, sexual assault, and murder.[15]

These facts lead us to the conclusion that in peripheral economies, as well as in the lower walks of life in developed countries, there is still much to be done in order to ensure that women benefit from basic human rights.

6.

From a civil rights perspective, women everywhere still have a long way to go to reach the same opportunities that are offered to their male colleagues in the corporate world, in public office, and in international organizations. The guarantees of nondiscrimination have not been enforced to the extent of ensuring to well educated and capable women access to power positions. They still lag behind and quite often are overthrown by less qualified males. This is not a vain statement. It is backed up by serious research and analysis. Opportunities for career advancement are dismal, even in countries where standards for women are high. For that matter, we should listen to the findings of an Australian researcher.[16] She named her paper "Glass Ceilings and Sticky Floors." The first expression defines the vertical sex segregation in organizations;[17] the second that there may not be career movement beyond the initial entry job. To these she adds another barrier, which she dubs "glass walls," referring to occupational segregation. Although Australian authorities invest serious efforts in fighting discrimination and even as the research took place in the finance industry, one of the major employers of women, the findings are that they would rather be confined in part-time work (94.5 percent of the total part-time employees are women) where training and career options are generally poor. As a consequence, only 15 percent of women were classified as managers and administrators. For the United States, the *Washington Post* published in 1998 a series of five articles that analyzed a national survey whose results showed that "the executive suite remains disproportionately male: . . . only 1 in 10 corporate officers and fewer than 3 percent of all chief executive officers are women." [18]

It is not different in civil service. Only 15 of the 187 countries that were assessed by the United Nations Division for the Advancement of Women (data of 1996) could boast more than 20 percent of women in ministerial positions. Forty-eight countries had none. Albeit, the inclusion quite often only hides the reality of exclusion and pays lip service to political correctness. Not even in developed countries does reality correspond to goodwill. When admitted, women are usually relegated to positions of no strategic importance for their countries. The social area is usually their destination. No wonder that this is exactly where budgetary cuts are first made when facing economic crisis. In 73 percent of the countries where this research took place, women had no role in economic areas, not even at the subministerial level.

Analyzing data furnished by the Division for the Advancement of Women (UN), we verify that in some instances even these ministerial positions are illusory and don't reflect conditions of sustainable access for women.[19] It's no use just to fill a quota with ill-prepared females, for their bad performance will create a backlash against other competent women who may be toiling their way upwards. The same with women who are not sensible to or aware of gender issues, for they take their accomplishments as individual success and may not be willing to work for the advancement of women.

The economic affluence of a country seems to have little to do with the share in power that is allotted to women. Examples are Japan with a very poor rate;[20] Kuwait, one of the highest per capita income rates of the world with no woman in a ministerial position;[21] and the United Kingdom, reigned by a queen and governed until recently by a strong woman, still showing rates that are only slightly over the global average.[22]

It also doesn't seem like exclusion has any relation to political ideology, for in countries strongly imprinted with egalitarian theories averages of access are very low, as in Russia[23] or in Cuba.[24]

Even in countries where illiteracy rates are subaverage, access to power positions may vary widely. This is the case of Argentina, with no women in ministerial positions, a minute[25] participation in the intermediate level, and illiteracy barely reaching 1.5 percent of women less than twenty-five years of age and 4.9 percent of those over twenty-five. With a similarly low illiteracy rate,[26] Chile boasts 14.3 percent women with ministerial status.

Latin America offers some dramatic examples of exclusion if we compare the share of women in the total labor force (paid work) and their representation in high office. In Uruguay, where 41 percent of the labor force is represented by women, only 6.7 percent have access to top government jobs and only 16.7 percent to the middle level. In other countries of the same region the numbers are somewhat blurred due to the fact that the informal economy is largely the realm of women.

Although in most countries the right to vote has been extended to women, its counterpart did not follow as easily. Women are underrepresented in parliaments everywhere, and the recommendation of the Conference of Beijing goes unfulfilled for that matter. Similar situations can be verified in the academic world where few women rise to the level of associate professors. The same exclusion is also to be verified in the international scene. We can see no women in decision-making bodies like the

UN, the OAS, or in international courts in The Hague, Luxembourg, and Costa Rica.

7.

Law has been a powerful trendsetting instrument all throughout the last century. Awareness of women's issues and of the need to access them percolated from international treaties and conventions to national legislations all over the world. We have seen ongoing progress that like a wheel set in motion cannot easily be turned back. It is very important to set those high standards even though, as we well know, their full implementation is still a far cry from reality. It is necessary that the international community takes a stand in their defense for this is a factor that adds a decisive incentive for national governments to put up specific policies and programs that support women's human rights.

In the terms of the Treaty of Rome for the creation of the permanent International Criminal Court (ICC), rape, sexual slavery, enforced prostitution, forced pregnancy, and enforced sterilization are considered as war crimes and crimes against humanity. On this basis, the International Criminal Tribunal for Rwanda, for the first time punished sexual violence in a civil war and considered rape as an act of genocide. Also, the International Criminal Tribunal for the Former Yugoslavia (ICTY) indicted twenty-seven men for gender-based offenses.

The influence of the Conference of Beijing is quite clear. It resulted in significant progress in various countries.[27]

But good legislation in itself is not enough. It is also necessary that those who interpret such texts are sensible to women's human rights. That's the reason why our judges, male and female alike, should receive in their training programs solid information about the cultural biases that may affect women's rights.[28] The role of the courts is deemed to be increasingly important in setting the pace for progress in this area, even more so when it means the rulings of international courts with its persuasive authority over local governments.

One step further is the continuing effort that is necessary to make cultural changes that are needed everywhere so that the future generations may benefit from a renewal of the feminine image—more human and whole, no longer demonized, no longer idealized. We should insist on having woman depicted as a full human being, in all its dignity, whose will is to be respected, whose potential is to be acknowledged and developed, and whose contribution for building a new world order of peace and plenty for all cannot be done without.

For that matter, much expectation relies on the media, the marketing, and the entertainment industries, who have their share of responsibility in the maintenance and diffusion of demeaning feminine stereotypes. Hopefully we shall see a time when the vast majority will be outraged to see women portrayed as objects, in stupid or subservient roles. These pervasive models still shape the fantasies of women and girls and channel their aspirations. School and family have a hard time conveying higher values and often lose ground to the appealing techniques used for the diffusion of new products.

And of course, much depends on how we raise our sons and daughters and prepare them for life in a century that we all wish to be better than the one just finished. There is no good and permanent change for "those who hold half of the sky"[29] without the participation of the other half. The fight for women's rights is not confrontational, is not exclusive of men, and is not a quest for supremacy. In their plights women represent the aggression of human values that is perpetrated over large segments of humanity.

8.

For the next century the feminine question will remain a civil rights issue for women in developed countries and for those women at the top of the socioeconomic pyramid in developing countries. And it will still be a human rights issue for most women in the third world and for those in the lowest tiers of the socioeconomic pyramid in the developed countries. Bare survival for these will be the first and only worry; famine, disease, ignorance, and the need to ensure their actual physical survival will be very present for them. For the ones in the top echelons as well as for most women in countries of strong economic presence in the world, the big issue will be access to power.

The twentieth century was a time of awareness about civil, human, and women's rights. For the first time in history large international assemblies convened to share their concerns over these issues and to set down minimum standards to be complied with. The recognition that, to this day, not all women enjoy the protection established by national and international norms should not discourage us. It should encourage those of us, both men and women, who are in vantage points to accept the responsibility of carrying the banner of full implementation of women's human rights for all. Together we can improve our less than perfect society and make this world a healthy and secure place for humankind. Women in high positions around the globe should use their influence in order to obtain from governments and international organizations a switch from rigidly cost-effective planning to social and human-effective policies. More female leadership can only be beneficial for humankind, for women would bring along characteristics that have been lacking and are severely needed in conducting the world's business and politics. Progress accumulated through the length of civilization should not be the share of just a few. The acceleration of scientific knowledge and the end of international nuclear stress must result in better quality of life for humanity as a whole. Caring for people and creating a safe and healthy environment for the family have always been women's roles.

Women's Roles and the Promise of American Law

Kenneth L. Karst

In 1909 Herbert Croly, a leading theorist of the Progressive movement, published a book entitled *The Promise of American Life.* Croly challenged the American people to join in a national enterprise to found a community that was truly national, transcending their regional differences and their religious or ethnic divisions. In today's perspective, many of Croly's specific proposals seem unappealing,[1] but his title captured something enduring in our society. From the "pursuit of happiness" celebrated in the Declaration of Independence to modern articulations of the American dream, the idea of promise has been central in defining the meanings of America, and in the self-definition of individuals. As a group, Americans are often said to be open to change, future-oriented, and optimistic. To speak of the promise of American life was—and is—to evoke a set of aspirations for individuals and for a people.

This afternoon we are concerned with women's roles, and I am to discuss that subject in relation to American law. A concern for aspirations is very much to the point, for a social role is the sum of norms linked to some social position (such as the position of an American woman) and a norm is a cluster of expectations of appropriate behavior.[2]

The title of today's session, referring to "cultures" in the plural, reminds us that the roles socially permitted to women are not given in nature but vary from one culture to another. So as soon as we ask about women's permissible aspirations, we have to recognize that there has been no single and universal promise of American life. In the first place, realistic aspirations have never been equally distributed over the whole population. The expectations of American women often have differed according to their race or ethnicity, their economic class, or their sexual orientation.[3] Even if we were to lump all American women together, we should have to recognize the persistence of a gap between the realistic aspirations of women as a group and of men as a group.

At least two dimensions of cultural variation are worth our attention. First, every culture is dynamic, changing over time. Here I emphasize cultural change in the years since the Second World War. Second, American society has always been multicultural, and it is important today to keep in mind that American women of color often have distinctive concerns. Another aspect of our cultural diversity is visible in recent political conflicts specifically focused on defining proper social roles. The perspectives of time and cultural difference come together in today's "culture wars," where the main actors see themselves in a struggle to define women's roles not only for now but for the future. On all sides, leaders who seek to shape cultural norms for women's behavior are resting a major part of their hopes on the promise of law.

In 1945, a few months before the end of the Second World War, the Michigan state legislature enacted a law requiring the licensing of bartenders in cities with populations of 50,000 or more. Only males over twenty-one were to be licensed, except that a woman could be licensed if she were "the wife or daughter of the male owner" of the bar. The law thus discriminated against women owners of bars and against women bartenders.[4] Valentine Goesaert, a woman who owned a bar in Dearborn, and her daughter Margaret, whom she had employed as a bartender, challenged the law as a denial of the equal protection of the laws. The Supreme Court rejected this claim in 1948. Justice Felix Frankfurter, writing for a 6–3 majority, said that the Michigan legislature might have believed "that the oversight assured through ownership of a bar by a barmaid's husband or father minimizes hazards that may confront a barmaid without such protecting oversight." Because such a belief was "not without a basis in reason," he said, the Court could not "give ear to the suggestion that the real impulse behind this legislation was an unchivalrous desire of male bartenders to try to monopolize the calling." [5]

Today this patronizing opinion irritates the eye, and perhaps you will agree with me as I applaud a 1976 Supreme Court opinion specifically disapproving the bartender decision.[6] The 1970s were a watershed for the modern American women's movement, and for the bodies of law that most directly influenced women's roles. Since then, formal legal restrictions on women's liberty and equality have mostly been discarded, and the status of American women has noticeably improved.[7] In 1948 it would have been hard to imagine that before the end of the century women would constitute about half of the nation's law students, women would constitute more than one out of five members of state legislatures, and women would be flying combat aircraft and attending Virginia Military Institute.

A few years ago, Deborah Rhode, a feminist legal scholar who is no Pollyanna, said, "The progress toward gender equality over the last three decades rivals that of the three preceding millennia. Women's control over the terms of their own destiny has never been greater."[8] One aspiration that American women can realistically entertain is the hope for further strides toward gender equality in the next three decades. In contrast, consider the words of Abby Liebman, director of the California Women's Law Center in Los Angeles, as she contemplated the persistence of sexual harassment, domestic violence against women, and the feminization of poverty: "We are trying to bring a huge change to the whole culture. To do that, you have to be content with setting smaller goals and celebrating the little changes."[9] As these two quotations make clear, formal legal equality for women is essential, but it can never be more than part of the story of women's equal citizenship.

Although the Michigan bartenders case no longer serves as a precedent, it will serve us as an illustration of two themes that have been central in the modern women's movement and in the law's recent contributions to sex equality. One theme is equal access to positions in the public world, including the world of work. Another theme is the emancipation of women from male control in the family and in other intimate relationships. This case shows how each of these themes is a counterpoint to the other. The bartender law reflected the premise that Woman, by virtue of her sex, is weak and vulnerable, in need of Man the protector—and the Supreme Court not only accepted the premise but reinforced it. In this article I discuss the interaction of law and other instruments of cultural development in transforming the roles that are socially permissible for women, first in work, and then in their intimate relationships. Both of these transformations of women's status have produced unease among substantial numbers of Americans—enough of them to form a major political constituency—and so I conclude with a brief look at the place of law in this arena of the politics of cultural counterrevolution.

I. Law and the Culture of Women's Work

By 1948, when the Supreme Court decided the bartender case, many of the women who had filled the employment void caused by the wartime draft had gone back home—as they were urged to do by public officials who wanted to assure returning servicemen that jobs would be waiting.[10] Even during the war, the traditional view of household life as "woman's place" had exerted a gravitational drag on women's prospects. Often women had been paid wages lower than men's, and often they had been channeled into work that had a "domestic" feel. Yet, as Alice Kessler-Ross has shown, the increase of women working outside the home was not just a fulfillment of patriotic duty; it also carried forward an earlier trend of growth in the proportion of women in wage work. Mainly, it manifested the "latent tendency of women to seek wage work when normative pressures to stay at home are removed."[11] Experience has its own acculturating power; many women who had found fulfillment in wartime jobs returned to housework with a frustration generated by dashed hopes. Even those who were more accepting of the return to domesticity surely came home with an enhanced sense of their own capacity.

In the postwar years the proportion of women working for wages continued to grow steadily. The first major antidiscrimination laws were not enacted until the 1960s, when women already constituted one-third of the work force.[12] Meanwhile, sex discrimination continued to be the order of the day. Job markets were segmented by gender, with women overrepresented in "helping" work (nurse, teacher, clerical worker); women's work, more often than men's, was part-time or temporary work; pay for women still lagged behind pay for men; trade unions resisted enrolling women workers. At the same time, however, colleges were graduating unprecedented numbers of women, and many of them were going on to graduate and professional schools. By the 1960s women in small but significant numbers had begun to enter the building trades. A culture of consumption gave new legitimacy for a married woman to take a job outside the home, to increase the family's power to consume.[13] A critical mass of employed women now constituted something a politician could recognize as a constituency, and officeholders were hearing calls from women for equal treatment in the work force. Congress passed the Equal Pay Act in 1963, the same year that Betty Friedan published her book *The Feminine Mystique.* The 1963 law prohibited pay differences for men and women doing the same work— but, significantly, did not cover agricultural workers or domestic workers.

A general law forbidding sex discrimination in employment seemed beyond political reach. Then President John Kennedy was assassinated, and President Lyndon Johnson gave a high priority to the Kennedy civil rights bill. While Congress was debating the proposal to forbid racial discrimination by employers, a highly placed southern senator proposed that the employment discrimination provisions of the bill be extended to forbid not only racial discrimination but sex discrimination. This proposal was intended to derail the whole project by extending it to absurdity. The pending bill was so amended, with strong southern support. When a committee then sought to delete sex discrimination from the bill, a woman senator and a woman in the House threatened to tie up the whole civil rights bill if the deletion were carried out. So Congress backed into the wording of Title VII that remains today—and sex discrimination became illegal for any business employing at least twenty-five (today fifteen) workers.[14]

It would be an oversimplification to describe this legal prohibition of sex discrimination in employment as a case in which law merely ratified a cultural change that had already taken place. But this important advance in women's legal status took root in a cultural ground that was well prepared. The presence of so many women in the work force contradicted the earlier view of women as weak and domestic. And although politics had not reached a point where one might expect the enactment of a freestanding law forbidding sex discrimination, politics had placed some women in important public office. Without the growth in women's employment and the placement of women in Congress, surely the extension of Title VII to sex discrimination would have been deferred to a later time.[15]

In the years since 1964, however, undeniably Title VII has had an important acculturating power of its own. Employers and employees by the millions, men as well as women, today take for granted the general proposition that sex discrimination in employment is wrong. It is worth our while to try to suggest how this process might be working. Part of Title VII's force as an agent of cultural change is that it stands as a public symbol, an official declaration by the United States—not just by "the government" but by the polity.[16] A more important influence on the culture of the workplace and the wider national culture is the impact of antidiscrimination law on the day-to-day behavior of employees and workers. Title VII is a high-visibility law; the very name "Title VII" has a high recognition value, and not just among the college educated. Part of the reason for this visibility is that the law is not only enforced but seen to be enforced. Workers in the plant know when a Title VII suit is filed, and they know how the case comes out. The educative power of this law, in other words, is strong. Furthermore, when the law is enforced, moving women into jobs from which they have traditionally been excluded (electricians, plumbers, metal workers, shop supervisors), those women help to reacculturate their coworkers every day, just by showing up and doing their work.

A vital aspect of women's access to work is the workplace environment. If the office or the factory floor is inhospitable, women's legal right of access to the work may be merely theoretical and not real. One long-standing behavior that makes the workplace inhospitable to women has been sexual harassment—a practice so common that it escaped the notice of most men, including federal judges.[17] The text of Title VII generally forbids an employer to "discriminate" against an individual because of sex, but it does not address the harassment problem explicitly. The first judicial entry into this territory came in the late 1970s, when two federal courts interpreted Title VII to forbid conduct we now call sexual harassment.[18] The breakthrough came in 1979, when Catharine MacKinnon, in her book, *Sexual Harassment of Working Women*,[19] made three crucial contributions: first, she popularized "sexual harassment" as a name for the practice; second, she argued compellingly that harassment of women on the job, although common ever since women went to work outside the home, was neither a joke nor a "natural" behavior of men but a harm to be taken seriously; and third, she made a convincing legal case that sexual harassment on the job was actionable sex discrimination in violation of Title VII. A number of lower federal courts, and then the Supreme Court, were persuaded.[20] The importance of establishing the name was twofold. In the first place, law, to be carried out by judges and to be followed by ordinary citizens, needs categories of conduct that bear labels. Furthermore, the term "sexual harassment" entered the common speech of employers and employees—indeed, entered a nationwide vocabulary, influencing perceptions of gender relations well beyond the domain of work.

Unfortunately, as Vicki Schultz recently made clear, most courts have tended to limit the idea of sexual harassment to sexual advances, minimizing the discrimination inherent in other forms of abuse of women workers when they seek to perform roles previously reserved to men: picking on them, constantly denying their competence, denying them opportunities for work experience needed for promotion.[21] More is obviously needed if the courts are to carry out the basic nondiscrimination command of Title VII. But bringing the legal remedies of Title VII to bear on harassment by employers and supervisors has also changed the everyday experience of millions of Americans on the job, contributing to the acculturation of men and women alike to new understandings about the behavior that is per-

missible in the workplace. In turn, the behavior teaches both those who engage in it and those who see it.

Title VII, of course, also forbids racial discrimination in employment, and a discussion of this law is a good place to raise more general questions about the ways in which culture and law interact in shaping the conditions of women of color. Some feminist writing has been criticized by African-American and Latina feminists for assuming that the experience of American women fits a "white-European" model and for ignoring differences in the lives of women of color.[22] More specifically, the critics worry that general analyses of women's condition may fail to notice that women of color often face forms of discrimination that can be harmful in ways distinct from either race or sex discrimination, perhaps more harmful than the sum of those two parts.[23] As the critics understand, any rule of law necessarily generalizes. They do not object to a general law forbidding sex discrimination in employment. What concerns them lies below the surface of any legal rule, in the application of general (assumedly race-neutral) legal principles to the particularized facts of women's lives.[24] Here, at ground level, a major irony abounds: The cultural fact of race[25] is capable of infusing—even dominating—perceptions of women of color when general policies are made by private actors and by government officers, but it is also capable of disappearing from official view when judges and other officers decide individual cases. The incongruity is apt to be exacerbated, and the difficulty of coping more acute, when the women of color are poor.

In some early Title VII cases, black women failed to win certification as a class of persons ("black women," fittingly enough) entitled to relief and were denied the right to serve as representatives of a class *either* including both black and white women *or* including black men and women.[26] (In a class action, the plaintiff is supposed to represent a group that has homogeneous interests.) In such a case, black women who could not "conclusively say that 'but for' their race or 'but for' their gender they would be treated differently" would remain outside the law's effective protection.[27] In later cases, however, other federal courts have concluded that it is possible to find discrimination against black women even though proof has not been made of discrimination against either white women or black men.[28] Still, American labor law, including not only Title VII but the legal structures for determining union representation, leaves women of color with a series of difficult choices among strategies emphasizing inclusiveness and strategies emphasizing their separate needs.[29] Cultural diversity comes to the fore when we consider the bilingual Latina worker in the Southwest who confronts her employer's English-only rule for the workplace; she may find that, for purposes of securing useful interpretations of Title VII, she has more in common with bilingual Latinos than she has with other women.[30]

These are sobering reminders, not just about cultural variations in what American women can realistically find in the promise of law, but more generally about the limitations of law. Still, if cultural change is a change in the meanings assigned to behavior,[31] Title VII, considered as a whole, has contributed mightily to cultural change. Little by little, local traditions of excluding women are giving way to more egalitarian cultural norms governing work. That is the good news. The bad news about gendered cultural norms is that they are embedded in the way we all think about social relations, so deeply embedded that they influence attitudes toward sex and gender that lie below the level of conscious decision. The psychologists' term for such a cluster of meanings is a gender schema,[32] and one consequence of the schema is political. Given that sex stereotyping is pervasive, it comes to be seen not as acculturation but as an aspect of "reality"; thus a sex-based system of dominance[33] is made invisible, and criticism of the hierarchy is made to seem "a request for special protection in disguise."[34]

In this light, three more gender inequalities in the area of work need to be taken into account. First, although the wage gap is narrowing, especially among younger workers, the wages for women's work still lag behind men's wages.[35] Part of the cause for this historic disparity is the continuation of the old assumptions, sometimes hidden and sometimes not, that a number of jobs have genders.[36] It is fair to say even today that a women who wants a blue-collar job almost certainly faces an uphill struggle; a "real woman," say the men who surround her at work, would not want such a job.[37] In other forms of employment, too, it is sometimes said—in court—that if women are underrepresented in some type of work, the reason is that the work is something women prefer not to do.[38] Given the persistent strength of cultural stereotypes, the very idea

of choice is blurred, and the degree to which gender-based segmentation of a given workforce reflects women's choices (rather than constraints imposed by employers or by other factors, such as perceived family obligations) is—literally—beyond measure.[39] Even when jobs are plainly open to women, in large proportion the jobs are still designed for an "ideal worker" who has no child responsibilities and can work until midnight when it is necessary—all on the assumption that someone else is home with the children. In short, the ideal worker, on the traditional model, is a man.[40] A woman colleague of mine says, "What I need is a wife."

Second, consider the scarcity of women in top management positions. Here the metaphor of the "glass ceiling" is almost perfect; a barrier exists, but it isn't visible. I cannot think of any company with a formal rule that the chief executive officer must be a man. In today's Air Force, no regulation prevents a woman from being a high-level commander of a combat unit, or even chief of staff.[41] Women lawyers, in theory, should be as likely as men with similar qualifications to rise to partnership in law firms.[42] What limits women's expectations of reaching all these high positions is not the sort of explicit policy of discrimination that is easily redressed by the law of equal employment opportunity. Indeed, at least some of these results are not explainable by anyone's conscious decision to exclude women from leadership. Surely, though, the traditional gender schema is at work here. No doubt many a male leader, called on to select his successor, will match the competing candidates against his own internalized picture of what it means to "look like a leader." It isn't that he will limit his search to men; rather, his mental picture will feature traits that his culture has taught him to associate—unconsciously—with masculinity.[43] Here, too, women of color are even more likely than white women to be forgotten in the search for leaders.[44]

A third inequality results from continued cultural expectations that women, working or not, must perform domestic duties—and this although "[t]he wife economy is as obsolete as the slave economy."[45] The issue is not new; earlier incarnations of the women's movement sought changes in law to recognize women's contributions to the household economy, first (unsuccessfully) by claiming that housework justified laws to afford joint ownership of marital property, and then (successfully) by promoting laws to give women control over their own earnings.[46] Neither of these law reform strategies would challenge the generally held assumption that home and family are primarily women's work. Nor can this assumption be dismissed as a stereotype that has died out. In a famous passage, George Lakoff remarked on the vitality of this assumption, which provides the cultural context for the expression "working mother." [47] And, to bring us up to date, a 1999 poll of parents in California showed strong agreement—68 percent among fathers and 69 percent of mothers—with the following proposition: "It is much better for a family if the father works outside the home and the mother takes care of the children."[48] When the married mother does work, typically she is expected to continue to take primary responsibility for child care and also for housework,[49] and typically she takes that responsibility. Married women do about four-fifths of the housework and two-thirds of child care.[50] Part-time work is no answer, for the pay is too low—and married mothers are mostly working full time.[51] In the aggregate, these inequalities effectively exclude many women from equal citizenship.[52]

The double bind of work and family has been especially acute for young, poor women of color in the inner cities. They are damned if they accept welfare benefits because they are seen to be lazing around instead of earning their keep. But they are also damned if they leave their children with someone else during the day, denying them motherly nurturance. Although this double bind may come to bear on any mother who works outside the home, a long-standing cultural assumption among white Americans gives the expression "welfare mother" a black or brown face.[53] In 1992, when Vice President Dan Quayle launched his famous attack on the irresponsibility of unwed motherhood, he tapped into this racial stereotype, as well as an ancient stereotype of black people as sexually promiscuous.[54] He announced that "the narcotic of welfare," as consumed by immoral single mothers who bore children outside marriage, was responsible for such evils as urban riots. This ploy was attuned to a political program of cultural counterrevolution, a subject revisited in the last section of this article.

The wage gap, the glass ceiling, and the double bind of work and family all reflect the staying power of cultural norms the Supreme Court has branded as "archaic and stereotypical notions" about women and men.[55] Even so, in the absence of governmental involvement or provable violation of civil rights laws, there is nothing in any of these conditions that law can readily grasp. The easy case—today typified by the Supreme Court's invalidation of the Virginia Military Institute's former all-male admissions policy[56]—is the case in which government plainly and deliberately discriminates against women. That action is routinely held unconstitutional.[57] In the more usual case, however, an official discriminatory purpose is hard to prove, and so a "neutral" law—even when it systematically harms women—is not considered sex discrimination at all. Rather, the harm is ascribed to some larger social or economic condition for which the government agency in court is not responsible.[58] This very conclusion has become the Supreme Court's theme song for the constitutional law of sex discrimination.[59] One risk in identifying pervasive cultural norms as a source of the subordination of women is that when we look around to locate responsibility for the subordination, no one seems responsible. Any lawyer will confirm that "the culture" is an unpromising defendant.

To say that a pervasively gendered culture will not yield readily to transformation by legal means is not to deny that the law has a role to play in cultural change. As an essay in cultural agency, the application of Title VII in expanding women's realistic aspirations in the world of work is, on the whole, a success story.[60] The success is not just that women have more and better work opportunities—even among married women of working age, some three-fourths are in the work force[61]—but that the enforcement of the law has some influence on the way men view women, and the way women view themselves. In this sense there is a cultural connection between the public world of work and the private world of intimate relations, and the law governing work is a link in the connection. As we shall see, a similar acculturating process has attended the uses of law governing the intimate relations themselves.

II. Law, Culture, and the Control of Women's Sexuality and Maternity

From the time of the earliest known legal systems, men's legal control over women's sexuality and maternity was a crucial foundation of the patriarchal family.[62] "The first gender-defined social role for women was to be those who were exchanged in marriage transactions," [63] and it was men who did the exchanging. For much of human history a woman's social status and economic class depended on her remaining under a man's protection and control—above all, control over her sexuality and maternity. The legal controls to accomplish this end were pervasive, including the law governing marriage, marital property, divorce, control over children, "illegitimacy," abortion, contraception, prostitution, and rape. From the mid-nineteenth century on, when women sought the vote, one principal goal was legislation that would increase their control over their own private lives,[64] and when women in the modern era spoke of "liberation," they continued to pay attention to the private domain. In that domain single, heterosexual women typically could control conception and childbirth only by a strategy of denial, and married women remained under the legal control of their husbands as to those intimate matters. Women had to wait until the 1960s and 1970s before their right to control their own sexuality and maternity received constitutional recognition—a recognition promoted by a generalized egalitarian shift in American politics following the successes of the movement for racial equality.[65]

In a series of famous cases the Supreme Court recognized constitutional rights to be free from state prohibitions on access to contraceptive devices and to abortion. From the 1965 contraceptives decision in *Griswold v. Connecticut*[66] to the 1973 abortion decision in *Roe v. Wade*,[67] the Court's opinions were written in the language of individual autonomy, but it soon became apparent that the unifying theme of these decisions was the validation of women's claim to equal citizenship.[68] What was at stake was more than the freedom to avoid conception or childbirth. It was the capacity to participate fully in the public life of the community, including the public world of work. Absent control over conception and maternity, a woman's access to this public life could be blocked not only by a formal or informal rule of exclusion but also by an unwanted pregnancy. This denial of access, multiplied by the number of women so denied, had its own acculturating effects, instructing men as well as women that women could not realistically aspire to

"the freedom of the city."[69] If the right of reproductive choice seems to some critics of *Roe v. Wade* to be a "super-protected right,"[70] the justification for strong protection is that the right is a necessary condition, not only for an individual woman's sense of self and equal citizenship, but for the equal citizenship of women in general.

The question of abortion rights offers an illustration of the interaction between law and other forms of acculturation. The *Roe* decision would have been inconceivable to the justices who decided the case of the Michigan bartender law a quarter century earlier. By 1973, however, the contraceptive pill was in wide use, offering women an important control over their sexual expression, and the Court had given that control constitutional recognition. Furthermore, by 1973, the modern women's movement had attained new political strength and had achieved its first judicial successes in making sex discrimination a serious constitutional issue.[71] No woman had yet been appointed to the Supreme Court. Indeed, Justice Byron White, dissenting in *Roe v. Wade*, remarked that the question of a woman's right to choose to have an abortion involved "issues over which reasonable men may easily and heatedly differ."[72] It is true that none of the justices had themselves lived at "the raw edges of human existence"[73] experienced by women who would choose to have abortions, but the justices were closely acquainted with upper-middle-class white women, the group that formed the early core of the modern women's movement. In 1973 then, *Roe v. Wade* seems to have been more a result than a cause of political and cultural change.[74]

In a number of states, abortion politics quickly took a turn toward restrictive legislation, and national politics soon followed. Laws to restrict abortion rights became a central goal of a nationwide "social issues agenda," designed to appeal to a constituency that favored a cultural counterrevolution.[75] For a generation this constituency of social conservatives has carried great weight in a number of state legislatures and in the Congress. Although the constituency's influence on presidential politics declined, it remained strong enough to influence the appointment of justices. Not surprisingly, the strength of *Roe v. Wade* as a precedent began to weaken as a reconstituted Supreme Court majority upheld one after another law cutting back abortion rights. By 1991, the possibility seemed real that the *Roe* decision would be overruled,[76] and in 1992 the Court was presented with a clear opportunity to accomplish that result.

The case was *Planned Parenthood of Southeastern Pennsylvania v. Casey.*[77] Pennsylvania had adopted several laws restricting abortion, including a rule that a wife seeking an abortion must notify her husband, and a rule that a doctor must not perform an abortion until he had provided the woman with some literature counseling against abortion and a twenty-four-hour waiting period had passed. At the Court's conference, a majority of the justices evidently voted to uphold all the laws; four justices were prepared to overrule *Roe,* but Justice Kennedy preferred simply to uphold these laws and to consider future abortion restrictions case by case. In the event, however, Justice Kennedy was persuaded to change his vote on the husband-notification law and to join with Justice O'Connor and Justice Souter in a joint opinion recognizing a woman's right to choose to have an abortion but allowing abortion regulations that did not "unduly burden" that right. This plurality joined with Justice Blackmun and Justice Stevens (who would have reaffirmed *Roe* in its entirety) to form a 5–4 majority that struck down the husband-notification rule. Although the other regulations were upheld, the basic right of a woman to choose to have an abortion was reconfirmed.[78] Justice Kennedy's preferred case-by-case evaluation will now go forward as the courts determine which state burdens on a woman's choice are "undue."

Casey's reaffirmation of the woman's right of choice was by no means a simple decision to follow precedent.[79] It is more fittingly seen as a reflection of the influence of *Roe v. Wade* on the larger culture, an influence the majority justices in *Casey* chose not to ignore. All three of the plurality justices, in the parts of the joint opinion they initially drafted,[80] took explicit notice of the issue of women's roles that lies at the heart of the abortion right. Justice O'Connor remarked that the husband-notice rule "embodies a view of marriage consonant with the common-law status of married women but is repugnant to our present understanding of marriage and of the nature of rights protected by the Constitution."[81] Justice Kennedy, discussing due process liberty, referred to a woman's suffering and sacrifice associated with pregnancy and concluded: "Her suffering is too intimate and personal for the State to insist, without more, upon its own vision of the woman's role, however dominant that vision has been in the course of our history and our culture."[82] And Justice Souter, taking note that "an entire generation [of women] has come of age" understanding the promise of *Roe v. Wade,* said that "for two decades of economic and social developments, people have organized intimate relationships and made choices that defined their views of themselves and their places in society, in reliance on the availability of abortion in the event that contraception should fail. The ability of women to participate equally in the economic and social life of the Nation has been facilitated by their ability to control their reproductive lives."[83]

So, among the many lessons of the last generation's struggle over abortion rights is a lesson about law as a cultural product and as an influence on cultural change. The story of abortion rights from *Roe* to *Casey* illustrates how law, like any other cultural form, not only is constituted by prevailing meanings but also plays a role in constituting meanings. Constitutional law by definition develops as courts respond to the products of the political world, but *Roe* shows how the nature of the judicial response depends on a larger cultural context in which politics is only one among many active ingredients.

No culture stands still; "social life," says Renato Rosaldo, "is both inherited *and* always being changed."[84] The cultural setting for American public life has always been strikingly dynamic. Because the Constitution has been seen as a repository of hallowed abstractions such as liberty and equality, constitutional law has been an important cultural arena for efforts to change the status of social groups. Legal claims have been not only a means of mobilizing women but also a means of giving concreteness to women's articulation of their own experiences.[85] Of course, changes in the law affecting group status relationships do not occur in a social vacuum; the existence of a vigorous women's movement stirred up the cultural pot, offered alternatives to traditional assignments of meaning to behavior, and gave women's claim of abortion rights new plausibility as a legitimate aspiration. As J. M. Balkin points out in analyzing the role of law in changes of group status, "law generally works most effectively in assisting the breakdown of a system of social meanings that has already begun" and "when some group has already imagined and acted upon the promise of a better world."[86]

Once *Roe v. Wade* was decided, the right of choice was no longer just a claim in a political contest about the roles that were appropriate for women. Now women's constitutional right to control their own maternity became a cultural icon symbolizing their emerging status as equal citizens; the *Roe* decision itself was a rallying point for the women's movement. The promise of *Roe* was that a woman's unwanted pregnancy would not necessarily imply her exclusion from the public life of the community. This promise of equal citizenship resembled other guarantees of expectations embodied in law, but it had a special poignancy: Equality of status offered a woman not just access to greater opportunities for material gain but an enhanced sense of self. Partly as a result of *Roe,* by 1992 women's equal citizenship could be seen as a "vested" status, in a sense roughly comparable to a vested property right. The possibility of an overruling of *Roe* must have seemed to millions of women to threaten their own status gains as well as their control of their lives. Justice O'Connor's sharp reference in *Casey* to the repugnance of married women's subordinate common-law status suggests that even she may have been acculturated by the promise of *Roe.*

Barriers to women's access to abortion remain, even when there are no direct governmental restrictions on the procedure. One barrier is cost; the federal government, and most states, will not fund abortions for poor women.[87] On the whole, the states that deny funding are the same ones that have enacted a series of restrictive laws, most of which have been held invalid by the courts. In these places the dominant culture envisions an image of the young woman seeking an abortion, an image featuring self-centeredness and promiscuity. This image is projected in the legislative halls and in the minds of those who protest outside birth control clinics: "She brought it on herself," and "if she can't pay for an abortion, well, so much the worse for her." In such a state, a poor woman's choices are bleak, for the minimum cost of an abortion exceeds a whole month's welfare benefit for a family of three.

Whether or not state funding is available, many a woman seeking abortion has no nearby place to turn. In about 85 percent of the counties in America, there is neither a hospital nor a clinic where the procedure is performed[88]—a percentage that may grow as

religious hospitals merge with nonreligious ones. Even in California, where the MediCal program funds abortions for poor women, some counties have no doctors who will accept MediCal patients.[89] In its *Casey* decision the Supreme Court, in theory, left the door open to reconsider the possibility that a twenty-four-hour waiting period requirement might unduly burden the right of choice. For women of limited means in many rural counties, the burden is unquestionably severe, but it remains doubtful whether the law's burden in any individual woman's case will be enough to persuade the Court that the law, in its general application, "unduly" burdens the right of choice. To contemplate this type of case is to recognize that no legal right enforces itself; every right, to be effective, requires an institutional framework and, ultimately, a culture of compliance.

When we view the subjects of women's control of their sexuality, maternity, and intimate relationships in the perspectives of women of color, we see even more clearly that applications of the relevant bodies of law may differ dramatically from one cultural setting to another. Black women's sexuality, so long in the shadow of the white male patriarchy maintained in the slave system, bears a special burden even today. As Barbara Omolade puts it,

> Black woman could not be completely controlled and defined by her own men, for she had already learned to manage and resist the advances of white men, earning and internalizing a reputation for toughness and strength, for resiliency and resolve, that enhanced the myth of her as both matriarch and wild woman.[90]

The previously noted irony[91] thickens and takes on a legal-doctrinal significance: Peggy Cooper Davis, bringing to light the neglected stories of slavery's ruinous effects on family integrity and reproductive autonomy, has argued persuasively for a historical grounding of claims to liberty and equality as to these basic intimate choices in the antislavery origins of the Fourteenth Amendment.[92]

Legal rights in these fields, such as they are, necessarily extend to all women, whatever their race or ethnicity. But the rights thus far recognized by the

Supreme Court, vital as they are in defining women's permissible social roles, are strictly limited: rights against government interference with access to contraception and abortion. For any woman, genuine choice depends on a great deal more than noninterference by the state, as a poor woman learns when she cannot afford to pay for an abortion. But funding is only one concern here. The expression "reproductive choice" evokes meanings for women of color that may lie outside the worries of many other American women.[93] Not the least of these meanings is the choice to have the baby. Dorothy Roberts, who has explored this field more thoroughly and more usefully than any other legal scholar, has highlighted a number of issues concerning sexuality and maternity that poor, young, inner-city women may face, issues either ignored or minimized by current law: lack of information about birth control; subtle and not-so-subtle pressures to engage in unprotected sex; reluctance to seek medical advice if they have taken drugs, for fear of prosecution; the absence of work opportunities, making motherhood the only path to self-realization in sight; the lack of adequate prenatal nutrition or health care; inability to earn enough to care for a child; pressure to submit to sterilization; lack of funds for an abortion.[94] Public policy on questions like these, as expressed in legislation and day-to-day administration, makes talk about a right of reproductive choice seem hollow, indeed, for these young women—and current constitutional law, with its narrow focus on direct state coercion, looks on all these questions with supreme indifference.

One grave limit on women's freedom in the sphere of intimate relations is the staggeringly high risk of domestic violence.[95] The risk is increased for women who are pregnant.[96] For an appallingly long time, married women have almost entirely lacked effective legal protection against their husbands' assaults, including rape. In the nineteenth century, American courts and legislatures formally repudiated the husband's common-law right to chastise his wife by corporal punishment, but as Reva Siegel showed a few years ago, for a century the courts remained reluctant to intervene in wives' behalf, lest they disrupt the "domestic harmony" of the family. Even more recently, the same notion of domestic privacy has been used to shield violence from judicial scrutiny—for exam-

ple, in the doctrine that immunized a spouse from tort damages in a lawsuit by the other spouse.[97] This attitude is not a relic of the dead past; it lives even today.[98]

The law governing domestic violence, like the law more specifically regulating reproductive choice, is properly neutral as to race and ethnicity. But this subject, too, is an aspect of the intimate sphere in which women's experiences can and do differ according to the subcultures in which they live. Women of color are more likely to be rape victims than are other women.[99] And, given that average prison terms for rape are lower when the victims are black, surely ancient cultural stereotypes about sexuality are still affecting prosecutors and judges, if only at levels below conscious awareness.[100] (After all, the protection of "white womanhood" was a central theme of racist politics—and lynch law—throughout the Jim Crow era.)[101] Black women who are battered often report that police officers are skeptical and hospital staffers relatively unresponsive—with the result that they and their friends become progressively more reluctant to seek official help when they are battered.[102] A black woman or a Latina who seeks official help outside the community—indeed, from institutions widely seen as oppressors of the community—may find that her action is viewed as a form of betrayal.[103] A Latina or an Asian woman whose immigration status is precarious may fear deportation, and thus refuse to report beatings to any authority. And if English language proficiency is required for a battered woman to have access to support services, then women who lack that qualification may be unable to escape the men who are beating them.[104]

Domestic violence, of course, lies beyond any direct remedy in present-day constitutional law, which is interpreted to address only governmental conduct.[105] But it does not lie beyond the capacity of state courts and legislatures to provide civil or criminal remedies, nor does it lie beyond the power of Congress to provide a remedy. In 1994 Congress enacted the Violence Against Women Act,[106] authorizing civil remedies (damages and injunctions) in cases of rape, sexual abuse, and other crimes of violence "motivated by gender." The latter term was defined restrictively to cover only cases of gender "animus" so as not to cause "disruptions" in divorce and other domestic relations cases—not a surprising development given the strong influence of social conservatives in both houses of Congress.[107] Even this modest venture into protecting women against violence is under constitutional attack in a case that has now reached the Supreme Court.[108] The outcome is hard to predict, but it is possible that the three justices who joined the plurality opinion in *Casey* will recall Justice O'Connor's portion of that opinion with its emphasis on the risks of domestic violence inherent in the husband-notification rule. In that case the plurality squarely rejected an argument founded on "domestic harmony," correctly seeing the argument as an appeal to an attitude toward women's roles that is unacceptable for government in a society in which women are equal citizens. One reason for believing that a decision to uphold the 1994 act lies within the realm of possibility for those three justices is, in the fullest sense, cultural. The world of domestic relations has taken a turn or two since the 1970s; the women's movement has educated women and men—occasionally, even justices—to the ways in which the invocation of "domestic harmony" has historically served as a form of "doctrine abuse" masking spousal abuse.

III. Law, Women's Roles, and Cultural Politics

Status politics is an old story in America; racial, ethnic, and religious groups have always been useful as cultural "enemies" at election time, but in the last three decades the political backlash against the women's movement has represented a great cultural divide.

The "enemies" technique was developed into a high art during the 1980s by the managers of the "social issues agenda" when they mobilized Americans who were alienated by social changes of the 1960s and 1970s. Race was one major polarizing factor, and gender was another, with a religious overlay to the whole agenda. The agenda emphasized law, and especially the uses of law to express group status dominance.[109] Under the banner of "family values," the social issues agenda proposed legal measures to reestablish a strong gender line in a society in which men would be men, women would be women, and there would be no room for homosexual orientation except as a symbolic enemy. A

"voting index" issued by a Christian political action group listed these evils as evidence of the national culture's slide into immorality:

> planned parenthood, the pill, no-fault divorce, open marriages, gay rights, palimony, test-tube babies, women's liberation, children's liberation, unisex, daycare centers, child advocates, and abortion on demand. A man is no longer responsible for his family; a woman need not obey her husband. God has been kicked out and humanism enthroned.[110]

This lament invokes a cultural tradition in which women were seen either as maternal objects, delicate and in need of protection, or as sexual objects. In either case, they must be kept under control. In the words of one leader of the new Christian Right, "Christ was not a lamb, but a ram!"[111] In short, the social issues agenda spoke to the anxieties of manhood, in language prescribing traditional sex roles as the will of God.

A great many recent topics could be used to illustrate the theme of law as a central object of cultural politics—prominently including the law of pornography, where social conservatives are joined by one wing of the feminist movement.[112] Here I limit myself to one illustration: legal control of abortion. This issue was, and remains, at the emotional heart of the politics of cultural counterrevolution. Proposals to overturn *Roe v. Wade* by constitutional amendment abounded, right through the 1980s. The issue of criminalizing abortion, long a question of state law, became a political space where presidential candidates were expected to stand up and be counted. Congress banned the use of federal money to fund abortions, and for years, in some states, legislatures adopted new laws restricting abortion at every session. Then, some months after the *Casey* decision reaffirmed the right of choice, in the midst of the 1992 presidential campaign the Bush-Quayle organizers discovered that this portion of the "family values" agenda was driving away more votes than it was attracting. They rang down the curtain on the abortion issue, and from that point on the conventional political wisdom has been that no candidate can win the presidency unless he or she is willing to live with women's right of choice.

Activist women on both sides of the abortion issue have tended to invest the issue with symbolism relating to their own choices of social roles. Most "pro-choice" activists have entered the public sphere in roles that used to be reserved to men; most "pro-life" activists have defended a domestic role for women.[113] This lineup, which partly reflects economic class differences,[114] represents not just a contest over status between cultural groups but agreement on both sides that women's control over their intimate lives—their sexuality and maternity—is closely related to their other freedoms, and particularly to their emergence from a state of dependence on men. Another word for that emergence would be liberation. But liberation itself, most especially the sexual liberation of young women, can be seen as a threat to a traditional cultural view of the sexual order that used to keep sex in the shadows and to "link sex for women with reproduction and sex for men with *self*-expression."[115]

The average age of marriage for women has increased to twenty-four years; meanwhile, partly because of improved nutrition, the average age of sexual maturity for girls has moved lower. As a result, young girls can look forward to about ten years negotiating what Kristin Luker has called a "reproductive minefield" while they are sexually mature and single.[116] Because teenage pregnancy occurs with greater frequency among girls of color, Luker points out that the term "teen pregnancy" has the political advantage of seeming to be race-neutral while it calls to mind images of youngsters disadvantaged by class and race.[117] But the emotional energy in a symbol derives from its ambiguity. Rosalind Petchesky has in mind quite a different response to this symbol when she says that legalized abortion "is seen to reveal sex; it is a signifier that makes sex *visible* . . . . Above all, it helps identify and categorize a new sexual subject [that is, actor]: the 'promiscuous' white teenage girl."[118]

A signifier is something that expresses meaning, something that contributes to cultural stability or cultural change, or perhaps both. The political dispute over abortion raises passions because the law of abortion is a complex signifier, touching the sense of identity of millions of Americans. Middle-class adult women who are economically independent do not need *Roe v. Wade* to have access to abortion; they can afford to travel to places where abortion is lawful and safe. For them, as for their main political antagonists, conflicts about abortion law are, above all, disputes over public symbols. If the practitioners of cultural politics have promised to use the power of government to rewrite the law, the main appeal of that promise is law's expressive power. Although law is a reflection of a cultural context, law can also serve to define the social status of groups and thus actively to shape individual identities.

Undoubtedly the changes in law governing women's control over their sexuality and maternity were possible because of a cultural change already in motion, the expansion of women's realistic aspirations outside the home. In a recent book Robert Max Jackson concludes that the rise in women's status was inevitable and will inevitably continue.[119] Changes in cultural beliefs, politics, and law, he says, are merely reflections of a more basic reorganization of productive resources over the last 150 years.[120] Production has moved away from households—long the foundation for systematic male advantage—and into business and industrial firms. The firms' economic interest have favored increased access of women to positions, and as a result, within families, sex role differentiation has eroded.[121]

Most theories of cultural change are thin,[122] and today I have offered no such grand theory; instead, we have looked at some particulars. To speak of cultural change, after all, is to impose a label, after the fact, on the aggregate of myriad individual beliefs and actions over some length of time. The idea of an improvement in women's status can have meaning only in the lives of individual women. It is no accident that an important method of the modern women's movement has been "consciousness raising"— women in small groups, sharing experiences, not just for moral support but to grasp their situation as women in American society. "The personal is political," these women said.[123] Perhaps there are large and impersonal market forces at work, tending to produce sex equality—that is, equality in general and in the very long run. In the here and now, however, when particular concrete advances or setbacks for women's condition are in issue, I have no doubt that cultural beliefs, politics, and law will all play their parts in determining immediate results. In 1915 Justice Oliver Wendell Holmes Jr. said, "The mode in which the inevitable comes to pass is through effort."[124]

It has taken effort—and not just by lawyers—to effect the changes in American law that have invigorated the aspirations of women to participate in the public world. The law of employment discrimination, along with judicial decisions like *Roe* and *Casey*, have inscribed new cultural meanings into an official, authoritative definition of the moral order. Illustrating "the role of legal norms in the art of composing identities,"[125] these legal changes have contributed to a change in what it means to be a woman.

Shannon Lucid, the astronaut who lived on the space station Mir for six months, was asked by a journalist, "If you were able to travel back in time, what era would you choose?" She answered, "Right now is the best time for a woman to live."[126] There is a lot of sunlight in space, and it would be unfair to ask her to restrain her exuberance just because other women, who live and work in dimmer surroundings, have aspirations that are more limited. To recognize that women still face obstacles to their full attainment of equal citizenship—and that the obstacles are most daunting for poor women and for women of color—is, in one perspective, simply to accept the fact that some cultural forms die hard. In another perspective, though, this recognition implies a challenge, not just to makers of law but to all Americans. The personal is political; the challenge to women and men,[127] at work and at home, is to make the effort to help the inevitable come to pass—and, not incidentally, to fulfill the promise of American law.

Redefining Muslim Women's Roles in the Next Century

Azizah Y. al-Hibri

Introduction

The new millennium is blowing winds of change over the Muslim world. After centuries of relative seclusion, Muslim women have awakened to their critical role in society and are demanding their right to full participation in the public square.[1] Patriarchal customs are being rejected, laws are being revised, and women are increasingly participating in various aspects of public life. Foremost in the struggle for greater roles in society is the revision of antiquated personal status codes (family laws) that have often deprived women of essential liberties. Revising these codes is not an easy matter because they rely primarily on religious law. Attempts to revise them leave the forces of reform open to charges ranging from sacrilege to secularization.

The recent change in Egyptian law is a case in point. After years of attempting to revise the personal status code for Muslims in Egypt, some basic revisions were both proposed and passed in January of this year.[2] The process of revision took nine years and involved religious as well as legal scholars.[3] Nevertheless, when the revisions were publicized they generated significant opposition.[4] Claims of secularization and submission to Western pressure were among the charges levied against the Egyptian government.[5]

Muslim countries watched this development intently. One reason for this interest derived from the tense atmosphere that surrounded the passage of the law and raised the question of possible political ramifications. Another reason was rooted in the fact that Egypt is a leader in Islamic jurisprudence. This fact gave its proposed revisions added significance. For example, the revisions contained a special provision facilitating the right of the woman to divorce her husband (*khul'*).[6] Years ago, a Pakistani judge issued an opinion that provided Muslim women with certain divorce rights similar to those in the new Egyptian provision.[7] His well-reasoned opinion went mostly unnoticed. Now that Egypt has adopted a similar position in the revised code, the situation has changed drastically.

The difference lies in the fact that, in an important sense, Egypt is the heart of the Muslim world. *Al-Azhar ash-Sharif,* the oldest Islamic educational institution in the world, sits quietly beside a bustling modern Cairo. For centuries it has provided leadership and guidance for Muslims around the world. In January, however, this venerable institution was divided upon itself. Grand Imam of *al-Azhar ash-Sharif,* Muhammad Sayed Tantawi, and many other distinguished religious scholars gave their stamp of approval to the new revisions of the code.[8] Thirty-one other religious scholars, however, issued a strongly worded statement denouncing the revisions as contrary to Islam.[9] The parliament quickly passed the revisions, which have now become law.[10]

But the battle of the personal status code may be far from over. During the administration of President Anwar Sadat, Law No. 44 was passed hastily by the Egyptian parliament in an attempt to improve women's legal status.[11] It was referred to by some Egyptians as "Jihan's law," a reference to the efforts of Mrs. Sadat in having it passed.[12] That law was rejected soon after the death of President Sadat.[13] Will the new law face a similar fate ultimately? It all depends. In understanding this answer lies the key to predicting the way the winds of change will blow in the Muslim world to define the roles of Muslim women in the information age.

Obstacles to Change in the Muslim World

In Muslim countries, personal status codes reflect religious law. Religious law, however, is intricately interwoven with deep cultural interpretations and influences.[14] Colonialist rule, which intensified Western legal influence in colonized countries, understood that tampering with the existing configuration would present quite a challenge to occupying authorities.[15] For this reason, it excepted from its ambit family law, naming it in the process "personal status law." Even today, changes in family law continue to evoke a great deal of resistance if society views them as attacks on religion, culture, or family. As a result of the legacy of colonialism, which often destroyed the infrastructure of Islamic education, many Muslims became less educated in religious matters, such as *fiqh* (religious jurisprudence).[16] Struggling to preserve their freedom of conscience, they often opted to cling to tradition rather than venture into new areas of change that may inadvertently be inconsistent with their religious beliefs.

Another complicating element in introducing change is rooted in current geopolitical conditions. Where a third world society (as most Muslim countries are) views change as being imposed by international bodies, foreign governments, or foreign-based or financed NGOs (nongovernmental organizations), it is usually inclined to reject it. For example, this past summer both Pakistan and Egypt cracked down on NGOs they viewed as tools of foreign powers.[17] NGOs have generally succeeded in globalizing various women's and human rights issues. Unfortunately, however, they have been often insensitive to cultural and religious differences. As a result, a great deal of resistance was created abroad to the women's rights movement, which often appeared as a foreign intruder attempting to destroy the family and complete the work of the colonialist.

Muslims have also rejected change that appeared to be imposed upon them by their own rulers. The parliamentary defeat of the right of the Kuwaiti woman to vote was unfortunately as much an expression of defiance in the interest of democracy as it was a rejection of a basic right of women.[18] For this reason, commentaries after the vote both condemned the defeat of Kuwaiti women's rights and celebrated the assertion of the right of the people to a robust democracy.[19] It is quite unfortunate that women's issues are often caught in the middle of other political struggles.

Nevertheless, there is great room for change in the Muslim world. Change has always had its internal rules there. Muslim women and men can go quite far by utilizing these rules. For this reason, the recent Egyptian change in family law is promising as it appears to have utilized some of the better methodologies to bring about change. What the next few years will determine is whether these methodologies were properly applied and adequately pursued.

Challenges Facing Muslim Women

Problems facing Muslim women are diverse. After all, Islam is the faith of over a billion people on this earth. Also, despite common belief to the contrary, most Muslims are not Arab. In fact, the largest Muslim country is Indonesia. As a result of this ethnic and cultural diversity, it is not possible to generalize about "the problems facing Muslim women." Rather, one must take into account the specific country under consideration. For example, while Afghanistan has denied women adequate education, some universities in the United Arab Emirates boast a female student population approaching 80 percent.[20] Also, while honor killing is a priority issue in Pakistan and Jordan, it is not practiced in Tunisia or Malaysia. Voting is a priority issue for Kuwaiti women, driving for Saudi women, but Muslim women in other countries have voted and driven for many years.

Despite this rich diversity, some personal status codes have exhibited conceptual similarities on issues that present significant difficulty for women. These issues have subtle but deep-rooted justifications that resonate in other parts of the codes. Uncovering these justifications requires attention to complicated jurisprudential matters. As early as 1992, I pointed out three major issues common to various Muslim personal status codes: (a) the right of the woman to execute her own marriage contract, (b) the requirement that the woman obey her husband, and (c) the woman's right to divorce. Of these, only the third was addressed in the recent Egyptian law, but not without controversy.[21] Underlying all of these issues is a single justification based on a particular interpretation of the Qur'anic concept of *qiwamah* combined with certain gender-based assumptions.[22] In most traditional jurisprudence, that Qur'anic concept has been interpreted to refer to the "superiority" of men over women.[23] Underlying this interpretation is the cultural patriarchal assumption that women are weak and irrational while men are strong and rational.[24] This interpretation has also been used to justify various restrictions on women.[25]

What is stunning about both the interpretation and assumption is the fact that they fly in the face of early Islamic history, which is replete with examples of women who were natural leaders, being neither weak nor irrational. To begin with, Khadijah, the first wife of the Prophet, was a successful business woman who employed the Prophet as a young man.[26] She was hardly a weak and passive woman, even in her own private life. Despite being twenty years older than the Prophet, she proposed to him in marriage, and the two lived happily together until her death.[27] Khadijah was the first Muslim and the Prophet's intimate advisor.[28]

Khadijah's female descendants were no less assertive or accomplished. Denied her inheritance under the theory that children of prophets do not inherit, Fatimah gave a major, well-reasoned speech in support of her claim.[29] Fatimah's daughter, Zainab, gave an even more challenging speech in the palace of Yazid after the latter's army executed all but one of the male descendants of the Prophet.[30] Um Salamah, another member of the House of the Prophet, provided him with valuable advice that prevented a major schism among Muslims.[31] 'A'ishah, a third member, was viewed as a major source of *hadith* (reports of the words of the Prophet) and also engaged in jurisprudence.[32] Furthermore, after the death of the Prophet, 'A'ishah led a faction of Muslims into a major battle.[33]

Activism and scholarship, however, were not limited to the House of the Prophet. Many Arab women of that time fought by the Prophet's side, attended discussion sessions with him, provided religious education, and engaged in business.[34] In fact, one of them was appointed by the Prophet to lead Muslims in prayer from her own house.[35] After the death of the Prophet, other women distinguished themselves in *hadith,* jurisprudence, literature, and even governance.[36] Hence the patriarchal assumption adopted by Muslim jurists flies in the face of the very facts that existed during the life of the Prophet and after his death. Since the Prophet was the model Muslim, one is entitled to point to his life, his respectful interaction with women, and approval of their lifestyles to raise important modern questions about current laws.

There are other issues. For example, many codes restrict the Muslim woman's right to free movement, thus requiring her to obtain her husband's permission for activities ranging from social visits to travel.[37] The originally proposed Egyptian law contained a provision that eased the travel restriction through judicial action, but that provision was dropped due to severe opposition.[38] It was viewed as an attack on the husband's prerogative.[39] In many Muslim countries women are required to travel with their husbands or with a male *mahram* (a close relation who is legally prohibited from marrying the woman, such as her father or brother). Saudi Arabia requires women entering the country for *hajj* (pilgrimage) but who are not part of a pilgrimage group to be accompanied by a *mahram.* Yet 'A'ishah argued centuries ago that since *hajj* is a religious duty, women may go to *hajj* without a *mahram.*[40] Furthermore, she argued that since women are permitted to go to *hajj* unaccompanied by a *mahram,* then they should be able to travel to other destinations without a *mahram* if they fear no *fitnah* (a rich word with meanings ranging from turmoil to temptation).[41]

Another common form of mobility-restrictive laws requires the wife to obtain her husband's permission to work outside the home.[42] Clearly, this form is susceptible to serious abuse and places enormous power in the hands of the husband over his wife's economic independence. Interestingly, however, economic and social changes in some Muslim countries have recently forced legal changes. Some modern Muslim jurists developed a less restrictive jurisprudence that provided the under-pinnings of the revised laws. Today, many codes permit women to engage in "legitimate" work, without the husband's permission, "so long as the work is not detri-mental to the family."[43]

Incidentally, the mobility-restrictive laws, even in their most confining form, do not mean that Muslim women are homebound without careers. Many are doc-tors, teachers, and engineers. Nevertheless, it is signifi-cant that the legal system places limitations on the mobility and employability of Muslim women, regard-less of actual practice. These limitations become impor-tant when there is a disagreement between the spouses and the husband attempts to limit the wife's options by relying on these laws. The new Egyptian laws have addressed such situations by ensuring that the wife has recourse to the courts to demand justice.[44]

Many women would like to see basic changes in per-sonal status law, as opposed to mere remedial action. The critical issue, however, is what would such changes entail. According to my conversations with Muslim women in various Muslim countries, I found them to be hesitant to demand change if that would entail a departure from their religious beliefs. After all, personal status codes are based on religious law, and Muslims are bound by every word in the Qur'an. So, contemplating the passage of laws in contradiction with the Qur'an's letter, or even spirit, is at least as serious as contemplating the passage of an "uncon-stitutional law" in the United States. Not only would it not work; worse yet, it would be sacrilegious.

Given the lack of adequate knowledge of the Muslim woman's history, the Arabic Qur'anic text, and the assumptions and arguments made by many traditional jurists, most Muslim women are in no position to dis-cern legitimate change from sacrilegious one. Generally, they do not have the tools to separate patriarchal cul-tural arguments from religious arguments, nor do they have the tools to develop their own gender-equitable jurisprudence. Unless this situation changes, the progress of Muslim women will continue to be severely ham-pered. The status of the Muslim woman in many Muslim countries is so much at odds with the rights granted her by the Qur'an that recently even male jurists have rejected aspects of patriarchal thinking and declared their support for women's rights.[45]

We can now see the complexity and seriousness of the problems associated with the call for Muslim women's rights. Pious women would rather suffer than sin. Some Muslim men are trying to help, but the movement to liberate Muslim women must emanate from within women's ranks. Western NGOs offer mostly irrelevant secular solutions. Patriarchal voices claim religious foundations for existing patriarchal laws. Everyone is talking past each other, and global politics is not far from the conversation. All of this creates a less than ideal environment for bringing about change.

Using Internal Rules for Change to Promote Progress

Traditional societies, however, have their internal rules for change, and Muslim societies are no exception. While using these internal rules can help accelerate acceptance, defying them can derail one's efforts. By the same token, radical change may require revision, if not destruction, of some of these rules themselves. These facts raise impor-tant questions: Dare women destroy some of the rules? If not, how could women use patriarchal internal rules to achieve their goals? Asked in the abstract, these questions seem daunting. Focused on specifics, answers become quite possible. In either case, it is important to think about these questions, if only to understand the chal-lenges facing Muslim women. We, therefore, turn to a brief overview of how these rules work.

Internal rules of change vary somewhat from one country to the other. Muslim societies are informed by both religious and cultural values, principles, and assump-tions. While the former set provides a common ground among all these countries, the second usually does not. Furthermore, because of the interaction of religious inter-pretation with cultural assumptions, even religious inter-pretation often reflects variations from one country to the other. These are significant facts given that demands for cultural change are not sacrilegious and that commit-ment to cultural norms can be overridden by religious principles or even social development.

To understand the full significance of the previous assertions, we need to understand better how personal status laws, which are founded on Islamic jurispru-dence, work. There are many schools of jurisprudence, and each country has historically adopted that school of jurisprudence that best suited its society.[46] Islamic schools of jurisprudence represent particular interpretations of the Qur'an, in light of the *sunnah* (words and example of the Prophet) and sound rules of logic. On some matters, clearly delineated by Qur'anic revelation, the difference among the schools is negligible. On others, where interpretation is a major element, differences may be quite significant. Understanding the difference between the two is critical. Confusing them is a sure path to failure.

Tunisia has properly understood this distinction. For this reason, it and other Muslim countries refrained from revising Islamic inheritance laws in response to international pressures by parties concerned about the laws' fairness to women. As one Tunisian judge stated, inheritance laws will remain unchanged in Tunisia until an Islamic solution to this matter is found.[47] This statement may surprise many non-Tunisian Muslims who view the Tunisian personal status code as influenced by French secularism. After all, it prohibits polygamous marriages and no longer requires obedience by the wife.[48] A closer look at the Explanatory Memorandum of the Tunisian personal status law, however, reveals the robust Islamic jurisprudence on which it relied. This example also helps illustrate two more facts: Islamic jurisprudential interpretations can vary significantly, and there is no single inflexible interpretation that informs all Islamic legal systems.

There are general rules for adequate and proper interpretations, and most are rules of logic, such as *qiyas* (argument by analogy) and the requirement for internal consistency.[49] No interpretation is considered worthwhile if it runs afoul of basic rules of logic because the Qur'an repeatedly defines Islam as a religion based on reason.[50] Other jurisprudential rules for assessing the applicability of a certain law to a specific situation admit such other practical considerations as public interest (*maslaha*) and avoidance of harm (*la darar wala dirar*).[51] These two sets of rules provide a rich base for diverse interpretations and laws.

Additionally, there are several juristic principles that govern *ijtihad* (Islamic jurisprudential reasoning). Two important ones deal with custom (*'urf*) and change.[52] The first principle permits the jurist to include in his or her jurisprudence laws and assumptions derived from custom, so long as these do not conflict with Islamic law.[53] This principle has permitted broad legal diversity in the Muslim world. While this flexibility is valuable, it has opened the door at times to laws that are gender biased. Although the Qur'an itself is gender-equitable, it is hard to see how a patriarchal jurist who is oblivious to his own biases could recognize the incompatibility between a gender-biased custom and basic Qur'anic principles.

The second principle recognizes the fact that laws change with changes in time and place.[54] Thus, what is suitable for a country in the tenth century may not be suitable for that country today. Countries have been known to change the school of thought they follow. For example, Egypt used to be a Shafi'i jurisdiction.[55] More recently, it opted to follow the Hanafi jurisprudence, which it deemed more suitable for its people.[56] Imam al-Shafi'i himself revised his own jurisprudence when he moved from Iraq to Egypt because the old jurisprudence did not suit the new milieu.[57] Furthermore, what is suitable for Egypt may not be suitable for Pakistan. *Ijtihad*, in other words, is a continuous thinking process that takes into account the very milieu in which it occurs.

Unfortunately, as a result of various historical factors, *ijtihad* shriveled in the Muslim world.[58] The time has come, however, to revive the best of the Islamic intellectual traditions—that of freedom of conscience and thought, that is, freedom of *ijtihad*. Such freedom, however, cannot be cabined to women's rights. If a society is to encourage freedom of *ijtihad* in pursuit of more gender-equitable laws, then that society must also be prepared to reap the consequences of such freedom in areas such as those of human rights, democracy, and civil liberties. This is why the issue of change is such a delicate one in Muslim countries. It concerns not only patriarchy but also general political authority.[59] Once the floodgates of freedom of *ijtihad* are open, the long-term effect would metamorphose all of society. For this reason, many men are willing to stand by women in their search for better laws and conditions, and many countries seek gradual measured change that ensures stability.

This short discussion of the basics of Islamic jurisprudence makes clear that Islamic jurisprudence is a highly flexible endeavor, sensitive to a full range of considerations, whether religious, social, political, cultural, or even contextual, that could arise at any time or place.

For this reason, given all these facts, it is hard to imagine that any serious Muslim scholar would deny the propriety of reviewing old jurisprudence in light of the demands of the modern age. The challenge, therefore, is how to perform such a review competently without creating unnecessary resistance and turmoil.

This is a tremendous challenge requiring thorough knowledge of the Qur'an, *sunnah,* Islamic law and jurisprudence, as well as the conditions in the country at hand. The strength of the recent Egyptian approach for legal change lies in the fact that the scholars involved took the time necessary to examine carefully earlier jurisprudence. Also being sensitive to the social milieu, they developed new jurisprudence suitable for Egypt, resting on firm Islamic ground and utilizing traditional Islamic methodology. This is one reason the new law passed and why it may even survive future challenges. If indeed it does, it may very well spread to other Muslim countries.

Opening the Doors of Jurisprudence to Women

The Egyptian approach worked well in part because of the enthusiastic support of some distinguished male jurists, but women played an active role as well.[60] Women in Egypt are more comfortable with religious text and tradition than many Muslim women in other countries. There are various reasons that explain this state of affairs. Among them is the fact that the Arabic language is the native language of Egypt. Also, the educational system is wide open to women. Even *al-Azhar* opened its doors in the last few decades to women. Furthermore, there is a strong tradition of women's involvement and assertiveness in Egypt.[61] All of these factors made Egyptian women an active part of the process of change.

This is a key point. If change is going to occur in the Muslim world, it cannot occur without the active participation of women. If change is going to be fundamental, it cannot occur without the leadership of women. Preparing women for this important task is paramount. They need to be educated generally, but also especially in the field of Islamic jurisprudence. Such preparation will lay the objective foundations for the emergence of a new kind of jurisprudence, one which understands firsthand women's concerns and challenges.

From a religious point of view, this educational requirement is not exceptional. After all, the Qur'an clearly advocates knowledge, and the Prophet himself stated that seeking knowledge is the duty of every Muslim, male or female.[62] Consequently, educating women is not only an option in Muslim societies, it is a duty. Unfortunately, as we all know, some countries have not taken this duty seriously.[63] In fact, they have ignored it, relegating the education of women to the bottom of their priorities.

The reasons for such a travesty are many. However, since many of the countries that limit the rights of women use religious or pragmatic justifications for their actions, the emergence of a class of Muslim women jurists across the Muslim world who would critique such unsound justifications would significantly alter the situation. Even traditional Islamic jurisprudence can be used in arguments refuting both religious as well as pragmatic claims by patriarchal regimes. With respect to pragmatic arguments, Muslim women could rely, for example, on the traditional principle of avoidance of harm, thus making it relatively easy to show the harm befalling more than half the population when restrictive interpretations of women's rights are adopted.

The integration of Muslim women in the religious educational process has taken place in many Muslim countries, among which are Lebanon, Syria, Morocco, and Iran, a fact which appears very promising. The way this integration was achieved differs from one country to the other. Integration alone, however, is not enough. Some women I talked to were confused or frustrated by the patriarchal jurisprudence they were being taught. They did not know how to evaluate critically the information provided. This fact underscores the importance of women's presence as educators and leaders, and not only as students, in the area of Islamic jurisprudence.

It is amazing how many of the quasi-religious arguments used to limit women's rights rely on assumptions that have been refuted in our American society and early Islamic societies time and again. Today, these assumptions are still widely accepted as fact in many countries. Some Muslim women have told me that women were weak and irrational. Muslim women

who have internalized their own oppression can benefit from Muslim women who have rejected it. Many
American Muslim women, who were participants and
beneficiaries of the American feminist movement, have
rejected oppressive assumptions about themselves and
other women, but they are also committed to the tenets
of their faith. Thus, they make excellent leaders for
change within a Muslim context.

American Muslim women can provide valuable leadership, along with their Egyptian, Moroccan, Saudi,
Gulfi, and other sisters who are already trying to bring
about change, each to the extent possible under their own
local circumstances. The advantage American Muslim
women enjoy over all others is that they are in fact removed from the pressures of local quasi-religious politics.
They also live in a society that broadly recognizes women's
rights, a society that has refuted many patriarchal assumptions still lingering elsewhere. This is a distinct advantage,
because in studying traditional Islamic jurisprudence we
become clearer about which assumptions are cultural,
refutable, and patriarchal. Once we eliminate that unnecessary baggage, we can then concentrate on a serious discussion of religious issues.

This recommended jurisprudential activity, however,
leads to many questions: May Muslim women engage
in *ijtihad?* May Muslim women lead their societies? Are
American Muslim women in a position to assist Muslim
women of other cultures, given that Muslims are entitled to reflect their own specific cultures in their laws?
I now examine these critical questions.

The Role of Women in Religious Tradition and in Society

Since the Islamic faith is based on the Qur'an, it is helpful in answering our questions to establish the Qur'anic
view of gender relations. The Qur'an, which is the revealed word of God, states that all humans, male and
female, are created from the same soul.[64] It also describes
spousal relationships as based on affection and mercy
(not domination).[65] The Qur'an itself addresses specifically female believers as well as male believers, and it
imposes on all of them similar religious duties and obligations.[66] The Qur'an further states that female believers and male believers are each others' *awliya'* (guardians

or protectors).[67] These Qur'anic assertions are inconsistent with the patriarchal assertion that men are superior to women. Yet it is this very patriarchal assertion
that jurists rely upon in interpreting the concept of
qiwamah mentioned in the Qur'an.[68] Since Muslims
believe that Qur'anic verses interpret each other as one
integral whole and that the Qur'an is a thoroughly
internally consistent revelation, then one could see how
existing patriarchal interpretations would be vulnerable
to serious religious critiques.[69]

Given the gender-equitable Qur'anic view, one may
wonder, therefore, about the glaring absence of women
from Islamic jurisprudential circles. As stated earlier,
women were not absent from these circles in early
Islam, and many of their contributions have survived to
this day, especially through citations by men on such
matters as *hadith*.[70] The contributions of women to *ijtihad*, however, have not fared as well, and there are efforts
now to rediscover those still in existence. Muslims have
generally understood that there is no Qur'anic bar to
Muslim women engaging in jurisprudence. Many,
however, do not await such contributions enthusiastically given the patriarchal assumption that women are
weak-minded. Incidentally, many of the men who
espouse patriarchal assumptions have no problem being
led in *sufi* orders by women.[71]

Since there is no bar to women engaging in Islamic
jurisprudence, it is important that they do so in order to
change the intellectual landscape. Historically, however,
male as well as female jurists were discouraged in their
endeavors or even prevented from pursuing them by the
arm of an authoritarian state.[72] Yet the Qur'an clearly
protects freedom of conscience and human rights;[73] so
does our international community. It would thus be
much harder to hinder these efforts in modern times.
Furthermore, American Muslims do not have to concern
themselves with fear of retribution or repression. Protected by American First Amendment jurisprudence,
they are free to pursue their own *ijtihad*. Consequently,
they have a relatively safe enclave to work from and an
important leadership role to play in developing a new
Islamic jurisprudence firmly based on the Qur'an and
fully suitable for the information age.

If Muslim women, along with supporting Muslim
men, succeed in questioning existing authority, then

they would open properly the door to a new era in Muslim societies, one which is closer to the society of Madinah headed by the Prophet himself.[74] In that society, matters were decided by elections (bay'ah) and consultation (shura).[75] Women made their voices clearly heard, to the amazement of Makkan men.[76] They participated in both elections and consultations.[77] They attended discussion sessions with the Prophet.[78] They prayed in mosques and engaged in business.[79] In general, they took their personal, social, financial, and political rights seriously. The assertiveness of women in Madinah was in fact preserved in one instance by a whole Qur'anic chapter about the woman who argued with the Prophet.[80] While it is clear that Muslim women may participate actively in society, the question remains: May Muslim women lead?

This question has been answered differently by different Muslim populations. Pakistan and Bangladesh appear to have responded affirmatively to the question.[81] But in both cases, the rise of women to power there was based upon the power of a male relative (usually deceased) and reflected cultural reactions rather than religious judgment.[82] Thus, even in those societies, the religious aspect of this question remains open. Women themselves are unclear about the answer. In a meeting with young university women in a particular Muslim country, I learned that the majority of female students agreed that Muslim women are entitled to political participation but not to leadership roles. In other words, if there is a "glass ceiling" in Muslim countries, then it is in part the result of many Muslim women believing in its appropriateness. These women have internalized gender-biased worldviews, even as some major traditional Islamic scholars have recognized the right of women to lead.[83]

While the majority of scholars argue against women's leadership, Muslim history is replete with examples of women leaders, such as Queen Arwa of Yemen, Shajarat al-Dur of Egypt, and Fatimah Sultan of Qasimov.[84] The Qur'an itself mentions positively the example of the Queen of Sheba, a wise woman who consulted her people before taking important decisions.[85] It also contains no prohibition against women's leadership. As stated earlier, the Qur'an describes men and women as each other's protectors and guardians.[86] On the other hand, the Qur'an contains other verses that have been inter-

preted as limiting leadership to men, such as the verse containing the concept of qiwamah, which I have already described as having been misinterpreted. So, let me explain that concept and verse briefly.

This concept of qiwamah is generally understood as establishing a hierarchical relation between men and women.[87] Yet the complex grammatical structure of the Qur'anic verse in which the concept occurs is not one of generality ('aam) but of specificity (khaass). Various words in the verse indicate that the verse applies only to some men who are related to some women in two specific ways: (a) they support them financially and (b) are preferred by God over these women at certain times in certain matters.[88] The latter condition refers to situations where a man (who is financially supporting a woman) may be more sophisticated than the woman he is supporting in some financial, social, political, or other matter. So long as he remains more sophisticated than the woman in that matter while being responsible for her financial support, the man is entitled to advise (be qawwam over) the woman in that matter. Once either condition ceases to exist, the verse no longer applies and the man has no right to interfere in the woman's decision making, even as an advisor. In other words, in a patriarchal world where men constantly interfered in the lives of women, this verse was revealed to limit that interference, not to encourage it.[89] Unfortunately, traditional interpretations overlooked that fact.

The fact that this verse applies only to specific situations would have been quite clear in early Islam when many women engaged in business and were not in need of being financially supported.[90] Furthermore, Islam gave the woman financial independence even within her marriage.[91] Thus, while the husband is obligated to support his wife, her assets remain hers and are totally separate from the marital property.[92] The husband may not touch them. Furthermore, if he refuses to provide support to his wife (even if she is rich), the wife may seek severe judicial remedies that could include divorce.[93]

However, in authoritarian societies in which jurists were arguing in favor of obedience by the masses of their ruler, even if he were unjust, the concept of qiwamah within the family was also interpreted in an authoritarian fashion.[94] The burden of the loss of democracy and human rights in Islamic history that was felt by the whole population was therefore felt doubly by Muslim women. As women were increasingly relegated to the home in later periods of Islamic history, they became more dependent on the financial support of men. This meant that the first condition of the Qur'anic verse was almost always satisfied.

To further bolster their view, traditional jurists interpreted the second condition of the Qur'anic verse discussed above as referring specifically to the physical superiority of all men over all women, an assumption that they viewed as generally true.[95] This interpretation ensured that the second condition of the Qur'anic verse was also always true. The limited domain of the Qur'anic verse was thus generalized to cover all men and women by using patriarchal jurisprudential interpretations backed by patriarchal restrictions on women in public life.

Jurists buttressed their interpretations by citing other Quranic verses, such as the law of witnessing and inheritance laws.[96] Their arguments again reflected a profound bias in understanding the divine wisdom behind these laws by reducing them to patriarchal advantage. For this reason, Muslim women's jurisprudence is now a necessity. But before it can be effective and accepted by society, it has to address all these issues in a pious, rational, and convincing detail. The task is daunting, given the great minds that developed Islamic jurisprudence over a period of almost fifteen hundred years. Fortunately, these same minds can offer some succor. Many of their arguments, when understood properly, could work in favor of developing a liberating jurisprudence. Very often, these honest jurists themselves stated clearly their cultural and patriarchal assumptions that led them to a specific interpretation. This valuable information facilitates the task of a modern jurist. As noted earlier, Muslims are not bound by the patriarchal or cultural assumptions of other cultures. They are bound only by the Qur'an. Hence, they are entitled to reject the cultural parts of a traditional jurist's arguments and replace them with ones that are more in keeping with our times and our culture. With these revised interpretations, it would be possible to revive the tradition of Muslim women leaders.

We are thus left with the last question: Are American Muslim women in a position to assist Muslim women of other cultures, given that Muslims are entitled to reflect their own specific cultures in their own laws?

The Role of American Muslim Women

Regardless of culture, American Muslim women are as bound by the Qur'an as all other Muslims. Consequently, whatever Islamic jurisprudence is followed by Muslim communities in the United States, it must be Qur'anically impeccable. The jurisprudential interpretations themselves may be colored by local customs, experiences, and culture, just as the interpretations of others were similarly colored. But so long as these interpretations comply with *usul al-fiqh* (the basic principles of traditional jurisprudence) they should be acceptable, even if in disagreement with other established interpretations.

This may be surprising to a non-Muslim, but jurists have always maintained an ethic of difference among them.[97] Recognizing that no human is infallible, no jurist claimed for his views the status of absolute truth. Rather, well-known jurists always ended their exposition with the phrase "*wallahu a'lam*" (God knows best).[98] For similar reasons, the Great Imam Malik bin Anas said: "I am a human being, who is sometimes wrong and sometimes right; so look into my views and take what accords with the Qur'an and *sunnah*. Discard that which does not." [99] The other Great Imam Abu Hanifah said: "Do not emulate me, or Malik or al-Shafi'i, or al-Thawri, and seek [your guidance] from [the sources] they sought." [100]

Developing an indigenous American Islamic jurisprudence is not only desirable but also necessary. Jurists of the past recognized the need to change laws in light of changing times, circumstances, and milieus. Unfortunately, the jurisprudence followed today has not been properly revisited since medieval times. It has been simply adjusted or recombined with customary and colonialist jurisprudence, leaving behind a strange mixture of tribal custom, patriarchal bias, and even European culture.

American Muslims are not bound by tribal custom of faraway places nor by values of past colonial powers. For this reason, a patient study of existing jurisprudence is necessary to uncover all these nonreligious assumptions on which it rests and that have either become obsolete or are unsuitable for our society. An American Muslim female attorney or investment banker is likely to find the assumption that women are naturally weak and irrational unacceptable, especially if all her female friends are successful working women as well. This single assumption, if removed, would alter significantly many laws in existing personal status codes.

For example, the argument for requiring a *wali* (guardian) to execute the marriage contract of a woman on her behalf would lose force.[101] In such a case, jurists may return to the jurisprudence of Abu Hanifah on that point. He argued that the *wali* (who may be the father) has only advisory powers, but the woman executes her own contract.[102] His argument in support of this position was very simple: If Islam gave the woman full independence in financial matters, he noted, how could it be conceivable that it would give her less in matters of greater importance, such as the choice of a husband?[103] Abu Hanifah, nevertheless, gave the *wali* the power to annul the contract, if the woman married an unsuitable man.[104] This condition reveals very clearly the impact of local culture on Abu Hanifah. He defines an unsuitable man as one who is not suitable economically, professionally, or in some other similar way.[105] This is a departure from the Prophetic tradition, which states that all Muslims are suitable for all other Muslims, regardless of class or race.[106] The defining consideration is simply that of piety.[107]

This example shows the constructive role traditional jurisprudence can play in formulating a new jurisprudence. It also shows the need to be careful in sifting through the various positions in order to adjust them to one's society. One part of one position may be acceptable, but another part may not be. This conclusion is not new. Muslim countries reached it decades ago when they started applying the doctrine of *takhayyur* (selectivity) in formulating their own laws.[108] This doctrine permitted them to borrow from each school of jurisprudence those laws that best suited their societies. When utilizing the method of *takhayyur,* a jurist must be very careful and cognizant of the overall effects of the choices made. In the above example, the resulting position that permits the woman to execute her own marriage contract while adopting the pristine Islamic definition of "suitability" combines elements from two

schools of thought, the Hanafi and the Maliki. Hence it is Islamically unassailable. It also reflects the realities of the American Muslim woman's independent lifestyle.

By developing Islamically sound jurisprudence suitable for the United States, American Muslims illustrate to the Muslim world the flexibility of Islam that was revealed for all times and all places. They also provide a prototype of a jurisprudence that is liberating, modern, yet authentic. Such a prototype will no doubt invigorate those Muslim women who labor under the impression that their oppression is divinely decreed. It will also open the door to the critical examination of other pressing issues, such as civil rights and representative government. These developments would usher a new age of reform to the Muslim world.

Many non-Muslims, biased by the stereotypical image of Islam as oppressive, may wonder whether the attempt to reinvigorate the religious intellectual life of Muslims is worth the effort. They may find it hard to believe that such an approach would ultimately lead to full liberation. This point of view invites to two observations. First, Muslim women in the West have an added burden in their struggle for a gender-equitable jurisprudence. For one, their efforts are treated by other Americans with skepticism, suspicion, even rejection. One glaring example of this unfortunate state of affairs is illustrated by an incident that took place a few years ago in our own capital. Muslim women wearing head scarves were not welcomed to a feminist demonstration in support of Bosnian women. Furthermore, Muslim women do not receive the same sort of moral and financial support that secular women from Muslim cultures receive, despite the fact that the latter group has little, if any, grassroot support.

Conclusion

All over the Muslim world, Muslim women are exploring new roles in public life and new interpretations of Islamic law that are in keeping with the times. They are often assisted in their efforts by men who are interested in advancing the cause of democracy and human dignity. The success of Muslim women in their endeavor requires deeper understanding of and increased participation in Islamic jurisprudential activity. The road to full participation by women in the public square is long and difficult, but Islamic history is replete with precedents of strong and active women. These historical role models offer both inspiration and validation in the face of entrenched patriarchal forces. Patriarchal forces, whose views are rooted in patriarchal cultures, appropriate religious language and symbols to achieve their purposes. Educated Muslim women can disarm these forces and expose their cultural biases by developing a sophisticated understanding of Islamic jurisprudence and its liberating potential. In the end, the winds of change blowing over the Muslim world will bring in freedom, justice, and democracy to everyone.

Conceptualizing Women's Rights

Eva Cantarella

It is not easy to comment on three papers offering such an amount of stimulating material for discussion. Therefore, I apologize for not taking into account all of the issues laid out by the authors. After some general considerations, I will concentrate on the more general problems they raised and shall single out a number of specific issues among the many explicitly or implicitly mentioned.

In reading and listening to the three papers I was struck by the remarkably different ways in which they all contribute to the development of concepts about the issue of women's rights and roles. This issue, today, is seen in an increasingly wider perspective that involves the definition of some basic concepts such as justice, rights, and democracy.

The problem of justice is clear: Is it just that women (even when they are totally "equal" to men on the books) continue to suffer discriminations? There is no point in minutely listing here the gender discriminations still observable even in the most developed and democratic countries. They have already been listed. Even in countries where women have formally equal rights, gender stereotypes exist and, as the three previous papers pointed out, create disadvantages concerning two basic aspects of women's life: work on one side; family life and sexuality on the other.

Hence, among others, a first, basic problem: how to offer equal opportunities to individuals who have been culturally constructed as different.

Issue 1. Gender Stereotypes and Equal Opportunities

As it is well known, in the United States the answer has been the politics of affirmative action and quotas for minorities. I am not going to repeat the story of these politics. It would be impossible to concentrate in a few words such a complicated and controversial issue. Suffice to recall a milestone: the Bakke case (1978). A white student was not admitted to the medical school at the University of California, Davis, because the school had set aside 16 out of 100 available positions for minorities. The Supreme Court decided that the university had violated Bakke's rights to the equal protection granted by the Fourteenth Amendment. Race can be taken into account only "as a plus"; it cannot be a factor determining the admission.

The philosophical debate concerning the definition of a just society that followed is also well known. As Ronald Dworkin said, in the selective processes merit is often associated inadvertently with other factors. Therefore, in order to promote a more just society, it may be legitimate to consider together with merit associated factors such as race or gender and to reduce the advantages of privileged individuals in favor of others who are disadvantaged. Justice must not be seen only as individual justice but as part of a wider social justice.[1]

Today this nonindividualistic notion of justice, although recently restated by Dworkin,[2] seems more difficult to accept. In the current scenario the rights of minorities are increasingly seen in a perspective of entitlement to specific rights, tied to an increasing number of different and multiplying identities, to a degree independent from the criteria of a large structure of disadvantages.

In this scenario the politics of affirmative action have been widely discussed and frequently opposed. In California in 1996, Proposition 209 forbade state institutions to adopt a different treatment for race, sex, and other factors. In the same year, the affirmative action program of the University of Texas Law School was condemned by the court of appeals. What is the future of these remedies? If their critics prevail, can we imagine other different ways to fight gender stereotypes?

In my opinion it could be interesting to widen the current discussion in this country through the quotation of two recent European experiences.

The first is an Italian law on sharing care approved February 22, 2000.

In 1971 an Italian law granted to all women workers the right to five months of compulsory leave (two before, three after delivery), while retaining 80 percent of their wages. The law also offered an additional six months of optional leave during the first years of life of the child, with 30 percent of their wages. But this law, as all protective laws, proved to be a disadvantage for women, and the new law changed the rules: Starting from February 22, 2000, in some circumstances the three months of leave granted after delivery may be asked not only by the mother, as it used to be under the old law, but also by the father. The father may also ask for the optional leave, in addition to the mother's. Furthermore, fathers asking for the new "paternity" leave receive as a bonus an extension of one month of leave.

Will the new law make Italian men more willing to share the caring role? Time will say. Anyway, in my opinion, this law represents an interesting attempt to offer equal opportunities to women through the activation of countermechanisms aimed at neutralizing or minimizing gender stereotypes.

The second example is a modification of the French Constitution proposed by Prime Minister Jospin and approved on June 22, 1999. The new rule stated that, starting with the municipal elections in 2001, half of the candidates in the election must be women. But the discussion of this rule, while it could prove very important and stimulating, would take us beyond the limit of our topic. In fact, though very interesting, this rule is not aimed to offer the same opportunities in their careers to women and men. Its aim is the introduction of a descriptive representation, inspired by a controversial model of direct representation, rather conflicting, and in my opinion highly debatable.

Issue 2. The Role of Law and Its Interaction with Culture in Shaping and Changing Women's Roles

As Professor al-Hibri writes, in the Muslim world Egypt has recently put in place a far-reaching reform of family law that cancelled some of the strongest discriminations suffered by women, namely, the former practical impossibility for wives to divorce without their husbands' assent. Today, a woman will be able to divorce her husband, with or without his assent, and she will also be able to call on the Egyptian government to garnish her husband's wages if he refuses to provide for her.[3]

In an interview given to the *New York Times,* the assistant justice minister who drafted the law, Fathi Naguib, declared that law was a shock for Muslim culture. I must say I was surprised by this statement. In her paper, Professor Al-Hibri says that the strength of the new code lies in the fact that the scholars involved in it developed a new jurisprudence suitable to Egypt and resting on firm Islamic ground. As far as I can understand, this code introduced novelties that could culturally be accepted, and this seems to me a very wise legislative approach. History offers too many examples of laws never enforced because they were culturally shocking. Let me give one example from Roman law.

In 18 B.C. Emperor Augustus passed a law on adultery. From the founding of Rome in 753 B.C. until that moment, punishment of adultery was a family and not a state affair, and the husband who caught his wife committing adultery was allowed to kill her with impunity. Under the new law, adultery became a crime that could be punished—with the exception of some special cases—only after a regular public criminal trial, upon indictment by any Roman citizen. But this law was so unacceptable to the Roman mentality that during the following century only about a dozen women were accused. A very small number indeed compared to the probable number of adulteries committed during a century! The *lex Iulia* was so blatantly a failure that it became the typical case for a theoretical question: Under which conditions is a law, intended to provoke a cultural shock, an effective device or, on the contrary, the occasion for a backlash?

When laws are changed, there are two possible models. One is the shock model, in which elites impose by law more and more progressive behavior. The other is a more developmental model, which would maintain that laws can perform effectively as acculturating factors only when they are based on previous and ongoing social mores.

As an example of the second model Professor Karst recalled the legal prohibition of sex discrimination on the job, prepared by a profound cultural change. This prohibition led to a generalized moral condemnation of sexual harassment, and in turn this led to the affirmation that this behavior was an actionable sex discrimination in violation of Title VII of the Civil Rights Act of 1964. This leads me, leaving aside the general problem, to pose a specific question concerning the ongoing debate on sexual harassment.

Issue 3. Should We Reconceptualize Sexual Harassment?

In recent years, the conceptualization of sexual harassment has been criticized by some scholars. Basically, the critique consists of this:[4] According to the most generalized interpretation, harassment must take the form of a sexual conduct (usually an advance) to be "sexual harassment." This created the problem of defining what is sexual. As is well known, the cases are teeming with controversies. Some years ago, Judge Posner drew a sort of line of separation, writing that "On one side lie sexual assaults, other physical contacts, whether amorous or hostile, for which there is non-consent expressed or implied; uninvited sexual solicitations, intimidating words or acts, obscene language and gestures; pornographic pictures. On the other side lies vulgar banter, tinged with sexual innuendo, of course, of boorish workers."[5] Yet what counts as a sexual advance remains uncertain.

A second critique concerns the consideration that the focus on sexual conduct reflects the idea that sexual relations were the primary producer of women's oppression. This adds another controversial issue, which gives rise to a host of questions: Are we really willing to state that any expression of sexuality in the workplace is presumptively illegitimate? Isn't such an approach paternalistic? Doesn't this involve a very low esteem of female agency? Furthermore, very often harassment in workplaces assumes a form that has little or nothing to do with sexuality but has everything to do with gender. Professor Karst gives some examples: constantly denying the competence of women workers or withholding the training and the information necessary to do the job in a better way.

According to some scholars, such as Katherine Franke, these behaviors are actionable under Title VII because they are manifestations of a "technology of sex-

ism" that perpetuates gender stereotypes in the workplace.[6] As a consequence, sexual harassment should be reconceptualized as "gender harassment," a reconceptualization that would have the further advantage of returning Title VII to its original focus on dismantling job segregation.

Would this reconceptualization be useful and appropriate? This question is very important not only because of its possible consequences in the United States but also for its potential effect on the European way of dealing with this problem. Sexual harassment was conceptualized as illicit behavior in workplaces in the United States, and many European countries consider the American concept a model and in part base their legislation on the American example. This is at least partly the case in Italy, where a debate is going on concerning the first proposition of law on this issue and where "sexual harassment" is defined as sexually characterized behavior. Should the American concept change, would this influence the European approach?

Issue 4. The Relation between Economic Development and the Condition of Women

In general, the three papers agree on assigning a positive role for women's improvement to economic development. However, Judge Northfleet recalled that globalization and segmentation of the labor market had on one side the effect of increasing the number of women workers, but on the other it provoked the growth of job volatility. This is one of the side effects of globalization confirmed by scholarship. As Richard Sennett writes, "flexibility in organisations is a double-edged sword and it can lead to increased pressure on the productivity of the individual worker, albeit in ways that are different from the traditional ones of direct control in the factory."[7]

Furthermore, Judge Northfleet recalls that globalization has gender-related effects, in some cases exacerbating gender-based discriminations, especially in the less privileged areas of the planet where the condition of women is not a problem of civil rights but of human rights. To use her words, "slavery still exists in the twenty-first century."

But this problem is not limited to the poor countries. If, as Judge Northfleet writes, "one to two million women and girls are trafficked annually around the world for the purpose of forced labor, forced prostitution, servile domestic labor, or involuntary marriage," the data refer to developed countries as well. And Italy offers a very telling example. Traditionally a country of emigrants, Italy is now the destination for millions of immigrants coming from other European countries as well as African and Asian countries. There is no doubt that this means that our country offers better economic opportunities. But as Saskia Sassen writes, asymmetry in economies becomes a push factor in immigration only when it is activated by an organized recruitment of the labor force.[8] But in the case of women, these organizations are often composed of pimps and slave traders. And the phenomenon concerns not only women migrating from traditional sub-Saharan societies but, increasingly, in recent time also those arriving from impoverished Eastern European countries or from areas affected by local wars or political turmoil, such as the Balkans.

This supports and in fact amplifies Judge Northfleet's points, signalling that even in a rich European country like Italy the growth of wealth, in addition to creating novel discrimination causes, is gender typed, offering specific occasions for the overexploitation and humiliation of women.

Finally, here is a last consideration concerning the relation between women's condition and economic development. In a note of her paper Judge Northfleet quotes an interview given in 1995 by Betty Friedan, who wonders "how, at this time of global economic insecurity, women could even maintain their gains, much less continue to advance." Friedan's answer is: "I've realized that they can't—not as long as they focus on women issues alone or on women versus men. The problems in our fast changing world require a new paradigm of social policy: transcending all 'identity politics'—women, blacks, gays, the disabled. Pursuing the separate interests of women isn't adequate and is even diversionary. Instead there has to be some new vision of community. . . . Women's issues are symptoms of problems that affect everyone." [9]

Is this opinion to be shared? Or would we rather maintain that in every state of economic development, even in the most underdeveloped countries, there are specific gender issues that must be approached as such?

Issue 5. Women's Role in the Process of Dismantling Gender Stereotypes

Basically, the three papers agreed that without women's contributions and efforts, gender stereotypes and discrimination would not have lost their strength and that women's contributions are necessary for future improvements.

Professor al-Hibri, in particular, put great emphasis on the role of women. Speaking of the necessity for a change in Islamic laws performed with the proper methods of juristic interpretation, she said that in some countries of the Islamic world, women educated in the field of Islamic jurisprudence now possess the tools to criticize patriarchal interpretations. These learned women, therefore, may open the road to a new nondiscriminatory juristic interpretation, firmly based on Qur'an, giving birth to a new Muslim society closer to the Medinah society headed by the Prophet himself where women participated actively.

This seems to me a very important point, but I wonder about the relative strength of these women when arrayed against the strength of the women who, as Professor al-Hibri writes, have internalized their own oppression and share and defend the arguments used by the traditional jurists to limit women's rights. Of course, I do not intend to minimize the role of feminine juristic interpretation. In my own country, where women were allowed to be judges in 1961, feminine jurisprudence has since been a very important factor in developing new, more equitable principles.

Nonetheless, recalling what happened in the United States and in Europe during the feminist revolution, I wonder how effective an elite feminine Islamic movement can be. This elite movement, as far as I know, cannot rely on a strong mass movement, such as the feminist one in the Western world. Of course, this is not a critique: I am aware of the fact that Muslim feminists are different from us. As Professor Al-Hibri stated, they even have a different idea of liberty. While the exploration of this idea would make even more interesting what Professor Al-Hibri can tell us about this movement—its strength, its strategy, and its agenda—what intrigues me most is the relation of juristic interpretation to ethical principles and mores. In the Western tradition the development of human and civil rights, among which are those concerning women's opportunities and equality, were part of the same process that separated law from religion. What is the role of juristic interpretation in systems where religious and legal norms are not separated, and religion supports values and practices that are contrary to those values considered an essential part of the universalistic principles supporting women's rights?

Issue 6. Abortion

The abortion issue has a fundamental importance and a special value in showing how dangerous generalizations about "women's rights" may be and how different the response of law to the expectations of women may be in different historical and cultural contexts.

Let's start with the first point, clearly connected with a debate still raging in Europe concerning the relations between "difference" and "differences."

The difference (singular) is, of course, the feminine difference: What makes women different from men. According to supporters of the "difference theory," the difference between the sexes (beyond the biological ones) is not completely created by society and culture, as the feminists of the first wave maintain (suffice it to quote Simone de Beauvoir). There exists also a real difference between the sexes in psychology and, for some difference-feminists, even in the mind, that is to say in the mode of reasoning (modus ponens). These theorists, therefore, maintain that women must not and cannot ask for equality.

On the other side, a great number of feminist scholars point out that stressing "the difference" (singular) means to go back, in fact, to the old idea of a feminine "essence." And even if today this "essence" is identified by women (and not by men, as in the past), to speak of the "difference" (singular) involves the idea that women adhere to one unique gender model and prevents the recognition of the differences among female individuals.[10]

Professor Karst attracted our attention to this point when he said that a general analysis of women's condition may fail to notice, for instance, specific discriminations suffered by African-American women. He recalled that some African-American and Latina feminists have criticized American feminists for assuming that the experience of American women fits a white European model and ignoring differences in the lives of other women.

As I said, abortion is the typical example. At least in the United States and in some European countries, abortion has become a sort of symbol of women's possibility to make their life choices. But a number of African-American feminists some years ago, in attacking the *pro-choice* feminist movement, said that their problem was not the right to abortion but the right to medical care allowing them to give birth to children. For some women in some African or Asian countries, abortion should not be considered a right. And even in the countries where abortion is a right, the foundation for that right may be different.

In the United States, as Professor Karst recalls, from the 1965 contraceptive decision in *Griswold v. Connecticut* to the 1973 abortion decision in *Roe v. Wade,* the Court's opinions were written in the language of individual autonomy. Later, the unifying theme of these decisions was the validation of women's claim to equal citizenship. Without control over maternity a woman's access to public life could be prevented, not only by a legal rule but also by a fact, such as an unwanted pregnancy.

In Italy, none of these principles has been considered as a possible basis for granting the abortion right. In 1987, the law that decriminalized abortion stated that a women may perform an abortion only in a state of necessity, that is to say if a medical doctor attests that she faces a clear and present danger (both physical and psychological) in giving birth to the child.

Of course, this provoked strong discontent in the feminine world. But a law considering abortion a woman's right would never be approved by the Italian Parliament, still deeply influenced by the power of the Catholic Church. The law that was approved was a compromise, and, as I said, it was very controversial.

Nonetheless, the fact that abortion was not recognized as a general right of women had, paradoxically, positive consequences on the problem of ensuring the real possibility to abort.

What happens, in fact, is on one side that medical doctors, as a rule, certify the state of necessity simply upon request of the woman; and on the other side, considering abortion a necessity, the law requires public hospitals to guarantee the presence of a doctor available to perform it. As in Italy access to public hospitals is universally granted and free, this had the paradoxical effect to make abortion available to a wide number of women, even among the poorest. Of course, also in Italy we have problems (basically, the public heath system is lacking, especially in the poorest regions of the country). Nonetheless, in spite of the continuous attack and the recurring attempt of the Catholic Church to change the law, this law is still in force and enforced. While in the United States the affirmation of a strong principle faces a number of challenges in practice, in Italy a weaker legal principle (not contemplating at all the right of choice) permits the introduction of a social principle in practice.

With this I end my comments. It is beyond the scope and the brief of them to draw general conclusions. I want nonetheless to agree with the three panelists when they write that much remains to be accomplished. But it is undeniable, as Professor Karst states, that women have conquered more rights and freedom in the last thirty years than in the previous three millennia. Because

ancient law is my specific field of interest, I deeply appreciate this observation, and I would like to close by recalling the first Western law, going back to the Athenian lawgiver Drakon (seventh century B.C.).

Though directed at homicide, Drakon's law also regulated women's condition, offering a legal basis for the oldest and still existing stereotype concerning women. Prohibiting the ancient system of revenge, stating that homicide was a crime, and establishing the penalty for that crime, Drakon also stated that in some cases a man could still be killed with impunity. A man caught while having illicit sexual intercourse with the wife, the sister, the daughter, or the mother of an Athenian citizen—in other words, with a woman who was a wife or whose social destination was to become a wife—could still be killed. In these cases the homicide of the accomplice of the lady—whose virtue had to be protected—was considered "legitimate."

But the life of the man having intercourse with other women was not endangered: Killing him would have been punished as homicide. In other words, the first Western law divided women in two categories: wives and whores—women to be respected and protected, women to be used. It would be fascinating to elaborate the psychological and social basis of this division, following its history and its effect over the millennia. But it would exceed our time and, perhaps, the topic of our discussion.

Closing Remarks

Ruth Bader Ginsburg

Thanks to our panelists for stimulating our thinking. Ellen Gracie Northfleet has emphasized the intolerable waste of valuable human resources in suppressing those who hold up half the sky. At the same time, she has constantly recognized that there can be no pervasive, enduring change in women's stature without educating and enlisting the participation of men in the endeavor. To the image of the glass ceiling, she has added perhaps the more problematic sticky floor (the inability to move from entry level jobs) and glass wall (occupational segmentation). Feminization of poverty is a reality worldwide, she underscores. For the good of all, she has invited us to aid in changing that sad reality. Government can be a way paver, she observed. Hopeful signs in the United States include the fairly recent appearance of women in top policymaking posts, for example, Madeleine Albright as secretary of state, Donna Shalala, who headed the Department of Health and Human Resources, and Janet Reno, our former attorney general. Ellen Gracie Northfleet has also encouraged us to learn about what our neighbors are doing in order to borrow solutions that may work for us, too. She mentioned in her paper, among many illustrations, legislation in Argentina to encourage men to support their children—laws providing, inter alia, for nonrenewal of drivers' licenses and withdrawal of permission to leave the country while child support is in arrears.

Ken Karst has eloquently developed two themes: women's access to all manner of work done in our world and their emancipation from man's control in family and other intimate relations. He has noted the large progress made in the United States in evening out the rights and responsibilities of men and women and has reminded us of the staying power of certain equality-inhibiting conditions: the wage gap, the scarcity of women in top managerial jobs, and the continued cultural expectation that women will perform the lion's share of domestic duties.

Azizah Y. al-Hibri has given us a picture of the large size and diversity of the world's Muslim population. She noted, however, certain issues common to personal codes, particularly, whether women will have the right to execute their own marriage contracts, to petition for divorce, to be free from the requirement that the wife must obey her husband. One could not fail to note the resemblance of those issues to similar concerns in other cultures. She approached with candor and sensitivity the question of the helping (but not imperious) role persons and organizations outside the Muslim world might play in advancing women's stature in Muslim communities.

Finally, Eva Cantarella's bright commentary has demonstrated how very wrong Voltaire was when he said: "Ideas are like beards, women and young men have none." Our commentator and panelists have offered papers and presentations bristling with ideas that may enable us in the century just dawning to draw on the talent of all of humanity, not just select segments of our societies.

It is fitting to close these remarks with the words of a brave lady, written in 1900. That year, Susan B. Anthony wrote of her anticipation for the then dawning century:

> The woman of the Twentieth Century will be the peer of man. In education, in art, in science, in literature; in the home, the church, the state; everywhere she will be his acknowledged equal, though not identical with him. . . . The Twentieth Century will see man and woman working together to make the world better for their having lived.

May Susan B. Anthony's expectation, now flowering, see its full working out in the starting decades of the twenty-first century.

Kosovo survivors of massacre. *Source:* © Hautu/SABA, 1998.

Session 3

Multiethnic and Multiracial States

Editors' Note

Since World War II, violence traceable to ethnic and racial divides within countries has replaced the historically more common wars between nation-states as the primary cause of armed conflict. While the roots of such eruptions are varied and complex, the struggle to reduce their number and to mitigate their severity requires strong democratic institutions to be built in multiethnic and multiracial states. The problem is endemic; despite the proliferation of new states based largely on racial or ethnic identities, few if any countries today contain people of only one background. Civil wars along ethnic or racial lines have become a major focus of international mediation and peacekeeping.

The panelists all recognized that the tensions created by ethnic and racial diversity, including language differences, afflict countries of all continents, sizes, and histories. They also observed that long periods of assimilation of minorities, such as Jews in Germany, or seemingly peaceful ethnic coexistence, as among Croats, Moslems, and Serbs in the former Yugoslavia, do not guarantee future peace. With this background, the panelists described political structures and techniques that promote democratic institutions and provide justice to members of different ethnicity and race. They also addressed issues that have long required creative solutions, such as native peoples in the United States, Australia, and elsewhere, and the Roma (gypsies) of Europe and immigrant minorities in many countries. The problems discussed in this session are among the most imperative that the new century will confront.

Ethnic Strife and Democracy

Kogila Moodley

I. The Limits of Legal Intervention in Ethnic Conflicts

The law can influence ethnic strife in multinational states, but good laws are no guarantee for containing or minimizing, let alone solving, ethnic violence. One must guard against legal hubris. Many a failed state in the world is littered with admirable, progressive constitutions. They did not prevent the ethnic unraveling of states, because attitudes cannot be legislated. Even if the expression of hostile behavior is criminalized, for example, by outlawing hate speech or extra punishment of bias crime, it often only drives intergroup resentment underground and makes the dormant, nonrecognized aggressive potential even more dangerous.

In order to devise constitutions that address potential ethnic strife effectively, familiarity with the country's cultural specifics and particular history is needed. Above all, a thorough understanding of the nature of ethnic antagonism is required. Western liberal democracies, based on the rights of individual citizens and used to the lures of atomized consumerism, are constantly surprised by the ferocity of ethnonationalist mobilization for sacrifice in other parts of the world. Communal attachments and loyalties to a national family are underestimated.

A recent example of such self-deception was the genuine assumption by NATO leaders at the beginning of the Kosovo intervention that Milosevic would yield after a few days of bombing Belgrade. Earlier, the Ramboillet ultimatum, demanding a Kosovo referendum and access of foreign troops to the whole of Serbia, was formulated in such a way that no nationalist leader of a sovereign state could accept the terms, short of committing political suicide. Western opinion failed to understand a society where the overwhelming majority of the populace, including the

democratic opposition, supported the intransigence of the authoritarian leadership toward outside threats and either their indifference toward or support for the oppression of denigrated Kosovars. Either the Western ultimatum was deliberately designed to provoke a military confrontation, which is vehemently denied, or the negotiators were naive and ignorant about ethnonationalism.

Walker Connor has reminded us that realistic attempts to peacefully resolve ethnic conflicts necessitate an appreciation of the emotional and elusive nature of ethnic identity. Understanding conflicting perspectives has to precede ascertaining reality. In this vein of total subjectivity, divorced from reality, one of the wittier definitions of a nation is that of "a group of people united by a common dislike of their neighbors and a shared misconception of their ethnic origin" (E. Mortimer 1999, 2). "Probing these matters requires not a knowledge of 'facts' but of commonly held perceptions of facts."(Connor 1999, 174). Indeed, "facts" on Kashmir look remarkably different through Pakistani eyes than the same facts viewed through Hindu eyes and again turn out to be different from a Kashmiri point of view. Kurdish inhabitants of Turkey appraise their conflict with Turks from totally different angles. Kurds, a sizeable minority of up to 25 percent of the population, do not even exist for Turkish nationalists, as did Palestinians for some previous Israeli leaders, while the very state of Israel constitutes a religious insult for Islamic fundamentalists.

Antagonistic communal perceptions are outside the reach of state law, and many a law in a multinational state may well reflect the bias and interests of the dominant group. Whose laws for whom is a frequently asked question of subordinate groups. When people feel themselves to be second-class citizens in an ethnic state, the very legitimacy of common laws is at stake.

Skepticism is also warranted towards the practical significance of international law in human rights. While the increased universal jurisdiction over violations at the expense of state sovereignty is to be praised—particularly if the proposed International Criminal Court is operational in the distant future—human rights advocates often take their noble declarations for reality. The Preamble to the Universal Declaration of Human Rights begins with the statement that "recognition of the inherent dignity and of the equal and inalienable rights of all members of the human family is the foundation of freedom, justice and peace in the world." However, as analysts of migrants, refugees, or asylum seekers the world over have noted: "Violations of the inherent dignity of persons occur continually simply because such persons do not have political citizenship in the country in which they reside" (V. Leary 1999, 262).

Another reason why human rights "on the books" are not enforced lies in state expediency and economic interests overriding moral concerns. When Western leaders deal with economically powerful dictatorships, most democratic politicians are under pressure not to jeopardize business deals by embarrassing their blood-stained guests or hosts. At the most, human rights concerns are raised "privately," not so much to achieve an improvement but to satisfy liberal public opinion at home. Even when enforcement of international laws on the books does not cost anything, it is often not implemented. Moreover, as a typical example from South Africa demonstrates, this neglect occurs by a government that came to power campaigning for human rights and being committed to universal human rights observance.

The South African constitution expressly incorporates customary international law with a right and a *duty* to exercise jurisdiction over crimes against humanity. Yet Pretoria blatantly faulted on this duty in a widely publicized incident. The former Ethiopian dictator Mengistu was shielded by Mugabe in Zimbabwe since the early 1990s. When Mengistu visited South Africa for medical treatment, the South African government was urged by foreign and local human rights organizations as well as the Ethiopian government to either extradite him or, in order to avoid Ethiopia's death penalty and notoriously unfair justice system, charge him before a South African court. Unlike Britain's arrest of Pinochet, Pretoria did nei-

ther. After a long embarrassed prevarication, it let the mass murderer of 100,000 forcibly relocated peasants quietly slip back into Zimbabwe in December 1999.

Coming from the interdisciplinary social sciences without legal training, I shall therefore interpret my task here as, first, dispelling some common liberal fallacies about the causes and remedies of ethnic strife, second, clarifying the nature of multinational democracies comparatively and, third, critically reviewing the commonly proposed solutions in the literature, from Arendt Lijphart's consociationalism to Donald Horowitz's electoral and constitutional engineering, with particular reference to the debate about Quebec in my adopted home country, as well as the lessons from the negotiated revolution in my birthplace, South Africa.

It seems worthwhile to start with extreme cases. In their stark revelation of human atrocities they shatter common myths in liberal democracies that take their state of affairs as normal and "natural." Genocide and ethnic cleansing are neither events of a dark past, historical aberrations of pathological national characters, nor confined to less developed countries in Africa or Asia. A better understanding of human capacities for evil may also sensitize more innocent individuals in Western liberal democracies to the warning signals in their own sheltered environments.

II. Fallacies about the Causes and Remedies of Ethnic Strife

During three months in early 1994, about 800,000 people were massacred in Rwanda at a rate that surpassed the industrialized death camps of the Nazis, despite mostly low-tech killing by machete. "These dead and their killers had been neighbors, schoolmates, colleagues, sometimes friends, even in-laws," notes an American journalist in a moving account (Philip Gourevitch 1998, 180). The majority Hutu population and the minority Tutsis speak the same language, belong to the same (mostly Roman Catholic) religion, and lived side by side.

A similar social integration existed in Sarajevo, which was once one of the most cosmopolitan European towns with integrated neighborhoods and high degrees of intermarriage between Serbs and Croats. They also share the same language and are indistinguishable to any foreigner. Yet the long historical bonds between the ethnic groups in former Yugoslavia together with forty years of Tito's policy of "Brotherhood and Solidarity" did not prevent the violent ethnic cleansing of the state when civil war broke out in 1991. These two examples alone should dispel several cherished liberal myths and conventional wisdoms.

1. Social Integration, Interethnic Mixing, and Even Successful Assimilation of Minorities into Majority Cultures Do Not Guarantee Intergroup Harmony

Another example demonstrates this. Before the rise of the Nazis, secularized German Jews were fully integrated into German society, indistinguishable in lifestyles, outlook, attitudes, citizenship, and appearance from other Germans. Yet like Tutsis in Rwanda, they were singled out by a self-proclaimed different majority for genocide on the basis of an assumed different ancestry and an imagined global conspiracy.

2. Whether a Minority Has Been Singled Out for Unequal Treatment Has Little to Do With Its Own Behavior

It is often targeted, regardless of its desires to assimilate or separate. Therefore, we must look at the collective predisposition of the dominant group to explain why one segment can be easily mobilized to turn against another segment of the population. Above all, the actions of political elites and opinion leaders are crucial in inciting aggressive behavior. Elite theory that blames civil wars solely on the egoism of power-hungry leaders, however, must always keep Leo Kuper's (1981, 50) reservation in mind "that whatever the responsibility of elites, they are working with social forces present within the society, and not creating a genocidal situation out of a vacuum."

3. It Is Also Not the Degree of Difference That Causes Ethnic Conflict

Even in so-called religious strife about incompatible interpretations of doctrine, religion functions only as a label. Neither are IRA bombers active Catholics nor are unionist marchers more than ritualized churchgoers. In fact, the greater the similarities between groups, the more intense the antagonism displayed. Psychoanalytic theory refers to this as the "narcissism of small difference." It reasons that in the absence of objective or visible difference, imagined pseudo-differences are magnified in order to reinforce an uncertain identity (Ignatieff 1996). However, indifference to difference and official failure to recognize claims of minorities can exacerbate tensions.

4. Ethnic Antagonism Is Also Not Caused by High Numbers of Perceived Strangers

All too easily an economic reductionism lists heightened competition or conflicting material interests as the real causes of ethnic strife. While discrimination obviously benefits some and shortchanges others, it would be misleading to reduce ethnic antagonism to material privileging alone. For example, former East Germany experienced many more incidents of violent xenophobia despite a relatively small number of resident foreigners (100,000) compared with West Germany with a forty-five times greater population of foreigners (4.5 million) competing for scarce jobs. As a Polish saying goes, there can be virulent anti-Semitism without any Jews left in a country.

5. Unfortunately, Different Political Ideologies and Different Economic Systems Would Seem to Make Little Significant Difference in Manifestations of Bigotry

After being exposed to communist versus capitalist socialization for forty years, East and West Germans were united in the content of prejudices, though they differed in their readiness to vent commonly held stereotypes. Likewise, U.S. and Canadian attitudes toward immigrants hardly differ, despite different state ideologies, according to survey evidence by Jeffrey G. Reitz and Raymond Breton in their study, appropriately titled " The Illusion of Difference." The American historian George M. Fredrickson (1999, 37) concludes: "Despite the myths that Canada is a "mosaic" and the United States a "melting pot," racial prejudice and xenophobia exist to about the same extent in both countries."

6. Attempts at Cooptation of a Separatist Adversary Are Far from a Foolproof Remedy

This is the historical experience of the rest of Canada's dealing with Quebec. With short interruptions of a few months, all Canadian prime ministers since 1967 originated from Quebec, comprising 25 percent of the country's population. French-Canadians are overrepresented in the federal bureaucracy, particularly in the diplomatic service and army. The separatist government receives large transfer and equalization payments from the richer provinces. Bilingualism in the civil service is actively promoted and subsidized.

Yet all these measures of accommodation have not guaranteed that Francophone Quebecers are content with anything less than independence. Sixty-one percent of Francophones support secession, and a second 1996 referendum on sovereignty was only narrowly defeated with the help of the 10 percent English-speaking and 10 percent Allophone ("ethnics") residents in Quebec. Although survey evidence indicates a slight decline of separatist support since, fickle public opinion swings frequently and the government is committed to a third referendum "when the time is ripe." Politicians from Quebec in the service of Canada are not viewed as representatives of an unrecognized people but as traitors to the cause. Pierre Trudeau or Jean Chretien enjoy the lowest popularity in their home province.

7. Similar Reservations Apply to the Effect of Greater Political Autonomy or Economic Clout for a Homeland

The global evidence is inconclusive. Devolution of power and political decentralization has diffused Scottish, Basque, and Catalan nationalism but failed in Quebec and the former Soviet Union.

Within a maximalist federalist state, Quebec has additional special jurisdiction over immigration and social programs. It has even entered into bilateral agreements with foreign countries. A self-confident Quebecois economic class has achieved world recognition with some highly successful manufacturing and technology companies. The language of the workplace has become French; non-English immigrants must send their children by law to French-language schools, and a special language police guard language laws that forbid English-only public displays. French as a home language has not declined during the last century, although the province is exposed to the U.S. cultural imperialism as much as the rest of the country.

Yet the federal government is still widely viewed as an oppressive foreign power akin to colonial occupation. In Quebec, car plates remind the French of the defeat by the British loyalists at the battle on the Plains of Abraham in 1766. An independent Quebec would rather rely on the United States than on Ottawa across the river.

8. Historically Oppressed Groups Do Not Necessarily Eschew the Same Behavior Once They Have Gained Power Themselves

Historical victimhood does not immunize against repeating similar abuses of others. Israel, the sanctuary of a long prosecuted people, treats its Palestinian population with an ethnocentric mind-set not too different from apartheid South Africa, with whom Israel closely collaborated. Palestinian activists in positions of power with the newly established Palestinian authority tortured fellow countrymen with the same methods learned in Israeli prisons. Closer to home, many guilt-ridden North Americans idealize and romanticize native people. Yet their conquest, marginalization, and historical disadvantage does not preclude First Nations people from behaving as exploitatively as their colonizers, given the opportunity. Quebec separatists insist on self-determination as a right of distinct, historically disadvantaged people but balk at Cree natives in Quebec when they claim the same right of national self-determination.

In short, there are no people that by history or nature would be exempt from inflicting injustices on others. Sociologically speaking, we have to look at the social conditions that restrain the aggressive potential in humans as well as the incentives that trigger solidarity and reciprocity in a society.

One of the most persuasive explanations of ethnic hostility universally has been provided by psychoanalytic theory. It also reveals the limits of legal efforts to contain ethnic antagonisms. The psychoanalytic explanation, first explicated in the seminal research on bigotry and anti-Semitism in "The Authoritarian Personality" (Adorno et al. 1950), established empirically that an individual who is prejudiced towards one group usually also holds negative attitudes towards other minorities, sometimes even fictitious groups. Bigotry as a syndrome comprises racism, homophobia, xenophobia, anti-Semitism, parochial ethnocentrism, misogyny, and other forms of denigration of outgroups. Recently, analysts of ethnic strife in this tradition like Michael Ignatieff (1996) or the Cypriot psychiatrist Vamik Volkan (1997) have further elaborated the crucial correlation between early socialization, ego development, and later attitudes toward collective attachments.

The Indian psychoanalyst Sudhir Kakar gives an account of Hindu-Muslim riots in India. Kakar, following Freud and Erikson, reminds us that the community in which we are socialized is always part of our personal identity. Its myths, history, rituals, and symbols are idealized by the young child "in the enhancement of self-esteem for belonging to such an exalted and blessed entity" (Kakar 1996, 189). However, the internalization of necessary social rules (culture) also clashes with a person's natural drives. This conflict is solved through projection of "bad" representations onto others. "First projected to inanimate objects and animals and later to people and other groups—the latter often available to the child as a preselection by the group—the disavowed bad representations need such 'reservoirs' as Vamik Volkan calls them. These reservoirs—Muslims for Hindus, Arabs for Jews, Tibetans for Chinese, and vice versa—are also convenient repositories for subsequent rages and hateful feelings for which no clear-cut addressee is available. Since most of the bad representations arise from a social disapproval of the child's animality, as expressed in its dirtiness, and unruly sexuality, it is preeminently this animality which a civilized moral self must disavow and place in the reservoir group" (Kakar 1996, 189).

This psychoanalytic account explains why in every ethnic hostility the other group is ascribed sexual licen-tiousness, drunkenness, and other forbidden behavior. In short, we tend to project onto others what we have to suppress in ourselves.

Strong ethnic attachment and bigotry is attractive to people in search of an identity. They can borrow strength from the glory of the group. Some people find their self-esteem in religion and the hope for afterlife, others in work and professionalism, others in sport or consumerism or even from the type of car they drive. Uncritical communalism and ethnonationalism is on offer among many bases of identity. The less fulfillment and sublimation is guaranteed in an uncertain work sphere, the more attractive becomes the ethnic ingroup. Because of the common socialization experience, associated with early security and comfort, individuals fall in easily with "my people" at the expense of solidarity with others in a crisis.

We can distinguish four ethnic relations situations according to (a) historical origin, (b) forms of stigmatization, (c) strategies and motivations of the subordinate group involved, and (d) relationship to the dominant group and the state. The four distinct contexts can be labeled (1) diasporic minorities, (2) immigrant minorities, (3) indigenous minorities, and (4) national minorities. Each situation requires different policy responses. They will be sketched in turn.

III. Dilemmas of Immigrant Minorities

Diasporic minorities originated from the migration of different ethnicities into host societies a long time ago. Either through rejection and ghettoization by the dominant group or through voluntary separation in the case of religious minorities, cultural assimilation did not take place or was not sought by the minority. Historically, the transplantation was mostly *involuntary*, as in the case of slavery, induced by extreme poverty, as in the case of indentured laborers, or due to religious or political persecution in the country of origin. Despite centuries of residence, the minority is still viewed as an alien element by the majority and is scapegoated and stigmatized, if not actively prosecuted. Due to the limited economic opportunities as a result of formal and informal discrimination, minority members were frequently relegated to economic niches. Here they often excelled, but they also made themselves visible. This cultural division of labor gave rise to an accusation of exploitation and resulted in renewed restrictions. Minority members have responded to this sociopolitical insecurity by emphasizing educational credentials of children, second passports, or contacts abroad, which again triggered charges of disloyalty.

The classical case of a diasporic minority are Jews worldwide, Roma (gypsies) in the Balkans, African Americans, or what sociologists (P. L. van den Berghe 1983) have called middle-men and trading minorities, such as Indians in East Africa or Chinese in Indonesia. All these groups differ from national minorities in their relatively small numbers scattered throughout the state rather than concentrated in their own historical territory. Although no threat to the far stronger state, some of the worst pogroms have been carried out against these defenseless people, as is well known from the long history of anti-Semitism.

Insistence on human rights and an effective criminalization of offenders would seem the main avenue of progress, particularly if the proposed International Criminal Court succeeds in establishing universal jurisdiction over perpetrators of atrocities. Even more needed would be a world forum where a threatened minority could appeal against its own government *before* it has become a victim.

From diasporic "minorities by force" in the past we can distinguish recent economic "immigrants by choice" not only by their voluntary migration but also in the lesser degree of stigmatization and easier incorporation into the mainstream.

Immigrant minorities are sometimes also called ethnic minorities (Banting 1999, 116). However, this term is avoided here because it feeds the common misperceptions that only immigrants possess ethnicity. Dominant group members, too, are "ethnics," although they falsely use the term for "othering" different newcomers. Most contemporary immigrant minorities originate from individual choice to seek improved economic opportunities abroad or escape repressive conditions in their home country. Whether immigrants arrived legally or illegally as independents, sponsored family members, or "refugees," they primarily strive for integration and personal betterment and not autonomy or special treatment as in

the case of national minorities. Immigrants do not aim at establishing a new state or foster a counternationalism. The generalization is doubtful that "they normally resist full assimilation: they seek to preserve their traditions and customs . . . they are often unwilling to surrender their ties to their original homeland" (Banting 1999, 116). The very opposite seems much more common in North America: with length of residence ties to origin fade, particularly among the foreign-educated second generation, except among some strongly religious communities with a critical mass to enforce conformity. Peer pressure to adopt mainstream cultural habits and conform to mainstream norms and fashions together with an all-pervasive media indoctrination frequently generates conflicts with parental traditions.

However, many professional immigrant families also lead an increasingly transnational existence. Economic globalization, multilingualism, and cross-cultural experience has made this group of internationalists a growing asset to a trading economy. With their network of global contacts and familiarity with other cultural traditions, they have a clear edge over homegrown competitors. They represent the future of mobile world citizens in demand by international conglomerates regardless of nationality. It is this corporate denationalization of top management that more than any laws makes ethnonationalism an outdated, parochial, and noncompetitive attitude. Ambivalent identification with any country characterizes transnational perpetual migrants.

Politically, it is crucial whether a host society allows new arrivals easy access to citizenship. Permanent resident rights and citizenship entitle social rights, from health care to old age benefits, education, or disability allowances. Western Europe restricts its access to social programs by increasingly tighter immigration rules but treats citizens and legal foreigners alike. In contrast, traditional immigration societies (United States, Canada, Australia) grant comparatively more liberal access to residency and citizenship rights but make it harder for immigrants (particularly illegals) to qualify for social benefits. Given the global migration, passports therefore function less as documents of political allegiance or national identity but as entitlements to social privilege in the industrialized capitalist countries. Insiders and outsiders increasingly confront each other in ethnic terms that disguise the underlying economic cleavage between a rich European/Japanese part and an impoverished black/brown part of the world.

The image of immigrants as eternal trespassers who import crime, diseases, drugs, political violence, and other unsavory habits particularly sticks to the racially different. In Germany, France, or Japan with its *ius sanguinis,* even their native birth does not always erase the notion of stranger, culminating in the assumption-laden question "Where did you come from?" To be sure, most immigration societies have made strides in educational representation and political empowerment of non-Europeans. Unlike Europe, which mainly attracted poor or rural migrants from less developed countries, North America is creaming off the economic and professional elite from many states. Yet even this privileged status of newcomers does not always exempt them from encounters with racism. While racism in Europe denigrates ethnic others on the basis of lower class, Canadian or Australian rejection expresses itself sometimes as envy of better off "others."

Western citizens are split on how they should receive a growing number of illegal migrants, often smuggled by criminal gangs into the country and falsely claiming persecution at home. There is no doubt that most illegals are desperate to escape poverty and improve their life chances abroad. If the migrants are mere economic refugees, they do not qualify for asylum, which in the case of genuine refugees is supported by an overwhelming majority of North Americans. Canada admits on average 57 percent of refugee claimants, compared with Europe's 6 percent. However, a great majority of Canadians also doubt that the country can afford open borders for millions of poor in the world, and therefore they support, like the United States does, stricter border controls and speedier processing of refugee claimants.

The attitude to unwanted immigrants has often been denounced as "a new racism." However, the everyday "racism" is proud of its tolerance. When Canadians are asked to identify the best word to describe themselves, 38 percent chose "tolerant," while the second most popular choice was "polite" at 26 percent. A majority of Canadians now think that homosexual marriages should be legally recognized. Such attitudes cannot be labeled old-style prejudice. Traditional racism includes all members of an outgroup, regardless of their standing or behavior. The new normal "racism" celebrates individuals from the other side as proof of its broad-mindedness. Most of the staunchest previous supporters of apartheid in South Africa genuinely love and admire Mandela. This phenomenon merely confirms that class and ideology transcends race, unlike the Nazi's anti-Semitism that did not make exceptions or differentiate among the outgroup. A perceptive paragraph in a book by the German critic Hans Magnus Enzensberger (1994, 120) points out the often neglected class and status dimension of racism: "The better qualified the immigrants, the fewer reservations they encounter. The Indian astrophysicist, the star Chinese architect, the Black African Nobel Prize winner are welcome all over the world. The rich are also never mentioned in this context; no one questions their freedom of movement. For businessmen from Hong Kong the acquisition of a British passport is no problem. For immigrants from any country, Swiss citizenship, too is only a matter of price. No one has ever objected to the Sultan of Brunei's skin colour. Where bank accounts look healthy, xenophobia disappears as if by magic. But strangers are all the stranger if they are poor."

Therefore, does it make sense if we lump rich and poor together under the label "visible minorities" who qualify for preferential treatment regardless of need?

In short, contemporary Western racial attitudes display considerable inconsistencies. Racist exclusion can exist together with respectful humanness toward the outsider. Often the same person disdains, envies, and admires aspects of the other simultaneously. Rather than generalizing about monolithic group attitudes, theories of contemporary racism and antiracist policies have to come to grips with these contradictions.

The legal response to the problems of immigrant minorities in both Europe and North America has been a growing support for various forms of multiculturalism, which has been official state policy in Canada and Australia since the early 1970s. Multiculturalism is rejected by national minorities because it levels their claim to prior rights as charter nations or aboriginal land ownership. In the United States multiculturalism has mainly concerned itself with revising educational canons. Affirmative action programs imposed and later abandoned school integration through busing and other preferential treatment for the historically disadvantaged, and designated groups can also be subsumed under the label.

In Canada and Australia, with official multiculturalism as the state's self-concept, a much more elaborate program has evolved that includes recognizing and subsidizing self-defined ethnic groups as well as implementing equity and antiracism programs.

Antiracism is held up as a more radical approach than liberal multiculturalism. On the other hand, multiculturalism's conservative critics (Bibby 1990; Bissoondath 1994) deplore an imagined divisiveness resulting from the official state policy that is said to undermine national unity. Left-wing critics point to the manipulation that pretends power and class differentials in a common consumer society can be overcome by the celebration of diversity and mutual tolerance. Both perspectives ignore valuable benefits of official multiculturalism. Psychologically, multiculturalism levels the traditional cultural hierarchy. Official multiculturalism includes the newcomers in the cultural construction of Canadianess. Multiculturalism makes immigrants officially welcome at little cost to the state. The symbolic acceptance prevents the official status of permanent strangers, both in the definition of "the other" by the dominant majority but even more important in the eyes of the newly arrived themselves.

At the same time, the official tolerance patronizes. The tolerant majority and its state wallows in a self-congratulatory confirmation of its open-mindedness. The graciously accepted others are expected to be thankful for the multicultural generosity. As Vijay Agnew (1996, 35) has pointed out: " Multiculturalism offers compensation to the powerless by 'accepting' them but not by giving them power or privilege. Rather than challenging Canadian political and social structures, it reinforces them." Such a challenge can hardly be expected from official state policy, unless its targets exploit its contradictions.

All opinion surveys reveal substantial approval of multiculturalism and at the same time some anxiety among a large minority about the pace of ethnic transformation. In a 1996 Angus Reid poll, 80 percent agreed with the statement: "Canada's multicultural make-up is one of the best things about this country." However, 41 percent also approved that "Canada is changing too quickly because of all the minorities we have now" (*Weekend Sun,* July 6, 1996).

Visible minority members are confronted with the majority attitude that they "own" the country. The "visibly different" are expected to be forever grateful to be let in. They are seen never truly to belong because the sense of belonging includes the imagined prior ownership in which the visibly different immigrants do not partake of the very history of initial European settlement. This makes the "visibles" eternal trespassers, both in the view of the dominant group but also sometimes in the eyes of the "intruders" who internalize majority attitudes toward them. Multiculturalism is intended to ensure equity through representation by highlighting origins elsewhere. At the same time, origins of dominant white groups wane into irrelevance as they exercise dominance and a "natural" claim to ownership. Only non-English/French origins are considered ethnic. However, the more the cultures of the others are celebrated, the less their claim to the local is emphasized.

The proprietary self-confidence shows unwittingly in the language used, what is said and how it is said, the humor, and even the body language. Himani Bannerji writes of a commonsense racism. Everyday ways of seeing embody locations of imagined ownership. Racism becomes a systemic, "normal" way of perceiving the world. "Its banality and invisibility is such that it is quite likely that there may be entirely 'politically correct' white individuals who have a deeply racist perception of the world" (Bannerji 1996, 45). Bannerji overstretches the concept and narrows its occurrence at the same time. She overlooks the situational racism by ascribing it, uncritically, to white people only. In parts of Africa and especially Asia, a similar ethnocentric normalcy pervades black or brown majority attitudes toward outsiders. The implied assumption of antiracism is absurd, as F. Palmer (1986, 149) stated, "that *all* white people and *only* white people are, and cannot *but* be racists." The discrimination in the Hindu caste system, the attitudes of Tutsis toward Hutus, or Japanese toward Koreans hardly differ from the nineteenth-century European social Darwinist ideology of natural inferiority and superiority. However, this old racism has now been substantially discredited and replaced by a new everyday ethnocentrism of difference.

Antiracism has been imported into Canada from the British discourse. British society had to cope with the fallout from the loss of empire. The Indian and Caribbean immigrants were seen as intruders who, despite their British citizenship, soon were graded according to descent. Being really British still means being white. Nonwhite immigrants—now comprising 6 percent of the population as a whole but frequently the majority in some British city quarters—were tolerated at best and discriminated and harassed at worst. If there ever was a chill factor—an atmosphere of not belonging and not being welcome—it can be experienced in the class-conscious British society. Antiracism programs were to make permanent outsiders into normal insiders.

Canada is not burdened with this legacy of empire because it never ruled over distant colonies. Canada practised internal or domestic colonialism in the spirit of empire. As a British/French settler society, it developed a different political culture, far more tolerant of difference, even to the extent of some color-blindness. As some of its early settlers were non-Europeans and the newcomers had to interact with the aboriginal inhabitants as well as 30 percent French speakers, unlike Britain before decolonization, multiethnicity and multiracialism were built into the fabric of the emerging state. Strident attempts to emulate the colonial power by "keeping Canada white" were doomed, despite head taxes and immigration restrictions. The massive influx of surplus peasants from Eastern and Southern Europe to cultivate the prairies during the first half of the century already had laid the foundations of multiculturalism, simultaneous Anglo conformity pressure notwithstanding. It is this culture of immigration and multi-identity, that could be at the core of the new Canadian self-conception. Antiracism falsely assumes that Canadian society is obsessed with British-type yardsticks of retaining a racist culture of empire. Both racism and antiracism are negative concepts. They appear to be refraining from something but lack the capacity to mobilize for a positive vision.

While uncovering the hidden systemic discrimination of a traditional order amounts to an advance toward equality of opportunities, the implied guilt or supposed ignorance of the beneficiaries is strongly resented. Antiracism would be more successful if it were to appeal more to positive contributions toward justice to be made rather than negative behavior to be penalized or ostracized. A new language has to emerge that concretizes Canadian identity in terms of equal citizenship and pride into the Charter of Rights. Human rights abuses, ascribed barriers to individual life chances, and particularly racial discrimination would each be "un-Canadian." Instead of having Canadianess associated with a romanticized past of European settlement, the new identity would stress the enrichment through diversity, the basic decency of all citizens in a model democracy where all can find unrivalled opportunities by cooperation rather than social Darwinist competition. The new identity would strive to preserve and strengthen these characteristics of a unique Canadianess.

Alan Cairns has argued that after the collapse of Western and Soviet empires it is time to turn our attention to "the imperialism of single identities." Bigots display single identities, indeed. Cairns (1999, 21) points out, "single identities are psychologically wrong. They mislead us by ignoring our complexities. They are politically wrong, because they exacerbate our divisions. They are ethically wrong, because they stifle empathy and allow us to do horrible things to each other with an undisturbed conscience." One could add that they also are economically dysfunctional for a globalized corporatism where the "united colours" of consumerism increasingly set the tone. Canada could be in the forefront of multiethnic societies that devise policies and institutions that affirm multiple identities, reward cooperative diversity, encourage respect for difference, and ostracize violations of cosmopolitan literacy. Canadian multiculturalism, its many shortcomings notwithstanding, is to be recommended as a promising beginning.

IV. National Minorities and the Democratic State

Indigenous minorities (almost extinguished San/Pygmies in Africa, 2 percent Aborigines in Australia, 11 percent Maoris in New Zealand, up to 5 percent native Indians in the United States and Canada, and Inuit in the North) distinguish themselves from all other minorities through constitutionally recognized "aboriginal rights." Indigenous minorities perceive themselves as the conquered owners of the original land. However, they lack the voting strength or economic clout to achieve their aims through common power and usually appeal through the legal system to the self-definition of liberal democracies. This symbolic power as "First Nations" or, in some cases, based on broken treaties with the colonial authority, can severely embarrass liberal states.

Even when indigenous people represent sizeable minorities, as in Mexico and other Latin American states and in some regions in India, modern states often suppress the protests of "tribal" people, if necessary by renewed genocide. In more liberal democracies, state policies towards the legitimate grievances of subjugated natives have wavered between forced assimilation in residential church-run schools in Canada, with often widespread sexual abuses of children, legal suppression of cultural traditions, and conversion by missionaries in what amounted to "cultural genocide" (Harold Cardinal), or simply benign neglect and welfare colonialism. Aborigines were treated as immature wards under state tutelage. More recently, limited autonomy and self-rule in education and policing on reservations were granted. This corresponds with a cultural revivalism and ethnoexclusivism stressed by once nearly extinct but now growing and politically conscious aboriginal minorities, who do not always consider themselves bound by the laws of the state of which they are "forced citizens."

Western democracies that ignore the justified legal claims of aboriginal groups and do not negotiate in good faith land claims or mineral or forest rights run the risk of encouraging an IRA-type terrorism in their very midst. Examples of indigenous rebellions against multinational oil companies in Nigeria, Sudan, and several Latin American states—using sabotage, kidnapping of foreigners, and other violence—is a foretaste of what could also happen in North America if frustrations of an increasingly sophisticated and militant indigenous leadership are not addressed.

National minorities are settled in defined territories that they consider their historical homeland. Although they owe their incorporation into multinational states to conquest or colonial boundary drawing, they differ from indigenous minorities in their population size, economic autonomy, and possibility of viable unilateral secession. Self-conscious as distinct people, they have

developed separate institutions and frequently already form ministates within states. Claims to self-determination are backed up by real power of numbers and capital control, unlike the symbolic power of the politics of embarrassment and legal claims practiced by indigenous minorities. Fed on strong ethnonationalist sentiment and resentment against the dominant center, common citizenship, constitutional patriotism, and pride in the overarching state are meaningless for people who define their primary identity in subnational or regional terms.

Worldwide, fewer than 200 sovereign states contain some 3,000 homelands (Cairns 1999, 7), although most national minorities do not aim at full independence. The weakening of nation-states through globalization and supranational agencies has facilitated regional ethnonationalisms, as did the ideological vacuum created by the collapse of the ideological master narratives in a postmodernist era. Many a civil war resulted from the tension between the conflicting claims to self-determination and nation-building by centrist elites, which sometimes amounted to nation-killing in many artificial colonial states.

Power sharing in an elaborate consociational democracy of an elite pact has been proposed by political scientists (Lijphart 1977) for such ethnically divided societies while others (D. Horowitz 1983) bank on electoral systems and constitutional arrangements to force dominant groups to compromise and guarantee minorities a stake in the central state. However, even a genuine federalism and a high degree of regional autonomy does not necessarily diffuse separatist sentiment, as the case of Quebec clearly demonstrates. Perhaps multinational states are best served by constitutionally recognizing the moral right of national minorities to secede (as few constitutions do) but laying down clear conditions for a mutually recognized and negotiated partition, as the Canadian federal government in the wake of a Supreme Court decision currently attempts.

At the instigation of the center, in 1998 the Supreme Court of Canada laid down conditions for a legitimate secession. The Court ruled that "a clear majority vote in Quebec on a clear question in favour of secession would confer democratic legitimacy on the secession initiative which all of the other participants in confederation would have to recognize" through "principled negotiations." Although the court claimed only to be acting in an "advisory role" giving but an opinion, which nobody is obligated to follow, it also decreed contradictorily: "the obligations we have identified are binding obligations under the Constitution of Canada."

Thereby judicial activism created a new constitutional amendment without any legislative or popular approval. Moreover, the Supreme Court deliberately did not clarify what a "clear majority" and "a clear question" concretely means but left this "for the political actors to determine . . . in the circumstances under which a future referendum vote may be taken."

In response, the federal government introduced the Clarity Act, which further specifies necessary conditions for secession. The Quebec government, however, views this as an assault on its democratic right to determine these issues unilaterally. The negotiated consensus of political actors implied in the Court decision does not exist because the secessionist party does not believe that such consensus is even required. Many analysts conclude that the legislation of a political issue, meant to regulate if not contain secession, assisted in reviving declining separatist sentiment. The bitter debate again demonstrated the limits of legal intervention in ethnonationalist disputes.

The problem of civic nationalism in a multicultural democracy lies in the lack of emotional glue that constitutional patriotism provides, compared with the ethnic nationalism of the myth of common kinship and culture. If sociobiologists are to be believed, kin preference provided an evolutionary advantage in the development of the human species, resulting in a genetic conditioning for nepotism. However, intraethnic conflicts can often be more intense than interethnic tensions. Economic interdependence, reciprocity for mutual advantage, and rational choice decisions can outweigh communal attachments, as the peaceful negotiated revolution in South Africa proved (Adam and Moodley 1993).

Arend Lijphart (1994, 228) has coined the interesting concept of "self-negating prediction," which emphasizes human agency and open-endedness of predicted events being turned around by conscious efforts. "In divided societies, political leaders may have the wisdom not only to foresee, but also to forestall the 'undesirable events' of violent conflicts and democratic failure by turning to power-sharing." This explains part of the surprising "miracle" of peaceful change in South Africa.

V. Consolidating Democracy in Multinational States

There are three further issues that have bedeviled the relationship between democracy and multiethnicity. They can be labelled (1) ethnic voting, (2) popular rejection of leadership compromises, and (3) the question of justice versus amnesty in newly emerging democratic states.

Ethnic Voting

The literature on so-called divided societies doubts democratic possibilities because of permanent minorities and majorities. As people vote along ethnic lines, elections amount to a "racial census." Without a floating vote, governments are not rotated. Despite numerous parties competing freely, the smaller parties lack the capacity to ever replace the ethnically strongest block and lose interest in political participation. The state evolves into what a recent South African study labels a "one-party dominant state" (Giliomee and Simpkins 1999). Not necessarily a one-party state, the ethnically frozen democracy nevertheless lacks "institutionalized uncertainty" that Prseworski (1992, 12) argues is the hallmark of a democracy. According to most democratic theorists, such a system does not deserve its name when there is "majority rule in perpetuity." Because of primary ethnic identity "Members of Group A *uniformly* support Party A. Members of Group B support Party B (Horowitz 1985, 83–86; 1991, 96). The two leading American theorists on multiethnic democracies, Lijphart and Horowitz, strongly disagree on how to engineer minority influence under such conditions. Lijphart advocates strengthening the centrifugal forces by reinforcing the autonomy of the partners in the prescribed ethnic grand coalition. Horowitz aims at the opposite by engineering participation through complex electoral choices and incentives, including a prescription that the state's chief executive can only hold office if he receives at least some support among major constituent groups in return for concessions. Both agree that South Africa is the typical example of a deeply divided society with all the democratic flaws outlined previously. Both Lijphart and Horowitz may well be wrong on this score, at least as far as expected electoral behavior is concerned.

In the two democratic South African elections in 1994 and 1995, the three minority groups, whites, coloreds, and Indians, split their vote between historically black and white parties, while only Africans voted overwhelmingly for traditionally black parties. However, if the ruling ANC with 66 percent of the vote eventually splits, which many observers predict (Johnson and Schlemmer 1996, 97), normal fluid democratic politics will emerge. There is also much evidence that Africans do not vote for the ANC not because of racial identification but because the party is viewed as representing their interests and ideological affinity as a broad-based liberation movement. Surprisingly for theorists of primordialism, all major political parties in South Africa are multiracial and vie for voters across the racial spectrum save some small racist white and black extremists.

Mandates and Approval of Compromises

It is often argued that pacts between competing ethnic elites must be endorsed by their constituencies in order to last and be considered legitimate. Therefore, referenda are frequently called to either give group leaders a mandate to negotiate controversial compromises or to ratify a historic deal.

The Canadian example shows unforeseen risks of this populist strategy. Agreed-upon leadership deals between Quebec and the federal government were twice derailed. The Meech Lake and Charlottetown Accords about the constitutional recognition of Quebec as a "distinct" society with special charter rights were vetoed because special interest groups (First Nations, women, unions) demanded similar recognition and resented being excluded from the negotiation process. One can therefore conclude that unless competing ethnic elites are able to impose their accord on the rest of the population, it is not worth the paper written on in light of a skeptical electorate. Conversely, the relatively smooth partition of the former Czechoslovakia highlights a case

where the political elites in both Slovakia and the Czech Republic separated without a referendum, although surveys indicated that the majority of the population favored the continued unity of the state.

On the other hand, a referendum may be necessary to allow ethnic compromisers to start negotiation in the first place. This was the case with the last all-white vote in South Africa, in 1992, in which 68 percent of voters gave de Klerk a mandate for the slogan "Negotiation Yes, Surrender No." Without that popular legitimacy the National Party would have easily been out radicalized by intransigent right-wing parties who realized only later that de Klerk's soft-liners had in fact negotiated the hardliners out of power. In the authoritarian hierarchy of Afrikaner nationalism, rank and file members trusted their leaders blindly (Adam and Moodley 1993). Unlike among Northern Irish unionist leaders whose internal democracy makes them accountable to a large working class base, the embourgeoisment of urban Afrikaner civil servants allowed the elite of the volk a free hand. For example, before de Klerk announced to parliament the release of Mandela and the unbanning of the liberation movements in Febraury 1990, he had not found it necessary to inform his caucus. Even more surprisingly, none of the 160 parliamentarians of the National Party protested or left the party over so fundamental a decision.

The risk of populist rejection also hangs over a Middle East peace deal since Barak promised a referendum on the result of negotiations. Most likely, an endorsement hinges on support from Israeli Arabs. However, once a perceived outside adversary holds the balance of power and defeats ethnonationalist hard-liners on their own turf, it exacerbates ethnic tensions within.

Compromising soft-liners are accused of betraying "their people" but utilizing "aliens" to achieve their goals. When Quebec separatists narrowly lost the 1996 referendum on sovereignty, the former premier Parizeau burst out with the separatists' rage against "the ethnics" responsible for the defeat.

Embittered Memories: Justice or Amnesty?

It has been suggested that divided societies, above all, need a shared interpretation of history. If only Serbs and Croats could achieve consensus on their mutual atrocities during World War II, the new generation would be spared the recriminations of their parents. Truth commissions are supposed to deliver the historical consensus. Members of the much praised South African Truth and Reconciliation Commission have stated that "South Africans desperately need to create a common memory" (Boraine 1997). Others aimed at establishing a "publicly sanctioned history" that can be "taught in schools."

However, as Heribert Adam (1999, 146) has rightly stressed, this noble goal is naive and dangerous because official history negates pluralist interpretations of the past. Adam views history "as a never-ending argument," whose suppression does not establish common ground among warring factions. Tito's attempt to silence bitter memories with the slogan "Brotherhood and Unity" may well have contributed to the vengeful outbreak of violence once the authoritarian control was lifted.

Indeed, honestly grappling with an unsavory, divisive past in the way Germany has admirably managed *Vergangenheitsbewältigung* may prove to be a more effective route to nation-building than official amnesia. Ironically, truth commissions initially may well deepen divisions and undermine short-term reconciliation by airing historical acrimony. Witty observers have pointed to the discouraging lessons from proceeding in divorce courts. However, while divorced spouses live apart, national minorities must live together in the same state. The moral basis of their coexistence is strengthened, not weakened, by a truthful history of their conflict. It is poor advice when philosophers (Will Kymlicka 1995, 189) opine: "To build a common identity in a multination state probably requires an even more selective memory of the past."

It is also risky to push for justice at all costs if trials of nationalist hard-liners were to destabilize a fragile peace. This was the classical predicament South African negotiators faced in 1990. By trading off justice for disclosure of past crimes, they found a wise formula to prevent further civil strife and yet expose the human rights violations of the past. Just as plea bargaining in the United States serves justice by solving otherwise unsolvable cases, so amnesty in return for confessions may serve the ideal of restorative justice, though remorse or even material compensation was not required for the societal pardon. Unsatisfactory as amnesty may seem for the judicial fundamentalists (see A. Neier 1998), the pragmatic compromise holds alive the possibility of reconciliation or at least a more modest peaceful coexistence of all identities in a multinational polity.

One should not be dismissive of laws aimed at reducing or managing ethnic conflicts and promoting human rights. Like educational efforts, human rights laws are a necessary but not sufficient mechanism to deal with a far deeper problem. There is the danger that the removal of discriminatory laws is mistaken for the solution of racism. For example, in South Africa the abolition of apartheid lets many overlook the continuing legacy of a racial past. Nominal legal equality also blinds us from recognizing new and more subtle forms of ethnoracial inequity, which is almost easier to combat when it is open, institutionalized, and on the books rather than hidden behind legitimate concepts of self-determination and cultural minority rights.

On the question of multiculturalism, of course there are cultural practices, such as clitorectomy and other violations of gender equality, that no multiculturalism can justify. It is important that widely accepted human rights are upheld and that violations are criminalized, accusations of Eurocentrism and spurious claims of postmodern relativism notwithstanding. The universality of human dignity needs to be reasserted against cultural relativists.

However, American advocates of universal rights must be particularly sensitive to the charge of "moral imperialism." They must also be conscious of the blatant inconstituency in U.S. policy to enforce human rights: While NATO bombs Milosevic for his atrocities toward Kosovars, NATO member Turkey gets off scot-free and without criticism for its oppression of its Kurdish minority. After all, it is the United States, together with a few unsavory regimes such as Libya, China, and Russia, that opposes an International Criminal Court for fear of having its own sovereignty curtailed and its own generals indicted for war crimes. These are double standards that undermine the necessary delegitimization of dictatorial regimes.

Secession for ethnic minorities is rarely benign, Czech and Slovakia's peaceful partition notwithstanding.

But it is better to have constitutional rules in place that hopefully regulate secession than have it squashed violently after a bitter civil war—as happened in Biafra, Chechnya, Sudan, and Sri Lanka—or succeed after India's bloody independence and Bangladesh's murderous split from Pakistan twenty years later. Rules about legitimate negotiated secession can also deal with the vexed question of minorities within minorities.

The psychological roots of the appeal of ethnonational identity need to be recognized. This allows policies to be devised that offer alternative identities to ethnic nationalism, particularly in dealing with xenophobia or the relatively mild quarrels about the status of Quebec. At present, at least no lives are lost in Montreal, though several dozen people died in nationalist-inspired bombings and kidnappings in 1970. Indeed, not all ethnic conflicts are of the same magnitude. Psychoanalytic explanations are of little use in the competition for scarce resources in the violent nationality conflicts in impoverished Africa, Turkey, or the Caucasus where political and economic accommodation occupies first priority.

Democracy and the State in Multiethnic Societies in Conflict

Perspectives from Sri Lanka

Jayadeva Uyangoda

Introduction

The historical experience of a host of multiethnic nation-states, particularly during the last quarter of the twentieth century, has brought to sharp focus a question that perhaps touches the basic foundations of contemporary political civilization. It concerns the inadequacy of the existing forms of the nation-state to address the historical tendency within political societies to disintegrate along ethnoidentity formations. The modern nation-state, in all its organizational forms ranging from centralized unitarism (Sri Lanka) and quasi federalism (India) to confederal devolutionism (Canada), has been challenged by minority ethnic communities who seek political alternatives ranging from autonomy to separate sovereignty. Meanwhile, impulses for monoethnic statehood have been so strong among communities in some states that, as in former Yugoslavia, even relatively advanced forms of federalism have not provided a framework or model for other, less federal, state forms to emulate. The point is that in the face of sovereignty-seeking political mobilization among minority ethnic communities, the federal mode of political association has been proved untenable as has the unitarist state. While in a number of instances the existing forms of the state, unitary as well as federal, have been crumbling, the emerging tendency has been for the setting up of monoethnic ministates with no willingness to accommodate pluralism and devolution of political power within them.

Indeed, it is a political irony that ethnic nationalists, who claim discrimination under larger multiethnic states, are generally driven toward establishing highly centralized and, where possible, antidemocratic states of single ethnic communities. Given the monoethnic nature of these new states, there is hardly any theoretical possibility at the moment for them to offer alternatives to centralization of state power.

This paper intends to discuss some of these paradoxes of the modern nation-state in relation to the experience of Sri Lanka. Its central focus will be on suggesting a possible way out from the seemingly inescapable crisis of the nation-state. As I will argue in this paper, one fundamental feature of this crisis is the inability of ethnic majority as well as minority communities to extricate themselves from the crisis that propels them to seek unilateral solutions. The most extreme stage of this scenario is reached when, as the Sri Lankan case once again represents, interethnic relations are militarized and the repoliticization of ethnic relations has escaped the sphere of constitutional and legislative politics. In such an extreme stage of ethnic relations, even when bilateral approaches are possible and therefore initiated, there is the ever present possibility of monoethnic nationalist movements, through their powerful military wings, succeeding in thwarting attempts at conflict resolution through compromise. The point is that in militarized ethnic conflicts, the possibilities for continuing reproduction of the conflict are greater than the opportunities for its resolution. A feature in the current stage of Sri Lanka's ethnic conflict is that the war between the government and the Liberation Tigers of Tamil Eelam (LTTE) has assumed a life of its own, relatively autonomous and separated from the political process.[1]

Against this backdrop, and in relation to the concerns of this conference, a host of complex political problems may confront the analyst. Central to these concerns is the link, as well as disjuncture, between democratic constitutionalism and the nation-state in crisis in multiethnic societies. This problem is grounded in a paradox inherent in the modern democratic state's ability, as well as inability, to deal with ethnic pluralism. Liberal democracy, in its classical form à la Mill, could hardly admit ethnic diversity into its domain of theoretical and philosophical concerns. Nor could it imagine pluralism in an ethnocultural communitarian sense. No wonder that the unitarist legal order of the modern state, with its centralized legislative, executive, and judicial institutions, evolved in England. And that legal order, based itself on a particular historical version of sovereignty in which the political will of a homogenous political community called a nation, could best be concretized in the centralized state. But North American and continental European reworkings of the modern state deviated sharply from that Anglo-Saxon modular form of the state and developed a political-legal order in which the state power could be decentered and sovereignty shared by the units that constitute the nation and the state. In this second model of the modern state, which is called "federal," ethnic diversity is supposed to be contained through political and constitutional recognition of pluralized sovereignty. Indeed, and in a historical sense, the federalist model rescued the democratic state by revising one of its fundamental tenets: sovereignty of the nation and the state can be parceled, shared, and decentered.

Meanwhile, there is now a fascinating problem for theoretical contemplation, posed in the present historical moment, but not adequately acknowledged in political and legal philosophy; it is the possibility of the emergence of a postplural form of the nation-state. In this paper, I will call this form of the state the "monoethnic ministate." One of the metapolitical claims I wish to make in this paper is that, in a historical sense, old forms

of the nation-state have come to an end and new forms are emerging. Unitarist as well as federalist forms of multiethnic nation-states are now giving way to monoethnic ministates in which ethnic diversity and political pluralism are delegitimized and violently expelled from the domains of juridico-constitutional concerns. Harbingers of this historical transition of political reorganization of the humankind are already there in former Eastern Europe, Africa, and in South Asia. Sri Lanka, indeed, is one of the most striking examples of this emerging historical tendency of state formation.

In this paper, my task is partly to treat Sri Lanka as a case study of the political context for the possibilities toward monoethnic ministates. In this exercise, I will be occasionally making the claim that Sri Lanka's experience is not an isolated, exceptional one but a condition that can be generalized and universalized. Then, in the second part of the paper, I will try to present a fictional account of a political future for the humankind in which pluralism and diversity of the nation-state would be rescued and reinstalled in a new form of de-ethnicized political order. In writing this futuristic political fiction, which may also have the potential of being universalized, I will treat Sri Lanka as the unit of reflection.

"Nation" in Political Imagination

Sri Lanka represents one of the key paradoxes present in the experience of modern nation-state formation in many other societies: the dichotomy between the multiple ethnic constitution of society and the unitarist organization of political power. Sri Lanka's unitarism of the state was indeed based on the constitutional principle of the European/British unitary state, which enunciated a model of political organization in which legislative and executive powers were centralized and decentralization of administration was accommodated only for municipal and local government.[2] Unitarism of the state, with centralized structures of legislative and executive power, is perhaps suited for societies with ethnic, linguistic, and cultural homogeneity or for societies with an ethnic diversity largely due to very recent migration of populations with no political claims to state power. However, as Sri Lanka's case very clearly demonstrates, for societies made up of historically evolved communities with distinct identity claims and competing perspectives for gaining access to economic resources, the unitarist nation-state has offered a thoroughly inadequate model of political organization.

After several decades of conflictual ethnic politics, and now confronted with a protracted internal war, it has become quite clear that the original political sin of Sri Lanka's modern state lies in its blindness to the multiple ethnic constitution of its polity. There are occasional examples of the modern state—India is a good case in point—where the structures of state power were reconstituted within a few years after independence in order to accommodate its ethnic and regional diversity at the level of the state's constitutional foundations. Sri Lanka has represented a different historical path to postcolonial nation building and state making. The political elite that became the managers of the postcolonial independent state in the second half of the last century—Sri Lanka obtained independence from the British in 1948—were drawn from the majority Sinhalese community. Their dominant nation-building project based itself on a refusal to accommodate the multiple ethnic constitution of Sri Lankan society. Its vision of political power has always been posited in the imagination that the Sri Lankan state should be a specifically unitary one in which political structures are defined in a highly centralized manner. Any demand for reforming the centralized state ran the risk of being characterized as dividing the country. There has also been a peculiar dialectic of majority-minority relations that reinforced the majoritarian commitment to a highly centralized unitary state. The demand for reforming the unitarist state along federalist lines was made by the political leadership of the Tamil minority on the premise that the Tamils in Sri Lanka represented a nation as much as the Sinhalese did. For Sri Lanka's Tamil nationalists, the Tamil community constituted a nation with an alienable political entitlement to national self-determination. In this context, the majoritarian ethnic mind could understand the ethnic minoritarian clamor for recognition as a nation only in adversarial terms. Indeed, the majoritarian suspicion of reforming the unitary, centralized state emanated from

the fear that if any local autonomy was granted to the Tamils, it would be the beginning of an inevitable process toward political division of the country.[3]

We may draw from the above experience in Sri Lanka an important lesson that has some universal validity. Once the politics of ethnic communities gets enmeshed in a relationship of mutual suspicion and hostility, it could develop a specific political ontology that could govern the entire process of nation-state formation in an irreversible direction of internal fragmentation. When the political vision for nation building is constructed exclusively around the nationalist ideology of the majority ethnic community, the political integration and unification of different ethnic groups within the emerging state becomes illusory and difficult. This has been and continues to be a key political lesson to be drawn from Sri Lanka's postcolonial as well as the contemporary experience. In the dominant ideology of state in Sri Lanka—the ideology of Sinhalese nationalism—the majority-minority dichotomy has enunciated a specific kind of political relationship among ethnic groups. That relationship was one based on a strictly demarcated hierarchy in which only the ethnic majority could give meaning and relevance to the political independence of 1948. In other words, the only political force that could legitimately and authentically make the postcolonial state in Sri Lanka was the majority Sinhalese. According to this ruling ideology of the state, the ethnic minorities had neither political desire nor political authenticity to take part in the nation-building and state-making enterprise because they had no permanent commitment to building a strong polity. The immediate consequence of this postulation was the elevation of the majority Sinhalese—more accurately, Sinhalese Buddhist—community to the status of the sole historical agency of making the postcolonial Sri Lankan state.

This denial of agency to ethnic minorities presupposed a particular reading of history as well as future of Sri Lanka while granting to the present a specific moment in history, a moment that should be occupied only by the majority. Indeed, it is this denial of the present to the minorities that constitutes the kernel of ethnic majoritarian politics. In an objective sense, the nation-state formation in multiethnic societies can have better historical chances of success if there is recognition of the historical principle that there is a multiplicity of ethnic agencies in nation building and state making.

Construction of "Nations" in Ethnic Terms

The outcome of the process described above has been the construction of competing nation projects in Sinhalese and Tamil ethnic formations. Indeed, a single nation-state had to negotiate two nation projects' politics, the dynamics of which has been mutually contradictory and exclusivist. This in a way represents yet another problem of the modern state, the outlines of which may be set out as follows. When multiple nation projects emerge within the political structures of a single and unitarist nation-state and when the existing political structures are not radically reformed to facilitate the coexistence among them, the irreversible tendency has been for the structures of the unitary state to turn into fetters for further political progress of that society. Under such circumstances, the internal disintegration of the existing state may become a historical possibility. To prevent disintegration, imaginative reforms of the existing political structures may also become an objective political necessity.

As decades of accumulated evidence from the experience of modern nation-state formation across the world indicate, the emergence of diverse and multiple "nationist" projects in multiethnic nation-states is a clear indication that the conventional single-nation-building model has lost its historical validation as well as political utility. In such contexts, the conceptualization of "nation" has assumed a new historical form that goes against the logic of "nation" in the traditional nation-state sense. The conventional project of nation building/national integration meant the creation of one single "nation" within the territorial boundaries of the sovereign state. In ethnically diverse or multiracial societies, the establishment of such a single nation also meant the concretization of a juridical category of citizens, the collectivity of which was supposed to constitute the transethnic or transracial category of the nation. The assumption then was that within a nation there could be more than one race or ethnic group, but the collectivity of them should constitute the nation, the central identity marker of which should be the political state. The modern state was thus seen in the conventional national integration model as both the agency and consequence of nation making.

In multiethnic societies where the project of nation making through state making has failed, the discursive category of "nation" has entered a process of redefinition, which is indeed an indication of the complexity of the relationship between the state and ethnic communities. At one level, the conceptualization of the basic category of "nation" has become a thoroughly contested exercise. Almost every ethnic group making claims to political autonomy within the nation-state prefers to define itself in the language of nation. At another level, multiple nationist imaginations point to the fact that the phenomenology of both the nation and the state has radically changed and it requires recognition in the juridical and political discourse of the modern state. Simply put, the question here is that the modern state needs to alter its discursive as well as structural foundations to facilitate the coexistence of multiple nationist imaginations.

But, as Sri Lanka's experience demonstrates—this is also an observation that can be universalized—such reworking of the discourse and structures of the modern state has not been a terribly easy exercise. Indeed, in Sri Lanka, pluralistic nation building has not been a part of the official policy discourse. A clear disjunction has existed between the theoretical category of "nation" and "nation building"—derived as it is from the modernization paradigm—on the one hand and the policy discourse of the state on the other throughout the postcolonial political history. This discursive difficulty has been a major obstacle to the possibilities of alternative imaginations of the nation or the state. The Sinhalese political category of nation is one with very little discursive flexibility. Indeed, the Sinhalese term *jathiya* has a range of restricted meanings that in no way approximate the assumptions of pluralistic nation building. The widest possible meaning of *jathiya* is a racial or ethnic group, while it also signifies still more restrictive group identities as caste, clan, and kin group. When a person refers to "our *jathiya*," its socio-existential signification can be either our race or our caste, the distinction being predicated on the context in which the reference is made. In most South Asian languages, this linguistic problematic goes beyond linguistics. Rather, it touches the essential relationship between identity imagination and projects of nation-state building. What it unveils is that there has been, and continues to be, a disjunction between the restrictive, ethnicized imagination of the nation and the state as the political association of many ethnic communities. It also demonstrates that the political discourse of "nation" as enunciated in the ideology of the majority community has no flexibility to transcend the limits of its own imagination of nationhood. This disjuncture is acutely evident in an attempt to translate the construction "nation building" into Sinhalese in order to convey what it entails. *Jathiya godagangeema* in the Sinhalese political idiom has only one meaning—the building of a nation in the ethnic sense, not a nation in the juridical sense of a pluralistic Sri Lankan state.

The problem, which we have just identified, is at one level a discursive anomaly in modern politics of nation and the state. Yet at another, more fundamental, level the anomaly is overtly political. It reflects one of the key problems of modern state formation in multiethnic societies; that is the tendency towards majoritarianization of the nationist imagination. In postcolonial contexts like Sri Lanka, India, Burma, and Malaysia, this tendency has been rationalized on the quasihistorical argument that the colonial rule had systematically favored ethnic and cultural minorities at the expense of native and indigenous majority. In Sri Lanka, for example, when the British colonial rulers left the island, it was easy to imagine the postcolonial state as the supreme instrument to be utilized for correcting the historical injustices that the Sinhalese-Buddhists majority community was thought to have suffered under the colonial state. With this instrumentalist view of the state, the immediate idea that entered the center of the Sinhalese nationalists' enterprise soon after independence was to redefine and reconstruct political relations of the state in such a way that ethnic relations would be reordered in a new hierarchical pantheon. In the new order, the Sinhalese-Buddhist community was to occupy the apex of the ethnic pantheon, while all other minority communities, ethnic as well as religious, were to be placed lower down in the hierarchical order. The majoritarian nationalist forces thought that the real meaning of political independence could be realized only when ethnic relations were reconstituted at the

political level in such a way that the state could be an instrument of discriminatory public policy.

Ethnic Differences and Democratic Politics

The dialectic of discriminatory ethnic politics in multiethnic societies is that dominant ethnic majoritarianism produces its own negation in the form of radical ethnic minoritarinism. Once again, Sri Lanka provides a paradigmatic example. Political mobilized ethnicity reinscribes and reinforces group differences with vigor and vitality. Ethnic groups are usually differentiated, or prefer to think of themselves as unique communities, in terms of language, culture, or religion. But in ethnic politics, ethnic differentiation is a highly politicized process. It is not just identity markers—language, religion, or culture—that produce and reproduce differences among ethnic groups. It is the question of state power that constitutes the central criterion of demarcation between ethnic communities. The discovery of differences among ethnic groups is a part of the political process in which they become aware of themselves as modern nations in the sense of their being communities with an inherent right and claim to political power. Claims to political power are then perceived and made in a revitalized discourse of difference. In the historical experience of nation building in many multiethnic societies, we may see how different ethnic groups, big or small, have made claims to political power from the starting point of each community being distinct and special. To be a distinct ethnic group is to emphasize differences vis-à-vis others while arguing for a share of the state power by virtue of being different. It has been an extremely interesting point in the process of state formation in multiethnic societies that often state violence against minorities or majority-minority ethnic riots have brought ethnic communities to qualitatively new phases of mutual understanding, a hypersensitized understanding of differences. It is in this sense that ethnic riots involving Sri Lanka's Sinhalese and Tamil communities in 1958 and 1983, and violence among Hindu, Muslim, and Christian communities in India, have to be seen as more than moments of breaking down peaceful ethnic relations. They are rather historical moments in which ethnic majorities and minorities have begun to rediscover each other in new terms of enmity.

As the Sri Lankan experience since independence illustrates, the assertion of ethnic differences by Sinhalese and Tamil nationalist groups in order to demarcate their own sphere of politics within the nation-state has been a major facet in the process of postcolonial state formation. There has been a variation, however, in the technology of self-differentiation employed by the two ethnic formations. The Sinhalese nationalists had access to state power, directly as well as indirectly, and they could use it as an instrument in order to translate their demands into state policy. Tamil nationalists, meanwhile, developed a self-understanding for the entire community in the idiom of an oppressed, yet separate, nation whose claims to a complete nationhood could be realized either through self-government or separation. (The term "right of self-determination" has signified both these ideas.) The minority Tamil nationalism also imagined a nation, a territory and a sovereign state, for its community.

Sri Lanka's postindependence politics thus evinces an underlying theme of two nations—one nation determined to possess and protect the existing state and the other aimed at changing or breaking away from the state. The two nations could not reconcile with each other, and they have been locked in a self-destructive war for nearly two decades. Sri Lanka's present crisis is a truly intractable one, not only because of the protracted nature of the war but also because the majoritarian and minoritarian nationalist projects seek ethnic solutions to the crisis. Sri Lanka is perhaps a paradigmatic example of the impossibility of ethnic solutions to ethnic grievances. One of the fundamental lessons that the humankind ought to learn from the contemporary experiences of ethnic conflicts is that ethnonationalist politics can highlight, in a larger-than-life fashion, ethnic grievances and injustices but can rarely offer solutions. Ethnic conflicts require democratic solutions. And it demands de-ethnicizing of all visions of political emancipation.

This, by no means, is an easy task. It requires the tireless working for reimagining the Sri Lankan state based on a new set of normative principles. These normative principles can be derived from Sri Lanka's accumulated negative legacy of the postcolonial past. Fairness and justice to all identity communities, ethnic and social egalitarianism in the distribution of the benefits and entitlements of democracy, associational cooperatism enabling democratic curtailment of sectarian aspirations of ethnic communities, and pluralistic democratization of communitarian desires are some of those historically necessary normative ideals. These principles necessitate a norm-based political agenda, the broad outlines of which may be formulated as follows. Firstly, there should be a fresh envisioning—indeed, reenvisioning—of the state as a voluntary democratic political association of all ethnic and other identity groups. Secondly, the reenvisioning of the state should be a cooperative project among all identity communities in which categories of political imagination should be derived from the future possibilities of greater democratization and political voluntarism and not from the preindependence or precolonial past inhabited in the historical unconscious. This presupposes, at least for the sake of a new political imagination, the erection of a veil of ignorance concerning most of the past of interethnic encounters from yesterday backwards. Thirdly, political and social emancipation of all identity communities as well as individual citizens should be inscribed in all spheres of state and civil society interventions. Fourthly, and finally, is the redemocratization of the politics of Sri Lanka's Tamil society, which is crucial to sustaining the democratic impulses of Sinhalese and Muslim societies. Sri Lanka's Tamil society has lost its democratic bearings in the context of a protracted and destructive war. As long as the politics and everyday life of Tamil society remain militarized, democratic impulses in both Sinhalese and Tamil societies are most likely to remain weak and vulnerable.

A new democratic agenda, as suggested above, will have to immediately confront and politically engage with two powerful nationist fantasies produced by two energetic appropriative desires of the Sri Lankan state: the Sinhala-centric unitary state and the Tamil-centric separate state.[4] Being ethnic fantasies, these two projects cannot reconcile with each other in the real world of democratic politics. Defantasizing these nation projects is therefore fundamentally important for Sri Lanka's democratic political future. But who will defantasize Sri Lanka's future? In a polity where the ruling class groups have abdicated their key class responsibilities, the question of the historical agency for democratic reenvisioning of the state should come to the fore in any serious discussion on Sri Lanka's political tomorrow. Similarly, there is also the need for a modernizing collective fantasy of democracy, around which the mass political energies can be remobilized. This is indeed where the social emancipatory ideals of democracy need to be summoned back to the terms of political imagination.

My analysis provides both despair and hope for a future that may be enunciated as follows: Although there are objective conditions for state reforms in Sri Lanka, state structures are unreformable under existing political circumstances and discursive possibilities. However, there is space for discursive reappropriation of the Sri Lankan state. The project of reenvisioning of the state that I have suggested above is essentially one of seizing state power through democratic reappropriation by all communities—jointly, cooperatively, and justly—of the language, the terms, the rules, and the dreams of the state. In brief, the task today and tomorrow is to germinate state-appropriative desires of cooperative, contractarian democracy. In the next section of this paper, I will try to develop a contractarian fantasy for Sri Lanka's democratic future.

Consociational Constitutions for Ethnically Divided Societies

Arend Lijphart began to use the term "consociational democracy" in the early seventies to propose a set of steps appropriate for societies that were ethnically divided and facing problems concerning democracy. As Lijphart accurately observed, the central problem of democracy in ethnically divided societies was the phenomenon of majoritarian democracy. Particularly in societies that had parliamentary governments of the Westminster model, majoritarian democracy had meant the rule of ethnic majorities. Lijphart also noted that the ethnic majoritarian democracy had tended to exclude ethnic minorities from the political process. To manage the conflicts that have arisen out of the contradictions of the majoritarian democracy, Lijphart

suggested a four-point formula on which the governments could be rearranged:

1. The creation of a grand ethnic coalition of all ethnic groups. This meant to facilitate coalitions not among political parties but among ethnic groups with the aim of managing ethnic conflicts.
2. Powers and the offices of the government should be proportionately shared and distributed among ethnic groups.
3. Each ethnic group in the coalition should have the power to veto public policy in order to safeguard its own ethnic interests.
4. The guarantee of ethnic autonomy in a system of federalism or devolution.

Lijphart's original idea of consociational democracy has been revised and expanded by a number of political scientists who were keen to develop conflict resolution models. Eric Nordlinger, for example, provides five conditions for a model of ethnic conflict resolution:

1. The presence of a stable ethnic coalition.
2. Proportional representation in the government for each ethnic group.
3. "Mutual veto" available to each ethnic group in the coalition so that it could vote against unfavorable government policy.
4. Agreement among coalition partners that the government would not directly participate in public debates on controversial matters in order to "depoliticize" such controversies.
5. Commitment of the majority community to a policy of working towards the benefit of minority ethnic groups through compromise and concessions on particular issues or on a package of issues.

To understand the consociational approach in its conceptual totality, we need to move toward the margins of political theory. As I have already mentioned, Lijphart and Nordlinger formulated their consociational schemes from the perspectives of conflict management. The conflict management approach—which emerged as a branch of social sciences in the seventies—is premised on a very important assumption. It is exceedingly difficult, according to conflict management adherents, to resolve conflicts in deeply divided societies where conflicts are often seen as intractable. Should enlightened or pragmatic leaders wait for all favorable conditions to emerge for a lasting resolution of conflicts? The conflict management perspective answers this question in the negative. It argues for the management of the conflict instead of waiting for the unpredictable final resolution. This premise of conflict management is further buttressed by another set of assumptions that can be summarized as follows:

1. It is appropriate and meaningful for ethnically divided societies to accept and live with, instead of ignoring, the fact that ethnic divisions are a social reality. Ethnic cleavages are an inescapable reality, and therefore it is only prudent to design the system of government and public policy to deal with that reality.

2. The task of conflict management should start from the top, with leaders of ethnic groups. Understanding and accommodation among leaders provide the best starting point for a movement toward ethnic unity. It is much easier and even pragmatic for leaders, than for the followers, to accommodate.

3. It is wrong to suggest that democracy is unworkable in societies with ethnic cleavages.

4. Building political institutions is crucial for both democracy and conflict management. Federalism and proportional representation are meant to promote political institution building.

Donald Horowitz, in his book *Ethnic Groups in Conflict* (1985), has developed a sympathetic critique of the consociationalist model, and I agree with his main line of criticism. Horowitz in particular questions the democratic viability of the "Grand Ethnic Coalition." He writes:

In democratic conditions, grand coalitions are unlikely, because of the dynamics of intra-ethnic competition. The very act of forming a multiethnic coalition generates intra-ethnic competition—flanking—if it does not already exist; what is more, the Asian or

African regime which declares that it has a grand coalition probably has, not a consociational democracy, but an ethnically exclusive dictatorship.[5]

We should not dismiss Horowitz's warning because of its Western bias. The grand ethnic coalition could easily become a grand authoritarian alliance. Seemingly, consociationalist authoritarianism can come in a variety of forms. Malaysia is a case in point. Malaysia has an ethnic coalition as the ruling alliance; it also has a semifederalist governmental structure. Yet the ruling alliance is a corporatist entity with its own version of Asian democracy. The primary characteristic of the Malaysian corporatism is the premise that only the ruling alliance has a legitimate claim to rule the country. There is hardly any reason for us to underestimate the authoritarian potential of grand ethnic coalitions.

Consociationalism is essentially a utilitarian enterprise; it premises that the political institutions can and should be manipulated for the maximum benefit of the largest possible number. This is a dangerous premise, both politically and philosophically. The consociational alliance and the sharing of power among leaders of ethnic communities are pragmatic enterprises, which may often lack lasting moral bases required for and by the polity. They are also devoid of explicit moral and normative links between the ethnic leaders and the society. Similarly, the consociational approach, as it has been conventionally conceptualized, does not say why the minority leaders should trust the majority leaders.

This is not to deny recent advances in the theory and practice of consociational politics. South Africa provides a refreshingly new example of it, which combines the idea of grand ethnic coalition with the immediate goals of conflict resolution. And one important aspect of the South African experience is that the consociational alliance is a transitional arrangement, organically linked with a political process of conflict resolution.

From Maximalism to Rational Choice

Is a consociational alternative feasible in Sri Lanka as a measure of ethnic conflict resolution? Before we examine this question, it may be useful to briefly discuss the nature of solutions available in Sri Lanka's present political debate. There exist a variety of prospective "solutions" to Sri Lanka's ethnic conflict, and all of them can be divided into two main categories: solutions emanating from maximalist considerations, and solutions suggested from a rational choice perspective.

The Ethno-Maximalist Approach

This is the dominant model of solutions offered by ethnonationalist projects in both Sinhalese and Tamil societies. Indeed, despite their politics of mutual hatred, extreme nationalists of competing ethnic formations think and act in terms of maximalist totalities. Sinhalese nationalist maximalists have been arguing for a total military victory over Tamil separatists as a precondition for peace. They are militantly opposed to any move by the state to negotiate with Tamil nationalist forces in search for a nonmilitary solution to the ethnic question. Similarly, the LTTE, from an ethno-maximalist perspective, claims that Sri Lanka's Tamil people have no option but establishing a separate state in order to protect their political and cultural rights. These two maximalist nationalist goals have been formulated in such a way that any retreat from that ultimate goal is viewed as totally antithetical to national interests of each community. In the maximalist mind, there is little or no room for negotiation and reconciliation of conflicts; even when negotiations are initiated, they are often treated as opportunities for tactical maneuvering in order to continue the war in other means. The paradox, and of course the tragedy as well, of maximalism is that one's enemy is one's foremost ally in reinforcing and protracting the conflict. As many examples of maximalist ethnic projects in the contemporary world would testify, ethnic maximalism is a gigantic political trap, an escape from which is not easy to find. It is a trap that ensures mutual annihilation of communities that are pitted against each other, on the ethno-romantic argument that for the sake of the nation and its sovereignty there should be no limit to human and material sacrifices that the nation should be prepared to make.

Rational Choice Approaches

All those who seek a negotiated political settlement to the conflict based on a reform package may be in-cluded in this category. Negotiated settlements in this sense mean the working out of a solution that falls much short of the ultimate goals that the movements have initially formulated. They envisage compromise among ethnic leaders and communities and a commitment to redress ethnic grievances that have led to the conflict. The basic moral premise in the rational choice approach is that the protraction of the conflict runs counter to the vital interests of all communities in the conflict. Working out of a system in which violence is reduced, political institutions and processes restored and reformed, and conflict controlled or reconciled is the goal of the rational choice approach to conflicts.

Rational choice alternatives to the ethnic conflict in Sri Lanka have been proposed and promoted by groups active in the democratic civil society, the international community, and even by regimes that want to bring the war to an end. It may also not be unrealistic to assert that there exist in Sri Lanka general conditions favorable to creating space for negotiated alternatives to the ethnic conflict. This space exists irrespective of the fact that ethnic maximalists of both communities have often occupied the center stage of the political debate.

However, a defining feature of the present stage of Sri Lanka's conflict is the fact that neither maximalist nor rational choice approaches seem to be possible as a means to end the conflict. The war, which has reached its seventeenth year, has entered a qualitatively new phase where the military process has assumed a considerable measure of autonomy from the political process. Linked to this development is also the rather disquieting fact that the warring sides, the state and the LTTE, have demonstrated a remarkable military resilience in the face of substantial military reverses in both human and material terms. In the military sense, the conflict is in a stalemate in the sense that one side cannot defeat or weaken the other side militarily so as to be able to impose on the adversary any political terms concerning a possible termination of the conflict. The conditions, then, are for the conflict to protract as a war for many years to come.

Amidst the possibility of a protracted war remains the unresolved political question of how to handle ethnic relations through political—that is, constitutional, legal, and negotiational—means. This is where the question of ethnic conflict resolution poses itself with a new urgency. As I have argued elsewhere in this paper, it also underscores the need to think beyond the mere restoration of the stability of the state. Ethnic conflict resolution in a deeply divided society like Sri Lanka calls for a fresh reorganization of the bases of political association among different identity communities. It indeed requires a new social contract to provide the moral and political bases for the postconflict state.

A New Social Contract

The notion that the authority and legitimacy of the state are defined in an original social contract has found many expressions in Eastern as well as Western political thought. The contract as the basis of the state came to the center of European political thought in the seventeenth century. John Locke presented the most democratic representation of the contractarian theory of social and political association while Immanuel Kant argued for normative and ethical dimensions of the contract. The essence of the Lockean contractarianism is that the government is a trusteeship arrangement among equal citizens. The Lockean contract also posits the notion of limited government organized on the principle of representation.

The classical contractarian theory, particularly the one formulated by Locke and Kant, has received a new impetus in recent years with some new interpretations. John Rawls, the leading contractarian philosopher of this century, initiated the new discussion on justice-based contract with his seminal work, *A Theory of Justice,* published in 1971.[6] Modern contractarian formulations are addressed to people who are deeply persuaded on the point that there are standards of justice for judging institutional arrangements in a polity. The contractarians are also egalitarians for whom an acceptable theory of justice must reveal a sense in which all individuals and communities owe equal consideration. Imagining society as the product of a social contract is the principal philosophical technique for putting rights-based equality to work in the evaluation of basic social and political institutions. The framework of contractarian ideas developed in this paper are related to this tradition.

Let us briefly consider what it should mean by a social contract in the contemporary historical context. The classical theory said that men and women formed the state after arriving at an agreement among them.

The conditions of the prestate society were so chaotic and disorderly that men and women as rational and equal beings decided to end that state of nonstate. The "contract" in this theory is a conceptual imagination, a metaphor to signify the moral bases of the political and legal order called the state.

The modern appropriation of the contractual notion of the state is located in liberal reformist politics. We do not live in a prestatal state of nature; yet we know that moral authority of the state has so collapsed that many political associations—the states— are facing disintegration. There seems to be a fundamental failure of the state in multiethnic societies, whether it is in the former Yugoslavia or in Sri Lanka. In societies that have internal rebellions and separatist movements, there are sections of the society who do not accept the moral authority of the state. They refuse political obligation to the state and, in fact, project disobligation as the legitimate response to the state. The willingness to disassociation from the state by communities is, paradoxically, one of the major problems of the modern state. And, those disassociationists often happen to be ethnic minorities.

It is in this context that we talk about political reforms and conflict management. To my mind, any political reform project in a society where the state is in deep crisis should have two essential components. First, it should aim at restoring, repairing, and creating democratic political institutions. Second, it should restore the moral foundations of the polity. Reforming the state in this sense is more than mere conflict management and social engineering. Any consociationalist project in a deeply divided society that would not compel the polity to rewrite the terms of political association is primarily a social engineering exercise. The political fantasy, which I wish to develop in this paper, is aimed at transcending the limits of consociationalist social engineering. I wish to see conflict management/resolution projects placed on firm contractarian foundations.

In the contractarian imagination, the state is a political association, the membership of which is obtained by all individuals—we may add, by all ethnic groups too— as moral equals and equally valuable agents. The state should be an association that is both fair and just so that each individual and ethnic group is to have an equal right to the most extensive basic liberty compatible with a similar liberty of others. Using John Rawls's notion of the general conception of justice, we may argue that "all social values in the polity—liberty and opportunity, income and wealth, and the bases of self-respect—are to be distributed equally, unless an unequal distribution of any or all of these values is to every one's advantage."

Ethnic Fairness and Justice

Borrowing from the general ideas of John Rawls, I will now explicate two reasons for ethnic fairness and justice to constitute the moral bases of a new social contract.

First, it is important for any society to formulate a set of moral and normative standards against which the institutions and processes, which are created for conflict resolution, can be evaluated and their performance appraised. For instance, what would be the normative basis of the grand ethnic coalition as proposed by consociationalists? Such pragmatist considerations as the saving of public expenditure annually spent on the conflict and the political stability necessary to attract foreign investment, although they are good enough reasons for people to make a rational choice, are not by themselves capable of being characteristics of a conciliatory polity. For ethnic peace, the polity needs normative principles, and the two notions I have proposed—ethnic fairness and justice—are meant to provide a moral purpose to the polity.

The second reason is linked to the political appeal of the claims to fairness and justice. As we know, secessionist movements always claim legitimacy to their politics on the arguments of fairness and justice. They project themselves as champions of wronged communities. The moral argument of any secessionist minority group is that leaving the existing political association with the majority ensures justice and fairness to the community. The majority community, I wish to reiterate this point, has a responsibility to present to secessionist minorities a strong moral argument for reassociation with the state. The task of persuading minorities to change their mind from political disassociation to reassociation is indeed a moral one.

My main argument in this regard is that any consociational solution needs to be located in a contractarian polity. With that objective in mind, the deeply divided societies need to search for normative principles that would enable the minority communities to join the polit-

ical association as absolute equals. Ethnic fairness and justice can very well provide the normative framework for the terms of an egalitarian ethnic/social contract.

I would at this point like to define briefly what I mean by my formulation, ethnic fairness, and justice. In order to manage and resolve Sri Lanka's ethnic conflict, it is essential that the terms of association with the Sri Lankan state are redefined for the ethnic minorities. It means that all ethnic groups in the polity are moral equals and equally valuable. When the ethnic groups join the association of the state through this contract, they do not consider their ethnic identity; to be equals and equally valuable, they disregard whether they are Sinhalese, Tamils, or Muslims. The communities enter the contract with the privilege of ignorance of their ethnic identity. To use John Rawls's philosophical language with some modification, they become participants to the contract behind a veil of ethnic ignorance. Thus, the privilege of ignorance enables them to choose the principles of ethnic justice/injustice while being in a position to define "fairness" untainted by ethnic interests or prejudices. And this stage of ignoring ethnic identities to enter into the contract for political association is analogous to the "state of nature" in the classical contract theory and to the "original position" in Rawls's theory of justice.

The second task of the contract is to define ethnic justice from the position of fairness as described above. In ethnically divided societies, the notion of justice is often understood and interpreted in exclusivist ethnic terms. Ethnicized notions of justice make the political and public policy processes extremely volatile and exceedingly contentious. The task then is to arrive at norms and standards of justice by which (I am using the Rawlsian language):

1. Each ethnic group is to have an equal right to the most extensive total system of equal basic liberties compatible with a similar system of liberty for all.

2. Social and economic inequalities are to be arranged so that they are both (a) to the greatest benefit of the least advantaged, and (b) attached to offices and positions open to all under conditions of fair equality of opportunity.

3. All social goods—liberty and opportunity, income and wealth, and the bases of self-respect—are to be distributed equally unless an

unequal distribution of any or all of these goods is to the advantage of the least favored.

In this perspective of ethnic justice, the insistence is that just institutions and practices could be the object of a unanimous agreement among affected communities. In a grand ethnic coalition of this kind, each contractor is represented as having a veto over any institutional configuration of society unresponsive to its vital interests. This approach to group justice will help us to de-ethnicize the notion of social and political justice.

My plea is that at this stage of the contract ethnic groups need to formulate just institutions by ignoring their ethnic identities and perhaps by locating each group in the ethnic identity of another. For example, a Sinhalese agent to the contract may think as a Tamil or a Muslim, a Tamil agent as a Sinhalese and a Muslim, and a Muslim agent as a Tamil and a Sinhalese. If this capacity to claim for oneself the ethnicity of another is achieved by all ethnic groups in their search for just political institutions, I am sure that new and hitherto unknown possibilities for justice and reconciliation can emerge. Once the ethnic justice is defined and just institutions identified, ethnic groups can go back to their respective identities. And politically, this is perhaps one available means to radically subvert the culture of an "ethnic other" constructed in adversarial imagination in multiethnic societies.

As I said earlier, a social contract is not a document that all individuals and groups put their signatures on. It is a philosophical metaphor of imagining the society as a political association of equals. The contractarian approach to politics and society may strengthen the moral, ethical, and normative bases of conflict management and resolution efforts. Some implications of this approach for the present political circumstances in Sri Lanka may be outlined as follows:

1. The process for constitutional reforms and conflict resolution should be transformed into a process of bargaining for and negotiating a new social contract.
2. The constitution should be a charter of ethnic fairness and justice. It should also be a peace treaty among ethnic and political communities in conflict.[7]
3. Sharing and devolution of state power, its institutions of governance, just electoral processes, and public policy—the ultimate standard to measure their validity and performance should be the contract arrived at by all ethnic groups acting as equals.

Conclusion

The discussion developed in this paper is based on a host of critical and unconventional premises on the state, citizenship, ethnicity, ethnic politics, constitutionalism, and legal order. A few may be restated as follows in order to recapture the flow of my analysis and argument. The existing forms of the nation-state as models of political association are becoming historically outdated. New forms of political organization are likely to emerge out of nation-states in crisis. Among the forms of the state likely to emerge are monoethnic ministates in postconflict societies. But this form of the state is unlikely to offer a democratic alternative. A key challenge that any new form of the state will be compelled to confront and negotiate concerns the democratic accommodation of ethnic plurality and diversity. But there remains a larger issue that has not been adequately dealt with in political thinking. It concerns whether ethnic politics could offer democratic alternatives for political emancipation of identity communities.

The argument in this paper is that political emancipation requires democratic solutions to ethnic questions. But working out democratic solutions will also mean a reconstitution of the modern state by reforming it from within its foundations. In deeply divided societies, it also means bringing conflict resolution to the center of the political reform agenda. Hence the need to reimagine the project of the state in contractarian terms. Contractarian reimagination of the state, as constructed in this paper, presupposes de-ethnicizing the bases of political association. To use a slightly Hegelian language, the ethical moment of the modern state can perhaps be recovered by establishing ethnic justice and ethnic fairness behind a veil of ethnic ignorance.

Factors of Stability in Multiethnic States

The Bulgarian Example

Nadezhda Mihailova

The conflicts that shook former Yugoslavia and affected the development of the whole region of southeastern Europe during the last decade were based on the false interpretation of nationalism as an ideology and policy contrasting one state to another and one ethnic group to the rest.

Within such difficult and tense surroundings, Bulgaria has successfully established itself as a factor of stability, for, without any hesitation, it sticks to the ideas of democracy and its values and follows steadily the principles known as the rule of law. Therefore, it is of considerable significance that there is a complete understanding of the position of the Republic of Bulgaria on the problems related to the rights and freedoms of the individuals belonging to ethnic, religious, or linguistic groups.

The Republic of Bulgaria stands on the ground adopted by most European states, namely, that the rights of individuals belonging to various ethnic, religious, or language groups are an inseparable part of the entire complex of human rights and freedoms.

The question of the fate of minorities in Europe was posed with explicit acuteness in the late nineteenth and the early twentieth centuries, and it was further intensified by the two world wars that brought as a result the reshaping of the European map. Such was also the fate of Bulgaria, which, on a number of occasions after the liberation of 1878, has lost parts of its territory. That is why we consider the fate of Bulgarian minority groups abroad to be among the priorities of our contemporary foreign politics.

Bulgaria considers the problems related to guaranteeing the rights of those individuals to be of excep-tional importance and directly related to both the issues of the domestic political stability of every state, as well as the regional and international peace. Apart from humanitarian and legal dimensions, those problems also have complex and delicate political aspects.

The experience of our country indicates that an approach based on the values of democracy, the obser-vance of human rights, as well as the supremacy of law guaranteed by the constitution and the laws are the best grounds for solving the emerging problems.

Our country maintains the view that the protection of minority groups could be effected through the com-plete guaranteeing of the individual rights and freedoms of the persons belonging to the separate ethnic, reli-gious, or linguistic groups. That protection should be carried out on the basis of guaranteed equality of every-one before the law: complete implementation of the principle of nondiscrimination on an ethnic basis; the necessity for prohibition of a forceful assimilation of the individuals subject to the various ethnic, religious, or lin-guistic groups and the need to create prerequisites and conditions for the complete integration of those groups into the social life of the countries citizens of which they are; and the necessity for development of tolerance and understanding among the various ethnic groups, as well as the achievement of a balance between the interest of the majority and the minority groups, which is to be sought for on the basis of the observance of the princi-ples of sovereign equality, territorial integrity, and polit-ical independence of the respective states.

In considering these issues we also take into account the fact that international juridical theory and practice have not accepted a standard definition of the term "national minority," as well as that the presence of certain language, religious, and cultural differences does not necessarily lead to the establishing and/or existence of national minorities. In this line we also defend the view that the international legal acts being elaborated should take precise account of the interests of the existing minorities.

Bulgaria supports the vision that every state should have the opportunity, on its own choice, to take additional measures and to determine the respective means for protecting the ethnic, religious, linguistic, and cultural identity of the minority groups residing in its territory according to every particular situation and the specific needs of every single group. However, the fact should not be ignored that those population groups are dynamic in their nature, and each of their members should be guaranteed the right to decide freely and independently the problem of his/her belonging to such a group. By applying that principle in practice, Bulgaria sticks to the conviction that Bulgarian citizens should determine themselves their appurtenance to one or another ethnic, religious, or linguistic group, and the protection of their rights and freedoms is accomplished on the basis of strict observance of the principle of equality and nondiscrimination.

The end of the cold war and the integration processes ongoing in Western Europe created the unique opportunity for the steady and democratic solving of the minority problems so that they are no longer a source of tension or a part of the "play of force" on the international stage.

In recent times, and especially within the context of the Kosovo conflict in Europe, the so-called Bulgarian "model" for solving minority problems is increasingly being discussed. The advantages of the Bulgarian model consist in, first, the protection of the civilian peace and, second, in the solving of the problems arising from the interethnic relations within the framework of the existing institutions and using the instruments of pluralistic democracy and law. In an international aspect, the balance and stability achieved in Bulgaria are estimated as an important stabilizing factor for the region and as a prerequisite for a change in the way of political thinking in other Balkan countries, too.

Upon the collapse of communism, nationalism has assumed extreme forms in the Balkans. Being adversaries to the principles and norms ruling the world of modern democracy, the nationalists have tried to demonize the Euro-Atlantic integration. It has been presented as an impediment to the realization of the national interests, as well as a new loss of sovereignty for the countries that had just averted the Soviet sphere of influence. The purpose of the nationalists, who actually sprang up from the circles of former communists, was the establishment of new dividing lines in the societies in order to prevent the accomplishment of real changes. They could have kept their influence in the societies only under the conditions of confrontation.

On a large scale the concept was advanced that the great Western powers were to blame for the unresolved problems in southeastern Europe with the purpose of inciting the people against the participation in the Euro-Atlantic community in their settlement. Enemies of the changing world order presumed that in this way the principles of Euro-Atlantic solidarity would remain unfamiliar to the societies in our region and that southeastern Europe would be isolated from the common development of the processes of democratization on the continent.

Even today some circles in the region present the policy of opposition to nationalism as opposition to the national interests. However, such an approach seems to be doomed to failure. The modern world of democracy has already shown the way to how the national interests could be achieved not by means of nationalism but by consistent implementation of the principles of European and Euro-Atlantic solidarity.

Today, nationalism in southeastern Europe remains dangerous not only because it creates a false idea of itself as being the only way for protection of the national interests, but also because it undoubtedly constitutes a wrong mechanism for their accomplishment in general. A look at the events from the last decade in the region reveals how the interests of one of the countries were doomed to failure exactly by nationalism. The more the Serb ruling party imposed the slogan "All Serbs in One State" onto the society, the more the state moved to its disintegration.

One of the manifestations of ethnic nationalism in southeastern Europe is the ungrounded claim that compatriots in the neighboring countries should be given rights that their mother state is not willing to grant to all ethnic groups in its own territory. Nationalists in the region declare their adherence to human rights, however, only to human rights in the neighboring countries. Thus, they aim at breaking through the policy of their neighbors and providing mechanisms for influencing them. So the problems related to the minority groups turn into an instrument for interstate confrontation, which ultimately serves the interests of nationalists in the neighboring countries. Figuratively speaking, nationalists in the region join hands and mutually support each other in their efforts toward gaining public influence.

At the same time, the wars to the west of Bulgaria proved that aggressive nationalism, which generates chauvinism and opposition, has no future in a new democratic world order. Nowadays, the international community does not accept and will never tolerate a policy based on destructive nationalism. Sharing a common stand on the Kosovo crisis, the peoples in southeastern Europe rejected the obsolete concepts and pseudoideals for ethnically clean states and ethnicities. Furthermore, we rejected the attempts to impose ethnically clean states by means of flagrant and massive violations of human rights. Bulgaria actively contributed to the creation of that common position of the states in the region. Since the end of the war, Bulgaria has been striving to maintain the unity among the frontline states, thus providing the most favorable regional environment for the complete settlement of the remaining problems westwards to its border. The inference can be drawn that, on the whole, a number of countries from southeastern Europe are yet far from stability and, hence, from economic growth. For a lot of people outside our region, it still remains a synonym of instability.

The change in that situation strongly depends on the states in the region, that is. on the way we will work together for the solving of our common problems. In this way we could create conditions that would allow the international community to expand its engagement to each of us and to the region as a whole. This would facilitate the accomplishment of our clearly defined priorities—reunion with the European and Euro-Atlantic integration processes, or in other words, a complete overcoming of the dividing lines on our continent.

Evidence is available of the capability of our countries to overcome the prejudices from the past and to carry out an open mutual dialogue on the problems that are common for the region. The existing formats of regional cooperation could be considered as a favorable basis for future successful actions in this area.

However, the resolving of the problems in southeastern Europe would require an overall approach aimed at the long-term stabilization of the region. Following namely that belief, we supported the concept of the Stability Pact as early as its very process of formulation. It is hardly necessary to emphasize that the goals of the pact coincide with our foreign political priorities for peace, security, and prosperity of the region as an integral part of the European continent.

It is our view, however, that what has been done so far for the achievement of those goals is insufficient. The initial period of establishing the structures and working mechanisms of the Stability Pact, of determining the priorities and coordinating the basic documents, extended longer than we expected. What is needed now is that the general vision for the pact is structured in time and receives the respective financial support.

Our countries already avail themselves of particular proposals, the accomplishment of which would actually have a rapid, positive effect with respect to the regional stability. These are projects of a common regional significance in all three major spheres of action of the Stability Pact—democratization and human rights, economic reconstruction and development, and security issues. There is an exceptionally great impatience for a faster transition toward the stage of accomplishment. Let us keep in mind the fact that this would serve as a clear sign of the decidedness of the international institutions to fulfill their obligations to the region and would also have a serious preventive effect from the viewpoint of regional stability as a whole.

We are completely aware of the fact that the slow rate of development of the Stability Pact is mainly due to the lack of financial resources for the carrying out of the projects. Therefore, we once again appeal for the best possible preparation of the coming Financial/Donors' conference to be held at the end of

March 2000 in Brussels. In our opinion this conference should become a turning point in the whole activity within the Stability Pact. We expect particular decisions for project financing, which could connect our region with the rest of Europe and would make the process of European integration irreversible.

Within the present discussion, I would like to send to our partners from NATO and the EU an important message, namely, an appeal for a more significant participation of the countries from the region in the mechanisms for decision making in the process of establishing and accomplishment of the projects of the Stability Pact. It is our opinion that this position corresponds to the spirit of the generally accepted vision of the pact as an initiative meant for the countries of southeastern Europe and aimed to favor the development of the region. In this line, of special importance is the achievement of a complete transparency of the reconstruction activities.

All of these views are related, above all, to the activity of Working Tables 1 and 2 on democratization and human rights and on economic reconstruction and development. Special emphasis should be put here as we consider the ranging of priorities to be of primary significance under the conditions of limited resources. The situation in the region clearly indicates that the leading part should be assigned to the economy. The success in this field is to serve as a good starting point for the activities related to improving the structures of the civil society and to security in general.

The Stability Pact takes into account the necessity for investments for carrying through the changes desired in the region. That principal position should be supported by practical actions that could prove the conviction of the international institutions that every investment in the region is going to be repaid many times. I personally believe in that. I also believe that success is possible if only foreign investments are accompanied by mobilizing our own strength, that is, if we all work together—both we, the countries from the region, and the international institutions.

At the constituent meeting of Working Table 1 within the Stability Pact, Bulgaria proposed the establishing in Sofia of an Information Centre for Democratic Development of southeastern Europe. The idea is that the Centre should contribute to the development and strengthening of democracy and civil society in the countries of the region, the deepening of the process of reforms, the assertion of a climate of trust and mutual understanding, as well as the prevention of future crises and conflicts in the region. The Centre could also play an important role in the processes of democratization of the Federal Republic of Yugoslavia, as well as in the search of a solution to the Kosovo problem. The Centre intends to organize the work on projects related to problems to which the states of southeastern Europe should find solutions. It could also have its part in the carrying out of the democratic reforms and the establishing of a market economy in the states of the region. The intentions are that the expertise provided by the Centre should assist the governments of the states in the region in finding optimal solutions to the problems. The functioning of the Centre could result in bringing closer the conditions in the states of the region, as well as of achieving a more favorable and homogenous environment. Nongovernmental organizations are envisaged to take an active part in the accomplishment of the project.

Bulgaria has expressed its willingness to host a regional conference on democratization, the main purpose of which would be to consolidate and channel the support for the efforts for democratization in Serbia.

Bulgaria takes an active part in the initiatives of the Stability Pact in support of the opposition mayors and the democratic forces in the Federal Republic of Yugoslavia (FRY)—the Szeged Conference (Hungary), the decision for establishing the so-called "twinning of cities." These actions allow for the establishing of close contacts with leading political powers and personalities as well. On the whole, these initiatives have the potential to enhance the democratization in the FRY, which is of a crucial importance for the stability in southeastern Europe.

On November 12–14, 1999, Bulgaria hosted a conference within the Graz process that reviewed the educational programs in the states of the region from the viewpoint of their adapting to the conditions of a good neighborhood and the exclusion of the elements of nationalism from them. Bulgaria plays an active part and contributes to the enhancement of the Graz process, which was highly appraised during the OSCE summit in Istanbul.

We express our support for the Slovenian Task Force on Human Rights for improvement of interethnic relations and its implementation through the establishing of a special delegation of representatives of the Council of Europe and the OSCE Office of the High Commissioner for the National Minorities. In December 1999 the delegation visited Croatia, Bosnia and Herzegovina, Macedonia, and Albania. A report was prepared containing comprehensive recommendations for improvement of the interethnic relations in southeastern Europe.

Bulgaria supports the efforts and takes part in the preparations for the signing of the Charter for Media Freedom, which is coordinated by the United Kingdom. The elimination of aggressive nationalism from the media space is an important and sometimes even leading factor for the rejection of the negative notions about "the other one" that exist in societies and, in the final account, for the overall and sharp improvement of the interethnic relations in the region as well. We could express our satisfaction with the fact that, in this respect, our country has achieved the highest standards established.

In the field of successful management, with the leading part of the Council of Europe, a discussion has started of a set of initiatives aimed at improving the local self-government, transfrontier cooperation, enhancing the efficiency of administration, as well as establishing the Office of the Ombudsman. Further initiatives envisage the adoption of a Model Code of Conduct for Civil Servants, as well as rendering assistance to the institutions from the region that deal with the problems of human rights. On December 6,1999, the Council of Europe held an informal meeting in Strasbourg to exchange information on the existing multilateral and bilateral programs, projects, and activities related to the local self-administration and transfrontier cooperation in southeastern Europe. The meeting was a stage of the preparation of the coming regional forum "Decentralization, Democracy, and Stability," Bucharest, February 21–23, 2000. In April 2000 Thessaloniki will host a forum on the problems of administrative reforms and the development of the states in the region.

The parliamentary dimension of the Stability Pact, in its aspect of democratization and human rights, will evermore be accomplished through the Royaumont process. On December 16, 1999, in Brussels, the participants in the Royaumont process discussed the project of an action plan with the leading part of the European Parliament, prepared by the International Democracy Institute in Strasbourg.

The Bulgarian position is to render an active support to Hungary in its copresidency and organization of the Working Table on Democratization and Human Rights (since January 1, 2000, Hungary has taken that presidency for a period of six months). We also appreciate the January 24, 2000, Budapest meeting of all working groups within Working Table 1 and the survey of the projects launched so far by the states of southeastern Europe in the fields of democratization and human rights. We supported the report of the Slovenian delegation on the work within the project for holding a ministerial conference in Ljubljana on the problems of the national minorities of the states in the region. A positive effect could also be expected from the discussion and popularizing of the existing "good practices" and the ongoing "good processes" for the assertion of the multinational and multicultural societies in the countries of the region. The acceptance of a final document that should specify the particular obligations of each state in this respect would prompt activity in that field.

The joint and decisive efforts of the international community toward stopping Milosevic in his aggressive nationalistic adventure proved the importance of democracy and of the rule of law being fundamental without alternative principles for the organization and regulation of international relations in a changing world order. The Kosovo crisis put to the test the democratic foundations of the international community and its ability to assure protection to human rights. The international community gave proof of a remarkable maturity while interpreting and implementing international law in the context of the dynamic vision of the United Nations Charter, proposed in 1947 by eminent lawyers such as H. Lauterpacht. Special emphasis was put to the fact that some affairs could not be considered to be of the exclusive internal competence of a state when they relate to matters regulated by international law. The reference to human rights made by the UN Charter, as well as the established relationship between human rights and peacekeeping, confirm the view that these matters have been regulated by universal international law. These matters possess international juridical dimensions, and the international community, therefore, has its own competence to interfere and to protect human rights as a value of priority significance.

Ethnic nationalism should be completely rejected in southeastern Europe. The only way for strengthening the nations that have restored their sovereignty after the end of the cold war is through establishing stable and prosperous democratic societies that already exclude ethnic opposition. Only the efficient exercise of human and minority rights guarantees the stability of the states. The use of ethnic minorities abroad against the interests of the neighbors finally reflects on the very state that attempts at doing it because it is impossible to produce nationalism only for export. Eventually, that nationalism starts to disintegrate the society in that same state.

Undoubtedly, by rejecting nationalism we do not reject the national idea but search for ways that lead to its accomplishment in the modern world. I have always said that the Balkans need no new boundaries but more democracy. Genuine democracy offers those appropriate means of policymaking according to which equality is established by the rule of law that assures the necessary balance of rights and commitments belonging to individuals, states, and societies. It is exactly the way of democratic development that leads to the elimination of the aggressive nationalism from the process of settlement of the complicated ethnic problems in the region. The alternative to that political behavior is the emergence of new conflicts like the one in Kosovo, new victims and pains, and, last but not least, slower integration of the whole region into the European and Euro-Atlantic structures.

For a long time Bulgaria was proud of itself as an island of stability in southeastern Europe. It is, of course, a great achievement. The Kosovo war proved that it was not enough to remain an island of stability but also to work toward the creation of a stable regional environment. It means to be surrounded by prosperous and democratic neighbors. Otherwise, Bulgaria might become a hostage of their problems.

From the very start of the Kosovo crisis we established the Bulgarian position on the universal principles of international law: nonviolation of the state boundaries and respect for the territorial sovereignty of the states. We take a firm stand on that position of ours in terms of an active foreign political behavior based on our national interests and within the context of the efforts of the basic international factors in the region and out of it.

The first thing I would like to point out is the fact that the objective reality and the interests of Bulgaria tend to lead us to the conclusion that Kosovo remains an unfinished element in the process of stabilization of the Balkans. In this line, in order to make the Stability Pact a working and active formula, it is necessary that Kosovo find its ethnic and social equilibrium based on the contemporary values of democracy. On the basis of the understanding of that necessity, a meeting on January 29, 2000, was organized between the Bulgarian prime minister and Mr. Hashim Taci, president of the Party of Democratic Progress of Kosovo.

That meeting, as well as the foreign policy steps taken with respect to the Kosovo problem, are completely marked by the sign of preventive diplomacy. The purpose is that Kosovo sees those principles and values being steadily established, the accomplishment of which would prevent the danger of renewing that fireplace of instability in southeastern Europe. I mean the multiethnic coexistence, democratization, the establishing of the structures of civil authorities and of acting democratic institutions, and respect for the human rights of all individuals residing in the region regardless of their ethnic or religious appurtenance.

Within the context of that preventive democracy is to be considered the demand posed by the Bulgarian state for the fast finalization of the inquiry of the tragic death in Pristina of the Bulgarian citizen Valentin Krumov, as well as the case with the missing Bulgarian from Bosilegrad, Stamen Genov. The same should also be the context for our demand for extension of the KFOR mandate, whose presence is a necessary and key prerequisite to create conditions of security, and for the development and guaranteeing of as complete and stable process of political regulation. We insisted on a maximum cooperation on the part of Kosovo Albanians for the KFOR troops, as well as for the UN civil administration in Kosovo. At the same time, we expect representatives of the Serb community in the region to take part in the interim Administration Council of Kosovo.

Being a primary political factor in the region, Bulgaria has certain responsibilities to the efforts of the international community for its stabilization. Just as when it played the key part during the period of the Kosovo humanitarian crisis, now it plays another key part by contributing through its authority and through its contacts in southeastern Europe for the establishing of such a social model in Kosovo, which would reject the ideas of both a Serb and Albanian ethnically pure Kosovo. It should be completely clear that a state that strives at playing a key foreign political part could not but contact with the key political factors in the region.

These contacts are carried out within the framework of our understanding that the outcome of the Kosovo crisis does not coincide with the military capitulation of the Belgrade regime but with the capitulation of the model of ethnic cleansing and ethnic confrontation.

Hence, in order to carry out our stabilizing role in southeastern Europe, we cannot afford to take a stand in any of the schemes for ethnic opposition. Our position is not and cannot be either pro-Albanian or pro-Serb. It can only be pro-European. This is the basis for all our contacts with representatives of various political factors in the region and out of it.

We are deeply concerned by the persisting attempts to impose the idea of an independent Kosovo, as well as of changing the boundaries in the region. At the same time, however, we are willing to get an insight into the essence of those social processes in Kosovo that create the public environment for the imposing of that idea. In this respect, we consider of extreme importance the establishment of stable democratic institutions in the region with the participation of all ethnic groups. That problem was a special focus of the talks of Prime Minister Ivan Kostov and Mr. Taci.

The achievement of a comprehensive political decision of the Kosovo problem with the active participation and contribution of the states from the region remains a major factor for the stabilization, reconstruction, and further development of southeastern Europe.

We shall continue our work in this respect, being convinced that only a stable and prosperous southeastern Europe, having accepted the common European morale and values, could have chances for a fast and successful European and Euro-Atlantic integration.

On the initiative of the Bulgarian prime minister, Mr. Ivan Kostov, from January 21–22, 2000, in the Bulgarian town of Hisarya, a Working Meeting was held by the prime ministers of the states neighboring the Federal Republic of Yugoslavia—Albania, Bosnia and Herzegovina, the Republic of Macedonia, Romania, Hungary, Croatia, and Bulgaria. In that meeting also were the Supreme EU Commissioner on the Common Foreign Policy and the Security Policy, Javier Solana, as well as NATO's deputy secretary general Sergio Balandzino.

The main aim of the meeting was to give the participants a chance to discuss in an informal atmosphere the problems in southeastern Europe and to send a clear and comprehensive message to the international community in order to reflect the different views about the way in which the peace in the region should be established. It was the will of the participants in the meeting, which, in fact, is turning into a process, to demonstrate that the states in southeastern Europe could initiate solutions to the problems remaining in the region.

The meeting discussed issues such as:

- The risks to the regional security within the context of the up-to-date development of the situation in Kosovo, the issue of the future status of the province and its effect on the inter-state and interethnic relations in southeastern Europe.
- The influence of the situation in the Federal Republic of Yugoslavia on the general climate in the region, the perspectives for its evolution, programs for humanitarian aid for the people in the Federal Republic of Yugoslavia, for example, EU's Energy for Democracy.
- The Stability Pact for Southeastern Europe—the problems for its implementation, financial resources, defining common priorities and projects, the problem of the renewal of free navigation on the Danube.

The main points in the position of the Republic of Bulgaria promoted at the meeting included:

- The democratization of the Federal Republic of Yugoslavia, which is at present generating instability, is of key importance to the security and stability in southeastern Europe.

- The solution to the Kosovo problem should be sought for in granting Kosovo a wide autonomy within the internationally acknowledged boundaries of the Federal Republic of Yugoslavia; Bulgaria will not tolerate any moves toward the establishing of an ethnically pure zone; it is necessary to preserve the multiethnic nature of Kosovo; concern about the continuing pressure for independence of Kosovo.

- The democratization of the Federal Republic of Yugoslavia should be considered not only within the context of the Serb opposition but also within the integration of the minorities in Serbia in the political process in that country.

- The necessity to precisely focus the sanctions against the Federal Republic of Yugoslavia in view to improve their efficiency so that they are aimed at Milosevic's regime and not the common people in Serbia—for example, the gasoline embargo does not affect the regime, yet it brings about mafia structures in fuel trading and allows Milosevic to claim that the sanctions are punishing all Serb people.

- The political dimensions of the Stability Pact cannot be defined without settling the problem about the future of the Federal Republic of Yugoslavia; the need of a financial support for the democracies in the region in view of their faster assertion as an alternative to Milosevic's regime.

On its part, Bulgaria quickly managed to regulate its internal ethnic contradictions, which had been inherited from the previous regime. The Constitution of the Republic of Bulgaria has promulgated as a supreme principle the protection of human rights, human dignity, and security. The rights and freedoms of all citizens are being exercised according to the provisions of the constitution and of the national legislation.

With an understanding of the deep relations between democracy and the rule of law in a changing world order, I would like to expand in detail the acting national legislation in Bulgaria that regulates the status of the persons belonging to minority groups.

In the first place, I would like to analyze the action of international laws.

The Republic of Bulgaria is a party to the basic universal international legal instruments providing for human rights, including the International Pacts for Human Rights, the International Convention for Rejecting All Forms of Racial Discrimination, and the European Convention on Human Rights. At the same time, Bulgaria is also a party to the basic European international legal instrument in this sphere after having ratified in 1999 the Framework Convention of the Council of Europe for the Protection of National Minorities.

According to Art. 5, Sec. 4 of the Constitution of the Republic of Bulgaria, the international agreements ratified by order of constitution, promulgated and effective for Bulgaria, are a part of the country's national law and have supremacy over those norms of the national law that contradict them. Furthermore, according to Art. 85, Sec. 1, It. 6 of the Constitution, the National Assembly ratifies by a law the international agreements referring to the fundamental human rights and freedoms. These two texts of the Constitution guarantee the supremacy of all international agreements referring to the fundamental rights and freedoms of man, including the rights of groups belonging to ethnic, religious, or linguistic groups, over those norms of the national law that contradict them. Being a part of the national law, they are a direct source of legal norms in the sphere of human rights (that is, everyone has the right to quote certain international agreements in search for defense).

The Constitution of the Republic of Bulgaria guarantees and promotes the development of democracy in a state of law.

The fundamental rights and freedoms of the citizens are provided for in Chapter One (Essentials) and Chapter Two (Fundamental Rights and Freedoms of the Citizens) of the Constitution. Those texts are based on the main international agreements (universal and regional) in that area, and the majority of their provisions are directly reproduced in the Constitution. From the texts of the Constitution, especially related to the rights of persons belonging to ethnic, religious, or linguistic groups, are the following:

Chapter One:

- Art. 1, Sec. 2—nonadmission of discrimination based on race, gender, nationality, ethnic appurtenance, language, etc.;
- Art. 11, Sec. 4—prohibition to establish parties based on ethnic, religious, or creed principles;
- Art. 13—freedom of religion and creed, division between the church and the state, prohibition to use religion and creed for political purposes.

Chapter Two:

- Art. 36, Sec. 2—the right to study and use the mother's language if different from the official language;
- Art. 37—freedom to choose religion and creed plus obligation on part of the state to provide for tolerance and respect among believers from various denominations, as well as among believers and nonbelievers;
- Art. 44, Sec. 2—prohibition of organizations inflaming racial, ethnic, national, or religious hatred;
- Art. 53, Sec. 5—right to citizens and organizations to establish private schools;
- Art. 54, Sec. 1—right for everyone to develop his/her culture along the lines of his/her ethnic origin.

Of special significance are the norms of law that refer to some essential rights of the persons belonging to ethnic, religious, or linguistic groups.

Such is the 1990 Law for the Names of the Bulgarian Citizens. In particular:

- Art. 7 postulates that a child's first name is to be chosen on the free will and mutual accord of the two parents;
- Art. 17 postulates that the use of threat, compulsion, force, fraud, or abuse of power, or any other illegal action for deciding, keeping,

changing, or regaining of a name, is subject to prosecution by the criminal law (such an act, regardless of whether it is performed by an official or not, is considered a crime and not a casual violation);

- Paragraph 2 of the Transitional and Final Provisions postulates that Bulgarian citizens whose names have been forcefully changed are allowed on their own will to regain their previous names.

In the present times of globalization and development of the information society, of special importance are legal norms in the spheres of education, science, and culture. The 1991 National Education Law has the following provisions:

- Art. 4, Sec. 2—nonadmission of any restrictions or privileges in the exercise of the right to education on the basis of race, nationality, gender, ethnic and social origin, religion, and social status;
- Art. 8, Sec. 2—students for whom Bulgarian is not their mother's language, apart from the obligatory study of Bulgarian, have the right to study their mother's language in the municipal schools under the protection and control by the state.
- The 1999 Law for the Degree of Education, the General Knowledge Minimum and the Curriculum defines in Art. 15, Sec. 3 that the obligatory optional subjects include the study of the mother's language, according to Art. 8, Sec. 2 of the National Education Law.

The Rules for Applying the National Education Law (1992) (Art. 5, Sec. 4) define the mother's language as "the language used by the child for communication in the family, prior to its starting school." That basic range of problems is further expanded through the 1995 Law for Higher Education. Its Art. 4 prohibits privileges or restrictions related to race, nationality, ethnic appurtenance, gender, social origin, political views, or religion.

A special decree, No. 183 of the Council of Ministers of 5.9.1994, defines the study of the mother's language in the municipal schools of the Republic of Bulgaria through:

- Art. 1—the mother's language is to be studied from the first to the eighth year in the municipal schools as an optional subject and up to four classes per week;
- Art. 2—those willing to do so should apply to the principal of the school. Afterwards, having started their course of education, they are allowed to resign from it;
- Art. 3—children who are not fluent in Bulgarian are enrolled in a one-year preparatory preschool course, organized by the principal of the school and agreed upon with the mayor of the respective municipality;
- Art. 4—the textbooks for learning the mother's language are not to be paid by the students;
- Art. 5—the municipal budget provides for the financing of the education.

Order No. Dé-14-72 of the Ministry of Education and Science of October 7, 1992, allows the establishing of a Secondary Islamic School seated in the town of Momchilgrad for the schooling of religious officials. Students are enrolled at the school after their eighth year in general schools and the term of education is four years.

Another important trend in the development of democracy and the implementation of the principles of the rule of law is the norms in the spheres of civilian and criminal law.

The Criminal Code of the Republic of Bulgaria treats the above-mentioned range of problems in Chapter Three:

- Section One, Crimes against the National and Racial Equality—Arts. 162–163 classify as crimes the preaching or inciting to racial or national feud or hatred, or racial discrimination, as well as the use of force over the personality or property of a person for reasons of his/her belonging to a certain race, gender, nationality, religion, etc., membership in organization or group, participation in a crowd with such purposes or actions;

- Section 2, Crimes against Creed—Arts. 164–166 classify as crimes the preaching of hatred on the basis of religion or the impediments imposed by means of force or threat on persons to exercise their faith or to perform their religious rituals and services in which they do not violate the laws of the country or the public order, as well as the duress to engage in such services or rituals.
- According to Art. 169b, subject to prosecution are actions that impede the performing of political rights guaranteed by the constitution.
- Art. 172 classifies as a crime the conscious creation of impediments for starting a job or the compulsory resigning from it for racial reasons.
- Arts. 416–418 of the Criminal Code levy heavy punishments for cases of genocide and apartheid—murder or injury; prevention of birth; placement in unbearable conditions, incitement of genocide; and the establishment of suppression by one racial group over another.
- In particular, the Criminal Process Code envisages in its Art. 10 for equality of the citizens in the criminal trial and nondiscrimination for reasons of nationality, religion, gender, race, origin, education, social, or material status.

Under the law for recovery of the ownership over real estate of Bulgarian citizens from a Turkish origin who had taken steps to depart for the Republic of Turkey during the May–September 1989 period (passed 1992), their ownership of the real estate is regained in case they were bought out by the state, municipalities, public organizations or their firms, or by cooperatives, unless those citizens had not been compensated in another way or had not transferred their rights to relatives of ascending or descending line, spouses, or the lateral branch of the family up to the fourth degree (first cousins); the agreements used by the above-mentioned legal subjects for the transfer of the property to private physical persons are annulled. Of special interest are the practices of the legislative, executive, and legal bodies of the state power in the Republic of Bulgaria in this respect.

Through a declaration of the National Assembly on the national question, passed on January 15, 1990, a critical analysis is done of the policy on the national question carried out by the communist regime, and the inference is made that a deep gap has emerged among the various ethnic groups; the free choice of a name is proclaimed, as well as the free use of the mother's language in everyday life and interpersonal relations; prohibition is imposed on the propaganda of ethnic feud; special protection by the state is declared (in the spheres of labor, satisfaction of material, cultural, religious, and social needs, everyday servicing and provision, property-legal relationships) for population groups that are of a minor numbers in ethnic respect in a certain region of the country, in a municipality, or a village.

By Decree No. 449 of the Council of Ministers of December 4, 1997, a National Council on Ethnic and Demographic Matters was established as a consulting body under the Council of Ministers in order to assist the collaboration and coordination between the government bodies and nongovernmental organizations and to carry out the governmental policy with respect to ethnic and demographic matters and migration. That council comprises officials of the various state ministries and institutions and representatives of the public organizations of the ethnic groups and the Bulgarian diaspora. Associated members of the National Council are representatives of different institutions, research institutes, and nongovernmental organizations. Among the main functions and tasks of the National Council are the promotion of the implementation of active social, demographic, cultural, and educational policies according to the requirements of the European social charter. It also studies, analyzes, and works out proposals; assists the balancing of interests of the separate social groups; and keeps contact with international governmental and nongovernmental organizations with similar activity.

Of special significance are the decisions of the Constitutional Court on matters related to the rights of individuals belonging to ethnic, religious, or linguistic groups.

Decision No. 4 of April 21, 1992—on the constitutionality of the Movement for Rights and Freedoms (DPS)—postulated that DPS was established and functions not within the restricted framework of a group formed on an ethnic and/or creed principle. It does not exist only because of that group and does not build up

its political platform on values and ideals belonging to a closed community alone; it is rather an open organization and therefore does not contradict Art. 11, Sec. 4 of the constitution.

Decision No. 5 of June 11, 1992—explaining the constitutional right to choose one's creed and religious views—defines that this is an absolute, personal, essential, and infringible right without which civil society would be impossible. It includes the following powers: the right to a free choice of creed, the possibility to exercise freely one's religion by means of word, press, or association. Restrictions to that law are only admissible under Art. 13, Sec. 4 and Art. 37, Sec. 2 of the constitution when that right is used for political purposes or is aimed at the national security, public order, health and morale, rights, and freedoms of the rest of society. This is a comprehensive listing and it cannot be considered in a broader sense or be complemented through a legal procedure. No interference by the state is admitted in the intraorganizational activities of the religious communities and institutions, as well as in their public actions, with the exception of cases when the above-mentioned provisions of the constitution apply.

Bulgaria is a party to all fundamental UN conventions in the field of human rights, as well as to some other twenty-nine international documents of the Council of Europe in this field. Among them are the Framework Convention for the Protection of National Minorities of the Council of Europe, ratified by the National Assembly on 18 February 1999, Protocols NN 6, 4, and 7 under the European Convention on human rights, as well as the European Social Charter (revised), which is to be ratified soon.

It is my strong belief that over the last few years the Bulgarian public model of ethnic tolerance and constructive coexistence of the minorities with the majority has been consolidated. It became possible thanks to the consistent efforts toward development of the democratic processes in the country and reinforcement of the democratic institutions.

I would like to illustrate this by presenting some data and practical measures in line with the acting legislation, which are aimed at guaranteeing the rights of individuals belonging to ethnic, religious, or language groups.

After the general election for the 38th National Assembly (April 1997), the Union for National Salvation (a part of which is the DPS Movement for Rights and Freedoms), won places for eighteen MPs. The National Assembly has as its member a person from Roma origin, elected by the United Democratic Forces list. The persons belonging to the various ethnic groups are widely represented in the local authority bodies. They have established their clubs and associations; they use their language and have their own specialized editions.

According to the acting legislation, the mother's language is studied in the municipal schools within the obligatory optional curriculum. The following table illustrates the numbers of students, groups, and classes for study of the mother's language toward the end of 1999:

Mother's language	Number of students	Groups	Classes
Turkish	38,684	3,175	–
Armenian	292	21	–
Hebrew	394	–	40

Of special interest are the practical steps taken for the resolving of certain problems that are relevant to the Roma population in Bulgaria:

- The Ministry of Education has published textbooks in three gypsy dialects. Special preparatory language courses were organized for children of the Roma community whose mother's language is not Bulgarian.
- By a decree of the government in October 1994, the payment of allowances for children in cases of two unemployed parents was renewed.
- In the second largest city in Bulgaria—Plovdid, where a large number of Romas reside—a council was established to assist the work of the mayor and his administration, and representatives of the Roma people are members of it; such a council is under construction in Sofia, too.
- In 1992 Sofia University and the New Bulgarian University launched special courses of lectures on the history of the Roma culture and folklore.
- The government passed a decree for granting land to Bulgarian nonland owners, which is mostly the case with Romas in Bulgaria.

- Within the National Council on Ethnic and Demographic Matters and with the participation of representatives of a number of Roma organizations, a Framework Program was worked out and passed in 1999 by the Council of Ministers for equal integration of Roma people into Bulgarian society; it envisages a number of measures to be taken in the spheres of employment, social support, land provision, health care, education, and protection of the ethnic originality and culture of the Roma people.
- In 1999, in fifteen of the twenty-eight regional administrations in the country, Roma experts were appointed, and such experts are to be appointed in the remaining thirteen regions as well.
- In the regions with compact groups of Roma population (Sliven, Pazardzhik, Plovdiv, Shoumen, Stara Zagora, Pleven, etc.) measures are to be taken according to the specifics of the region—provision of earmarked funds for supporting acute social problems, opening of additional job places, educational discussions either through lectures or personal talks aimed at improvement of the interpersonal and interethnic relations. A special public relations group was established within the Ministry of Interior, which provides contacts and feedback information with individuals and social groups that address particular demands to the Interior offices, including problems of the Roma population.

The borderline between the two millennia opened a new horizon in front of Bulgaria. The invitation we received for starting negotiations for EU membership completely made our country part of the European and Euro-Atlantic communities of nations that share the values of individual freedom, political liberty, and the rule of law forming the basis of all genuine democracy and guaranteeing the observance of human and minority rights. Now Bulgarian citizens have the chance to carry into effect their European identity in the context of the perspective given by the membership to the European Union. Europe is a common but also a personal project in which all people, notwithstanding their nationality and ethnic origin, can share their own perspective.

Today, more than ever, southeastern Europe needs a successful model, an example of a prosperous state in the region. Bulgaria offers such a model to destroy the vision that nothing good can happen in the Balkans and that ethnic nationalism is the only matrix determining the relations both among the states and within the societies. In such a way Bulgaria best shows that it shares the European and Atlantic values and supports the Euro-Atlantic community in its efforts to build a better and fair world.

Here, I would like to remind you of the extremely precise words and definitions made by U.S. president Bill Clinton during his visit to Sofia in November last year:

Let me say to the people in the United States, Europe, and all over the world who will see this tonight on television: This is a wonderful country! Come here and help Bulgaria build the future! And let me add this: the cold war was fought and won by free people who did not accept that there could be two Europes in the twentieth century. Now, we must not, we will not accept that there could be two Europes separate and unequal in the twenty-first century. If you stay the course, Bulgaria will be a place where young people can make their dreams come true. Americans and Bulgarians, together, will help to build a Europe that is undivided, democratic, and at peace for the first time in all human history! When that vision of the future was threatened by President Milosevic's brutal campaign in Kosovo, you stood with NATO. I know it was very hard for you to do. But I ask you to think about what would have happened if we had not stood

up. This entire region would have been overwhelmed by refugees. And a message would have been sent to the rest of the world: stay away from southeastern Europe, for here dictators still hold power by exploiting human differences and destroying human lives. I thank you for standing your ground with us against that evil! And I also want to thank you for setting a very different example here in Bulgaria. You have preserved a multiethnic society. As President Stoyanov has said, you chose to stand with and for civilization two years ago. But you also made that choice fifty years ago, when you helped Bulgaria's Jewish community to survive World War II and the Holocaust. On behalf of American Jews and Jewish people everywhere, I thank you for that! When you saved Bulgaria's Jews, it was one of the proudest moments in your history. And tonight, as you stand for freedom, it is one of the proudest moments in your history. But now we have work to do. We must help all of southeastern Europe choose freedom and tolerance and community. We must give all the people in this region a unifying magnet that is stronger than the pull of old hatreds that has threatened to tear them apart over and over again. You may be young democracies under a lot of economic difficulties, but because you know how it feels to be insecure, you know what it means to sacrifice for common security; because you know how it feels to lose your freedom, you know what it takes to defend freedom. And so, even though you paid a great price and you are not yet in the heart of Europe, you have Europe and its values in your heart!

Minority Rights in Multiethnic and Multiracial States

Ann Elizabeth Mayer

International human rights law has taken the importance of group rights into account, albeit somewhat belatedly. Early documents like the 1948 Universal Declaration of Human Rights centered on the rights of the individual, and many would still argue that the best way to ensure that the rights of members of minorities are protected is via ensuring that the rights of every individual are protected. At a later stage of the development of international human rights law, the United Nations saw a need to make special provision for the group rights of minorities. A significant initiative was the 1992 UN General Assembly Declaration on the Rights of Persons Belonging to National or Ethnic, Religious, and Linguistic Minorities. Among other things, this declaration provides in Article 1, Number 1, that "States shall protect the existence and the national or ethnic, cultural, religious and linguistic identity of minorities within their respective territories and shall encourage conditions for the promotion of that identity." Article 4, Number 1 says that "States shall take measures . . . to ensure that . . . minorities may exercise fully and effectively all their human rights and fundamental freedoms without any discrimination and in full equality before the law." However, the declaration and other international law instruments are far from affording us anything like a reliable, comprehensive blueprint offering tidy solutions to complex disputes about how to realize the group rights of ethnic or racial minorities in all the widely varying contexts in which such disputes arise. Even the most expert scholars of international law struggle to define exactly what group rights should comprise or precisely how group rights are to be vindicated in ways most consonant with democratic values. Referring to the same set of legal principles, they may wind up in significant disagreement.[1]

We have no definitive guidelines for what we should do when minorities insist that their rights can only be vindicated by a process of self-determination that may or even must culminate in secession from existing states. The 1992 declaration asserts in its preamble that "the promotion and protection of the rights of persons belonging to national or ethnic, religious and linguistic minorities contribute to the political and social stability of states in which they live." That is, it assumes that states are stabilized by advancing and protecting minority rights. Of course, the record does show that infringing minority rights tends to exacerbate interethnic resentments and that this can lead to clashes that fragment states. However, in actual cases when minorities make demands for their own separate states, we can often foresee that the process of secession could provoke instability and undermine peace. Even calls for an extensive range of group rights may seem to threaten stability by institutionalizing differences between ethnic groups within a country, effectively walling them off from each other in ways that could impede their understanding each other. This brings us back to the controversy over how we are to balance our concern for maintaining peace against our concern for respecting the rights of ethnic minorities. Depending on the situation, one may be able to make plausible arguments that maintaining the peace must be our overriding concern and should therefore justify placing certain limits on the autonomy of minority groups where to do otherwise risks provoking warfare.

The complicated politico-historical backgrounds of the many contemporary disputes over minority rights stand in the way of devising all-purpose legal models for regulating the political status of minorities. Where disputes about group rights are concerned, one needs to take into account the peculiar characteristics of specific cases in order to assess whether proposed solutions are workable or fair. Furthermore, as both Professor Moodley and Professor Uyangoda underline, the emotional and psychological factors underlying a particular ethnic conflict may have at least as much impact as political forces on its potential solvability. Thus, this panel is obliged to wrestle with a diabolically difficult subject. Not surprisingly, given the complexity of the problems that they are grappling with, our panelists do not agree on the feasibility of using law to address these problems. Minister Mihailova stresses law and constitutionalism as vital tools for reshaping not only polities but the outlooks of the parties affected. Laws, she proposes, can channel developments in a way favorable to the realization of human rights and ethnic harmony. Professor Uyangoda offers a probing analysis of the Sri Lankan case, which includes exposing how the wrong laws and insensitive policies exacerbated interethnic grievances. He also accords weight to constitutional and legal methods for dealing with ethnic conflict and proposes that a constitution can effectively serve as a kind of peace treaty among ethnic and political communities in conflict. Both of these panelists look to constitutions, laws, and respect for human rights standards as potential ways of alleviating ethnic conflicts and establishing a democratic foundation for majority-minority coexistence. In contrast, Professor Moodley in her wide-ranging discussion displays profound skepticism regarding the capacity of constitutions and laws to contain ethnic antagonisms and expresses doubts about the utility and meaningfulness of international human rights law.

Although a desire to add balance to this panel might normally tempt me to join forces with Professor Moodley, my own inclinations dispose me to lean heavily on law as a means of addressing ethnic and racial conflicts. I am attracted by Professor Allott's vision that law must be central to humanity's self-remaking. I see the need for recourse to law to buttress democracies in ways that do justice to group rights, and I believe that, notwith-standing all the trouble we have applying it to complex political controversies, international human rights law provides a viable framework for regulating the political status of ethnic minorities. However, perhaps I can reach a modus vivendi with Professor Moodley by concurring in part with her assessment. I am prepared to concede that law, by itself, is manifestly insufficient to cure problems or to deter self-seeking rulers from embarking on courses of action that are nefarious for human rights and democracy. I am also ready to acknowledge that we cannot calculate with mathematical certainty which legal models will work or confidently predict that any particular legal formulas will successfully and definitively resolve ethnic disputes. Notwithstanding this, I would still maintain that just laws informed by a sensitivity to ethnic grievances give us the chance to reduce conflicts and manage those that persist relatively well. Furthermore, I note that, via examination of the laws that have in the past shown the propensity to aggravate ethnic strife, we can identify categories of measures that should not be taken if interethnic warfare is to be avoided.

Professor Moodley seems ready to accept that ethnic minorities have a right to regulated secession, perhaps leaning toward the idea that resisting demands for such secession may only amount to a delaying action. Of course, when one contemplates the implications of Quebec seceding from Canada, one confronts a prospect quite different from the mayhem that has been occasioned by ethnic separatism in the Balkans. In Canada's model democracy, secession, if it occurs, is unlikely to bring with it the horrific consequences that the world witnessed as the former Yugoslavia was broken into new geopolitical chunks that supposedly corresponded to ethnic units. In North America, one would expect a carefully orchestrated, peaceful separation along the lines of Slovakia's decorous divorce from the former Czechoslovakia.

Minister Mihailova and Professor Uyangoda are less inclined to accept the right of secession as a logical consequence of a commitment to upholding minority rights. Minister Mihailova stresses the importance of strong protections for human rights within existing states. Minister Mihailova offers us her mantra about the Balkans, that what is needed is not new boundaries but more democracy. Surveying the results of the savage ethnic warfare in the former Yugoslavia, one is disposed to concur, noting that the proliferation of new statelets in the wake of its violent breakup has led to wrenching dislocations without producing an overall enhancement of human rights and security for most of those living in the affected areas. Professor Uyangoda proposes that if the moral argument of a secessionist minority group is that it must leave the existing political association in order to secure justice and fairness, those resisting secession must meet this moral argument by protecting minority rights within the existing state. A system must be established in which all ethnic groups are morally equal and equally valuable. As he says, the polity must have a moral purpose, and the constitution should be a charter of ethnic fairness and justice.

Recent Spanish history suggests that the right constitutional provisions do have a positive impact on interethnic relations. As it happens, Professor Moodley does occasionally refer to Spain, but she does not seem to draw the same lessons that I do from the Spanish experience. Constitutional patriotism, she warns us, does not provide the kind of emotional glue that ethnic nationalism affords. Now, Spain is a country where substantial goodwill and relative harmony have been achieved in a multiethnic state after a traumatic twentieth-century experience of civil war and dictatorship and severe interethnic strains. In its preamble the Spanish Constitution embraces the notion of a multiethnic polity, providing that the Spanish nation proclaims its will to: "protect all Spaniards and peoples [*pueblos*] of Spain in the exercise of human rights, their cultures and traditions, languages and institutions." Article 2 advises:

> The Constitution is based on the indissoluable unity of the Spanish nation [*nacion*], the common and indivisible homeland [*patria*] of all Spaniards, and recognizes and guarantees the rights to autonomy of the nationalities [*nacionalidades*] and regions that make it up and the solidarity among all of them.

That is, it establishes political association on the basis of an acknowledgement that Spain is inhabited not only by Spaniards but by groups that are variously called "peoples" or "nationalities"—the terms being used for minorities being inconsistent, as is so often the case. At the geopolitical level, there is one nation, Spain, but this nation allows autonomy to regions and respects the various cultures and languages of its "peoples." The Spanish Constitution has had sufficient time by now to shape the way Spaniards of various ethnicities think about their political community. It accommodates difference within a vibrant democratic order that provides strong guarantees for both individual human rights and minority rights and that inspires confidence among all groups.[2] Of course, Spain has not eliminated ethnic conflicts, but it has significantly reduced them. Today, when Basque separatists resort to terror to register their rejection of the Spanish system, their actions provoke vigorous condemnations and protests in the Basque region itself. The Spanish Constitution deserves credit for creating an environment where Basques, Catalans, Galicians, Spaniards, and others can share a common patriotism, even as they consider themselves as distinct "peoples" with their own national identities and are legally recognized as such.

The Canadian legal framework embodies another attempt to accommodate difference. It makes a conscious attempt to satisfy French Canadians' aspirations to maintain their group identity, and it seems well-designed to accommodate Quebec's demands for preserving French culture. Despite this, as Professor Moodley's trenchant assessment reminds us, Quebec nationalists are still not appeased. However, while conceding that secessionist demands are still voiced in Quebec, I would argue that the Canadian case demonstrates the positive impact that good laws can have. Unlike the violent conflict in Sri Lanka that is dissected in Professor Uyangoda's paper, the quarrel between Quebec separatists and the Canadian federation has remained relatively civil and is most likely to be resolved peacefully, regardless of the ultimate outcome. It seems that Canada's enlightened and equitable legal framework, including sundry constitutional acts and strong human rights protections, has enabled the country to avoid the worst kinds of violence. This is no mean accomplishment! Furthermore, despite the secessionist clamor, the federation may yet survive. Many in Quebec, including a large proportion of French Quebecers, believe that remaining within the federation is in their best interests. That Canada is cold does not mean that it is moribund.

Quebec is one of many cases where secessionist arguments are based on the premise that secession is a means to redress historical wrongs. Where deep-seated resentments over events in centuries past still fester, well-intentioned designs for accommodating demands for group identity within current state boundaries may prove inadequate. International law has no mechanisms for calibrating how ancient wrongs to an ethnic community are to be factored into evaluating its contemporary claims for justice. Focusing on past grievances, ethnic nationalist politicians may insist that territorial sovereignty, entailing secession, is the way—and the only way—to redress historical wrongs. As Professor Moodley observes, Quebec separatists dwell on the eighteenth-century defeats of the French of North America at the hands of the British, speaking as if secession would compensate for these French defeats. This brooding on past losses is embodied in the Quebec provincial slogan "je me souviens." A recent newspaper article mocked this attitude, asserting that, with this slogan emblazoned on their license plates, modern Quebecers are driving into the twenty-first century still smarting over eighteenth-century events.[3] Having this mind-set, Quebec separatists may not be amenable to reason grounded in the political realities of the present day.

Benedict Anderson's term "imagined communities" has by now become familiar, but we need to bear in mind that the imagining behind these communities may be delusional. Professor Uyangoda refers to what he aptly labels "ethnic fantasies." In this category, I would place the fantasy that, once Quebec's ties to Canada ties are severed, French culture will be better protected than it is in bilingual, pluralistic Canada. The preservation of French culture is an eminently laudable goal, but it is doubtful, given its geographical setting, that an independent Quebec will be more successful in warding off the inroads of English. I estimate that an independent Quebec surrounded by larger, more powerful, and far richer Anglophone countries—including the English-speaking colossus to the south, with its seductive youth culture—will turn out to be more vulnerable to Anglo-Saxon encroachments than the province of Quebec now is as an influential player within Canada, which backs its demands for the preservation of French culture.

Among other things, if it ever does secede, Quebec will be distracted from the task of preserving French language and culture by having to deal with its own internal ethnic conflicts, which are sure to be intensified by any secession. As Professor Moodley notes, Quebec secession is opposed by the non-French minorities within Quebec. These groups feel that their rights will be better guarded in a larger Canadian federation, where ethnicity is not the glue that holds the nation together. Thus, Quebec secession may incite other ethnic groups like the restive Cree Indian minority to demand a right to secede from the newly independent state. Once ethnicity has been put forward as the basis for one secession, it is hard to stop it from becoming the basis for another. The recent history of the Caucasus and the Balkans reminds us of how the promotion of ethnic separatism may launch a wave of fissiparous tendencies, with one split provoking new infighting and conflicts over proposed subsplits. That is, when one draws up new boundaries that are supposedly congruent with ethnic divisions, one often confronts a new set of demands for self-determination as yet more ethnic groups seek to delineate their own territories. Depending on the geopolitical setting, serious harm to regional stability can result.

As all three papers note, even the best laid plans can go awry due to the machinations of irresponsible ethnic nationalist politicians eager to exploit communal grievances for their own personal agendas or to establish themselves as relatively bigger fish by creating smaller ponds. Thus, one can devise a constitutional scheme like the Canadian one that should work and see its promise threatened by relentless separatist pressures engineered by politicians of the caliber of the separatist leader Jacques Parizeau. If we scrutinize the stances taken by Quebec separatists, we uncover hints that some may be aiming at an ethnically pure Quebec, a goal that could not be pursued within the Canadian federation with its stringent rights protections. We see their tendency to exalt ethnic purity in their public glorifications of "pure wool" [*pure laine*] Quebecers, whose families can trace their ancestry to before the 1759 British conquest. Of course, invoking the notion of ethnic purity in any form should set off alarms. Those of us who watched the outburst of Jacques Parizeau when he lost the November 1995 referendum on Quebec secession will be unlikely to forget the moment. His angry lambasting of "the ethnic vote," coming as it did from a fervent ethnic nationalist, was a usage that might have sounded comic had it been uttered in less menacing tones. His embittered vow to take revenge on those opposing Quebec independence was chilling. Even though Parizeau has since been sidelined and replaced by more diplomatic spokespersons for the separatist cause, non-French minorities within Quebec have grounds for feeling nervous about their future if the province ever attains independence.

Being attuned to such developments, Professor Uyangoda warns that politicians pressing for ethnic separatism tend to have antidemocratic agendas. He proposes that ethnic nationalists are drawn to establish highly centralized and even antidemocratic states consisting of single ethnic communities. In the wake of the success of certain ethnic nationalist movements and separatisms, we now have monoethnic ministates in which ethnic diversity and political pluralism are delegitimized and expelled from the domain of juridico-constitutional concerns. Such conditions are unhealthy for democracy.

If Canada shows us what kinds of laws *should* be adopted in a multiethnic democracy, examination of the Sri Lankan record teaches us what should *not* be done in a state riven by ethnic cleavages, presenting examples of measures that could only heighten mistrust between ethnic groups. The Sri Lankan government has adopted precisely the wrong policies, thereby widening the gulf between the Sinhalese majority and the alienated Tamil minority. From the Sri Lankan example and other analogous cases we learn that certain types of laws should be ruled out. Some precepts come to mind: Do not adopt constitutions and laws that enshrine one ethnic identity as the national identity; do not make laws that reinforce the privileged status of one ethnic group at the expense of another; and eschew government measures that embody an ethnocentric outlook and constitute a direct affront to the values and feelings of the minority. Failure to adhere to these precepts is a built-in recipe for the aggravation of interethnic hostility.

Turkey provides an apposite comparison. The modern Turkish republic was born, of course, in circum-

stances that meant that building the nation-state was associated with fighting against a European plan to dismember the territory remaining in Turkish hands after the staggering Ottoman defeat in World War I. Having barely saved their nation from dismemberment at the outset of the Turkish republic, Turks have been drawn to a strong unitarist state and ideology. As Professor Uyangoda notes, this unitarist model is an inadequate form of political organization for a country comprising more than one major ethnic community. It has been hard to move beyond this original model of a unitarist state to one that acknowledges that Turks share Anatolia with a large Kurdish community. This in turn impedes coming to terms with Kurdish demands for group rights. Now, to be sure, many individual Turks have a clear-eyed grasp of the Kurdish issue and are quite prepared to reach sensible accommodations with Kurdish aspirations for group rights and respect for their distinct culture. But at the level of Turkish law and officialdom, one encounters a rigid refusal to make concessions to this restive minority, some of whose members might be content with expanded opportunities for expressing their cultural identity within Turkey, whereas others would insist on establishing a separate Kurdish state.[4]

At a formal level, the official Turkish stance has been to pretend that a separate Kurdish minority with its own ethnicity, culture, and language does not exist. If Kurds inconveniently insist on revealing their presence, such as by demanding to use Kurdish, criminal sanctions may follow. Consulting the Turkish Constitution, one sees an instrument fashioned around the ethnic nationalist ideology of the majority Turks. The Turkish Constitution refuses to move beyond the fiction that all citizens of Turkey are Turks. Furthermore, Turkish laws set up a scheme for repressing and punishing discussion of the minorities issue; even asserting publicly that there *is* a minorities problem can expose one to criminal prosecution. The Turkish example shows how ill-conceived laws can block realistic efforts to come to terms with the claims of a large, disaffected ethnic minority, thereby sowing the seeds of further conflict.

Now, Turkey obviously has an unusually acute security problem because Kurds do not live in Turkey alone but are spread across the region, including populations in Syria, Iraq, and Iran.[5] Other powers in Turkey's dangerous neighborhood have tried to manipulate Kurdish groups for their own ends. Turkish government policy, largely dictated by security concerns, has been to clamp down harshly on any signs of Kurdish nationalism and to deploy military force to repress Kurdish separatism. The result has been exacerbated ethnic antagonisms, protracted guerrilla warfare, and savage terrorism and counterterrorism. The bloody war being waged to suppress rebellious Kurdish groups in southeastern Turkey has cost $100 billion, according to a recent *Financial Times* estimate.[6] After observing all these years of fighting to make the Kurdish problem go away, one has reason to ask: Are the policies of repression and attendant denials of rights to the Kurdish minority actually working to advance Turkish security? Or are they ultimately counterproductive, dooming Turkey to insecurity and encouraging patterns of rights violations that inevitably spill over beyond the confines of the Kurdish population?

It seems time to ponder Professor Uyangoda's assessment of the Sri Lankan case. Like Minister Mihailova and Professor Moodley in their assessments of the problems of ethnic nationalisms, he emphasizes how certain ways of conceptualizing political association can impede constructive approaches to ethnic conflicts. He shows us how a project of nation-state building can shape the identity imagination, and how, under the influence of a certain image of the nation-state, the majority community may come to lack the flexibility to transcend its restrictive ideology of nationhood. (Of course, in the case of Sri Lanka, the Tamil minority counters with its own vision of an ethnically exclusive Tamil nation.) Sclerotic modes of imagining the political community afflict many milieus in Turkey, just as they do in Sri Lanka.

However, when Turks' perceptions of the equities in disputes about minority rights are not beclouded by their entrenched nation-state ideology, they appreciate that ethnic minorities deserve protection for their cultural identities. Thus, for example, Turks immediately grasped the unfairness of the treatment meted out to members of the Turkish minority in Bulgaria when this minority was persecuted in the late 1980s by the faltering Bulgarian Communist regime. Bulgaria's Communists, fearing that they were no longer masters of the game, groped about for some winning card, finally opting—as Serb politicians caught in a similar dilemma would subsequently

do—to play the ultranationalist card. I happened to be in Istanbul in June 1989 at the time of massive public demonstrations protesting Bulgarian initiatives designed to obliterate the identity of the large Turkish minority. In their efforts to eliminate manifestations of ethnic difference, Bulgarian officials had gone so far as to resort to coercion to recast all Turkish Bulgarians as Slavs—even forcing them to take Slavic names. Turks demonstrating in the streets of Istanbul expressed outrage at these measures, denouncing them as human rights violations. Of course, the Bulgarian policies that were being attacked in Istanbul had certain parallels to what the Turkish government had been doing in suppressing the identity of the Kurdish minority in Anatolia.

Minister Mihailova's paper reminds us how dramatically Bulgarian politics have altered since the collapse of Communism. As Minister Mihailova shows us, the Bulgarian state has been reimagined on a basis of democratic values, pluralism, and respect for human rights, including stringent protections for minority rights. By adopting the human rights tenets of the European system and embracing principles ensuring justice and equality for all, the current Bulgarian model offers a way to appeal to the moral imagination of Slavs and Turks alike. Placed in the European context, Bulgaria's new approach, affording human rights to all its citizens regardless of ethnicity, is not seen as a sacrifice or capitulation to minority demands but as a positive initiative from which all stand to benefit.

Among its many strong protections for human rights, the Bulgarian Constitution now specifically provides in Article 7 that a child's name shall be freely chosen by the child's parents and makes it a crime (Article 17) to use threats, force, or other illegal actions to determine or change names. In our interconnected world, one in which people study the constitutions of other countries, Turks in Turkey will read this provision, and they will be struck by the dramatically changed rights philosophy that it embodies. I like to think that many Turks will draw inspiration from Bulgaria's unequivocal repudiation of the old Communist techniques of suppressing ethnic difference in the interests of upholding the fantasy of a monoethnic Bulgaria. If Turkey borrows ideas from the Bulgarian constitutional model, a new approach more favorable to recognizing the rights of ethnic minorities in Anatolia might result.

Like Bulgaria, Turkey is attracted by the prospect of becoming part of the European Union. Because Turkey has started moving forward—albeit in fits and starts—toward membership in the union, Turks have an incentive to rewrite their own constitution to meet European standards for protecting minority rights in multiethnic states. Of course, meeting the European standards that Minister Mihailova discusses will entail radical revision of Turkish policies on ethnic minorities, but doing so in the context of integration in Europe may make this adjustment more comfortable. As Minister Mihailova proposes, issues of minority rights should be placed in a regional framework. When they are, the benefits of the European model seem more obvious. Among other things, by visualizing the problems of ethnic minorities in a wider, regional setting, Turks can grasp how the millions of Turks now living outside of Turkey will benefit from a system guaranteeing minority rights. That is, it will not seem so much like a loss for Turkey's Turks if they recognize Kurdish rights at the same time that they join a system that ensures that Turkish ethnic minorities elsewhere will have strong protections for their rights. Turkey stands at a juncture where it is possible to commence reimagining the terms of political community within a broader European framework and rethinking the question of ethnic minorities in ways that may enable Turks to see the equities of the Kurdish question in a new light.

In what may prove to be a milestone in Turkish politico-legal history, Judge Ahmet Necdet Sezer was elected as the new president of Turkey on May 5, 2000—too late for the significance of this development to be considered by our panel. Formerly the president of Turkey's Constitutional Court, Judge Sezer had a record of outspoken criticisms of the deficiencies of Turkey's constitution, the restrictions on democratic freedoms, and the ban on teaching the Kurdish language. On April 25, 2000, he spoke on the thirty-eighth anniversary of the Constitutional Court, proclaiming: "A pro-freedom liberal and pluralist constitution which brings to life the principle of a state based on the rule of law is necessary [for Turkey] to be able to join the international community of modern democratic states."[7] That someone who had publicly enunciated this iconoclastic position could be elected

president shortly thereafter suggests that Turkey's ingrained resistance to reconsidering its policies of suppressing ethnic difference is breaking down. It hardly seems coincidental that it was a jurist immersed in constitutional law who came forward with bold proposals for revising Turkish law to meet modern international standards. Judge Sezer's approach dovetails with views articulated during our panel in support of the notion that sound principles of constitutionalism and the rule of law should inform our efforts to devise just solutions to controversies about minority rights.

Turkey's policies vis-à-vis the Kurdish minority may have been wrongheaded and even counterproductive, but at least, if one accepts certain premises, they may be said to have aimed at an intelligible goal—preserving intact the Turkish state. Especially with the regime in adjacent Iraq having launched two major wars in the last two decades and with the situation in northern Iraq being so explosive, Turkey can make an argument that according greater autonomy to the Kurdish minority, which is concentrated on a strategically sensitive border, would open the way to subversion and more violence. That is, it can point to elements in its peculiarly perilous geopolitical setting to explain its curbs on minority rights. In contrast, we witness some governments undertaking policies that have no relation to the national interest and that can only be characterized as criminally stupid—at least if their authors do have any concern for holding their states together and avoiding devastating interethnic warfare. In societies already strained by ethnic rivalries, we sometimes encounter governmental initiatives that are so poisonous to ethnic relations and so catastrophic in their implications for peace that no responsible political actor would ever pursue them. Minister Mihailova decries the destructive impact of the rash pursuit of short-sighted ethnic nationalist agendas that ultimately culminate in turmoil and death. She naturally focuses on the Balkans, but those of us who observe African developments see disturbing parallels there.

The Sudan, enmeshed in a devastating civil war since 1983, provides an apt example of the havoc and misery that can be wrought in a multiethnic and multiracial state by foolhardy government initiatives that are guaranteed to magnify intercommunal antagonisms. A country divided between a largely Arab Muslim North and a largely African Animist and Christian South, which constitutes about one-third of the population, the Sudan is a highly unstable polity. It was a thuggish and unpopular military dictator, Ja'far Nimeiri, who in 1983 decided suddenly to impose Islamic law as the law of the land. It would be simplistic to see his Islamization campaign as a mere instance of Islamic fundamentalism run amok. Nimeiri was not a pious Muslim but a nervous dictator in search of a gimmick that would shore up his tottering regime. He decided to risk measures that he hoped would impress the powerful local Islamic fundamentalist constituency, including the movement that was headed by Hassan al-Turabi. Lacking any empathy for the feelings of the African minority, Turabi and his followers had been pressing for establishing the Sudan as an Islamic state and making Islamic law the law of the land.

Professor Uyangoda aptly notes how the question of state power affects perceptions of ethnic difference. Because promoting Islamic law was identified with the ascendancy of the Arab majority, the Islamization program was not only taking a position promoting one religion but also taking sides in an ethnic and racial quarrel, proclaiming that the government would be endorsing an Arabo-Islamic identity.[8] Southerners rightly apprehended that the North would attempt to stamp all Sudanese with this identity. When the national government in Khartoum endorsed Islamization, this crudely underlined and exacerbated the differences between Arabs and Africans and provoked the Sudan's second civil war, which has outlasted Nimeiri's dictatorship and a brief democratic interlude and now continues under the Bashir military dictatorship.

The primary response of the South has been to insist on an inclusive polity and to fight to force the North to roll back the Islamization measures. That is, in the Sudan, it is the ethnic minority that champions the cause of a democratic, pluralistic state under a constitution that affords equitable treatment for all groups. This provides a neat contrast to the Canadian situation, where it is the national government that embraces pluralism and inclusiveness, whereas the Quebec separatists press demands based on a narrow ethnic identity. Living in a region comprising a multiplicity of ethnicities, Southerners with a grip on local political realities appreciate that ethnicity cannot serve as the basis for viable

political organization. The Southern perspective was highlighted when John Garang, the most important of the Southern leaders, engaged in an exchange of letters in the period December 1999–January 2000 with the Northern leader Sadiq al-Mahdi, who was not directly implicated in the Islamization measures but whom Southerners accuse of supporting the Islamization agenda and betraying Sudanese democracy. Showing impatience with Northern attempts to impose unilaterally various formulas that were supposedly designed for achieving peace, Garang forcefully laid out Southern demands. He insisted the South was struggling for justice, equality of all nationalities and cultures, fair play, an even political ground, and equality of opportunity for all irrespective of religion, race, or gender. He also denounced the monstrous idea of an Islamic constitution in a multireligious and multicultural country like the Sudan and decried the efforts at forcible Islamization and Arabization.[9] Whether the deep wounds caused by this prolonged, merciless war can be healed is an open question, but heeding Southerners' protests and seeking to address their demands for justice and equality via a democratic process would be a positive beginning.

The Sudanese situation is tragic enough, but recent developments in Nigeria provide special cause for dismay. One of the saddest things to see is officials who have had an opportunity to learn from experiences of neighboring states what they should *not* do taking precisely the steps that are *most* likely to maximize interethnic resentments and conflict. For those of us who have watched appalled as civil war has ravaged the Sudan, the implications of the Islamization measures recently inaugurated in northern Nigeria are troubling. Like the Sudan, Nigeria is an artificial concoction of British colonialism that joins together a variety of ethnicities under one roof, and their uneasy coexistence means that this state is particularly fragile. Nigerians have endured decades of tensions among major ethnic groups, like the predominantly Muslim Hausa-Fulani ethnicity, which is concentrated in the North, and the predominantly Animist or Christian Yoruba and Ibo ethnicities, which are dominant in the South. These tensions have flared up in occasional clashes and have already led to the bloody civil war of 1967–1970, when the Ibos fought unsuccessfully to secede. Subsequent misgovernment by a string of military rulers and massive corruption degraded Nigeria's national institutions. However, after suffering for years under Sani Abacha's egregiously kleptocratic dictatorship, Nigeria was freed in 1999 by the sudden demise of the despotic Abacha and then blessed by a return to democracy. The new president, Olusegun Obasanjo, comes from the South and has shown a commitment to democratic principles and reform. But, soon after taking power, the new national government had to confront some preliminary Islamization measures, which were taken in Zamfara state in October 1999. These were shortly followed by the imposition of Islamic law as the law of the land in various other states in the North in February 2000. These Islamization programs do not have exactly the same connotations that Islamization has in Sudan because they are being imposed by state governments, not by the national government, and in a country where all the competing ethnic groups are racially African. (Of course, as Professor Moodley reminds us, it is not the *degree* of difference that determines the intensity of ethnic conflict!)

The imposition of Islamic law by Northern states has been read as throwing down the gauntlet to Nigeria's non-Muslim ethnicities. Lethal rioting has broken out in which one ethnic group has been pitted against the other. Violent reactions and counter-reactions have spread around the country, from the North, where non-Muslims are in the minority, to the South, where the situation is reversed.[10]

This bodes ill for the future. As Professor Uyangoda observes, majority-minority riots make for a "hypersensitized understanding of differences," and in the course of riots, ethnic groups "rediscover each other in terms of enmity." The long-term consequences that this bloodletting could have for Nigeria are frightening to contemplate.

The authors of Nigeria's national laws had anticipated how sectarian favoritism could disrupt the new democratic order and had sought by prudent prophylactic measures to prevent this. After the restoration of democracy, the Nigerians devising the 1999 national constitution sought to prohibit the state from becoming too closely associated with any one religion. Both the Nigerian federal and state governments are legally bound to treat all religions equally, and Section 10 of the Nigerian Constitution states that the government of the federation or of a state shall not adopt any religion as the state religion. Of course, by opting for Islamization of their legal systems, the northern Nigerian states were effectively signaling that they were adopting Islam as the state religion and thereby endorsing Islam as their ideology. In doing this, they flouted the constitutional provisions designed to preclude such governmental promotion of any particular religion in a context where this would inevitably be associated with favoring a particular ethnicity at the expense of others. Now, I concede that Professor Moodley's assertion that antagonistic communal perceptions lie outside the reach of state law may have some validity—at least insofar as she means that such perceptions cannot be automatically altered for the better by state law. However, the Nigerian example shows how antagonistic communal perceptions can be intensified by enacting precisely the wrong kind of laws. Again, I would argue that this proves that law is far from a negligible factor in determining relations between ethnic communities.

Analysis of the Nigerian case suggests that it may be one of the instances when ethnic conflicts have been artificially engendered by politicians seeking to profit from the resultant strife. As has happened elsewhere when ambitious politicians exploited intercommunal tensions or sought to inflame ethnic hatreds to further their personal agendas, Nigeria's Islamization measures may have been deliberately encouraged in order to provoke mayhem as a way to destabilize the new democratic order. Members of the Northern military elite, disappointed at losing their places by the lucrative troughs that had for years abundantly satisfied their grandly mercenary appetites, may have cynically calculated that intensified ethnic conflicts would give them an opportunity to sideline the democratically elected government and return to power, either as rulers of Nigeria or of breakaway states that could be converted into personal fiefdoms along the lines of the Serbia of Slobodan Milosevic.

Yes, political actors' propensities to pursue short-term political goals do mean that the goals of laws devised to establish peace and secure justice in multiethnic states may be thwarted. Nevertheless, we still need to make every effort toward enacting the laws and devising the constitutions that are best calculated to promote peace and secure the rights of ethnic minorities, treating these as two goals that may sometimes appear to be at odds but that we should strive to render compatible. While recognizing the merits of Professor Moodley's vigorous critique and granting that we have seen much over the last decades giving us cause for acute pessimism, I nonetheless maintain that because law has the potential to do a great deal of harm or a great deal of good it behooves us to work to ensure that it does the latter.

In this connection, I turn again to the Balkans. When we survey the devastation that has befallen Sarajevo, formerly an oasis of multiethnic harmony, it is tempting to despair. But when we turn our eyes further eastward to Bulgaria, we see that developments on that once cheerless political terrain have moved in precisely the opposite direction, from egregious denials of minority rights and persecutions of persons because of their ethnicity to an incorporation of the most exigent European human rights standards and protections for the human rights of ethnic minorities. How unlikely it would have been for any of us back in the 1980s to project that Bulgaria would shortly move into the company of countries like Canada and Spain, becoming a proponent of enlightened democracy and maximal protections for the human rights of its ethnic minorities! Contemplating this remarkable transformation, we have grounds for heeding Professor Allott's admonition that we must open our minds to the prospect that everything could be otherwise.

Political Status and Democracy in Multiethnic and Multiracial States

Stanley N. Katz

This was an unusually stimulating session, and it was particularly interesting to me because it has ranged from what I take to be the pessimism of Professor Moodley to the optimism of Minister Mihailova. The fact that we have witnessed such extremes bears testimony to the fact that democracy and the rule of law come under very different pressures, and take very different forms, in the multitude of countries that constitute the modern world.

We learned one thing, at least, that was not intuitively obvious to me before this session, which is that the Bulgarian model of democracy and constitutionalism is something that we ought to put front and center. Too few of us are adequately informed about the post-Communist legal experience in general, and the Bulgarian case in particular. I am grateful to Minister Mihailova for her spirited presentation. But the session touched upon an admirably wide range of different parts of the world. Professor Moodley's emphasis on Canada has been particularly useful, since in thinking about multiethnic and multiracial states we must not forget to deal with situations that do not necessarily reflect overt strife and that seem more or less hopeless. We have now been given a couple of examples of conflictual situations in which there is reason to be quite hopeful that ethnic and racial conflict can be turned in positive directions. These obviously are situations from which we might learn.

It is a little surprising to me that, while we talked so much about ethnicity, more emphasis was not placed on religion and especially on language as sources of social and legal conflict. I am also sorry that we did not attend more to economics, although we verged on the subject at the end of our discussion. It can be argued, after all, that ethnic and racial harmony depend at least in part on a certain level of economic well-being in a society. I was, however, impressed by the extent to which several of the participants referred, in one form or another, to regionalism. The prospects for regionalism or at least supranational structures as a means to resolve what are now thought of as internal problems is a lively topic of debate these days, and we could have taken the idea further.

And we didn't discuss at all the antithesis of liberalism, group rights and the reconceptualization of the state and of constitutionalism around groups as opposed to individuals, although Professor Uyangoda mentioned it. The notion that the nation is, or should be, built around groups rather than individual rights is a serious argument in many places, and it is occasionally a reality at the constitutional level. A related matter, the question of multiple racial and ethnic identity, also came up only at the very end of our exchange. My impression is that multiple identity is becoming a more and more important problem in all parts of the world and that it is one that may require some rather fresh thinking.

Of course, there are many, many other questions that we might have addressed, but there simply was not sufficient time in this very lively session. I am particularly sorry that we did not find time to speak of the need to provide the legal constitutional structures necessary to create and sustain the organizations of civil society, for we need to know much more about the interrelationship of constitutionalism and civil society. But each of the presentations was superb, and the questions were very good.

I feel, however, that I must conclude on a sad note. As I listened to this fascinating discussion, I could not help but remember the days when we first began planning this conference. It saddens me, and I know many others who were present, that Neelan Tiruchelvam, who had been invited to be part of this conference, was assassinated in the summer of 1999. Neelan is a martyr to the goals that everyone who took part in the session shared—especially in his lifelong struggle to bring the power of law and compassion to bear upon the resolution of ethnic, religious, and linguistic disagreement. I can only hope that the proceedings of this conference will further Neelan's commitment to a fully democratic, constitution-abiding world.

The Supreme Court building, Washington, D.C. *Source:* Library of Congress.

Plenary Sessions

Editors' Note

Two crucial questions seemed so pressing to us, given the needs of new democracies in several regions of the world, that we organized sessions with a format to permit more interaction among the panelists and questions from the audience.

The first plenary session asked the question: Do democracy, legitimacy, and the rule of law necessarily go together? While it is clear that in American experience the three concepts are closely linked and that, as Thomas Franck argues, they are the three essential components of good governance, the history of other cultures suggests that no necessity binds these concepts together. Electoral democracy does not guarantee either the rule of law or legitimacy, as some modern "illiberal" or bogus democracies illustrate. Free and fair elections do not necessarily lead to governments that follow due process or permit judicial review of government acts. Elected majorities can be intolerant and despotic. The Chinese, as Daniel Fung makes clear have known legitimate government for centuries, if not millennia, but they have not experienced either democracy or the rule of law (as contrasted to rule *by* law). In recent years, Hong Kong has enjoyed the rule of law, although the legitimacy of its government has been threatened and challenged. What is required for good governance is a balance among the three concepts, what Rosalyn Higgins calls "these mutually reinforcing limbs of the essential trilogy." We live still in a world where national sovereignty protects against international inquiry into all but the most egregious and murderous lapses from the standards of good governance, but such international standards are slowly evolving as the democratic ethos becomes more firmly rooted in more countries.

The second plenary session asked the question: Can law be used to hold the past to account? A spirited divergence of views appeared. The principal difference of emphasis turned upon the importance accorded to remembrance, retribution, or reconciliation. Shlomo Avineri, who, having been born in Krakow, lost almost his entire family in the Holocaust, cited the precedent-setting character of the Nuremberg trials as the basis for German acknowledgment of Nazi barbarities but questioned Nuremberg's applicability in, for instance, the union of East and West Germany. He emphasized that for him the crucial act was remembrance. Working to keep alive the memory of what happened and why it happened made a different future possible. In this, the positive German example stood out in contrast, for instance, to Japan's unwillingness to face its past. Luis Moreno Ocampo was a prosecutor in the Argentine trials of the generals responsible for the regime that led to thousands of "disappeared." He sees the investigations and public trials of those accused as essential to the society's acknowledgment of its past. The information and debate made possible by the trials led to a civil society committed to democracy. "Politically and emotionally, the trials were critical to Argentina's attempts to serve justice." Without the information revealed by the trials and the judgments of guilt, it would not have been possible for Argentinians to live together, to acknowledge the past and move to the future. They needed a civil society that could function without the cancer of continual accusation. Alexander Boraine, vice chairman of South Africa's Truth and Reconciliation Commission, agrees that "for stability and the restoration of dignity to victims there must be accountability for the past." After a review of the possible options, he describes the South African model "with its emphasis on restorative justice and its unique approach to limited amnesty and victim hearings. . . . Where there exists a need for peaceful coexistence, justice must become something more than punishment; it must become inextricably linked to revelation, truth, and redemption." The stories of forgiveness are a powerful glue in a reconciling society, but a victim must know *whom* to forgive and *for what*. Truth must be personal and not merely abstract.

Democracy, Legitimacy, and the Rule of Law: Linkages

Thomas M. Franck

The Three Concepts Defined

Democracy, as its etymology makes clear, concerns the role of the people in their governance: the right of persons in a political community to participate meaningfully in the process by which they define and implement values, priorities, and policies. Thus, at its most basic, democracy can be symbolized by the polling station and voting booth.

Legitimacy can be symbolized by Robert's Rules of Order. It is the aspect of governance that validates institutional decisions as emanating from right process. What constitutes right process is described in a society's adjectival constitution or rules of order, or is pedigreed by tradition and historic custom. When a statute is openly debated in Congress after public hearings, passed by a majority of duly elected members of both houses, and signed by the president, it may be said to be legitimate. This legitimacy makes it more likely that those to whom the law is directed will feel a pull toward compliance with it.

The *rule of law* can be symbolized by a judge's gavel. It manifests itself in the willingness of all actors in a political community—citizens, corporations, unions, legislators, regulators, judges, and national and local political leaders—to defer to what H. L. A. Hart has called the community's agreed primary "rules of recognition," the "grund-norms," to use Hans Kelsen's term, around which the community, its institutions, and liberties are organized and justified. These "primary rules of recognition" are available to test the validity of any disputed instance of governance or exercises of authority.

The rule of law need not invariably involve courts. At its most basic, the rule of law may also be seen as per-sonified by the corner traffic light. Cars on a busy intersection stop and go in obedience to a normative, albeit mechanical, allocator of rights and duties in accordance with an agreed definition of fairness and equality. Cars at the light stop or go on its signal rather than, for example, in accordance with the democratically or politically expressed preference of those at the intersection itself.

At a more sophisticated level, the rule of law implies that courts—applying legitimate law made by democratically elected legislators but themselves isolated from democratic will and political discourse—determine whether a proposed exercise of power is procedurally legitimate and accords substantively with fundamental rules of fairness agreed by the democratic process.

Instinctively, one feels that these three constituents of a free and just society—democracy, legitimacy, and the rule of law—must be conceptually linked and inter-dependent. The 1776 Declaration of Independence claimed for citizens of the United States the right to be governed by those deriving "their just powers from the consent of the governed." In 1789 the French Declaration of the Rights of Man, too, proclaimed the "natural and imprescriptible" right of every citizen to liberty, equality, property, and security. With magnificent self-assurance, these foundational documents assume a linkage between democracy, legitimacy, and the rule of law.

In the 200 intervening years, the strands of good governance—democracy, legitimacy, and the rule of law—have strengthened, become more firmly intertwined, and lengthened to extend far beyond America and France.

Especially dramatic has been the recent vitality of the democratic entitlement.

Speaking to the 1999 UN General Assembly, President Thabo Mbeki of South Africa said, "I believe it would be correct to say that the overwhelming majority of countries in the world have opted for democratic forms of government. Having learnt from their own experience, the nations have turned their backs on dictatorship."

Note that the president's formulation makes democracy tantamount to repudiation of dictatorship. But for a society to turn its back on dictatorship, its embrace of democracy is not enough. It must also embrace legitimacy and the rule of law. These may be linked, but they are not so inextricably linked as to constitute a "package deal."

The Three Concepts Distinguished

If the three concepts are examined closely, it immediately becomes clear that their symbiosis cannot be taken for granted.

It is possible to have the kind of democracy symbolized by the polling booth without either the legitimacy symbolized by Robert's Rules of Order or the rule of law symbolized by the judge's gavel. Consider the following hypothetical.

The state of Aurora has just conducted an election. The principal issue between Aurora's three political parties is the role of women in society. The Hard Party has campaigned for the disenfranchisement of women—their exclusion from the professions, higher education, and public life. The Medium Party has taken the position that women currently enfranchised, in the professions, higher education, and public life, should be allowed to remain but no new women should be admitted. The Soft Party has campaigned to retain the status quo, which admits women to the franchise, professions, higher education, and public life on terms of complete equality with men. The campaign also turned on several other unrelated issues such as the escalating price of bread and the high rate of unemployment.

In the event, in a free and fair election, the results were as follows:

Hard Party:	38 percent of the presidential poll and thirty-eight seats in Parliament;
Medium Party:	32 percent of the presidential poll and thirty-two seats in Parliament;
Soft Party:	30 percent of the presidential poll and thirty seats in Parliament.

Accordingly, the newly elected Hard Party candidate becomes Aurora's president and forms a minority government. Legislation fully implementing the Hard Party's program disempowering women is introduced into Parliament. By Auroran constitutional law, legislation can be passed only on receiving at least fifty votes in the 100-member Parliament. With the Medium Party split and with three of its members abstaining, the vote on the proposed law is forty-nine for and forty-eight opposed. The president then signs the bill into law despite its failure to garner the requisite fifty votes. Thereupon, Aurora's army overthrows the elected government, suspends the constitution, and declares the law on women repealed. It establishes a junta to rule for five years, promising, thereafter, to hold democratic elections.

In this scenario, a democratically elected government has violated the procedural rules that support its own legitimacy, thereby provoking a suspension of the rule of law.

Our scenario decouples democracy from legitimacy and the rule of law. That these three are not inextricably linked is readily apparent when one observes the recent phenomenon of what Fareed Zakaria has called the "rise of illiberal democracy." Zakaria argues that "for almost a century, in the West, democracy has meant *liberal* democracy—a system marked not only by free and fair elections, but also by the rule of law, a separation of powers, and the protection of basic liberties of speech, religion, and property." But, he notes, while the rise of procedural legitimacy and the rule of law in the West may have coincided with the rise of electoral democracy, these are not "immutably or unambiguously linked" and are "coming apart in the rest of the world." [1]

Democracy

As of 1999, it is estimated that approximately 120 of 190 national governments are legally committed to holding open, multiparty, secret-ballot elections with universal franchise. This is an unprecedented global endorsement of electoral democracy. While a few of these democracies may be more democratic in form than substance, most are, or are becoming, practitioners of meaningful political choice through a formal, periodic process of open electoral consultation.

This is a transformation of historic significance. Unfortunately, however, as our Aurora hypothetical and the realities in much of the world make all too clear, electoral democracy does not necessarily ensure either governmental legitimacy or the rule of law. Before considering that problem, however, it is necessary to note that free and fair elections themselves are not even sufficient conditions of electoral democracy.

True, there has been remarkable progress in ensuring that people have a say in free, periodic, secret, and multiparty elections. This progress, however, has become ubiquitous only in the past decade and still stretches the credulity of people accustomed to voting booths not as symbols of real participatory democracy but as a sham accoutrement of Potemkin's village. To mitigate this deep-seated skepticism, many national elections are now monitored by observers from the United Nations, the Organization for Security and Cooperation in Europe, the Organization of American States, and the Organization of African Unity. These observers have monitored the actual vote counting and, in some instances, have overseen the election campaign itself. After an election, these monitors have certified whether it was "free and fair" in accordance with standards established by the UN General Assembly.

While this is progress toward real electoral democracy, certification by international monitors that an election was "free and fair" may mean no more than that the registered voters were allowed to vote and their ballots properly counted. Democracy requires more. In particular, it requires that the elections be the culmination of a process—free and fair procedures of nomination, unfettered debate, equal access to media and to public spaces—that precedes and conditions the actual polling of voters. The electoral process, in fact, is likely to be free and fair only when it is the culmination of an ongoing democratic process and not its surrogate: For example, when the society has established a tradition of free press, religion has been disestablished, and oligarchies of class, gender, and money have yielded to equality of opportunity.

In this deeper sense, democracy is not nearly so universal a phenomenon as we may like to think. In the words of Martin Kilson and Mitchell Cohen, "What you see is not always what you get; democratization can produce regimes ostensibly democratic but substantively plutocratic."[2]

Seemingly free and fair elections may even become obstacles to democracy when—as recently in Bosnia—

they, and the crude campaigning that precedes them, tend to polarize the citizenry. Secretary-General Kofi Annan, contemplating the extremists recently elected in several ethnically divided societies, has ruefully observed: "democracy would be a wonderful thing, if only it weren't for the elections." Elections—even when free and fair—have sometimes seemed to approximate the conduct of civil wars by other means. Jamaica, for example, while maintaining a democratic parliamentary system, saw its rival political parties arming youth wings, turning "grass roots politics into block-by-block warfare. . . ."[3] Elections may also conduce to majoritarian totalitarianism. Recent elections in Kazakhstan, Peru, and Venezuela have cautioned us to recognize that a majority of today's voters, like those of Germany in the early 1930s, may deliberately choose government by illiberal populists. Party politics itself may turn illiberal. Elsewhere, the lure of winner-take-all politics has become so irresistible that election victory is seen to be worth any price by those bullying or buying their way to power. The phenomenon is by no means limited to the third world. A recent study of the effects of corruption on democratic politics in Italy concludes: "By attacking two of the fundamental principles on which democracy is based, the equality of citizens before institutions and the open nature of decision-making, corruption contributes to the delegitimation of the political and institutional systems in which it takes root."[4] Free and fair elections may make the problem of corruption worse, although under different conditions it may also make it better.

The worsening is likely to occur when the spoils of politics—over export licensing, for example—are uncontrolled by legitimate checks and balances and unreviewable by an effective judiciary. When public office provides the only good jobs, or when profound ethnic antagonisms become the basis for poisonous political parties, then murder and money, although deployed in formally free and fair balloting, result in bogus democracy and contribute to the corruption and delegitimation of power.

Legitimacy

The legitimacy of governance is determined by the degree to which those chosen to exercise power do so in compliance with the checks and balances of right process.

In practice, this means that those who are chosen to govern by democratic elections do so as the bona fide representatives of the people in a manner that promotes open discourse.

How responsive should the elected be to the will of those they represent? Societies and political philosophers disagree whether the elected elite should mirror the preferences of their constituents or give weight to the dictates of conscience and party.[5] It is clear, however, that legitimate representative government precludes the making of governmental decisions by deception, stealth, bribery, and other forms of venality. It excludes government in violation of prescribed parliamentary procedures, as was the case when Aurora's president signed a bill into law that had failed to receive the requisite majority in Parliament.

Government is also illegitimate—no matter how free and fair the process of its elections—if disproportionate powers are vested in unelected officials or if key officials are in practice publicly unaccountable. Finally, governance is illegitimate if elected representatives owe their mandate to grossly unequal electorates—what used to be called "rotten boroughs."

Illegitimacy in governance undermines public order and peoples' acquiescence in being governed. It promotes anomie, a popular belief that persons must look to their individual well-being without relying on officials who, even if democratically elected, act for special interests.

Even in the democracy that is the United States there is widespread unease about the legitimacy of governance. It is appropriate to feel unease at the control of U.S. foreign policy by one senator whose leadership is based solely on seniority and who was elected by voters with ten times the voting power of a Californian. Likewise, there is unease at the control exercised by lobbyists and the consequent distortion of the public interest.

This unease is reinforced by some of what our democracy produces. The Center on Budget and Policy Priorities in Washington, D.C., has recently concluded that the "gap between rich and poor [in the United States] has grown into an economic chasm so wide that this year the richest 2.7 million Americans, the top 1 percent, will have as many after-tax dollars to spend as the bottom 100 million. . . . [the richest] will have about $620 billion to spend" while "four out of five households, or about 217 million people, are taking home a thinner slice of the economic pie today than in 1977. When adjusted for inflation . . . these [eighty percent of] households' share of national income has fallen to just under 50 percent from 56 percent in 1977." While the national income has grown sharply in the past twenty years, "[m]ore than 90 percent of the increase is going to the richest 1 percent of households, which this year will average $516,600 in after-tax income, up from $234,700 [in constant dollars] in 1977."[6]

How can a democratic system featuring universal suffrage produce a distributive regime so heavily tilted toward the interests of a tiny minority of the enfranchised? MIT economist Frank Levy has concluded that the extraordinary recent reconcentration of income growth at the top is a consequence of the tax rules enacted by Congress "and those rules right now are shaped by money."[7]

We are all aware that the political power of money perverts our democracy directly by sloping the electoral playing field in favor of rich candidates. That undermining of the ballot box, however, is the least remarkable aspect of the problem. More insidious is the erosion by money of the legitimacy of Congressional lawmaking. Suspicion of opaque backroom dealing and drafting by money-wielding lobbyists has undermined the consent of the governed as surely as, if more subtly than, ballot box stuffing or military rule. It is not merely our electoral democracy that has fallen under suspicion. It is the very legitimacy of our parliamentary system that is now seriously at risk.

Sen. John McCain, R-Ariz., commenting on the power of special interests to block regulation and write legislation favorable to their interests—tobacco, the National Rifle Association, the petroleum industry—has observed that Congress is "gridlocked by special interests who control us with their big money."[8]

So widespread is the impression that money speaks far louder than votes in shaping the American political agenda that, in most elections, barely half the eligible voters bother to exercise their franchise. Worse, only about 20 percent of Americans between the ages of eighteen and twenty-four voted in the past two presidential elections.[9] In a system that features national elections every second year in which billions are spent to attract voter attention, many now believe that casting their ballot is essentially irrelevant to the lawmaking process. The result undermines not so much formal democracy as democratic substance and popular belief in the legitimacy of parliamentary governance by those elected. In the words of Justice Souter of the Supreme Court, "Most people assume, and I do, certainly, that someone making an extraordinarily large contribution gets something extraordinary in return." The nation needs "a political system in which there is some basic level of confidence on the part of those governed."[10]

After thirty years in Congress, Rep. David R. Obey, D-Wis., recently concluded that the U.S. electoral system, although formally democratic, has lost its legitimacy. "The democratic system in this country," he said recently, "is in crisis as never before in my lifetime. It's the ultimate destruction of the legislative process."[11]

The remedy is obvious. The legislative and executive process needs to be reformed by laws that reestablish the legitimacy of our institutions of governance, making them once again representative of the people's, rather than special interests', will and restoring the openness of the government's consultative and deliberative processes.

Even if accomplished, however, that alone would not cure all doubts about legitimacy. Even a governing process in which the will of the people was more perfectly represented in legislative outcomes might yet produce illegitimate laws. For example, recently, in wealthy, bankrupt Nassau County, New York, the federal government has had to initiate legal action alleging that the county's property assessment system levies higher taxes on black and Hispanic residents in poor neighborhoods than on those in wealthier, mostly white districts.[12]

Nassau County illustrates another way a formally "free and fair" electoral democracy may undermine the legitimacy of governance. There, the county tax rolls have been challenged on the ground that the representatives of a white voting majority have used their lawmaking power to skew the property tax system in favor of preponderantly white neighborhoods at the expense of nonwhite ones. If true, the duly elected legislature, openly representing the will of the majority, will have violated legitimacy's most basic rule: that the law treat likes alike.[13] That principle of legitimacy is not guaranteed by elec-

toral democracy. Indeed, Madison and others have argued that democracy has a penchant for factionalism and majoritarianism that readily puts it at variance with the principles of legitimacy.[14] To illustrate this tension, Professor Albert O. Hirschman has pointed to France's early (1793) introduction of male universal suffrage as a determinant cause in the extraordinary delay—until 1944—in extending the franchise to women.[15]

If legitimacy of governance is a problem in wealthy Nassau County, it is a much graver problem in the fledgling electoral democracies of Nigeria, Bosnia, Azerbaijan, Georgia, Benin, and Zambia, to name but a few where free and fair elections have not guaranteed legitimacy of governance. If those elected by free and fair elections use their legislative authority unfairly to maximize the goods allocated to "their" interest group or tribe, then democratic majoritarianism is all too likely to become a tool for oppression of minorities.

Rule of Law

To counteract the tendency of democracy to corruption and illegitimacy, societies have sought relief through the rule of law. Symbolized by the judge's gavel, the rule of law establishes a means of "accounting for and regulating legislative activity."[16]

Consent of the governed depends not only on formal electoral democracy but also on legitimacy of government and its fidelity to the rule of law. Absent a general belief in a system's legitimacy and in fidelity to the rule of law, even demonstrably free and fair elections come to mean very little. In particular, even electoral democracy cannot save the legitimacy of governance if significant portions of those governed have reason to believe that the rules made applicable to them by the majority are not those they would have chosen to have imposed on themselves were they the minority. In other words, a democratic legislative system that regularly produces outcomes that cannot be justified by reference to neutral principles of the rule of law in time will conduce to widespread public disaffection, cheating, noncompliance, and, in extreme cases, civil insurrection.

Precisely to avoid that latent propensity in democracy to illegitimate governance by manifest preference for the interests of voting majorities—or, worse, for moneyed interests that sway voting majorities and its legislative representatives—most mature political systems have provided one form or another of the rule of law to balance both the principles of electoral democracy and parliamentary supremacy. In the United States, reliance on the rule of law is embodied in the federal constitution and the practice of the federal judiciary since *Marbury v. Madison*.[17]

The need to balance democracy and safeguard legitimacy through implementation of a rule of law has been widely recognized in the recent global resurgence of democracy. UN Secretary-General Kofi Annan has cautioned that states fail when their ruling regimes no longer meet the minimal, legitimate expectations of their people. This is most likely to happen when there is a tendency of political elites to equate "democracy" with a form of "majority rule," which, in effect, licenses the suppression of opposition and the weakening and disempowering of civil society.[18] The result is a loss of civil balance. Professor James Paul adds that in "these states the existing constitutional order has, in effect, been embezzled by predatory elites ... and governance has been converted into a despotic system increasingly geared to private gain. ..."[19] There is no mystery about how to prevent this: by a careful balancing of electoral democracy, legitimate parliamentarism, and judicial review. The need for this balance is recognized not merely as a political but also as an economic requisite for social cohesion and progress. In the words of Alan Greenspan, chairman of the Federal Reserve Board, "The guiding mechanism of a free market economy ... is a bill of rights, enforced by an impartial judiciary."[20]

When such balance is lost, all may be lost. Unregulated electoral competition, naked parliamentary supremacy, or unbridled judicial intervention will destroy that quality of governance that earns public acquiescence. It thus becomes clear that while democracy, legitimacy, and the rule of law are different, they are bound together as utilitarian requisites that, when in balance, guarantee governance that induces people willingly to participate and comply.

There is no objective standard for prioritizing or balancing the powers of the ballot box, Robert's Rules of Order, and the judicial gavel. That they are each necessary to the other is demonstrable. That they are, to a degree, adversaries is inevitable. Robert Filmer in 1648 illustrated the dilemma: "if the King be judge, then he is no limited Monarch. If the people be judge, then he is no Monarch at all. So farewell limited Monarchy, nay farewell all government if there be no judge."[21] One might add that, if the judge be judge, farewell democratic will and parliamentary governance. In a mature, stable, and liberal society, the voters, legislators, and judges must know, instinctively, that only through an equilibrium between them can there be the social order that signifies popular acquiescence in governance and facilitates progress. That balance requires restraint, a conscious abnegation of each party's strongest claims.

The Road to Good Governance

During the early years of decolonization and the cold war, there were some who believed that good governance—democracy, legitimacy, and the rule of law—were gifts bestowed on a people only when, through economic and social development and in the fullness of history, they had earned them. By this reasoning, totalitarian rule could foster the day when a people were ready for these gifts by expediting economic and social transformation. This "mobilizational" view is now generally rejected both by scholars and by political leaders. Economic and social development, we now know, derives from good governance in accordance with the principles of democratic participation, legitimate exercises of institutional power, and the rule of law. Conversely, the absence of good governance causes economies to atrophy and societies to splinter.[22] It is right for nations, and for the international system, to address conditions of electoral democracy, governmental legitimacy, and the rule of law without distinction between nations' degrees of economic and social development because these latter are dependent variables of the former, not the other way around. As former secretary of state James Baker has said, "legitimacy flows not from the barrel of a gun but from the will of the people."

This makes it appropriate for the global system to address all three aspects of good governance in societies without excessive deference to Westphalian notions of state sovereignty. As Secretary-General Kofi Annan has confirmed, the problems of nations' economic and social deprivation must first be addressed as problems of political governance, of constitutionalism. Moreover, the ill effects of grossly bad governance are also global: environmental degradation, massive flows of migrants, diffusion of deadly diseases, terrorism, growth of the narcotics trade.

As it happens, both economic and social development on the one hand, and politico-constitutional development on the other, depend equally on the same prescription: universal recognition of the ineluctable and equal rights of all to personhood. To quote once more Secretary-General Annan:

> State sovereignty, in its most basic sense, is being redefined by the forces of globalization and international cooperation. The state is now widely understood to be the servant of its people, and not vice-versa. At the same time, individual sovereignty—and by this I mean the human rights and fundamental freedoms of each and every individual . . . has been enhanced by a renewed consciousness of the right of every individual to control his or her own destiny.[23]

In other words, the quality of governance is the essential determiner of the quality of a people's economic and social life. This quality of governance can be measured by certain key indicators: Does the society hold periodic elections? Does it have a deliberative parliament? An independent judiciary? But these institutional indicators—the ballot box, Robert's Rules, and the judge's gavel—must be understood not only in formal structural terms but as instruments for the advancement of individual autonomy. Do all voters really have equal and autonomous weight in the electoral process? Do all citizens have genuine, equal, and autonomous access to the legislative and administrative process? Do all claimants have ready access to, and effective representation before, principled and independent judicial tribunals? Polling stations, Congressional records, and judges' gavels are forms and symbols but not the substance of good governance.

Globalization of Good Governance

To get beyond the formal, institutional indicators of good governance to the essentials of real democracy,

legitimacy, and the rule of law requires that all three elements be deployed substantively and concurrently in the constituting of states' sociopolitical architecture. Linkage is not automatic; they are not dependent variables. Yet linkage is essential if the three elements are to succeed in generating good governance. That essential linkage must be planned, deliberately executed, and protected against uncoupling.

In recent years, we have seen a globalization of this planning, execution, and protection of linkage between democracy, legitimacy, and the rule of law. Globalization is powered by growing realization that, first, the consequences of failed governance are felt globally, and, second, that there is a global convergence as to standards of good governance. Today, almost everyone knows, or could know, the essential elements of good governance. Accordingly, a universality of standards is being acknowledged and implemented without excessive fastidiousness for older notions of state sovereignty. It has dawned on us, in the words of Professor James Crawford, that "we need some form of collective democratic security."

This widespread, acknowledged need creates, equally, opportunity and danger. Both emanate from what Secretary-General Annan has called the current redefinition of sovereignty. When the fundamental rights of individuals—to life, liberty, and equal and meaningful participation in governance—are grossly denied, the international system now tends to react. When democracy, legitimacy, and the rule of law are subverted in a society, the victims of such subversion increasingly seek and find outside recourse. An example is the successful campaign of Letty Scott, an Australian Aboriginal woman, to arouse the world's conscience to her complaint against her government for the treatment of Aboriginals after her husband had committed suicide in a Darwin prison.[24] She sought and obtained help from the rich Pequot Indian Nation that runs Connecticut's Foxwoods Resort Casino, the biggest in America. They paid for Ms. Scott to take her cause to members of Congress, English nongovernmental groups, and the United Nations human rights subcommission. These made Letty Scott's case a global issue of good governance.

On the cusp of the new millennium it is timely to review the development of this new kind of transnational recourse. More than two centuries have elapsed since the signers of the U.S. Declaration of Independence endorsed two radical propositions: that citizens have "unalienable rights" and that those who govern derive "their just powers from the consent of the governed." Both these propositions expound a right of persons within their state, a right enforceable through national institutions and processes. Connected to these, however, was a third, even more radical proposition: that a nation earns "separate and equal station" in the community of states by exhibiting "a decent respect to the opinions of mankind." This suggests that states, in upholding the rights of their citizenry, are also accountable externally to "mankind."

Today, it is becoming more commonplace that governments, to be entitled to sovereign prerogatives, must acknowledge the inalienable rights of their own people. More to the point, governments increasingly acknowledge that they owe the obligations of good governance to their own populations, but also to *all* governments, *all* people, *erga omnes*. While democracy, governmental legitimacy, and the rule of law have long been the formal rights of persons in some nations, enshrined, however imperfectly, in their constitutions, processes, and institutions, it is only very recently that good governance is becoming a global entitlement recognized by international law, monitored by international institutions, and implemented through collective measures. When, a quarter century ago, the international system, acting through the UN, took responsibility for enforcing the democratic and equal rights of all the people of South Africa and Rhodesia—by blocking trade, investment, arms shipments, and sports matches with those racist societies—something fundamental changed in the old Westphalian canon of state sovereignty.

How a government governs is no longer a matter to be determined exclusively by each governing elite. Rather, it is increasingly recognized that all people are legally entitled to minimal standards of democracy, legitimacy, and the rule of law, and, increasingly, compliance with these emerging global standards is being monitored by intergovernmental and nongovernmental, judicial or quasi-judicial, international or regional institutions. At least in the most egregious instances of the violation of these norms they are being enforced by cultural and economic ostracism and, as in Kosovo and Sierra Leone, by occasional recourse to "collective measures."

The Emergence of Global Standards

The emergence of transnational standards of good governance is evidenced by at least twenty global and regional treaties and half a dozen tribunals before which violations can be brought to the world's attention. These standards cover all three components of good governance.

For the sake of economy, let us consider the instance of the globalization of the democratic entitlement.

The International Covenant on Civil and Political Rights,[25] now virtually universal in application, guarantees all persons freedom of thought (Article 18), expression (Article 19(2)), association (Article 22), and the right to "take part in the conduct of public affairs, directly or through freely chosen representatives [and to] vote and to be elected at genuine periodic elections which shall be by universal and equal suffrage and shall be held by secret ballot, guaranteeing the free expression of the will of the electors" (Article 25). Similar provision is made in Article 5 of the Charter of the Organization of American States, which requires the member states to promote "the exercise of representative democracy." Article 23(b) of the American Convention on Human Rights provides that every citizen "shall enjoy the [right] . . . to vote and to be elected in genuine periodic elections, which shall be by universal and equal suffrage and by secret ballot that guarantees the free expression of the will of the voters."[26] In Europe, Article 3 of the First Protocol to the European Human Rights Convention obliges the parties to "undertake to hold free elections at reasonable intervals by secret ballot, under conditions which will ensure the free expression of the opinion of the people in the choice of the legislature."[27]

Implementation of the International Covenant is overseen by the Human Rights Committee of elected, independent experts. In our hemisphere, implementation of the American Convention is entrusted to the Inter-American Human Rights Commission and Court. In Europe, more than a thousand cases have been brought by individuals—usually against their own governments—before the European Commission and Court of Human Rights. A significant number deal with the nuts and bolts of electoral democracy: for example, the right of a Swiss parliamentary candidate to run for office under her maiden name.

The emergence of this democratic entitlement, enunciated in international and regional law and monitored by transnational judicial and political institutions, is the most important single transformation in the global system since the end of the Second World War. It represents an emerging consensus that the quality of governance within states directly affects world peace.[28]

In recent years we have seen two striking examples of transnational enforcement of the right to good governance. One is the use of military force under authority of the Security Council to restore the elected government of Haiti after its overthrow by a military junta.[29] In the 1990s OAS enforcement machinery has also been invoked to block juntas' attempted assaults on constitutional governments in Paraguay and Guatemala.[30]

The second example is the use of force by the North Atlantic Treaty Organization in a successful effort to prevent the Federal Republic of Yugoslavia from meeting the demand for self-determination in Kosovo by expelling or killing a large majority of its population.

Such use of military force to compel sovereign states to adhere to international standards of good governance creates its own problems of potential abuse of power and hegemony. Paradoxically, it raises new questions of democracy, legitimacy, and the rule of law in the increasingly empowered institutions of global and regional governance. There can be no turning back, however, from the pursuit of democracy, legitimacy, and the rule of law, both as a global and equal entitlement of persons everywhere and as an aspiration increasingly supported by international as well as national laws, institutions, and morality.

Three things have become clear in this time of millennial transition. First, it is individuals, everywhere and equally, who are entitled to good governance as a widely recognized aspect of their inherent personhood. Second, good governance is constituted by a balance among electoral democracy, legitimacy, and the rule of law. These elements are not inherently linked or naturally symbiotic but must be conjoined and balanced through constant, deliberate effort. And, third, the entitlement of persons to good governance is no longer confined by old notions of state sovereignty but is recognized as tenable everywhere, in accordance with universally accepted standards that are increasingly implemented, where necessary, by transnational institutions and collective measures.

Legitimacy and Two Upstart Concepts

Daniel R. Fung

A cursory examination of the concepts of democracy, legitimacy, and the rule of law reveals how far the two brash young upstarts (namely, democracy and the rule of law), essentially products of Western civilization and culture, have joined the senior citizen legitimacy (long having been universalist in its application to political order and government) in being considered the indispensable building blocks of modern civil society.

Although democracy, or rule by the masses (at least insofar as the notion applies to free men), as a modality of government was known 2,500 years ago in the Greek city-states, modern political democracy has a pedigree of less than 200 years. The concept has enjoyed less than half the life span of the nation-state, historically postdating the Peace of Westphalia by at least two centuries.

The rule of law incorporating notions of predictability, transparency, and accessibility is even younger. Case decisions of the European Court of Human Rights and the United Nations Human Rights Committee on what may properly be considered "law" under, respectively, the European Treaty of Human Rights and the International Covenant on Civil and Political Rights are less than thirty years old. Other definitions of the rule of law as being the antithesis to the rule of man and embracing the principle of equality before the law, the idea of an independent judiciary, are somewhat older, tracing their lineage back to the eighteenth-century doctrine of separation of powers expounded by Montesquieu.

The notion of legitimacy, on the other hand, is arguably as old as human society. The idea of righteous rebellion against a tyrant or the overthrowing of an "illegitimate" foreign conqueror is as old as human civiliza-tion. In the East Asian context, the political doctrine that held sway from 221 B.C. to A.D. 1911 that the emperor of China ruled only through the mandate of heaven exemplifies this concept. The withdrawal of the mandate of heaven (evidenced variously by famine, floods, and foreign military depredations) would indubitably legiti-mate a rebellion and the ushering in of a new dynasty, the latest instances occurring in 1644 and 1911.

Transposing these three concepts to modern East Asia, one can immediately see that while one or other of the notions of Western progeny have been enthusi-astically embraced by some nations (for example, de-mocracy or at least elections by Japan, South Korea, and Taiwan in contradistinction to, say, rule of law by Sing-apore), no single sovereign state can validly claim an existentialist adoption of both.

This phenomenon is particularly marked in the Sinocentric world where two out of three components of Greater China, arguably the outer periphery, have each embraced one or other of the Western concepts (namely, Taiwan, democracy, and Hong Kong, rule of law) while the cultural core (the mainland portion of the People's Republic of China (PRC)) has arguably remained true only to the traditional notion of legitimacy.

Taiwan embraced electoral democracy for the first time in the late 1980s as a result of American prodding following the eclipse of the Chiang Kai-shek dynasty. Hong Kong has long enjoyed an ersatz rule of law under British tutelage, and while the quaint notion of a colo-nial rule of law may appear oxymoronic, the rudiments of the rule of law were sufficiently robust to allow for a maturing of the concept after the Sino-British Joint Declaration triggered the running of the sands of time from September 1984 through to June 30, 1997.

On the mainland the rule of the Chinese Communist Party (CCP) is deeply rooted in the notion of political legitimacy historically coalescing around the CCP's resistance to Japanese military incursions from 1931 to 1945 in contrast to Nationalist inaction, ineptitude, and corruption. Such legitimacy suffered an almost fatal body blow following the failure of the Great Leap Forward and, more importantly, the horrendous depredations of the Cultural Revolution. More recently, the CCP has pulled off a spectacular partial redemption in delivering, since the launch in 1978 of Teng Hsiao-p'ing's Four Modernizations Movement, over two decades of close to double-digit real economic growth throughout the country and, in the southeast coastal province of Guangdong (particularly the Pearl River Delta abutting Hong Kong), actual double-digit real growth throughout the 1990s prior to the onset of the Asian financial crisis in July 1997.

Today, each of these separate notions of legitimacy on the Chinese mainland, democracy in Taiwan, and the rule of law in Hong Kong are confronting crises of various degrees of gravity. On the mainland, increasing economic prosperity has triggered, inevitably, ever greater demands for freedoms of a personal, proprietary, and political nature. This has engendered, in turn, periodic backlashes, most recently exemplified by state suppression of the Falun Gong. Coupled with endemic corruption in the civil service, a grotesque and growing discrepancy in the standard of living between the prosperous coast and the impoverished hinterland, and the rise of Islamic fundamentalism in Xinjiang bordering former Soviet Central Asia, a crisis of legitimacy has confronted the rule of the CCP. Truly, Alexis de Tocqueville's dictum that the most dangerous moment is not when the totalitarian boot is firmly in place but rather when the same is slightly eased off has returned to haunt us!

In Taiwan the corruption of money politics, in particular the extraordinary wealth and efficiency of the Kuomintang machinery, has raised a question mark over the efficacy of the democratic electoral system in giving voice to the people's real concerns. Not surprisingly, the same issues of the role of money in electoral politics confront the people of Taiwan as they do those of the United States.

In Hong Kong the perceived confrontation of the judiciary by the Central People's government through the National People's Congress Standing Committee's interpretation of the Basic Law after a decision by the Hong Kong Court of Final Appeal has, rightly or wrongly, raised a question mark over the integrity of the rule of law in Hong Kong.

Each of these recent developments on the mainland, Taiwan, and Hong Kong are reasonably predictable. The challenges raised are difficult, but none insuperable. On the mainland, if the putative success of WTO accession could be balanced by controllable levels of consequential unemployment, if the Internet revolution could trigger a technology leap by China moving straight to wireless application protocol (WAP) technology while skipping the PC stage, the resulting prosperity will, in China as in the United States, lead to muted political opposition.

In Taiwan, if the specter of money politics could be mitigated by the successful presidential candidate resisting fanning the flames for Taiwanese independence in favor of maintaining sensible equilibrium in all the all-important cross-straits relations with the PRC, stability will flow.

In Hong Kong self-restraint by both the Central People's government (which has, thus far, behaved in exemplary fashion) and, perhaps more importantly, by the SAR government in vigorously guarding the principles of autonomy enshrined in the Basic Law and the Sino-British Joint Declaration, would ensure that the rule of law has a fair chance not merely of surviving but prospering.

Beyond these issues, much more important is the question whether each one of these three separate concepts of democracy, legitimacy, and the rule of law would be sufficient to ensure plain sailing by each component of Greater China in the twenty-first century. The answer must be an emphatic no. On the mainland both the leadership and the people recognize that without the rule of law the country would encounter extraordinary difficulties in further development. In other words, legal democracy must constitute the fifth modernization. This entails a profound transformation of mind-set and political will. The jury is still out as to whether such change is forthcoming.

In Taiwan whoever emerges as the victor in the March presidential elections will have to confront the issue of voter legitimacy in balancing the conflicting demands of stability in relations with the PRC and those agitating for greater centripetalism.

In Hong Kong the asset of an independent judiciary has long been recognized as an insufficient substitute for democracy and legitimacy. Although the Basic Law makes plain that questions of a fully elected legislature and a chief executive returned by universal adult suffrage cannot be structurally addressed until after 2007, these important questions have already surfaced in public debate and can-

not be postponed for another seven years. The SAR government is fully cognizant of these conundra.

Whether any of these difficult issues will be successfully tackled depends very much on political will, continued economic prosperity and stable cross-strait relations between Taiwan and the PRC, and, above all, stable geopolitical relations within the strategic triangle of China, Japan, and the United States. Nevertheless, the prognosis appears reasonably clear that without all three components—democracy, legitimacy, and the rule of law—no society can develop its full potential within the globalized economy of the twenty-first century.

Our "Virtuous Trilogy"

Rosalyn Higgins

It is a very great privilege for me to be invited to speak at this splendid symposium, in these marvellous surroundings, and to be participating under the chairmanship of Justice Kennedy.

The two papers from Thomas Franck and Daniel Fung provide us with the best possible intellectual framework. They are the catalyst for my own observations. Professor Franck's analysis of what precisely underlies the concepts of democracy, legitimacy, and rule of law is both brilliant and persuasive. He speaks of democracy as the right of persons to participate meaningfully in processes by which they derive and implement values and priorities. He speaks of legitimacy as the validation of institutional decisions by virtue of the fact that they emanate from "right process"—a process that, in turn, he identifies as being the constitutional rules of order or tradition and historic custom. As for the rule of law, the third element of our "virtuous trilogy," Professor Franck perceives it as lying in the deference of actors to primary rules of recognition by which disputes are authoritatively tested by those who stand distinct from those who are immediately elected. Mr. Fung, essentially agreeing with this typology, convincingly demonstrates that it is entirely possible for each of these elements to exist without the other in a given society. He uses Taiwan, the Republic of China, and Hong Kong to illustrate this point and to explain how these variables have come about.

It seems to me that we can all agree on two key points: that the three elements of our theme together maximize the aggregate of welfare to individuals, and that democracy is a necessary element for that outcome but is insufficient alone.

I hope in my remarks, when examining this triptych, to add some European and international perspectives.

Democracy

The democratic process must be meaningful and not encumbered with too many negative or qualifying elements.

Entry into and exercise of the electoral process must not be controlled by financial excesses or requirements that place an unacceptable barrier to real entry into the process and lay the way for domination by interest groups in its exercise. I have always thought that the crown jewel in the British democratic system is the severe financial limits that are placed upon the electoral process. Each individual member of Parliament may not spend more than about £8,000 in the election campaign. The election campaign is itself limited strictly in length, about three weeks being the norm. These provisions allow people from all walks of life to enter into the elected body politic. And if more than a pence over the statutory limit is found to have been expended, that person will forfeit his or her Parliamentary seat. These controls really are exercised and these outcomes really do happen.

Of course, there are still problems, as elsewhere, concerning the general funding of political parties, and these matters are among those under review in the Political Parties Election and Referendum Bill currently before Parliament.[1]

The financing of democratic elections is a global problem, as debates and events in Germany, Japan, Canada, the United Kingdom, and Australia, as well as the United States, clearly demonstrate. For the United States there appears to be a special problem in reconciling national perceptions on freedom of speech and the financing thereof with the manifest need for accountability and real opportunity to participate in the political process. The global need for democratic states to successfully address these problems cannot be overstated.

Democracy has to be more than the ability of the electorate to rid themselves of those who are elected. There have to be checks and balances in operation also *between* elections. Even in certain European countries, which we certainly deem democracies, there is still a culture of inordinate state power, with its impact on both the judiciary and the rights of individuals in the periods between the elections. It manifests itself in particular by an overly deferential attitude by courts to the state and by great difficulty in securing counsel at the bar to defend causes or persons known to be unpopular with the government of the day. Yet in such countries, whether in Europe or elsewhere, democracy is felt to be satisfied by the fact that if the public are dissatisfied they can get rid of the government at the next election.

It is absolutely essential for us to nourish the democracy we have. It goes without saying that one cannot afford corruption of the sort that we see in many corners of the world, notwithstanding democratic government. We fail at our peril to maintain the standards in public life that democracy requires. In the United Kingdom, for example, a certain public disenchantment exists side by side with an undeniable and great democracy. Through what has been passively allowed or positively encouraged to happen in the last two administrations, the public has come too often to identify politicians with "sleaze" (that is, with behavior unbecoming of those for whom we vote) and with "spin" (that is, with too great a priority being given to how news is presented to the public). The maintenance of full Parliamentary scrutiny has an important role to play for ongoing democratic control between elections.

The nourishment of democracy requires that government is not seen to act on behalf of only certain interest groups. And another very important element, especially relevant in countries where there is proportional representation, is for us to learn how to deal with the reality that the democratic voting system so often results in a constant return to office of the very same people with essentially the same policies. One party may rise in numbers and one may fall somewhat, a policy may be trimmed, or it may be expanded, but at the end of the day there is a considerable risk of alienation because when the electorate look back over twenty years, they feel that, notwithstanding the exercise of their right to vote, nothing has really changed and they have been offered no real choices. They have essentially been getting more of the same, and their vote, they feel, is counting for little. I think we cannot doubt that these elements have been felt rather keenly, particularly in Italy in the fairly recent past, and very recently in Austria. In the discussion on women's rights this afternoon, reference was made in this context to party lists. In the United Kingdom the introduction, for regional and European voting, of the "party list" of candidates is a phenomenon that is quite new. To some it is deeply alienating, as it seems to give too much power to the political parties and too little to the voter. Of course, the party list seems quite normal to other European countries. It is all a matter of political culture.

Finally, but certainly not least, we cannot afford in a democracy to fail to think about the duty to deliver economic equity and opportunity. Without that, we have an underclass that has its impact in the long term on democracy. Those deprived of the benefits of democracy, and those who care about them, understandably become contemptuous of it.

Tom Franck raised an interesting problem: that of the situation when the public itself votes for a limitation of constitutional freedoms. We heard this morning, of course, in the context of the question of return to constitutional rule in South America, that sometimes the retention of certain powers by particular elements is taken as the precondition for a return to democracy. Chile was a case in point. There is, of course, a further range of possibilities: public referenda to affirm certain self-imposed limitations, the revisions of the constitution, again put to a public vote, and periods where the courts have been put aside on the basis—not always without truth—that they are corrupt or unable to act in all the prevailing circumstances. The recent histories of Uruguay, Argentina, and Peru attest to the many variations on this particular theme. And we have seen the phenomenon in sharp relief in Algeria where a party that was publicly committed to limiting future elections was voted into power and then the result of that election was set aside by the outgoing military government, which continued to govern. And we are all wrestling today with the agonizing problems of Austria. In Europe there are certain requirements imposed on internal choice by European Union requirements. Yet, at the same time, we still have to ask ourselves the question of whether one can, in a democracy, exclude 27 percent of the persons who have taken part in the election under proportional representation from participation in government by virtue of the fact that it was the Freedom Party that got that 27 percent of the vote. While we may certainly feel we are entitled to offer our views on events occurring within other countries when they seem to impact upon human rights, the underlying question still remains. And the answer, I think, is far from easy.

It is easy to see that democracy requires nurturing, between elections as well as during them. But that exercise can itself present many difficult questions.

Legitimacy

Legitimacy is the second limb of our "virtuous trilogy." Professor Franck has put to the symposium the difficult question of how responsive those elected should be to those whom they have been elected to represent. Here, again, political culture has a large role to play. Referenda on a vast range of issues routinely held at federal and local levels, in Switzerland and the United States for example, would be unthinkable in the United Kingdom. In the United Kingdom there is still heavy debate on the circumstances in which referenda should be used, with consensus only on the fact that they may be needed to sustain legitimacy where issues of major constitutional departure are concerned. European Union entry, potential Euro participation, and devolution British style are examples. Even as regards these overarching questions there is the attendant problem that they involve the understanding of prodigiously complex technicalities. Some of the electorate feel that it is their elected representatives who are better placed to study and absorb all the elements, while others nonetheless insist upon an entitlement to participate directly.

At the philosophical level, the issue is one of reliance or otherwise on the old Burkeian principle of representative government rather than government by delegated powers from the electorate. The answer, which should be one of high principle, is complicated by the reality that—in my country at least—parliamentarians can often be more progressive than the electorate at large. If

I take the example of capital punishment, in the United Kingdom the majority would undoubtedly be in favor of capital punishment. But Parliament votes consistently against capital punishment in all of the various formulas in which it is sought to be reintroduced (including that of being limited to terrorist offenses).

At the end of the day, I think the exercise of a representative judgment is the best guarantee against majoritarian excesses—though care still has to be taken that the Parliamentary debates are reasoned, open, and intellectually accessible to the public if the concept of legitimacy is not to be undermined.

Professor Franck has characterized legitimacy as decision by "right process." Mr. Fung has shown how that understanding plays out in certain countries in Southeast Asia. Past history in, for example, resistance to the Japanese in World War II, or in delivering economic progress, are for him part of what constitutes perceptions of legitimacy.

There is perhaps a further question to be asked about legitimacy. Is the concept of "right process" to be measured only by such internal criteria or also by reference to external criteria? That issue, I think, is particularly relevant here in the United States, which for reasons of its very size, power, and geographic separateness has been disinclined to test "right process" and legitimacy by reference to international standards—even if it is party to instruments stipulating such standards. I refer to such instruments as the International Covenant for Civil and Political Rights. Looking outwards for the test for legitimacy can have the salutary effect of making one query one's own national processes that one has long taken for granted. In particular, it can bring into sharp relief the question of the relationship of a separation of powers to perceptions of legitimacy. For example, in my country we have a system where the head of the judiciary, the lord chancellor, also sits in Cabinet and occasionally also sits as a judge in the House of Lords. When one looks outwards one begins to perceive that what we in the United Kingdom treat as routine may to others look anomalous. In the United Kingdom the law lords, judges of the final superior court, also sit in the upper house of the legislature but by tradition limit themselves in that capacity to participating on legal matters. But even that is, and correctly in my view, today under debate and perhaps may shortly come to be regarded as inappropriate to a proper separation of powers.

The role of British home secretary in extradition matters has been very visible recently in the Pinochet cases. Of course, very many countries have a political input into the otherwise legal process of treaty extradition. That in itself can perhaps be queried, but in any event, that is a rather widely shared phenomenon. In the United Kingdom that role is, I think, rather less political and more quasi judicial than most. By that I mean that the home secretary takes no political advice on the matter at all, and the matter is not even discussed in government. But in all these examples—and many more could be given—the line between the executive and judiciary is often not nearly as clear cut as might be expected of states that accept in principle a separation of powers.

The Rule of Law

The rule of law requirement presents a series of problems of concern for us. It is often said, and particularly in countries undergoing certain political difficulties, that the exercise of a robust judiciary is, at the end of the day, undemocratic because it entails overruling what the elected representatives have decided to do. I think we have frankly to say that judicial recourse *is* "undemocratic" in that particular sense of the term and to acknowledge also that democracy carries the seeds of a majoritarianism. Democracy is one of the elements of our virtuous triptych, but not the sole or even superior element. So there is this inevitable tension, and this tension has to be minimized by ensuring a great public confidence in those who carry out this rule of law function—very often the judiciary. That in turn leads to a series of issues as to how judges are chosen: whether they are elected or nominated by Parliament or the president, whether they are selected by the head of the judiciary or selected by other means. The Committee on Human Rights, under the Covenant on Civil and Political Rights, although it had many firm views on many things, never took a formal stance on the issue of how judges should be selected because it was realized there are many possibilities that can, at the end of the day, turn out to be rule-of-law compatible. Nonetheless, all the many variations merit close scrutiny and reflection, and some are clearly more hazardous than others.

A related question is the pool from which judges are selected—from within the legal profession or from outside (with the attendant risk of selection being perceived as a return for favors rendered). There is the further dilemma that the tabloid press—an essential element for democracy—can pander to prejudice by constantly referring to judges as all coming from the same social class, with set views of society. This phenomenon is much in evidence in Britain. These assertions, usually far from the truth, merely exacerbate the built-in tensions. Is the answer parliamentary confirmation of judicial appointments? Clearly, there are significantly different practices as to the issue of how much the public needs to know about a judge before his or her nomination. Americans may well feel the British system is a very closed system, while the British will feel the U.S. system, at the end of the day, entails allowing the legislature to try to preselect in order to get certain outcomes within the judicial process itself. There are undoubtedly elements of truth in both of these perceptions.

Last night Chief Justice Rehnquist emphasized the importance of judicial review in countries that have written constitutions. In countries without a written constitution, such as the United Kingdom, judicial review does not serve to strike down legislation; there is no constitution by reference to which that can be done. But it serves to review the legality of the acts of ministers and public servants by reference to the test of manifest unreasonableness. Breadth of standing in judicial review cases is thus very important indeed. Breadth of standing in the United Kingdom in judicial review is very much wider than in the substantive legal actions themselves. So it was that Belgium, for example, was allowed to be a party to the successful judicial review action relating to the exercise by the home secretary of his discretion regarding the confidentiality of the medical reports of General Pinochet, though Belgium was not a party at all to the bilateral extradition treaty between Spain and Britain. The judicial review judgment required the secretary of state to release to the judicial review applicants the medical evidence that he had hitherto undertaken should remain private.

Under the new Human Rights Act, the hitherto external standards of the European Convention on Human

Rights become in England the yardstick for rule of law consideration of legality. Even so, so far as legislation is concerned, the courts still will not be able to strike down offending legislation; but they will be able to declare that the legislation is incompatible with the European Convention and it will go back to parliament for a fast-track procedure for reconsideration.

My final observations are on the issue of globalization and the requirement of good governance. Professor Franck has elaborated on this. I think we have to be very careful not to overstate where we now stand on legal expectations. Professor Franck spoke of new international consensus favoring reaction of the international system in certain circumstances. He suggested, for example, that NATO had engaged in a "successful effort to prevent the FRY (Federal Republic of Yugoslavia) from meeting a demand for self-determination in Kosovo by expelling or killing of the large majority of the population." But one could have a long debate about whether self-determination was at play there at all. I read things very much more narrowly. I think there has long been a right of intervention that predates globalization—that is, intervention through word of mouth—in human rights issues. For several decades now we have known there is no national sovereignty a state may invoke to exclude critical observation by other countries. But I believe that only where there is a large scale loss of life, genocide or the most heinous and visible expulsions, have we seen any predisposition to intervene physically. But for the other components about which we have today been speaking—that is, equal and meaningful participation in elections and public life, legitimacy, rule of law—I see no tendency yet to intervene in the absence of these entitlements. One only has to look around the world to see all of those states with whom we maintain friendly relations who do not provide these mutually reinforcing limbs of the essential trilogy to see how very limited the new developments are. This is not at all to say these developments are unimportant, but their scope of application should not be exaggerated.

Recent tendencies in globalization suggest two key things so far as rule of law requirements are concerned. The first is to ensure access to the international decision makers. Once we have participants and players, other than states, then there necessarily has to be a reference to external criteria of legitimacy. And the rule of law function must be elevated to this international plane. It follows that there is a pressing need for the international judiciary that reviews legitimacy to be endowed with an automatic jurisdiction. Secondly, there has to be a ready willingness by states and other international actors to comply with their decisions. Until these two things happen (which requires a certain moral and political leadership), we will continue to have an immature international system. And that immature system will confirm that while democracy is essential for the realization of the good society, alone it is not enough.

Historical Memory and Transitional Justice

Shlomo Avineri

1. In a literal sense, the obvious answer is no. The past cannot be held to account; only people can—this is true even more so when we relate to the law, which can be aimed and used only against persons. Even corporate entities—organizations, parties, security services—cannot be held to account apart from the individual people who make up their membership and composition. The "past" cannot be made responsible for anything; only people can.

2. But obviously, this is not a satisfactory answer. The question posed to us is, of course, wider: To what extent can one use the law and the judicial process as an instrument to hold former regimes—always after their defeat, disintegration, or demise—responsible for what appear to be inhuman and unacceptable acts by initiating legal action against some or all of their leaders and accomplices? This raises of course the issue of retroactive justice, selectivity, scope, and the very aim of the process thus undertaken. By calling the process "transitional justice" the major issues are not overcome.

3. The Nuremberg trials are the watershed in this respect. They clearly exemplify all the dilemmas involved: retroactive justice, a victors' trial, the problematic participation of the Soviet Union in the trial. However, the enormities of Nazi atrocities against civilian populations, the systematic eradication of designated ethnic groups, the scope of the extermination—all suggest that it is reasonable to argue that given the conditions of 1945 there might not have been any other way. It was the crimes committed by Nazi Germany—and not strategic considerations—that also made the Allies decide to push for a German unconditional surrender and the total dismantling of the Third Reich,

lock, stock, and barrel. The alternative to the Nuremberg trials would have been to shoot the Nazi leaders out of hand, but this, obviously, would have raised even more complex questions.

4. When we move from such enormities as Nazi mass murders to other cases—be they internal transitions in Eastern Europe, South Africa, Latin America, or recent developments in the former Yugoslavia, Rwanda, and East Timor—the issues are far more complex. Here the issue is to find a balance between keeping an historical memory as part of the national narrative, making individuals pay for acts that by any universally accepted standards were criminal (even if they were not criminal according to the law of the land when perpetrated), and last and not least, how to integrate all these considerations into a political project that at least partially aims at national reconciliation. To this one should add that in most cases of transition, yesterday's dictators turned over power peacefully, not voluntarily (they were, after all, forced to do so by the political circumstances), but in various ways—whether in Poland, South Africa, or Chile—the transition was part of a negotiated settlement. At the end of the day, Jaruzelski, de Klerk, Pinochet, and Honnecker participated actively or at least acquiesced in the transfer of power and the transition to democracy.

5. Let me state quite clearly that the issue of historical memory is to me much more important for future democratic development than the issue of transitional justice. The crimes of iniquitous regimes should be remembered in the national narrative: in schoolbooks, public monuments, in the calendar—in all the spheres of public space. Germany, for one, has been particularly

successful in this due to the fact that the German body politic was totally smashed by the Allies and a reconstructed Germany had to work hard to gain legitimacy in the family of nations. Japan (as recently shown in Ian Buruma's study *The Wages of Guilt*) never went through a similar process, and the consequences are showing. For that matter, the recent resurgence of a xenophobic and racist party in Austria has equally to do with the fact that Austrians never had to undergo the kind of internal process of facing their own past that characterized post–World War II West Germany. Austrian schoolbooks stop at World War I; phenomena like Waldheim and Haider would not be conceivable in the German context, paradoxical as it may sound. "Never Again," in all its variations, should be central to the political culture, but political memory and narratives achieve this more than the instruments of law.

6. I am much less sanguine about prosecuting leaders and accomplices of repressive regimes after a peaceful transition. I will limit my examples and arguments mainly to Central and Eastern European cases with which I am more familiar than Latin American ones.

7. Should one put on trial former Communist leaders and security service operatives? Should one introduce lustration? I have my doubts, and my philosophical and political position is similar to that of Adam Michnik. The cases of Erich Honnecker and Egon Krenz are a case in point, bringing out the ambiguities and moral inadequacies of a prosecutorial mind-set. While Honnecker was in power he was courted by West German leaders, and Chancellor Kohl even saw it as a justified achievement of his own policies when a state visit of Honnecker to West Germany was feted as an apex of a politics of reconciliation. Kohl himself played the generous host to Honnecker, and for years West Germany subsidized the economy of the GDR for reasons that were accepted by the whole West Germany political establishment. The vindictiveness with which the Kohl government then persecuted and prosecuted Honnecker all over the globe (chasing after him to Moscow and Santiago de Chile) is, at best, distasteful. Perhaps Kohl should also have been indicted as an accomplice given the fulsome language—and subsidies—he showered on his guest

Honnecker during his visit to West Germany. Similarly, the incarceration of Krenz—who, after all, was responsible for bringing down the Berlin Wall—is equally distasteful. When one remembers that some Waffen SS veterans get state pensions in West Germany—as did, until her death, the widow of Reinhard Heydrich—the sheer vindictiveness of West German justice is problematic. Nor did it help to create solidarity with the new democratic system among many former GDR citizens.

8. Lustration in Poland and the Czech Republic raises similar problems, especially as it is based on the archives of the former internal security services. The Gauck Commission in Germany is tainted by a similar burden. People who held high positions in the Communist system do not labor under any limitation, but sometimes unwilling or frightened collaborators with the security services are ostracized and their lives and careers totally ruined.

9. Should people then who were responsible for atrocities go scot-free? I do not think so, and perhaps the truth and reconciliation commission method is the best way to balance values of justice, remorse, and reconciliation. I am sure Alexander Boraine will be able to enlarge on this.

10. One final word about the international tribunals set up under UN auspices for the former Yugoslavia and Rwanda. I will limit my comments to the indictments connected with Bosnia (the Kosovo case is still wide open). This was not a victors' court, but in my view it was tainted and compromised by two other circumstances: First, it was set up clearly as an alibi by the UN for not doing what should have been done during the brutal Serb aggressions in Bosnia: use force against Belgrade. It was a placebo, an attempt to assuage the conscience of (mainly) Western democracies for sitting by during the years of the siege of Sarajevo and later the massacre in Srebrenicia. Secondly, by not bringing to court the major war criminals (Karadzic, Mladic) while prosecuting relatively minor figures, it basically undermined the legitimacy of the whole process.

11. As you can see, I am reticent in viewing the juridical system as an effective vehicle of either doing justice (in the sense in which we usually use the term to denote

the equal application of universal norms) or in keeping memory alive. Memory is central; it is hard work, mainly educational, and has tough political costs. Even in the case of Germany, where I do not have problems with the Nuremberg trials, what made Germany into the decent democracy it is today (vindictiveness towards the GDR notwithstanding) are not the Nuremberg trials but the constitutional, political, ideological, and educational continuing efforts of the Bonn Republic. If current winds of change in the so-called Berlin Republic would go in another direction, this would be a problem, but it is a political, not a legal, issue.

Beyond Punishment: Justice in the Wake of Massive Crimes in Argentina

Luis Moreno Ocampo

The history of power politics is nothing but the history of international crime and mass murder (including it is true, some of the attempts to suppress them).

—*Karl Popper*

In Argentina, between 1976 and 1983, thousands of people were secretly kidnapped and tortured in hundreds of detention centers throughout the country. More than 10,000 people were murdered by a military regime that took control with widespread national and international support.[1]

Argentina's military dictatorship came to power through a coup d'état to combat leftist guerrillas and attempt to solve the nation's severe economic crisis. The military dictatorship lasted until 1983, when a renewed economic crisis and Argentina's defeat in the war against England over the Malvinas/Falkland Islands ushered in a transition to democracy. Public trials were held in 1985 and 1986 to hold military officials responsible for the tortures and killings they committed. In all, 481 military and police officers were indicted; sixteen were tried—eleven of whom were top-level officers—and eleven were convicted.

The intent to extend the trials to some of the younger officers generated severe political tension and four military rebellions between 1987 and 1990 and strong manifestations in favor of democracy. Two laws to limit the outreach of the judicial investigations were dictated, and in 1990 President Ménem ordered that these officers be pardoned and released.

As a prosecutor in the trials of those responsible for state-sponsored "disappearances" and systemic torture, I realized the limits of using a criminal justice system to prosecute gross violations of human rights. Crimes like those committed in Argentina during the so-called dirty war were more complex than regular crimes: instead of upholding laws, authorities ordered them violated; law enforcement agencies committed crimes instead of preventing them; criminals were not isolated by society, rather they were supported by the elite; and finally, groups that the regime deemed problematic were systematically eliminated with no respect for their human rights.

Massive crimes require massive legal and societal solutions, solutions that extend beyond judicial remedies. Law enforcement agencies and judiciaries are not enough to establish the law. The information about the crimes generated by the trials is as important as the punishment. Punishment is just one part of the criminal justice system, and its application does not guarantee the reformation of the society or its authorities.

Civil society was strengthened through the investigations and public trials, which increased its commitment to and respect for democracy—a free press and free and open public debate. Stories about kidnapped children, atrocious tortures, and people being thrown from navy airplanes to their deaths at sea became household information. Knowledge about the violence employed by the military to fight "subversion" provoked a reevaluation of the past, and the military's claim of victory in the fight against communism was supplanted by humanitarian and legal judgments. As society expressed its increased investment to its commitment to democracy, the military lost much of its credibility and power.

As in past centuries, the active participation of citizens is required to establish a legal system that in turn protects and by which they feel represented. To improve the relationship between society, the elite, and the law, facts about the past must be uncovered and dealt with through institutions, public debate, and free press. Societal conclusions and consensus must in turn be reintroduced into the institutions.

Based on the example of Argentina, I propose four points:

1. The rules that were governing in Argentina were not the law but other rules.
2. The rulers were not only Argentineans. The decisions adopted by the U.S. Congress in 1959 and 1960 had defined the strategy.
3. The control of the information and its management were key both to be able to commit the crimes that were committed as well as for being able to stop and punish them.
4. Law enforcement agencies do not suffice to establish the law. The trial was the culmination and result of collective action headed by civil society groups.

1. The Rules That Were Governing in Argentina Were Not the Law but Other Rules

The functioning of a state-run organization reveals the limited scope of punishment. While individuals might act out of hate or passion against the guerrillas who are killing their comrades, such motivations can be more readily ascribed to the state apparatus ultimately responsible for the commission of those crimes. The perpetrators were not people used to breaking the law; on the contrary, they were members of the military and security forces that followed orders. While breaking the rule of law, those officers were acting with another set of rules in mind, namely the military rules, that ordered for undercover actions to be executed. This denotes the limited scope of punishment.

In September 1975 the military establishment secretly debated and approved a plan to fight and eradicate sub-versive communist movements once and for all.[2] They decided to implement an offensive strategy to stymie the guerrillas' attacks. To break the sworn silence among guerrilla members they decided to use extra-judicial methods of kidnapping and torture.[3] They planned to execute prisoners, based on the military's fear that the kidnapped victims would be released upon the slightest change of political power. In turn, Argentina's solution came in the form of clandestine executions—avoiding, they thought, an international backlash similar to what had transpired in Gen. Augusto Pinochet's Chile. The military needed absolute power to implement their plans.

On 24 March 1976 the armed forces staged a coup d'état. Legal authorities were removed, Congress was dissolved, and members of the Supreme Court and federal judges were dismissed. The chiefs of the army, navy, and air force formed a military junta that concentrated constitutional and political power in its hands.

Support came from all sides, including the business sector, which had been one of the main targets for guerrilla violence. According to the *New York Times,* there were more than 170 kidnappings of foreign businessmen reported in 1973.[4] The 1976 coup was either silently accepted or overtly supported, and virtually no political party tried to mobilize society in defense of the democratic system. The coup was not simply a case of the military imposing its will upon a reluctant civil society, it was the result of a civic-military alliance with foreign backing.

The junta established military courts to try civilians accused of supporting the guerrillas and often unspecified charges of subversive activities. While these courts were authorized to issue the death penalty, not one prisoner was officially sentenced to death.[5] In parallel to its own set of rules, the military established another set of rules "to make possible full control of covert operations."[6] This planning indelibly marked the kind of operations carried out, because no member of the armed forces was able to avoid taking part in the operations.

Argentina was divided into five zones and a general commanded each one. Each of these five zones was then subdivided and controlled by a subordinate general. These subzones were then divided further still into areas and then subareas.[7] Each zone commander was responsible for the operations that took place under his jurisdiction, reporting weekly to the commander-in-chief of the army. These reports included the number of people detained, their place of captivity, transfers, liberations, and executions.

At the disposition of each commander were intelligence groups dedicated to singling out suspected subversives and carrying out the eventual detention of these "targets." These intelligence groups used great discretion in identifying possible targets because the orders established that "whoever sympathizes or collaborates with subversive elements is as menacing as the members of a subversive group."[8] Under this argument, human rights groups and other civil society groups who denounced the crimes were targeted as subversives. The regime kidnapped parents of the disappeared for making public the fate of their loved ones.

The prisoners were systematically tortured in a secret center to get information. Zone commanders not only approved and controlled the detentions and tortures but also guaranteed the kidnappers' impunity by ordering that the information about those actions not be given to any authority.[9] Also, no other part of the security forces was to investigate or impede the detention, torture, or execution of the targets. Decisions about the fate of the kidnapped were made at military zone headquarters. To keep the disappearances secret, the corpses were either thrown into the sea or buried in unidentified graveyards.[10]

The military approach and the technical language employed to write the orders allowed those who planned and approved the actions to think of these as war strategies instead of common crimes. The authors of the laws did not attend torture sessions, nor were they forced to look into the eyes of people singled out to be killed. They attempted to clear their consciences by remembering that every war has innocent victims, that it was the necessary price for victory.

The illegal orders issued by the military generals meant that criminal law no longer acted as a deterrent. When a young officer was given the order of throwing a prisoner out of a navy airplane, he did not see any risk of being sentenced to life by a judge—but he did see the threat from his superiors should he disobey the criminal orders.[11]

Nevertheless, since Nuremberg it is clear that due obedience—the terminology that protects lower-ranking officers against superiors in the ordering of heinous crimes—cannot be used as a legal criminal excuse. But in order to protect human rights, preempting the organization of such a murderous bureaucracy is more important than trying to stop its crimes while they are being committed.

2. The Rulers Were Not Only Argentineans—the Decisions Adopted by the U.S. Congress in 1959 and 1960 Had Defined the Strategy

The rise of Argentina's murderous military regime also had its roots in the cold war. Under the direction of Fidel Castro and Che Guevara, and with support of the Soviet Union, there was a push throughout Latin America to export the Cuban model of seizing power through guerrilla warfare. To confront the threat of communism, the United States established U.S. military missions within the highest echelons of every Latin American army, a move that impacted millions of people throughout the hemisphere. Beginning in 1959, the U.S. military organized meetings of these Latin American armies with the specific objective of combating the internal communist threat. In Fort Benning, Georgia, and in Fort Gulick in the American zone of the Panama Canal, the United States trained thousands of members of Latin America's armed forces. The Argentine armed forces hired veteran French officers from Algeria as professors to give lectures and write articles about how to combat guerrilla warfare.[12]

The collaboration of military forces transformed the debate of how to manage the communist threat. The Argentine army was waging a war against an international army, using clandestine and unconventional methods. The constitutional rights of both the victims and the perpetrators were not to be considered.

The Argentine army's mission of internal control was officially introduced in 1964 during a speech at the U.S. Military Academy of West Point by General Onganía, then Army chief of staff: "It is absurd for us to continue preparing to enter the war of 1914. It is absurd for us to continue organizing heavy artillery . . . The main objective of the army is currently to prevent subversive communist activities."[13] The decision of the U.S. Congress was executed sixteen years later. As the rulers did not represent Argentine society, their constitutional guarantees did not have to be taken into account.

3. The Control of the Information and Its Management Were Key Both to Be Able to Commit the Crimes That Were Committed as Well as for Being Able to Stop and Punish Them

The military junta was able to build consensus by stressing its commitment to society's common goal of ending guerrilla violence while hiding the means—torture and illegal executions—to achieve it.

To hide the fate of its victims, the military government committed itself to manipulating the media both in the country and, less successfully, abroad. What amounted to a media blackout enabled the military government to execute its plans without resistance. Censorship and direct government control of television stations in the absence of international networks played a key role in keeping the state's actions secret.

The generals used language to convey an unambiguous commitment to patriotism and the defense of a beleaguered nation. According to Marguerite Feitlowitz, a Harvard professor who writes on the language of terror and Argentina's dirty war:

> The takeover is described as the result of "serene meditation," suggesting that the new leaders are clear both in mind and conscience. Further on, the junta pledges to "fully observe the ethical and moral principles of justice . . . [and to act in] respect of human rights and dignity." The new government will be devoted to the most sacred interests of the nation and its inhabitants.[14]

Argentine civil society, frightened by the guerrillas and misinformed by the military government, did not oppose what was happening. Censorship was absolute, and people tended to believe that the seized prisoners were actually guilty.

For example, a so-called task force from the navy kidnapped two nuns and Azucena Villaflor, the president of *las Madres de la Plaza de Mayo* (Mothers of the Plaza de Mayo), a human rights group. The navy officers took a picture of them with a banner of the guerrilla group "Montoneros" on the background and ran it in newspapers, attributing blame to the guerrillas for the action.[15]

Starting in 1977 the Argentine generals faced a most unlikely foe: the White House. Under the Carter administration, human rights became a primary foreign policy focus, and gross violations of human rights were condoned in neither friendly nations nor in the interest of fighting communism in Latin America.

Based on human rights reports, Carter curtailed and later called off military aid to Argentina, making the country a case study for how the United States would use human rights as critical foreign policy criteria. In 1977 he sent Patricia Derian, assistant secretary of state for human rights, to Argentina three times to get an on-the-spot view of what was happening. A special office in the United States embassy in Buenos Aires was set up to deal with human rights issues, and Secretary of State Cyrus Vance presented a formal complaint to the military junta about the thousands of disappeared people. After years of indoctrination by U.S. officials on the imperative fight against international communism, the Argentine generals, who considered themselves the vanguard in the so-called Third World War, were confounded by the dramatic shift in U.S. policy.[16]

The attention to human rights extended past the work of the Carter administration. While the disappearances were coupled with the suppression of information about what was happening, local human rights and civil society groups, initially formed by the victims' relatives, formed to seek answers to the multitude of questions that were slowly emerging. Meeting in state offices and army barracks, they found out that they had a common plight, and the *Madres de la Plaza de Mayo* was formed to work with groups related to churches and political parties to uncover the truth. Every Thursday they gathered in the Plaza de Mayo, in front of the presidential palace, to march in protest.

Argentina's Permanent Assembly for Human Rights established a fact-finding task force that would become the basis for further probing. The Center for Social and Legal Studies, another human rights association, initiated thousands of court actions to spur the media into publishing, albeit briefly, reports about the cases.[17]

The country's human rights groups were forced to act in appalling solitude, and only international backing spared them from being eliminated. All their members underwent serious risks, and some were imprisoned, tortured, or killed by the military. But they succeeded in getting their claims noted in debates at the United Nations and the Organization of American States. In 1979 the publicity prompted in situ research by the Inter-American Human Rights Commission (IAHRC), which under the direction of Tom Farer came to Argentina in the heyday of the military dictatorship and closed the remaining concentration camps.[18]

4. Law Enforcement Agencies Do Not Suffice to Establish the Law—the Trial Was the Culmination and Result of Collective Action Headed by Civil Society Groups

Repression reached its peak in 1977.[19] By 1980 most of the detention centers had been closed.[20] The military junta thought itself prestigious because of its success in fighting the subversive threat. General Vaquero, then the army's chief of staff, proclaimed on 18 November 1980 that no kind of investigation into the actions against terrorism would be permitted, in the present or future.[21] The regime's goal was to capitalize on that prestige and establish a political model in which the armed forces would retain control over Congress and the executive branch, as was done in Chile following Pinochet's presidential rule.[22]

Then in 1981 the generals got good news: Ronald Reagan was elected as the next president of the United States, and the superpower went back to business as usual with the Argentine military. Once again, the foreign policy objective was the eradication of the subversive communist threat. In 1981 Gen. Leopoldo Galtieri became president of Argentina and closed a deal with the United States under which his military officers would receive U.S. funding to train contras in Central America to fight communism in the region.[23]

But the economy imploded. It was under these conditions that the military junta decided to invade the Malvinas/Falkland Islands to recapture political support and rebuild a civic-military alliance.

The chiefs of the armed forces thought they would be able to garner support for the military action through continued manipulation of the mass media. Nationalist propaganda was employed with a broadcast of images of Argentina's victory over colonial Britain in its victorious 1806–1807 battle. Newspapers ridiculed British prime minister Margaret Thatcher. Military "experts" explained that five British invaders were needed to counter a single Argentine soldier defending the islands. Broadcast news showed sinking British aircraft carriers and make-believe heroic actions by local servicemen. Until 14 June 1982 Argentina was winning the war—and then suddenly it lost.

A few days later the junta resigned. Army general Reynaldo Bignone assumed the presidency with the sole objective of calling elections and handing over power.

The military debacle marked the end of the military's control over public information, and reports of the atrocities committed by the regime started appearing on television. There was, for instance, the discovery of a mass grave of 300 corpses, each shot through the head. The military tried to prevent information from being broadcast, but their threats were useless.

The military debacle also signaled the end of the junta's project of sealing a political deal to grant the armed forces impunity for its crimes. Military officers secretly debated what to do. Most of the younger officers feared being prosecuted and made claims for an amnesty law. The generals, seeing themselves as heroes, asked for medals and did not want to be treated as criminals. In 1980 General Viola declared that the "Armed Forces would not review any of the acts against terrorism. To try those who with honor defended the peace would be treason."[24] Less than a month before the 1983 general election, the military regime decreed its own long-awaited amnesty.

This amnesty spurred society into action. Several judges considered it unconstitutional, and Raúl Alfonsín, the Radical Party's presidential candidate, pledged to declare it null. He promised that a trial would be held to bring the officers responsible for the crimes to justice. Italo Luder, the Peronist Party's candidate, on the other hand, said that the amnesty could not be repealed. Based on his promises of justice, Alfonsín won the election with 52 percent of the vote.

Based on information provided by human rights groups and disseminated by the media, Argentine society started to demand both an investigation of the past and conviction of the criminals. Alfonsín understood that claim, promising to reestablish the rule of law.

The first law passed by Congress under the Alfonsín administration declared the amnesty null.[25] The almost unanimous vote included sectors that had traditionally supported the military.

Unlike the Chilean case, where Pinochet retained a tight grip on power, 1983 marked a turning point for Argentina with the establishment of democracy. Under the direction of civil society and a determined human rights commission, the country's darkest chapter would be opened for investigation and prosecution. With no transitional agreement, Argentina would forge its own path of justice. Alfonsín's government went forward with two measures many had never dreamed possible: the prosecution of the former members of the military junta and the creation of an independent commission to investigate the truth.

Two days after the presidential inauguration, and in his first act of government, Alfonsín requested the prosecution of the first nine members of the military juntas, all of whom had ruled with absolute power and three of whom had been presidents. To show that political vengeance was not the foundation of the juntas' trial, Alfonsín's administration also prosecuted exiled guerrilla leaders.

In response to demands from civil society and in the interest of preserving the country's stability, President Alfonsín created the National Commission on Disappeared People (CONADEP). The purpose of the commission was to collect testimony from all those willing to give it. Originally mandated to function for six months, CONADEP's term was extended to one year. CONADEP was chaired by the novelist Ernesto Sábato and included members of the media, clerics, intellectuals, and university lecturers. For the first time, the state tackled Argentina's disappearances.

The commission received about 50,000 testimonies from victims and relatives of the repression, asked for thousands of reports, and conducted inspections into the detention centers. From this, a television special was aired and a final report printed in the form of a book, *Nunca Más* (Never More), was released, exposing the generals' extermination campaign for the first time.

The book, which provided the basis for further investigations, became a best-seller. In a market where publishing between 4,000 and 10,000 copies was the norm, its 20,000-copy first edition came out in December 1984 and sold out in just a few days. One month later, four new editions (110,000 copies) were sold.[26]

Nowhere in the world was it common to put generals on trial. Traditionally in Latin America, the law had been a tool for those in positions of power to punish their subjects.[27] In this case, however, it was a means for protecting the weakest members of society.

Politically and emotionally, the trials were critical to Argentina's attempts to serve justice. The trial also presented substantive technical and legal challenges.

A six-judge panel was in charge of the case. They joined the Federal Court of Appeals of Buenos Aires with jurisdiction over the junta and Zone 1 members. The judges, selected by the executive and appointed by the Senate, made every effort to respect the rules of due process while attempting to solve the cases as quickly as possible. The panel did not want to use international laws covering genocide or crimes against humanity because they wanted to avoid further complicating an already complex case. Instead, the foundations for the trial were national laws punishing torture, theft, kidnappings, and murder.[28]

The preliminary investigation was made informally by a team of two prosecutors. The chief prosecutor was Julio Strassera, and I was the assistant. We selected 709 victims that we thought would best demonstrate the pattern of the secret operations implemented by the former junta members. We faced uncommon difficulties. For example, we could not ask for collaboration from the police because they had also been part of the execution of crimes, nor could we offer plea bargains or immunity in exchange for information. For three months, the victims and/or their relatives were called upon to accumulate evidence.

We had to prove three things beyond a reasonable doubt: first, that every victim had suffered a crime. To do this we could only issue charges of homicide when we had the body of the victim as evidence and thus could not issue such charges in the thousands of cases where people had been disappeared. Second, we needed to prove that the criminal in question had been a member of the armed forces or the police. Third, we had to show that their task formed part of a plan established and supervised by the top commanders. This way each commander could be found responsible for the crimes they were accused of.

The public hearing of the trial began on 22 April 1985. In what was the first public demonstration before the court in Argentina's history, thousands of people marched to the Central Court building to demand justice.

During the trial, 833 witnesses gave testimony.[29] The media printed and televised dramatic testimonies about mothers giving birth while handcuffed and fifteen-year-olds being killed by medieval torture tactics such as *empalamiento*—a form of torture in which the victim is seated on a spear fixed to the floor, which tears apart his/her entrails. During the eight-month trial, newspapers—even those that had supported the military dictatorship—published one or two pages with victim and witness testimony every day.

On 9 December 1985 the verdict was handed down: five defendants were convicted and four were acquitted. The judges ruled that each of the commanders—but not the junta itself—had masterminded a plan for illegal repression and was responsible for the execution of kidnappings, thefts, tortures, and murders.[30] Gen. Jorge Videla and Admiral Emilio Massera, chief of staff of the navy, were both convicted for life. Gen. Roberto Viola was sentenced to seventeen years in prison, Admiral Armando Lambruschini to eight years, and Air Chief Marshal Orlando Agosti to four-and-a-half years. The four members of the junta in power after 1980 were acquitted. One year later, the Supreme Court upheld this acquittal and reduced the convictions against Viola and Agosti.

The conviction reaffirmed the truth of the victims' testimonies, adding to it the legitimacy court rulings confer. The matter was given the force of a final judgment, but a final judgment that was soon to be damaged.

The massive publicity of the crimes committed during the military dictatorship and the subsequent convictions deprived the armed forces of the only prestige they thought they had won: respect for victory in the war against subversion. While dissemination of information strengthened society's commitment to the rule of law, it brought anxiety to the barracks.

President Alfonsín believed the ruling against the junta leaders was sufficient to serve society's thirst for justice without risking a military uprising.[31] The judges, however, acting in accordance with the law, opted to continue the investigations to include the remaining military chiefs and the lower-ranking officers. This meant that more than 1,000 officers faced the prospect of prosecution—an alternative considered unreasonable by the government. With the transition from authoritarian rule to democracy in its infant stages, the threat of military action remained.

The case for limiting prosecution to a small number of cases was not easy to make. Popular demand for justice was based on punishing all known culprits. But with so many, which principle would determine who would face prison and who would remain free? The armed forces's pyramidal structure compounded the problem: Lieutenants could not understand how they would be prosecuted while their captains and colonels would not.

Alfonsín tried to halt the trials with two new laws, but this did not impede that 400 more officials were tried, which in turn led to four military rebellions. His successor, Ménem, limited the outreach of those trials with pardons, and finally, in December 1990, he pardoned the commanders that had been condemned. These decisions were taken against the majoritarian opinion in society.

The combined effect of court hearings and its coverage by the media had a significant societal impact that cannot be erased or ignored. Breaking the walls of secrecy, facts were revealed, analyzed, debated, and disseminated through various media, including several movies, television series, and books. While civil society had already formed a strong pact with democracy, the information had the critical impact of convincing the ruling class elites that democracy was indeed the best path for Argentina to forge.

During the same month that the trial of the junta leaders began, the movie *La Historia Oficial* (The Official

Story) premiered, revealing what had happened in the years of the military dictatorship. More than five million people have watched *La Noche de los Lápices,* a movie based on the story of a group of high school students kidnapped by the army. By December 1998 the book *Nunca Más* had been reprinted twenty-one times, selling 276,000 copies, and had been translated into English, German, Italian, Portuguese, and Hebrew. Information became the most imperative healing tool.

Marking a clear difference with the attitudes prevalent during the last sixty years of Argentine history, the four military uprisings that took place between 1987 and 1990 were repudiated by society, political parties, businessmen, mass media, and most members of the armed forces, who chose either to reject the rebels or fight against them. In spite of many internal contradictions, society has condemned the military dictatorship and is deeply committed to democracy. In 1995, 89 percent of those polled nationally thought that democracy, albeit imperfect, was the best system of government.[32]

A second wave of investigations about the disappeared people began in December 1998, when both General Videla and Admiral Massera were imprisoned on charges of systematic appropriation of babies born in captivity. Cases of baby snatching were the only ones excluded from the scope of the Due Obedience laws, thus providing another channel for Argentina's demand for justice.

Conclusions

While Argentina's case is one of horror and tragedy, it is an important case to highlight the dramatic impact international policy can have on creating fear and the institutions to manage that fear. Argentina's military dictatorship—an organized bureaucracy that came to power with national and international support—organized and executed heinous crimes in the name of fighting for stability and peace. The means to this end were disguised; the ends were almost universally accepted.

The climate of fear that seized Argentina for almost two decades reveals the reach as well as the limits of utilizing the judiciary in handling these massive crimes.

But measuring the whole process by the number of convictions, the norms that limited punishment, or the pardons would be a mistake. The combined effect of court hearings and its coverage by the media had a social impact that cannot be controlled or erased: The dissemination of information allowed for public judgment.[33] The information about the crimes and the trials themselves effectively demarcated the line between dictatorship and democracy.[34] As this distinction became apparent, society increased its respect for the law and its commitment to human rights.

The Argentine case shows that the importance of national or international criminal justice should not be emphasized at the exclusion of civil society. An effective justice system requires citizens who are willing to establish and abide by laws and democratic institutions. In developing countries, we have to build both: Civil society still does not know the power of its voice, and democratic institutions are weak.

Economic globalization has both attenuated and exacerbated the dilemma. States, corporations, and individuals are increasingly intertwined, yet there are no world democratic institutions to monitor these relationships. New risks appear, and the media is as likely to be manipulated by boardroom executives as it is from government offices.

To increase national and international respect for human rights, we need to forge alliances between individuals, universities, nongovernmental organizations, multilateral organizations, and governments that actively support these values. Yet these alliances do not appear overnight. The development of national democratic institutions requires centuries. To do more in less time we will have to look toward the institutions of civil society—in particular the media—to demand their implementation, nurturing, and oversight.

Remembrance, Accountability, and Magnanimity

Alexander Boraine

Introduction

The underlying assumption in the question is that the past must be held to account. The past we are discussing relates to those countries that have either experienced a military dictatorship or an extreme authoritarian regime that involved gross human rights violations in the course of maintaining its repressive rule.

While it would be difficult to find anyone willing to defend these gross violations, there is wide disagreement as to how to deal with the past. On the one side, there are those who argue for remembrance. Judge Richard Goldstone, former prosecutor of the Hague Tribunal and Constitutional Court judge in South Africa, argues that "fundamental to all forms of justice is official acknowledgment of what happened whether by criminal process or by truth commission."[1] Many convincing voices have been raised in support of "doing something" about the past. Timothy Garton Ash reminds us that "there is the old wisdom of the Jewish tradition: to remember is the secret of redemption." And that of George Santayana, so often quoted in relation to Nazism: "those who cannot remember the past are condemned to repeat it."[2] Kathleen Smith, in her book *Remembering Stalin's Victims: Popular Memory and the End of the USSR,* quotes Lev Tolstoy along the same lines:

> People say why recall the past. What is the good of remembering what has been swept away? What is the good of irritating the nation? How can one ask such questions? If I suffered from a serious and dangerous disease and recovered or was cured from it, I would recollect the fact with joy. I would be disturbed by it only if I was still ill or if I'd taken a turn for the worse and want to deceive myself.[3]

On the other hand, there are powerful voices who urge that the way to deal with the past is to forget and to move on. To be fair to those who argue this way, for many of them it is not a question of ignoring the atrocities that have been committed so much as their concern to consolidate and protect the newly emerging democracy. Of course, there are those who simply wish to ignore the past because of their own involvement in it. But there is a defensible position that calls for moving on into the new future and not allowing the past to destroy or inhibit the new democracy. Timothy Garton Ash refers to this school of thought in his book *The File: A Personal History:*

> There is the profound insight of the historian Ernest Renan that every nation is a community both of shared memory and shared forgetting. "Forgetting," writes Renan, "and I would say even historical error, is an essential factor in the history of a nation." Historically, the advocates of forgetting are many and impressive. They range from Cicero in 44 B.C. demanding just two days after Caesar's murder that the memory of past discord be consigned to "eternal oblivion" to Winston Churchill in his Zurich speech two thousand years later, recalling Gladstone's appeal for a "blessed act of oblivion" between former enemies.[4]

Professor Bruce Ackerman of Yale has strongly criticized those who "squander moral capital in an ineffective effort to right past wrongs—creating martyrs and fostering political alienation, rather than contributing to a genuine sense of vindication."[5] Indeed, he says, "moral capital" is better spent in educating the population in the limits of the law rather than in engaging in a "quixotic quest after the mirage of corrective justice." He goes much further and cautions that any attempts to engage in corrective justice will generate "the perpetuation of moral arbitrariness and the creation of a new generation of victims because of the inevitable deviations from due process that would attach to trials."[6]

On balance, it is my view that the assumption underlying the question before us, namely that we have to be accountable to the past, is the right assumption. Firstly, to ignore the past is to perpetuate victimhood. Secondly, there are many examples of countries in transition that have strengthened their commitment to the rule of law and to the democratic culture by making a concerted effort to be accountable to the past. Thirdly, there are many other countries that have been haunted by their own past. Contemporary examples are Switzerland and the Swiss banks in relation to their own culpability toward the Holocaust, and Japan in relation to the so-called "comfort woman." Further, the furor surrounding the extradition of Gen. Augusto Pinochet has had an enormous impact on modern Chile, but the impact has been felt far beyond that country and there must be a number of present and former dictators who are decidedly uncomfortable at this turn of the events. There is also the challenge to the United States itself in relation to the residue of denial and contradictions flowing from the bitter experience of slavery that still has considerable impact on relationships within that country today. For the sake of justice, therefore, and for stability and the restoration of dignity to victims there must be accountability for the past. An added benefit would be that such accountability could deter further dictators. A more pointed question is what form that accountability should take, and it is to that question we turn.

How Do We Deal with the Past?

In his provocative and thoughtful book *Radical Evil on Trial,* Carlos Nino poses the critical question: "How shall we live with evil? How shall we respond to massive human rights violations committed either by state actors or by others with the consent and tolerance and consent of their governments?"[7] Following Kant, Nino argues that gross human rights violations are so abnormal and inexplicable that they can only be termed "radical evil." To describe, for example, the killing of more than six mil-

lion people and the unimaginable suffering of countless more in any terms less than "radical evil" is to insult the victims and contributes to the obscenity.

In trying to come to terms with genocide, crimes against humanity, and other massive atrocities, not only does our moral discourse appear to reach its limit, but it emphasizes the inadequacy of ordinary measures that usually apply in the field of criminal justice. Abnormal atrocities demand abnormal measures.

There is, however, no unanimity among politicians, lawyers, and philosophers as to what these measures ought to be. Nino leaves us no doubt as to where he stands: "I believe . . . that some measure of retroactive justice for massive human rights violations helps protect democratic values."[8] But this only begs the question: What is meant by "some measure of retroactive justice?"

Clearly, the question of retroactive or transitional justice remains uncharted, and there are far-reaching moral, political, and legal problems that deserve detailed study and vigorous debate. Despite these widely divergent views and the fact that impunity has been the norm rather than the exception, many countries and international agencies have sought accountability from those responsible for gross violations of human rights.

Transitional justice, the name given to the study of transitions from authoritarian rule to democratic consolidation, is emerging as an important interdisciplinary field with its own specialized literature and professional practitioners. A study edited by Neil Kritz, *Transitional Justice: How Emerging Democracies Reckon with Former Regimes,* has brought together major documentation of and contributions to this field, and many other research projects and international conferences are underway. The topic is related to but not distinct from human rights law and international law.

The traditional study and practice of law has a rather paradoxical relation to the problems of transitional justice. On the one hand, societies in transition faced with the problems of "dealing with the past" are increasingly looking to law to provide the mechanisms for doing this. On the other hand, "normal" law often cannot be applied in the extraordinary contexts of transitional justice, and there is a range of legal complications. For example, retroactive justice may often involve conflicts between the objectives applying the rule of law to past events and the fair procedures required in settling accounts.

Historical Precedence

The Nuremberg trials were a watershed case conducted by the victorious allies in November 1945 following the crimes committed by Nazi Germany during the preceding six years. Sentences for the accused were announced in October 1946 and included the death sentence for several of those found guilty. More than fifty years later discussion still rages as to the merits and demerits of the Nuremberg trials. But there can be no denial that the trials represent the first concerted action by the international community to deal in a systematic manner with what Nino describes as "radical evil." The Tokyo trials were equally contentious, and they were followed by trials held in many of the European countries that had been overrun and occupied by the Nazis during World War II.

Different countries made different choices as to how to deal with past violations. Argentina is especially interesting. A special commission was appointed to deal with "disappearances," and its report, *Nunca Más,* became a bestseller in Argentina. Several trials followed, which resulted in prison sentences for several junta leaders. In the main because of pressure from the military, President Alfonsín was forced to desist from further trials, and his successor, Carlos Ménem, pardoned those who were serving prison sentences. The recent arrest of military leaders relating to the kidnapping of children of dissidents indicates that the search for justice is not over in Argentina. Several countries in the region followed suit with similar commissions, the best known of which is the Truth and Reconciliation Commission appointed in Chile. With rare exceptions, trials were excluded from the options facing these countries.

Eastern European states responded in different ways to the demands for retroactive justice. Vaclav Havel, joined by the famous dissident Adam Michnik of Poland, advocated a spirit of tolerance and forgiveness. In the Czech Republic, the Law of Lustration dominated the debate. Havel was opposed to the pursual of former communist leaders who held office in public service, trade unions, and even parliament. Nevertheless,

he finally signed such a process into law. Many expressed their reservations because of the unreliability of the state security files.

One interesting theory as to why there were no truth commissions and few trials in Eastern Europe is that the nature of communism's teachings and practice robbed even the dissidents of initiative and the will to act against those who were in authority for so long. A further reason is that posttotalitarian transitions to democracy in former communist countries are characterized by the weakness or absence of civil society. There were no alternative legal, security, and bureaucratic elites. Consequently, any attempt to pursue retroactive justice that has to rely on the rule of law, due process, an impartial police, and state bureaucracy is extremely difficult. An exception is East Germany because of the transfer of trained jurists, policemen, bureaucrats, and academics from West Germany.

War Crimes Tribunals

The genocide and ethnic cleansing that took place in the former Yugoslavia provoked an international outcry, and, belatedly, the Untied Nations Security Council established an international war crimes tribunal based in The Hague. Six years later, after a very slow start, a number of those allegedly responsible for atrocities have been indicted and some arrested. For hundreds of years, Yugoslavia has experienced a recurring cycle of gross human rights violations. A major question is whether the cycle can finally be broken if the final word is punishment. It is interesting to note that in recent months many in Bosnia have been advocating the establishment of a truth commission, raising the question as to whether war crimes tribunals and truth commissions are contradictory or complementary.

In Rwanda there has been a similar cycle of ethnic violence over hundreds of years, culminating in the terrifying genocide in 1994 that left close to 800,000 people killed and many thousands injured and displaced. The war crimes tribunal set up to deal with the former Yugoslavia was given the additional responsibility of conducting trials in Rwanda. The situation in Rwanda is dire, with scant human or material resources to conduct trials let alone reconstruct a severely damaged economy and society. Surrounded by Burundi and the Congo, this stricken land is sitting on a powder keg. The situation is not helped by the fact that there are in excess of 120,000 people awaiting trial under the most dehumanizing and deplorable conditions. Again the question must be asked whether most of the international resources should be tied into trials or whether some new approach should be considered. Whatever else is true, there can be no doubt that punishment alone will not renew the Rwandan society.

There is very little certainty about how the international community and Cambodia itself will deal with its own violent past. It is difficult to believe that it was only twenty years ago that approximately two million people were put to death by the Khmer Rouge. Several of the leaders have now returned to Cambodia, and the initial response by Prime Minister Hun Sen was to greet the returning killers as heroes, presenting them with bouquets, hosting a lunch in their honor, and declaring that Cambodia should "dig a hole and bury the past." However, there still seems to be considerable controversy surrounding his initial approach, and he has made a number of other statements that suggest he's in favor of some means of bringing to account those who were guilty of human rights violations. The United Nations has recently concluded a study looking at options and there does seem to be a determination that some accounting has to be made.

While most of the international community have been in support of the ad hoc tribunals for former Yugoslavia and Rwanda, these tribunals are not without their major problems and limitations. Recently the retiring president of the Hague tribunal, Gabrielle MacDonald, made her report to the United Nations. In that report she records that in the period since 1993 until the present time only ten of those indicted have actually been sentenced. This is a very small number in relation to the expenditure of material and human resources. In Rwanda there has always been considerable disagreement between the Rwandan government and the tribunal itself, and recently this was highlighted by the tribunal's decision to release a key accused on the grounds that he had been held too long before being brought to trial. A more important question is the exclusive focus on punishment. The fact of the matter is that punishment per-

petuates itself; indeed, as Nino observes, "when I add the evil of the crime to the evil of the punishment, my moral arithmetic leads me consistently to believe that we have 'two evils' rather than 'one good.'"[9] As long as punishment forms our primary and only means of justice, then we can arguably expect a cycle of reinforcement of violence. Without some measure of forgiveness or pardon, is there any hope of restoring a community or a country torn apart by past divisions and hatred? If one looks at the former Yugoslavia and Rwanda, then there does seem to be a demand for other alternatives that seek to bring about not only accountability but also unity and reconciliation. The South African model could well make a major contribution in this area with its emphasis on restorative justice and its unique approach to limited amnesty and victim hearings.

Sociopolitical Considerations and Their Impact on Transitional Justice

Many scholars argue that in actual practice decisions made by transitional governments around issues of retroactive justice are not choices at all and, moreover, are little affected by moral or legal considerations. Rather, such decisions on the form that justice can take—be it trials, truth commissions, ad hoc international tribunals, or amnesty—are dictated by the mode and politics of the particular transition. Modes of transition can be defined by four categories:

1. Full defeat in an armed war (for example, post–World War II treatment of Germany);
2. Transition through a dictator's loss in an election (such as Chile);
3. Transition through compromise and negotiation (such as South Africa); and
4. Transition from a long-standing communist regime (such as Eastern European countries).

Each mode presents its own set of institutional and political constraints, which in turn delineate the form of justice, whether the most retributive model (prosecutions and trials) to more restorative models of justice (truth commissions and lustration) to no justice at all (impunity). In the context of military victory (category one), the only restriction is the victor's own sense of justice and long-term strategic considerations. For instance, Germany's military defeat in World War II was absolute in that it had lost both political and military power. The Allied victors thus had to check upon their ability to punish and opted for the most retributive model, the Nuremberg trials.

Where transitions from a totalitarian government occur after elections (category two), greater political restrictions arise. Very often, the former dictator maintains a strong power base (whether in the military or civil society) and has passed, prior to departure, laws to grant amnesty for past human rights abuses. The new democracies, faced with an unstable political and social situation and no clear legal remedy, often seek an amalgam of retributive and restorative models of justice via truth commissions, reparations, and limited prosecutions.

Where transitions occur through a process of peaceful negotiation between the democratizing force and the previous totalitarian regime (category three), the political constraints become even more heightened. Negotiation politics require, first and foremost, compromise; thus, in a country that is attempting to accommodate all factions in a new democracy, justice necessarily becomes a restorative project of establishing moral, if not legal truth. In such contexts, justice takes the form of truth commissions and limited amnesty. South Africa is a noteworthy example of this approach.

In the particular cases of transitions from totalitarian communist regimes to democracy (category four), political constraints all but preclude more retributive forms of justice. The nature of communism's teaching and practice arguably had two discernible consequences: (1) to rob even dissidents of initiative and will to act against those in authority for so long, resulting in a weakness or absence of civil society; and (2) to create a technocratic government of such pervasiveness in society that large numbers of individuals in communist countries achieved a level of complicity with the regime unparalleled even by other noncommunist totalitarian regimes. Posttotalitarian transitions to democracy in former communist countries are thus characterized by little retribution in the form of trials and little truth-seeking in the form of truth commissions. Instead, these nations took refuge in general laws of lustration, which only implicitly admit a history of misdeed by barring the guilty from future participation in government.

Thus, a country's particular mode of transition and level of political restriction surrounding the decisions of retroactive justice define the parameters of the choice between the competing theories of retroactive justice. The more that peaceful coexistence is a stated goal of transition, the greater the political restrictions faced by the transitional government. Moreover, history bears out that as the level of restriction increases, transitional societies turn away from retributive models and towards more restorative models of justice.

Importantly, then, retroactive justice forms the basis for transitions defined by the need to coexist in peace. In times of extreme conflict, the duty to prosecute is balanced by another duty to restore beyond punishment. In the words of Jose Zalaquett, "complete victors generally hand out a tremendous amount of punishment, but not necessarily justice."

Where there exists a need for peaceful coexistence, justice must become something more than punishment; it must become inextricably linked to revelation, truth, and redemption. Indeed, "Memory is the ultimate form of justice."

Concluding Remarks and a Way Ahead

The International Criminal Court (ICC) will regulate future acts of genocide, ethnic cleansing, and crimes against humanity. It will do so firstly by advocating norms that states are obliged to follow and secondly to act where states do not measure up to the requirements of international law. This will be a great improvement on the ad hoc tribunals that have been and may still be appointed to deal with current and future problems of conflict.

It is hoped that when the ICC comes into being it will not either by definition nor by approach discourage national state initiatives in trying to come to terms with their past. There are a number of unique circumstances that exist, and it would be regrettable if the only approach to gross human rights violations would be in the form of trials and punishment. What would be extremely helpful would be a new

and thorough study of retributive and restorative justice and to ascertain whether these two are always
contradictory or whether they could be regarded as
complementary. Hannah Arendt, the Jewish political philosopher, argues that societies can overcome
the evils in their past and change for the better
through promise and forgiveness in her book *The
Human Condition: A Study of the Central Conditions
Facing Modern Man.*[10]

> The remedy against the irreversibility and unpre-
> dictability of the process started by [human] acting
> does not arise out of another and possibly higher fac-
> ulty, but is one of the higher potentialities of action
> itself. The possible redemption from the predica-
> ment of irreversibility—of being unable to undo
> what one has done though one did not, and could
> not, have known what he was doing—is the faculty
> of forgiving. The remedy for unpredictability, for the
> chaotic uncertainty of the future, is contained in the
> faculty to make and keep promises.[11]

Arendt points in the direction that I believe the
current debate concerning transitional justice needs to
go. On the other hand, there is the recognition that
full justice is impossible, and unless there is something
beyond punishment, there is very little hope for the
restoration and healing of societies that have been
deeply divided and deeply wounded by the conflicts
of the past. On the second hand, her emphasis on the
need for a new contract, that is, a new commitment,
is a promise that the past will not be repeated and the
future holds promise of democracy, stability, and culture of human rights on a basis of commitment to the
rule of law. In our search for justice and reconciliation
we must admit that there are limits to the law, although
the law can and does and must play a central role in
accounting for the past. Perhaps the next step is to
engage in a serious evaluation of international interventions that have taken place post-Nuremberg, un-
derscoring the good that has been achieved but critically assessing where mistakes have been made and
focusing on prevention and peacekeeping as well as
acting in times of emergency when lives have already
been lost and property has already been destroyed.
Such an evaluation could assist the international community to deal more creatively with conflicts that are
bound to be with us forever.

Steel factory, Baltimore, Maryland. *Source:* R. Michael Jenkins, Congressional Quarterly.

Session 4

Natural Resources and the Environment: Individual Versus Community Interest

Editors' Note

The recuperation of stressed environments, the interaction of natural and man-made needs for health and diversity, and the functional integrity of ecosystems will surely be global priorities in the twenty-first century. Growing population pressure on existing environments exacerbates conflicts among community interests and often has distant deleterious effects (ozone holes, acid rain, nuclear fallout) far from the sites of the original problems. What are—and ought to be—our obligations to future generations? How should such obligations be secured?

The three papers presented approach these issues from varying perspectives. Richard Stewart deals primarily with the constitutional assumptions and structure of the United States, posing the essential problem as one between the liberty of action, change, and innovation and the liberty of security, constancy, and dependability. Both are important values for the environment and neither can prevail completely. Both represent crucial community interests, mobilized in differing ways. Stewart observes that money may distort the process and contribute to a substantial "democracy deficit," for which the cure is more careful judicial oversight of administrative procedures and the substitution of market-driven incentives for bureaucratic decisions.

Yuri Kostenko and Antonio Azuela write from national perspectives that strongly influence the approaches taken to environmental issues. Ukraine, emerging from forty years of misguided and wasteful policies that polluted environments and degraded human health, culminating in the Chernobyl disaster, has relied heavily upon new legislation and international agreements and treaties to put in place a forward-looking environmental regime, including the concept of European econets. In Mexico, the legacies of attitudes toward land established by the 1910 revolution are now being complicated and challenged by a mixture of ideas: the importation of common-law concepts, the involvement of national and international NGOs in social mobilization, and the devolution within Mexico of authority from the federal to the local and municipal levels. In both Ukraine and Mexico, the vitalization of civil society and increased democratic participation are seen as positive, though sometimes contentious, contributors to environmental values.

Sidney Draggan calls attention to two powerful trends in environmental policy: the escalating involvement of increasingly diverse stakeholders in discussions and resolutions of environmental issues, and the uses to which science may and can be put within an adversarial legal culture. Scientific views, he reminds us, are of necessity continuously tested, refined, or changed in ways that may be in advance of, or at odds with, accepted environmental practice. Koichiro Fujikura attests to the benefits and liabilities of the Japanese consensus-based environmental legislation when compared to Ukraine, Mexico, and the United States.

Environmental Law
and Liberty

Richard B. Stewart

I. Introduction

"Natural Resources and the Environment: Individual Versus Community Interests," implies a fundamental conflict between individual liberty and collective interests in environmental law. This misstates the fundamental issue. The most important conflicts that we face are those among different collective interests and values—most fundamentally, those associated with activity on the one hand and security on the other. In conceptualizing the issue as it does, the panel title echoes the rhetoric of the current property rights movement, which opposes most environmental regulation on the ground that it illegitimately curtails individual liberty.[1] To the contrary, properly designed legal measures for protection of the environment can enhance liberty. Conceptualizing environmental issues in terms of conflicts between individual liberty and the community will lead us astray from the important task of advancing liberty by balancing activity and security through the adoption of appropriate laws and institutions.

This essay first explains that liberty has two basic components: activity and security. The law must balance these twin elements of liberty at the collective, not the individual level. It then summarizes how the law, over the past 125 years, has come to give increased weight to environmental security and less to activity, explaining how this change has been accomplished by a shift from common-law litigation to administrative regulation. Next, the essay address the normative question of how we should strike the balance between activity and security. It examines a number of potential principles for doing so, con-

cluding that the divergent collective interests and values at stake must ultimately be resolved through institutions of democratic governance consistent with the rule of law. The essay then summarizes how during the past thirty years we have created a national "command and control" environmental regulatory state that has achieved significant progress in environmental protection but has also had significant drawbacks. Our top-heavy system of environmental central planning has also eroded the rule of law, spawned a pernicious form of factional politics, created enormous economic waste, and hindered environmentally beneficial flexibility and innovation. This system has also been attacked by property rights advocates on the ground that it has been abused by environmental interests and their bureaucratic allies to confiscate private property values. Finally, the essay considers three types of proposed solutions to these failings. The first, championed by property rights advocates, is for the courts to apply the takings doctrine of the Constitution to require government payment of compensation for the economic losses suffered by property owners as a result of environmental regulation, and to substitute private litigation for administrative regulation as the primary legal mechanism for addressing environmental problems. The second proposed solution is to enhance judicial review and control of agency regulatory decisions through administrative law and to develop higher-level administrative mechanisms to strengthen agency adherence to cost-benefit and risk analysis. The third solution is to develop new market-based regulatory instruments to achieve environmental objectives in place of command and control central administrative planning. The essay concludes that a combination of the second two mechanisms will appropriately enable us to promote environmental security while at the same time maximizing the benefits of activity.

II. Balancing Activity and Security Through Environmental Law

Activity and Security

The fundamental conflicts in environmental law are not those between individuals and collectivities but those between activity and security. Activity is endemic to human nature. It generates many benefits: economic development, experimentation and innovation, learning by doing, diversity, and mobility. On the other hand, activity inevitably creates risk, including environmental risks that threaten the security of persons, property, and ecosystems. Does the expansion of environmental liabilities and regulatory controls on activity inevitably result in a corresponding loss of liberty?[2]

As a first approximation, we may define liberty as freedom to do as one pleases. Liberty is served by activity. But it is also served by security. If I am made ill by pollution, if my property is destroyed by a neighbor's exploding boiler, if my recreational fishing is destroyed by an oil spill or by wetlands development, my range of advantageous opportunities is reduced. Environmental regulation may preserve or enlarge my opportunities and, hence, my liberty. Environmental law must decide how far activity should be curtailed in order to protect security. Liberty is at stake on both sides. Thus the liberty of both the property owners and recreationalists is at issue in a decision whether to prohibit filling of and construction on wetlands. While environmental controls may contract our freedom to do what we wish in some respects (for example, the operation of high-polluting automobiles may be prohibited or heavily taxed), they may enlarge our opportunities in other respects (such as enable us to see and enjoy distant mountains or live in Los Angeles without health risk). Thus, environmental protection through law does not necessarily entail a net reduction of liberty; the reduction of freedom from control of

activity may be outweighed by the enhanced liberty afforded by greater security.

Collective Interests and the Rule of the Law

The rule of law requires that government, in imposing controls or liabilities or distributing benefits, act toward persons pursuant to general rules or standards rather than on an ad hoc, particularized basis. This requirement of legal generality promotes impartiality and helps prevent decisions by government officials selectively to impose burdens on or distribute benefits to particular persons on the basis of friendship, cronyism, partisan affiliation, race, religion, or gender. It is also designed to ensure that the criteria for making such decisions are based on general public-regarding objectives. The requirement of legal generality implies that decisions as to what the law shall be must be based on a consideration of the collective interests of those affected.[3] These principles of generalities govern common-law decisions by courts. Suppose that both the plaintiff and defendant are individuals who own neighboring properties. One neighbor's activity on her land injures the other on his property. The court must decide in favor of the one individual and against the other, but do so on the basis of rules, standards, or principles of general applicability. Thus the court is not to decide the case on the basis of whether it favors the particular plaintiff or defendant but on the basis of the proper balance between the interests of property owners generally in making use of their property without incurring legal liability and the interests of property owners generally in security against injuries caused by neighbors' activities. This choice ultimately requires an evaluation of the collective interests in the two aspects of liberty. The collective character of the underlying evaluation and choice that the law must make is more explicit in the case of environmental regulatory programs, which impose controls on a class of actors in order to provide enhanced environmental security to a class of beneficiaries. Thus, the legislature that enacts or the administrative agency that implements an automobile pollution control regulatory program must consider and balance collective activity interests (automobile driving) and collective security interests (health harm, climate change) in determining the nature and extent of controls.

The property rights advocates like to paint environmental law as a conflict between David (the lone individual property owner who is prohibited from developing her property) and Goliath (the regulatory bureaucracy that adopts and enforces the prohibition). This example misleads in two basic respects. First, it is unrepresentative as a factual matter. As a result of industrialization and the large-scale organization of economic and governmental activity, the targets of environmental regulation are most often large corporations or governmental entities that have generated widespread pollution, wastes, and other forms of environmental degradation affecting very large numbers of people. Second, it ignores the law's collective character. While a regulatory enforcement proceeding may involve only a single landowner, the statutes and regulations being enforced apply, in accordance with the rule of law, to the relevant class of landowners in general. By the same token, the regulatory agency is acting to protect the interests of the general class of persons adversely affected by uncontrolled land use. The extent to which the statutes and regulations should limit land use must be based on a consideration of the collective interests of landowners in activity and of neighbors in security. It is accordingly a mistake to conceptualize environmental law as a struggle between the community and the individual.

Changing in the Law's Protection of Environmental Security from the Nineteenth to the Twenty-first Century

Today, property rights advocates complain that private property rights have been unjustifiably subordinated to environmental interests. One hundred twenty-five years ago the situation was the reverse. What we would today regard as environmental interests (including interests in human health and safety as well as ecosystem integrity) were often denied legal protection in preference to industrial and commercial activity interests. Because environmental, health, and safety regulation in the nineteenth century was rudimentary, the primary battleground was tort litigation in the courts. A fundamental

issue was whether the courts should adopt a rule of strict liability for accidental harms or a negligence rule that relieved those causing harm of liability unless the plaintiff could establish that they had failed to take due care. American courts almost uniformly adopted a negligence rule. Furthermore, judges often refused to allow juries to find a business defendant negligent for accidental harms, including environmental harms, out of concern that liability would unduly burden socially beneficial investment and innovation.[4] In doing so they followed a widespread sentiment summarized by Oliver Wendell Holmes Jr. In his 1881 lectures on the common law, Holmes opposed strict liability in tort, maintaining that it would chill "activity . . . that tends to the public good."

For example, in its 1886 decision in *Pennsylvania Coal Co. v. Sanderson,* the Pennsylvania Supreme Court rejected strict liability and denied recovery for a railroad's pollution of a stream. The court took into account the social value of the railroad's activities, holding that the railroad's conduct was not negligent.

> It may be stated as a general proposition, that every man has the right to the natural use and enjoyment of his own property and if, while lawfully in such use and enjoyment, without negligence or malice on his part, unavoidable loss occurs to his neighbor [the law will not hold him liable to compensate the neighbor] . . . We are of the opinion that mere private personal inconveniences . . . must yield to the necessities of a great public industry, which, although in the hands of a private corporation, subserves a great public interest. To encourage the development of the great natural resources of a country trifling inconveniences to particular persons must sometimes give way to the necessities of a great community.[5]

In a 1876 decision, *Losee v. Buchanan,* the New York Court of Appeals also refused to adopt strict liability and denied recovery to a landowner whose property was injured by a neighbor's exploding boiler. The court rejected the landowner's claim for compensation with the following logic:

> By becoming a member of civilized society, I am compelled to give up many of my natural rights, but I

receive more than a compensation from the surrender by every other man of the same rights, and the security, advantage, and protection which the laws give me. So, too, the general rules that I may have the exclusive and undisturbed use and possession of my real estate, and that I must so use my real estate as not to injure my neighbor, are much modified by the exigencies of the social state. We must have factories, machinery, dams, canals, and railroads. They are demanded by the manifold wants of mankind, and lay at the basis of all our civilization. If I have any of these upon my lands, and they are not a nuisance and are not so managed as to become such, I am not responsible for any damage they accidentally and unavoidably do my neighbor. He receives his compensation for such damage by the general good, in which he shares, and the right which he has to place the same things upon his lands.[6]

Both decisions effectively subordinate collective interests in environmental security to those in activity, which the courts regarded as of higher societal value. In these decisions and many others, the courts adopted and enforced general rules, standards, and principles that preferred collective interests in industrial and development activity over these in environmental security.

Today, the law has worked a radical change in the balance between production and development interests and environmental security. Due to the growth of technology and science, the adverse environmental consequences of wide-scale industrialization and development are no longer regarded as "trifling inconveniences." Further, it is generally no longer accepted that those suffering serious environmental injury must be denied compensation for the greater community good. Thus courts today routinely impose strict liability in damages for harm imposed by toxic pollutants and wastes. Thus, in a 1983 decision, *State of New York v. Schenectady Chemical Co.,* a New York court held that a landowner could be held strictly liable at common law, without proof of negligence, for the costs of cleaning up toxic contamination from chemicals stored on the site. The court noted that the "common law is not static," and should change in order to address new environmental problems created by "the modern chemical industry."[7]

Currently, however, the primary legal instrument of environmental protection is not judicially enforced liability for harm but far-reaching administrative regulation by federal and state agencies. Courts accord considerable deference to such regulatory programs. For example, in *Just v. Marinette County,* the Wisconsin Supreme Court in 1972 upheld a regulatory prohibition on filling of wetlands by a landowner who wished to build a home on the property:

In the instant case we have a restriction on the use of a citizen's property, not to secure a benefit for the public, but to prevent a harm from the change in the natural character of the citizens' property. [The court noted] the interrelationship of the wetlands, the swamps, and the natural environment of shorelands to the purity of the water and to such natural resources as navigation, fishing, and scenic beauty. Swamps and wetlands were once considered wasteland, undesirable, and not picturesque. But as the people became more sophisticated, an appreciation was acquired that swamps and wetlands serve a vital role in nature, are part of the balance of nature, and are essential to the purity of the water, in our lakes and streams. Swamps and wetlands are a necessary part of the ecological creation and now, even to the uninitiated, possess their own beauty in nature.

Is the ownership of a parcel of land so absolute that man can change its nature to suit any of his purposes? . . . An owner of land has no absolute and unlimited right to change the essential natural character of his land so as to use it for a purpose for which it was unsuited in its natural state and which injures the rights of others. The exercise of [regulatory power] must be reasonable and we think it is not an unreasonable exercise of that power to prevent harm to public rights by limiting the use of private property to its natural uses. . . .

The Justs argue their property has been severely depreciated in value. But this depreciation of value is not based on the use of the land in its natural state but on what the land would be worth it if could be filled and used for the location of a dwelling. While loss of value is to be considered in determining whether a restriction is a constructive taking, value based upon changing the character of the land at the expense of harm to public rights is not an essential factor or controlling.[8]

These examples are illustrative of the changes in environmental protection through law since the nineteenth century. The law has greatly increased its protection of the collective interests in environmental security. As a result of successful industrialization and large-scale development, technological advance, and greatly increased wealth, many of the adverse environmental impacts of production and consumption activities have increased, even though others have decreased. Science has educated us about adverse health and environmental effects that were formerly unknown or underestimated. These developments, along with public education, have led to widespread awareness that activity generates significant environmental risks and an enhanced appreciation of the benefits of security. Moreover, the wealth that we have developed through the process of economic development enables us to invest more in environmental protection. In short, because of the law's encouragement of activity in the past, we can better "afford" greater security today.

The Rise of Administrative Regulation and the Precautionary Principle

The enhanced protection afforded to environmental security by the law has been to a large extent accomplished by a parallel shift in the institutional means employed by the law in addressing environmental issues. Statutory systems of administrative regulation have largely supplanted liability awards by common-law courts as the primary legal instrument for environmental protection. Under common law, liability is generally imposed only after harm has already occurred. While the prospect of such liability undoubtedly gives actors incentives to prevent harm from occurring in the first place, these incentives have been judged by the political process to be insufficiently effective or reliable. Accordingly, legislatures have supplemented tort liability by adopting extensive "command and control" administrative systems to regulate conduct in order to prevent

harm. Pursuant to legislation, government agencies adopt specific prohibitions or requirements relating to pollution, wastes, resource management, land use, development, and other activities. These regulations are enforced against firms, government entities, and individuals through licensing and permit requirements, monitoring and enforcement actions, and sanctions for violations.

For a variety of reasons, tort litigation in the courts by private parties is inherently ill suited for addressing complex environmental problems affecting large numbers of individuals. For example, air pollution from a given factory may potentially affect very large numbers of individuals throughout an air basin. While each exposed individual may suffer some increased risk of harm from such emissions, it is virtually impossible to show that such exposure caused a particular individual's illness or property damage. Moreover, pollution in a given air basin or water body is often created by many sources, making the problem of establishing causal responsibility even more difficult. Litigation is costly, and the individual plaintiff's stake may be small. Litigation before generalist judges and juries is also a poor means for resolving recurring scientific, economic, and engineering issues presented in environmental controversies. Damage remedies are often inadequate because of the difficulties in tracing causation, quantifying injury, and dealing with harms with long latency periods. The public has accordingly demanded proactive controls on activity to prevent harm from occurring in the first place. Courts are institutionally unequipped to meet this need. Administrative regulation was adopted by legislatures precisely in order to overcome these institutional limitations of the litigation system. Administrative agencies have substantial resources. Unlike the courts, they do not depend on private initiative but are self-starting. Unlike common-law courts, they specialize in a given policy area and have expert staff that can conduct extensive information gathering and analysis. They can devise, enforce, and monitor the performance of regulations and other administrative measures to address large-scale environmental problems created by many sources and affecting many people.[9]

In the past, most environmental regulatory systems were generally adopted after the occurrence of serious environmental harms that common-law liability had failed to prevent. More recently, however, environmentalists have urged that we go even further, invoking a "precautionary principle," which would justify preventive regulation of activities that may pose some risk of harm even in the absence of proof that harm actually has or ever will occur.[10] Environmentalists have, for example, argued that the very fact that the health and environmental risks of genetically modified crops and foods is highly uncertain justifies their regulation. This approach, which represents a dramatic departure from the common law and earlier regulatory programs, is finding increasing acceptance.

The embrace of the precautionary principle reflects our developing understanding of scientific uncertainty and the inevitable limitations of data. In many cases, it is difficult or impossible to establish whether, for example, a given chemical substance will cause cancer in humans and, if it does, the extent of illness caused. Ecology and other natural sciences tell us that activities that do not appear to cause harm may have in fact have far-reaching adverse effects. Many of these effects are cumulative over time or have substantial latency periods. We accordingly deal in many cases with highly uncertain risks of harm. In deciding whether or not to regulate activity in order to reduce such risks we must balance two types of regulator errors: the error of regulating an activity that in fact turns out to cause harm (false negative), and the opposite error of not regulating an activity that does not in fact cause harm, wasting the societal resources diverted to regulatory compliance (false positives). A further option is to postpone a final decision on whether or not to regulate pending development of more information that may reduce uncertainty. Risk management consists in weighing these various considerations and making regulatory decisions in the face of considerable uncertainty. Today, much of environmental law is an exercise in risk management. Environmentalists concerned about environmental security assert that it is more important to avoid false positives than false negatives. Industry and others that place a higher value at the margin on activity take the opposite position. The law must choose. But how?

Principles for Striking the Balance Between Activity and Security

A history of environmental law, such as the capsule version given above, tells us how in fact the balance between activity and security has been struck at various points in time, but it cannot answer the normative question of how we, today, *should* strike the balance between activity and security. This section considers a number of substantive principles that might answer that question. The conclusion, however, is that none of these principles are adequate to the task and that the balance must be struck through democratic methods of decision-making disciplined by the rule of law, as discussed in sections that follow.[11]

Proof of Causation of Harm as a Limitation on Legal Control of Activity.

The common law limits the coercive imposition of legal liability or of regulatory controls to actors who have caused or threaten imminent, irreparable harm to the person or property of others.[12] Could this principle provide the solution to striking the balance between liberty and security? While at first glance intuitively appealing, further examination shows that the principle is neither workable nor sufficient.

With a few exceptions, tort law requires a plaintiff, in order to recover damages, to prove that the defendant's conduct more probably than not caused her to suffer harm. This requirement, however, is not dispositive of the liability issue, for there is the further question of the choice of liability rule: Should the rule be strict liability or negligence? The choice between these two standards as well as the determination of due care under a negligence rule, which must balance the benefits and burdens of precaution, reintroduces the necessity of choice between liberty as activity and liberty as security.

Furthermore, the common-law requirement of proof causation of harm has been abandoned by many contemporary environmental statutes, which authorize imposition of regulatory controls where an activity may simply pose some risk of harm. For example, the Clean Air Act empowers the administrator of the Environmental Protection Agency (EPA) to impose controls on emissions of air pollutants "which, in his judgment, . . .

contribute to air pollution which may reasonably be anticipated to endanger the public health or welfare."[13] Contemporary statutory programs of environmental liability, such as the Superfund program, also abandon traditional requirements for proof of causation of harm as a prerequisite for imposing liability.[14]

Such departures from the common law reflect factors already discussed in connection with the rise of administrative regulation: our developing understanding of scientific uncertainty and the inevitable limitations of data. The data and analysis in most cases generate fuzzy, continuous gradations of risk, without any sharp break that might serve as the threshold that triggers imposition of government controls. Even where it is decided that a risk is sufficiently significant to merit attention, there is the further question of how intensive regulatory controls or liability systems should be, which again reintroduces the fundamental choice between activity and security. For these reasons, we can no longer rely on causation of harm as a benchmark to determine when legal measures to limit activity are justified in order to promote environmental security. Accordingly, because risk is pervasive and uncertainty abounds, the prevailing contemporary risk management approach sets few inherent limits to the potential reach of legal requirements, especially if one follows a precautionary approach. Landowners such as the Justs complain that prohibiting a family's construction of a house cannot be justified as preventing harm without stretching the concept of harm so far as to abolish, as a practical matter, any limits on regulation. Also, those subject to regulatory controls often attack regulatory agencies' risk assessments as biased in favor of regulation. Yet it would not be appropriate to deal with such problems by reverting to the common-law requirement that harm be proved before the law can act. A workable basis for striking an appropriate balance between liberty and security must accordingly be sought elsewhere.

Welfare Maximization.

Welfare economics offers another potential solution to the problem of where the balance between liberty and activity should be struck. Environmental quality can be understood as a commodity whose value is determined by individuals' willingness to pay for it. For example, people pay more for houses in locations with a higher level of environmental amenity and spend money to travel to enjoy scenic areas. Also, to the extent that environmental quality is a normal good, we would want more of it as our wealth increases; the increased protection given by the law to the environment tends to confirm this hypothesis. If environmental quality were in all respects a commodity, on a par with marketplace products and services, the nature and extent of environmental controls could be determined based on our preferences for environmental quality (security) versus our preferences for other goods and services that would be produced in the absence of such controls because the resources devoted to compliance with environmental controls would be freed to produce commodities other than environmental quality (activity). In this way security and activity could be reduced to a common metric of value, set ultimately by individuals' willingness to pay for environmental quality versus other goods and services. Government, through some institutionalized system of preference aggregation, would determine the optimum level of environmental controls that would maximize the value of the two aspects of liberty-as-preference-satisfaction.[15]

There would, of course, be formidable practical problems implementing any such felicific calculus. But this approach has more fundamental flaws. Environmental quality is "special" in several ways. Environmental security is closely tied with human health and physical, psychological, ideological, and cultural integrity. Preserving the ecosystem is also an essential part of our legacy to future generations. Maintenance of diverse physical environments is central to the potential for experiential diversity that nurtures ethical and social development. Many hold that we owe moral duties to other species or to nature herself. Accordingly, environmental security incorporates many values that are noncommodity in character. On the other side of the equation, the benefits of activity are likewise not limited to the production of goods and services. They include such values as creativity, diversity, flexibility, experimentation, and learning. Thus, the balance between activity and environmental security implicates many qualitatively different values on both sides that cannot be reduced to a single commodity metric.[16] The balance must ultimately be struck through liberal democratic processes of decision conforming to rule-of-law disciplines.

Distributional Equity.

Regulatory decisions that determine the balance between activity and security also have distributional dimensions. In an ideal world, perhaps, the benefits and burdens of regulatory decisions would be equally shared and everyone would enjoy a net gain in liberty. In the real world, however, regulatory benefits and burdens are "lumpy" and unevenly distributed. The allocation of such benefits and burdens may thus raise issues of justice and equity. In tort litigation, the issue is treated as one of corrective justice; a defendant who has breached or has a legal duty to a plaintiff and caused her harm must pay compensation for the harm done and thereby redress the violation of her rights.[17] But risk-based environmental regulatory programs and liability systems like Superfund do not depend on the existence of a causal nexus between the conduct of a given actor and loss to another. Furthermore, many actors typically contribute to a given environmental risk, and many persons are exposed to that risk. In Los Angeles, for example, many millions of sources, mobile and stationary, contribute, to differing extents, to air pollution that affects millions of people, some (the aged, the young, the asthmatic, the ill) much more than others. Regulatory decisions thus typically have complex and far-reaching distributional effects that are polycentric, not bipolar, in character and therefore must be analyzed in terms of distributional rather than corrective justice.

In the main, the benefits and burdens of environmental policies have appropriately been treated as simply one instance of the distributional issues raised by government regulatory programs generally. Regulatory programs should be used to solve regulatory problems, not to promote other social objectives such as the equitable overall distribution of wealth that are the appropriate task of tax, social welfare, and other government programs. To the extent that environmental regulatory programs raise general questions of distributional equity, our constitutional system has appropriately remitted the determination of equity to the democratic political process. Thus, distributional justice is not a principle that can provide much assistance in determining the balance between security and activity in environmental law.

Two more specific points of distributional controversy have, however, arisen with environmental regulation. In each, an identifiable minority group complains that it has been unfairly treated by the majority. The first controversy involves the siting of locally undesirable land uses (LULUs), such as waste sites or nuclear facilities. The environmental justice movement asserts government decisions and policies that have resulted in LULUs being disproportionately sited in poor and minority neighborhoods.[18] This essay will not further consider the controversy, which presents special civil rights and other issues. A second focus of controversy has been the legal and political attacks made by landowners against environmental regulatory controls, such as wetlands, beachfront, and endangered species regulation, that significantly restrict their use of their land.[19] The situation that the landowners face in such cases is the reverse of that faced by the plaintiffs in the nineteenth century, in cases like *Sanderson* and *Losee,* where the courts ruled that the plaintiffs had to suffer uncompensated environmental harms because of the public benefit from activity. Today, landowners like the Justs complain that environmental regulation unjustly requires them to suffer serious uncompensated economic harm because of the public benefit in environmental security.

III. The Centralized Environmental Regulatory State

Constitutional Democratic Procedures for Striking the Balance Between Activity and Environmental Security

In our system of government, issues of environmental law and policy, like other issues of social and economic law, must be resolved through democratic processes subject to rule-of-law and other constitutional disciplines. Our federal government implements democratic principles and the rule of law through a system of lawmaking by elected representatives and an institutional system of separated powers. Laws must be enacted by one set of elected officials (the legislature) and enforced by a different set of officials accountable to an elected president (executive branch) subject to review for legality by a third set of officials (the independent judiciary). In addition to a system of horizontally separated but shared powers within the federal government, the Constitution establishes a vertical system of power sharing between the federal and state governments.

These arrangements are designed to promote wise laws that enjoy democratic legitimacy and advance public-regarding objectives. They are the processes through which environmental law is made, including determination of the balance between liberty and security, the choices among the competing interests and values at stake, and the resolution of distributional questions. These arrangements are also designed to secure the rule of law, including due process requirements that state power be exercised against persons only in accordance with general rules or standards that enjoy democratic legitimacy, that are knowable in advance of conduct, and that are enforced impartially. These due process requirements apply, of course, to government imposition of environmental regulatory controls or liabilities. Government enforcement of such measures does not present any distinctive liberty-related issues different from those presented in taxation or regulation generally. Since liberty consists of well-ordered opportunities, there are no grounds for supposing that environmental controls, established consistent with due process of law, will necessarily or even typically curtail liberty overall. The issue is whether we value the opportunities provided by environmental security more than other sorts of opportunities. Certain aspects of liberty may be curtailed, consistent with due process, in order to expand other aspects through the lawmaking system summarized above.

In addition to establishing a complex system of democratic government and basic rule of law disciplines, the Constitution includes specific provisions dealing with particular subjects like freedom of speech, criminal procedure, and civil rights. These provisions are primarily negative in character: They restrict the laws that government may enact and enforce, or otherwise limit the exercise of government authority. These provisions do not address environmental issues as such or have any particular implications for environmental law, with one exception, namely the Fifth Amendment's

prohibition on government taking of private property without payment of just compensation. Property rights advocates have, as discussed further below, made this provision a centerpiece of their attack on environmental regulation. Otherwise, protection of the environment as such has no role in our Constitution. A healthful environment and ecosystem integrity are regarded as matters of "positive" liberty or "affirmative" benefits, like welfare or social insurance benefits, education, physical security, and other advantageous opportunities provided or secured by government. Determinations regarding the character and extent of such goods, including environmental quality, is remitted to the political processes. In contrast, the constitutions of many other countries include affirmative provisions guaranteeing rights to a healthful environment and other social benefits; in some countries, the courts play a role in securing these rights.[20] The absence of such provisions in our Constitution, however, has not impeded the development of a vigorous national system of environmental protection through the political process.

The Achievements of the National Environmental Regulatory State

Madison identified domination by economic and ideological factions as the central problem in a liberal polity. He argued that such domination was more likely to occur in smaller, territorially limited units of government than in the proposed national government. An extended republic would encompass so many diverse and scattered factions that no single interest group could gain dominance, nor permanent coalitions be maintained. The separation of powers within the national government would provide an additional safeguard against domination by factions, prevent the growth of excessive and irresponsible central power, and further promote government in the public interest.[21]

The move from the common law to environmental regulation and liability programs like Superfund has resulted in a shift of primary lawmaking responsibility from courts to legislators and administrative agencies. It has also led to a shift from the states to the federal government as the dominant source of environmental law. In the period 1965–1990, Congress enacted sweeping new environmental, health, and safety regulatory programs. New environmental regulatory agencies, such as the federal Environmental Protection Agency and the Occupational Safety and Health Administration (OSHA), were created and invested with extensive powers.[22] The dramatic growth of regulatory authority in Washington reflected political judgments that states are often unwilling or unable to deal effectively with environmental problems because of inadequate administrative resources, the threat of industry flight to jurisdictions with laxer regulatory standards, the dominance of organized economic interests in local politics, and the problem of interstate pollution spillovers. Moreover, businesses, especially makers of nationally marketed products, often have reasons to favor federal regulation.

Our national environmental regulatory state has made significant progress in protecting human health and welfare and the ecosystem.[23] Discharges of many air and water pollutants have been substantially reduced. The growth in discharges of many other pollutants has been limited, although we have yet to begin to address emissions of greenhouse gases in any serious way. On average, air and water quality have significantly improved. The generation of toxic wastes has been sharply curtailed, and their storage, treatment, and disposal tightly regulated. After a very slow start, cleanup of toxic waste sites is gathering steam. Nonhazardous wastes, however, still present many problems that have yet to be addressed. In the area of natural resources conservation, the record is more mixed. The destruction of the nations' wetlands resources has been sharply curtailed. Progress has been made in expanding and improving the management of those portions of the public lands and of marine resources dedicated for wilderness and preservation purposes, but other areas continue to be over exploited for short-term commercial and bureaucratic gain. The record in protection of endangered and threatened species and fisheries is decidedly mixed. The conservation of habitat and biodiversity in an integrated, ecosystem-based manner poses an enormous challenge that we have just begin to consider. Yet overall progress has been good.

On Madisonian premises, the growth of these federal programs should be welcomed as an authentic expression of the public interest and an appropriate consequence of the national government's superior performance in promoting that interest. It also reflects the fact that many Americans regard environmental quality as an important national good that transcends individual or local interest. These manifestations are most powerful in the case of the Endangered Species Act, wilderness legislation, and other federal regulatory measures designed to protect natural resources of special rarity, beauty, or other significance. But public opinion and political support for other far-reaching forms of federal environmental regulation, including air and water pollution control and toxic waste regulation and cleanup, suggest that these aspects of environmental quality are also regarded as part of the national good.[24] From this perspective, our contemporary national environmental bureaucratic regulatory state can be regarded as "the stream of democratic desires."[25]

Notwithstanding the achievements of the national environmental regulatory state, it also has its darker sides. It has spawned a system of factional bureaucratic politics that subverts the law's public-regarding mission. It also creates enormous waste and inefficiency as a result of reliance on command and control regulatory central planning, which handicaps our ability to harmonize and realize both economic and environmental objectives. These deficiencies are discussed in the following two sections.

Madison's Nightmare

In textbook "good government," the directly elected Congress makes the basic regulatory tradeoffs between activity and security, delegating responsibility for the details of implementation to the executive subject to standards that limit its discretion in terms that the courts can enforce. In practice, environmental statutes veer to two extremes. One is excruciating detail. For example, the text of the Clean Air Act runs to hundreds of pages in the United States Code.[26] The other extreme is generality verging on vacuity. For example, Section 404(a) of the Clean Water Act authorizes the Secretary of the Army to "issue permits . . . for the discharge of dredged or fill material into the navigable waters."[27] It provides no standards or criteria for the exercise of this authority. Both approaches result in a serious loss of political accountability. Highly detailed legislation, framed in subcommittee, is typically comprehensible only to a few members of Congress, their staff, and the lobbyists representing specialized environmental, industry, labor, and other interests. Other members, the media, and the public are generally unable to understand or exercise oversight of their decisions. On the other hand, legislation that is framed in very broad terms shifts the responsibility to make the key tradeoffs to unelected administrators. Both of these circumstances constitute a serious threat to democratic principle. Although the problems created by excessively detailed legislation are serious, those created by broad delegations to regulatory agencies are even more severe and will be the focus of the discussion that follows.[28]

The legitimacy problems created by excessively broad delegations are exemplified by two federal regulatory programs that have been a focus of controversy. The first is based on Section 404(a) of the Clean Water Act, quoted above, which was originally adopted in 1974 and was originally designed to regulate and prevent obstacles to navigation by vessels. Prodded by environmental group advocacy and litigation, the Army Corps of Engineers and the EPA have erected a far-reaching national wetlands regulatory program on the basis of the Act's bare grant of authority to issue permits for the discharge of dredged or fill material. When it enacted Section 404(a) in 1948, Congress certainly did not contemplate that it would be used to establish a national system of land use planning and control. The second regulatory program is that established under Section 9 of the Endangered Species Act, which prohibits a "take" by any person of a member of an endangered species. The Department of the Interior, through the Fish and Wildlife Service, has by regulation extended this prohibition to include members of threatened as well as endangered species and has also defined "take" extremely broadly to go far beyond deliberate actions, for example, to capture or kill an animal, to include otherwise wholly legitimate activities such as farming and construction of housing that adversely affect the habitat of such species. The result, again, is a system of national land use controls that Congress never specifically authorized and could hardly have contemplated when it enacted the Endangered Species Act in 1973.

The exercise by an administrative agency of such broad and discretionary power naturally invites vigorous efforts by organized economic and ideological interest groups to influence the agency's decisions. Such groups mobilize political influence and deploy legal remedies in order to advance their agendas. During the 1970s, it became popular wisdom that regulatory agencies are typically "captured" by the industries that they are supposed to regulate. But other economic interests, including labor, government contractors, agricultural interests, state and local governments, and other client groups, also exert a significant influence over agency decisions. Moreover, industry makes extensive efforts to influence regulatory requirements in order to obtain an economic advantage over competitors. A variety of ideological interest groups, including organizations championing the environment, consumers, minorities, and other collective interests, have also risen to join the "regulation game." The interactions among economic and ideological lobby groups, key congressional members and staff, and the political/administrative officials who ultimately decide law and policy are often obscure and accountability is limited.

Understandably, the losers in this factual struggle may, especially if they represent a minority interest that tends to suffer repeated losses, attack the process as corrupt and illegitimate. Thus, federal environmental regulatory programs like those under the Endangered Species Act or Section 404 of the Clean Water Act have become a favorite target of attack by landowner interests that are the target of the regulatory controls. They assert that these programs abuse the democratic process because they impose confiscatory economic losses on property owners in order to shift collective benefits to environmental interests and enhance the power of bureaucrats.[29] One need not embrace all of their arguments in order to agree that these and similar examples of administrative exercise of broad lawmaking discretion raise troubling legitimacy problems.

The problems of the special interest state are exacerbated by a pervasive reliance on legalistic "command and control" strategies to achieve national goals. The command system requires the development and adoption of detailed requirements to control the conduct of those subject to regulation. For example, a command system of air pollution regulation requires detailed specifications of behavior for hundreds of thousands of industrial and command sources of air pollution that vary widely in character, as well as tens of millions of mobile sources. Although Congress sometimes enacts quite detailed statutes, in many cases it finds that it is ill-equipped to devise or politically unable to agree upon the required detail for command regulation and hands that task to administrative bureaucracies. The use of command regulation accordingly tends to inevitably involve a substantial shift of decision-making power from Congress and the president to federal bureaucracies, sidestepping federalism and separation of powers safeguards against the domination of factions. The rapid growth of federal regulatory controls has outstripped the capacity of Congress or the president to responsibly make the thousands of decisions required to dictate conduct throughout a vast and diverse nation with a dynamic economy. By delegating vital decisions about environmental risk management to a remote, opaque, and labyrinthine bureaucratic process, the command system necessarily runs a serious democracy deficit.

Not surprisingly, the political, administrative, and legal struggle among interest groups to gain advantage within the command system of regulatory controls often generates extremely bad public policy. Regulators broker deals that placate powerful interest groups but fail to promote public-regarding objectives. For example, the EPA adopted regulations imposing controls on new fossil-fuel, electric-generating plants in response to the pressures exerted by an "unholy" alliance of environmental and eastern coal interests. The regulations required plants to install intensive "scrubbing" technologies to remove sulfur dioxide from power plant emissions, suppressing the use of low-sulfur western coal. The eastern coal interests could continue to sell their product. Environmentalists favoring the expanded use of technological control mechanisms also had their way. The regulation, however, increased the cost of achieving limitations by well over a billion dollars as compared to alternatives that would have afforded sources greater flexibility, and also resulted in more polluted air in some regions.[30]

Madison associated the problem of factional domination with territorially limited government. The growth of the national regulatory welfare state, however, has spawned a new form of factional domination. Madison's

centralizing solution to the problem of faction has produced Madison's Nightmare: a maze of fragmented and often irresponsible micropolitics within the federal government itself, which invites the very domination of factors that Madison was so anxious to prevent.[31]

The Economic and Environmental Dysfunctions of Central Planning

Our system of centralized command and control environmental regulation also results in tremendous inefficiency and waste. Throughout the world, central planning of economic activity has collapsed because of its built-in limitations. Central planners are unable to gather and process the information needed to write directives that respond appropriately to the diverse and changing conditions of a dynamic economy by many actors. Central planning commands cannot provide the necessary incentives and flexibility to meet changing social needs and spur innovation. Command and control environmental regulation in the United States is a form of central planning that is plagued by these same fundamental and irreparable defects.

EPA regulation writers, for example, face insuperable difficulties in gathering information about the diverse circumstances of the millions of different facilities that they regulate and devising regulatory requirements that are responsive to these different circumstances. In order to economize on decision-making costs, regulators tend to adopt uniform, rigid measures imposing the same requirements on different facilities with different characteristics. Sources with high costs of pollution or waste control are held to the same requirements as those with lower costs. Great savings could be achieved by allocating more of the overall control effort to sources with lower costs. It would, however, neither be practicable nor equitable to achieve this goal within a central planning system. As a result, the costs of achieving a given overall level of pollution control under such a system can be twice or more what they would be under more flexible market-based regulatory systems such as pollution fees or tradeable pollution permits.[32] Given that the regulatory costs imposed by the EPA are approaching $200 billion annually, the current command regulatory paradigm wastes tens of billions of dollars annually. By shifting to more flexible strategies, these wasted resources could be invested in achieving higher levels of environmental quality or in meeting other societal needs.

In order to improve environmental quality while still maintaining economic growth, enterprises must constantly reduce the amount of residuals generated per unit of output. In order to achieve this goal, enterprises must be given both the incentive and the flexibility to devise and adopt innovative, resource-efficient methods of production. While command regulation can ensure adoption of existing technologies, it often fails to create appropriate incentives for the development of new technologies and production methods to further reduce pollution. Command controls are imposed on different pollutants into different media from different discharge points from different facilities within the same plant. Among the important innovations needed to meet environmental as well as economic goals is the development and adoption of integrated pollution and waste prevention and resource efficiency measures on a plant-by-plant or region-by-region basis. Inflexible command requirements not only fail to encourage such innovations but often prohibit them. Thus an EPA case study found that an integrated approach to pollution prevention and resource management at a major oil refinery, which involved some limited increases in some pollutants but much greater reductions in others, could dramatically reduce pollution and waste and also substantially reduce overall control costs. The EPA, however, concluded that the regulatory statutes that it administers would make adoption of such an approach illegal.[33]

IV. Redressing the Failings of National Environmental Regulation: Retrenchment, Reform, or Reconstruction?

As explained in the previous part of this essay, our centralized environmental regulatory state has made substantial overall progress in promoting environmental security, although there are areas of significant weakness. At the same time, the system of central regulatory planning by administrative agencies enjoying substan-

tial lawmaking discretion suffers from democracy deficits, unduly penalizes activity, and impairs flexibility and innovation in ways that thwart environmental as well as economic progress. This part of the essay considers three potential solutions to these failings: a strengthened regime of private property rights regulated by the common law, expanded judicial and administrative review and supervision of environmental regulatory decisions by administrative agencies, and the adoption of more flexible market-based regulatory instruments in lieu of command regulation. The conclusion is that the latter two strategies, and especially the third, hold the greatest promise for advancing the twin elements of liberty through environmental law.

Retrenchment: The Property Rights Agenda

Property right advocates do not believe that the failings of our environmental regulatory system can be cured by devolving regulatory authority from Washington, D.C., to the states, finding that state legislation often shares many of the objectionable features of federal legislation. Nor do they hold much faith in proposals for greater procedural rights before administrative agencies or more searching judicial review of their decisions, believing that such ameliorative measures do not do much to change the fundamental defects of environmental regulation and may instead simply serve to legitimate a fundamentally unjust and corrupt system. They offer two basic cures for the evils of environmental regulation.

- Greatly expanding judicial interpretation and enforcement of the takings clause of the Constitution in order to require government payment of compensation for regulation that diminishes the economic value of property.
- Substituting common-law litigation for administrative regulation as the basic legal tool for addressing environmental problems.

Property rights advocates thus call for a powerful role for the judiciary in restricting the reach of environmental regulation through constitutional interpretation and in leading a revival of common-law approaches to environmental problems. The two elements of its program are closely related. Expanded takings protection for property rights is designed to limit sharply the extent of administrative regulation of land and natural resource use, paving the way for predominant reliance on the common law. The property rights movement is supported by individual landowners, developers, and conservative conservationalists, as well as by libertarians. Its agenda has generally not been supported by industry, which tends to favor legal reform of the existing regulatory system.

Expanding the Scope of Regulatory Takings Protection of Market Property Value.

Property rights advocates assert that government should pay compensation for imposing environmental controls on the use of property that significantly diminish the property's value. To this end, they advocate broad judicial interpretation and enforcement of the takings clause of the Constitution as a weapon to deter regulatory expropriation or require payment of compensation to prevent distributional injustice.[34] There is merit to many of the property rights advocates' criticisms of command and control environmental regulation by administrative agencies. Also, the imposition of stringent environmental regulatory controls on individual landowners may in some cases present substantial problems of distributional inequity. The takings clause of the Constitution is not, however, an appropriate solution for these problems.

The Fifth Amendment to the Constitution forbids the government from taking private property for public use without payment of compensation. For the first 150 years of the Republic, this clause was enforced by the courts in cases where the government took physical possession or otherwise exercised ownership powers over property. With the rise of government regulation, however, the Supreme Court held that regulatory controls that limited an owner's use of real property and thereby diminished the property's value could amount to a "taking" for constitutional purposes. The Court, however, has given a rather restricted scope to constitutional protection against regulatory takings. Property rights advocates would extend its scope far beyond its present contours. Their objective is to discourage the

adoption or enforcement of intensive regulatory controls affecting property use.[35]

Broadened judicial enforcement of the regulatory takings doctrine would require the courts to engage in two highly problematic exercises in constitutional line drawing. First, when is regulation sufficiently justified by prevention of harm to justify what would otherwise be a compensable taking? The Supreme Court has held that no constitutional "taking" occurs when a regulation prevents harm of a sort that would be redressable under common law. Application of such a test in the context of a greatly expanded regulatory takings doctrine would, however, present many difficulties. For reasons already discussed, regulation may be necessary to deal with environmental risks that are too complex or elusive for the common law to handle effectively. How substantial must the evidence of risk and its magnitude be? In order to answer this question, the courts would be obliged, as a matter of constitutional law, to draw arbitrary lines between fuzzy gradations of risk. Second, what is the test for determining whether a regulation impairs property rights in a way that requires the payment of compensation? Is the test the type of limitation on property rights imposed? The diminution in economic value that results? Whether the regulation defeats legitimate investment-backed expectations (an essentially circular inquiry because expectations depend largely on the legal rules for payment of compensation)? The answers given by the courts are halting and often inconsistent.

Property rights advocates have introduced congressional legislation to deal with both of these line-drawing problems by requiring that compensation be paid whenever any regulation reduces the market value of property below a threshold percentage, such as 75 percent.[36] Such a crude and broadly applicable test would, however, require the government to pay for imposing many entirely legitimate regulatory requirements, giving property owners a wholly undeserved windfall. In addition, payment of compensation would create perverse incentives for owners to overinvest in improvements in properties likely to qualify for compensation. Further, in determining the economic impact of government regulatory requirements, account should be taken of specific economic benefits conferred on the property by government measures. These and other problems in implementing a statutory scheme for compensation led the United Kingdom to abandon such a system for reductions in property values caused by development controls.

Furthermore, the Court's decisional law firmly limits the protective scope of the regulatory takings doctrine to real property. Most property rights advocates do not quarrel with this limitation. There has also been no serious claim that takings protection includes industrial facilities subject to environmental regulation. Nonindustrial real property, however, represents only a limited subset of the wide range of property interests and wealth affected by environmental regulation. Why should it be singled out for special protection? While property rights advocates often invoke the rhetoric of individual rights and a Jeffersonian republic of landowning citizen-farmers, the reality is otherwise. Most of those who bear the brunt of environmental regulation of real property use are developers or large landowners with commercial interests. They cannot claim any special property-based liberty interests, nor do they deserve special protection against economic losses due to regulation. The cases of the small individual farmer or other individual landowner may present a different case. Such owners may have developed noncommercial attachments to their property based on what Margaret Radin terms "personhood" values.[37] Such values implicate special security-based liberty interests that arguably deserve special protection. The German Constitutional Court has accorded such interests greater constitutional protection than commercial interests, although our Supreme Court has refused to do so.

In addition to claiming potential personhood interests, an individual who owns land and uses it personally, and does not have other significant assets, is especially vulnerable to stringent environmental land use controls. Owners of personal property, especially capital assets, can hedge against the risk of loss-causing regulatory impositions by diversification, as can developers and other businesses with widespread interests in land. But the individual landowner may find it difficult or impossible to hedge against the risk of controls, for example, that prohibit any significant use of her land when an endangered or threatened species is found on it. She is likely in even a worse position than the plaintiff in *Losee*, who could have bought insurance against the property losses caused by his neighbor's exploding boiler; such insurance is generally not available for losses resulting from government regulation. Furthermore, the circumstance that government benefits all citizens, including landowners, in a general way does not justify imposing a serious, undiversifiable loss on a landowning individual for the sake of general regulatory benefit.

A statutory program for payment of compensation to small individual landowners whose use of their land is severely restricted by environmental regulation may accordingly be justified. Implementing such a program would involve difficult line-drawing problems. What counts as a "small" or "individual" owner? What types of uses are protected? Would an owner of a property who wishes to build a vacation home be covered? Would there be a means test? These issues, however, could be resolved legislatively. Payment of compensation, whether based on the Constitution or statute, would not fully protect the liberty interests of small owners; regulation restricting their use would still be allowed to proceed, and standard measures of monetary compensation would not adequately compensate for loss of personhood values. Nonetheless, compensation could avoid potentially severe distributional inequity toward owners who are unable effectively to hedge against regulatory risks. The property rights movement has not, however, supported a limited compensation regime. Moreover, such a program would make only a very limited contribution to remedying the failings of environmental regulatory central planning.

Reinvigorating the Common Law.   Thoughtful property rights advocates do not embrace outright laissez-faire because they recognize that unfettered market competition will produce excessive environmental degradation. But, why won't the market take care of the environment? The answer may be summarized as follows: Clean air, unpolluted oceans, scenic vistas, and other forms of environmental quality typically have the character of collective or public goods in that they are enjoyed in common by many individuals in ways that make it impractical to exclude some individuals from enjoying, for example, clean air, while allowing others to do so. This lack of excludability represents a form of market failure because it deprives potential suppliers of environmental quality of incentives to provide it. Since an industrial plant that emits air pollution and installs controls cannot limit enjoyment of the resulting clean air to those who pay for it, it will be unable to recover its control costs and will therefore not voluntarily adopt controls. The nonexcludability feature of many environmental benefits also inhibits individual beneficiaries from contributing voluntarily to the costs of cleanup due to free-rider problems. Each individual may reason that if others make such contributions, he can enjoy the resulting clean air for free. But if all reason in the same way, none will contribute, and controls will not be undertaken. Moreover, someone would have to incur the costs of organizing the myriad individuals affected in order to attempt to pool their contributions.[38]

Property rights advocates, who sometimes style themselves "free market environmentalists," are nonetheless optimistic that private law can solve this market failure by making firms or consumers pay compensation to those injured by the adverse effects of their activities. This model would require a strong system of private property rights in environmental resources, such as in-stream river flows or air quality, in order to mobilize private remedies to prevent harm to such resources. Strong property rights would assertively give the rights holders the incentive to invest in protection and enhancement of these environmental resources. Moreover, because these property rights could be freely transferred, free market environmentalists claim that they will end up being held by those who value them most. One of the reasons that property rights advocates attack environmental regulation is that it weakens property rights and therefore undermines the incentives for private actors to protect resources and ensure that they are held by those who value them the most.[39]

This strategy might be practicable for certain local resources, such as a small river, but is hopelessly unrealistic for dealing with most of our more serious environmental problems. How could a workable system of property rights and property markets be established for the millions of individuals who live and firms who operate in a given airshed like that of greater Los Angeles, which receives pollution from tens of thousands of stationary sources and many millions of motor vehicles?

For all those individuals affected by pollution of the Great Lakes or the oceans by numerous land-based and vessel sources? How could the problems posed by toxic waste handling storage and disposal be prevented through a system that relied exclusively on private law litigation imposing liability after the fact? Given the failures of the market with respect to preservation interests, how could a market-based system of private property rights ensure protection of biodiversity and ecologically valuable resources? Given the breadth of the collective interests at stake and the nature of the problems presented, courts could deal with such problems only through massive class actions procedures and sweeping awards of injunctive relief to direct and manage activity on a wide scale. This path would transform the courts into a far less effective and less democratically accountable version of administrative agencies. Some free market environmentalists are nonetheless optimistic that new information technologies will facilitate the development of sophisticated market-based systems of individual property rights in common resources like water bodies and air basins by enabling individuals and nongovernmental organizations to define, track, trade, pool, and manage such rights at very low transactional cost. At present, however, such proposals remain so vague and wholly untested as to lack credibility.[40]

Moreover, even if individual rights could be established and effectively enforced, it is most unlikely that they would be used in the socially most highly valued way or that such uses would be environmentally benign. Holders of small interests in common resources might not be willing or able to pool their holdings in order to secure long-run environmental goals given the alternative of a quick sale to industrial and developer interests who wish to use the resources to dispose of pollution or for other short-term, market-driven returns. Even if the system succeeded in driving resources to their highest-valued use as market commodity, the pattern of uses produced by the market is most unlikely to be that which is most highly valued in social terms because many of the values associated with environmental quality are public and noncommodity in character.

Accordingly, the property rights movement, in part because it misconceives the problem of environmental law as a conflict between individual liberty and community power, fails to provide a workable or appropriate contribution to the problem of constructing environmental law and legal institutions so as to promote both aspects of liberty, security as well as activity.

Reform: Enhanced Judicial and Administrative Review of Agency Regulatory Decisions

A quite different approach to curing the ills of the centralized environmental regulatory state is to preserve its basic apparatus while imposing legal mechanisms of supervision, review, and enhanced accountability in order to address its most serious shortcomings. One approach that has already been widely implemented seeks to cure the democracy deficit threatened by broad delegations of lawmaking power to administrative authorities by extending access to formal agency decision procedures and reviewing courts to all of the various collective interests potentially affected by the agency's decisions and requiring agencies to take all of those interests into account in their decisions. They also included strengthened mechanisms of administrative or judicial review of agency regulatory decisions for the specific purpose of improving and promoting greater agency attention to cost-benefit analysis and quantitative risk analysis. This approach is supported by many lawyers and also by industry interests seeking to ease regulatory burdens and costs. A third strategy, also strongly supported by many industry interests and some policy analysts, is to invalidate statutes that grant regulatory agencies very broad and important lawmaking authority as an unconstitutional delegation of legislative power or to construe such statutes so as to limit the scope of the delegated authority.

The Interest Representation Model of Judicial Review.
Litigants and the courts have already reshaped much of traditional nonconstitutional administrative law in service of the above agenda. Consistent with rule-of-law principles, we in the United States have long relied upon judicial review to check administrative power in order to protect individuals and their property against coercive impositions by government that were not legislatively authorized. Beginning in the late 1960s, as a result primarily of court decisions, the right to participation in agency decision-making procedures, including regulatory rulemaking, has been extended to individuals and groups representing environmental, consumer, and other "public" interests. This change was fueled by recognition of the extent to which Congress delegated broad discretion to regulatory agencies to make important decisions, the fact that agency choices were dictated less by bureaucratic expertness than by policy choices and the influence of political and economic interests, and that for a variety of reasons agencies were more responsive to the interests of organized economic interest groups than to the less well-organized public. The extension of agency participation rights and standing to secure judicial review was designed to redress this imbalance by giving "public" interests access to administrative decision-making procedures and to courts in order to make their concerns heard.[41]

In reviewing agency decisions, courts have not only ensured that agencies obey relevant statutes. In order to curb agency bias and promote decisions that are responsive to the full range of affected interests and values they have also reviewed administrators' exercise of discretion, requiring a detailed agency explanation supported by the administrative record of why an agency chose a given alternative and why it rejected others advocated by those challenging its decision. In short, courts have attempted to ensure that agencies take a hard look at the relevant evidence, analysis, and considerations of policy, as well as the legal arguments advanced by the contending interests, and justify the policy choices that they make. At the same time, courts generally refuse to dictate a particular policy choice unless it is rather plainly required by the relevant statute. If an agency fails adequately to justify its discretionary policy choices, the usual remedy is a remand for further administrative proceedings. Courts have used these techniques to require agencies to give greater consideration not only to environmental values but also to regulatory costs and burdens. Administrative agencies with specialized missions and constituencies tend to develop corresponding predispositions, biases, and "tunnel vision." One function of these procedural requirements and judicial techniques is to counterbalance these tendencies. Thus, in the case of development-oriented agencies, such as the Department of Energy or the Bureau of Land

Management in the Interior Department, these mechanisms may serve to provide greater access and voice for environmental interests. In the case of "pro-regulation" agencies such as the EPA and the Occupational Safety and Health Administration, they may be used to force greater agency attention to regulatory costs and burdens. Taken together, these innovations can be understood as establishing a system of interest representation and participation, guaranteed and supervised by the courts, that serves as a surrogate political process to promote greater agency responsiveness and accountability to the full range of social values and interests affected by their exercise of discretion.[42]

Despite its achievements, the new model of administrative law has drawbacks. Rulemaking proceedings are protracted and cumbersome. Litigation often follows. For example, the EPA issues several dozen major rules each year; over 90 percent of them are challenged in court. In a substantial number of these cases the court finds that the agency has failed to justify at least some portion of its decision and remands for a further rulemaking proceedings, which may be followed by a second round of judicial review. This process also tends to diffuse governmental responsibility and impair coordination of regulatory policy by treating each decision in relative isolation. Moreover, the process of representation through legal advocacy is hardly democratic. Agency decisions tend to respond to the interests that have the organizations and economic means to be represented in the process. Policy choices, which are often resolved by agency settlements with litigants who have brought legal challenges, may thus neglect more diffuse, less well-organized public interests. Moreover, this approach to reform cannot cure the basic shortcomings of central planning, and in some respects may make them worse by overlaying extensive legal procedures and case-by-case litigation on an already unwieldy and fragmented apparatus.

Cost-Benefit Analysis and Risk Analysis. Beginning with President Nixon, every president has maintained a system of centralized review by the Office of Management and Budget (OMB) of new administrative regulations that have a significant impact on the economy. The system was established in essentially its current form by President Reagan. President Clinton continued it with minor modifications in Executive Order 12866. The review system has been primarily applied to environmental regulations. It has been adopted and maintained by presidents of both parties because of concern that the EPA, OSHA, and other regulatory agencies often fail to pay adequate attention to the costs and burdens imposed by their regulations or to balance appropriately regulatory costs and environmental benefits. The executive order requires federal agencies to prepare a regulatory analysis that accompanies all proposed and final major rules. The analysis must consider the costs and benefits of the rule and of alternative means of accomplishing the regulatory objective in question. Agencies must also, "to the extent permitted by law," take into account costs and benefits in their substantive decision and adopt the regulatory alternative that maximizes net benefits. The regulatory analysis must be submitted to the OMB before issuance of the proposed rule and again before issuance of the final rule. The OMB often submits comments to the agency critiquing its analysis, which sometimes results in changes in the rule itself. In rare cases of persistent disagreement between an agency and the OMB over the agency's compliance with the executive order, the matter may be brought to the president for resolution.[43]

Many thoughtful observers believe that such a system of centralized review of regulations under the direct supervision of the president is necessary to counteract the powerful dispersion of power and accountability that results from a congressional form of government and the creation of a vast and uncoordinated federal bureaucracy exercising significant regulatory discretion. They also believe that the OMB review process has, on balance, improved agency decisions.[44] Some would like to see the OMB review process become even more systematic and professionalized, drawing on science as well as economics to promote better risk analysis and management by environmental regulatory agencies. There is also a clear need for a more systematic process of risk management. Some regulations involve a very high cost for achieving a regulatory benefit, such as reducing fatalities or illnesses. Other regulations achieve the same benefit much more cheaply. Regulations are issued on an uncoordinated, ad hoc basis. Critics rightly point out that we could achieve greater regulatory benefits by increasing the stringency of regulations that can produce benefits at low cost, while reducing the stringency of those that entail very high costs.[45] An expanded system of regulatory review based on the executive office of the president could deal with this problem.[46] By building its professional competence and prestige, such a system might evolve into an American version of the French Conseil d'État. Such an institution might well relieve courts of the felt necessity to supervise agencies' exercise of discretion as closely as they do under current "hard look" standards of review. But others dismiss such a possibility, arguing that such an institution would be entirely incompatible with American political structures and traditions.

The executive order establishing the current system of OMB review requires agencies to implement cost-benefit analysis in their decisions only to the extent that the applicable regulatory statute permits it. Many environmental regulatory statutes preclude or restrict the consideration of costs, or a balancing of costs and benefits of such factors. In addition, courts are without jurisdiction to enforce compliance with the executive order. Many policy analysts, along with industry representatives, believe that the current OMB review system has failed to do enough to prevent wasteful and unjustified regulatory requirements. The economist Robert Hahn, for example, conducted a review of a large sample of major EPA rules that were issued in compliance with the OMB review process. He found that even using the EPA's estimates of regulatory benefits, which are generally quite optimistic, most of the EPA regulations involved costs that far exceed their benefits. He also found that the EPA had failed to adopt alternative regulations that would have achieved most of the same regulatory benefits as the rule adopted but at much less cost.[47]

In order to strengthen existing cost-benefit and risk analysis mechanisms, various proposals have been introduced in Congress to impose a "supermandate" through generic legislation that would override particular environmental, health, and safety regulatory statutes; require all regulatory decisions to be made in accordance with cost-benefit principles; and authorize private parties to enforce compliance with this requirement through

litigation in the courts. Some proposals would also oblige agencies to undertake quantitative risk assessments to justify new regulatory requirements and impose other judicially enforceable requirements to control regulatory risk assessment and management. While these proposals attracted considerable support, they also encountered sharp criticism and were not adopted. The criticisms were voiced not only by environmental and labor interests but also by lawyers and policy analysts who concluded that they would impose tasks on the courts that they are ill-equipped to discharge and add a great deal of cost and delay to the already quite protracted and burdensome procedures for regulatory rulemaking. Some critics charged that the real purpose of the proposals was not to improve regulatory decision-making but to stall it completely with burdensome procedural requirements.

Nondelegation Doctrine and Clear Statement Principles. Another strategy for dealing with the problems of administrative discretion is for courts to invalidate general or vague regulatory statutes as unconstitutional on the ground that they violate the separation of powers principle by delegating to bureaucrats choices that should be made by elected legislators. The Supreme Court used this nondelegation doctrine principle to invalidate several New Deal statutes. Since then, it has rebuffed all efforts by litigants to strike down statutes for undue delegation, although it has indicated the principle is not completely dead. The D.C. Circuit Court of Appeals, however, recently struck down the EPA's adoption by regulation of new air quality standards for ozone and particulate matter under a provision of the Clean Air Act authorizing it to set such standards to "protect the public health . . . with an adequate margin of safety." In its decision in *American Trucking Ass'n v. U.S.E.P.A.,* the court found that the statute failed to provide any meaningful guidance on standard setting for pollutants, such as ozone, which the EPA has found to be "non-threshold" in character, in that any amount causes a risk of harm.[48] The court did not invalidate the statute outright, indicating that the EPA could save its constitutionality by adopting an "intelligible principle" to limit the discretion conferred but that the EPA had failed to do so. The same court also recently invalidated, as exceeding the agency's statutory authority and without reference to constitutional principles, a Corps of Engineers regulation under Section 404 of the Clean Water Act to include not only the deliberate deposit of dredged or fill material to fill wetlands but the "incidental" discharge of soil that is displaced and redeposited in place in connection with any dredging operation, thereby extending regulatory jurisdiction over dredging operations designed to drain wetlands without adding fill.[49] This decision can be seen as an instance of "clear statement" approach to statutory construction to limit broad assertions by agencies of expansive regulatory authority that have not been clearly authorized by Congress. The techniques in these decisions can, if applied carefully by the courts, serve to overcome the "democracy deficit" by promoting greater accountability on the part of agencies and Congress and promoting the rule of law by limiting agency discretion. It remains to be seen, however, whether the rulings in these cases will be upheld by the Supreme Court, which had previously upheld the Interior Department's expansive interpretation of the term "take" in Section 9 of the Endangered Species Act.[50]

Reconstruction: Market-Based Incentives for Environmental Protection

The reform strategies discussed in the previous section seek to ameliorate some of the failings of the current national environmental regulatory system without altering its basic characteristics. A more ambitious strategy that promises a much higher payoff is to shift to market-based regulatory instruments that address more directly the political, economic, and environmental shortcomings of the command paradigm.

Command and control central planning dictates specific operational and management decisions by actors in order to produce environmental quality, backed up by punitive sanctions for noncompliance. Alternatively, the government can use market-based incentives to achieve "strategic coupling" between the decisions of myriad market actors and environmental goals by imposing costs on those actors with inferior environmental performance and providing cost savings and competitive advantages for those actors with superior performance, without attempting to dictate particular outcomes on an individual basis. Command regulation fixes, directly or indirectly, the quantity of pollution or waste generated by each source or the manner in which a natural resource must be used. Economic instruments instead use prices to discourage the generation of harmful residuals or other socially disfavored resource uses. This reliance on the price system, if appropriately implemented, produces substantial cost savings and enhances flexibility and innovation, promoting both economic and enviromental goals. The command systems focuses, piecemeal, on preventing specific sources of pollution, waste, or environmental degradation. Economic instruments mobilize the market affirmatively in the service of more efficient and sustainable use of enviromental resources, which is the ultimate basis for enviromental security.[51]

For example, government can impose a tax or fee on pollution or issue a limited number of pollution rights and allow them to be bought and sold in the market. In addition, it could disseminate information regarding firms' environmental performance to consumers and investors who might use their market power to reward firms with superior environmental performance and punish those with poorer records. Government and industry could also negotiate environmental covenants providing for an overall reduction in pollution or wastes from a given facility or industry in accordance with an agreed timetable. Further, government could adopt deposit/refund systems to deal with hazardous wastes and postconsumer residues. Government would draw on this expanded portfolio of regulatory techniques. Command and control regulation would continue to play a role but on a reduced scale.

Economic instruments for regulation have, until recently, played little or no role in environmental policy. In the United States, as elsewhere, the overwhelming instrument of choice has been command and control regulation. Although the historical record may suggest that regulation "works," several decades of experience have made clear its fundamental limitations. The incentives that it provides for innovation are, at best, uneven and often counterproductive. The detailed requirements and short deadlines for compliance that are characteristic of command style regulation tend to stifle innovation by depriving firms of flexibility in meeting environmental goals. The proliferation of ever more detailed regulations has created problems characteristic of central planning: information overload, rigidity, lack of coordination and consistency among different requirements, and economic inefficiency. The Clinton administration has sought to address some of the drawbacks of the current command system by "reinvesting government" and "common sense" initiatives, including the EPA's Project XL program for regulatory flexibility.[52] The inherent limitations of central planning and the legal constraints imposed by existing command regulatory statutes, however, sharply limit the contributions that such "add-on" programs can make. What is needed is a fundamental shift in the regulatory paradigm.

Among the most market-based regulatory instruments are pollution fees and tradeable permit systems. These instruments offer important advantages over command and control regulation in dealing with widespread pollutants. They substantially reduce the costs of achieving given levels of pollution reduction by equalizing the marginal costs of control among different sources. Under a system that levies a fee on each ton, or other unit, of pollution emitted, each source will invest in pollution prevention and control to the point where the marginal costs of additional controls equal the fee. Since all sources must pay the same fee, their marginal control costs will tend to equalize. A similar result is reached under a tradeable permit system, where the right to emit a ton of pollution carries a market price. In addition to eliminating the enormous deadweight losses of the inefficient command system, these systems provide firms with powerful economic incentives for innovation to further reduce pollution and waste loadings. Those firms that are successful in innovation will either pay lower taxes or be able to sell excess pollution rights to others, thereby gaining a competitive advantage. Firms will have positive incentives to invest in environmental protection, in contrast to the current system, which leads firms to invest in lawyers in order to fight regulations. A further advantage is that fees or tradeable permits leave firms with broad flexibility to reduce discharges through any and all available means they please, including process changes and conservation, in contrast with the exist-

ing technology-based regulatory system, which tends to be based on "end of pipe" and other standardized technology controls.

Economic incentives can also be an effective way of steering the conduct of small facilities and individual consumers in directions that are environmentally protective through mechanisms such as pollution taxes on automobiles and tradeable risk permits for chemical and biological methods of addressing agricultural pests. Deposit/refund systems, which have already been used to promote recycling of beverage containers, can be extended to deal with postconsumer wastes generally or problems such as hazardous wastes.

Local air pollution and other environmental problems can be addressed by environmental covenants negotiated and agreed to by facilities and state or local governments. These contracts would use the risk levels established under existing federal and state regulatory requirements as a benchmark. Facilities would have the flexibility to depart from the specific regulatory requirements imposed on different waste streams and sources under existing law and could devise their own environmental management plans tailored to the circumstances of their particular facility and location, provided that the plan would achieve an equivalent or lower level of aggregate risk. The covenants would include specific commitments that would be monitored and enforced by the government.

The virtues of economic instruments for environmental protection are not merely theoretical; they have been and are being confirmed by experience.[53] In the United States there has been substantial use of tradeable permit systems to provide flexibility within the general air pollution control regulatory system, phase out lead additives in gasoline, and reduce sulfur dioxide emissions by 50 percent over a ten-year period. They have delivered environmental protection at costs that are far less than those of the command regulatory system. For example, the tradeable permit system for sulfur dioxide emissions involves issuance by the government to sources of a fixed number of emissions permits annually. Each permit entitles the holder to emit one ton of sulfur dioxide; the number of permits is decreased over time in accordance with a schedule for achieving an overall 50 percent reduction. Sources may not emit sulfur dioxide in excess of the permits that they hold. The system is achieving emissions reductions substantially ahead of schedule and, by providing individual sources with wide flexibility regarding the level and method of emissions control, is achieving these reductions at less than half the cost of the command and control alternative. Firms have strong incentives to reduce emissions because permits, being fixed in quantity, are economically valuable; surplus permits obtained as a result of emissions reductions can be sold in the permit trading market, transferred to other units within the same company, or retained for future use, Firms whose emissions exceed their permit holdings are subject to stiff penalties. Also, emissions are monitored on a continuous basis. Thus, the trading system has achieved significant environmental and economic benefits. These benefits, generated by the switch from command and control to market-based incentives, enabled political agreement to be reached in Congress, breaking a thirteen-year legislative stalemate between Midwestern states, where many emissions originate, and eastern states affected by acid deposition on measures to address the problem.

In Europe, a number of countries are relying on emissions taxes or fees to reduce discharges of various air pollutants. Fee or tax levels in several countries have been set at sufficiently high levels that they are already having a significant impact in reducing emissions. Use is also being made in the United States, Europe, and elsewhere of tradeable permit systems and taxes to limit water pollution discharges. Emissions trading and tax systems are best suited for addressing widespread air and water pollutants emitted by many sources in an air or water basin. They also have great promise for addressing greenhouse gases in order to deal with climate change.[54] The Kyoto Protocol to the Framework Convention on Climate Change authorizes a number of emissions trading mechanisms to limit greenhouse gases.

Deposit and refund systems are being used in Europe to deal with postconsumer wastes on a broad scale. European countries have also used environmental contracts or covenants with industry to deal with a variety of air and water pollution control problems. Industry has agreed to achieve, on a specific timetable, significant reductions in pollution discharges in emissions, going far beyond the cuts mandated by otherwise applicable

command regulations. In return, the government provides industry with flexibility in the means of achieving reductions and an undertaking not to impose additional controls during the commitment period, which gives industry the time to plan and implement more far-reaching capital investments and pollution prevention measures.

Transferrable development rights are a form of tradeable permit system that can be used to implement land use controls and preservation schemes. Landowners whose development rights are restricted for environmental reasons are given rights that can be transferred and used for more intensive residential or commercial development in adjacent areas. This technique responds to the equity claims of landowners and helps defuse political opposition to land use restrictions. It also encourages a regional approach to preservation and development planning. This technique has been used successfully in a variety of local settings, including programs to preserve farmlands in Montgomery County, Maryland, and to preserve undeveloped pine barrens in New Jersey and Long Island. Transferrable development rights programs would be a useful means of defusing the controversies, discussed previously, over federal programs for preservation of wetlands and endangered and threatened species habitat. Indeed, the Army Corps of Engineers has already fostered a wetland trading plan, and the Fish and Wildlife Service has helped to broker habitat conservation plans that provide for a version of transferrable pollution rights. The problem, however, is that these programs are Band-Aids on a command regulatory system and have no statutory basis. Both programs should be revamped by Congress to make market-based arrangements a foundational element. Use of market-based "carrots" in conjunction with regulatory "sticks" would enable the federal government to achieve natural resource management goals more effectively, eliminating much of the rancor and divisiveness that has compromised the current command system.

Regulatory systems using the various economic instruments described above have certain affinities with the proposals of free market environmentalists to address environmental problems through a system of property rights based on the common law. Both emphasize decentralized ordering over central planning. Both allow considerable flexibility to market-based actors and rely on market-based incentives to achieve environmental objectives. There are, however, fundamental differences between the two. Regulatory programs using economic instruments are established by legislation and administered by administrative agencies. The environmental goals to be achieved are established on a collective basis, through the political process, that takes account of the broad range of social and ethical values involved in balancing environmental security and activity. The programs are designed on a national or regional scale, dealing explicitly with the problems posed by large numbers of sources that affect many people. The responsible administrative agency monitors and oversees the program and its performance and can take corrective measures if necessary. Furthermore, the responsible administrative agency enforces program requirements, such as the requirement in the sulfur dioxide trading program that emissions not exceed a source's permit holdings. Thus, the program is established and enforced through collective means. The market serves solely as a means to achieve objectives determined through nonmarket processes.

Free market environmentalism, by contrast, involves a far more radical degree of decentralization. Property rights are not established, monitored, and enforced administratively but through litigation by private litigants. There is no collective determination of environmental goals; the overall level of environmental quality is the by-product of millions of individual decisions. For reasons already noted, it is most unlikely that such arrangements will give adequate weight to noncommodity values or provide the level of environmental quality that the public collectively wants. Free market environmentalists deprecate tradeable permit programs as "market socialism." The fact, however, that the goals of such programs are collectively determined and its implementation collectively overseen, while still allowing market-based flexibility and incentives to operate, are their great virtue. These and other regulatory programs that use economic instruments, if properly designed, can combine the best features of command regulation and private law property regimes without the drawbacks of either.

Accordingly, appropriately selective deployment of economic instruments to achieve environmental objectives can promote both socially beneficial activity and enhance environmental security. In addition, a major shift to economic instruments for environmental protection will help to deal with many of the governance problems created by the use of command regulation.[55] The use of economic instruments will remit to firms via the price system the vast number of complex and detailed engineering and economic decisions about limiting pollution and wastes and managing natural resources at particular sources and locations that are now made by government. Managers of firms are generally far better equipped to make such decisions than are government officials. This approach would also greatly lessen the need for the complex legal apparatus of procedure and litigation that has been developed to oversee and regulate the central planning effort. Government will instead be forced to focus on broad decisions about the overall level of pollution or waste or resource preservation. For example, under tradeable permit or pollution tax systems, the government would set an aggregate quantity limit on pollution or the level of the tax at the national or regional levels. Political transparency and accountability will be enhanced by thus shifting the focus of government decision making from a myriad of technocratic decisions to "bottom-line" decisions about the overall extent of environmental objectives, which are more likely to be made by the legislature. By relying on the price system, regulatory programs that use economic instruments generate current, accurate, and public information about the cost of environmental protection measures—an important consideration in any democratic decision-making process. Through environmental covenants and regional programs of transferrable development programs local risks will be dealt with by local decisions made by local communities and facilities, responsive to local conditions and needs, subject to a federal regulatory safety net establishing overall baseline levels of permissible environmental risk or resource preservation.

A shift to economic instruments for environmental regulation will not eliminate Madison's Nightmare. Factional struggles for influence will not disappear. Both at the legislative and administrative levels, interest groups will vie to shape the operational details of regulatory programs for their benefit, whether the program in question uses economic instruments or command techniques. But regulatory programs that use economic instruments provide far less purchase for factional domination than command systems. They remit most decisions about control of pollution and waste and resource management to the market, where rivalry works to benefit society. The most important of the remaining decisions, which government must make, will be generic in character and have substantial visibility, thereby enabling public and political mechanisms of accountability to function. Although Madison's Nightmare will not disappear, it will shrink substantially.

V. Conclusion

Environmental law is not, fundamentally, a zero-sum conflict between community interests and individual liberty. It is an undertaking to serve society by enlarging the liberty of its members. In order to do so, the law must simultaneously promote collective interests in environmental security while enhancing the collective benefits of activity. The law must be fashioned through democratic institutions, subject to rule-of-law disciplines, and give appropriate weight to the wide range of societal interests and values at stake in environmental protection policy. Our centralized command-based environmental regulatory state has made substantial but uneven progress in promoting environmental security. At the same time, it has unduly burdened socially beneficial activity and compromised democratic values. Strengthened methods for judicial or higher-level administrative oversight of the existing command system of administrative regulation can help to address these shortcomings. The adoption of economic instruments for environmental protection in lieu of many existing command regulatory programs would make an even greater contribution to promoting liberty and democratic values.

Building Bridges for People and Repaying Debts to Nature

Yuri Kostenko

The creation of nature reserves has allowed over a million hectares of natural land to be preserved for the state and for future generations of Ukrainians. This now constitutes a kind of golden investment fund helping to restore an environmental equilibrium, clean water and air, and increase the numbers of wildlife, medicinal grasses, and so on. A fundamental priority in the creation of nature reserves is their diverse function. First and foremost this means national parks. These allow the twin functions of nature preservation and sustainable recreation to coexist. It should be remembered that we did not inherit our biodiversity from our ancestors but "borrowed" it from our children. And what is borrowed obviously has to be returned. Today, mankind has a fine opportunity to return what has been borrowed and has begun to do this.

International Cooperation in the Context of National Environmental Policy

The international dimension is a necessary component of any environmental protection activity. It should be based on cross-border efforts to coordinate activities reducing global-scale human damage to the environment and on an incorporation of international experience, technology, and know-how as well as technical and financial assistance for solving internal problems. The following are important in this respect:

- Concluding and implementing bilateral cooperative agreements on environmental protection with Ukraine's neighbors and other countries where this would serve national interests and priorities;

- ratifying and coordinating the implementation of the terms of regional and global environmental agreements;

- developing national plans for the realization of those conventions relating to national priorities—first and foremost the UN framework convention on climate change, the Vienna convention on the protection of the ozone layer, the UN convention on biodiversity, the convention on the protection of cross-border waterways and international lakes, and the agreements on the protection of the Black Sea;

- coordinating efforts in implementing the Pan-European environmental policies developed in the An Environment for Europe, Health and the Environment, and Transport and the Environment processes and beyond, including preparing for the Pan-European ministerial conference, An Environment for Europe, scheduled for Kyiv in 2002; and

- developing and implementing a series of measures related to the decision to seek associated membership in the European Union.

Today, Ukraine is a party to eighteen regional and global environmental conventions as well as five additional protocols and amendments to these agreements. More than twenty additional international protocols, conventions, and agreements are being prepared for signing or ratification, or for Ukraine's participation. New agreements are also being drafted. These include one on biosecurity to supplement the convention on biodiversity; a protocol on water and health to the EU–UN convention on the protection and utilization

231

of transnational waterways and international lakes; and additional protocols on the reduction of nitric acid emissions and on unstable organic compounds and heavy metals to the convention on transnational atmospheric pollution.

One of the most basic and potentially most productive documents within this process is the Pan-European strategy for the protection of bio- and landscape diversity. It was developed by the Council of Europe with the help of the regional UNEP office and the EU environmental policy committee and was adopted by the meeting of EU environment ministers in Sofia in 1995.[1]

Ukraine took an important political step by signing and ratifying the following: the convention on access to information, public participation in the policy process, and access to legal recourse on environmental issues (Aarhus 1998); the UN convention on the preservation of migration routes of herds; the EU–UN agreement for evaluating the influence of transnational problems on the environment; agreements on the international trade in endangered plants and animals; and the international agreement for the protection of migrating Afro-European aquatic and marsh birds. Work has practically finished on preparing and negotiating with the appropriate ministries draft laws for ratifying or acceding to a number of other agreements and conventions, specifically, the UN conventions on preventing the desertification of those countries suffering from serious water deficits and/or desertification, particularly in Africa.

The international ecological agreements to which Ukraine is a party also enlarge the national environmental legislation base.

Initial Results and New Challenges

The following results have been achieved by implementing a consistent program of environmental reforms:

- The formation of a system of national ecological legislation and its harmonization with international norms through adherence to conventions and agreements and the adoption of European norms and standards;
- the introduction of the basic components of an economic mechanism for managing the environ-

ment that make pollution and excessive use of natural resources uneconomical;
- the development of national ecological programs that reflect the priorities of the National Action Plan;
- the balancing of the environmental budget's revenues and expenditures through the introduction of a rational economic mechanism for exploiting the environment;
- a one-third reduction in air and water pollution indicators; and
- the doubling in area of protected territories.

Intellectual and administrative efforts should focus on:

- Creating a mechanism that would ensure funds designated for environmental protection—whether at the national or regional level—are used for their specified purposes;
- improving regulatory functions;
- realizing priority state programs;
- developing environmental legislation that meets international, specifically European, standards;
- reinforcing regional and local levels in their efforts to pursue ecologically sustainable development;
- providing scientific and technical support for environmental reforms; and
- publicizing environmental policy at all levels of government and among a broad circle of social groups, including cooperating with nongovernmental organizations and other interested parties.

Building Green Bridges

The All-European Econet and the Experience with Creating National Econets in Europe

The concept of econets is integral to the preservation of bio- and landscape diversity. Such an idea is already quite well developed within Europe. A concept for the creation of an all-European (Pan-European) econet is practically complete.[2] A number of countries have already declared their intention to create national econets with trans-European elements. A Pan-European econet, in the shape of a significant physical network of natural and seminatural territories, is the major goal of the Pan-European strategy for the preservation of bio- and landscape diversity approved by the conference of European ministers of the environment held in Sofia in 1995. This strategy consists of the following elements:

- Ecocorridors for preserving the continuity of natural ecosystems (and, simultaneously, migratory paths);
- natural territories or nuclei (key regions) for preserving ecosystems, environmental habitats, species, and landscapes that have Europe-wide significance;
- regions of renewal for the renewal of disrupted components of the ecosystem, environments, habitats, and landscapes of European significance;
- "satellite" natural areas (principally for migratory species); and
- buffer zones that contribute to the strengthening of the network and assist in its defense against negative external influences.

The legal basis for defining the core of the Pan-European econet are two European Union directives: Council Directive 79/409/EEC on the conservation of wild birds and Council Directive 92/43/EEC on the conservation of natural habitats and of wild fauna and flora. Among the other legal underpinnings of the econet are the global conventions comprising the system of international environmental law. These include the Bonn convention on migratory species and agreements on bats, small whales, and Afro-Eurasian migratory routes, as well as the convention on aquatic and marsh environments of international significance, chiefly for aquatic birds (the 1973 Ramsar convention). The law on accession to these conventions, as well as the Berne convention, was passed by the Ukrainian parliament on 29 October 1996.

The organization of natural core areas, buffer zones, and corridors is accompanied by the integration of conservation policy with other national policies. These include agriculture and forestry (the support of extensive, traditional management practices), tourism (supporting village tourism while taking into consideration

the interests of the local population), transport (through cooperation in defining corridors), fishing (based on principles of ecologically balanced development), landscape planning (the creation of "green lung" zones that take into account urbanization and the requirements for locating econets), legal policy (through the provision of suitable legal norms), and evaluations of the state of the environment. The basic element of the European integrationist idea is the creation by 2005 of a Pan-European econet based on national econets.

In the national econet program the natural areas that are part of the Ukrainian natural reserve fund will perform a variety of functions—from serving as natural core areas to ecological corridors and buffer zones. According to Ukrainian environmental law, holiday and health resorts, recreational, historical, and cultural sites, agricultural lands, and those designated for transport and communications all form part of the econet. The "environmentalization" of government activity deserves attention. So does the improvement of a system of limiting environmental damage that tries to preserve the protectional function of forests, especially as havens for a variety of species, and the introduction of a form of continual and sustainable utilization.

On September 22, 1994, the Ukrainian parliament adopted a resolution on a program for the future development of nature reserves that improved the legal basis for this development. This was done specifically through a proposal "to develop and to adopt legislative acts on a system of territories subject to special protection" (and the need to legally combine the network of all of the natural and seminatural territories into one single system). This can take the form of a new law on econets or on the stabilization of the country's ecosystem. Or initially, it might be sufficient simply to amend existing legislation, specifically the laws on the protection of the environment and the nature reserve fund of Ukraine. Another aspect is the need to develop interdepartmental cooperation, and to improve and unify policies for the maintenance of all legally protected natural territories, particularly unique natural complexes, landscapes, and environments that contain species of endangered European and Ukrainian flora and fauna.

Existing strategies for the protection of living nature and those conventions dealing with the individual and territorial protection of, first and foremost, species do not take a holistic approach. Only in the convention on biodiversity is there mention of the need to protect other organizational units of life forms, such as ecosystems and landscapes. But even this document is not comprehensive enough to cover every type of collective grouping of living organisms since it essentially seeks to protect their gene pool and conditions for existence. The idea of renewing the integrity and unity of the planet's living membrane was not the aim of the convention. All of current nature reserves are localized and isolated. That is why within the framework of the Pan-European strategy for preserving biological and landscape diversity it was decided to create a Pan-European econet based on the idea of holism—the integrity of natural systems, mutual interdependence, and the indivisibility of the constituent subsystems. Ecocorridors are spatially elongated configurations linking natural core areas and include all types of biodiversity and their environments as well as territories requiring renewal. Their principal function is to facilitate breeding, the diversification of the gene pool, migration, the geographical spread of species, enhance their survival prospects, and to ensure the stability of the ecosystem.

On the Analysis of Econets as a Synthesis of Theory and Practice, a Compromise Between Individual and Collective Needs and the Legal Safeguarding of Their Enlargement (the Socioeconomic Significance of the Econets)

The approach to econets is characterized by a general tendency to try to create a universal socionatural structure that would address both the need to protect flora and fauna, as well as their environments, and be socially and economically beneficial to the human population by raising living standards and thereby laying the foundations for an ecologically balanced development of the region as one of its key components. The econet is of particular importance for environmentally fragile and degraded areas whose ecological potential has been largely exhausted and where extreme conditions exist. In such cases, they offer the only short-term means for improving the situation.

Some Advantages of Econets and the Conditions Under Which They Are Created

First, the creation of an econet requires a comprehensive examination of the territory using ecological and social indicators in order to identify those factors that threaten its future development and, on this basis, a means for dealing with any negative elements. Second, an econet regenerates neglected areas and increases their productivity by providing food for animals and woods, mushrooms, berries, medicinal grasses, and other productive plants for the population while also providing it with additional benefits either directly or through licensing arrangements. Those branches of government dealing with forestry, rural, and aquatic issues can play a leading role. They are beginning to reorient themselves to a balanced form of exploiting the land and resources. Almost ideal in this regard are woodlands and waterways. They provide almost every type of resource and service, ranging from hunting, fishing, and relaxation to the scientific and educational. Tourism—focusing on the natural core areas that are rich in history as well-planned excursions—is extremely important given the numbers of people involved and the funds it can generate. Third, the econets improve the environment by regulating the hydrological system, controlling erosion, regulating the microclimate, lowering pollution levels, improving soil quality, and generally maintaining the ecological balance. Fourth, econets contribute to the preservation of the historical heritage and to the further development of traditional, less intensive forms of farming such as beekeeping, fish farming, the rearing of livestock, and so on. Fifth, they improve the overall infrastructure by rationalizing the relationship between the areas of different usage and their locations—principally in agriculture—and facilitate a comprehensive, rational use of natural resources and objects such as large rivers, lakes, and estuaries. Finally, the realization of such a program would assist in helping to create a more rational distribution of population, thereby increasing employment, income, and lifestyles and raising the level of education and national self-awareness.

With regard to the legal aspects of creating an econet, there already exists in Ukraine a developed legislative base, primarily in the area of natural reservations and nature reserves. It can be further developed and improved, specifically to accommodate the econet, and these improvements will determine the nature of the task and the level of funding. Therefore, the most important factors today are the organizational, financial, and technical aspects. Resolving this type of problem obviously requires a three-tiered approach: The creation of a general legislative base for the econet, the development of normative regulatory documents, and negotiations with local populations concluding in concrete agreements.

The econet could, to one degree or other, become self-financing and thus contribute to addressing the financial problems associated with its creation and functioning. This could be achieved particularly through a more economical use of bioresources, the various properties of landscapes, and the creation of a favorable economic and legal climate in industry. The main source of income could be funds from the utilization of fish resources, hunting, forests, and medicinal herbs. All of these resources would be available to the user for a certain fee that, although rather symbolic for the individual, would represent a fairly large income to the budget. The important thing would be to guarantee that this is then used as designated, to monitor the income and expenditure of these funds carefully, primarily to reopen the bioresources and introduce nonexploitative technologies for working with the environment. Fees should also be introduced for the use of other mineral, aquatic, recreational, and land resources.

Arguments for the creation of an econet can be both moral and material. The moral arguments are based, for example, on calls to renew the natural landscape as a natural-historic environment for the development of the nation and the state; the implementation of constitutional norms for environmental equilibrium and safety, and also other normative-legal documents ensuring the purity of water, soil, and air; the creation of new recreational zones; and guaranteeing the quality of the environment and the quality of life—all things that academics, scientists, and writers call for. This also means upholding certain laws (the basic law on the protection of the natural environment, the laws on the natural reserves and on wildlife, and so on).

Some of the important achievements in the creation of an econet are:

- making use of natural resources through an insignificant initial investment, specific principal investment, low depreciation, and long-term profits;
- making considerable reductions in the future costs of ensuring environmental safety and of cleaning contaminated waters on the territory of the econetwork;
- reducing human health expenses as a result of an improvement in the quality of the environment;
- integrating financial and human resources for the purpose of implementing a coherent program instead of wasting resources on numerous separate and unrelated programs and popular initiatives, as is currently the case; and
- making use of the potential for receiving international financial assistance as compensation in the form of, say, "value-added" from the Global Environmental Foundation.

An important source of funding for the econet program could be funds collected at the local level for the purpose of dealing with environmental problems, the creation of an ecobusiness infrastructure for encouraging joint financing of projects. Today, unfortunately, the ecological problems caused by the disappearance of small rivers and springs, erosion, and salinization can be found in any populated location and on every kind of territory. All of these problems obviously require solutions. Since the idea of an econet coincides with the solutions to each of the above-listed problems, it can therefore provide a basis for cooperation between national, regional, local, and local state authorities as well as public organizations and institutions, thereby simultaneously assisting the democratization process.

Given the social value of this project, another strategic-level socioenvironmental program could be proposed under the provisional name of A Green Ukraine—2000. This program could throw down a challenge to unemployment as well as ecological problems and could provide a synergy between the efforts of society and state for their solution.

(An explanatory note on the program A Green Ukraine—2000: It is well known that many countries have had experience with public works projects. This was particularly the case with the United States in the 1930s during the Great Depression and in the Federal Republic of Germany in the late 1940s as it tried to overcome the socioeconomic problems of the postwar period. The essence of these public works projects lies in drawing upon the temporarily unemployed for the construction of infrastructure projects. It would seem to make sense that Ukraine, which has a 4 percent official unemployment rate (and a hidden rate probably close to 20 percent), should draw on this kind of experience and direct its public works programs into the environmental sphere. This could lead to the creation of a first-rate econet and temporarily overcome the problem of unemployment. Time would also be gained for the introduction of other socioeconomic programs for reducing unemployment and for the expansion of the econetwork itself. An additional effect of such a program would be a growing ecological awareness within society through practical education in accordance with Pestalocci's golden rule of learning through observation. Of course, it would be necessary to make sure that such a program does not simply become the latest plan for the transformation of nature and retains its systematic and socioeconomic essence.)

The above-mentioned sketch provides a more or less holistic image of a novel approach to solving some eternal problems confronting humanity, which grow more acute with the passage of time and are approaching a critical point in mankind's relationship with nature. This scheme arises from the convention on biodiversity as well as the Bonn and Berne conventions and attempts to reflect the various means suggested for solving the numerous manifestations of this crisis in the social, economic, ecological, genetic, and even spiritual aspects. This is not a straightforward path in many respects, and there are many questions that will require further research and clarification. First and foremost, this concerns the problem of a rational choice of region when all of the indices might not agree, and they then have to be prioritized according to the environmental con-

ditions and state of a particular region, including its management structures, direction and degree to which its natural resources are being exploited, the social conditions, and so on. Mention should be made here about certain legal difficulties relating to the still insufficiently developed legislative base for the organization of international preservation projects. Beyond this the biggest problems are posed by the general economic situation in the country, the transformation of the economy to a more traditional, nonexploitative mode of production, and an insufficient awareness of the need for a swift resolution of this problem by officials at all levels as well as the population at large, as well as the little time that remains for implementing such a project. Therefore, there is much hard work ahead if the concept of an econet is to be realized.

Uniting Efforts

There is no such thing as a national ecological problem. In working on the ecological problems of its Polissya region, Ukraine is helping to renew the "green lungs" of Europe. In improving the aquatic environment of the Azov and Black Sea regions, and by working intensively on the environmental renewal of the Dnipro basin, Ukraine contributes to the amelioration of both regional and global problems. An environmentally clean, economically stable, and democratic Ukraine is not only the dream and aim of Ukrainian citizens, but it is also a full-blooded, future part of Europe and the global community.

Instead of a Summary

The following should be key instruments for the cooperative development of environmentally friendly societies:

- A coordinated system of environmental laws based on decisions reached in Rio in 1992 and global conventions;
- political support for environmentally sound forms of development (through, for example, the "environmentalization" of technical assistance;
- environmentalization of the world financial, economic, and banking spheres;

- development of international ecological institutions that will try to encourage a synergistic form of development;
- development of regional ecological accountability, including legal;
- technological reorientation; and
- the "greening" of local communities.

A breakthrough in thinking is required, primarily by the everyday pressures on developments. Thus there are fewer fishes in the rivers and seas, fewer animals in the forests, and fewer grasses—including medicinal ones—in meadows. There are fewer forests, and this has led to erosion and the southward movement of deserts in parts of the world; the natural, environmental means for purifying the air and for the stabilization of the hydrological cycle, and, ultimately, the climate, have been degraded. This sad list could be continued, but, finally and importantly, contemporary society has begun to understand that it is more beneficial to garner and have natural, primarily living, resources than to lose and then try to restore them, if this is at all possible. It is perhaps appropriate therefore to recall a saying of the Cree Indians: "Only when the last tree will be felled, only when the last stream will be poisoned, only when the last fish will be caught, only then will you understand that you cannot eat money." This kind of understanding is also coming to Ukrainian society.

Property Rights, Environmental Regulations, and the Legal Culture of Postrevolutionary Mexico

Antonio Azuela

Introduction

The purpose of this paper is to analyze recent developments in Mexican law regarding the definition of property rights to land in the face of the emerging environmental interests of society and in the context of globalization processes. In particular, I will try to explore those developments in the context of Mexico's legal culture. The main question is the way in which global developments influence the balance between community and individual interests in the regulation of the use of land and the way Mexican legal categories (as read by operators with the legal culture of postrevolutionary regimes) can absorb that influence.

The tension between individual and community interests has been a classic subject for legal thinking about property for more than a century. After communism predicated the abolition of private property as the center of its political program, those societies that did not choose to follow that program had to redefine old liberal theories on property. In spite of deep intellectual and ideological diversities, many countries where a social pact allowed for some form of redistribution of wealth adopted a doctrine to account for a limitation to private property rights in the name of social needs and interests. The names of Henry George, Richard Tawney, and Leon Duguit should be enough to illustrate this.

In Mexico dominant legal ideas about property occupy a central position in legal culture as they embody

the program of social reform that emerged from the 1910 revolution in two crucial subjects: control over natural resources and agrarian reform. The first section of the paper presents a summary of the constitutional doctrine on property as the context in which recent developments in land use regulation in the country are taking place. As will be seen, in some respects those developments are consistent with that constitutional doctrine, but in others they represent a departure that it is interesting to consider.

In order to establish the relationship between globalization processes and the new ways of regulating land uses (and therefore property rights) in Mexico, I follow a cultural approach to consider legal institutions.[1] The emphasis is not on the technical aspects of legal institutions but on their meaning beyond the world of lawyers and judges. One of the main theses in the paper is that the influence of globalization upon the Mexican legal system is important not so much because of specific changes in legal norms but in the fact that Mexican legal culture becomes exposed to new legal ideas. The presence of these ideas in the debates about property in Mexico, as promoted by new social actors—most notably NGOs—is a cultural change that deserves attention because it is the social context within which the law makes sense to society.

It is important to make clear that by emphasizing the relationship between globalization and new forms of land use regulation in Mexico I do not mean to affirm that the main force behind those regulations is globalization. Certainly, it is important to be aware of overrating the impact of globalization.[2] As we will see, some of the new developments in Mexican law emerge from internal developments such as political reform. However, there are aspects that would be difficult to explain in terms of social changes taking place only within Mexican borders. Those aspects are worth the emphasis.

Environmental Regulations and the Social Function of Property

In order to understand the way Mexico is facing the tension between individuals and the community in the regulation of property rights, it is important to bear in mind that one of the most salient features of Mexican law after the 1910 revolution refers precisely to the ownership of land and natural resources. Article 27 of the 1917 Constitution has been a source of pride for Mexican jurists and politicians as it embodies the doctrine of the "social function of property," a doctrine that has provided legitimacy to the regulations of property relations. The opening words of that article establish that all lands and waters in the national territory belong "originally" to the nation, which has the right to transfer the ownership (*dominio*) of those lands and waters to individuals (*los particulares*), thus establishing private property. The corollary of this doctrine is that all property rights held by individuals are a mere derivation of a superior right that originally rests in the nation.

Regardless of the merits of this doctrine, it is beyond doubt that it has played a major role in shaping the legal culture that has surrounded the treatment of property rights in Mexico throughout the century. It provided the foundation for, inter alia, an agrarian reform that lasted for almost seventy years and involved the compulsory acquisition of more than half of the national territory and its distribution among peasants; the nationalization of the oil industry in the thirties; and the state control of the private appropriation of natural resources such as mining, water, and forests. It is easy to see the relevance of Article 27 in shaping not only domestic arrangements on property but also the international position of Mexico in strategic economic issues.

In order to accommodate our law of property to Continental legal doctrine, Mexican jurists have accepted that the constitution follows the thesis that property is called to fulfill a "social function,"[3] which means that the needs of society represent a limit to private property rights. The degree to which this doctrine has been accomplished in real life is, to put it mildly, very variable, and it is outside the scope of this paper to consider that question. However, it is a remarkable feature of the Mexican arrangement that, on the whole, the doctrine has not been questioned. That is, neither the courts' decisions nor serious legal writing have offered an alternative view of property relations in Mexico. From this it seems easy to conclude that, in the same way that Mexico's is the only social revolution in the world that still enjoys its original reputation,[4] the social pact behind the property doctrine remains intact.

However, that image is to a large extent misleading. It is only in appearance that Mexican law allocated private property a social function. In practice, the program of social reform that marked postrevolutionary governments was pursued through expropriations and/or state control of natural resources rather than through the regulation of private rights over those resources. Certainly, Article 27 states that the nation is entitled to "impose restrictions on private property that the public interest may require, as well as to regulate, for the benefit of society, the use of those elements of nature that can be the subject of private appropriation." So the constitutional foundation for land use regulation has been there since 1917, but that sort of regulation did not develop until the eighties for urban and suburban areas, and only recently for the regulation of nonurban areas of environmental interest.

In fact, the main ways in which the constitutional doctrine on property have been translated into law and government practice refer to three distinctive forms of government intervention in property relations. First, agrarian reform gave access to land to millions of peasants. Land distribution created almost some 28,000 agrarian communities (mostly *ejidos*) that today hold 52 percent of the national territory. This entailed the creation of a new form of property rather than the regulation of a preexistent property arrangement.

A second way of pursuing collective goals has been to maintain certain strategic natural resources (such as oil) as state ownership (*dominio directo de la Nación*). Thirdly, access to other natural resources (such as metallic minerals) by private individuals is regulated under the principle that they belong to the nation. All this did not prevent the formation of an entrepreneurial class that developed a large part of Mexico's current industry; in fact, that was only the other side of the coin. But in constitutional doctrine (and therefore in legal culture), private interests were always seen as secondary to national interests as represented by state powers.

In short, state interventions in property matters that were typical of postrevolutionary Mexico were more directed to define who owns the land and natural resources rather than to establish legal limits to property rights. The role of government as a "property giver" (and taker) created a strong legal culture around property issues.[5] Octavio Paz chose the image of a "philanthropic ogre" to describe the Mexican state in this respect. The fact that our postrevolutionary state not only created a new form of landownership (the *ejido*) but also nationalized the oil industry from foreign companies created, in cultural terms, a sort of legal identity involving a very interesting element of national narcissism.[6] This allowed its supporters (bureaucrats, law professors, PRI leaders) to ignore debates on property coming from abroad. In fact, lawyers who believed in the social function of property had to be suspicious of "foreign" ideas. It is against this backdrop that new debates and legal changes on the role of property can be better understood.

Much of the current discussion over property relations in Mexico refers to the fundamental changes that the postrevolutionary formula suffered in the last years: hundreds of state-owned companies have been privatized since the mid-eighties; on the other hand, agrarian reform (land distribution) was ended in the early nineties. Again, this is not the subject of this paper. The point here is that, at the same time, a less notorious development is gaining force: something like Mexico's silent revolution in land use regulation. During the last fifteen to twenty years, Mexican law underwent two major developments in the definition of property rights to land. First, there has been an increase of regulations involving limits to property as a result of urban and environmental law. Second, the situation of agrarian communities (*ejidos* and *comunidades*) has changed dramatically as land distribution came to an end. The question is no more how to give land to peasants but how to regulate the use they make of it. Let us now consider these two developments. In the following analysis of these two developments I will try to emphasize the way they put into question some of the main features of the Mexican postrevolutionary arrangement.

Urban and Environmental Land Use Regulations

With the development of urban and environmental planning and environmental impact assessment procedures, Mexico now has an institutional framework to deal with the tension between individual and community interests in the search of environmental goals. As we will see later, the problem now is how to define what exactly we mean by "the" community and who has the right to represent it—the usual dilemmas for any modern society, by the way.

The first comprehensive legislation that tried to regulate land development came about in the mid-seventies.[7] Parallel to the first World Summit on Habitat (Vancouver 1976), President Luis Echeverría promoted a "General Act for Human Settlements" that provoked a furious reaction from the private sector.[8] It was the first time that government powers to control land use, so familiar in Western countries, were made explicit in the Mexican statute book, with an explicit reference to the social function of property. However strange it may seem now, one of the aspects that aroused the private sector's opposition to that legislation was that it gave local authorities powers to impose land use restrictions through urban plans.[9] That was in fact the first step towards decentralization of urban management.

One decade later, more than one hundred Mexican cities had published urban plans containing restrictions on the use of property. Nowadays, these plans establish the conditions to develop land and/or the prohibitions to do it in certain areas for environmental or safety reasons. That generation of urban plans provided the first legal support for citizens' organizations that fought against certain urban developments they found harmful to the environment.[10]

However, urban plans are far from being enough, mainly because they are poorly enforced. The main form of noncompliance with their land use regulations is the proliferation of "irregular settlements"' both in urban and rural areas. More than half of Mexico's urban growth takes place outside the law. Environmental risk in the country is growing, not because of the creation of new industrial sources of pollution, but because of the irregular urbanization of places where people become exposed to some form of risk: from industrial sources to landslide, flooding, hurricane, and so on. It is important to point out that irregular settlements concern environmental organizations only insofar as they threaten natural habitats; it is the job of urban planners and NGOs working in the field of housing to worry about the problem. I will come back in the last section to the implications of this division of labor.

A more ambitious set of land use regulations came about with the environmental legislation of the late eighties. The General Act for Ecological Balance and Environmental Protection, or LGEEPA (1988),[11] was the first single piece of legislation that integrated pollution prevention with national protected areas and the environmental effects of certain land uses. By establishing the need to submit an environmental impact assessment (EIA) before the national environmental authority for an important number of works and developments, federal law was doing two things. First, it was creating an administrative procedure specifically designed to look at the environmental effects of certain "works and activities." Nowadays more than one thousand projects are submitted every year to that procedure. Second, it is a federal agency, the National Institute of Ecology, which has the power to authorize works that were previously within state or local authorities' jurisdiction. I will come back to the implication of this to decentralization policies.

A comprehensive reform of Mexican environmental legislation in late 1996 reinforced the instruments for land use planning with environmental ends. On the one hand, through the establishment of natural protected areas of various categories[12] the federal government has the power to impose restrictions in the use of areas with outstanding biodiversity or other natural values. On the other hand, a new category of regulation,

"ecological land use planning," (*ordenamiento ecológico del territorio*) allows local authorities to establish restrictions on land use in rural areas.

In short, in the last two decades, through different legal techniques, environmental protection has given the rationale for new restrictions on landowners' rights. Nowadays, no one disputes the legitimacy of such regulations. For the moment, we seem to be free from anything like the Lucas case syndrome. Not only because we inherit from our constitutional tradition the doctrine that property rights must perform a social function, but also because in Mexico there is now a very important social support for the protection of natural areas. One example is the Caribbean coast of the Yucatan. To the south of Cancun, there is a 100-mile strip with very detailed land use regulations that establishes building densities and conservation areas. Those regulations are always subject to the scrutiny of both government agencies and NGOs.[13]

On the whole, all these new regulations are consistent with a doctrine that was already in the Constitution. Their purpose is precisely one that Article 27 proclaims: to regulate, for the benefit of society, the use of those elements of nature that are subject to private property. At the same time, they represent a clear departure from legal culture and government practice that characterized postrevolutionary Mexico. This departure has three aspects: the fact that it is reducing government's discretionary powers through legal rules, the growing importance of NGOs, and the role of state and local authorities in the definition of property rights. Let us take a closer look at these three features of the environmental regulation of property rights in Mexico.

First, there is a process of "juridification"[14] of land use control that imposes restrictions upon the exercise of state power on property owners. This does not mean to say that before this landowners could develop their lands with no restrictions from the part of government. The latter did on occasion impose restrictions, but it used to do it in a more arbitrary way. Almost any development project could be prevented by government agencies without specific legal reasons. In many cases, private (and indeed public) works were discouraged or promoted just for "political" reasons. This does not mean to say that public authorities never served private interests (quite the contrary). It means that the exercise of public power was less subject to legal rules. Nowadays, as land use control itself is subject to other legal restrictions (such as processes of public participation), there has been a clear reduction of the discretionary powers of bureaucracies (Azuela 1997). To a larger extent than before, public power is exercised according to a rational-legal framework that is typical of the modern state. Urban and environmental planning, decrees of natural protected areas, and EIAs are the most relevant rules and procedures that perform this function.

As to the forces behind this process, it can be said that, on the whole, it has been an internal phenomenon, that is, a result of changes within Mexican society. Political parties, social organizations, and a stronger public opinion have put the rule of law at the center of the agenda of our transition to democracy. At the same time that political pluralism has brought with it a closer surveillance over those in government, the latter has been subject to more stringent rules on its daily operation.[15]

During the nineties, these "internal" forces have been coupled with developments in the international sphere. It is worth mentioning a couple of legal aspects of the North American Free Trade Agreement (NAFTA), which mean new commitments for the Mexican state. On the one hand, as with trade liberalization in general, NAFTA reinforces the legal protection of foreign investors.[16] On the other hand, one of the most salient obligations established in the "side agreement" on environmental issues[17] refers precisely to the enforcement of environmental law. There is a cost for Mexican authorities if they exercise their power against foreign corporations *ultra vires,* but they can also pay a high price if they do not enforce environmental law, which frequently involves affecting corporations' interests. In other words, NAFTA also contributed to reducing the discretionary powers of authorities as to the compliance of land use regulations.[18]

A second feature of recent land use control mechanisms in Mexico that involve a departure from the traditional model of the postrevolutionary regime refers to the role that social groups outside government (NGOs) are playing in the implementation of the new regulation.

As part of our long transition to democracy, large sectors of society became aware of the possibility of acting outside the system (the sphere of what used to be the official party) but at the same time within the law. It was of course not only a question of awareness; when political reform began in the late seventies, Mexico was much more complex than the predominantly rural society out of which the postrevolutionary regime had grown up in previous decades. The Institutional Revolutionary Party (PRI) was not capable anymore to give room to every political expression of society.

Civil society, an idea that used to be almost absent from Mexico's public life, grew stronger during the eighties,[19] particularly as a result of the social mobilization aroused after the 1985 earthquake in the capital city. Since those times, NGOs have assumed an unexpectedly relevant role, and the environment has become one of its main fields of action.[20]

As in other countries, NGOs in Mexico are extremely varied, and it is almost impossible to generalize anything about them. The fact is that some of them have been able to influence public policy to an extent that very few would have imagined two decades ago. In order to underscore this development it suffices to say that during the last five years there has been no major social conflict over land use issues in which an NGO did not play a relevant role.

By far the most important participation of NGOs has been in relation to the reforms to the environmental legislation (the LGEEPA) in 1995–1996. After ten months of public participation around the government's project, a large group of NGOs were not satisfied, and it was obvious for all political parties in Congress that passing the law without their blessing would result in a bad environmental record for them. In the end, the reforms were approved unanimously (in both houses) right after the project was satisfactory for NGOs.

In the following section I will refer to the cultural implications of this development. Here the point is that a second salient feature of the current Mexican discussion on property rights is that the definition of the social function of those rights ceased to be the exclusive responsibility (and privilege) of government. Citizens acting from outside the state apparatus (and very often against them) are now participating in the definition of the public interest. And they do so using the law as an argument.

There is a third feature in Mexico's recent land use regulation that is important to recognize: the role of state and local authorities in the context of decentralization trends. As many other countries, Mexico adopted decentralization policies in the early eighties. An amendment in 1983 to Article 115 in the Constitution gave new powers to local authorities, particularly in relation to urban planning and land use. At the beginning, land use issues were not noticed as a central question in the decentralization agenda. For the most part of that decade, the dominant idea in the public debate on decentralization was that local authorities would play a major role in economic policy. Land use was important only for a few federal civil servants who tried to convince local authorities to develop their urban plans.

During the nineties there was a dramatic shift in this field: Environmental problems began to be linked to land use issues at the same time that opposition parties began winning elections at local and state levels. Most of the emerging social protest around environmental issues in recent years has focused on a number of notorious cases of works and developments, and part of the debate is on the legal status of the project according to land use regulation. Urban plans became important because there was a social mobilization (through NGOs) against a particular development, and the responsibility for it happened to be on the local authorities that approved an urban plan (or failed to do so).

Urban plans began to attract the attention of grassroots organizations and local politicians. Just to give an example, in 1993 the mayor of one of the municipalities of the Monterrey metropolitan area organized a referendum to solve a land use conflict. The number of people that voted in it was larger than the number of people that had voted in the municipal election.

It is worth mentioning that political pluralism is now a reality in the landscape of local and state governments. The vast majority of larger cities are now governed by what used to be opposition parties. More importantly, the same happens with the governors of nine out of thirty-one states and the federal district, the eight million inhabitants of the capital city. Since the end of the revolution and until 1989, all state governors had been members of the PRI.

These days it is not strange that, when it comes to conflicts on land use, state and/or local authorities, regardless of their political party, take a different position from that of the federal government. Moreover, two of the most notorious conflicts between states and the Union in the last years involved PRI governors. In the case of the Golf Course of Tepoztlán, in the state of Morelos, the governor supported a project that was shut down by the federal attorney for environmental protection. In a very different case, the PRI governor of San Luis Potosí took the side of local groups and Greenpeace, which opposed the opening of a hazardous waste landfill that had been authorized by the federal government.

It is tempting to see the new role of subnational authorities as part of what is supposed to be a global trend: the weakening of the nation-state (Held 1995). However, in Mexico that does not seem to be the case, as the federal government is more active than ever before in the field of land use regulation. Rather than a shift from one level of government to another, what we can see is an increasingly intense participation of all levels, with the new company of nongovernmental participation.

It is worth mentioning that state and municipal authorities are not always backed by NGOs. In fact, we are seeing all sorts of situations. At one extreme, NGOs acting in the name of global interests oppose certain projects that are supported by local authorities. The most notorious case today is that of a large coalition of national and international NGOs against a salt works facility at Baja California in the name of the protection of whales. At the other extreme, we see the typical NIMBY syndrome in cases like the aforementioned hazardous waste landfill in San Luis Potosí in which Greenpeace and a local group managed to stop a project that seemed to be good for national interests, as there was only one hazardous waste landfill for the whole country.

The fact that there is a wide variety of situations does not mean there is no general trend in the role of NGOs vis-à-vis decentralization: When it comes to the legal debate about the distribution of powers between national and subnational authorities for land use regulation, NGOs have opposed the idea of decentralization, as they think state or local authorities would be more permissive than the federal government. Thus, they see it as a way of "dismantling" environmental leg-islation. In fact, that was one of the hard issues in the discussion of the 1996 reforms to the LGEEPA. Oppo-sition by NGOs blocked the decentralization process—for the good or for the bad—and the subnational lev-els of government cannot exercise all the power that the Constitution gives them to regulate the use of property. Paradoxically, a typically "global" process (decentraliza-tion) is prevented by another typically global trend: the emergence of NGOs.

In this context, the conflict between individual interests and those of the community in the use of property cannot be solved in a simple way as there are several versions of what the community is because there is a plurality of actors (within and outside governments) that claim the representation of collective interests that range from those of the neighborhood up to those of the entire globe and even reach the future generations. Centralized bureaucracies (in the name of national communities) may think there is a need for a hazardous waste facility, but the local community (represented by authorities elected by worried voters) might oppose it. Finally, an NGO (representing the global community) can tip the scales in favor of any of them—for the good and/or for the bad, I must insist.

The Reform of Ejido Property

It is clear, then, that environmental protection in Mex-ico is now recognized as a community interest that jus-tifies restrictions on private property rights. This is a worldwide trend, but it takes different forms accord-ing to the prevailing land ownership system of each country. In Mexico, as a result of agrarian reform, more than half of the nation's territory belongs to agrarian communities (95 percent of them having the category of *ejidos*). It is interesting to see the consequences of the specific form of our agrarian reform for the regulation of the use of land.

The creation of *ejidos* was the way of giving peasants access to land and thus advancing the program of the revolution. To the extent that a more numerous class of peasants substituted the old landed classes, the *ejido* was the mechanism to materialize the "social function" of property. Once land distribution has come to an end,[21]

the problem is to accommodate the interests of *ejidos* as landowners within the wider interests (particularly the environmental interests) of society.

The original institutional design of *ejidos,* through laws and procedures established in the thirties, focused on the access to land, that is, in the creation of a new form of land ownership without considering that the use of that land would have to be regulated at some point in time. It is interesting to note that, in Mexican legal culture, *ejidos* belong to a sector of the economy that is separate from both private and public institu-tions. The Constitution itself establishes three sectors of the national economy: the public, the private, and the social sector.[22] *Ejidos,* the most relevant representa-tives of the social sector, are thus seen as a world on its own, and it somehow escapes from the public-private dichotomy, which is typical of modern societies. In other words, the categories of Mexican legal culture make possible that *ejidos* appear as is they were free from both the obligations of private corporations and the account-ability of public authorities. This institutional isolation was irrelevant as long as urban and rural societies were also relatively isolated from each other. However, as a result of population growth, urbanization processes, the recent development of environmental legislation, and the end of land distribution, there is a need to estab-lish the status of agrarian communities as property rights holders, that is, their rights and obligations vis-à-vis public authorities.

Let us briefly summarize the main elements of this form of agrarian community. The typical *ejido* is a cor-poration with an average of 100 members that holds an average extension of 3,500 hectares. Lands are divided into three uses: common use lands for pasture, forest, and other uses; parceled lands, that is, parcels that are held individually by the members of the *ejido* (called *ejidatar-ios*); and lands for the human settlement, that is, the vil-lage where *ejidatarios*—and other neighbors—live.

During the past three decades, *ejidos* have undergone important changes in their relation to urban life. On the one hand, *ejidos* located in the periphery of cities have been absorbed by urban growth. According to offi-cial figures, two-thirds of that growth takes place at the expense of *ejido* lands. When we see this from the rural perspective, this means a loss of agricultural land; from the urban point of view, the urbanization of *ejido* lands is one of the greatest problems of town planning as local governments find it very difficult to enforce their regulations on lands that, according to our legal culture,[23] are thought to be outside their jurisdiction. This is the social sector, and its relation to government is only through agrarian—federal—authorities. In many states, *ejidos* do not even pay property taxes. Thus, millions of urban dwellers live in *ejido* lands where the urban authority cannot exercise its land use power.[24]

On the other hand, there is a large number of *ejidos*, distant from large urban areas, in which there has been an urbanization process. Thousands of *ejido* villages, which are considered rural because of their size, have obtained certain public services that were almost nonexistent when those villages were created. An elementary school, piped water in at least part of the town, a small medical center, a couple of sport facilities, lighting in the main streets and maybe a bridge over the neighboring stream—no matter how modest they may seem—constitute an ensemble of public goods that have to be administered by the internal authorities of the *ejido*. The life of the community consists of more than merely agricultural issues. Being an *ejidatario* means more than just being part of a corporation that owns land for cultivation; it means the ability to participate in decisions that affect the community life because they refer to their basic public goods and services. At first glance, this seems the ideal self-sufficient rural community. The problem is that the system excludes two sets of actors who would like to be part of the game. On the one hand, those who are not *ejidatarios* (called *avecindados* or neighbors) cannot be part of the *ejido* assembly. If four or five decades ago most dwellers of an *ejido* village were at the same time *ejidatarios* (with full rights to participate in decisions affecting the community) today, after a spectacular population growth, the majority of those dwellers are not entitled to any form of participation. This would not be a problem if a public authority elected by all citizens administered the public goods of the village. The problem is that local (municipal) authorities are precisely the second kind of actors who have difficulties in ruling over the internal decisions of an *ejido*.

The result is that *ejidos* are now more than corporations of landowners; they perform functions that correspond to local authorities. It is a fiction that they constitute a third sector (the social sector) apart from the private and the public. That view ignores that they are a de facto form of government based on the ownership of land. The origin of this is quite simply centralism, one of the main features of the postrevolutionary arrangement. Agrarian reform was carried out by the federal government while municipal and state authorities did not play a relevant role in land distribution—in most cases they even opposed it.

Let us look at this phenomenon from the point of view of Mexico's transition to democracy: It was hard for opposition parties to win state and local elections, and now that we have the political pluralism we are so proud of, local and state authorities find it very difficult to govern over half of their territories (and the vast majority of the rural population) because there is a corporate enclave that prevents them from doing it.[25]

The tension between *ejidos* and public authorities gets more intense as the latter try to develop environmental regulations affecting the use of land. When private individuals own the land, the social function doctrine helps precisely to control private interests on behalf of the public good. But when it comes to *ejido* lands, it is difficult for their members to understand that there are restrictions on the use of land in the name of the environment. *Ejidos* are seen only as "beneficiaries" of government actions, and it is an alien element to postrevolutionary culture that their rights over land are subject to restrictions as much as private property.

However, all this happens in a context that allows for some optimism. As land distribution came to an end in the early nineties, property relations in rural Mexico tended to stabilize.[26] Only ten years ago, groups of landless peasants still had the right to demand the creation of an *ejido*, even if there were no more *latifundios* (landholdings exceeding the legal limits) to distribute. The end of agrarian reform was, and in some regions still is, a hard thing to admit for those who thought that the original program of the Mexican Revolution could continue without changes forever. Beyond that nostalgia, it marks a change in the function of *ejido* property: From being a way of access to land it is now an established form of landownership that gives security to its owners and at the same time is subject to land use regulations.

One of the promising avenues of the stabilization of rural landownership is the registration of the *ejido* lands held in common. *Ejidos* now have the opportunity to regulate the use of those resources by its members. The challenge is to develop internal regulations that do not clash with regulations coming from public authorities—the three levels of government.

Legal Changes and Cultural Exposure

As I have described in previous sections, there have been a number of important changes in the treatment of property rights in Mexico in the last two to three decades. Let us look more closely into the implications of recent developments for the legal culture of postrevolutionary Mexico. This is important because it is that culture that has provided most of the legitimacy to the treatment of property rights in our country.

The main contention in the following pages is that Mexican legal culture has been exposed to global cultural developments in different topics: the environment, property rights, democracy, human rights, and so on. As a result of this exposure, new rules and legal ideas are being adopted that challenge the assumptions of the postrevolutionary model. For almost eight decades after the revolution it was possible to maintain the hegemony of the political and legal culture that emerged from it. That is why it is interesting to ask ourselves how this exposure is taking place.

In order to answer that question I suggest that we can identify different "routes of exposure," a term I borrow from the sort of environmental analysis that seeks to determine the specific ways in which a given population enters in contact with a given substance. I will refer here to two major routes of exposure: the new legal ideas of economists and the legal ideas of the new social actors—NGOs.

Economists and the Culture of Legal Pragmatism

A silent academic phenomenon has been taking place during the last twenty years or so: Mexican economists who undertake postgraduate studies in U.S. universities are going back to Mexico with new legal ideas, ideas that enrich Mexican legal culture. This happens because of the rise of institutional economics (the New Institutionalism), which has placed rules (and therefore the law) at the center of economic science. In the end of many economic debates there is a legal issue. "Getting the institutions right" has become a new task for economists.

This is certainly a novelty for economic thought in Mexico,[27] but the consequences for the legal culture are far reaching. To begin with, lawmaking ceases to be the privilege of lawyers, and the ideas behind new laws are quite different from what we used to teach in law schools. Suddenly, Ronald Coase and the law-and-economics movement take the place of the ideals of the Revolution. There is a clear symptom of the presence of these new ideas in the parlance of Mexican civil servants and policy analysts: When they talk about *derechos de propiedad* (property rights, in plural) instead of the usual Continental expression, *la propiedad* (in singular), one knows they are talking from another culture—the common law, which is the legal language of the new institutionalism.

Some of the most important pieces of legislation and regulatory policies of the nineties have been drafted within this new economic approach.[28] Of course, the traditional Left has criticized what they call the "Chicago Boys" for the privatization and liberalization policies, but it is not the purpose of this paper to enter into that debate. The point here is that this kind of economic thought (which is also a form of legal thought) is based on a theory that puts a great emphasis on the question of property rights in order to explain economic development. It recognizes in law not only the embodiment of values that a society supports but also normative arrangements with a specific social effect. It is a pragmatic way of thinking about the efficiency of different property arrangements.

New Institutionalism is a departure from the postrevolutionary tradition not only because it recognizes a positive role for private property rights (an ideological issue on which much has been written); it is new because it uses an extremely sophisticated theoretical apparatus for the design of public policy. There is a contrast between the social function of property doctrine that social sciences were able to produce a century ago and the methods of New Institutionalism today. Obviously, as with every theory in social science, New Institutionalism cannot be declared as the winner. However, it is clear that it is among the most advanced scientific proposals to understand the role of property in society.[29]

Unfortunately, few of the critics of the new economic thought recognize that it helps not only as a support for privatization policies. The truth is that it is also being used for proving that, under certain circumstances, common property arrangements can be more efficient than those dominated by private property, as the work of Elinor Ostrom (1990) has shown.

Now the problem of using institutional analysis for lawmaking and policymaking in Mexico is not only a question of ideological choice. There is also a cultural problem in that the categories of Mexican law are those of European Continental civil law (or the Roman-Germanic legal family), whereas the legal categories of institutional analysis are those of the common-law tradition. Our legal system does not recognize "bundles of rights," the doctrine of "estates," and so on. There is even a temptation to blame our legal institutions because they follow the Continental legal categories,[30] a view that takes us back to the old Anglo-French rivalry and that amounts to accepting Sir Frederick Lawson's argument about the superiority of the common law, a rather heavy burden for our already troubled Mexican lawyers. Anyway, the corollary would seem to be that we not only have to change the content of our rules on property, we have to think about these problems with different legal categories. The problem of operating a legal system with the categories of another legal system is that legal systems are made of nothing but categories.[31]

Of course, as a "cultural issue," this does not seem to affect anyone beyond professional circles. It appears as a problem only for lawyers and economists who draft our legal texts. But if we assume that those texts are to mean something for society as a whole, thinking about this is not so irrelevant.

Besides, it is important to recognize that legal categories are more than neutral professional tools; as we have seen, rules on property (most notably Article 27

in the Constitution) are linked to a strong nationalist feeling. For most legal professionals, switching from their legal culture to another one (particularly if the latter comes from the United States) represents what psychoanalysts call a *blessure narcissiste* (a "narcissist wound").[32] Thinking beyond our own legal tradition without feeling guilty of treason is a problem for Mexican public lawyers and policymakers in general. Of course, institutional economics are not the only way of reasoning the establishment of restrictions to private property rights, but the search for an altogether different alternative, just to satisfy our national narcissism, would perhaps be the most irrational of all positions.

NGOs and the Culture of Human Rights

The second route of exposure to new legal ideas, and one that has been felt well beyond professional circles, refers to the ideas that NGOs have made so popular in the last years. It is well known that they are now playing a relevant role in the definition and implementation of environmental laws and policies, including the definition of legal restrictions that collective interests should impose upon private property rights. In spite of the contradictions I will refer to below, they have enriched Mexican legal culture, even at the expense of our traditions.

It is useful to give an indicator of the spectacular growth in the importance of NGOs in Mexico. In 1976, during the discussion of the Human Settlements Act, COPEVI,[33] one of the first NGOs of Mexico—an organization created to help housing projects for low-income groups—was the only one to issue a declaration regarding the project. Newspapers did not notice that declaration and it was completely ignored in the discussion of the law. This discussion was between the executive (the only one who interpreted the national interests) on the one hand and private interests on the other; the usual version of the individual versus collective tension within our legal tradition.

Twenty years later, in the reform of environmental legislation, Congress members waited until environmental NGOs approved the project before they voted—and they voted unanimously in favor of it. Without signals from NGOs, political parties did not show an interest in environmental legislation, and, therefore, legal restrictions on property rights for environmental reasons depended more than ever on the views of NGOs.

The most important legal contribution of NGOs to legal culture refers to the introduction of contemporary ideas about human rights. Mexican legal culture was never overtly hostile to human rights. As a subject in international law, the country was always ready to support international conventions covering the whole range of human rights as they appeared. However, within the national agenda, the set of rights that official discourse used to emphasize were mainly those of workers and peasants, and as long as the representation of those rights rested in government, independent social organizations were always looked at with suspicion.

The first cultural change that NGOs have brought about is that the rights they defend are not in the hands of bureaucrats. The idea that a group of citizens can represent the interests of the public is another narcissist wound for those who think that only government officials are entitled to represent them. The community right to know and the possibility to conduct class actions that were opened in the 1996 reforms to the LGEEPA were no doubt the most important achievement of the NGOs' participation in the process.[34]

The most serious challenge for Mexican legal culture in this context is the possibility that foreign NGOs may have the same rights as Mexican citizens. As one commentator puts it: "the environmentalist movement has spawned a number of international organizations that have sought to establish an international standard of duties and obligations. Similarly human rights are perceived as international in their reach" (Entrikin 1999). The nationalist character of our postrevolutionary tradition makes this an extremely delicate issue. Mexico is considered among the five richest countries in biodiversity, and it is easy for Mexicans to proclaim that we have a responsibility before the entire world to preserve it. The problem arises when a group of NGOs, in the name of global interests, demand the Mexican government to take a different course of action than what it had decided in terms of its development strategies.

In political theory and in jurisprudence, one of the more salient discussions nowadays refers to the idea of a "global citizenship" (Held 1995). This would mean that citizens of one nation-state have rights vis-à-vis another nation. This does not have to happen in legal practice in order to become a real issue, because it is already happening as a cultural phenomenon with political consequences. In Mexico, NGOs (both national and international) have obtained important victories in the realm of law without obtaining favorable resolutions from law courts. Their influence comes through the media and due to the support they are able to obtain from international organizations and from personalities of different circles, from the movie industry to the European nobility.

Thus, the impact of this new form of social power is far beyond the narcissist wound we have already mentioned. NGOs now influence decision-making processes. In the same way it is important to underscore their positive contributions, it is also necessary to recognize that they pose some serious problems. I have already mentioned the problematic position of NGOs against decentralization. But maybe the main problem has to do with the priorities in their agendas.

Most NGO activities have to do with the protection of ecosystems, particularly wildlife, against works and developments. This usually brings into the discussion the dilemma between progress and conservation (a false dilemma in most cases). But it is not that dilemma that I want to indicate but the fact that in Mexico, as in many other countries, there are still some serious environmental problems that are being almost completely ignored by NGOs.

In an agenda of environmental priorities built from a national point of view, most people would agree that public health and risk problems should come first. Many Mexicans are still exposed to industrial pollution, water pollution from an uncontrolled urbanization process, and, above all, to the vulnerability of the very location of the place they live in. If environmental risks have caused deaths and injuries in the last years, it has been mainly from natural disasters (flooding, landslides, hurricanes) that in the end are not so natural to the extent that they could have been avoided. Thus, preventing human settlements in unsafe locations is an environmental goal as important as the preservation of natural habitats. Unfortunately, these issues are not part of the agendas of NGOs.

A dramatic example of this happened in early 1999 when the most serious case of lead poisoning was discovered in the northern city of Torreón. The operation of the largest smelting facility in the country (which produces 95 percent of Mexico's silver exports)[35] had caused more than one thousand cases of children with high lead levels. That was the hardest case in many years for Mexico's environmental authorities, and there was not a single environmental NGO—national or international—following the case.

The reason for this is not that NGOs care more about wildlife than human health. Real people's intentions are hard to guess anyway. But the fact is that pop stars, European aristocrats, and other world citizens are more prone to give their signature for a letter to demand protection to whales than for brown issues. In the legal culture of international environmentalism, there is a very well-established idea in the concept of "world heritage." From this it follows that every human being has a right to protect a pristine environment; there is nothing equivalent about the health and security problems in people's environment.

Of course there are international NGOs that specialize in health issues. *Médecins sans frontières* is an obvious example of people working in the field of health. But then the problem is precisely that human rights become subject to a process of specialization. If human rights are important in the history of ideas it is because they constitute a normative synthesis of human needs. They are a way of thinking about a legal order from the point of view of human experience as a whole. In practice, NGOs and other international organizations tend to look at one human right and ignore the rest.[36] It is remarkable that in the end human rights become a series of fragmented, specialized fields just like governmental bureaucracies. Moreover, debates as to what human rights should come first are marked by prejudices between groups of NGOs interested in different issues. A clear example is the position of NGOs working in the field of housing rights against environmentalism.

Even if we see the human rights discourse of NGOs as a civilizing message that comes from the global village, it is a message that arrives to Mexico—and surely to any other country—in a rather fragmented and sometimes rarified form. There is no guarantee that the agendas of NGOs are more rational than national or local ones.

In the end, it is important to recognize both the constructive and the problematic aspects of the impact of NGOs in Mexican legal culture. What cannot be denied is that they are playing a role that very few people could have foreseen only twenty years ago.

Conclusion

Environmental protection is an area in which the legal culture of postrevolutionary Mexico has been exposed to new legal ideas in a process that becomes more intense as globalization goes on. In the regulation of property rights vis-à-vis environmental concerns, new ideas refer more to the question of who is entitled to impose restrictions on property holders than to the principle that community interests should prevail over private ones. It is important to stress that, apart from legal developments that can be attributed to globalization or to economic integration with North America, there have been crucial changes in Mexican society itself. Just to name one, transition to democracy is the result of the growing diversity of society.

One of the alleged aspects of globalization, the waning of the nation-state, is simply not in sight in Mexico. Federal authorities are more active than ever before in the regulation of property rights in order to attain environmental goals. The real change is that they now have to interact with all sorts of emerging actors that did not use to play a part in the discussion on the limits to property rights. Local authorities, NGOs, and *ejidos,* to name a few, constitute—along with federal authorities—a dense network where competing views are discussed.

Again, it is not that nationalism has disappeared from Mexico's public life. It is only that the new legal ideas are reaching fields that had been dominated by the nationalist tradition: lawmaking and, in particular, thinking about law. It is clear that there has been an important influence of globalization.

By looking at the specific ways through which Mexican legal culture has been exposed to global ideas about property and the environment, it is easy to see that there is nothing like a single and coherent global doctrine. What we find instead is a collection of different, and in many ways competing, legal ideas. Apart from the obvious tension between pro-development and anti-development approaches, there is a fragmentation of environmental issues as a result of the specialization of both NGOs and international organizations. Most of those who "think globally" do it in respect to some environmental issues at the expense of others, and this creates distortions in policy agendas. Depending on factors such as the way international funds of different origins are distributed, the debate in one country may be dominated by housing rights while in another country the priority can be palm trees or dolphins. National governments seem to be the level at which those distortions should be dealt with. In the case of Mexico, constitutional doctrine provides the foundation for putting the environmental needs of community before the interests of private property holders. Here is an aspect in which Mexico's legal culture is still alive and meaningful.[37]

The recognition that the nation-state still has a relevant role to play in the definition of property rights before environmental interests does not mean to ignore the enormous challenges it faces. In Mexico, the notion that citizens and their organizations—and not only public authorities—can represent the interests of community as a whole puts into question one of the assumptions of Mexican postrevolutionary legal culture. Thus, in spite of recent changes in legislation that recognize those new ideas, in legal practice few things have changed. In fact, some important environmental conflicts have been solved not through legal procedures but with social mobilization and the use of the media. Of course, in every society there is a limit to what the law can accomplish, and there is not a universal formula as to where that limit is.[38] But the Mexican legal system has a long way to go in the recognition of emerging social interests. The challenge is to design new legal procedures that involve a more formal participation of citizens' views and a stronger role of the judiciary while at the same time avoiding the risks of adversarial legalism that is so familiar to other countries.

With all the difficulties I have described, it is possible to conclude with an optimistic note. The exposure of Mexican legal culture to new ideas in the context of globalization not only enriches our public life; it is helping to keep our debates within the realm of law. It does not matter how confusing the landscape of legal ideas can get, thinking in legal terms will still be better than falling into the temptation of advancing one's views and interests outside the law.

Environmental Governance and the Uses of Science

Sidney Draggan

Setting Some Boundaries

When first given this assignment, and even before receiving drafts of this session's presentations, I felt an immediate need to first review and understand, and then address, a term pivotal to this bicentennial symposium. That term is "democracy." Democracy, I think that all here will agree, is a convenient label for an extraordinarily multifaceted approach to social governance. There is no single, correct, or easy-to-follow approach to the pursuit of democracy.

Several years ago, in 1993, I took part in what I saw as an intriguing workshop on science, technology, and democracy.[1] That workshop focused on finding workable bases for the conduct of scientific research on issues of governance and change. We recognized that the scope and pace of scientific, technological, and social or cultural changes challenge notions of democratic governance continually. The workshop's participants agreed, therefore, to look broadly at issues by referring to "structures of democratic governance" rather than using the term democracy loosely. An important, generalized finding of that workshop was that:

> [a]ttempts to translate the social structures for [individual or community interest] governance from one society to another, or to modify it in existing ones, go awry because the human dimensions of that interface are poorly understood.

As evidenced clearly by each of the papers presented during this session, notions of democratic governance—and the spheres of individual and community interests—vary as do the many sovereign nations that have embraced its practice. Given these warnings, we—

contributing to this session—move forward cautiously; but we do move forward.

A second term, which is in my mind crucial for the presentations and the considerations of this session, "Natural Resources and the Environment," and that needs some agreement on its definition—as well as the scope of that definition—is "community." Community is defined in many ways, but for the context of this session a definition that highlights and embodies the extent, or spatial dimension, of community seems relevant. That is, we need to focus our attention broadly from the intimately local level of a grouping of individuals to the wider ranging grouping of nations that comprise one level of "community" of our biogeosphere.

Looking at community along a spectrum also raises the opportunity for us to extend our understanding of the term beyond humankind. In doing that, we allow a place for other organisms that exist in our environs as well as a place for those living ecological systems that provide vital habitats for humans and fellow organisms. I leave this suggestion open for more thorough discussion among ourselves during this session.

The subject area of this session and the focus of its presentations suggest that it may be instructive to revisit such past work as Garrett Hardin's "Tragedy of the Commons"[2] and "Living on a Lifeboat."[3] Reading these works—and others like them—again may help us to evaluate whether their central assumptions continue to be fully relevant to the changes we are trying to recognize and address during this bicentennial symposium. Since the appearance of Hardin's works, I believe that today there are some extremely fundamental, unexpected, and unsettling shifts in the ways that law and society operate and information (or knowledge) flows. These shifts—of necessity—

influence how we are driven to look at and handle the interests of individuals and the interests of communities. This is particularly true within the apparently boundless realm that encompasses all of the known influences and phenomena that make what we understand currently to be "natural resources and environment."

Being an ecologist, I must admit that thinking about the specific issue area of individual versus community interests in the context of natural resource and environmental governance does not always keep me awake at nights. That specific issue area does, however, arise more often than expected in my work. It continues to have substantial impact on how legislation, policies, and decisions in the environmental arena are considered, made, and implemented.

For example, this very day I expect that the House Judiciary Committee will continue its debate on and markup of what has been characterized as a controversial property rights bill (that is, H.R. 2372). The short title of the bill is the Private Property Rights Implementation Act of 1999 (the official title runs to ninety-nine words!). The bill, as I understand it, would allow individual property holders to take directly to federal court cases claiming that federal, state, or local governments have deprived them of the ability to do as they wish with their land. Proponents say the bill would help property owners receive compensation, and receive it in a timely fashion. Opponents charge the bill would remove decision-making authority from elected officials for many environment-related issues, and they claim the measure unfairly favors development interests while undermining community interests. Last week, the bill's debate became stalled over discussion on an amendment that would broaden its scope by making its expedited appeal processes apply to other constitutional rights, for example, in civil rights cases. As I have mentioned, debate on H.R. 2372 is scheduled to continue today in a chamber not far from here. This current debate should provide healthy grist for our session's analysis today.

Some Common Threads

The three presentations in this session have dual foci: one that is predominantly national in scope and a second that hopes to recognize the global nature of the perceived ten-sion between individual and community wants and needs, rights and responsibilities. Each author to some extent addresses the history—and the limits—of highly centralized, command-control approaches to natural resource and environmental governance. Each vividly portrays the warts of these approaches. We should remember, however, that natural resource and environmental governance (as understood and practiced today) is a social activity as yet in its infancy. This type of governance is changing dynamically along with growing information about and understanding of the natural and physical sciences, economics, and sociology. Novel and innovative proposals to streamline, economize, and make these approaches more comprehensive are part of the natural evolution of their practice.

One recent U.S. effort worth noting is the Enterprise for the Environment Initiative. This effort convened stakeholders (a pivotal term, to which I will return) to work on formulating a set of recommendations for fundamental improvements to the U.S. system of environmental protection, starting with the underlying environmental statutes. Early in 1998, after considerable consensus-building among "stakeholders," the effort released an instructive report, *The Environmental Protection System in Transition: Toward a More Desirable Future.*[4] Recommendations were focused on: (1) transforming [the Nation's environmental] regulatory system; (2) increasing the use of economic and other incentives to encourage continuous environmental improvement; and (3) promoting higher levels of responsibility, accountability, commitment, and stewardship in the private sector.

Another thread evidenced to some extent in each of our papers is the growing role of stakeholders not involved traditionally in natural resource and environmental governance (or for that fact, in any official policy or decision-making capacity). Whether it is greater individual sophistication gained through acquisition of wealth or knowledge, the collective forces of globalization, or the making of uncommon political alliances is not important. What is important is that more of our citizenries feel obliged—if not empowered—to become involved in issues that hold potential to directly affect their health and environs as well as the well-being and environs of such wider communities as those among other nations, or other organisms or distant ecological systems.

Under such a changing mind-set of the populace there are inevitable alterations to what are viewed as the boundaries between individual and community and what are the accepted norms for who "decides." There is a presumption of full and open access to the administrative decision-making process that has developed an increasingly strong formal basis in the United States. Interestingly, in other nations, where such access is not codified, nontraditional stakeholders enjoy, nonetheless, an unexpected level of leverage in the functioning of decision processes. Increasingly communities, at whatever spatial scale, are looking at and framing concerns, questions, and issues from a globally influenced perspective while recognizing that real solutions will require local, concerted action. We can expect this phenomenon to continue to blossom. An insightful study of this phenomenon is "Using Stakeholder Processes in Environmental Decisionmaking: An Evaluation of Lessons Learned, Key Issues, and Future Challenges" by Terry F. Yosie and Timothy D. Herbst.[5] While the phenomenon of stakeholder involvement in environmental decision making is inevitable and will continue to expand, it will not be without internecine strife among stakeholders and among "power clusters" of stakeholders. For example, some scientific and risk experts have voiced frustration about the emphasis governments are placing on the use of stakeholder-inclusive decision-making processes.[6] These experts feel that this emphasis is leading to less reliance on empirically generated technical and scientific information in decision making.

As reflected by these "expert" sentiments, a second phenomenon accompanying the growing role of stakeholders in the design and implementation of natural resource and environmental regulation involves growing calls for the use of scientifically based information, methods, and opinion. Here, empirical data and evidence, and such approaches as cost-benefit and risk analysis, are being highlighted as important adjuncts to processes for development of policy, decisions to act, or regulations. This arises from the growing recognition of the often unexpected complexity and uncertainty associated with the forces driving natural resource, human health, and environmental events and processes. But science is not the solution to the problem; it serves as only one of the tools that can prove useful in problem solving and in decision making or regulation.

While debates about our ability to link the requirements of good science with those of good law have gone on for many years, it is appropriate to revisit the gist of those arguments. Among many others, this revisitation was done in a recent article by David Case and Jeffrey Ritter (based on an earlier talk given by Peter Kalis to the advisory board of a major scientific professional society publication).[7] They restate the truism (neither widely recognized nor accepted among all stakeholder groups) that:

Science seeks to explain the physical world and the processes that govern it. Scientists attempt to reach those explanations by considering a broad range of hypotheses, subjecting those hypotheses to experiment, and excluding those hypotheses shown to be incorrect. Scientific conclusions are thus subject to perpetual revision, both in detail and sometimes in the fundamentals. In contrast, legal truth seeking typically occurs in the context of the discreet resolution of competing claims based on an analysis of evidence presented by adversaries.

This "disconnect" between science and law parallels the dysfunction that becomes evident when science must become part of decision making, policy, or regulation. This dysfunction is used, sometimes knowingly and sometimes innocently, by stakeholders to bolster a position on a contentious issue. Even when the highest standards are used in the generation of scientific information, and even when this information is evaluated independently, it is often viewed as less than credible for whatever reason.

Conclusions

I believe that these two themes, the rising voices of non-traditional stakeholders and the use and misuse of "science," have been acting as wedges in the handling of natural resource and environmental governance. They need not. Perhaps we might consider suggestions made by Robert Costanza in a recent article.[8] He notes that:

The most critical task facing humanity today is the creation of a shared vision of a sustainable and desirable society, one that can provide permanent prosperity within the biophysical constraints of the real world in a way that is fair and equitable to all of humanity, to other species, and to future generations. . . . Science and economics as applied to policy are in conflict more often over alternative visions of the world than purely "scientific" disagreements. Likewise, governance has gotten bogged down in mediating short-term conflicts between special interests rather than its more basic role of creating broadly shared visions that can guide dispute resolution.

Perhaps, I think, we are looking for a problem where there is, in fact, none. Looking at the title of this session we need to realize that we have pitted "individual" against "community" interests. Is there another way to look at this? I think there is little problem, just ample opportunity. In a democratic system of governance should there not be a constant balancing act between these two interests? Individuals, groupings of individuals at the local level, and groupings of nations are all in a constant state of self-reevaluation. They are always reexamining their needs and wants and, therefore, are continually shifting their interests among various spheres of influence.

I suggest that rather than suffer, democracy builds from this foment.

Closing Remarks

Koichiro Fujikura

Professor Richard Stewart thinks the subtitle of the session misstates the fundamental issue because it implies an underlying conflict between individual liberty and collective interests in environmental law. The important task for environmental law, according to him, is to advance liberty by balancing activity and security through the adoption of appropriate laws and institutions. He sees that the law has come to give increased weight to environmental security and less to activity. He argues, however, that the United States has created a national "command and control" environmental regulatory state and a top-heavy regulatory system of environmental central planning, achieving significant progress while producing economic waste and inflexibility. He proposes to adopt a more market-based regulatory approach. He focuses on the need of: (a) compensation for the economic losses suffered by property owners as a result of environmental regulation, (b) cost-benefit and risk analysis for decisions made by regulatory agencies, and (c) utilizing such regulatory instruments as tradeable permits, effluent fees, taxes, and charges on polluting activities. I find these points very relevant to Ukraine, Mexico, and Japan.

Both Dr. Yuri Kostenko's presentation and Mr. Antonio Azuela's paper bear well the central theme and concern of our session, which is that the divergent collective interests and values at stake must ultimately be resolved through institutions of democratic governance consistent with the rule of law.

Dr. Kostenko notes that the Ukrainian "command-administrative" economy was centralized and displayed huge structural disparities during the Soviet period. The inefficient Soviet system, according to him, encouraged an irrational use of resources and an excessive consumption of energy by emphasizing only production without creating any incentives for preserving either resources or the environment. He points out that the advantages of countries with transitional economies like Ukraine lie in their high intellectual potential and the fact that they are still at the early stages in their development. They could manage by adopting proper regulatory regimes and approaches to prevent further environmental destruction. Since the Chernobyl tragedy, Ukraine, in cooperation with the European Union and the G-7 governments, has joined the regional environmental regulatory regime by complying with European standards. I believe that there are ample opportunities for Ukraine to experiment with market-based regulatory instruments as proposed by Professor Stewart.

Mr. Azuela states that the tension between individual and community interests has long been a "classic subject for legal thinking on property" and still is in postrevolutionary Mexico. He analyzes this tension, interestingly and persuasively, in the context of the Mexican legal culture. The social function of property was traditionally recognized and recently reemphasized by the government to regulate and control land use. Because of industrialization and urbanization, the traditional units of society have been undergoing a period of rapid and drastic changes. Active participation of many and diverse NGOs in the political process also has contributed to the increasing tension. A strong impact of the law and economics school is also felt among the Mexican legal academics. He points out that a dilemma is "how to define what exactly we mean by the community and who has the right to represent it." This is a universal dilemma we all share in any modern state. He sees the challenge to design new legal procedures that "involve a more formal participation of citizens' views and a stronger role of the judiciary, but at the same time avoiding the risks of adversarial legalism." Also, in Mexico, a coming trend may well be the environmental regulatory approach based on the market.

I can say that the same trend has been taking hold in Japan. However, the move toward a market-based regulatory regime in Japan may be prompted by quite different reasons from the United States as analyzed by Professor Stewart. The environmental regulatory approach in Japan has largely been consensus based. Once national goals have been set, officials usually implement their policies without resorting to legal coercion or overt enforcement. Implementation of national policies relies largely upon voluntary compliance by the regulated industries. The central government often provides tax incentives and financial assistance in order to achieve defined goals and to assure compliance by regulated entities, but it also often works closely with them, gathering information and providing necessary guidance and protection. Environmental legislation sets general standards and delegates a wide range of powers to administrative agencies to implement. Government agencies in charge of carrying out legislative mandates have used informal "administrative guidance" to induce voluntary compliance by the parties regulated. A pretense of the consensus approach is that the regulators and the regulated have agreed to whatever regulatory goals and standards through consensus-forming negotiations.

The major advantage of a consensus approach is that practically no enforcement costs are needed. Once a consensus is reached, it is assumed that the regulated parties who agreed to the consensus will honor and carry out their part of the obligation. The disadvantages are, of course, a lack of transparency and accountability of the consensus-forming as well as implementing process, especially unfairness to those who could not participate in the process. The consensus-based regulatory approach may work where the major actors to be regulated are limited in number and well identified. This approach, however, may be ineffective where many and diverse actors are involved. For example, it worked in the case of ozone layer protection, quickly achieving the treaty goals regarding production and use of certain CFCs. Major producers of CFCs are few in number and well defined. Yet the same approach proved totally ineffective in controlling CFC emissions and retrieval, where implemen-

tation necessarily involved controlling many users of diverse products. (James V. Feinerman and Koichiro Fujikura, "Japan: Consensus-Based Compliance," in *Engaging Countries: Strengthening Compliance with International Environmental Accords,* ed. Edith Brown Weiss and Harold K. Jacobson, MIT Press, 1998.)

I attest to Dr. Sidney Draggan's statement that nuclear technology is very safe, but human elements involved in using technology are not. A recent nuclear accident in the Tokaimura reprocessing plant (September 30, 1999) illustrates what could happen in the absence of regulatory inspections. In the plant, bypassing the standard equipment and process, the workers manually carried radioactive uranium fuel by using a bucket and overfilled a storage container, thereby creating a nuclear fission. The two workers later died from the exposure. Many people in the town were exposed to radiation, and 120 of them have been placed under periodic medical monitoring. No compliance officers visited the site for the past seven years. There exists a terrible and frightful price for the lack of enforcement efforts.

Japan, like Ukraine and Mexico, is facing the need to change traditional regulatory approaches. Japan has to resort to a more active use of law and legal means to implement international and national environmental policy objectives more effectively, calling for more citizen participation and greater involvement of local governments. A more imaginative use of the market mechanism is not only effective but also a necessary means of implementing environmental regulatory aims. Because of its traditionally weak law enforcement structure and resources, it is necessary for Japan to rely more upon economic incentives of all the actors involved. Also, in the context of the global environmental protection, the consensus-based approach as well as the market-based approach are necessary because no international enforcement structure and regime have yet been developed. For both national and international environmental control, however, a positive use of law is essential for making the official process of environmental policymaking and of implementation more transparent, accountable, and efficient.

The Golden Temple, Amritsar, India. *Source:* Library of Congress.

Session 5

Religion, Culture, and Governance

Editors' Note

In almost all societies, ancient and modern, the relationship among religion, culture, and governance is intimate. In theocratic societies, religion has dominated the state apparatus, with government power dependent on the authority of religious leaders. Even where such dominance is absent, the force of religious ideas and institutions, deeply entwined with national culture, has significantly influenced public policy. This has been true in the East and West, and in all historical periods. Only since the Enlightenment of the late eighteenth century have secular concepts of the state been able to compete successfully in a few places. We felt the conference required a session devoted to the interactions between culture (including religion) and the governance of society.

The authors of the papers that follow come from countries with particularly long and complex histories, and they illuminate the subject in different ways. In India, the ties between religion and politics are apparently so deep that they cannot be intelligibly separated. Despite the internal problems of political parties, the overriding public goal of providing service to the people—itself part of the Hindu tradition—is credited with sustaining India's democracy for more than a half century. Turkey's situation is different; its inheritance of an Islamic culture while simultaneously facing the West and being nurtured by Western philosophy has led to singular tensions that will require working out over generations. And post-Communist Russia represents another model. Seeking to establish a democratic tradition that would be new to its culture, and to do so in a highly uncertain economic climate, Russia must rely on a largely untested legislative process to develop a system that will earn wide public support.

The Culture of Public Service

Inder Kumar Gujral

The Republic of India has been a democracy since its inception. This single feature distinguishes it from all the other 120 nations that together make up the developing world and account for the greater majority of the world's six billion people.

India's experience with democracy has not been totally faultless. The mid-seventies witnessed the agonizing interregnum of the Emergency, when Prime Minister Indira Gandhi suspended constitutional and civil liberties to propagate a personality cult. But even in those days, the strong public protest made Mrs. Gandhi realize that India would not surrender before the whiplash of authoritarianism that easily. Poor our county certainly was, but never pliable. Over the years, the free, democratic, and pluralistic essence of Indian society has often been tested, yet in the end rarely found wanting. The chief justice of South Africa, Ismail Mohamed, when asked to judge the temper of India pronounced it thus, "Passionate argument and intense debate, incessant intellectual effervescence and vigorous dissent, fluctuating discourse and continually unfolding horizons, endless consultation and mutating states of consensus, thesis, antithesis and synthesis are central to the Indian character."

What makes for this fortunate exception? Why did India's faith in the grand anarchy of democracy not crumble and break as most others in Asia, Africa, even in her own South Asian backyard did before the tanks and serried ranks of military might? Why has the collective Indian psyche so utterly rejected totalitarianism of every type and form, whether it posed in religious, cultural, artistic, or any other guise? Political pundits in the developing world are still wont to say that the unlettered masses will accept tyranny as long as this serves to keep their bellies full. The Indian experience unequivocally reveals this self-serving hypothesis to be both barren and false.

National characteristics do exist, indeed, I would say that nations are much like human beings in that they are all similar in certain basic ways yet each also has an unique individuality and a personality all of their own, coming from a certain historical background and experience. I think it can also be said that culture and religion are the factors that most profoundly impact on the character of a nation and on the manner in which politics and governance evolves therein.

As one looks at the map of the world, it is possible to demarcate a Christian world, or what in the parlance of multilateral diplomacy is referred to as the developed world. A product of Christianity, tempered by the Renaissance, the Reformation, and the Enlightenment, this stretches from Western Europe, its birthplace, to North America. This is the West, the birthplace of modern day democracy, the industrial economy, and all the scientific and technological achievements of the eighteenth, nineteenth, and twentieth centuries, in a nutshell, the center of world civilization as it is presently projected.

Then there is Asia, the ancient continent, with its own great history and civilization and a sprawling land mass home to roughly half of the world's population. For all its sprawl and variety, the people of Asia still share commonalties enough to warrant the coinage of the term "Asian values," a feature that is also supposed to distinguish Asian society from the West, in particular from the latter's stress on individual rights and liberties. This term reflects an unease with democracy and is used mainly by those wishing to justify the benign despotism—or what President Soekarno of Indonesia once called the guided democracy—that is accepted by many countries of this continent—India excepted.

Then there is the Islamic world with its glorious history, but conscious also that its future is under a cloud unless it can find a way around its present situation: the internal weakness that sometimes gets reflected in authoritarianism that impedes indigenous democratic impulses. In most of the remaining parts of the world, namely in Latin America, Eastern Europe, and Africa, there are still dialectical struggles between the forces of democracy and those ranged against it.

Such evident linkages notwithstanding, many difficulties remain in analyzing the interplay between culture and governance in any sort of scientific manner. We are, after all, dealing with intangibles. Neither laboratory experiments nor mathematical proofs are possible. We can only attempt a case study approach, using parables, anecdotes, and historical examples to try and identify, illustrate, and hopefully establish the general characteristics of case histories and experiences that will enlighten and illuminate the subject at hand. I approach the subject from the Indian experience, firstly in view of its relevance. The added advantage is that this allows me to apply the full weight of my experience—a lifetime spent in Indian public life and in a wide variety of political capacities, including that of prime minister, the highest elective position in the nation—to the subject at hand. This approach may provide a foundation, something that is particularly useful in dealing with a slippery subject.

One Western concept that is not easily transferred to the Indian context is the distinction between religion and politics. The concept of a secular society in which religious beliefs and practices are a matter of free individual choice, one in which the instruments of the state do not intrude or interfere in any manner, has come to be taken for granted in the West, certainly in the United States and probably also in most of Europe. India too professes to be a secular society and justifiably so given the commitment of successive governments ever since independence to follow the ideals of Mahatma Gandhi and Jawaharlal Nehru. Yet despite this tradition, despite free India's unswerving commitment to secularism, and despite the genuine secularization of India's elite, even so we find from time to time that sectarianism, or what in India goes by the name of communalism, is seen rearing its ugly head from time to time.

The 1980s were truly a trying time for Indian secularism. The Punjab crisis began as a center-state row over the devolution of political power and the apportionment of resources. It stemmed from resentment, not uncommon in other parts of the country disaffected by a distorted and overcentralized federal polity and their own humiliatingly subordinate status vis-à-vis an apathetic, unresponsive, and overbearing state apparatus in New Delhi. Events took an ominous turn as political parties stirred sectarian passions in order to extract quick political gains. Soon, what had begun as a political argument between Punjab and the federal government in New Delhi was to assume the color of a religious conflict between the Sikhs and the Indian state.

At the time of the Punjab crisis one question that was frequently asked of the politicians of Punjab was why they did not keep issues of religion separate from those of politics. The journalists who asked these questions were typically youngsters from Delhi, freshly graduated from university and the products of a public school culture that had ingrained in them all the essential tenets of Western intellectual thought. To them it was entirely natural to assume that all sensible people kept matters of religion from those of politics and governance. The gray eminencies who were asked these questions were hardened veterans of Punjab's public life who had survived and grown in politics by learning to keep their finger close to the pulse of the people. "We cannot keep religion separate from politics," they would reply, "because for us religion and politics are one and the same thing."

A huge gulf had been created. Here were these young representatives of modern, Western-educated, urban India on one side and the grizzled veterans of tradition and conservatism on the other with a vast intellectual chasm separating the two. And although the Punjab crisis has since blown over, this particular intellectual divide remains unbridged, the contradiction between the religious and the secular having been absorbed, as such convictions often tend to be, in the vast contradiction of India itself. And yet as I reflect on it I observe that the conservatives had a point. For if one were to look at India's own philosophical traditions as distinct from Western-derived ones, it becomes more difficult to hold that religion and politics in India hold nothing in common.

The two great epics central to Hindu religion and mythology, the *Ramayana* and *Mahabharata,* deal as much with issues of statecraft as they do with religion. The story of the *Ramayana,* for example, culminates in the establishment of the perfect society, Ram Rajya, wherein humanity flourishes under the rule of God incarnate, Lord Rama himself. The *Mahabharata,* the longer and more involved of the two epics, goes further, delving into the various dilemmas and riddles of statecraft in minute detail. It investigates the duties of monarchs and their obligations to their subjects, the role and responsibilities of warriors and princes, of priests and advisers, indeed, one could well say that in this great religious epic governance is a central issue, for as the *Mahabharata* observes: "The people are rooted in Governance and Governance is rooted in Truth."

The essential contribution of the Indian philosophical tradition was in introducing and emphasizing the concept of service in statecraft. In the West, which is to say in the Christian tradition, the imprint of religion on governance is most readily apparent in the concept of human rights. Christianity endowed the West with the belief in the essential, equal, and inviolate dignity of the individual. This philosophical concept translated into political discourse—liberty, equality, and fraternity—which of course is the foundation of all modern day democracy.

By contrast, in the Indian tradition such an egalitarian concept of human rights never really existed. There were no bonds of Christian brotherhood to bridge the divide between the all-powerful monarch and his powerless subjects. How then does one prevent the lion from turning on the lamb? In a fragmented society how does one ameliorate the hierarchies of unequal wealth and power to create an unity of interests, the common bonds that make a civil society possible?

The answer, in the Indian tradition, is found in the concept of service. Service before self is a notion common to many a religion, but Indian philosophy was perhaps the first to elaborate on this at length. Its importance was stressed to the extent that the fulfillment of the obligations arising out of one's situation and status in society, without reference to any personal gain or loss, became a religion complete and self-contained unto itself. The word "Dharma," which serves to convey this concept, has no exact English counterpart. The literal translation of this Sanskrit word would be "foundation," or "basis." Its sense is in moral obligation or duty, and it is also used to convey righteousness or virtue.

The Dharma of the monarch lay in dispensing justice and ensuring that the person, property, and the general welfare of the citizens were protected. The king had a moral obligation, a religious duty, to ensure that these ends were served. And it was only in fulfilling these duties and obligations, in serving Dharma, that the monarch gained legitimacy and moral authority himself. As long as Dharma was observed, social order would be maintained and the welfare of both monarch and people preserved. By contrast, egotistical rulers who disavowed any notion of service to their people would inevitably bring great suffering upon themselves as well as others around them. There was a mutuality of interest that had to be respected, even if it could not be readily perceived, for ultimately it was only in serving his people that the king really served himself. "Yatha Dharma tatha jaya," where Dharma is there is victory. It is this philosophical discovery that the *Mahabharata* retells time and time again.

I use the word discovery advisedly. The rules and processes of Dharma were not an invention of the philosophers, like grandmothers' tales meant to keep errant children in line, but an existential reality. If Dharma was complied with, people progressed and peace and prosperity followed. Where Dharma was violated, suffering was inescapable. There was this moral logic underlying the universe that had to be respected, for even if its workings and varied manifestations were unfathomable, its reach was infinite and inescapable. This, in a nutshell, was the message conveyed in the grand politico-religious epics of Indian mythology.

By contrast, it is taken for granted today that individuals as well as nations live in pursuit of their particular self-interest, indeed, that it is entirely natural and justified for them to do so. Modern day economic theory serves to reinforce and validate such self-centered behavior in its assertions that individual decisions, however selfishly motivated they appear to be, will nevertheless take us to a collective optimum, and the engine of human selfishness, however narrowly focused or greedily obsessive it may appear, will be guided by an invisible but fortuitously benevolent hand to join the bountiful mainstream of the common good.

Yet, as we have argued, the opposite more often than not proves to be true. For while selfishness has always existed as a human motive, it is only those societies that were able to temper and condition this selfishness, that were able instead to instill the creed of obligation, who were able really to achieve any sort of progress. This is something we arrive at not only in reading the philosophy of the *Mahabharata* but in surveying the history of contemporary Europe as well. Max Weber, in describing the uneven progress of the industrial revolution across Europe, observed that its progress had much to do with social conditioning and motivation. Indeed, one of Weber's main observations was that communities in which individual greed was unfettered remained poor on the whole. In Weber's words, "The universal reign of absolute unscrupulousness in the pursuit of selfish interests by the making of money has been a specific characteristic of precisely those countries whose bourgeoisie capitalistic development measured according to occidental standards has remained backward."

Those societies that were able to instill a sense of obligation on the part of the individual to society progressed. In these regions of Europe, Weber observed that one thing was unquestionably new: the valuation of the fulfillment of duty as the highest form that the moral activity of the individual could assume. The only way of living acceptably to God was not to surpass worldly morality in monastic asceticism but solely through the fulfillment of the obligations imposed upon the individual by his position in the world.

The individual will be well served in deferring to the group, in subordinating his interests to the interests of the society in which he lives. This is a paradox that religion, whether Hindu, Christian, or any other, asks us to accept. But this paradox also has a twin, a mirror image that fortunately is far more easily seen and accepted. For it is equally true that the interests of the group are served in deferring to the individual. This latter paradox reciprocates the former. The group progresses not by asserting itself but in asserting the individual, which is to say the rights and liberties of its citizens. This second paradox is of course the revelation of modern times in the aftermath of the collapse of

Communism and the totalitarian state, which has shown once again that only those human societies that are founded on the bedrock of individual freedoms and human values are protected from decay and ruin.

So we come to this dual paradox whereby the interests of the individual are served in deference to the group while the interests of the group are served in deference to individual. The reality of the situation, both for the individual as well as the group, is that neither is served in asserting themselves; each is served in asserting the other. Both the individual and society itself must learn to transcend themselves if they are to succeed. And it is managing these confusing paradoxes, the double interdependence of the individual on society and the society on the individual, that governance essentially is all about.

One for all and all for one must be the motto for the individual and society to prosper together. It would appear that there are few forms of social organization that are capable of reconciling such widely disparate interests, but a little reflection will reveal that the most common form of human society, which is to say the human family, lives precisely by such a sentiment, and this is true of human families everywhere in the world with few distinctions. But to generalize such a sentiment beyond the family into the wider society as a whole is far more difficult to achieve and something I do not believe really succeeds without the assistance of religious values.

Christianity, through its message of piety, compassion, and human brotherhood, could build a society in which the reciprocal obligation, the mutual support and solidarity that characterizes the family, found expression in the wider social context. By emphasizing both the essential dignity and freedom of the individual and at the same time the individual's civic obligation to his fellow man, both the individual and the group could grow and prosper together. And this is what democracy is really all about. For a democracy is more than just a society based on the cold, clinical application of the rule of law and due process. It may also be seen as a society imbued with the spirit of family in which both the individual and the group grow and prosper together on mutual support and understanding. That is what religiosity makes possible. And that is why religious beliefs and democracy through the ages have been so closely associated, such as modern democracy with Christianity, but even earlier, starting from the eighth century A.D. when Europe was still in the Dark Ages and the grand sweep of Islam revolutionized and democratized Arab society, enabling its glittering achievements in the scientific, cultural, military, and political spheres.

Individual rights and civic obligation—both hang together or not at all. One side of the equation cannot be stressed to the exclusion of the other, but this has not stopped such claims from being made. It is still said, for example, that within Asian culture and tradition the individual has few inherent freestanding rights and liberties and that it is necessary for the stability and progress of society that individual liberties be curtailed and the individual made to conform with the group. This is, of course, the so-called Asian values theory referred to earlier, which has come to be used to justify the authoritarian regimes prevalent in a number of Asian countries.

I do not believe that such an hypothesis can stand scrutiny, certainly not in terms of the analysis presented in the preceding paragraphs. If an ideal society is modeled on the lines of the family, as indeed would appear to be the case, then there must always be a reciprocal obligation on the part of the group to the individual. It is impossible to visualize any well functioning society built on the denial of civil rights and liberties for the simple reason that it is impossible to visualize a functional family, whether in Asia or in any other part of the world, where the individual has no rights or standing of his or her own. While the group is important too, the Asian values theorists, in stressing the importance of the group before that of the individual, cannot even claim to be half right. Half the facts are not half the story. I would not like to belabor this point but simply illustrate it with a story, turning for a moment to Europe in the earlier part of the twentieth century.

From 1939 until 1941, which is to say in the early days of World War II, Nazi Germany was able to inflict quick military defeats in rapid succession against its neighbors—Poland, Czechoslovakia, France, and even Russia initially. The stunning speed with which the German military machine was able to steamroller its neighbors became possible largely because of their military organization, the tremendous capacity of the Ger-

man General Staff to deploy, coordinate, and synchronize the use of widely dispersed military resources—whether land, sea, or air—and focus them all on the chosen area of combat. Their skill in this deployment was such that the German army often did not have to engage the defendants in combat, rather they were able to overwhelm them through the sheer weight of the military machine that they were able to concentrate and bring to bear at the vulnerable points in their adversaries' defenses. Nazi Germany's triumphant military juggernaut, in other words, was built more on its mastery of logistics and planning rather than its actual fighting or combat record.

The people who did all this planning and coordination, the brains of the Wehrmacht so to speak, were the General Staff. This was the crème de la crème, the supra-elite of the German army. Identified by a distinctive stripe on their uniform, members of the General Staff were deferred to by even senior commanding officers in the Wehrmacht, that is, the army proper. When the Great War was finally over and Germany lay in ruins, the systems and techniques of the General Staff were analyzed by the victorious Allies in some considerable detail. How was the General Staff manned? what qualities did the men appointed to the General Staff possess? the Allies queried.

The officers of the General Staff were selected not on the basis of the traits they possessed, came the reply, but on the basis of the trait they did not. The main criterion for those selected to be officers of the General Staff was that they be free of the taint of personal ambition. Only those soldiers who met this criterion could hope to gain entry into the top elite of the Nazi army.

It was this lack of personal ambition, their selflessness and complete identification with the interests of the group, that enabled the strategists of the German General Staff to work together as a team, as a smoothly oiled machine, and pull off such stunning victories against their unfortunate adversaries. But the ultimate tragedy of the situation was that while the individuals themselves were selfless, the ultranationalistic state that they had the misfortune to serve was fatally flawed. The tactical brilliance of the General Staff may have given it a powerful engine of propulsion, but the Nazi state was so blinded by its own arrogance and the evil it nursed within that it lacked any antennae to navigate. And so you have the picture of these selfless men brilliantly directing a flawed nation toward utter disaster.

A sense of service is required for the integrity of both the individual as well as the organization. The question that the votaries of Asian values should actually be asking therefore is not whether the individual should serve the state, which of course he must. The question really is what values and objectives must the state serve. The state cannot merely serve itself, its own self-aggrandizement, for that way, as history has shown time and again, lies disaster. Rather, the very survival of the state demands that it must be defined in terms of service to its people, and no state that purports to serve the people can really set itself above the people.

India has been a democracy since its inception. This, as I observed in the beginning of this article, is a unique record, one in which every citizen of India takes some measure of pride and justifiably so, given the unpromising raw material that the founders of the republic had before them. In 1947, at the time of independence, India had less than 5 percent literacy, persistent hunger, and recurring famine. To many outside observers, India was nothing more than a bewildering melange of clashing cultures, languages, and dialects, all mired in poverty, superstition, and dark beliefs. The British prime minister, Winston Churchill, said at some point that India was no more a nation than a purely geographical entity such as the equator. Broken by religion, fractured by caste, trapped in feudalism, and revealed by its own history to be a weak and divisive society, India in 1947 was—as Nehru said in his Independence Day speech—a country still in deep slumber.

For all these handicaps, democracy in India has survived and grown. What is the reason for this unlikely success? Many would say that it has much to do with the temper of the country—tolerant, even broadminded, certainly open to the invigorating influences of dissent and diversity. It is said that the Indian ethos has two distinctive traits. One of them is pacifism, or what we call Ahimsa, or nonviolence. The other is its ability to assimilate new ideas and influences, even those quite alien to the soil of India. Both these traits would have greatly favored the growth of a democratic culture in the country.

There may be something in this "Hindu temper" theory, but I for one would not invest it with too much significance. For one thing, the great modernizers who took it upon themselves to reform Indian society and make it capable of self-rule, people like Raja Ram Mohan Roy in the nineteenth century and Mahatma Gandhi and Jawaharlal Nehru in the twentieth century, all had to face tough battles with the forces of religious conservatives. Indeed, for Mahatma Gandhi, the freedom struggle was as much about reforming Hindu society and freeing it from its internal evils—its abominable treatment of its weaker sections, especially its scheduled castes—as it was about freeing India from the British.

The foreign influence on India's modernizers was considerable though varied. Without such exposures I doubt that they would have become the great reformers that they did. Mahatma Gandhi and Jawaharlal Nehru both spent their formative years outside India training as lawyers in British jurisprudence. Gandhi's nearly twelve years in South Africa confronted him with the inhuman and uncivilized face of a modernized state that made him a deep humanist trying to evolve the basic concepts of humane governance. After returning to India, he spent as much of his time in confronting Hindu religious conservatives, who were deeply upset at his attempts at reforming and cleansing Hindu society, as he did in confronting the British. Gandhiji remained a devout Hindu till the very end—in times of trouble, "I turn to the Bhagavad Gita as a child turns to his mother," he would say—but his efforts to rid Hindu society of its gross injustices always saw him on the opposite side of his conservative co-religionists.

For Gandhiji, this freedom struggle was as much about reclaiming the lost soul of India as it was about evicting the British. His great success was in investing the movement with high moral purpose. The spirit of the Indian freedom struggle threw up a political class imbued with a spirit of idealism, service, and a commitment to peaceful and consensual means. This spirit and the people who represented this spirit lived on even after independence was won, ensuring our democracy would survive and grow strong roots. If there is one single factor that more than any other accounts for Indian democracy it is to be found in the spirit of the Indian freedom struggle—the universal values of love and brotherhood that this movement stood for—plus, of course, Gandhiji's special emphasis on the use of peaceful and correct means.

Today, fifty years after independence, Indian democracy has moved beyond the drawing rooms of the elite to permeate the length and breadth of the country. It is genuinely now a people's movement, no longer just a game that the rich and the powerful play among themselves. Indian society itself has changed over the years to become somewhat more egalitarian, educated, middle class, and cohesive, less burdened now by the various taboos and restrictions that fettered it in the past. The winds over India now carry the heady fragrance of freedom, and they may not easily go, but one still has to be cautious, for not all the trends or forebodings are positive.

The unfortunate fact is that over the past fifty years of independence many of our vital institutions have atrophied and are in danger of withering away. The administration underperforms, the law-and-order machinery is under a variety of strains, the courts are clogged, and the political class is generally lacking respect. The aspirations of the people on one hand and economic limitations on the other, along with the slow pace of social change, are causing widespread frustrations and disillusionment with the system. Anyone who comes to occupy high offices quickly loses his shine. This has given rise to a uniquely Indian political phenomenon, what our political analysts term the anti-incumbency factor. Its rough import is that the incumbent in any race for public office is ipso facto unpopular, and hence always at a disadvantage. Such widespread public disaffection may not be witnessed elsewhere but it is certainly disturbing.

Another weakness is that Indian democracy is sustained by political parties that are not internally democratic. Almost all of them are captives of a caucus or a dynasty. Some still project a narrow sectarian outlook and beliefs that negate the very foundation of our composite polity, which leaves limited space for dissent or ideological inquiry. The methodology and practices of Indian democracy do correlate with precedents of democracies elsewhere. There is nothing wrong in it. All the same, most of the political ideas and ideals are a legacy of the freedom struggle. Secularism, equality,

social justice, and federalism are supported by an incipient nationalism, but these are not enough because many in India have yet to imbibe deep understanding of what democracy is all about. If you ask an average Indian what makes for democracy, he or she will say majority rule. This is true only in part, for democracy must make special provision for minorities, the weak, and the underprivileged. Others might say that democracy means popularly elected government, but by that token Germany's infamous Nazi regime would be the epitome of democracy. Sometimes it is said that democracy is all about the peaceful transfer of power, but that too is patently incorrect because this would include all the erstwhile Soviet-style Communist regimes.

We are still learning to appreciate that democracy is all about the rule of law, a system of justice and due procedure that applies equally to everybody. For any democracy to survive, the people, and particularly the politicians and those who occupy public office, must respect and abide by the laws; they must believe that just laws provide the only sure means of finding order in an unruly world and that no society can be strong without a deeply ingrained respect for the law. Neither the wealthy nor the powerful may be allowed to escape the rigors of the law; its reach must be all-pervasive, impartial, and firm. For it is only the rule of law that allows equality, dignity, and freedom to a society. As Aung San Suu Kyi unites in the Burmese context, just laws do not merely prevent corruption by meting out impartial punishment to offenders, they also help to create a society in which people can fulfill the basic requirements necessary for the preservation of human dignity without recourse to corrupt practices.

In India, unfortunately, over the years we have come to witness a willful disregard for the law, especially on the part of public officials entrusted with its maintenance. No longer seen as an instrument of justice, the law has become an enfeebled instrument, one that is debased and eroded by its own custodians and seen as a pliant handmaiden of the rich and the powerful. Few of our officials and politicians understand what democracy is about, and hence few realize that in showing an arrogant disregard for the law they are merely undermining the basis of their own authority, like the man cutting the branch of the tree on which he is sitting.

But even this is not the core of the problem. The basic difference between Indian democracy and Western democracy is at heart one of religious cultural training. It has to do with what our notion of obligation to one's fellow citizens is all about. In Western democracy the notion of obligation exists in an impersonal sense, which is to say that one has a civic duty to society—to keep the streets clean, to drive safely—irrespective of whether one knows the people concerned or not. In India, such an impersonal notion of duty has yet to stabilize. Such obligations are mostly confined within a closed circle of family, relatives, and friends. The notion of having a civic duty of obligation to someone one does not know or has never met is something to be imbibed at a wider scale.

The idea that the world at large is but a single family, "vasudhaiva kutumbukam," is part and parcel of our faith. It is quoted in books, verses, and speeches; it is inscribed in the Central Hall of Indian Parliament. This motto provides the foundation of civic society because it implies that one has the same obligation to society at large as one has to one's family. This has particular importance for all those who hold a public position, for if they are to honor and fulfill this position they can no longer keep any place for personal ambition, either for themselves or for their family and friends. Society is due an equal loyalty as family, and a public person particularly has to be empty of all clannishness so that the greater good of society can be fulfilled.

Such notions of justice and governance have to be emphasized in building the civil society. In the older democracies such impersonal notions of civic obligation hold, and fewer politicians have been accused of exploiting the position to benefit their family. The social backgrounds, the evolution of the nation-state, and the ending of the feudal attitude provide the needed background for the stabilization and extension of the civil society. In most of the former colonial countries that is still an unfinished or partly finished task. In the meantime, narrow family loyalties undermined civic duty. I am not speaking about corruption; the very fact of a public person having a personal agenda should be deemed corruption in itself. And the unfortunate fact is that there will be very few who look beyond the interests of their family to the interests of the nation.

Nor is the politician or the public official himself to blame for he too as an individual is merely reflecting the prevailing social lacuna and bias. In India there is a good chance that people who become perfect democrats will be criticized rather than praised for shirking their responsibility to their family. There is the famous episode in the Ramayana when Lord Rama, at the behest of a commoner, asks his wife, Sita, to undergo an *agni pariksha,* the fire test. This action of his is not held up as exemplary of a true democrat, the self sacrifice that Ram Rajya necessarily entails, but rather attracts criticism for the apparent lack of fealty displayed towards Sita.

It was India that gave the world the very concept of service before self. It is our religious texts that propagate the virtues of detached and selfless service. It is in our tradition to regard all humanity as but a single family. Though we have still to go a long way to practice what we profess.

Whatever position a public person holds—whether he is a junior civil servant, a minister, or a managing director in a large public company—his situation in the scheme of things can be viewed in either of two alternative ways: I occupy this position in order to sense the general welfare by doing the assignment as it is best done, or my position is my personal privilege to exploit and do with whatever pleases me most. Both these options are open, the former promising jam tomorrow, and the latter urging jam today. The path one takes, the attitude one adopts, is a product purely of social conditioning, the imprint of religion or culture on the mind.

Obligation or privilege? The answer to this question is fundamental. A society or organization that is able to invoke the former sentiment will grow and prosper while the latter spirit will inevitably bring forth regression and decay. To hark back to nineteenth-century Europe, the successful development of the industrial economy there depended on the new attitudes that the Protestant culture brought with it. To recall Weber once again, labor must, on the contrary, be performed as if it were an end in itself, but such an attitude is by no means a product of nature. It cannot be evoked by low wages or high ones alone but can only be the product of long and arduous education. Today, capitalism, which is in the saddle, can recruit its laboring force with considerable ease. In the past this was in every case a difficult problem.

Obligation or privilege? It is the former course that the Indian religious texts extol, but we notice that people in public life focus on the obligation they bear to society. None forgets the privilege that they deem to be their due. The very term public service or public servant attracts opprobrium and disapproval as being something below the dignity of a person of good breeding.

Not long back there was a long debate in the Indian Parliament as to whether members of Parliament were in fact public servants because many members were against such an appellation. The question of course is that if senior people in public life do not serve the public interest, then what do they serve? And if they do not serve the public interest, then why should those organs of government that do serve, at lease in theory, some public obligation—such as the army, the police, the administration—listen to them? Without this fundamental obligation of service the whole apparatus of the state and the governing machinery lack legitimacy, and, as we have seen most recently in neighboring Pakistan, when this legitimacy is lost the rule of the tyrant begins. The fact is that democracy does not hold without the foundation of public service. As the new millennium dawns, the recently issued *Human Development Report of South Asia* warns, "South Asia has emerged by now as one of the most poorly governed regions in the world, with exclusion of the voiceless majority, unstable political regimes, and poor economic management. Their systems of governance have become unresponsive and irrelevant to the needs and concerns of people."

It proceeds to say, "Though the country's GNP has grown and is important for achieving Human Development, it is believed that the main reasons for South Asia's colossal human deprivation are not just economic. These problems go hand in hand with social and political factors rooted in poor governance. How does governance relate to people and what has been its impact on human development, this is the central question?"

In the last analysis an effective democracy requires democratic culture and values that emphasize consensus and power sharing. Frequent elections within political parties are as crucial as regular elections at the national level. Internal democracy holds leaders accountable to their own party and workers. When internal democracy is absent, individuals become more important than political parties and popular confidence in the political system is gradually eroded."

I conclude, sharing the report's belief that "Humane governance is governance, indeed good governance, which is dedicated to securing human development. It requires effective participation of people in state, civil society, and private sector activities that are conducive to human development. It further enjoins the state, civil society, and the private sector to help build capacities that will meet the basic needs of all people, particularly women, children, and the poor. Humane governance will also ensure that human development is sustainable. Governance must enable the state, the civil society, and the private sector to further broad-based economic growth and social development. Ownership, decency, and accountability are the bedrock principles underlying humane governance."

Secular State and Muslim Society: The Case of Turkey

Nur Vergin

Years ago I lectured on religion and politics. Very soon it became obvious to my students and to me that we were at the core of the essential problem that shapes the Turkish sociopolitical reality. Lecturing on the theoretical sources of the relationships of the state and religion, I soon realized that we were in fact sailing toward the very questions that Turkish society has been trying to answer adequately for the last decades. These lectures are over now but the dilemmas driven from the Western political thinkers and the Turkish reality do not seem to come to an end.

Relationships between state and religion are, of course, a tremendously vast subject that I am not going to relate in this paper. My aim will only consist of inviting all those interested in the subject to think on two main topics that create much turmoil in the social and political life of Turkey. One of these topics is related to some of the perspectives on this issue. For the sake of sounding more academic we may also call them theoretical models. The other topic I want to focus on is secularism, a topic that creates a real polarization within the Turkish society, especially since the electoral success of the now banned religious party (the Welfare Party) in 1995. This polarization is aggravated by the unexpected emergence of new fundamentalist religious communities within the last two or three decades.

State and Religion Relationships

Before analyzing this topic within the framework of the Ottoman society and Turkey, I will take the risk of being a little didactic and relate some of the models that the Western thinkers developed in the past with the emergence of the modern state. These models, I believe, are crucial for understanding the relationships between state and religion in Turkey.

The European thought on state and religion relationships lies mainly along four axes. One of these, designed by theologians like Calvin, Luther, and Bossuet, contends that the state could not have an autonomous existence apart from religion and that the norms and principles of the state should be directly derived from religion. A state should exist only through the power that religion would confer it. State and religion were but an organic whole, inseparable and indivisible. The state was in fact an emanation of the church and God's reflection upon the earth.

But this approach that vulgar political science has commonly named theocratical is not our concern here. Another approach, qualified as instrumentalist, fits our topic better. Many notable political theorists like Machiavelli, Hobbes, and Rousseau, to name only a few, have advocated it. These authors argued that politics and the state had priority over religion. They thought that religion should be subordinated to the state. Although not concerned with religion per se, Machiavelli discovered the power of religion, which should be at the service of the society and the state. He rejected the servitude of the Medieval state to Christianity and thought that the state should declare its independence from religion and the church. He claimed that the state should get rid of the passiveness and plainness that Christianity had been preaching for centuries. But how? By assuming that religion does not exist any longer, or by rejecting it? Neither of these ways fit with what he wanted to achieve. Religion would persist, and the state should attach religion to its own will and make it serve its own political interests. Machiavelli saw in the magnificence and the political power of ancient Rome this wise use of religion. He thought, for example, that Emperor Numa Pompilius had been able to turn an extraordinarily rebel people like the Romans into an obedient one by making them believe that he had religion and the gods on his side. Machiavelli therefore came to the conclusion that political obligation could be obtained through religious allegiance. The creation of a "state religion" was necessary for the formation of a united state in Italy. So church should not be rejected but should be transformed into a "state church" that would act on behalf of the state interests.

In the same vein, Hobbes writes in the *Leviathan* that in ancient Rome as well as in the Jewish tradition, religion is an element of politics. In both societies politics includes religion and at the same time directs it. His conclusion is categorical: Religion is not only necessary to the individual but to the society as well, especially to the state. There should be fusion between religion and the political power. Political matters and religious matters should not be dissociated.

Hobbes wanted these principles to reign in his own country. If not, war, tears, conflict, and divisions would never cease. So the state should be a Christian state and Christianity should naturally be bound to the Crown—a national church at the service of the state. Only under these conditions would religion cease to be a threat to the state. On the contrary, the religion preached by a national church would only help in consolidating the state because such a religion would also give the state the sacredness it otherwise lacks.

The theorists of the absolutist state are not alone in using this argument. Rousseau, too, although celebrated as the precursor of the democratic theory, set forth in the *Social Contract* the notion of "civil religion," that is, a religion that would serve the needs of the state. Rousseau's claims for union made him coin the concept of civil religion that would meet society's needs and help the development of patriotic sentiments within the society. Adepts of this civil religion would be good nationals and trustworthy citizens. He thought that by melding state and religion one could reach unity in the society. Contrary to other eighteenth-century *philosophes,*

Rousseau believed that a powerful religion was an indispensable asset for stability in politics. As a good instrumentalist, he urged for a state-bound religion.

But the French Revolution could as well be the end of these approaches that lead to the consolidation of the state through religion. In fact, with the Revolution, the absolutist state was now relegated to the past. Liberal theses were flourishing and religious freedom was required. Locke had indeed already written on toleration, and he had argued for the separation of religion and politics as well as for the autonomy of the church. But his ideas, which then remained unheard, have found echo after the French Revolution. De Tocqueville and other adepts of liberal democracy thought that the state was not competent on religion; they wanted religion to be free and to constitute an autonomous sphere within the social system.

De Tocqueville's studies on the American society helped further more liberal suggestions on religion and state relationships. He stressed the importance of religion, but in his opinion such an important and perennial institution should not be linked to the state, which, by definition, was time and space bound and could thus only be variable and relative. Besides, the state was not competent on religion, which should be completely autonomous. He also thought that the dissociation of religion from the state would be favorable to the former. He claimed that only under these conditions could religion adjust to new social institutions. Thanks to its capacity to adapt to new social structures, religion could preserve its influence on society. The separation of state and church would free religion from being the symbol of counterrevolutionary and reactionary forces. It would also cease to be considered as the instrument of conservative institutions and politics. Apart from these considerations on behalf of religion, de Tocqueville also claimed that the separation of religion and the state was necessary for democracy.

One may assert that de Tocqueville had been deeply influenced by Thomas Jefferson, as limitless freedom and limitless pluralism were his motto. In this respect, the following sentence of the writer of the Virginia Constitution is worth noting: "the fact that my neighbour says that he believes in twenty gods or in any one at all, does not cause any prejudice to me." The key word here is, of course, prejudice, and it needs to be underlined. The idea is that those individuals' beliefs and opinions cannot be detrimental to the rest of the society. Yet the question arises whether it was possible to form a society with individuals torn apart between so many different ideas and beliefs. Was it possible to make people develop a sense of togetherness and feel the need of being united when they hold different religious beliefs and divergent opinions? De Tocqueville's answer to these questions is positive. This was possible because to form a political union and to be part of the political community having socially valued virtues and being oriented toward collective life was sufficient. Whereas, thought de Tocqueville, religion was a personal matter and it had nothing to do with the public sphere.

At this point, before continuing with Comte's contributions to the theory of the state and religion relationships, I want to take a pause and recall the situation in the Ottoman society as far as the fusion theory and the instrumentalist approach are concerned. It is widely known that the Ottoman Empire has usually been considered a theocratic state. All the numerous political writers and scholars in Turkey who said that "the source of power and authority in the Ottoman state was God, and secularism came and the source of power became the nation" seem to have nailed this opinion down in our minds too with undeniable success. Thus the Ottoman Empire being a theocracy became in Turkey a scientific credo for generations. This contention was even upgraded to the status of official knowledge, sponsored by state officials and academic discourse. Who is responsible for this false judgement that has been spread around is of no importance. What is important is that so many Orientalists and Islamologists and more recent Turkish scholars like I. Arsel have accustomed us to think this way and make us accept this view as a sacrosanct premise.

There are, of course, a few exceptions. For example, Ç. Özek, in his voluminous book dedicated to state and religion relationships, says, "there is no way to say that the Ottoman State was a theocracy." And he adds, "Contrary to the principles led by theocracy, the 'state affairs' have always been considered superior to those of the religion in the Ottoman social order, and customary law that was not based upon religion has always existed for the sake of good governance of the 'state

affairs.'" This indicates that the famous principle of the "reason of the state" that Machiavelli later cherished so much had its advocates already in the Ottoman Empire. To be quite fair, I want also to refer to N. Berkes, for he too argued that the Ottoman sultanate was not a religion-based state and believed that the attribution of theocratic government to the Ottoman Empire is totally groundless, at least for the period up to the nineteenth century. It seems that confusion concerning the nature of the Ottoman state stems from the fact that we often take the existence of an official state religion for the existence of a theocratic state. For example, the Fundamental Law in 1876, a first attempt at constitutional government, said, "the religion of the Ottoman State is Islam." This article makes all of us who are not sensitive enough to nuances jump to the conclusion that since state and religion were not separated, the Ottoman political system was not secular. Consequently, it could only be the opposite of it, that is, a theocratic system.

We all know for sure that for a state to have a state religion and to have it stamped in an official state document does not mean that this state is necessarily a theocratic one. Furthermore, we all know also that the first constitution of 1924, just one year after the proclamation of the Kemalist Turkish Republic, also stated that "Islam is the religion of the state." A hurriedly made logical assertion can also lead to the conclusion that the Kemalist state, when first formed, was not secular. This is why it is a must for more intelligible analysis to avoid interpretation based only on official documents. Therefore, the argument that the Ottoman Empire was not theocratic and that it had in this respect very few similarities with the European "church states" that existed at that time is a plausible one and should be considered.

Nonetheless, if an analogy has to be made with Europe, it is possible to assert that there was in the Ottoman state a "state religion" such as Machiavelli, Hobbes, and even Rousseau along with other instrumentalist thinkers dreamed of for the good government of their societies. Evidence can be found in the writings of the historians of the Ottoman period, and for empirical support I want to turn to these sources and refer to the analyses of F. Köprülü, H. Inalcik, and O. L. Barkan. Köprülü as well as other prominent historians provide us with a great deal of factual knowledge about the relationships of state and religion in the Ottoman Empire. Many of them assert that even before the Ottoman period Turks had formed the first real absolutist state on the borderland between Asia and Europe. The politics of state and religion relationships as conceived by Machiavelli and Hobbes had already been launched in this Islamic state on the marches of the European continent. The requisites of the Machiavellian *raison d'état* had already been set up through the public policies implemented by the Ottoman administration under the ideological formula of "world orderliness" (*nizam-i alem*).

F. Köprülü, a major Turkish historian of the Ottoman state formation, writes, "Medieval Turks have given the first example of an Absolutist State regime." He says that the pre-Ottoman Turkish states' laws concerning the public order were decreed by the sovereign himself and not dictated by the Koran. Islam was already the dominant religion and had even been "elevated to the status of state religion" as Köprülü notes, "especially in matters concerning public order secular customary law promulgated by the state was rigorously obeyed." This is why "beside the Islamic tribunals, secular tribunals succeeded, which were competent on public law affairs."

The Turkish Muslim states did indeed have their own specificity, and Köprülü makes the following comment that sheds light on our argument: "The Gaznevi Sultans have always observed the customary laws for matters concerning state affairs." And these sultans were never accused of misleading their subjects and betraying Islamic precepts. Sultan Mahmut, sovereign of a former Turkish state, the Gaznevi Sultanate, is portrayed by Köprülü as a sovereign who never confined the authority of the state within the boundaries of the Islamic law and used religion only as an instrument for his "imperialistic politics." Practicing instrumentalism in religion and state relationships was a matter of political instinct more than a deliberate doctrine. Sultan Mahmut never had the chance of reading Machiavelli and other political thinkers who lived and wrote centuries after he died, and it seems that in this example practice did anticipate theory.

Inalcik, too, notes the same historical facts in his article entitled "Islam in the Ottoman Empire." He states that the Muslim Turkish dynasties led a very active and elaborate politics of religion. He says, "what they sought by espousing the 'just' cause was in fact legitimacy." On the other hand, he also indicates that these dynasties set forth a totally independent public legislation in order to strengthen their political power. To strengthen their power, they were cautious enough to refer to Islamic concepts derived from the Koran, and thus, by justifying the newly established states, they were able to gain the trust and the collaboration of the Muslim jurists. Consequently, Mawerdi, a leading jurisconsult, acknowledged the right for the sultans to enact customary "laws" in order to maintain the public order and to preserve the interests of the state, as long as these "laws" conformed to the essentials of the Shari'a, the Holy Law. As the result of these policies, the concept of a religion-free state law started to gain ground. Ghazali, a notorious authority, also supported this view in Islamic jurisprudence. Ghazali's position was clear: A bad social order, disorderliness, and even an "unjust" order is better than anarchy. The function of the political power is to safeguard the religion, and religion cannot be preserved and glorified if the social order is in peril. So anyone who wants to defend his or her religion has the primary duty of submission to the political power.

But if we turn back to Inalcik's statement, we must recall that he argued that the Ottoman state has been more insistent than its predecessors in establishing an entirely autonomous public law. Mehmet the Conqueror was the first Islamic sovereign making laws on the sole basis of his political authority. These laws "stemmed entirely from his free and independent will." Inalcik recognizes that later, during the reign of Soliman the Magnificent (called the "Lawgiver" in Turkish historiography), a new impetus was given to the re-Islamization of the Imperial (customary) laws and that Soliman tended to emphasize the primacy of the Shari'a. But, nevertheless, he too maintained the autonomy of the public laws. These findings can, no doubt, turn upside down our mental comfort and the stock of our knowledge. Academic circles as well as the political class in Turkey have so far shaped our beliefs in such a way that we are usually bound to think unimaginable the separation of Islam from politics. Too often, dissociation between religion and politics when Islam is concerned appears to be simply unthinkable. And surprisingly enough, there is a strange convergence between this view and the radical Islamists' declarations. This is exactly what a lineage of thought from the Egyptian Muslim Brother leader S. Kutup to Khomeini, which we call political Islam, has taught us for the last decades.

But it is true that other Muslim political thinkers are more sensitive to nuances and take a less maximalist position than those mentioned above. One of the major contributions to this liberal approach is due to M. Arkoun, who claims the existence in Islam of a distinction between religion, worldliness, and the state (*din/dunya/devlet*), three spheres that need not be brought together. Another modern Muslim scholar argues that in Islam there is neither a total amalgamation of religion with the state nor an indissoluble separation between the two. Thus, the Turkish Muslim states and more especially the Ottoman state cannot be qualified as unorthodox and even less heretic if we consider that the Ottomans' customary law did not defy the religious precepts. They simply designed the society according to the interests and needs of the public sphere.

The Ottoman political system, far from being a theocratic system, was actually a system that incorporated religion in order to maximize its legitimacy in the most Machiavellian way. Historical data collected by Barkan also verify this proposition. He notes that the leading religious authority of the Empire, the *Seyhlulislams,* never challenged the sultan's right to govern on the basis of the customary law. He also writes that not only did the *Seyhlulislams* not deny the sultan's right to legislate, but they simply refused to interfere in matters they considered being "high level state affairs and political matters." Furthermore, Inalcik's studies give us much evidence with regard to Ottoman governance, which was perceived by the subjects as conforming to the Islamic political theory. Perception, more than the real and objective situation, is of course sufficient enough for a political system to be recognized as fully legitimate.

The instrumentalists, we have seen, have stressed the necessity of a national religion that would function in the favor of the state. The data provided by Turkish historians on the other hand, point out that this position occurs to be in harmony with the Ottoman outlook. Now I want to refer to the approach launched by A. Comte. Not for the sake of reminding his too-well-

known prescriptions for good society but because his concept of state and religion relationships enables us to give account of the present Turkish experience.

In one of his major books, *The Positive Catechism,* Comte says that a society without priesthood not only cannot preserve itself but that it cannot develop adequately. It may sound like a paradox but it is true that the founding father of positivism thought that moral force was necessary for the society. He argued that being no longer capable to represent that moral force, Christianity had ceased to be functional. Thus, a new religion to replace the older one was necessary for the public welfare. He also forged a name for the new religion, which he called the "religion of the Humanity." This new religion was attributed the same functions with the old religion but its nature would be totally different. This is an entirely secular religion and in that respect excludes all reference to transcendental categories.

The new religion does not acknowledge any source of power superior to human reason for it is a godless creed that it does not have to comply with God's will or any kind of deity. Comte is definite on this subject as he says that "humanity has now taken the place of God for ever, but of course, it does not forget the services that He gave in the past." Can what Comte is talking about be taken for a real religion? Some scholars comment that this is an "atheistic humanism" that aims at usurping the status of religion. Sociology has now taken the place of the Medieval theology. The new religion has also its distinguished sacerdote—its calendar, its temples, its rituals—and it provides the humanity with its specific sacredness. Comte assesses that the religion he conceives is only related to the moral sphere and is definitely separated from the political power. But it seems that this separation is true only when action is concerned, for Comte also displays an instrumentalist spirit when he says that the state should have predominance over religion. Religion then is a mere auxiliary for the state's interest and requirements. On the other hand, as religion without deity is not liable to be a finality for itself, the religion professed by Comte should found its principles on society's welfare. According to Comte, the new believers are now expected to act and behave not for the sake of God but for the sake of society. The deification of society is a matter of necessity, and religion has the duty to serve the society. As long as it helps to evict the "moral anarchy" that Comte observes in the industrial society, this religion is a *positive* religion that should be maintained.

Secularism

These ideas have had an immense success in Brazil and especially in Turkey at the eve of the Kemalist revolution where they gave way to the formation of political organizations and parties such as the Union and Progress. It is also interesting to note that the promoter of the Union and Progress, though starting from entirely different theoretical premises, has ended up joining the idea that societies cannot reach the ultimate goal of progress unless they are motivated by faith and belief.

One cannot say, of course, that Comte's ideas have been a central interest all around the world. But the brief overview that I have presented is extremely familiar to any student of Turkey. Comte's claims have indeed been the motto of generations of Turkish secularists. It is true that the same views have been expressed in 1945 under the appeals for "religious reform" and later have been adopted during the single-party regime by the Republican People's Party (RPP) in 1947. The politics of the RPP concerning state and religion relationships and the ideology it diffused stemmed directly from Comte and Durkheim's positivism.

Appeals for "reform in religion" that the RPP thought indispensable for secularism to be set up were in fact a quest for the creation of a new religion based on Comtean argumentation. The reforms the Turkish ruling class requested were in fact an attempt to adjust religion with the necessities of the new Turkish society and the nation-state. The Kemalist elite considered religion as an asset to meet the demands of the new Turkish social and political reality as they figured them out to be. The difference between the Turkish reformists and the "pope of the new positive religion" was that the religion devised by the latter was supposed to be established on universal principles. This religion addressed all of humanity, while the RPP's leading staff thought of a religion that needed to be reformed only for the particular needs of Turkey. This is the reason why perhaps they lectured people for a religion that would suit the "Turks' spirit."

During all this period of tension between the progressive and the reactionary forces, T. Z. Tunaya, a leading figure of Turkish secularism, raises once again the issue of the necessary reforms and argues that even the edifices dedicated to religious services should be designed according to the Turkish tradition. Consequently, they should look like the "People's Houses" where the members of the Republican People's Party used to gather to indoctrinate the partisans. One may wonder whether this unfulfilled intention of replacing the traditional mosques with those houses supposed to fit with the "Turkish soul" was a simple fancy. But it undoubtedly gives account of the general state of mind prevailing during that period—a state of mind very much inspired by the Comtean devices.

But what is essential for the understanding of religion/state relationships are not only the attempts of the single-party regime at reforming Islam for Turkish purposes. We need to know more about the scientism that has penetrated the political class a generation earlier, during the first years after the founding of the republic. This is important because it gives account of the fact that these ideas, which have subsisted up to now, were not accidentally generated by conjunctural events. It will not be wrong to point out that the background of the peremptory sociologism of the RPP advocates lies in a text published in 1928 and entitled the *Proclamation for Reform and Amendment of Religion*. The authors of the *Proclamation* consider religion as a "social institution" and as such argue that it should be obliged to evolve in the course of the social development and comply with the ever changing needs of social life. According to the new methodology, this meant that religion is no longer going to guide society and politics but is bound to change perpetually when new social needs come out. The Turkish laicists wanted a religion that conforms to political and social demands and that they could order at their ease when the necessity arises. The Turkish instrumentalism goes far beyond the instrumentalisms set forth by Machiavelli and others, and it displays a very controversial *raison d'état* concept subject to much criticism and objection. In fact, the *Proclamation* argues for the setup of "a new conscience for religion." This means a new religion for the new society. This is a line of thought that has incessantly come to present days, which I have called *laicism* in order to separate it from lay thinking and secularism. Laicism stands against the notion of secularism (or *laïcité,* in its French version) as it is conceptualized in Western societies. It cannot be assimilated with the rationale that lies behind the notion of secularism, and instead of standing merely for a means or a method for social peace it is an *ism* itself—a doctrine more than a political and judicial method.

Attempts at implementing this atypical form of militant secularism have given way to tensions between the supporters of state-centered politics and those who defend liberal views. Without wanting to take the part of any of the parties, I can still advance that much of the religious intolerance witnessed in this country originates partly in this laicist system of thought. This system of thought engenders social tension because the "new religious conscience" that the authors of the *Proclamation* as well as the RPP wished for the Turks to develop simply did not convince the people. Only a limited group of bureaucrats and the political class as a whole favored this approach, but, nonetheless, this has become the hegemonic official discourse because their advocates are the leading figures of the Turkish politics and the state. This has enabled it to become the hegemonic ethos of Turkish politics and to last up to present days. But as recent events of political violence and acts of terrorism perpetrated by political Islamists indicate, this ethos has failed to totally penetrate the civil society.

The fact is that contrary to the expectations of the resolute secularists just mentioned, Turkish society was reluctant to accept the laicism professed by the reformist ruling class. Consequently, when the politics of amendment or adjustment of Islamic faith to the needs of the new Turkish society failed, these militant secularists suggested other interpretations. They started to say that religiousness, the way it continued to exist in Turkey, is residual "primitiveness" that should be swept away if society was going to make any progress. In this line of thought, a prominent Turkish sociologist wrote in 1989, "while in civilized societies religion has become totally outdated it is surprising that it still operates as an active force in the Turkish society and politics." Discussing whether the observation made on the so-called "civilized" societies is adequate and if this observation is supported by serious evidence is beyond my scope. But what I must emphasize here for my purpose is the inadequacy of the logical relation the author establishes by equating civilization with the fading away of religion. This is important because from this equation there is only one step to jump to the conclusion that Turkish society can righteously be evaluated as un- or precivilized. This is important also because in the core of the sentence quoted above we can see the prototype of the position that I qualify as laicist. This sentence not only summarizes the laicist attitude toward religion, but it also warns society on the following points: (1) religion is an anachronism, (2) this is due to the requisites of civilization, (3) religion is not only the cause but also the result of backwardness, and (4) we should all make efforts to avoid it. It is interesting that this argument has not only been asserted in the past years but continues to be put forward in the present by some of the adamant advocates of positivistic secularism. Many politicians and intellectuals persist in this uncompromising determination. They claim that this is actually what secularism is about and urge Turkish society to understand it. But the truth is that, as we will see later, this argumentation has very little to do with the conceptual and/or historical foundations of secularism as it has developed in Western societies. One of the main reasons for the incongruity of this argumentation is due to fact that it does not acknowledge that secularism is precisely the raison d'être of religion. In this argumentation there is no recognition of religion, or any respect of it. This thought entails the determination to banish religion on behalf of science and of a dubious concept of civilization. This is an attempt at the ejection of religion out of society and a flagrant distortion of secularism. As such, it is called laicism.

To refer to Lenin's well-known metaphor, laicism is the "childhood disease" of laïcité, or secularism, a deviation and a recurrent pathology that originated in France. Turkey, under the influence of the French ideologists early in the nineteenth century, has started to experience a very peculiar type of secular politics, which instead of settling the ground for tolerance and social peace became one of the main causes of social and political unrest. D. Martin, in his book on the different secular governance models, relates that the supporters of the French model, besides advocating adversity toward the religious institutions and the church, pleaded also for the progressive erosion of the religious beliefs. Apart from the principle of state and church separation, historical and political conjuncture made the French state fight against religiosity, and this is why this model cannot be taken as an adequate model for secularism. The militant secularism professed by the French has strong laicist connotations, and the secularism that they wanted to preserve as one of the Republican values was in fact not only confronting fanaticism and religious intolerance but religion itself. While it may be true that nobody in France advocates the refounding of the religious state, many French want the religious values they share to be more conspicuous within the society, as, for example, to be taught in schools.

This demand would obviously not damage secularism and would in all probability have no political consequences. Though nobody advocates today the foundation of a religious political state, the French laicists believe that this a turning away from Republican values. Therefore, in the name of secularism and with the aim of protecting it, this demand is violently rejected. It is a known fact that the disunion of secularism and laicism in France has led to polarization and conflict, both of which are directly contradictory to the basic idea of secularism—peace and social integration. It has been said that however much the ideals of 1789 and the Enlightenment have become part of the social fabric, there is no need for the laicist doctrine of the Third Republic and that this ideology has been eliminated, one still cannot maintain that French laicism is an issue belonging to the past. This ideology preached state neutrality in the religious sphere, and this idea was suited to nation-state ideals. It had visible simplicity, but nevertheless included tacit and open political aims to destroy the principle of state neutrality. The secular state, supposedly neutral in religious affairs, was also guilty of laicist deviance. The laicist approach is actually entrenched in the school, which as Althusser noted, is an "ideological state apparatus." This is, no doubt, the reason why the school has been the battleground on which the war to gain ideological hegemony is fought. In fact, even though by definition the secular school had

respect for different religious beliefs, it still orientated the pupils in a specific ideological direction. On this subject J. Ferry, a prominent figure of French laicism, could not conceal his true aims: "Yes, . . . with respect to religion we promised neutrality, but we did not mention anything about philosophy or politics." In fact, the function of secularism is not as the ideologists of the Third Republic would have it—forcing nationalist ideology or making itself philosophy or state ideology—but rather developing and granting freedom to all philosophy and thought systems within the context of plurality. The acceptance of plurality, a necessity for freedom and human dignity, not as a barrier or flaw but as a positive "given," is the only philosophy on which secularism can be based. Yet the reality is the position of the Third Republic ideologists and that of Ferry mentioned above.

This state neutrality and even aloofness from religion (*laicité*) has determined the ethos of the French Republican tradition and brought the state under the yoke of militant understanding (*laicisme*). This militant thought, inspired by positivism and influenced by Marxist and Marxian ideology, while becoming hegemonic has never really become the official state credo. But it did become hegemonic among the French intelligentsia. Today it is apparent that some feel embarrassed about it and prefer to consider it as only a memory in the Third Republic history. Nonetheless, laicism continues to exert its influence on France, and as one French sociologist has said, "the monster often haunts us." Thus, the fluctuating debates of the 1980s between Catholics and laicists and the problems of the head scarf of the "covered" immigrant families today show that France is still an arena of controversy and division on the subject of secularism and laicism. Also, laicism, despite having lost its political and legal domination as a type of Third Republic ideology, still raises its head when important choices are debated, and by taking its place in these discussions shows its persistence. It is interesting to see that secularism, which aims to be integrative, has in the French context become laicism, that is, an ideology characterized by struggle and the creation of divisions in this country. While secularism sees the church as its target because it leads to social divisions and disagreement, laicism takes up a position against what the church preaches, namely religion, and as the nineteenth-century French poet Peguy said, the real objective of laicism is "to promote atheism to the status of state metaphysics."

French secularism with its laicist deviation not only seems to fulfill Weber's idea of "disenchantment of the world," but it is even speeding up the exit from a godly world. The process of disenchantment, which Weber pointed to, gives time to create judicial-political solutions. However, this is not the function of secularism, and in sociopolitical systems where secularism exists people can continue to be religious and freely maintain their loyalty to the religious community in which they belong. As opposed to what is commonly thought in Turkey, secularism was in fact a principle supposed to protect the religious citizen under the reliance assured by law.

At this point I would like to stop for a while and mention two issues concerning the memorized understanding that prevails in Turkey on the term "laic" (in Turkish, *laiklik*). Turkish political scientists and analysts generally like to point to the etymological origin of this term and over the decades have made this etymological history seem crucial and capable even of solving the problem of secularism, a problem that has haunted Turkey down through the years. These political thinkers insist on referring again and again to the Greek term "*laios*," meaning "people." They also inform Turkey that the term "laic" means "nonclerical" (information that is probably found to be very enlightening). But with time, and thanks to this tenacious instruction, Turkey has also been able to understand that due to the semantic changes that occurred, the term also refers to a system or person that has no connection with religion or religious institutions whatsoever. This is how Turkey understands it because this is how prominent and influential teachers have presented it. While elaborating about the history of the term, nobody mentioned to the people in Turkey that in the Christian world, where the term originated, a layperson is a noncleric—a believer and faithful Christian. The real problem in Turkey is the irrelevance and lack of information that lead to nonsense and idle discussions over questions such as Is the state secular or the individual? The problem that we witness in the Turkish secularism experience is obviously neither connected to the etymology of the term

nor it being Turkish or foreign. The problem in Turkey is the nature of the relationship in a secular sociopolitical system of secularism with religion and the religious. It is the problem of the social and political situation of religion and the religious, or in other words, the question of the status of religion and the religious in the secular system.

By defining the problem this way we can say that what Turkey has to learn and worry about is not the semantic adventure through time of the term "laic" but rather why and in which context it gained its particular meaning. If we look at it from this angle Turkey has to realize that as an ethos of public order the term "laic" is very new and has only emerged a little over one hundred years ago.

In fact, as the pioneering thinker of the Third Republic, F. Buisson, says in his book, published in 1887 and constituting a kind of manifesto for the laicist school, "this is a new term . . . not yet in general use. Yet I find this neologism necessary since no other term can so precisely express this idea." This means that the place occupied by secularism in Turkey is exactly that expressed in the idea itself, an idea that is a product of the thought system created by those known as the "1860s generation," mostly agnostic and who dreamed as J. Ferry did of creating a "Godless and kingless world." This is the final stop on the semantic route of the term secularism in its French version—*laicisme*. And it is this final stop only that interests Turkey because secularism understood in this sense as laicism has already taken effect not only in public life but also shaped the course of the political life in Turkey. This specific meaning of secularism has created what we commonly know as "Republican values" in both France and Turkey.

When the principle of the separation of church and state is put forward, the real issue concerned is the differentiation of religious authority (clerical *auctoritas*) and political power (the king's *potestas*). This differentiation , according to L. Dumont and other contemporary political thinkers and historians, is made possible only by the "cultural" feature, which is dualism in Western civilization and Christianity. Because of this dualism St. Paul's formula of "power belongs to God and earthly power emanates from and is granted by Him" ruled supreme until the Middle Ages and was able to undergo change with the answers developed by St. Thomas Aquinas. Until that time the Church was not a state among states. It was the state itself in accordance with the theory of papal supremacy (*plenitudo potestatis*). However, after this time the Church would never be all-powerful, and in matters concerning public order the clergy would be subject to the king. Furthermore, the paradigm did not only consist of this. According to the Thomist view that emerged in the fourteenth century, autonomy of the state was possible, religiously acceptable, and therefore should happen. Events sweeping through Europe at the time and historical conjuncture also created fertile ground for such a dissociating mentality. Time itself became a breeding ground for secular ideas and the rise of nation-states. It is an interesting paradox that while St. Thomas was preaching the duality of the spiritual and the worldly, the structure of the state was beginning to become unitary, a movement that reached its peak in the nineteenth century. St. Thomas did not forget though to mention that this was the will of God and therefore it was necessary to behave, produce, and think according to His will. These ideas proclaimed the good news of an autonomous public sphere and a political power to order that sphere. This was the baptism ceremony of worldly politics.

With this differentiation the first seeds of secularism were broadcast, because the autonomy of the state meant that the worldly power, the king or the emperor, made laws on earth and thus created public order. The differentiation of the worldly and religious spheres also caused power sharing to come into being, and so the king or emperor, guided by reason and abiding by the contract, became the one responsible for creating the "good life" here and now. The legality of the state would be found in itself because of his monopoly in the autonomized political sphere. This rational legality would be identified and evaluated by taking into account the satisfaction of the general good and the ability to provide law. Being the power in the political sphere, the king's reference point was the general good of the individual while the church would continue to be imprisoned as the representative and protester of its believers' existence and interests.

We know that this differentiation became more pronounced in the fourteenth century. The debate became harsher between the emperor's followers and those defending the absolute power (*plenitudo potestatis*) of the pope. The followers of the emperor, without disregarding the superiority of the Church, argued that the foundation of the two separate and individual powers had been granted and willed by God. They proposed a new system to bind together and harmonize the worldly and the spiritual. With respect to this system, L. Dumont stated "their proposed system reminds us of Hinduism. In the spiritual sphere the State bows to the Church and in worldly matters the Church to the State." This was the only way to reach the ideal of unity. The separation of church and state was in fact strengthening rather than disregarding the principle of *cuius regio eius religio*. According to this interpretation people were bound to the dominant religion of their country, and even if political power was not bound in the same way to the church there was still a resemblance between the relationships. In this way the secular power of the king was conferred the sacredness it would otherwise miss. There was no doubt in the mind of the ruled about political power, and thus the legality of the rulers was ensured.

There is no doubt that a theory that systematizes church-state relations in this way is based on the idea of a single-religion homogeneous society in a state. It is a fact that no such homogenous society exists and even more true that religious communities vary. Varying creeds and religious practices existed under the umbrella of the state, leading to a situation in which religious groups constantly competed with each other and struggled for distinction and superiority. All these developments were deeply affecting society and bringing weaknesses of the state to the fore but also creating an environment leading to a growth in the search for new strategies for living peacefully together. I see Marsile of Padua as one of the pioneers of this search, still going on today, with his book *Defender of The Peace,* which contains, though embryonic, the first systematic thoughts on secularism.

Marsile considered the principle of *cuius regio eius religio,* that is, the intersection of church and state, as unrepresentative of reality and anachronistic. His aim was more than freeing political power from religion. It was also, just as his predecessors and his contemporary, Occam, searching for ways to bring into the state those sects and religions that had different views of God from that preached by the pope. He was trying to reconstruct social peace, which had started to show signs of collapse. All these discussions on the nature of the power emanating from God to popes or kings were creating discomfort in the minds and agitating the consciences of the people of the Middle Ages and presaged the coming religious wars. Marsile's search for ways to build and protect social peace was the first stage of a process, which many years, actually centuries later, was called secularism. According to Marsile the oppressive actions of the Church were unjust, and the only way to abolish this injustice was to transfer all worldly powers to kings. We know he is not the first one to make this proposal, but what makes his problematic unique and familiar to us is not the proposal of separating the worldly and the spiritual but rather his emphasising the civil unity and voluntary nature of the communities that organized themselves within the framework of religion. What is modern for us is that the basic concern was social peace and his evaluation of church-state separation as a prerequisite factor in creating a solid base on which this could be built.

However, Marsile's modern relevance does not only consist of this. He also advocates that just as freedom from the church is necessary for civil and political life, so must civil life be directed from within society itself. This in fact means that the source of political power is within society, and thus the aim and function of this power must be to create and maintain worldly happiness, of which surely the first priority is social peace. This is the function of politics, and as it is a worldly function it must therefore be nonreligious. Marsile, in 1324, created the philosophical foundations of the contemporary system of representation in politics. He wished for the building of a secular state, totally worldly oriented, and it was very different from the ideas of St. Thomas Aquinas. Society would not consist of a community of believers as part of a belief system ascribed to God but rather as a totality in which people could live happily and have their needs met. What would make this society a totality would be civil law. It is at this point that Marsile offers us a new understanding of legality and a new order that would be protected by civil law, the source of which would be the people. The source must be the people or their representatives. So the epistemological rupture is complete: Lawmaking is given to the people, the sole source of legitimacy. Because of the autonomization of political life, the hegemonic power of the state is recognized, and as a natural result peace will be able to hold sway in society.

With our contemporary understanding it can be seen that the autonomization of politics and secularism as a means to create social peace go hand in hand. Of course Marsile's search in the fourteenth century for a system of peace does not have freedom of the individual at its center. Yet thinking retrospectively we can see that secularism, emerging from the freeing of politics from religious institutions when looked at not from a macrosociological analysis but on an individual level, is still a method on the road to both freedom of religion and conscience for the individual. Within this framework secularism still holds its ground as a method, and because of this it has been bound up in our consciousness with the administrative system of democracy in a way which P. Bourdieu called *habitus*. The fact has to be accepted that secularism, whether looked at on an individual or societal level, is not a philosophical finality; it is a method to be used to reach a certain goal—freedom. Therefore, secularism appears not as a container for ethical values but as tool or a concept that supports the construction of freedom, which is an ethical value. Because of its nature secularism takes different forms from society to society, and in each society it has a different historical background, appearance, and way of being constructed. Because of this we can talk about French secularism, English secularism, or the American version, which nowadays fascinates many observers in Turkey as it did de Tocqueville in the past. Of course, insofar as it has freed and exempted itself from the level of laicism that I was trying to explain, we can, without doubt, talk about the specificity of Turkish secularism in its laicist form and its unique aspects. We can also talk about using a method in a specific way. I will come back to this point again.

But before this, I would like to mention a fact that is of vital importance and has a great deal to do with secularism because it too is an active leading factor in the creation of social peace and the practice of individual freedom. But while secularism is a judicial-political method that envelops society, tolerance, which I will now speak about, is a mentality, an attitude or a way of life more specifically related to the individual. Because of this, it is an attitude that is located at the heart of the secular judicial-political method and makes this method function and gives it impetus. The proposal comes from Locke. Concerned by the scenes of religious fighting he witnessed in his country, Locke decided, as I mentioned at the start, that the only solution lay in church-state separation. He also asserted that such a separation could only bring positive results for both state and church. For Locke, the important issue was that the church gaining freedom from the state, as any state whose policy is religious control, would by its very nature be inclined towards despotism and interventionism. For the state this would be a naturally justifiable problem, but the problem was the acceptance or rejection by the ruled of such an interventionist state. As opposed to Hobbes, Locke felt that the way to peace did not lie in the fusion of church and state. He proposed that such an amalgam of the worldly and the religious would not increase the ease of administration but would lead only to greater tension and divisions. This road would only lead to civil society being deprived of peace, and for Locke all his theoretical effort and ultimate direction of his political philosophy was the creation of social peace.

A solution had to be found to the obstacles to social integration. One of the solutions for civil peace was limiting state power so this had to be the target, and this target could be reached through tolerance. The creation of an atmosphere of tolerance would lead to a situation in which social peace could be built, and, furthermore, tolerance itself, by shaping the attitudes and behavior, would allow a new worldview and an approach to valuing differences to take root. In order to reach this there had to be revision in the state, and the first step toward this goal is not allowing the state to have the function of organizing religious affairs.

When Locke talks about the necessity of tolerance he founds his ideas on the notion of freedom of thought. His problem is not the resurrection of human rights. As G. Mairet has pointed out, in the eyes of Locke tolerance is an ingredient, and because of this quality it is the ethical basis of the liberal state. The goodness of tolerance lies not in its quality of easing consciences but only in its being a phenomenon that brings about civil peace. It represents a connective medium between the functioning public order and the good life. Otherwise, how

can we comment on Locke's proposals on the classification of tolerance? How can we understand Locke's doubts and lack of tolerance for atheists, whom he finds untrustworthy and dangerous to the maintenance of order, and Catholics, whom, because of their swearing allegiance to another sovereign—the pope—he finds politically disloyal. For him, because these have the capacity to weaken the basis of social peace they have to be considered outside the limits of tolerance as they are themselves in opposition to the existence of tolerance, which has peace as its aim. Any approach that will weaken the peaceful influence and divert the aim of tolerance must not be allowed to survive, even in the name of tolerance. This may be creating the historical basis for the approach of the twentieth century, which is "no freedom to the enemies of freedom." Seemingly, in the eyes of our liberal thinker it is necessary to show that one is taking part in the peace process to gain the right to tolerance and deserve it. The aim is not to create goodness or a mystical goodwill. It is to eliminate social conflicts and divisions. These conflicts are not the result of variety in thoughts and religious beliefs, and especially not the outcome of sectarianism in the Christian world, but are the result of the denial of tolerance by the church and state. So at the end of this long narrow road, when tolerance is ensured, what will happen? Locke's answer is clear on this point: Social peace will have been created. Social peace! Now we come face to face with that magical shimmering chimera that immediately moves us emotionally and mentally. But I feel it is necessary to stop for a moment and think about the true meaning of this exciting term. The first question that comes to mind is what will happen in an environment where social peace has been established, in other words, in an order where the state can tolerate tolerance.

Will differences disappear? Will we picture a paradise on earth where all factions walk hand in hand in peace? In order to answer this question I will suggest the conclusion of a liberal philosopher. I would like to read one of Oakeshott's statements. He tells us that societies in which tolerance grows will not be perfect rose gardens: "in the system of contemporary states, the states are not allies, but yet neither are they enemies; maybe they are in the same position as England and France in the sixteenth century, they are sweet enemies." This means that in lands where the social peace method is applied and the idea of tolerance has grown we still find ourselves in the half light. The light is somewhere else above.

Turkey is faced with uncountable proposals in its efforts to reach the light, and in this respect one can but congratulate the proponents. But when I examine the relationship of religion and the state and the particular forms of this relationship, I see that some of the proposals have no place in the ethos of the society and are in fact alien to it. They are unacceptable for the establishment of social peace and from the point of view of governance. If we put what I have shown to be the inappropriateness and confusion that is laicism to one side, we can distinguish two sorts of proposals. The first one is the expression of an imagined religious orthodoxy in which objections and discontent toward the state are put forward. In this view the state is considered irreligious because of its secularist position. The second group of proposals consists of statements in the name of secular orthodoxy. While the first group demands that the state organization should be in accordance with religion, the others want the state and religion separated by clear, sharp lines, never to approach each other. They are both mouthpieces for their own orthodoxies. With one exception, none of the proposals possess any concrete value or the qualities to make them applicable and have no place in ensuring social peace. Both groups want victory for their own theory, and in order to gain this they call out for the abolishment of the Directorate of Religious Affairs, an institution that makes Turkish secularism so atypical.

While the religious group looks at the state's running of religious affairs as harmful to religion, the second group is busy showing that this situation is creating cracks in the theory of secularism. As the first group desires public order to be under religious control, the second group is after the glorification of secularism. Their rhetoric is flawless. But I am afraid that these proposals, which do not intend to create social peace and are purely political and intellectual discussions giving way to more conflict, take us further back beyond Oakeshott's tart statements that I mentioned before.

Despite my concern, my opinion is that Turkey, with its tradition and experience in balancing state and religion relations, can find its way out of this dimness. One of the ways out for Turkey means giving the Directorate of Religious Affairs a role in establishing the spirit of tolerance within the society. In accordance with both society's demands and the prerequisites of secularism, this religious institution should be totally revised. It should be transformed in order to abolish the overpowering status of established religion. It should be reorganized to justly serving, without discrimination, all religious groups and communities within Turkey. What Turkey must not do is lose time on maximalist proposals or waste energy trying to rule them out. Instead, in order to create a social climate prone to tolerance and social peace, it has to reawaken its historical balancing capacity. Turkey should conceive another politics of religion, away from the excessiveness of laicism and capable at the same time of dismantling the militant and/or terrorist religious organizations, which have in the Turkish society a growing and threatening role.

The Trophy Art Law as an Illustration of the Current Status of Separation of Powers and Legislative Process in Russia

Alexander N. Domrin

Russia is a country of extremes. James H. Billington symbolically titled his interpretative history of Russian culture *The Icon and the Axe,* and George F. Kennan called contradictions the essence of Russia: "West and East, Pacific and Atlantic, Arctic and tropics, extreme cold and extreme heat, prolonged sloth and sudden feats of energy . . . ostentatious wealth and dismal squalor . . . simultaneous love and hate for the same objects. . . . The Russian does not reject these contradictions. He has learned to live with them, and in them. To him, they are the spice of life . . . The American mind will not apprehend Russia until it is prepared philosophically to accept the validity of contradiction."[1]

Evaluations of Russia, of her cultural and spiritual heritage, are often extreme as well. According to a French poet, "even if everything dies and only the remains of Ancient Greece and the Russia of the 19th century endure, then nothing will be lost," (Paul Valery) whereas an American scholar alleges that Russia and her people have no "cultural capital" at all (Richard Pipes).[2]

As Harold J. Berman has observed, contemporary legal systems are only surface expressions of deeper, broader forces of cultural evolution: "Law cannot be neatly classified in terms of social-economic forces. A legal system is built up slowly over the centuries, and it is in many respects remarkably impervious to social upheavals. This is as true of Soviet law, which is built on the foundations of the Russian past, as it is of American law, with its roots in English and Western European history."[3]

The "Scythian complex" of Russia—the dialectical dichotomy of being an inseparable part of the European civilization and historically being in confrontation with it,[4] attraction toward the West and alienation from it, enthusiastic receptivity to all cultures, natural and absolutely organic multiculturalism (*vsechelovechestvo,* in Pushkin's and Dostoevsky's terms),[5] and traditional Russian suspiciousness, the two-headed eagle as a historical symbol of Russia with one head turned toward the West and the other one toward the Orient, a centuries-long dialogue between those who in the early nineteenth century became known as "Westernizers" and "Slavophiles"—manifests itself in various forms of social life, including contemporary Russian legislation. Among these is the Trophy Art Law, those circumstances in which the law was drafted and adopted and the collision between all three branches of government in respect to that law.

Indeed, if there is any particular Russian legislation that in the years of the Second Russian Republic[6] has stirred major controversy in Russia and abroad and made the biggest number of headlines in Western media it's probably the federal Law on Cultural Values Transferred into the USSR as the Result of the Second World War and Remaining in the Russian Federation, also known as the Trophy Art Law.[7]

Apart from the context of Russian–German relations and international property rights, which have been quite extensively studied in a number of works (although with a rare exception in English legal literature,[8] exclusively from anti-Russian positions[9]), the controversy around the Trophy Art Law is extremely important for a more adequate understanding of peculiarities of the current status of separation of powers, legislative process in the Russian Federation, and the role of all three branches of government in it.

It is recognized that the Russian Constitution of 1993 clearly violates the doctrine of separated powers by granting the president disproportionate leverage.[10]

Whether the president and parliament adhere to the Constitution depends largely on the effectiveness of judicial enforcement.[11] So it was inevitable that President Yeltsin's constitutional coup in September–October 1993 was aimed not only against the federal legislature but against the third branch of government, too.[12] Simultaneously, with the violent dissolution of the Russian parliament, President Yeltsin, in his Decree No. 1400, On the Gradual Constitutional Reform in the Russian Federation (September 21, 1993), also "advised" the Constitutional Court "not to convene" until after the elections (Article 10). The same night the Constitutional Court of Russia, in an emergency session, voted 9–4 that the president's action violated the Constitution and might justify impeachment. The court stated that the president violated Article 121-6 of the Constitution, according to which the president couldn't use his powers "to dismiss, or suspend the activities of, any lawfully elected agencies of state power." Otherwise, the president's powers "are discontinued immediately." Originally, it was an article of the law, On the President of the RSFSR (of April 1991), that introduced the presidency in Russia and that later (in May 1991) was included in the Constitution.

On October 7, 1993, President Yeltsin formalized his assault on the power of constitutional review in the country and signed Decree No. 1612, On the Constitutional Court of the Russian Federation, stripping the only constitutional watchdog in the Russian Federation of its key powers and virtually suspending its functions. As admitted by the New York-based Lawyers Committee for Human Rights, the only fault of the court was

that it obeyed the Constitution but was unlucky and "ended up on the losing side when Yeltsin emerged victorious from the bloody events of October."[13] It was only eighteen months later that the new Constitutional Court of Russia resumed its work.

Besides shutting down the Russian federal parliament, regional legislatures,[14] and the Russian Constitutional Court, President Yeltsin introduced censorship, closed fifteen independent periodicals, and pushed a new draft Constitution while simultaneously warning the Russian citizens to refrain from criticizing the draft.[15]

The new Constitution, whose actual adoption by the Russian population is doubtful and still disputable, provided for one of the strongest presidencies in Europe, "superpresidentialism" or "a modern-day czar," and was described as placing Russia, once again, under something similar to an authoritarian rule.[16] As a "victor's Constitution,"[17] the new Russian Constitution introduced presidential supremacy and placed the executive above the other branches of government.[18] Among other things, the 1993 Constitution granted several areas of traditional court jurisdiction, like protection of civil rights and freedoms (Article 80.2), to the president.[19] Such a delegation of authority to the executive to protect constitutional rights "not only violates separation of powers doctrine, but may give him or her a claim, albeit tenuous, to usurp the Court's jurisdiction, and suspend judicial review in a time of crisis."[20] That is the context within which the trophy art act was drafted, debated, and adopted.

The legislative history of the law is really dramatic. The original version of the bill was passed by the Duma in the fall of 1996 but rejected by the Federation Council.[21] By February 1997, when the Duma passed a revised version of the law, gubernatorial elections had been held in about fifty out of eighty-nine regions of the Russian Federation. The elections increased the independence of governors, who, unlike in the past, could no longer be appointed or dismissed by a president's decree.[22] Since governors form one-half of the Federation Council, the upper chamber of the Russian parliament got a better opportunity to reassert its position in the system of separation of powers in the Russian Federation. On March 5, 1997, the bill declaring that the art taken from Germany during and immediately after World War II would be the "sole property of the Russian Federation" was adopted by the Federation Council.

If signed into effect, the law would make it practically impossible for Germany to reclaim the remains of the trophy art seized from the Nazis by Soviet troops at the end of World War II and subsequently would have a negative effect on German-Russian relations. In an attempt to appease the largest creditor of Yeltsin's regime and arguably its closest ally in the West,[23] on March 18, 1997, the Russian president vetoed the bill calling it (in a letter to Chairman Yegor Stroev of the Federation Council) a "unilateral decision" made "without regard for generally accepted norms of international law," and adding that it did not differentiate between the art works of Germany and its allies in World War II and art valuables originating in the nations of anti-Hitler coalition and Nazi-occupied countries. As a result, according to Yeltsin, the bill "weakens Russian positions in difficult negotiations now under way with France, Germany, Liechtenstein, Poland, Hungary, the Netherlands and other countries" (ITAR-TASS, March 19, 1997).

Strangely, a correct statement of the president that the law in that form, as it was adopted by the Federal Assembly in February–March 1997, "would hinder efforts to retrieve artworks seized from the Soviet Union during the war" was accepted by Western media as an "apparent bid to somewhat appease the nationalists."[24]

Although, as it was revealed in an opinion poll conducted by the Public Opinion Fund in late May 1997, the law was supported by 53 percent and disapproved by only 23 percent of respondents,[25] Western observers have been persistently demonizing the supporters of the Trophy Art Law and associating the bill exclusively with "Nationalists and Communists" in Russia and its parliament.[26] In reality, the Trophy Art Law is quite consistent with the views and feelings of most Russians who never forgot that in the days of what we call the Great Patriotic War (1941–1945), German Nazis and their allies destroyed 1,710 Soviet cities and towns, more than 70,000 villages, 32,000 plants and factories, about 100,000 collective and state farms, approximately 65,000 kilometers of railroads (one-and-a-half times the length of the equator), and the country's national wealth diminished by 30 percent.[27]

Just as during a previous European invasion of Russia in the nineteenth century, when Napoleon's soldiers were making stables in Russian churches, Hitler's soldiers looted and destroyed 427 museums, 1,670 Russian Orthodox churches, 237 Catholic churches, 532 synagogues, 43,000 libraries, 6,000 hospitals, and 82,000 schools. According to incomplete data, in the seventy-three richest museums of the USSR 564,723 exhibits were destroyed or looted by Nazis; the fifteen richest museums lost 269,515 exhibits.[28] As Lynn H. Nicholas wrote in her remarkable book: "Everywhere in the USSR special attention was given to the trashing of the houses and museums of great cultural figures: Pushkin's house was ransacked, as was Tolstoy's Yasnaya Polyana, where manuscripts were burned in the stoves and German war dead were buried all around Tolstoy's solitary grave. The museums honoring Chekhov, Rimsky-Korsakov, and Tchaikovsky received similar attentions, the composer of the *1812 Overture* being particularly honored by having a motorcycle garage installed in his former dwelling."[29]

After liberation of the occupied territory, the Soviet army, as a rule, could find "nothing of value left in the museums of its recaptured cities. They found instead burned and defaced buildings, ruined laboratories, books reduced to pulp."[30] The whereabouts of most art objects that were looted and taken away by Nazi aggressors (like an invaluable historical Smolensk archive or the Amber Room) are still not known. An American prosecutor at the Nuremberg trial called the Nazi policy on the occupied Soviet territory a "deliberate destruction of Russian culture."

Ultimately, 26.5 million Soviet people (or 11.5 percent of the USSR population in 1941), most of them civilians, were killed by Nazis, exterminated in German concentration camps, or died as a result of wounds. The combined number of Soviet citizens who were killed or crippled during the Great Patriotic War was equal to over forty million.[31]

As a form of reparations for the damage that had been done by Nazi Germany to the Soviet Union, if one can speak about any possible reparation that could compensate for the loss of millions of lives, the USSR, among other things, evacuated from Germany approximately 2.2 million artworks and about 3 million archival files.

Between 1955 and 1969, as a manifestation of its goodwill, the Soviet Union handed back to the German Democratic Republic the lion's share of art objects that had been taken away after the Second World War: more than 1,922,000 pieces of art (or 87.4 percent of what had been originally evacuated) and almost all three million archival files. Among the art treasures returned were Raphael's *Sistine Madonna* from the Dresden Art Gallery, a collection of artworks from the Berlin National Gallery, the famous Pergam Altar, masterpieces by Titian and Botticelli, and a collection of antique sculpture from the Albertinium Museum. Naturally, after 1990 all those artifacts belong to the unified Germany.

In 1994, Doris Hertramf, counsellor for cultural affairs of the German embassy in Russia, estimated that between 30,000 and 100,000 artifacts were still in Russian museums.[32] By 1997 the German side had raised the question of a return of some 200,000 to 300,000 pieces of art from German state-run and private collections. Most of them are the monuments of numismatics (175,000 coins and medals) and archaeology, as well as about 55,000 paintings, including works of French impressionists and postimpressionists (Monet, Matisse, van Gogh), masterpieces of Goya, Rembrandt, Rubens, and Delacroix, a fifteenth-century Gutenberg Bible, and the 5,000-year-old Trojan gold collection discovered by German archaeologist Heinrich Schliemann.[33]

Insisting that the law does not rule out the possibility of "cooperation" with third countries (looted by Nazis) on a bilateral basis, the state Duma disagreed with Yeltsin and on April 7, 1997, with 308 against and 15 votes in favor, effectively overrode the presidential veto.

The April 16–17 session of the Federation Council coincided with President Yeltsin's visit to Germany during which the Russian president was to hold talks with Chancellor Helmut Kohl and receive an award from a German media organization. Although prior to the visit the president's aide listed at least seven major matters on the agenda (the draft accord on Russia–NATO relations; problems of European security and cooperation; Russia's "full membership" in the Group of Seven, World Trade Organization, and the Paris Club of Creditors; economic cooperation with Germany; and the restitution of World War II trophy art) (ITAR-TASS, April 16, 1997), in reality about 80 percent of the summit time was given to just two questions: Russia–NATO relations and the issue of art objects moved to the USSR at the close of World War II. When meeting with his

German counterpart, Yeltsin, in a "gesture of friendship and openness," handed him microfilmed archives of the Central Committee of the former GDR ruling party (Socialist United Party of Germany), eleven files from the Rathenau Archive,[34] an inventory of artworks and other materials taken to the USSR at the end of the war, as well as a letter from Patriarch Aleksy II of Moscow and All Russia with a list of property the Russian Orthodox Church wants Germany to return (ITAR-TASS, April 17, 1997).

Quite illustrative is the detail that although in an interview with *Stern* (published a day before the beginning of Yeltsin's visit to Germany) Yeltsin said he would bring "some pieces" of the cultural treasures seized during World War II (ITAR-TASS, April 15, 1997), a Russian foreign ministry spokesman told ITAR-TASS that the "ministry knows nothing about Yeltsin's plans to take cultural valuables to Germany."[35]

Hardly by coincidence, in the midst of the argument over trophy art in Russia and on that very day (April 16, 1997) when the Federation Council overrode the president's veto, two items apparently belonging to the Amber Room (a fragment of mosaic and a lacquered wooden cabinet) were "unexpectedly" found in Germany.[36] The German government used those "discoveries" as a chance to reciprocate President Yeltsin's veto by pressing the search for the Amber Room's remains.

The composition of the Federation Council is different from the U.S. Senate or Rajya Sabha in India: It is composed of the heads of administration and legislature of each of the eighty-nine constituent subjects of the Russian Federation, convenes not more than twice a month for two to three days each time, and, unlike the state Duma, can hardly be considered a permanently working legislative body. Long Russian distances and urgent regional matters often prevent senators from attending sessions of the Federation Council. In an attempt to provide even missing deputies with an opportunity to cast their vote (negative or positive) regarding the president's veto, the Federation Council decided to follow a rare voting procedure and to use written ballots ("questionnaires") that were mailed to deputies who couldn't attend the current session.

By May 14, the Federation Council received ballots back and announced that it obtained votes of more than two-thirds of the total number of its members necessary to override the veto.

On May 22, Yeltsin again returned the Trophy Art Law to the parliament without signature claiming in his statement that the law had been adopted "with violations of the constitutional procedure." Russian prime minister Chernomyrdin was also critical of the Federation Council's voting, calling it "an emotional approach" and reminding that "Russia owes but is also owed seized art objects, and more at that" (ITAR-TASS, May 16, 1997).

On June 10, the Federation Council de facto for the second time overrode the president's veto and by 121 votes to 9, with four abstentions, voted to return the Trophy Art Law to President Yeltsin for signing. In its resolution sent to the president, council deputies correctly argued that only the Constitutional Court can determine whether parliamentary voting procedures violate the constitution and stated that "the President of the Russian Federation has evaded the fulfillment of responsibilities within his competence to sign and publish the law" (ITAR-TASS, June 10, 1997). Three days later, the state Duma by 351 votes to 1, with one abstention, approved a similar appeal to Yeltsin stating that he was exceeding his constitutional authority by not signing an act properly adopted by the Federal Assembly.

Indeed, the superpresidential Constitution of Russia of 1993 gives the president great powers but does allot to parliament certain countervailing prerogatives.

Article 107 of the Russian Constitution (Chapter 5, The Federal Assembly) unambiguously and in explicit terms determines the veto procedure of the president. According to the Constitution, an adopted law shall be sent to the president for signing and publication within five days. The president has two options: to sign a law and publish it within fourteen days, or veto it and send it back to the Federal Assembly. In that case, the state Duma and the Federation Council may either take into account the president's comments and criticism and work out a new draft or, with two-thirds of the total number of deputies of both chambers, override the veto and approve the law in its original version. After that the law shall be signed by the president within seven days and published.

The Constitution is silent, however, as to whether the legislation becomes law in the event the president refuses to sign the previously vetoed bill. In this respect, Russian constitutional law does not contain any provision similar to the principle of U.S. constitutional law saying that the president may not use executive powers to thwart the expressed will of Congress (see *Youngstown Sheet & Tube Co. v. Sawyer,* 343 U.S. 579 (1952)).

Although back in March Yeltsin's representative in the Duma, Kotenkov, warned the Federation Council that if the president's veto is overridden by the upper chamber Yeltsin would have to appeal to the Constitutional Court to block the law, it didn't happen. On June 30, 1997, President Yeltsin, in violation of his own Constitution—but "courageously," in the eyes of the *New York Times*[37]—imposed his second veto on the same law, arguing that both houses of the parliament used unconstitutional procedures to override his first veto: proxy voting in the state Duma and mailed ballots in the Federation Council. The argument was particularly disingenuous since Yeltsin had signed numerous other laws passed with exactly the same voting procedure in the Duma. The Federation Council, in an unanimous vote on July 4, filed with the Constitutional Court an inquiry against Yeltsin's actions arguing that the president lacks the authority to declare parliamentary voting procedures unconstitutional.

The legal collision was particularly unusual because proxy voting is a common procedure in the Duma and because it was not the first time the chambers of the Federal Assembly were overriding the president's veto. That had happened at least three times before. On October 25, 1994, eleven months after the adoption of the new Constitution, the Federation Council (following a similar procedure in the Duma) overrode Yeltsin's veto of the Russian budget bill. On November 15, 1995, the upper chamber of the Russian Federal Assembly overrode President's veto of the Law on the Subsistence Minimum. And on August 7, 1996, the Federation Council overrode Yeltsin's veto of a law defining budgetary classifications.

After several postponements for procedural reasons caused by an illness of coreporter Judge Vladimir Strekozov, the problem was finally decided in the Constitutional Court. The Court did not address the issue of trophy art itself but considered legal processes and the question of the president's "obligation" to sign into effect a law after his veto had been overriden by both chambers of the Federal Assembly. On April 6, 1998 the Court supported the parliament's claim that Yeltsin had failed to meet his constitutional responsibilities by refusing to sign the law. In its decision the Constitutional Court ruled that the president could not simply ignore a parliamentary vote to override his veto of a bill and ordered him to sign the trophy art bill into law immediately.

The decision was assessed by observers as "unusually independent."[38] Indeed, it was a rare case in which the Court, suspended by Yeltsin in October 1993 and restored in March 1995 with limited powers, disagreed with the president and "put their rubber stamps away." In a characteristic manner, Yeltsin considered such disagreement reflected in the Court's decision "a good slap in the face" and in a subsequent meeting with the Constitutional Court chairman, Marat Baglai, scolded him for the fact that "something is not quite right with our Constitutional Court" (Interfax, June 2, 1998).

The president signed the bill and appealed to the Constitutional Court to consider the constitutionality of the law. More than a year later, on July 20, 1999, the Constitutional Court struck down as unconstitutional several provisions of the Trophy Art Law, but not the act in its entirety. The Court upheld Russia's right to keep cultural valuables seized from Nazi Germany that are not to be returned to former "aggressor-countries" (like Germany, Italy, and Hungary). These artworks are rightly regarded as the federal property of Russia, the court said.

Significantly, even in that case, some artwork can be transferred to Germany—within the framework of cultural exchange programs between the two countries as a goodwill gesture on behalf of Russia.

At the same time, according to the Court, the law improperly lumped all trophy art into one category and didn't allow for claims by individuals whose art had been stolen from them by the Nazis or by the Soviet Union's wartime Allies such as France, from which the Nazis looted many objects and brought them to Germany where they were in turn taken by Soviet troops. Thus, the Constitutional Court confirmed the right of the Nazis' victims and citizens of the countries of the anti-Hitler coalition to get their property back.

Another provision saying that trophy art of an unknown origin cannot be reclaimed was pronounced as violating the Constitution. The court ruled treasures of unknown origin can be reclaimed within eighteen months if an owner comes forward.

The court also considered Yeltsin's objection about the voting procedure in which some lawmakers in the Duma voted for absent colleagues. Proxy voting is allowed by the state Duma regulations; it has been used when adopting most Russian laws, and the president has never had a problem to sign those laws into effect.

The court agreed the procedure was improper but decided to refrain from voiding the vote, saying that an incorrect voting procedure may become a reason to reject laws in the future.

The law was sent back to parliament for a revision, and on April 26, 2000, the Duma passed the law in its third reading. A new consideration of the Trophy Art Law in the Duma became just another corroboration that the statute is supported by the whole spectrum of political forces represented in the parliament. The vote was truly unanimous: 355 deputies voted in favor and zero opposed.

As expected, adoption of the law does not preclude the Russian authorities from holding consultations with the German government regarding exchanges of cultural values. On April 28–29, 2000, the Russian minister of culture, Mikhail Shvidkoi, returned to Germany 101 paintings from the Bremen Art Museum. His German counterpart, Michael Naumann, handed over to Shvidkoi a fragment of the Amber Room (an amber chest).[39]

Apart from the particular provisions of the Trophy Art Law itself, the whole legislative process in which the law was drafted, rejected by the Federation Council, redrafted, adopted, vetoed by the president, readopted, and especially two Constitutional Court decisions regarding the law, can be considered a test case for the constitutional mechanism of checks and balances and separation of powers in the Russian Federation. The Trophy Art Law as an illustration of the current legislative process in the country indicates that the process has acquired features of a legal and civilized character. The Constitutional Court has revealed a hidden democratic potential of the Russian legal system, even within the limits of the "superpresidential" Constitution, which is definitely a sign of hope for Russia standing on the edge of a post-Yeltsin era.

Some Questions

Stephen Holmes

I will limit myself here to a few brief comments on each of these fascinating contributions to our symposium and on some unanswered questions they jointly and separately raise.

Professor Nur Vergin's excellent paper corroborates the common perception of outside observers that contemporary Turkey is a painfully cleft society. What makes her approach unusual is that she lays a large portion of the blame for the self-divided condition of her country on the militant secularism that Turkey's state-building (Kemalist) elite borrowed from the French tradition of atheistic republicanism. To heal the excruciating split between its secular state and Muslim society, she believes Turkey needs a new politics of religion. She leaves deliberately vague the contours of this new politics of religion, but she does say that it should take a leaf out of the Ottoman playbook. Contrary to some Western historians, the Ottoman system was not a theocracy, she explains. It certainly involved no fusion of state and religion. The relation of the Ottoman state to Islam was much more instrumental or Machiavellian than this. And the modern Turkish state would do well to adopt an Ottoman-style instrumental attitude toward Islam rather than to continue self-destructively in its French Revolutionary–style antagonistic attitude.

In developing this point, Vergin draws guidance from what can be called the liberal raison d'état tradition, namely, the thesis of Locke, Montesquieu, and other European liberals that domestic peace and prosperity (and therefore state strength) can be fostered most effectively by a policy of religious toleration. In the United States, this idea has been recently pressed home by John Rawls, who argues that social stability can be achieved most effectively if citizens all agree on "penultimate values" (such as justice) while leaving individuals and groups free to differ on "ultimate values"

(such as the path to salvation). Providing leeway for the social expression of religious and nonreligious beliefs, so long as sectarian groups abstain from violence, is more compatible with social cohesion and coherent governance than a secular campaign to keep religion down. Vergin's parallel conclusion for Turkey is that accommodating Islam, rather than trying to repress it, is the most promising path to political stability. (Repression will only increase Islam's capacity to attract militant adherents.)

My questions to Professor Vergin are the following: Can the Western liberal tradition, which grew out of religious civil wars in a sect-torn Christian Europe, offer pertinent guidance to those seeking to moderate religious-secular strife? Americans who want to study religious-secular conflict usually look to Israel where the split (if not enmity) between Jerusalem and Tel Aviv, between tradition and modernity, between priests and soldiers, seems fairly intractable if not downright archaic. The question in the Israeli case is this: Can secular liberals tolerate, and even subsidize, religious communities that are incubating a form of life that aims eventually to extinguish secular power? Is it really prudent to address confrontationalist fundamentalism with an accommodationist "new politics of religion?" What if zealously antisecular forces are embarked on a "combat mission" to colonize the junior officer corps? Should secular authorities respond with concessive mildness? (Even in the United States, we have a pale version of the Turkish/Israeli dilemma, since U.S. law will not accommodate the wishes of newly immigrated Moslem fathers to arrange marriages for their eleven-year-old daughters. In this case, be it noted, American liberalism dictates not accommodation but prohibition.)

Finally, Professor Vergin's search for a new politics of religion assumes that Turkey's principal problem today lies in the conflict between a militantly secular state and a deeply Islamic society (which can be either enraged or cooperative, depending on how despotically or liberally it is treated). But what if we describe the problem differently? For example, does not an urban-rural conflict underlie Turkey's secular-religious conflict? Does not the crisis of the Turkish state stem from a democratic backlash by humiliated and neglected rural voters? Thinking about the problem this way suggests that what Turkey needs is not a new politics of religion but rather an invigorated policy of rural development. Or why not focus on state incapacity? Turkish authorities, somewhat to the surprise of outsiders, recently refused to allow Islamic relief agencies to deliver earthquake aid despite the urgent needs of the quake victims. (The state's rationale was presumably that any "private" service-provision agency will legitimize itself in the eyes of the populace at the expense of the state, and that the prohibited relief agencies were nursing a not-so-hidden antisecular agenda.) Does this not suggest that the challenge that Islam poses to the secular Turkish state should be met not by a new politics of religion but rather by persuading the business community that increased tax revenues to improve public services—in the countryside as well as poor urban areas—is a valuable investment in Turkish secularism?

As former prime minister I. K. Gujral argues in his interesting paper, India's democratic traditions are almost unique in the developing world. And he invokes the vivacious, talkative, rambunctious, and pluralistic "essence" of Indian society to explain his country's stubborn refusal to submit to authoritarian rule. Nevertheless, he admits that India today suffers from unresponsive government. Its political elite is marked by a kind of self-serving clannishness and Orientalism that often takes the form of corruption. Family values, we might say, often override national interests. And this degeneration has occurred despite the great Indian philosophical tradition that places "service before self."

Although Gujral is preoccupied with discovering cultural genealogies for different styles of governance, he also warns us to be skeptical of such attempts. The simple existence of a philosophical tradition in a country's past does not guarantee the emergence of political practices informed by it. For instance, one and the same

German philosophical culture was able, in the course of a century, to sustain a monarchy, a republic, Nazi rule, and a second republic. Similarly, Confucianism has proved compatible with both distressing economic stagnation and astonishing economic growth. This flexibility suggests that, although it is surely always a factor to be reckoned with, culture does not rigidly "determine" styles of political or economic behavior.

Indeed, culture has proved irresistibly attractive to would-be historical determinists precisely because it is so rich: If you look closely enough you can find foreshadowings of everything that comes to pass. Indeed, "cultural legacy" explanations routinely confuse analogy with causality. "Things are the way they are today because they remind us of the way they used to be." In other words, cultural genealogy substitutes the false pleasure of pattern recognition for the true pleasure of causal explanation.

It is not especially surprising, in any case, that contemporary Indian politicians fail to live up to the principles enunciated in the *Mahabharata*. Yet the *Mahabharata* contains a treasure of wisdom that any politician, Indian or otherwise, would benefit greatly from considering. Gujral draws attention, in particular, to the proposition: "where there is Dharma, there is victory." Formulated differently, when Dharma is missing, defeat will likely follow. Gujral translates this maxim to mean that unresponsive and irresponsible government is self-defeating and even self-endangering. Public officials who are brazenly corrupt and publicly flout their own laws can defeat themselves by inadvertently breeding a dangerous disrespect for law among ordinary covens. The normal difficulty of governing a country as large and diverse as India turns into an impossibility when politicians are exposed as grossly corrupt and self-seeking. Where Dharma is missing, defeat will follow.

Developing this insight, Gujral identifies the key to democratic governance in the idea that a government can strengthen itself by managing to respond coherently to the needs of society. A responsive government is stronger than an authoritarian government (one that quashes the voices of the ruled) because the former can mobilize the voluntary cooperation of society in formulating appropriate policies and carrying them out. A democratic state that regularly engages in consultative relations with society can both identify and solve common problems more rapidly than a hovercraft state that insulates the political class from a voiceless society.

And yet democracy, Gujral concludes, can produce serious problems of its own. Selflessness is not always good for the simple reason that selfless people can be stupid, unobservant, incoherent, or fanatical. Similarly, democracy is not always good because ill-timed appeals to the people can sometime exacerbate social tensions and instability. Modern India might even be compared to modern Europe in this respect. The modern and Western-educated elites of New Delhi, writes Gujral, find it nearly impossible to understand the anxieties and aspirations of the majority of Indian voters living in tradition-bound and conservative rural India. Democracy guarantees that this gulf of incomprehension between a hypermodern political class and a still-traditional society will breed politically destabilizing movements: Hindu nationalism in India, alpine populism in Europe. My only question to Prime Minister Gujral picks up on this point. Can he explain to us in greater detail how Hindu nationalists managed to use India's democratic institutions to climb into power?

Finally, I come to Professor Alexander Domrin's useful paper on trophy art. As he makes clear, Germany's request for the restitution of artworks removed by Soviet forces after World War II does not stir much sympathy among Russians, for whom the victory against the Nazis remains a living and vital national myth. Rather than commenting directly on this case, which Domrin has explained exceptionally clearly, I will merely say a few words about the way Russians today experience the "justice" of property claims. This is the most illuminating context, I believe, in which to view the more specific, and politically marginal, issue of restitution.

While the heart of the Soviet regime was the KGB, the heart of Russia's new "democratic" regime is the privatization agency. To study post-Communist Russia is to study the emergence and consolidation of, and to some extent rivalry among, predatory-redistributive networks. These networks are more deeply entrenched in Russian society than either market mechanisms or state authority. What we have witnessed over the past decade has been a grabbing by stealth and force, and a parceling out among insiders, of the public assets of the collapsed Communist state.

Nether Lenin nor Marx help us understand the new way in which Russia's strong trample upon Russia's weak. It resembles neither political repression nor economic exploration. It has been called "corruption," but that term, accurate as a first approximation, is too bland, having been developed in social contexts where most of the economy was not corrupt.

Lenin remarked that the bourgeoisie would never voluntarily relinquish its property, which would therefore have to be ripped away by violent revolution. But the expiring Communist state did not resist wild privatization. The assets that were expropriated were unowned, or diffusely and collectively owned, and hence no tightfisted kulaks had to be intimidated or liquidated in order to seize their property. Unowned assets were scooped up, clandestinely and without resistance (except from rival expropriators), because the only people capable of resisting the theft of state property were exactly those best positioned to carry out the plundering unobserved.

And if Lenin is no guide, neither is Marx. The new Russian elite has not waxed rich by depressing the wages and increasing the output of Russian factory workers. Since 1991, Russia's "oligarchs" have invested little in domestic productive industries (which would create jobs). The typically post-Communist form of abuse is not the exploration of surplus labor power, therefore, but the sale abroad of natural resources and accumulated inventories removed from former state factories (using a small specialized workforce, export monopolies, and other means) by a well-positioned and well-organized few. What Russia's new elite is doing, in other words, is "exploiting the dead," feeding off the carcass of the defunct Soviet regime. The thieves who steal an electronic circuit board from a hydroelectric power plant and melt down the precious metals for sale on the black market are doing in miniature what "the oligarchs" are doing on a grand scale. They are neither tyrants nor exploiters, but scavengers at an airplane crash. They unjustly expropriate the fruits of the cooperative efforts of earlier generations who are no longer around to protest (or who are too old to protest effectively).

This new style of abuse has rendered useless some classic strategies for protecting the weak from the strong. Under the old regime, a reliably enforced bill of rights would have sheltered the abused from their abusers. That is no longer the case. Russia's 1993 Constitution contains a fairly standard bill of rights. But it is not well-adapted to protecting ordinary citizens from the typically post-Communist form of abuse, namely the stealing of the country's collective patrimony. Indeed, after the collapse of Communism, rights (especially property rights) are more likely to help the abusers defend themselves from those they abuse than vice versa. What was previously sought as a shield for the weak has become, on obtaining, a shield for the strong. This alchemy goes a long way toward explaining public cynicism about the "justice" of property claims in Russia and elsewhere.

In effect, the private siphoning off of formerly public assets (the typically post-Communist style of abuse), is legitimized by the new redefinition of justice and injustice. Under the old regime, private property was considered unjust, while under the new regime private property has officially become just. "Justice" is redefined, inhabitants of the entire region can reasonably conclude, when power changes hands. This realization alone would explain a pervasive public cynicism about just ownership. Indeed, if the moral crisis of post-Communist society has a theoretical source, it lies in the following paradox: While private property has become "just" (in a legal sense), the privatization of property has been flagrantly "unjust" (from the moral perspective of most citizens). This head-on collision between official creed and public sentiment complicates the entire transition to liberal democracy, casting doubts on its basic legitimacy. And, needless to say, it also helps explain the scorn with which Russians in general greet Germany's solemn requests for restitution of the art that Germans previously "owned."

Closing Remarks

Jean Bethke Elshtain

Although each of the three broad topics under discussion in this panel were huge and nearly unmanageable, the paper givers succeeded admirably in bringing lucidity and coherence to the interlocked themes. They did so by observing, whether explicitly or tacitly, the fact that the separation of church and state and the distinction between religion and politics are not the same thing. That is, the logic of church-state separation—a staple of North American jurisprudence—does not by definition and need not in actual practice translate into a radical bifurcation between religion and politics. In practice, this is nearly impossible to do in any case because too much of the same territory is claimed by religion and politics respectively, including the following: normative ideals of human flourishing; the meaning of community and membership; and claims of duty, service, honor, and commitment—on and on.

Prime Minister I. K. Gujral noted as much in observing that "culture and religion are the factors that most profoundly impact on the character of a nation, and on the manner in which politics and governance evolves therein." In other words, culture and religion afford the framework—the milieu—within which governance is generated and sustained. The Honorable Mr. Gujral also put on the table a broad topic of philosophic interest and perplexity that also poses daunting legal and political challenges, namely, how best to sort out national characteristics and the particular features of any culture from those imperatives that are universal in scope and application. He sees an intermingling of such imperatives, an always volatile and challenging task, as inevitable and, indeed, desirable.

Professor Nur Vergin's paper was itself an example of the interpenetration of the particular and universal in its unpacking of the question of faith in the Turkish context within a philosophic and legal framework provided by John Locke's famous *Essay on Toleration*. Professor Vergin insisted that it is possible to forge a workable compromise between strong religious devotion and commitment as a feature of a political culture, that is, that a culture need not go the route of either radical theocracy or radical laicism. Sorting this out is no easy matter, of course. Nor is it easy to derive a politics of constitutionalism out of a backdrop of authoritarian statism and, prior to that manifestation, orthodoxy fused with autocracy—the challenge taken up by Professor Alexander Domrin. His paper additionally raised questions about the distinctions between democracy on the one hand and representational constitutionalism on the other—a distinction pressed by commentator Professor Stephen Holmes.

In a world in which globalization proceeds apace, it is vital to pause and reflect on the terms under which this globalization operates. Summing up the contributions of the paper givers, it seems wise to insist that the most workable and just globalization is one that gives generous scope to the working out of the dynamics of religion and politics particular to every culture on our fragile globe so long as the outcome does not violate in any egregious way the general features of a by-now universal commitment to human rights. This is a tall but not an impossible order, especially in light of the fact that the Universal Declaration of Human Rights foregrounds religious freedom as a central feature of human freedom and dignity rightly understood.

Protestors in Washington, D.C., demonstrating for fair trade. *Source:* © Martin Simon/SABA, 2000.

Session 6

Corporate Power, National Sovereignty, and the Rule of Law in a Global Economy

Editors' Note

Few issues have engaged partisans so vociferously as the relationships between transnational corporations (TNCs) and the jurisdiction of host nations, whether to monitor activities, enforce damage claims, assert environmental or labor standards, protect financial institutions, or limit electronic transactions. Global finance, trade, and traffic occur at such an accelerating pace that the legislative and juridical responses of any single nation are not likely to be sufficiently timely or weighty enough to affect global trends for long. Thus the responses have tended to develop regionally and internationally. The papers here describe, from interestingly diverse points of view, the origins and consequences of the emerging legal regimes that apply to global trade and transactions.

Mr. Nariman, who was involved in the Bhopal case, inventories the changes in emphasis and perspective concerning TNCs in the past fifty years—from promoting investment to imposing duties to formulating rights—and discusses the present means of creating a legal framework to deal with them. He explores the benefits and limits of bilateral investment treaties, codes of conduct, and interstate linkages, pointing out that one of the consequences of increased international cooperation is the "disaggregation" of the state—"for instance, courts, regulatory agencies, departments of government, banking institutions, even parliamentary bodies are now seen working with their counterparts in other countries, creating a new web of relations."

Professor Tarullo discusses the range of international agreements that limit state regulatory discretion. While states may have given up little of their legal sovereignty (except in the case of the European Union), they have in many cases voluntarily turned to market mechanisms that make global transactions easier. These mechanisms also make transactions less subject to control (for example, banking regulations, money laundering, tax havens). When do international economic arrangements "run afoul of notions of accountability and democracy"— leading to the perception of a "democracy deficit" even if there is no formal loss of sovereignty? He suggests that the increasing convergence of domestic and international regulations may be one of the promising paths toward reconciliation.

Professor Trebilcock states the case for international trade against the objections voiced by some NGOs against the World Trade Organization (WTO) meetings in Seattle in late 1999. Concluding that most of the objections are specious or dubious, he recognizes that the WTO's dispute settlement process should be more inclusive and more open to be fully consonant with the expectations of the rule of law. Mr. Ko-Yung Tung, recently appointed as general counsel of the World Bank, makes clear that considerations of the effectiveness of the rule of law and systems of justice are infused throughout the World Bank's work in poverty reduction and comprehensive development. Impartial and honest judicial and legal systems are essential for development, as he illustrated from a number of World Bank assessments. Mr. Pitofsky emphasizes that we are now "moving from national to international markets and the consequences are enormous." After summarizing some key issues, he discusses the difficulties of international coordination and cooperation, a goal he nevertheless believes we must pursue. Judge Edwards reiterates the tough questions—especially whether national self-interest will always operate as an inherent limitation on the rule of law in a global economy.

The Globalization of World Trade and Corporate Power

Fali S. Nariman

I. Introduction

A capsule version of the history of mankind has divided its progress into three major periods:

In the first period (which was the longest), mankind used muscle power to survive, fashioned rough tools for himself, and learned the uses of fire. We then discovered that the capacity to develop, both physically and mentally, was an attribute only of human beings, not of any other living creatures. Mankind could thus subjugate the animal world, and it did.

The second period began with the advent of the industrial age in the West: The invention of machines facilitated mass production of goods of all kinds. But with the invention of machines, man's evil genius also invented sophisticated instruments for the destruction of human beings—on a mass scale. This led to conquests of people by people and notions of race superiority that parts of the human race at one place were superior to those living in other places. The industrial age brought with it the age of colonization. And with colonization came economic exploitation.

We are now living in the third period of this peephole view of world history. It began with the end of the Second World War and the formation of the United Nations. In its wake came freedom movements and political independence of the erstwhile colonies, new sovereign states and the looming specter of multinational corporations.

II. The Globalization of World Trade and Corporate Power

The manifold activities of these multinational (or transnational) corporations[1]—then known as MNCs, especially those based in the first world—were often criticized and commented on at the United Nations and in various other forums around the globe. In 1972 the Department of Economic and Social Affairs of the UN published a report called *The Multinational Corporations in World Development,* popularly known as the Secretary-General's Report. The report was compiled in order to facilitate deliberations of the Group of Eminent Persons, who were called upon to study the role of MNCs and their impact on the process of development of the same (under a resolution of July 28, 1972). The following year came the disclosure of the involvement of an American MNC—the International Telephone and Telegraph Corporation (ITT)—in a coup against the democratically elected Communist government of President Salvador Allende in Chile (an event that brought Pinochet to power). It was a sensational case involving an abuse of corporate power, which considerably influenced the outcome of the Final Report of the Group of Eminent Persons—the "eminent persons" from the developing countries differing from the "eminent persons" of the developed world in almost all the findings and conclusions recorded (in the Final Report). One of the few points on which the Final Report was unanimous, however, was in the following generalized statement (under the subheading Nation-States and Multinational Corporations: Sovereignty and Power):

> Most of the problems connected with multinational corporations stem from their distinctive transnational features in a world that is divided into separate sovereign States. . . . Multinational corporations have developed important capacities which can be put to the service of world development. Yet, these same capacities can also be used in ways, which may conflict with the interests of individual States. While Governments pursue a variety of economic and non-economic objectives to advance the welfare of their citizens, the chief goals of multinational corporations like those of all business enterprises are profit and growth. The differing objectives of nation-States and multinational corporations suggest that their respective decisions will not always be in harmony with each other. . . . It is in this context that countries may find their national sovereignty infringed upon and their policy instruments blunted by the operations of multinational corporations.[2]

The conclusions in the Final Report were soon overtaken by events. From the late seventies nearly four billion people entered into the mainstream of world trade (until then almost entirely controlled by the developed world). These four billion people formed the aggregate populations of China (and Taiwan), India, Vietnam, Pakistan, Bangladesh, South Korea, Malaysia, and Singapore—as well as of the constituent units of the former Union of Soviet Socialist Republics (USSR).

World trade became truly globalized—its levels sharply rising—doubling to an annual rate of $2 trillion in the decade of the eighties. It soared to $3 trillion in the first half of the nineties.

Of course, half of the world trade (or what is called "international trade") consisted of (and still comprises) cross-border transactions between different regions of the same corporation operating in different parts of the world, in other words, an internal transfer of goods and services. At the Singapore Air Show of February 1999, John Wolf, Executive Vice-President of the Douglas Aircraft Company, said that the McDonnell Douglas Corporation's MD-II had its fuel tank made in Japan,

its wings in Italy, its tailbone in Japan, and sections of the fuselage in Korea![3]

Meanwhile, multinational corporations kept growing in size and power, many of them transforming into global corporations, defined (in the secretary-general's report) as corporations having "such pervasive operations that (were) beyond the effective reach of the national policies of any country, and in the absence of supranational policy, free to some extent to make decisions in the interest of corporate efficiency alone." (Multinational, transnational, and global corporations are compendiously described in the rest of this paper as TNCs.)

TNCs have acquired great power; many of them have total assets that exceed the GNP of the countries in which they operate. A recent UN study revealed an alarming statistic: Among the 100 largest concentrations of wealth in the world, 51 percent are owned by TNCs, only 49 percent by independent sovereign states![4] Easier to comprehend is the fact that Mitsubishi is larger than Indonesia (the fourth most populous nation on earth), that General Motors is bigger than Denmark, that Ford is bigger than South Africa, and that Toyota is bigger than Norway.[5] The fact that TNCs operate across borders makes them more independent than nation-states and more difficult to control.

The way TNCs have been treated has changed with changing global perceptions of their role. Before the Second World War and in the decade after its end international organizations were preoccupied with protecting investors; there was an emphasis on issues like expropriation and compensation. Then during the seventies, due to pressure from the newly formed nation-states (former colonies), the emphasis shifted to prescribing the duties of TNCs and various international codes of conduct were fashioned such as the Organization for Economic Cooperation and Development (OECD) Declaration on Transnational Investments and Multinational Enterprises (1976) and the International Labour Organization (ILO) Tripartite Declaration of Principles Concerning Multinational Enterprises and Social Policy (1979). The United Nations Centre on Transnational Corporations (UNCTC) attempted to carry this forward and sought to frame human rights standards in a separate code. But the attempt was ill fated and given up. The UNCTC is now defunct. The decades of the 1980s and 1990s witnessed once again an emphasis on protection of TNCs and formulating rights for them. This was as part of a universal effort to promote free trade and "foreign direct investment." The World Trade Organization's (WTO) rules and the OECD-sponsored Multilateral Agreement on Investment (MAI) launched in September 1995 are more favorable to commercial freedom. The latter (MAI) aims at limiting the future domestic regulation of business, thus creating a free and predictable market for TNCs.[6]

III. International Legal Framework—Bilateral Investments Treaties as a Part of International Legal Order

Today, the accepted role of international law rules and processes in investment matters has considerably expanded. The substance of these rules is itself in the process of changing, chiefly in the direction of further liberalization. The legal framework for foreign direct investment as it exists today consists of a wide variety of national and international principles and rules, of diverse origins and forms, differing in specificity. These operate at several levels, with extensive gaps in their coverage of issues and countries. In this framework, national legislation is still of paramount importance.[7]

However, independently of the WTO there was put in motion fifteen years ago a strong silent current operating in the sphere of multilateral trade relations. It was based on "law"—not statute law, but "law" in the international sense—that is, treatymaking. This law was in the form of BITs (bilateral investment treaties). There are almost 1,000 such BITs in existence today. Many of these BITs have been signed in the last ten years in new areas of emerging markets.[8] They have given a stimulus to the globalization of the world economy by providing increasing investment opportunities to the developed world with corresponding advantages and benefits to the developing countries.

Such treaties are negotiated and signed between states, but they present future foreign investors in states the right to arbitrate a wide range of grievances arising from the action of a large number of public authorities within the state—whether or not any specific agreement has been concluded by the latter with the particular complainant. These bilateral treaties confer contractual rights on investors even though there is no direct contractual relationship (or nexus) between the investor and the state in which the investment is made nor with any of its state agencies. All this helps promote expansion of the global economy under the aegis of an international legal order.

This novel approach is different from the methodology of dealing with an aggregation of complaints brought by governments on behalf of their nationals before a preconstituted public body such as the World Trade Organization (WTO). The potential utility and efficacy of BITs was illustrated in the ICSID[9] case of *Asian Agricultural Products Ltd. v. Republic of Sri Lanka* (June 27, 1990).[10] In a BIT between the United Kingdom and Sri Lanka, Sri Lanka had undertaken to agree to the arbitration of claims by investors (in the United Kingdom and its dependencies) who made investments in Sri Lanka. In 1983, a Hong Kong company known as Asian Agricultural Products Ltd. (AAPL) made an officially approved investment in Sri Lanka in the form of subscribing to the equity capital of a Sri Lankan public company known as Serendib Seafoods Ltd. Serendib was incorporated to undertake shrimp culture. Serendib's shrimp culture farm was destroyed in January 1987 during a military action conducted by the Sri Lankan security forces against the installation—the installation having been previously taken over forcibly by local rebels and used as a guerrilla base. AAPL suffered a total loss of investment as a result of this military action. It claimed damages in the sum of $8 million (U.S. dollars) from the government of Sri Lanka through the International Centre for Settlement of Investment Disputes (ICSID). ICSID's jurisdiction was not challenged by Sri Lanka because the treaty (BIT) incorporated (Article 8) an undertaking by the government of Sri Lanka to have claims by investors arbitrated by ICSID. No dispute was raised or could be raised on the ground of contractual nonprivity. But since this was one of the first decisions of its kind, a high-powered team of international arbitrators appointed by the ICSID held (unanimously) as a matter of law that under the treaty AAPL (the Hong Kong company) became entitled to institute the ICSID arbitration proceedings against the government of Sri Lanka.

The case then went forward on merits and an award was made (by a 2–1 majority) in favor of the foreign investor, directing Sri Lanka to compensate for the destruction to the shrimp farm that had been occupied by the governmental security forces in violation of the Sri Lankan government's duty under the treaty to provide protection and security. Subsequent ICSID arbitrations, currently pending, have now been brought by investors in Western countries invoking similar BITs.[11] These have now created an international legal framework far beyond that envisaged in the New York Convention of 1958. Under the New York Convention for Enforcement of Foreign Arbitral Awards 1958, a foreign award arises out of a contractual stipulation contained in an arbitration agreement between an entity or an individual in the state of origin (party to the New York Convention) and another person or entity in another state (also party to the New York Convention). The foreign award rendered between these two parties is enforceable as a convention award in any of the New York Convention countries wherever assets of the judgment debtor can be found to satisfy the award.

But under the aegis of BITs, investors of a state (signatory to the treaty) are conferred direct rights of action against the other state (also signatory to the treaty) in which the investment is made without any contractual privity, the word "investment" being widely defined. Most BITs include obligations, claims, and rights having economic value. We now have (thanks to the ingenuity of the legal fraternity) a rule of law regime in which investors in foreign countries through the instrumentality of bilateral treaties can exercise direct rights of action against the state entity in which the investment is made—without contractual privity with it.

The latest instance of this is the Energy Charter Treaty signed by forty-nine states (in December 1994) including major countries producing and purchasing power in the energy field—like France, Germany, Italy, Japan, the Netherlands, Russia, Spain, and the United Kingdom. Article 26 of the Energy Charter Treaty is different from existing provisions made in BITs; it is

better drafted and should be a forerunner of what to expect from treatymaking in the future:

- An investor who is a national of a signatory state may use the mechanism for any claimed violation of Part III of the treaty (Investment Promotion and Protection).
- There is a cooling period of three months (relatively short in comparison to most similar provisions in BITs).
- If the investor is not satisfied within that period it has a wide range of options with respect to where it may seek redress: the courts or administrative tribunals of the host state, any jurisdiction provided for by a previous agreement, or arbitration under the treaty.
- If the investor wishes to avail itself of arbitration under the treaty, it has the further option of choosing among three sets of rules: either those of ICSID (that is, the Washington Convention 1965), the UNCITRAL Model Law (1985), or arbitration under the rules of the Stockholm Chamber of Commerce.
- Irrespective of the type of arbitration chosen, the dispute must, under Article 26(6), be decided "in accordance with the Treaty and applicable rules and principles of international law."
- Article 26(8) makes it clear that in the event that acts of a public authority are ruled to be in violation of the treaty, that authority may at its option pay monetary damages in lieu of any other remedy. In other words, arbitral tribunals will be effectively barred from annulling governmental acts or ordering specific performance or restitution against governmental action: a prudent limitation.
- Signatory states may make only two types of limited reservation to the Energy Charter Treaty, namely, to exclude disputes already submitted by the investor to a competent forum or to exclude claims under specific contracts between the defendant state and the investor.

The unmistakable thrust of Article 26 of this new Energy Charter Treaty is to eliminate procedural or jurisdictional wrangling by creating a regime that strongly favors the use of neutral arbitration to sanction violations of the treaty to the detriment of investors. This can be seen in the wide range of options granted to the claimant. Reference to the treaty and to international law as the source of norms to be applied by arbitral tribunals operating under Article 26 stands in sharp contrast to other laws or treaties, which either make the national law of the host state exclusively applicable or allow reference to international law only in an incidental fashion.

One great advantage of the BITs (as well as the Energy Charter Treaty of December 1994) over direct bilateral transnational arbitration between individual contracting parties is that it avoids the "force majeure" syndrome. A local contracting party (with a foreign investor) often attempts to avoid responsibility for claims arising out of a contractual breach by setting up its own government's actions and pleading force majeure. International law generally requires the relevant state government to defend the legitimacy of its acts, said to constitute force majeure, which is often in practice seen as an irritant in international relations. The possibility of direct action—international arbitration without privity, as the BITs now provide—allows the true complainant to face the true defendant.[12] This legal device has the merit of clarity and realism and helps ensure confidence in the legal process.

So much for the rights of and protection for TNCs and other investors in providing inducements for investment in developing countries.

IV. Codes of Conduct— Are MNCs and TNCs Regulated or Controlled?

But how are these multinational and transnational corporations regulated and controlled? The fact is that they are not. Various attempts to introduce internationally binding regulations on TNCs have been made since the early 1970s by the United Nations, the OECD, and ILO. The United Nations first tackled TNCs and sovereignty issues in 1974, commenced work on a code of practice in 1977, compiled a draft code of conduct in 1990, and completed a draft code of conduct for transnational companies (also in 1990). But negotiations for finalization

ground to a halt in 1992 as a result of opposition by TNCs and some Western governments.[13] At meetings of the UN Commission for Human Rights, the impact of transnational corporations is still being assessed but with little hope of progress (in the foreseeable future) toward the framing of a binding code of practice and procedure.

Since the 1990s, in the absence of regulation, there has been considerable worldwide activity in the development of voluntary codes either by organizations concerned by the activities of TNCs, by the TNCs themselves, or by other nonregulatory agencies. For instance, a text of principles for global corporate responsibility has been recently released and published by the ECCR.[14] It contains fifty-five detailed principles supported by more than seventy-six sets of criteria for assessing company policies and practices, and more than sixty-six benchmarks or reference points for assessing the performance of TNCs—an admirable beginning. There are also at least twenty different generic codes available for TNCs to choose and adopt. A number of major companies have voluntarily announced internal policies and procedures for dealing with social issues in the countries in which they do business. In the absence of binding transnational regulations, voluntary codes do play a positive role.[15] The negotiations over codes of conduct, whether or not ultimately successful, have been instrumental in defining areas of common understanding over the proper conduct of TNCs and in clarifying the standards for their treatment.[16]

In the *Human Development Report 1999* (12) it has been suggested that a task force should be established on global economic governance with representatives from ten industrial and ten developing countries, and also with representatives of private financial corporations. That task force would report to the key institutions of global governance: the Economic and Social Council of the UN (ECOSOC), the International Monetary Fund (IMF), the World Bank, as well as to the WTO.

V. Economic Globalization— Some Problems, Some Hiccups, and Some Advantages

Economic globalization has entered a critical phase. The world economy is going global in a way that national governments have not, and it is moving beyond any kind of democratic control.

The decade of the 1990s has seen the systematic reduction of barriers to the free flow of goods, services, and capital across national borders—particularly capital. The World Bank has estimated that 95 percent of the daily flow in currency exchanges around the world is speculative: only 5 percent relates to real trade. But it is fluctuations that make profits. Trading in derivatives is of such magnitude that a loss of only 2 percent in profits would exceed all the reserves of money in the world! This is the house of cards that the advanced economic powers have built, and the apprehension is that the ghost of the world's financial crash starting in Wall Street in 1929 has not yet been laid. Fukuyama, the proponent of modern global capitalism, is credited with the irreverent observation that "there is a lot of glob-aloney in the world today."[17]

While the free flow of goods and services has facilitated faster economic growth and greater prosperity, it has also posed new challenges. Developed and developing countries alike are now more exposed to dramatic shifts in their external positions brought about by rapid changes in market sentiment. Crises in the balance of payments have become an unwelcome but all too familiar feature of the global economic landscape. The Mexican peso crisis of 1994, the Asian financial crisis of 1997, and the more recent collapse of the Russian ruble in the summer of 1999 all point to the need for new mechanisms that will more effectively protect the stability of the international monetary system.[18]

The recent spectacle of bankruptcies among many of South Korea's leading conglomerates and the crash in the stock markets of Thailand, Malaysia, Indonesia, and Hong Kong has led to some readjustments in thinking about economic globalization. Many now doubt the wisdom of accepting the death of state capitalism and refuse to face up to the uncertainties of the free market. In itself, globalization of trade is a good thing, but globalization without an effective policeman is viewed with concern, especially in the developing world. The growth of the global economy requires some growth in global government. But economic globalization is without a government.

Global trade is certainly making the world richer, but not uniformly so because the benefits of global cap-italism remain unevenly distributed. While it is optimistically estimated that about a billion people now enjoy an abundance of affluence, it is also pessimistically recalled (in countries not so affluent) that more than a billion people struggle in desperation to live on a dollar a day!

One of the widely discussed features of globalization is economic integration. Barriers to trade and investment are disappearing. Borders are becoming less relevant, and goods, services, and capital flow freely around the world. Trade across national borders and prosperity within these borders have become interlinked. This is not because governments or powerful corporations have decided that it should be so. Integration has been driven by a wave of technological change that has reshaped communications and transport. The speed and low cost of moving goods, services, money, and information have virtually eliminated distance as an economic factor. Millions of people have gained access to long-distance communications and to computers: More computers are now being sold than motorcars. One of the most powerful tools driving the borderless economy is the Internet. With the costs of communications plummeting and with innovative tools becoming easier to use, people around the world have burst into conversation using the Internet, mobile phones, and fax machines. The fastest growing communications tool ever, the Internet had more than 140 million users in mid-1998. The number is expected to surpass 700 million by 2001. The world is certainly becoming smaller.

Clearly, not everyone is enthusiastic about the way our world is changing. Indeed, the pace and scale of change can be traumatic and have real-life impacts on families, nations, and communities.[19] Rapid change has altered the landscape for everybody. Companies are faced with increased competition. Firms and individuals have to adapt to new technology. Workplaces are changing. Strikingly, the greatest pressures from globalization are on low-wage, low-skill workers. The people who are most vulnerable are precisely those with the fewest tools to adapt. Even where job creation has been strong and unemployment is falling, many people are experiencing greater insecurity about their own employment. A striking feature of our times is that large numbers of people harbor deep anxieties about the future. There is a widely felt uncertainty about how these rapid changes in the world are going to play out in our own lives.

The suggestion that the global market-oriented economy toward which we appear headed "has been as much the product of choice *by* nations as it has been thrust *upon* nations"[20] is not a point of view shared by nations that regard themselves as "thrust upon!" The breathtaking "globalization of prosperity" side by side with a depressing "globalization of poverty" leaves some nations with but little choice except to go along in the "race to the bottom."[21] They go along, even when unconvinced of the success of corporate globalization!

Globalization has its good points—it helps sustain freedom around the world. For instance, imagine that in the Soviet Gulag or Nazi concentration camps there was one laptop computer. Information about what was going on would have been instantly available to people all over world. The oppressors would not have been able to do what they did. The technological revolution (involved in globalization) means that dictatorships of the economic, political, or military kind are going to be very hard to sustain.

At the same time there is also the downside: Criminals are reaping the benefits of globalization. Deregulated capital markets, advances in information and communications technology, and cheaper transport make flows easier, faster, and less restricted not just for medical knowledge but for heroin as well, not just for books and seeds but for dirty money and weapons. Illicit trade—in drugs, women, weapons, and laundered money—is contributing to the violence and crime that threaten neighborhoods around the world.[22]

Globalization opens people's lives to culture and all its creativity and to the flow of ideas and knowledge—a good thing. But the new culture carried by expanding global markets is often seen as a disrupting influence. Mahatma Gandhi once said: "I do not want my house to be walled in on all sides and my windows to be stuffed. I want the culture of lands to be blown about my house as freely as possible. But I refuse to be blown off my feet by any." Today's flow of culture, especially media culture and consumer culture, is heavily weighted in one direction—from rich countries to poor. It blows the poorer countries off their feet!

We need trade that respects and supports communities and families and safeguards the environment. We need trade that encourages countries to educate their children, heal their sick, and respect human rights. Progress must be measured by human development not gross product. This is the essence of corporate responsibility. The new corporate responsibility must say no to dealing with despots, drug peddlers, and torturers. Some supranational body perhaps may help ensure this, but that is more easily recommended than done. The "chromosomes of State Sovereignty" lie firmly embedded in the psyche of all nation-states.[23]

VI. From a World of Independent Sovereign States to a World of Interstate Linkages

We live in times when the walls of national sovereignty afford little protection against technological advances and movements (to and fro) of capital, information, and ideas. The traditional sovereign state is now penetrated in insidious ways, and, as mentioned in Daniel Tarullo's excellent paper, "alternative forms of sovereignty" have not yet surfaced. Judge Rosalyn Higgins of the International Court of Justice recalls, in an article published in the *Cambridge Law Journal*,[24] that when loans to developing countries in the sixties and seventies were often tied to preferential trade arrangements with donor countries, this was resented by the donees who characterized it as "economic colonization." But in the mid-nineties when loans, whether through the IMF or other international financial institutions, became conditioned upon "good governance," upon a certain measure of transparency, and upon observance of international human rights norms, this was not seen as unreasonable or oppressive by the recipient countries. Invocation of human rights considerations across national boundaries is no longer regarded as an intrusion upon the "internal affairs of state."

Besides, international law places the responsibility on individual states to ensure that transnational corporations do not violate human rights through their operations in their country. According to current human rights law, it is now accepted that the states that have ratified the International Covenant on Economic, Social, and Cultural Rights (ICESR)[25] are under an obligation to regulate the conduct of third parties in order to protect individuals under their jurisdiction against human rights abuses. The obligation to protect includes the state's responsibility to ensure that private entities or individuals, including transnational corporations over which they exercise jurisdiction, do not deprive individuals of their economic, social, and cultural rights. States are responsible for violations of economic, social, and cultural rights that result from their failure to exercise due diligence in controlling the behavior of such nonstate actors.[26]

This interpretation of obligations under the ICSER has been confirmed by the UN Committee on Economic, Social, and Cultural Rights.[27] There is, however, as yet no response from international law in other fields such as environment, fiscal regulation, or trade law having an adverse effect on economic and social rights of peoples.

Globalization has not meant the disappearance of the nation-state (as was once optimistically predicted). Rather it has led to the state "disaggregating" into its separate, functionally different parts. For instance courts, regulatory agencies, departments of government, banking institutions, even parliamentary bodies are now seen working with their counterparts in other countries, creating a new web of relations. It is believed that there is a power shift from "sovereignty" to "transgovernmentalism," which has now become the more widespread mode of "international governance."[28]

Most observers of international affairs have long regarded the Peace of Westphalia (1648) as of great analytical significance because it formalized a world of political systems composed of state actors exercising equal and exclusive sovereignty over defined territories. Each state strove for self-sufficiency, homogeneity, and concentration of authority and power in a single center. But major social changes engendered by increasing globalization have driven a paradigm shift from a world of independent sovereign states to a world of diminished state sovereignty and increased interstate linkages.[29] The nation-state is acquiring a new dimension: interdependence and heterogeneity, "the single center" being replaced by parts of a multicentered (transnational) network so necessary for survival in a globalized world. A kind of "new economic internationalism" is emerging in which national democratic institutions simply have to cooperate with like institutions in other countries to recapture the sovereignty that each has lost in going global.

It appears that a new world order is developing based on the same functional foundations as of the European Union. There are emerging new global confederal structures (like intergovernmental organizations) concerning a vast range of transnational activities in health, communications, environmental resources, capital, investment, intellectual property, and the like. People and polities continue to claim to be sovereign without claiming the right to be totally independent, reserving for themselves the right to decide how and in conjunction with whom they will exercise such of their powers that they are willing to delegate, always emphasizing that they have the sovereign authority to do so. But claims to a limited (not absolute) sovereignty cannot be overlooked even in such a closely structured unity like the European Union, as emphasized in a recent decision by the Supreme Court of Denmark (April 6, 1998).

The case arose out of a challenge to the second Danish referendum on the ratification of the Maastricht Treaty.[30] One of the arguments advanced was that the extent of sovereignty transferred under Denmark's Act of Accession violated the principle of democracy, which was implicit in the Danish Constitution. Denmark's national Constitution placed conditions on the transfer of legal authority to a supranational (or international) organization. The delegated authority under the Constitution had not only to be "specified" but "specified in some detail" (Section 20). According to the Maastricht Treaty, the European Community (EC) has the power and authority to issue regulations directly applicable to member states, and the European Court of Justice (ECJ) is the final arbiter on questions as to whether regulatory measures of the EC authorities are legally valid. Decisions of the ECJ have established that EC law prevails even over national constitutions. But if all this were to be accepted as definitive, national courts would be deprived of the possibility of enforcing constitutional limits on delegated powers. While holding that the provisions of Section 20 of the Danish Constitution were fulfilled (in the case at hand), the Danish Supreme Court, however, made it clear that Section 20 would be violated if the European Community were to specify its own powers. It was only on the assumption that it was Danish courts (and not the ECJ) that would definitively determine the (legal) competence delegated to EC organs by the state of Denmark that the Supreme Court ruled that the treaty did not violate the Constitution.

Under the formulation of the Danish Supreme Court, European legislation would be struck down by national courts in Denmark if it was certain that the application of the treaty went "beyond the surrender of sovereignty."[31] (The opinion of the German Supreme Court is no different.) It appears that the dream of Jean Monet and successor European constitutionalists of a common European demos—a supreme European constitutional order—is as yet unlikely to be accepted by the politicians and people of nation-states, even those that have ratified the Maastricht Treaty. As Chief Judge Harry Edwards said (in his closing remarks at the International Symposium), we must expect that "national self-interest will always operate as an inherent limitation on the so-called rule of law in the global economy."

Conclusion

In the end, whether we like it or not, globalization is not only the buzzword of the new millennium, it is going to be the watchword of the twenty-first century. The challenge of globalization is not to stop the expansion of global markets but to find rules and institutions for stronger governance—local, national, regional, and global—to ensure that globalization works for people and not just for profits. "We have underestimated its fragility," the UN secretary-general said in his address to the World Economic Forum in Davos, Switzerland in January 1999. Global markets are vulnerable to the backlash of too many *isms*—protectionism, populism, nationalism, ethnic chauvinism, and fanaticism. The common factor in all these *isms* is that they exploit the insecurity and misery of people who feel threatened and victimized by the global market. The truth is that the spread of markets has outpaced the ability of societies and their political systems to adjust to them, leading to an imbalance. That is why Mr. Kofi Annan advocated "global markets with a human face," a rounded, nice-sounding expression that must not remain a cliché but must be translated into reality. The *Human Development Report 1999* has emphasized the need for a new commitment "to the ethics of universalism set out in the Universal Declaration of Human Rights."[32] Our sights must be set on a spirit of universalism—a universality of attitudes, concepts, and aspirations—in a world of sovereign nation-states. Not for us as yet the fulfillment of Wendell Wilkie's dream of one world.

International Economic Law
and Democratic Accountability

Daniel K. Tarullo

In a liberal market economy, law has three basic functions: (1) to create a framework for private, consensual economic transactions; (2) to regulate private economic activity, at least nominally in the interest of the polity as a whole; and (3) to establish private property rights that are protected not just from other private actors but from the state itself. These functions frequently conflict with one another. It is, for instance, possible to argue that almost any government regulation of the economy is an infringement on property rights of some kind or another. In practice, each of the three functions is widely accepted as legitimate. Debates over the acceptable scope of each function and the optimal reconciliation of conflicts among them comprise a major part of economic policy discussion in market economies.

By contrast, the international economic law that evolved in the last decades of the twentieth century is principally concerned with limiting the prerogative of national governments to regulate certain forms of economic activity. This was not necessarily the intent of those who founded the International Monetary Fund (IMF), General Agreement on Tariffs and Trade (GATT), and other important postwar international economic organizations. Those organizations embodied what John Gerald Ruggie has famously termed the "compromise of embedded liberalism," under which states committed themselves to a more liberal multilateral order of reduced tariffs and currency convertibility but retained discretion to pursue the domestic economic policies of their choice (Ruggie 1981). Yet as tariffs fell and controls on current account and capital transactions were removed, a state's domestic economic policies

assumed greater importance as determinants of international economic activity. Today, everything from intellectual property law to professional qualifications to food safety standards to telecommunications services is subject to international agreement limiting state regulatory discretion.

In a sense, the concentration of international economic law upon limiting the prerogatives of states is unremarkable. Traditionally, international law has applied only between sovereign states, which acquire rights and obligations only as against one another, not with respect to private entities. Thus the very nature of international economic law tends to define state interests as opposed to one another. Promoting the interests of their companies in exporting or investing abroad, states have contracted with one another to forbear from restricting commerce originating from other states. Tariff agreements bind national tariffs at or below negotiated levels. International aviation agreements preclude participating governments from restricting the operations of foreign air carriers below specified numbers of international flights.

These reciprocal obligations to reduce government restrictions on commerce have permitted the expansion of international trade and capital flows that have helped fuel world economic growth. But events of the last few years have underscored concerns that the traditional emphasis upon limiting state regulation has produced an imbalance in the corpus of international economic law that is neither economically prudent nor politically sustainable. The global financial crisis of 1997–1998 attested to the importance of providing sound regulatory frameworks, both national and international, for the conduct of international transactions. The spread of illicit transnational behavior—from money laundering to price-fixing cartels to financial fraud—has demonstrated that, in the absence of effective international cooperation, some activities can escape effective regulation. The explosive growth of electronic commerce has revealed the need for common, or at least consistent, rules of contract, privacy, and tort to govern international transactions conducted over the Internet. Finally, as graphically evidenced in the street demonstrations during last fall's trade ministerial meeting in Seattle, domestic political interests have organized to reverse what they see as a tendency to fashion international economic law with only commercial interests in mind.

Thus, even as the importance and extent of international economic activity continue to increase, the legal and institutional frameworks within which that activity is conducted are far from stable. The legal arrangements that survive or emerge in the next decade will both reflect policy choices on the nature of the international economy and help define the feasible range of those policy choices. Legal arrangements will have to mediate between the autonomy of governments and the operation of an international economy. They will have to reconcile the differing regulatory approaches and capacities of the world's nations. They will have to resolve the legitimacy problems raised by the apparent encroachment of international rules into domestic polities. Most of these challenges will be met (or, less happily, not met) at the point of intersection between international arrangements and domestic law. It is at this point that the behavior of private economic actors can be affected, for good or ill. It is also at this point that issues of democratic accountability are most acute.

In this essay I explain the types of international governance arrangements that have evolved in recent decades and the possibilities for reforming those arrangements to address the issues noted in the preceding paragraph. As I hope will become apparent, the choice of international legal arrangements has enormous consequences both for sustaining international economic growth and for the shape of democracy in a rapidly globalizing economy. Before turning to this analysis, however, I begin with some introductory comments on the meanings and nature of sovereignty as applied to the international economy.

Sovereignty in a Globalizing Economy

The trend toward global economic integration has provoked much debate on the nature of sovereignty and the role of government. One view is that we are witnessing a disconcerting "retreat of the state." As concisely stated by the late Susan Strange in her book of the same name,

> the progressive integration of the world economy, through international production, has shifted the balance of power away from states and toward world markets. . . . That shift has led to the transfer of some powers in relation to civil society from territorial states to nonterritorial TNCs. . . . [and] to the emergence of some no-go areas where authority of any kind is conspicuous by its absence. (Strange 1996, 46)

A popular variation on this view from both the political left and the political right is that nations have lost their economic sovereignty to international institutions such as the IMF and the World Trade Organization (WTO). These views of a diminished or powerless state have been contested by other scholars, who believe that the emergence of a global, more market-oriented economy has changed, rather than reduced, the role of government in the economy (Weiss 1998). A radically different position agrees with Susan Strange that global capital markets are increasingly dictating the policies of governments, rather than the other way around, but finds the promise of great prosperity in this reversal and counsels governments to "stop worrying and learn to love the market" (Bryan and Farrell 1996, 252).

This debate, which includes many positions in addition to those just mentioned, is not likely to be resolved soon. Two points, though, seem both reasonably clear and reasonably important in formulating policy choices. First, with the important exception of member states of the European Union, nations have not surrendered their *legal* or *formal* sovereignty to multinational corporations, international organizations, or any other entity. Second, to a substantial degree, the trend toward a market-oriented, global economy is the result of conscious policy choices by national governments.

Discussions of sovereignty have been something of an academic cottage industry in recent years. Each scholar now seems inclined to create his or her own typology, so there are no consensus terms for very similar concepts. For present purposes it is sufficient to note that nearly everyone draws a conceptual distinction between formal or legal sovereignty on the one hand and effective sovereignty on the other (Krasner 1999; Reinicke 1998). The former refers to exclusive legal authority within a given territory and to mutual recognition of that authority by other sovereigns. The latter refers to the control actually exercised by the legal sovereign within its territory (or at the borders of its territory). Contrary to the arguments of some critics of the WTO, for example, no country has ceded any legal sovereignty to that organization. A finding by a WTO arbitral panel that the United States has violated a WTO obligation does not supplant U.S. law. If the United States fails to comply with the ruling, it may be subject to retaliation from the aggrieved country. But this is not very different from the situation in which a nation may find itself whenever it violates international law. The possibility of retaliation or reciprocal disregard of international obligations may, to be sure, make the policy choices more difficult for a nation. The international law obligations of states are not insignificant in shaping expectations and behavior. But this does not mean that nations have lost their legal sovereignty. Similarly, nations have not "lost" legal sovereignty to large corporations.[1]

An important exception to the preservation of legal sovereignty is found in the European Union (EU) where, with respect to matters within the competence of the European Commission and the European Court of Justice, member states do seem to have ceded an element of sovereignty to the Union. As those competencies have broadened, debate over the "democratic deficit" in the operation of the Union has loomed larger. Even so, because member states retain the right of withdrawal under the constitutive treaties of the European Union,

it is unclear whether they have ultimately "lost" sovereignty. Stephen Krasner has aptly grouped the EU with the British Commonwealth of the early twentieth century as situations where an "alternative bundle" of sovereignty characteristics prevails (Krasner 1999, 235). The long line of applicants for admission to the EU suggests that preservation of pristine legal sovereignty is hardly the ultimate aim of all countries. Although alternative forms of sovereignty may eventually develop in the world generally, the medium term seems unlikely to produce such a development.

The debate over whether nations have lost their "effective" sovereignty is an interesting and important one. This issue leads to the second point, which I believe is reasonably clear, that the global, market-oriented economy toward which we appear headed has been as much the product of choice *by* nations as it has been thrust *upon* nations. The development of global markets cannot be explained simply by the dissemination of new communications technologies or the strategies of large multinational enterprises. Governments around the world have created the conditions for truly global markets to emerge by themselves adopting market-oriented laws and policies. In fact, one could plausibly argue that a swing toward the market was the dominant economic theme of the last quarter of the twentieth century. From deregulation in the United States to privatization in Europe and Latin America to the abandonment of central planning in China and the formerly communist countries, market principles have driven policy. Japan and other East Asian countries, which had prospered through the 1960s, 1970s, and 1980s with variants on a state-coordinated form of capitalism, have begun their own tentative steps toward more market-oriented structural policies in the wake of the financial crisis of the late 1990s.

By and large, countries have turned to more market-oriented policies because of discontent with the economic performance yielded by existing policies. Consider the U.S. experience. One can surely find examples of deregulation somewhat forced upon the government by international developments, such as certain changes in banking and securities laws in response to the growth of the less regulated eurodollar and eurobond markets. But the deregulation of commercial aviation, railroads, trucking, telecommunications, and financial services was substantially motivated by the belief that efficiency and consumer benefits would be greater than under regimes regulating pricing and entry in those industries. The great Latin American drive toward market-oriented policies in the late 1980s and early 1990s similarly arose from domestic discontent with the economic consequences of the statist policies of the 1960s and 1970s.

Thus, to the degree that the state has "retreated," it has done so mostly of its own accord. To be sure, governments may have felt they had no choice but to adopt market-oriented policies in order to enhance prospects for economic growth and to satisfy a restless electorate. But governments—particularly those in democratic states—are constantly faced with choosing among policies that entail costs as well as benefits. Airline deregulation in the United States has led to substantially lower fares and more service on many routes. It has also led to crowded planes and airports, bad customer service, and the loss of scheduled carriers to some smaller cities. The country could not return to the pre-1978 situation— too much has changed in the last two decades. Massive re-regulation will probably not occur precisely because the costs to the average traveler would be so high. But if the costs of a deregulated airline industry were thought sufficiently high, some form of price or entry regulation could be reimposed. More likely, as already seen to some degree, proposals will issue for regulation targeted to specific problems.

The policy choices presented by a "deregulated" global market are somewhat parallel to those available following domestic adoption of deregulatory or other market-oriented policies. Nations, particularly large and powerful nations, could impose broad restrictions on flows of goods and capital into and out of their territories if they so chose. But the costs to Mexico of forgoing foreign capital, or to the United States of forgoing foreign automobiles, are considered sufficiently high as to make the option unattractive (except, perhaps, to groups that would particularly benefit from such a step). Again, more discrete or targeted forms of intervention remain potentially attractive policy responses. The parallel between global and domestic markets is far from perfect, however. There are at least three important distinctions that are relevant to the exercise of

"effective" sovereignty and the nature of international legal arrangements.

First, where markets are genuinely global, the efficacy of national regulation will depend to some degree on the cooperation and enforcement of other national regulators. Even where there is a rough equivalence of regulatory aims, the failure of one nation to pursue these aims effectively can create problems for other nations. For example, inadequate supervision by U.K. and Luxembourg banking authorities over the Bank of Credit and Commerce International (BCCI) led to losses for depositors around the world when the bank eventually collapsed. Countries hosting branches of BCCI were unable to remedy, or in some cases even discover, irregularities in the bank's practices. These troublesome practices could only be fully detected and countered at the hubs of BCCI's operations. In other instances, competent and congruent national regulation may still be insufficient to staunch illicit transnational activity. Special transnational cooperation may be necessary. Money laundering, for instance, can appear as legitimate financial activity in one nation (or, at least, cannot be proven otherwise) in the absence of information from authorities in the country where the funds originated. Similarly, without cooperation among authorities in multiple jurisdictions, it may be impossible to prove illegal price-fixing activity by international cartels.

Second, nations may not share regulatory aims with respect to economic activity affecting other countries, thereby complicating or frustrating achievement of those aims. Sometimes nations may self-consciously have adopted a looser regulatory scheme in order to attract business away from other nations. A clear example is the effort of small polities to establish themselves as tax havens, or as particularly lax regulators of banks or oceangoing vessels. This is hardly a new phenomenon. Small polities can profit simply from the registration fees of companies or ships that transact most of their business in other countries. Yet larger countries will occasionally engage in similar behavior. As mentioned earlier, the government of the United Kingdom has promoted London as a major offshore financial center by imposing looser regulations for transactions in foreign currencies than either the home countries of those currencies impose or the United Kingdom itself imposes for transactions in pounds sterling. The ongoing resistance of the United Kingdom to a common withholding tax on interest and dividends throughout the European Union is the latest manifestation of this overt competition for business.

More frequently, nations do not fashion their regulatory schemes for the express or principal purpose of luring investment or business away from other nations. But in a world of mobile capital and reduced trade barriers, one country's decision to reduce taxes or offer investment incentives or simplify a regulatory scheme will affect not only the domestic business environment but the trade and investment decisions of foreign companies as well. From the vantage point of the foreign countries, the motives or appropriateness of the country's decision may be less relevant than the fact that their companies may now be tempted to shift production overseas. This dynamic is the origin of fears of a "race to the bottom" in which regulatory regimes, social standards, and tax incidence on capital are placed under downward pressures by "footloose" corporations. While generalized fears of this sort are somewhat exaggerated, they are not without foundation. There does, for instance, seem to be evidence that the relative tax burden borne by capital (as opposed to labor) has headed downwards in a more integrated world economy (Rodrik 1997, 63–64). Additionally, it is almost certainly the case that companies make some decisions on locating production based upon lower cost structures, including regulatory requirements. In certain instances, large companies proposing employment-generating investments may overtly solicit "bids" of subsidies and regulatory relaxation from host countries hoping to attract the new facility.

The dilemma this dynamic poses for international economic law and governance is perhaps the most difficult to resolve. On the one hand, a nation may genuinely be limited in its regulatory options (including taxation) if other nations with lower requirements can host companies that can count on selling their goods or services back into the first nation because of open trade. On the other hand, an international requirement that *all* countries abide by a set of norms preferred by the first nation will limit the policy choices of those other countries. This

problem implicates the larger economic policy debate as to when regulatory competition among governments is desirable, deleterious, or unimportant. This debate frequently arises in the context of whether the U.S. government or the European Union should impose uniform or minimum standards on all U.S. states or member states, respectively. Notions of decentralization or "subsidiarity" are regularly at issue. Whatever the merits of those notions in particular domestic cases, decisions in those cases are made within a constitutional framework, unlike the situation internationally.

This last point leads to the third important distinction between domestic and international markets—the fact that international arrangements operate outside the presumptively legitimate political and juridical structures of participating governments. Of course, such arrangements are undertaken at the outset in conformity with domestic constitutional requirements. In the United States, for instance, most major trade agreements have been presented to, and voted favorably upon by, the Congress. But once the international arrangement is in place, it has some degree of autonomy from the domestic political processes of participating governments. In one respect, this autonomy is necessary. If, for example, each WTO ruling on the conformity of a nation's tariff levels and procedures were subject to approval in the domestic political process of that nation, there would be little meaning to the agreement. Expectations that nations would conform to their initial undertakings would be very weak indeed, with costly increases in uncertainty among economic actors. As international arrangements intrude further into domestic policy, however, the autonomy of an international arrangement can become highly problematic as a matter of domestic politics. A good example is provided by a ruling of the WTO in 1997, which held that European restrictions on the importation of beef that had been fed hormones violated WTO rules. The ruling itself was arguably consistent with the relevant WTO rules. The problem arises from the rules themselves, which require WTO arbitral panels to determine if there is adequate scientific justification for food safety rules, even those which are nondiscriminatory as between domestic and foreign producers. The outcry of the European public over this ruling was such as to prevent the European Commission from complying with the ruling. Instead, the European Commission accepted the alternative available to it under the WTO of retaliation by the United States against certain European exports.

The beef hormones example reveals two ways in which international economic arrangements can run afoul of notions of accountability and democracy. One is that politicians and legislators may resent determination of sensitive issues such as the safety of the food supply by the "unelected bureaucrats" of an international organization. The lack of accountability of those decision makers to the affected polity undermines the legitimacy of the decision. The second sort of problem is that these kinds of disputes may highlight for citizens the fact that the international arrangements have been negotiated largely on the basis of commercial interests of the countries involved. For example, the dynamic of trade negotiations and the relationship of trade negotiators to industries in their countries have traditionally emphasized the export interests of those countries and have undervalued noncommercial interests.

To sum up, the globalization of the economy has presented national governments with an additional, sometimes difficult, set of decisions as to the costs and benefits of pursuing specific economic policies. In some respects these decisions are familiar to any government. But there are ways in which international economic activity may limit policy choices by any single government more than purely domestic economic policy choices have been limited. Moreover, while concerns about the loss of legal sovereignty to international organizations are largely misplaced, international economic arrangements do seem at times inconsistent with the commitment to popular sovereignty that has come to characterize a growing number of the world's nations.

International Governance and the Role of Law

Let me now turn to the role of law in international economic arrangements. As I suggested earlier, law is increasingly called upon to mediate among nations and interests in these arrangements. Because private actors carry on most of the economic activity in modern market economies, the relevance of an international arrangement rests largely on how it affects private behavior. Generally speaking, international law does not create private rights and obligations. But arrangements that bind states can indirectly create or constrain opportunities for private actors. Thus the point of intersection between international arrangements and domestic law is of particular interest, for it is here that private conduct can be affected. Examination of this point of intersection reveals what behavior is being regulated, how the regulation is legitimized within domestic legal systems, and possibilities for modifying the arrangements to achieve different policy ends.

The international economic arrangements of the postwar era can be grouped according to the three approaches to governance variously embodied in them. The *basic contract* type, exemplified in international aviation agreements, creates binding obligations among participating states but provides little in the way of process for elaborating or enforcing those obligations. It depends upon a more or less continual assessment of the reciprocal benefits and obligations accruing to both sides. Because of its contingent, almost ad hoc quality, it yields few rules of general application and does not significantly penetrate into domestic law and policy. For these reasons, it is increasingly anomalous in global markets, which are oriented toward generally applicable rules or standards. Indeed, one can discern pressures building within the current system of bilateral aviation agreement for a global framework of rules so that, for example, an airline based in the United States would be able to reconfigure its Asian routes to meet market demands without a requirement that the U.S. government undertake negotiations with each country. Because of the limited role of law in basic contract arrangements, and because these arrangements are of diminishing importance, I will say no more about them here.

The *statutory/adjudicatory* type of arrangement, exemplified in the World Trade Organization, emphasizes rule adherence by states. The "statutes" are reasonably detailed rules for state behavior that are negotiated and adopted by WTO members. Until recently, these rules were mostly of the "thou shalt not" variety, such as forbidding tariff increases above certain levels, imposing import quotas, or the discriminatory taxation of foreign products. Some WTO codes negotiated in the last decade place affirmative obligations on governments, such as to provide certain intellectual property protections to foreign companies or to implement certain regulatory policies to assist foreign telecommunications companies attempting to compete with recently privatized telecommunications monopolies. In all cases, though, the behavior regulated is that of states, not private actors.

The "adjudicatory" part of the arrangement is found in the dispute settlement procedures of the WTO. Over the years, these procedures have been progressively refined into a quasi-adjudicatory process for applying WTO rules in specific circumstances. Disputes between nations over WTO obligations are now processed on a strict timetable, with decisions of dispute settlement "panels" binding on the disputant nations, subject only to review by the appellate body of the WTO itself. The combination of WTO rules reaching deep into domestic policy and binding dispute settlement has proven a volatile mixture. Although most dispute settlement decisions have been routinely handled and implemented, a few have involved clashes between trade and nontrade values. WTO decisions against certain features of U.S. laws protecting endangered species and, as described earlier, European prohibitions on importation of meat fed with hormones have been particularly controversial with the U.S. and European publics, respectively.

The WTO system has been quite successful in reducing tariffs and other border barriers to trade. The articulation of reasonably clear rules for states, coupled with an efficient and neutral dispute settlement process, has created an environment in which market actors conduct business with reasonable expectations that states will not raise tariffs or otherwise contravene their obligations. As a result, the WTO (and GATT, its predecessor organization) has played a major role in creating the certainty needed for growing international trade and investment. But the statutory/adjudicatory governance approach of the WTO has also been subject to vigorous criticisms in recent years. The emphasis on constraining state discretion that has become so familiar when applied to tariffs is more controversial when applied to domestic policies. Developing countries have complained that rules on intellectual property, for example, deny them the opportunity to fashion a legal regime most compatible with

their levels of development. Environmental and consumer advocates have complained that the WTO rules excessively limit the discretion of states to protect environmental and safety interests. Quite apart from the nature of the rules, the dispute settlement process has been criticized because it has not permitted submissions or participation by nongovernmental groups with a strong interest in the outcome. The process is also quite opaque, at least compared to judicial or administrative proceedings in many countries.

In a very general sense, these criticisms are linked by the belief that the statutory/adjudicatory system of the WTO is too exclusively focused on restraining state discretion, too oriented to the commercial needs of multinational companies. Developing countries feel that their interests are underserved, while citizens of developed countries believe that the social values for which they have waged political struggles at home are being threatened through removal of those issues to international fora. It now seems clear, in light of the debacle of the WTO's meeting in Seattle in December 1999, that the WTO system will be changed. One proposal is to open up WTO processes to public scrutiny and, perhaps, limited participation by allowing nongovernmental entities to file briefs in dispute settlement cases. Proponents of this change argue that a more open process will be better understood by the public and will incorporate more points of view into the decision-making process. Without a change in the rules, however, it is hard to see how process changes will redress the imbalance in the WTO legal system. While a change that allowed dispute settlement panels explicitly to balance trade against nontrade values would raise the chances of decisions in favor of environmental interests, it would also—ironically enough—entail committing more discretion to the politically unaccountable WTO panels.

A change in the scope of WTO rules is a second possible reform. Social activists and labor unions have proposed requiring each WTO nation to enforce minimal labor standards, an obligation that would be enforceable with trade sanctions, just like other trade rules. While this change would indeed respond to those who feel that the trading system is too weighted to corporate and commercial interests, it would do so by further intruding into the domestic political systems of member states, particularly the developing countries. The suspicion of those countries is that, in a trading organization, labor standards could be enforced for trade—that is, protectionist—reasons rather than humanitarian ones. They also fear that such standards could be as ill suited to their development needs as the intellectual property rules already included in the WTO. These dual concerns would be equally relevant if other social or regulatory aims were to be pursued through the WTO. Competition policy and environmental regulation, which in national governments are means of controlling private economic activity in the public interest, become instruments of national trade policy in a system that enforces rights among nations. The WTO, and the statutory/adjudicatory approach to international economic regulation generally, is thus faced with a dilemma. In seeking to broaden its scope beyond narrow commercial interests, it may intrude more, not less, into domestic policy decisions and the self-determination of discrete polities.

The *regulatory convergence* type of international economic arrangement is characterized by a system of structured international activities through which national laws and regulations are made more congruent, or the enforcement of similar laws is coordinated among states. This approach to governance is distinguished from the statutory/adjudicatory approach in several respects. First, as a matter of history (though not necessarily of logic) the regulatory convergence approach has taken root where states attempt a collective effort at regulating private economic actors instead of or in addition to collective efforts at self-restraint by states. It may or may not be grounded in a formal international agreement and, even where one exists, its provisions are elaborated exclusively among national regulators who implement agreements through their own regulatory practices. The approach relies upon shared regulatory ends and frequent personal contacts among these national regulators, which together can produce substantial trust and peer identification. Disputes do occur, of course, but they do not generally become public clashes as trade disputes often do. Though participating regulators are surely influenced by distinctive national interests, they tend to modulate those interests in pursuit of the common aim of protecting the citizens of their countries.

The regulatory convergence approach is not nearly so well-defined or pervasive as the statutory/adjudicatory approach. It has taken hold to a greater or lesser degree in competition policy, securities regulation, anti-money-laundering efforts, and pharmaceutical regulation. It is best illustrated through the Basle Committee on Banking Supervision. In the last twenty years the Basle Committee has effected greater coordination in the supervision of internationally active banks through the Basle Concordat and, more remarkably, has achieved substantial harmonization of national requirements for bank capitalization through the Basle Accord on Capital Adequacy. The accord, though quite detailed and often amended, is not even an international agreement in a legal sense, yet it has arguably had as great an impact on state behavior (for good and ill) as any formal treaty.

Like the statutory/adjudicatory approach, the regulatory convergence approach can engender greater certainty in the legal environment for international economic transactions. It does so, however, through coordinated regulation of private market actors rather than through prohibitions on such regulation. Thus it is more compatible with the regulatory function of law, which I suggested was largely absent in statutory/adjudicatory arrangements. It operates precisely at the intersection between international understanding and domestic regulation. National regulators generally have sufficient legal authority to implement these understandings and do so as a matter of their enforcement discretion. In practice, the approach provides for national variation within a harmonized framework based on the shared expectation that each participating regulator is substantially committed to their common aims. It can command domestic political legitimacy where citizens regard the international cooperation as designed to protect them. When U.S., Canadian, and European antitrust authorities cooperate to uncover and prosecute an international price-fixing cartel, the activity looks less like the loss of "sovereignty" and more like the recovery of governmental authority.

Variations on the regulatory convergence approach have the potential to help balance international economic law more successfully among the three functions of limiting government interference with property, setting a stable framework for private economic activity, and regulating private economic conduct in the public interest. One can, for example, imagine national officials developing and implementing common principles for the conduct of electronic commerce that include appropriate protections for privacy and other consumer interests as well as restraints on government taxation or other burdens on Internet business. Similarly, one can foresee an arrangement among national food safety regulators both to improve the safety of food in international commerce and to reach understandings on the reasonable scope of national regulation of food in the absence of clear scientific evidence of harm or safety. WTO rules prohibiting arbitrary or discriminatory regulation of food could then be implemented in light of the activities and understandings of the arrangement.

While promising and certainly underutilized, the approach will not be a panacea. A number of limitations may be encountered. First, a substantial, preexisting consensus on the need for cooperative regulation is necessary for a successful regulatory convergence arrangement. Even where such a consensus exists, other factors may promote or inhibit success: the extent of shared versus conflicting national interests, the relative levels of bureaucratic chauvinism or inertia in the particular subject area, the significance of differences in national regulatory approaches or capacities, and the presence or absence of external events that create a political imperative for response. For example, nearly all nations share a strong interest in controlling various forms of financial fraud. Hence it is not surprising that law enforcers from different nations have long cooperated and are doing so now in increasingly formal ways. Forty countries currently participate in an arrangement to combat money laundering. Even so, radical differences in style and enforcement priorities among various nations have retarded progress toward cooperation at several key junctures in recent years.

In other areas the impulse toward cooperation is obvious, but it is qualified by possible issues of national commercial advantage. Whether regulatory convergence is feasible in these areas may depend upon external events. The Basle Committee itself was formed following the spectacular, and system endangering, failures of the Franklin National Bank and the Herstatt Bank in 1974. Its efforts have been reinforced by subsequent collapses of internationally active financial institutions

such as BCCI and Barings. These incidents reinforced the sense of common interests among regulators and, perhaps, served as ballast to more nationally centered concerns about the relative competitiveness of each country's banks.

The hardest cases for regulatory convergence will be those in which nations perceive their interests to diverge significantly, even where each believes that some form of regulation is warranted. For example, labor standards are at least nominally regulated in nearly every country in the world. And while there have been many (weak) international agreements negotiated on the subject under the auspices of the International Labour Organization, there is little that constitutes regulatory cooperation. Particularly in light of the recent contentiousness surrounding discussion of labor standards in the WTO, it appears that countries believe their interests diverge more than they converge. In addition, debates over labor standards and policies are often particularly controversial domestically. The relevant national regulators may not command deference on these matters from the rest of their governments or possess the requisite legal discretion to implement informal international arrangements through changes in domestic enforcement practices.

Even if the requisite motivation for convergence exists, or can be developed, it may be hard to achieve broad participation in a regulatory convergence system. Insofar as governance depends on continual communication among national regulators, the system may become overloaded if too many nations participate. In contrast to the regular, manageable meetings of the Basle Committee—which consists of eleven financially important nations—imagine the logistical and practical difficulties of organizing meetings among 140 countries.

"Successful" regulatory convergence arrangements may also be problematic as a matter of policy or accountability. Compared to formally negotiated, legally binding agreements, regulatory convergence arrangements may be quite insular. The very sense of shared mission and expertise that binds such an arrangement even in the face of differing national interests can create a different set of problems. Many of these problems are encountered in domestic contexts because of the substantial discretion committed to administrative officials. Regulators may be "captured" by the industry they regulate. Alternatively, they may be completely inattentive to legitimate concerns of the regulated about cost or regulatory technique. The more independent the regulator from political oversight and control, the greater the potential for such problems to go unremedied, an ironic counterpoint to the rationale for administrative regulation as deciding matters on the basis of expertise rather than politics. An international arrangement is likely to be even less transparent than domestic regulatory activities. Moreover, once an agreement has been reached among national regulators on a certain point, the difficulties of changing that understanding will be much greater than in a single government. Thus there may be legitimacy problems in regulatory convergence arrangements—different from those encountered in statutory/adjudicatory arrangements—but potentially just as significant.

The existence of a global economy in a world of nation-states defines a major governance challenge for the indefinite future. There will be disagreements among, and even within, nations as to the right mix of national autonomy and coordinated policies. Where coordination is deemed desirable, the choice among international governance arrangements will significantly affect the development of the substantive aims of the arrangement itself. Thus the choice of arrangement can itself influence which of the three aims of law in a market economy is most important in circumstances where those aims may conflict. Finally, the strengths and weaknesses of the different kinds of governance arrangements may call for creative combinations of attributes of the different models to create an amalgam for a particular issue or area that best balances substantive policies, efficient governance, and political legitimacy.

Rivalry, Collaboration, and Policy

Like the last part of the twentieth century, the last part of the nineteenth century witnessed substantial integration of economic activity across national boundaries. Goods, capital, and even labor moved among nations in unprecedented amounts, notwithstanding the fact

that the emergence of national economies was still incomplete. As with most significant economic phases, economic trends interacted with political and technological factors to produce the nineteenth century's "global" economy (Polanyi 1944). But for a few interruptions, such as the Franco-Prussian War, the European balance of power system brought about an atypically peaceful period that allowed international transactions to multiply. The steam engine and telegraph facilitated international commerce. Industrialization vastly increased the appetite of European countries for raw materials from other parts of the world. The establishment of the gold standard provided a more or less stable environment for international trade and capital flows. The triumph of the market over tradition in most affluent countries was both a cause and effect of these other developments.

The trend toward global integration in the last part of the twentieth century is similarly the result of a complex interaction of political and technological change, as well as economic policies and commercial strategies. The end of the cold war, the turn to market-oriented policies, and the information revolution have all played prominent roles. A comparison of today's globalization with yesterday's provides useful perspective, not the least by demonstrating that international economic integration is far from irreversible. World war, the collapse of equity markets and the gold standard, and the Great Depression elicited policy responses that further constricted international economic activity. Together, these external and policy measures reduced international capital and goods flows so much that their levels in 1914 were not reached again until late in the century. While one hopes and expects that we will not experience such dramatic reversals in the foreseeable future, there are real policy decisions to be made. These decisions, particularly the degree to which states are willing to strengthen one or more elements of an international economic order, can vary significantly with the circumstances of the individual state relative to the rest of the world.

Foremost among these circumstances is how states elect to balance their mix of rivalry and cooperation with other states. The geopolitical context of this election has changed considerably in just the last decade. As they have had their regulatory capacities weakened by global market forces, there has been a tendency for the industrial democracies to intensify their economic rivalries with one another. Even before the end of cold war, the increased importance of international commercial activities to all nations had provoked conflicts among states vying for sales in foreign markets. With the collapse of the Soviet Union, an important counterweight to economic antagonisms among the political allies of the OECD countries has disappeared. Mindful that domestic prosperity depends more than ever on success in global markets, states compete more vigorously than ever to win foreign contracts or commercial advantages. To a great extent, U.S. attitudes have shifted the most, since in its exercise of postwar international leadership the United States had periodically been willing to forgo short-term commercial benefit for the long-term goal of a system compatible with its anti-Communist interests. In economics as well as traditional foreign policy, the United States is now tempted to act unilaterally and sometimes quite heavy-handedly.

When the United States *is* inclined toward more inclusive forms of leadership, its closest allies—not to mention other countries—are increasingly unlikely to follow. Just as the end of the cold war removed a major incentive for the United States to accommodate other nations in the interests of the anti-Soviet alliance, so it removed a major incentive for other countries to defer to the United States. Europe in particular has struck a more independent note. In addition to the dynamic just mentioned, the breadth and depth of European integration have fueled aspirations of equality with the United States. Other states share misgivings about unchecked American preeminence and, despite their own diverging interests, may resist U.S. overtures. Meanwhile, Asian countries continue to consider whether more distinctively Asian arrangements, political and economic, are not the best response to the influence of both Europe and the United States in the last century.

This geopolitical context matters for the future of international economic law. The United States may be tempted to propose arrangements on a kind of take-it-or-leave-it basis, constricted by domestic politics and confident that the rest of the world lacks the capacity to take on a leadership role. Other nations resist U.S. blueprints because they fear the resulting edifice will inevitably support American political, economic, and cultural influence. As one foreign official once put it to me, "One 'American century' was quite enough."

No one concerned with economic policy can disregard these factors in assessing international economic governance and proposing new arrangements. Those who believe the global economy will require a more sophisticated framework will need first to convince states that their shared interests in structuring and regulating private conduct are at least as pressing as their divergent interests in commercial advantage and geopolitical position. One modest step down that path is to promote arrangements that accentuate the shared interests rather than exacerbate national antagonisms.

Post–Seattle Reflections

A Qualified Defense of the WTO and an Unqualified Defense of the International Rule of Law

Michael J. Trebilcock

NGOs and the WTO

The public perturbations leading up to and surrounding the Seattle ministerial meetings of the WTO in late 1999, and the ensuing failure to launch a new "Millennium" round of trade negotiations, have confirmed dramatically, unambiguously, and probably irreversibly that trade negotiations and trade disputes have moved out of the quiet and obscure corners of trade diplomacy and become matters of "high politics." Despite the civil disturbances that attended the Seattle meetings, it is important to bring some measure of rigorous detachment to the evaluation of the criticisms that have been widely and vehemently directed at the WTO, especially by the NGO community. While there are, of course, dangers in scholars seeming to abandon the detachment of the academy for the passions of the acropolis to join issue directly with the critics, I believe that the stakes are so high for global welfare that there are larger risks entailed in trade law specialists simply disregarding these criticisms on the grounds that they are ill informed and ill conceived (which in this paper I will argue is mostly the case).

Rather than attempting to distill the essence of the NGO community's criticisms of the WTO from sound bites from the streets of Seattle, I have chosen to rely on three full-page advertisements published in the *New York Times* in three successive weeks in November 1999 immediately prior to the Seattle meetings and endorsed by over twenty NGOs as the source of the major criticisms of and claims about the WTO, which I analyze below.[1]

Claim #1: Economic Globalization Is Leading to a Global Monoculture

With economic globalization, diversity is fast disappearing. The goal of the global economy is that all countries should be homogenized. Institutions like the World Bank and the WTO promote a special kind of homogenizing development that frees the largest corporations in the world to invest and operate in every market everywhere. To these agencies and corporations, diversity is not of primary value; efficiency is. Diversity is an enemy because it requires differential sales appeal. What corporations love is creating the same values, the same tastes, using the same advertising, selling the same products, and driving out small local competitors. Mass marketers prefer homogenized consumers. . . . Every place is becoming every place else: monoculture. . . . What is the point of leaving home?

It is hard to know where to begin unraveling this argument. First, it must be said that it is crucial to the basic economic theory of international trade that countries exploit their comparative advantages in trade with other countries. Put differently, this means that mutual gains from trade derive from exploiting differences, not similarities, in production. If every country in the world were like every other country, there would be next to no international trade. Indeed, international trade enables countries to accentuate rather than minimize their differences by specializing in economic activities where endowments permit a degree of specialization that confers comparative advantages on them relative to other countries, who in turn should pursue a similar strategy of specialization, thus creating the potential for mutually beneficial trade. This is observable not only across countries but also within countries. In Canada, Saskatchewan specializes in wheat production (and would specialize in more of it but for trade protectionism that it faces in foreign markets); Alberta specializes in oil and natural gas; central Canada in a variety of manufactured goods and services; the Atlantic provinces in commercial fishing. Within the United States, Michigan specializes in automobile production; Florida in citrus fruits production and tourism; California in wine production and high-tech industries; Texas in beef and oil production. Largely unconstrained internal trade has not obliterated but rather accentuated these differences. Largely unconstrained international trade has had, and will have, similar effects on differences among nations.

Second, as to what exactly the litmus test is for the claim of increasing homogenization of culture is far from clear. Accompanying the advertisement in which this claim was made was another full-page advertisement comprising numerous photos showing urban traffic congestion in various cities around the world and inviting readers to guess whether the city in question was, for example, Manhattan or Bangkok. Urban traffic congestion seems a bizarre test of similarities or differences in countries' cultures. While it may be the case that certain aspects of popular culture such as mass entertainment and mass consumer products have achieved a degree of worldwide consumption appeal (as the advertisements claim), the claim that every place is becoming every place else and that there is no point even in leaving home is belied by the most casual observations derived from traveling in various parts of the world, such as Latin America, Africa, the South Pacific, Western Europe, and Central and Eastern Europe, where cultural, social, and economic differences in both production and consumption remain huge.

Indeed, these differences, in many respects, translate into disparities that are unconscionable in the modern world. As Amartya Sen argues in his recent book, *Development as Freedom,*[2] the basic goals of development can be conceived of in universalistic terms where individual well-being can plausibly be viewed as entailing certain basic freedoms irrespective of cultural context: freedom to engage in political criticism and association, freedom to engage in market transactions, freedom from the ravages of preventable or curable disease, freedom from the disabling effects of illiteracy and lack of basic education, freedom from extreme material privation. According to Sen, these freedoms have both intrinsic and instrumental values. While obviously different countries and cultures will seek to vindicate these freedoms in different ways, the challenge facing most poor developing countries in the world today is to realize these basic freedoms as most citizens of developed countries have already been privileged to do. While successful vindication of these freedoms may make citizens of poor countries more like us, they have no duty to us to preserve exotic but impoverished ways of life in order to provide opportunities for tourists from developed countries to indulge a desire for voyeurism. While Francis Fukuyama, in *The End of History,*[3] argues apocalyptically that the final triumph of economic and liberalism is occurring, and is generally to be welcomed, he worries that it may presage a material blandness and homogeneity and lack of engagement with great ideas that ideological conflicts in the past have provoked. However, it is far from clear that the apocalypse has in fact arrived given fratricidal ethnic and religious conflicts that, if anything, seem to be proliferating in many parts of the world. More homogeneity of values, especially liberal values, would seem a small price to pay for avoiding the huge human costs of these conflicts.

Third, the claim that diversity is the enemy of efficiency is false. While it may be true that in some industries, such as fast food and hotel chains (as the advertisements claim), many consumers want assurances of quality and consistency across multiple locations, in many, perhaps most, industries the most successful competitive strategy is to differentiate one's products from those of other providers, whether this is in men's and women's fashions, automobiles, consumer durables, or restaurants. Merely mimicking rivals' product offerings and then competing strictly on price and cost is often a recipe for economic oblivion, as opposed to offering consumers distinctive preferences for what they want. That corporations could or want to homogenize all consumer preferences globally is belied by the huge and proliferating diversity of product and service offerings that one sees in markets all over the world.

Fourth, it might be claimed (although the advertisements do not explicitly do so) that the WTO in its rules and trade dispute rulings has been unsympathetic to efforts by countries to protect culturally distinctive activities from foreign competitive encroachment, for example, domestic film, television, and magazine industries. Article IV of the GATT explicitly allows for quotas on foreign films. In addition, Canada negotiated for itself a more general, qualified exemption for its cultural industries under the Free Trade Agreement and NAFTA. While the WTO Appellate Body in the *Split-Run Periodicals* case struck down features of Canadian policies designed to promote the domestic magazine industry, its decision still leaves open to the Canadian government a wide range of measures to support this and similar culturally sensitive industries, indeed, superior mechanisms than those employed in the past, which have focused on subsidizing or protecting national inputs rather than subsidizing distinctive informational outputs.[4]

Finally, if one were really to avoid the consequences of cosmopolitanism, trade barriers would hardly be enough. There would also be a need for strict censorship laws, exit visas, limits on immigration and ethnic and religious diversity, and other measures aimed at maintaining the insulation of communities from external influences, with highly uncongenial implications for repressiveness and intolerance. As Sen argues, citizens in developing

(and other) countries should be assured of the right to freely choose which traditional cultural values and practices to preserve, which to modify, and which to abandon.[5] This is a freedom that others have no right to deny to them.

Claim #2: Trade Liberalization Exacerbates Inequalities of Wealth

Trade liberalization benefits corporations, their shareholders, and CEOs, but not ordinary citizens. The gaps between rich and poor within countries and among countries have grown because of the inequities of global trade. Even in the United States, the median wage of factory workers has fallen by 10 percent in the last two decades. While CEO's salaries in global corporations are rising sharply, worldwide real wages for most people have fallen. . . . The rising tide lifts mainly yachts.

Again, these claims are largely false. While it is true that the earnings of low-skilled American workers relative to high-skilled workers have declined in recent years, most empirical studies show that increased trade with low-wage developing countries may account for at most 20 percent of this reduction, and most of the increase in the wage gap between skilled and unskilled workers is attributable to technological change and rapidly declining rates of unionization.[6] Moreover, these data relate to relative inequalities. Between 1960 and 1990, the real value of wages and fringe benefits of production or nonsupervisory workers in the United States increased by 60 percent in absolute terms.[7] However, the returns to highly specialized human capital in an increasingly knowledge-based economy increased much more. In any event, it hardly behooves citizens in the United States and Canada, currently running the lowest unemployment rates and highest sustained growth rates in thirty and twenty years respectively, despite the economic adjustments entailed in the major trade liberalization initiatives of the past decade (the FTA, NAFTA, and the GATT Uruguay Round), to claim that trade liberalization is generally impoverishing these countries. Moreover, as Paul Krugman and many other economists have pointed out, the growth rate of living standards essentially equals the growth rate of domestic productivity—not productivity relative to competitors but simply domestic productivity.[8]

Even though world trade is larger than ever before, national living standards are overwhelmingly determined by domestic factors rather than competition for world markets. In the case of the United States, exports are only 10 percent of the GNP, which means that the United States is still almost 90 percent an economy that produces goods and services for its own use. Thus international trade has little to do with declining relative living standards of unskilled workers in the United States; to the extent that it does, an argument needs to be made as to why mostly poor, developing countries should be denied the opportunity of utilizing their comparative advantage in low-wage, low-skilled labor by investing in manufacturing sectors that capitalize on this advantage and in pursuing export-led growth policies. However, in recognizing this comparative advantage it is important not to exaggerate it. Data show almost a one-to-one relationship between labor productivity and labor costs in manufacturing in a wide range of countries.[9] Thus it is a fallacy to assume that low wages are the driving force behind today's global trade. This relationship also explains why internationally most firms are not seeking to relocate to Bangladesh despite its low wages, and why nationally (within the United States) most firms are not seeking to relocate to Arkansas despite its low wages. While international trade theory suggests that international trade will generate a tendency to factor price equalization, this is only true, inter alia, after adjusting for differences in factor productivity.[10] Nevertheless, international trade will tend to increase the incomes of workers of given skill categories (adjusting for productivity differences) in developing countries.

It bears remarking, in this context, that the outstanding examples of developing countries that (despite recent setbacks) have dramatically increased the average real incomes of citizens (often by factors as large as six or eight) in recent decades have been the so-called Asian Tigers, beginning with Japan and followed by countries such as Taiwan, South Korea, Hong Kong, and Singapore, all of which have pursued relatively open, export-led growth policies. In contrast, developing countries that have pursued extreme forms of import substitution policies have generally experienced disappointing and, in many cases, disastrous results.[11] These results have been exacerbated by the protectionist policies maintained by most developed countries toward goods of potential export interest to developing countries such as textiles, clothing and footwear, and processed agricultural and natural resources. Even today, tariffs against imports from developing countries are substantially higher than for imports from other developed countries. Economic estimates have found (reflecting a massive exercise in hypocrisy) that the costs of protection inflicted on developing countries by developed countries substantially exceed the entire value of foreign aid in recent years.[12] This is not to suggest that open trade and investment policies are sufficient in themselves to launch developing countries on a strong growth trajectory. As Hufbauer and Schott point out,[13] between 1975 and 1990 the dollar value of two-way trade between OECD countries and low-income countries tripled from $59 billion to $200 billion. Yet the per capita income gaps between OECD countries and low-income countries actually increased over this period (from thirty times higher to fifty-eight times higher), reflecting the higher productivity of labor in developed economies.[14] Clearly, a range of other domestic policies that promote higher levels of capital investment, investments in human capital, health care, and infrastructure, as well as high-quality public sector institutions, are important determinants of growth. Again, many of these policies have been important in the growth record of the high-performing East Asian economies. In addition, it is important to note that the benefits of growth in these countries have also been equitably distributed by virtue of policies of land redistribution, investments in public education, health care, and public housing, and the encouragement of small and medium-sized businesses (SMEs).[15] More generally, the empirical evidence suggests that extreme levels of inequality have a negative impact on growth at all stages of development[16] and that over a large sample of countries and over long time periods the income of the poor rises one-for-one with overall growth—a relationship that holds in poor countries as well as rich countries, in economic crises, and in open-trading regimes.[17]

A related claim that is often made (although not explicitly by the NGOs in the *New York Times* advertisements) is that trade and investment liberalization threaten to gut the welfare state that, not coincidentally it is argued, evolved in many developed countries in the postwar decades, along with progressive trade liberalization in order, in part, to provide a cushion for the economic instabilities and risks associated with the latter for many citizens.[18] Now the concern is that with increased capital mobility and increased mobility of highly skilled workers this social contract may be put in jeopardy as the better-endowed firms and individuals in the community exit or threaten to exit in order to avoid the taxes required to underwrite the social programs that are perhaps even more necessary in the present and the future than in the past to cushion shocks to less-advantaged citizens given the increasing speed of economic change and the transition costs it entails.[19] While I believe that these are legitimate concerns, the facts largely belie the claim that economic globalization has to date had major deleterious effects on the welfare state in most developed countries. Data show social expenditures in fact increasing or at worst remaining constant as a percentage of GNP in most OECD countries and tax levels rising in most of these countries. In addition, data show a dramatic increase in social regulation (environmental, health and safety, human rights, and employment regulation) in most of these countries over the past three decades, in part reflecting the fact that a cleaner environment and greater safety are normal economic goods, the demand for which rises with increasing prosperity, itself in part engendered by greater international trade.[20] Thus, there is no evidence to date of any significant contraction in the scale of the welfare state in most developed countries.

Claim #3: Free Trade Trumps All Other Values in the WTO

The central idea of the WTO is that free trade should supercede all other values. It views the laws of nation-states that protect the environment, small business, human rights, and consumers, labor as well as national sovereignty and democracy as possible impediments to trade. The WTO's victims include dolphins, sea turtles, clean water, clear air, safe food, family farms, and democracy itself. The WTO has never once ruled in favor of the environment. The composite effect of these rulings is "cross-border deregulation" which ratchets down standards for health, safety, and the environment everywhere, homogenizing laws in all countries to the lowest common denominator.

In evaluating this claim it is important at the outset to emphasize that only a tiny handful of cases have come before the WTO's Dispute Settlement Body that implicate environmental or health and safety concerns, and that the hundreds of thousands of regulations maintained by the 130-odd WTO members with respect to the environment and health and safety—a dramatically growing number of regulations as noted above—have never been challenged. Moreover, the empirical evidence strongly suggests that economic integration has a ratcheting-up rather than a ratcheting-down tendency in these areas.[21] Furthermore, the specific cases cited by the critics of the WTO of irresponsible or insensitive disregard by the WTO's Dispute Settlement Body of environmental and health and safety concerns for the most part do not justify the criticisms that have been made of them and in fact involved disguised protectionism or gratuitous restrictions on trade. By way of context, it is important to note that by virtue of successive rounds of GATT negotiations tariffs have now been reduced to zero or trivial proportions in many sectors (down from over 40 percent in 1947 to about 3 percent on average currently), so that remaining barriers to trade are often internal regulatory measures of member states. Unless one believes (implausibly) that such measures can never be manipulated or abused so as to provide a disguised form of a protectionism, the WTO is necessarily seized with the task of determining when a challenged regulation genuinely serves an environmental or heath and safety purpose, or when, on the other hand, it is a disguised restriction on trade. A recent doctoral graduate of mine, Julie Soloway, in detailed case studies of informal disputes in these areas in the three NAFTA countries, concludes that perhaps as many as twenty-four of the twenty-five cases of environmental or health safety regulation that she studied yielded no consumer welfare benefits but were merely disguised forms of protectionism.[22] Even if this assessment is unduly harsh, it suggests that this is not an imaginary problem.

Of the cases cited by the NGO critics of the WTO,[23] the *Reformulated Gasoline* case involved regulations under the U.S. Clean Air Act that entailed the progressive removal of pollutants from gasoline but imposed laxer (plant-specific) base starting points on U.S. gasoline refiners than refiners in Venezuela and Brazil exporting gasoline to the United States. The WTO Appellate Body held that there was no basis for differential treatment. In the *Thai Cigarette* case, a ban on imported cigarettes, not accompanied by any ban on domestically produced cigarettes, was held to be discriminatory and an unjustifiable restriction on trade. In the two *Tuna/Dolphin* cases decided by WTO panels before the creation of the WTO Appellate Body as a result of the Uruguay Round Agreement, the NGO community has more cause for criticism in that the panels ruled on narrow and unjustifiable grounds that an import ban on tuna caught by fishing methods that killed or maimed dolphin was unjustifiable because it was directed to environmental concerns outside the territorial jurisdiction of the United States or was predicated on changing another country's environmental policies. However, the NGO critics of the WTO fail to note that the Appellate Body in the subsequent *Shrimp/Turtles* case, in effect, overruled the two panels in the earlier *Tuna/Dolphin* cases and held that there was no territorial constraint on a country adopting environmentally related trade measures in response to another country's environmental policies (in this case shrimp fishing techniques that killed or maimed a particular species of sea turtle that was an endangered species under CITES). However, the United States was found by the Appellate Body to be in breach of its GATT obligations in that it had negotiated exemptions with some foreign countries and not with others from the ban on shrimp imports, but there was no rational relationship between these exemptions and whether countries maintained safeguards against shrimp fishing techniques that endangered sea turtles. Thus the United States had acted in an arbitrary and discriminatory fashion.

In the *Beef Hormones* cases, the EU ban on the sale or importation of beef that had been reared on certain growth hormones was struck down both by the panel and the Appellate Body because it was not based on a risk assessment as required by the WTO Agreement on Sanitary and Phytosanitary Standards (SPS). Alternatively, if the ban was based on a risk assessment, the available risk assessments at the time that the ban was adopted all indicated that there were no ascertainable risks to human health from this product. Similarly, in the *Japanese Agriculture* case, where imports of various fruits from the United States and elsewhere were banned because of a concern that they could spread disease through coddling moth unless they met various stringent border tests, both the panel and the Appellate Body found that these border requirements were based on no risk assessment at all and were thus in violation of the SPS agreement. Finally, in the *Australian Salmon* case, a ban on the importation of fresh, chilled, or frozen salmon was found to violate the SPS agreement both because the ban was based on no risk assessment at all and because, inconsistently, it allowed imports of other kinds of fresh, chilled, or frozen fish that presented at least as high a risk of spreading disease. Thus, with the exception of the two *Tuna/Dolphin* cases (in effect, subsequently overruled by the Appellate Body), all of these decisions by the WTO's Dispute Settlement Body seem to be sensible and restrained, unless one believes that the WTO and its members should give up entirely on the task of attempting to screen out disguised forms of regulatory protectionism.

I should add that, in addition to nondiscriminatory, environmentally related trade measures that address cross-border externalities or the protection of the global commons, I would also be prepared to contemplate bans on imports from countries guilty of gross human rights violations or systematic violation of core labor standards analogous to human rights (perhaps under the "public morals" exception of Article XX of the GATT), provided again that these are not discriminatory or disguised restrictions on trade.[24]

Claim #4: Self-Sufficiency Is Preferable to Dependency

Any nation's people are most secure when they can produce their own food, using local resources and local labor. This creates livelihoods, minimizes costly transport and waste, and solidifies communities. It also makes countries more self reliant. . . . Small farms have given way to miles of single-crop luxury monocultures, for export to foreign markets . . . Self-sufficiency is giving way to dependency.

This argument is unfathomable. First, if the case for self-sufficiency rather than dependency is well taken in the case of food, why should not the same argument extend to other necessities such as clothing, footwear, lifesaving medications, automobiles, or steel? Why is food special?

Second, if self-sufficiency is a good thing at the national level, why not also at the state, local, or family level? Within federations such as Canada and the United States, perhaps Texas should seek to produce not only beef but wine, wheat, and citrus fruit; California should diversify into beef and grain production; Michigan and Kansas should diversify into all of the above. Each member state of the EU should also aspire to be self-sufficient in food, fundamentally contradicting the entire European economic integration enterprise. Indeed, why not self-sufficiency at the level of the family so that each family produces all its own food (and other needs), returning us all to members of hunter-gatherer or peasant societies?

Third, even adopting a national perspective and focusing on food, it would be surprising if the social pathologies said to be afflicting the agricultural sector are due to international trade. Agriculture has been and remains the most protected sector in the international economy. Worldwide, about 90 percent of all agricultural production on average is consumed domestically. The empirical evidence suggests that agricultural protectionism in the United States, Western Europe, and Japan entails average costs of fourteen hundred dollars per household per year for the countries concerned—a large and regressive hidden "tax" on ordinary consumers of basic staples.[25] Apart from these costs to consumers, it is agricultural protectionism itself that has promoted excessive monocropping and use of fertilizers and irrigation, as most starkly exemplified by the European Union's Common Agricultural Policy, which over the postwar years has turned Europe from the largest importer of temperature zone agricultural products into the second largest exporter, accounting for some 60 or 70 percent of the entire annual budget of the EU in terms of subsidy costs. Moreover, it is not generally true that trade liberalization in agriculture benefits primarily corporate agribusinesses. Family farms in, for example, Saskatchewan, Kansas, New Zealand, and Australia are severely prejudiced by agricultural protectionism elsewhere in the world. It is important to remember that there are communities and farming families on both sides of the trade equation. Most importantly, the argument for national self-sufficiency in food, as in any other sector, centrally defies the entire theory of comparative advantage in international trade and argues for complete autarchy on the part of every nation in the international community. This is not only economically illiterate but if taken seriously would reverse the entire course of economic enlightenment and progress pursued (albeit often falteringly) by many countries around the world since at least the repeal of the Corn Laws in Britain in 1846 and would return us to some medieval form of Dark Ages,[26] fundamentally jeopardizing the dramatic real increases in living standards that most citizens, at least in the developed world, have enjoyed over the past century and a half.

If the critics are right, Canada should attempt to grow citrus fruits, tea, coffee, sugar, bananas and other tropical fruits, and fresh vegetables in wintertime; Saudi Arabia in turn should attempt to grow its own wheat. Obviously, such efforts at national self-sufficiency in food would vastly impoverish both nations. All that the theory of comparative advantage purports to demonstrate, in essence, is that international trade dramatically increases the scope of the contract opportunity set available to people. Or in Adam Smith's famous words in *The Wealth of Nations:* "The division of labour is limited only by the extent of the market." If the claim by the critics is moderated somewhat so that some international trade is all right but too much is not, then the critics need to produce a theory that tells us how much is enough and how much is too much. But not even the beginnings of such theory have been offered.

Claim #5: The WTO Is an Undemocratic and Unaccountable Form of Global Government

The WTO is emerging as the world's first global government. However, it was elected by no one. It operates in secrecy and its mandate is to undermine the constitutional rights of sovereign nations. WTO dispute settlement decisions are made in secret, closed tribunals—like the old "star chambers"—where unelected faceless bureaucrats sit in final judgement over the constitutional rights of nations. According to a European trade minister, "it's not undemocratic; it's anti-democratic." The dispute settlement operates in secret: no press, no public, no public interest organizations. Three bureaucrats (former corporate or government trade officials with no social or environmental training) make profoundly important judgments affecting human health, jobs, agriculture and food, and the environment.

At a quite fundamental level this claim is disingenuous, even incoherent. Every international treaty, whether it pertains to nuclear disarmament or nuclear nonproliferation, land mines, human rights, the law of the sea, or the environment, to the extent that the commitments made by signatory states therein are effectively binding, necessarily constrains domestic political sovereignty. But unless a lawless and anarchic world is preferable to a world where nations collectively agree to address issues cooperatively that entail ramifications beyond the exclusive territorial preserve of each of them, this should be seen as an extension of the domestic rule of law to the international arena. In the case of the GATT/WTO, all the obligations of member states (now more than 130 with most of the remaining countries in the world seeking membership) have been voluntarily assumed by members (until recently referred to appropriately as contracting parties), representing the quintessential form of government with the consent of the governed. While amendments to the GATT or covered agreements may be approved by two-thirds of the membership of the GATT, such amendments are not binding on nonconsenting members. Member governments represent most of the democratically elected countries in the world (as well as others with more dubious political pedigrees). And not only have all member states voluntarily agreed to the elaborate set of commitments entailed in membership of the GATT/WTO, they have also sensibly agreed that in order for these commitments to be more than paper commitments they should be effectively enforceable. In order for them to be effectively enforceable, countries

obviously cannot be judges in their own cause in cases of alleged noncompliance. Hence member states, almost from the genesis of the GATT, have agreed to neutral third-party adjudication of complaints by member states of alleged violations of commitments by other member states.

Initially, this process of adjudication took more a form of a diplomatic conciliation, but over the past half century since the creation of the GATT the dispute settlement process has evolved increasingly in the direction of formalized legal adjudication. The roster of panelists from whom panels are drawn in particular cases must be approved by consensus of all members. The seven members comprising the Appellate Body must be approved by consensus of all members. In the event of a member state failing to comply with a decision of a panel or Appellate Body once adopted by the General Council of the WTO, now applying a negative consensus rule (only a consensus of all members favoring rejection leads to nonadoption), retaliation by the aggrieved party may be authorized by the Council against the noncompliant party in the form of trade sanctions. The system has worked remarkably well over the decades in ensuring a relatively high level of compliance with decisions by panels and more recently the Appellate Body.[27]

Instead of seeking to eviscerate the WTO, NGOs who are critical of its effectively binding nature would seem well-advised to redirect their energies to ensuring that other international treaties of concern to them, such as those pertaining to human rights, war crimes, land mines, the environment, or international labor standards, are as effectively enforceable through similar evolution of parallel supranational dispute settlement regimes in these contexts. Thus I interpret much of the spleen vented by NGOs against the WTO's Dispute Settlement Body as a function of envy rather than legitimate grievance.

However, this said, some criticisms of the WTO's dispute settlement process are warranted.[28] Reflecting perhaps the diplomatic origins of dispute settlement under the GATT, the closed nature of current dispute settlement processes is inconsistent with a fully elaborated international rule of law. In particular, initial and subsequent written submissions of disputing parties (member states) should be made publicly available (with exceptions for confidential information) at the time that they are filed with the DSB, and the oral hearing component of the process should equally be open to the public (as has long been the case with other international dispute settlement bodies such as the International Court of Justice) with provision for *in camera* hearings for confidential information. In addition, nongovernmental parties, including NGOs but also including affected business firms and trade associations, should have limited rights of standing as intervenors (or amicus curiae) in dispute settlement proceedings as third-country governments do already (as the Appellate Body went some distance to recognizing in its decision in *Shrimp/Turtles*), at least to the extent that they are permitted to file short written submissions and respond briefly to any questions from members of the panel or Appellate Body in the oral proceedings by way of clarifying or elaborating on their written submissions (much as in major domestic constitutional litigation). Permitting private parties to initiate complaints before the WTO Dispute Settlement Body raises a host of much more complex questions, including the capacity of the dispute settlement process to handle a much higher volume of complaints, the potential for strategic abuse of the process by competitors, and the likelihood (from the perspective of NGOs) that private firms or trade associations are likely to challenge much more frequently environmental and health and safety regulations of foreign states. Thus the dispute settlement process should remain, for the present time, a state-driven process with provision for amicus briefs, which are likely to be a particularly important legitimation mechanism in trade and disputes involving major public policy issues.

With respect to the criticism that panelists and Appellate Body members lack expertise or sensitivity in matters relating to environmental and health and safety issues, it bears pointing out that the quasi-judicial review role played by the DSB is not markedly different from the judicial review role played by all-purpose courts with respect to specialized agency decisions in domestic administrative law and calls for a similar degree of substantial, but not complete, deference—in effect by requiring some minimum level of rationality

in agency decision making where disparate impacts on foreign suppliers are entailed. The Appellate Body in *Beef Hormones, Shrimp/Turtles,* and *Australian Salmon* has largely adopted this perspective by, for example, recognizing that a respondent need not undertake its own risk assessment but may base its measures on others' risk assessments, by accepting that it is sufficient that the risk assessment is supported by a respectable minority of scientists, and by applying a very narrow consistency requirement. In many respects the Appellate Body's approach resembles the proportionality test adopted in Canadian Charter jurisprudence. Moreover, under the rules governing the dispute settlement process both in general and in specific contexts (such as the SPS agreement), panels may appoint individual scientific advisors or advisory groups of scientific advisors, and have sometimes done so (but should do so more systematically). In similar vein, panels and the Appellate Body in disputes implicating environmental and health and safety issues should be more proactive in seeking the advice of other international agencies with major mandates in these areas where these exist. Again, WTO policy committees, such as the Committee on Trade and the Environment, should be open to submissions by NGOs and other interested private parties.

All of these changes can reasonably be viewed as incremental and as falling well short of what might be viewed as justifying turning Seattle into a war zone. However, it seems unlikely that many elements of the NGO community would settle for incremental changes of this kind. A fundamental contradiction in their position is revealed by claims that the WTO should be vested with a mandate to authorize or initiate trade sanctions against countries maintaining weak labor, environmental, or human rights standards. Paradoxically, the "constitutional rights of sovereign nations" to regulate as they please should be subordinated to external judgments and sanctions when their domestic standards are "too lax" but should entail immunity from external judgments and sanctions when they are "too stringent." The GATT/WTO TRIPS Agreement on Intellectual Property Rights thus becomes the harbinger of the future, where developing countries are forced to adopt the regulatory standards of developed countries in most contexts, often with devastating implications for their own welfare. Moreover, to invest the

WTO with a mandate so expansive would precisely be to risk reconstituting the WTO as the world's first global government—a prospect that the NGOs generally decry as nightmarish. On the other hand, to allow member states unilaterally to invoke trade or related economic sanctions against other countries on grounds of weakly framed or enforced environmental, health and safety, labor, and human rights laws, without some neutral third party adjudicating whether such measures are warranted, or whether on the other hand they are simply a pretext for trade protectionism or discrimination (especially against developing countries who have strong historical grounds for harboring suspicions in this respect), would return us to the international law of the jungle. For example, for the sake of argument, suppose that the United States lacks a domestic textile industry and freely admits imported textiles from particular foreign countries made with child labor, or that the United States possesses a substantial domestic clothing industry and bans imported clothing from other foreign countries made with child labor. Should the ban stand in the latter case given the absence of a ban in the former case? In offering an alternative vision of a world order subject to the international rule of law with an overriding normative commitment to nondiscrimination, among foreigners or between domestic interests and foreigners, without nontrade related justification, the GATT/WTO has been a beacon of hope and inspiration over the past fifty years. The mutually self-destructive economic factionalism of the interwar years and its consequences provides a salutary contrasting specter.

Another fundamental contradiction in the NGOs' position relates to the claim that the WTO is undemocratic. To the extent that this criticism is directed not so much at the dispute settlement process as at the negotiating processes among countries that give rise to trade agreements and obligations in the first place, then this criticism is misplaced and should not be directed to the WTO as an institution but to NGOs' own state policymaking processes. Here, indeed, there may well be room for improvements. Trade treaties, often negotiated over protracted periods of time and over a very wide range of complex issues, inevitably involve delicate political trade-offs across issues. Once an agreement has been reached, while ratification or implementation may

require legislative action in member countries, this cannot realistically entail picking and choosing among various elements of the agreement without serious risk of the entire agreement and the negotiating processes that led up to it completely unravelling (as recognized in the U.S. "fast-track" approval processes), rendering ratification or implementation actions an imperfect form of democratic accountability. Thus, in terms of public input into the negotiating positions taken by member states and revisions to these positions and trade-offs across issues as negotiations proceed, the negotiating positions of member states in the future will need to be more open to public scrutiny and input than in the past. In past trade negotiations in Canada a large number of industry-specific advisory groups have been constituted by the Canadian government to advise it during the negotiating process, but these groups are not inclusive of all relevant constituencies. However, negotiations themselves cannot be extended beyond government representatives to a host of nongovernmental and private sector actors from all over the world without reducing the process to a theater of the absurd (akin to negotiating in a football stadium)—and total functional paralysis. Thus while representatives of governments should remain the chief negotiators, this should not exempt them, and certainly will not exempt them in the future, from being more proactive and imaginative in structuring an appropriately inclusive domestic consultative process during negotiations. This imperative also has application to the development of government positions in dispute resolution proceedings and WTO Policy Committee deliberations. But, to restate the principal point here, this is not a concern that the WTO as an institution can resolve, but it is a concern that NGOs and other interested groups and citizens must resolve within their own political communities. That is to say, democratic decision making begins at home, not in Geneva.

Mostly Smoke and Mirrors

Calling oneself an NGO, or a public interest group, and setting aside questions of how spokespersons for these groups are elected, appointed, and financed and whether they in fact represent the constituencies on whose behalf they claim to speak,[29] should not entail any dispensation from conventional norms of veracity and coherence in serious public policy discourse. If the NGO community aspires to an enduring place at the table in trade policy debates and disputes, beyond the transitory prominence achieved in Seattle, criticisms of existing trade policies and institutions will have to acquire a veracity and coherence that they presently mostly lack. As I have attempted to show, most of the criticisms presently directed against the world trading system in general and the WTO in particular are either false, incoherent, or fatuous. This is especially true of criticisms of substance (the first four claims), while criticisms of process have some limited cogency (the fifth claim). But more open processes presuppose that these will facilitate valuable contributions of substance that may not otherwise have been articulated. NGOs, as spokespersons for elements of civil society whose perspectives have often indeed been seriously lacking from trade negotiations and trade dispute resolution in the past and whose values, concerns, and interests would illuminate, enrich, and legitimate these processes, surely owe more to their claimed constituencies on matters of substance than they provided at Seattle if they are themselves to avoid a crisis of legitimacy of precisely the kind that they allege of the WTO. In the end, the litmus test of NGOs' enduring contributions to the evolution of trade policy is likely to be the battleground of ideas, not street battles in Seattle or elsewhere.

The World Bank's Role in
a Global Economy

Ko-Yung Tung

Lest anyone fall asleep during my talk, let me start with my conclusion.

1. The World Bank is unequivocally dedicated to the rule of law.
2. The promotion of the rule of law is firmly embedded into the World Bank's activities in every corner of the world.

The definition of the rule of law may, like Justice Stewart's definition of pornography, be in the eye of the beholder. The rule of law in the eyes of the World Bank is unique and evolving within the specific framework of the Bank's mission, mandate, capabilities, and disabilities.

Today the eyes of the World Bank focus first on poverty reduction—our mission. We see:

- 6 billion people who live on our planet.
- 3 billion people who live on under two dollars a day, 1.2 billion of them who live on under one dollar a day in what we call absolute poverty.
- 2 billion people who don't have electrical power.
- 1.5 billion people who don't have safe water.
- 125 million elementary school-age children who can't go to school.
- Millions who die every day from preventable diseases.

Statistically, the rich are getting richer and the poor are getting poorer. To fight this pervasive poverty, we must first listen to the voices of the poor. We've just published the first of three compilations from a ten-year project to hear the voices of the poor:

- An old woman in Africa: "A better life for me is to be healthy, peaceful, and to live in love without hunger."
- A middle-aged man in Eastern Europe: "To be well is to know what will happen to me tomorrow."
- A young man in the Middle East: "Nobody is able to communicate our problems. Who represents us? Nobody."
- A woman in Latin America: "I do not know whom to trust, the police or the criminals. Our public safety is ourselves. We work and hide indoors."
- A mother in South Asia: "When my child asks for something to eat, I say the rice is cooking until he falls asleep from hunger—for there is no rice."

Other voices tell of problems with law and justice systems:

- It is difficult to get to the court. It costs 10 rands return by taxi from the farm to Patensie and then 3.50 rands from Patensie to Hankey.—South Africa 1998
- The leader of the collective farm was and remains a king; he does not obey the law; he does what he wants, when he wants.—Moldova 1997
- Since there is no self-owned property, we can't get loans.—Venezuela 1998

- Even if a woman is given a chicken or goat by her parents, she cannot own it. It belongs to her husband. A wife may work hard and get a chicken. If it lays eggs, they belong to the husband.—Uganda 1998
- Kinh people have been applying and writing papers for a year now and still haven't gotten anywhere. The land tenure situation in Vietnam is precarious without official recognition.—Vietnam 1996
- The most important strategy for finding either public or private employment is to use one's "connections" and pay a bribe.—Georgia 1997

Our challenge is to respond to the cries of the poor within the framework of the Bank's charter and within the resources available to the Bank.

Fighting poverty is our twenty-first-century articulation of the mission of the World Bank. You may know that the World Bank, formally known as the International Bank for Reconstruction and Development, was conceived on the eve of the end of World War II at Bretton Woods, New Hampshire. (Our birthplace and that of our sister institution, the International Monetary Fund, is remembered when we are called the Bretton Woods institutions.) With victory in sight, the leaders of the Allied powers met to map out the postwar landscape. The first order of business was reconstruction—at that time—of the devastated countries, economies, and societies of Europe. Secondly, an equally important though longer-term objective was the development of the economies of the so-called third world. These twin objectives are with us still as wars and conflicts continue to plague our member countries even as they strive for economic development.

Today the World Bank has 181 member countries. I should add that most of these countries are also members of the International Development Association (IDA), the Bank's concessional loan affiliate established in 1960 to provide development assistance to the poorest countries. The World Bank and IDA are each governed by a board of governors, representing each of the members, and managed by a twenty-four-member board of executive directors, which as a resident board meets regularly every Tuesday and Thursday of each week in Washington, D.C. When I refer to the World Bank here, I am including the IDA's activities as well.

The Bank's mandate comes from our Articles of Agreement, our constitution. The articles direct the Bank:

(i) To assist in the reconstruction and development of territories of members by facilitating the investment of capital for productive purposes, including the restoration of economies destroyed or disrupted by war, the reconversion of productive facilities to peacetime needs, and the encouragement of the development of productive facilities and resources in less developed countries.

(ii) To promote private foreign investment by means of guarantees or participations in loans and other investments made by private investors; and when private capital is not available on reasonable terms, to supplement private investment by providing, on suitable conditions, finance for productive purposes out of its own capital, funds raised by it and its other resources.

(iii) To promote the long-range balanced growth of international trade and the maintenance of equilibrium in balances of payments by encouraging international investment for the development of the productive resources of members, thereby assisting in raising productivity, the standard of living, and conditions of labor in their territories.[1]

Thus, the purposes are driven by economics. Within those purposes, the articles provide specific strictures for the Bank's financing and requirements for the activities it finances. Most relevant for today's discussion on the rule of law, however, are the parameters for the Bank's relationship to politics. In this regard the articles also provide:

The Bank and its officers shall not interfere in the political affairs of any member; nor shall they be influenced in their decisions by the political character of the member or members concerned. Only economic considerations shall be relevant to their decisions, and these considerations shall be weighed impartially in order to achieve the purposes stated in Article I.[2]

Thus, the Bank's articles specifically prohibit the Bank from interference in the political affairs of any member and exclude the political character of members as a grounds for decision making. Only economic considerations may be taken into account by the Bank, and political or other noneconomic influences or considerations must be disregarded.

Let me contrast the charter of the World Bank with that of the European Bank for Reconstruction and Development (EBRD). The EBRD was established in 1991 right after the fall of the Soviet Union. EBRD's mandate is to "foster the transition towards open market-oriented economies and to provide private and entrepreneurial initiative in the central and eastern European countries committed to applying the principles of multiparty democracy, pluralism, and market economics."[3] While the EBRD, like the World Bank, is focused on economic development, it is also mandated to foster democracy and strengthen respect for human rights and the rule of law.[4]

With its economically oriented purposes and restrictions on political considerations, how can the World Bank be directly involved in the rule of law and the promotion of social human rights? We have already seen from the "voices of the poor" that the World Bank's poverty focus encompasses issues of law and justice. Instinctively, we believe that the rule of law is essential for poverty alleviation, but for the World Bank we must establish the intellectual and programmatic framework for the promotion of the rule of law within our constitution.

From a legal point of view, the Bank's promotion of the rule of law has been accomplished through a series of "purposive" interpretations of the charter. As my predecessor as general counsel, Ibrahim Shihata, opined: "Subjecting the few provisions of these Articles to a strict reading which reflects only the circumstances of the time of their adoption can hardly enable the Bank to serve its objective fully under present and future conditions."[5] This kind of reasoning allowed the Bank to move, for example, from the bricks-and-mortar rehabilitation of bombed-out factories in France to the building in countries born since 1945 of soft infrastructure, such as education, health, and governance.

With this purposive interpretation, "governance" has also been broadly defined: "In its broad sense, 'governance' includes both the exercise of political powers and the overall management of human, natural, and economic resources."[6]

Today the World Bank is involved in every aspect of the rule of law, as well as social human rights, so long as and to the extent that they can be creditably proven to be reasonably intertwined with economic development. This is an area where legal scholars can—and I invite them to—undertake intellectual and empirical studies to deepen the understanding of the role of the rule of law in fighting poverty.

The World Bank is mandated to take only economic considerations into account, and the Bank cannot interfere with the political affairs of any member country. Yet it does, and indeed it must, take political conditions into account. While "only economic conditions, which are weighed impartially, are relevant to the Board's decisions . . . political events which have a bearing on the economic conditions of a member or on the member's ability to implement a project or the Bank's ability to supervise the project may be taken into consideration."[7]

Indeed, as Mr. Shihata argues elsewhere, certain other requirements of the articles: "could hardly be met if the Bank were deprived of the ability to take into account the degree of political stability in the countries where it operates, or if it were to lend in situations where, due, for instance, to military occupation or civil strife, the staff would be unable to appraise the project, supervise its implementation or evaluate its performance . . . the Bank must take into account whether, under the prevailing conditions of the country, prospects exist that the project can be implemented to achieve its agreed purposes and the borrower can service the loan."[8]

What is key for the Bank is to establish that the political aspects for its consideration have direct and obvious economic effects.

To illustrate how rule of law issues are addressed and infused throughout the Bank's work, let me take you on a brief survey of some of our principal instruments. We will look first at the Comprehensive Development Framework (CDF), an overarching compass that is being gradually introduced as the framework for everything we do. Then we'll look at the Bank's Country Assistance Strategy (CAS) for assistance to a given country. Next we'll follow two types of documents that assess the country's development needs in a CDF-driven context: a country's Poverty Reduction Strategy Paper (PRSP) and the Bank's

Social and Structural Review (SSR). Finally, we will examine the Bank's operational policies that help shape the projects we finance under our assistance strategy.

CDF

Let us look first at the Comprehensive Development Framework (CDF), a collaborative initiative launched by the World Bank last year. The CDF has four essential elements:

- Structural reforms
- Human reforms
- Physical reforms
- Specific sectoral development

With poverty reduction as the central goal, the CDF aims to create a holistic framework for each country's economic development by addressing—in discussions led by the government and including civil society, donor partners, and the Bank—a country's development prospects and priorities across thirteen interrelated sectors.

Why the CDF? The CDF stems from evidence that the pursuit of economic growth may too often have been at the expense of social development.

- Experience has shown that open, transparent participatory processes are important for sustainable development.
- The World Bank is committed to expand its partnerships, transparency, and accountability under the leadership of the government.

To achieve greater effectiveness in reducing poverty, the CDF rests on the following principles:

- Country ownership
- Partnership with the government, civil society, assistance agencies, and the private sector
- A long-term vision of needs and solutions built on national consultations
- Structural and social concerns treated equally and contemporaneously with macroeconomic concerns

Under the CDF, structural reforms rest on four principal pillars. The first pillar is good governance—

anticorruption. "If you do not have good governance, if you do not have good people in government, if you do not have a legal system that works, if you do not have an honest justice system, you can pour as much money as you like into a country and you do not get results."[9]

The second pillar is legal and judicial reform.

Without the protection of human and property rights, and a comprehensive framework of laws, no equitable development is possible. A government must ensure that it has an effective system of property, contracts, labor, bankruptcy, commercial codes, personal rights law, and other elements of a comprehensive legal system that is effectively, impartially, and cleanly administered by a well-functioning, impartial, and honest judicial and legal system.[10]

The third pillar is financial and regulatory reform, and the fourth is social programs. In addition to the four pillars of structural reform, the CDF also covers the social/human sectors (education and health and population), the physical sectors (water and sewerage, energy, roads, transportation and telecommunication, and environmental and cultural issues) and specific sectoral development strategies (rural strategy, urban strategy, and private sector strategy).

CAS

While the CDF represents a country's long-term view of its poverty reduction strategy, a Country Assistance Strategy, the so-called CAS, is a medium-term instrument that maps the Bank's strategy for assistance to a country. The CAS determines the overall priorities and parameters for the Bank's package of analytical and advisory work, technical assistance, and financing in each area. The CAS is prepared every three years with the direct and active participation of all stakeholders, including NGOs.

Within each country's CAS is an assessment of each relevant sector, including a country's legal and judicial systems. Let me show you how this happens in practice with two examples. Here we see a summary of the related points in the CAS done for Ecuador in 1996:

- The need to devote greater attention and resources to the provision of basic infrastructure and social services to the poor was highlighted.
- Modernization of the state—including judicial reform—became a key element as a means to improve service delivery to the poor.
- A heavily burdened and inefficient judicial system had become a constraint to economic development. Judicial reforms were also seen as a precursor to private-sector development.

Here is how a 1997 CAS for Morocco looked at these issues:

- The challenge of CAS was to accelerate growth and social development through strong reforms.
- Despite Morocco's impressive economic growth and fiscal health in the mid- to late-1980s, a weak judiciary and bureaucratic delays were signaled as the major hindrances to investment.
- Collaboration between the private and public sector was an important element of the passage of new commercial and company codes and led to further legal reforms.

PRSP and SSR

Developing the CDF and the CAS requires considerable assessment, analysis, and policy dialogue in each sector, and the World Bank works with each country using the modalities suited to its needs. A good illustration of how this interaction takes place and incorporates rule of law concerns is our Social and Structural Reviews (SSRs) and Poverty Reduction Strategy Papers (PRSPs).

The PRSP is a specific operational expression of the CDF. It recognizes that income poverty is a critical, but far from the only, handicap afflicting the poor and that fighting poverty requires a long-term and multidimensional approach. One of these dimensions, of course, is law and justice. Initially, we plan to encourage and support the development of PRSPs in countries involved in our debt-relief initiatives and those of the IMF. Eventually, the PRSP approach would extend to all IDA countries.

The SSR is used primarily for middle-income borrowers and was introduced after the Asian financial crisis to provide an integrated analysis (across different sectors) of the critical constraints on poverty reduction and long-term development in the country. The SSR was intended to help identify major sources of vulnerability or risk, particularly as countries continue to increase their integration with the world economy. Four broad areas are analyzed in the SSR. They are:

- Growth and income distribution. Growth is a fundamental condition for sustained poverty reduction but is not always sufficient to address income distribution questions.
- Delivery of key services (health, education, human welfare) is often essential to maintain the country's human capital.
- Risk and vulnerability.
- Voice, transparency, and accountability.

For both the SSR and the PRSP, an assessment is made of the country's legal and judicial systems (see Box 1).

Box 1

Key Points Covered in an SSR (Legal and Judicial Systems)

For legal systems
- Lawmaking process and capacity: institutional capacity for legislative drafting; public inclusiveness in lawmaking process; accessibility of laws; and systematization, codification, harmonization
- Legal education and training
- Legal profession: professional legal associations, provision of legal services to community and vulnerable groups

For judicial systems
- Impartiality and independence of the judiciary: structural and functional independence, decisional independence
- Accountability and transparency: checks and balances, selection and removal processes, public trust
- Professionalism of judges
- Efficiency of the judiciary
- Access to justice: financial affordability and adequate support, physical accessibility (location and structure of court houses), informational and psychological barriers (language, gender)

Operational Policies

Each operation carried out by a member country with Bank financing must strictly comply with a myriad of self-imposed Bank policies and rules. These policies and rules apply whether the Bank's support takes the form of a loan, grant, or technical assistance. We have eleven safeguard deficits: (1) Agricultural pest management, (2) Cultural property, (3) Environmental assessment, (4) Forestry, (5) Indigenous peoples, (6) Involuntary resettlement, (7) Natural habitats, (8) Pest management, (9) Projects in disputed areas, (10) Projects on international waterways, and (11) Safety of dams.

Box 2

Operational Policies: The Rule of Law and Human Rights

Indigenous Peoples

"ensure . . . full respect for their dignity, human rights, and cultural uniqueness . . . based on the informed participation of the indigenous peoples themselves." (Operational Directive 4.20, Indigenous Peoples 1991)

Involuntary Resettlement

When project requires taking of assets, affected people should be:

- Compensated (same as or better off than before)
- Assisted in moving
- Assisted in efforts to improve living standards (Operational Directive 4.30, Involuntary Resettlement 1990)

Gender

"improve women's access to assets and services . . . with due regard to cultural sensitivity." (Operational Policy 4.20, The Gender Dimension of Development 1999)

Environment

Environmental assessments take into account:

- Natural environment (air, water, land)
- Human health and safety
- Social aspects
- Global environmental aspects

(Operational Policy 4.01, Environmental Assessment 1999)

Box 3

Legal and Judicial Reform Projects in Six Countries

Ecuador Judicial Reform Project

(A program for law and justice providing small grants for civil society)

- Four pilot women's legal services centers where the majority of the cases involve domestic violence, children, or family issues.
- Mediators are being trained in communities where the nearest place for formal justice is seven hours away. The majority of the issues deal with land disputes, child support, inheritance, and intra-institutional issues within the community.
- Legal training and assistance for prisoners' organizations and prisoners' relatives to understand the judicial process.
- Justice for children's welfare—this activity is designed to increase awareness among children, their parents, and teachers about the rights that the new Ecuadorian Constitution recognizes for children.
- Design of teaching material on children's rights to be used by teachers, children, teenagers, and parents.

China Economic Law Reform Project

- Drafting economic legislation—putting comparative legal experience at the hands of local drafters.
- Training in new economic laws so that lawyers, judges, and regulators can implement.
- Institutional strengthening of key agencies (such as the Commission on Legislative Affairs).

Tanzania Financial and Legal Management Upgrading Project

- Legal task force developed five-year strategy with broad participation
- Training for lawyers, magistrates, and judges
- Legal reform

West Bank/Gaza Legal Development Project

(An example of extensive donor coordination)

- Unify and develop existing legal framework
- Judicial administration
- Training for judges
- Mediation for commercial cases
- Dissemination of legal information to the public

Continued box 3

Russia Legal Reform Project

- Legal drafting
- Collection and dissemination of legal information
- Legal education and public education campaigns
- Judicial reform

Peru Ombudsman's Office

(An example of holding government accountable)

- Institutional strengthening
- Improvement of users' knowledge of office
- Enhancement of access to services

Let me give examples of some of the Bank's operational policies that bear on the rule of law and human rights. Box 2 lists our policies on indigenous peoples, resettlement, gender, and the environment. Box 3 gives you some examples of the Bank's direct role in the rule of law in certain countries: Ecuador, China, Tanzania, West Bank/Gaza, Russia, and Peru:

In conclusion, we have seen that the World Bank's mission of poverty reduction and its economically focused mandate not only permit but require us to support the development of the rule of law in our member countries. Each of the ingredients in our own special blend of alphabet soup—CDF, CAS, PRSP, SSR, OP, OD—takes on the needs of a country's law and justice systems. The result, as you have seen, is that the World Bank plays a unique and critical role in the development of the rule of law in the developing world.

Globalized Trade and
the Rule of Law

Robert Pitofsky

Let me say how pleased I am to be included in this superb weeklong conference and to have an opportunity to comment on these very fine papers. On globalization, as you have heard, and as you have seen if you have read the papers, our panelists express rather different points of view turning on their different experiences. I would like to consider whether I can detect common ground among all the papers that we will discuss this morning.

It's not the easiest task I've ever set for myself, but I would like to state a few introductory principles. Either I found these principles expressed in the papers, or between the lines of the papers, or I happen to believe these things, and therefore I detect these principles in the views of others:

1. The expansion of cross-border trade is inevitable.
2. A rule of law to facilitate globalized trade is essential. To some extent a "hands-off international trade" approach by the international community is really not an option.
3. There is a bright side and a dark side to globalization.
4. Getting it right in terms of international agreements, and introduction of the rule of law, is essential to maximize the bright side and minimize the dark side.
5. The correct choice of various national and international devices and a correct allocation of power is essential.
6. Finally and most obviously, the decisions that we make now at the threshold of this vast new internationalization of trade phenomenon will have consequences for a long time to come.

In other writings I have compared economic development at the end of the twentieth century to the end of the nineteenth century, particularly in connection with my own areas of responsibility: consumer protection and antitrust. We moved from local to statewide to national markets at the end of the nineteenth century; we are now moving from national to international markets and the consequences are enormous.

Turning to the papers, unfortunately senior advocate Nariman is not here, but you have his paper. I say unfortunately because he strikes a theme that I believe is important. He writes that the primary challenge in introducing a rule of law to international trade and other issues is that the rule of law must work for people and not for profits. His concern is that great multinational corporations that bestride the world today will operate beyond the reach of national jurisdictions and may be a law unto themselves. If they are a law unto themselves, then perhaps it's inevitable that they will pursue profit alone and not be sensitive to historical and cultural differences, local values, and special local needs. My own view is that, to some extent at least, this paper exaggerates how powerless national governments are to deal with multinational corporations. If you were to put the question to a general counsel of a great international corporation and ask how easy it is to comply with the 6, 10, 20, or 40 rules of law that must be observed by the corporation doing business in that many jurisdictions, he or she would be surprised to learn that some believe national law is powerless to control the multinational corporation.

On the other hand, in a broader sense, if you examine the long-term goals of these corporations, their ability by threats of departure from a country to extract concessions and their political clout, it may very well be that these corporations do have extraordinary power—especially in smaller jurisdictions.

Vice President Tung discusses the very constructive role of the World Bank in technical assistance. The extent to which the World Bank has engaged in technical assistance throughout the world while at the same time remaining sensitive to cultural and historical differences for the most part is an underreported story. And it does seem to me the role they have played (with reservations discussed below) is highly constructive.

Turning to the last two papers, I agree with most of what Professor Trebilcock says. He argues that the criticisms of the WTO that have emerged out of the controversy in Seattle range from foolish to wrong.

I think one of the interesting aspects of this criticism is the fact that so much of it is not really directed at the WTO or GATT but is really directed at the growth of world trade, which I've already suggested is inevitable. It's criticizing the messenger for a message that must and will be delivered. The most extreme example is the criticism that self-sufficiency is preferable to dependency and therefore that increasing world trade on balance is an unwelcome development. The whole point of international trade is for companies to take advantage of their own comparative virtues. To ask Hong Kong to give up facilitating financial arrangements in favor of growing wheat seems to me the wrong approach.

Also, some of the criticisms are simply not true. It is not usually the case that world trade contributes to inequalities; if anything it helps the less-advantaged countries. In any event, Professor Trebilcock points out that differences in wealth, and they are pronounced in the world today, are probably more a result of domestic factors than of world trade.

The professor concludes with some concessions. He notes that the WTO's closed dispute settlement approach needs to be reconsidered. Dan Tarullo, I think, would add that there is another problem and that is the focus of the WTO exclusively on economics, on dollars and cents.

It seems to me there is more to arrangements to encourage world trade; there is more to world trade generally than lowering tariffs. There are issues of the environment and labor policy, among others, and they need to be addressed

successfully if the WTO is to continue to play what has been an immensely successful role up to now.

Let me turn to Dan Tarullo's paper. His scholarship is closer to my own work and therefore it's more comfortable for me to be discussing the pros and cons of his proposals. I admire Dan, in this paper and elsewhere in his scholarship, for his willingness to think outside the envelope.

He starts with the usual premises—that international law has expanded and that some of it encroaches on national law; that there are threats to national sovereignty, but national law remains exceptionally important. If we are to encourage a rule of law within a successful international economic system there must be coordination and cooperation between international groups and national institutions.

From my point of view he uses the perfect example, the Internet, which is a vast promising new medium that respects no borders and has consequences in many countries around the world.

Let me try to illustrate the point about national and international coordination with a practical example from my own experience. A few months ago the Federal Trade Commission (FTC) received an extraordinary number of complaints from consumers. They were browsing on various Web sites, such as looking for price quotes from Merrill Lynch or doing some legal research—clicking, for example, on the NYU Law Review—and suddenly they found when they clicked on the NYU Law Review they were transferred to a hard-core pornographic site with some very extreme ads on the site.

These people I suppose would have said to themselves "Well that's not the NYU Law Review that I have come to know and love (either that or the students have really taken over)." And they would then click the delete button and nothing would happen. They might click the back button, but nothing would happen. No matter what they clicked to exit this pornographic site, they were trapped in this site. How did this happen? First, a clever but unethical person living in Portugal had introduced lines of codes in thousands of Web sites in the United States that automatically kidnapped visitors from the intended site to a pornographic site. The pornographic site itself was operated by a sponsor in Australia, a relatively legitimate business, just one selling pornography. Now why would they do this? What was the point of it? The answer is that every time you clicked delete or back, every time you clicked anything on that site, a fraction of a penny went to the advertisers on that site. The money was collected by the advertiser's agent, paid to the Web site in Australia, and I assume the Web site sponsor in Australia shared the revenues with the code author in Portugal.

Now what can law enforcers in the United States do about a situation like that? What are we to do about it if the perpetrator is in Portugal and the collector of the money is in Australia? We can cancel the code introduced at the Web sites, and we did that immediately, but this person can introduce code at 10,000 or more Web sites designed to kidnap unsuspecting visitors.

This case is still pending in the Northern District of Virginia. We have had extraordinary cooperation from the government of Australia. We know who the party is, and I think we'll shut that person down. To date we have not had extraordinary cooperation from the Portugese government, and the jury is out as to whether we will be able effectively to deal with this kind of fraud. Without coordination and cooperation between government authorities there is no way there can be effective law enforcement. The only connection between that fraud and the United States is this is where the victims were. All the other parties were outside our borders, outside of our jurisdiction. The issue then is not the advisability of coordination and cooperation—it is essential—but rather how it is to be accomplished.

Dan cites three government structures, and it seems to me those are exactly what I have seen in my experience. First, countries can enter into bilateral arrangements, more or less like a contract, with respect to their commitments and responsibilities. These are on the decline, however, and probably not the wave of the future. A second possibility is detailed regulation and dispute resolution as seen with GATT and the WTO. To be sure there are occasional disputes, there are occasional flair ups, but it seems to me the WTO in the trade area serves the world and this country well. Although there are criticisms, as I mentioned earlier, and there is, I think, a need for reforms, this is a valued approach.

To me the most interesting part of Dan's paper is the discussion of regulatory convergence. In many ways it is the most efficient yet the most difficult of coordination efforts, and it will only occur if countries see that it is in their own interest to join in an effort that promises mutual shared interest rather than national advantage.

Let me refer again to my own experience in this area. On coordination and cooperation, particularly with respect to competition policy as opposed to consumer protection policy, we've made enormous strides with respect to procedural coordination. Attorneys at the FTC are on the phones working out arrangements with their counterparts in Tokyo and Brussels, in South Africa and Latin American, every single day. Cooperation is exceptional.

The question worth considering is Why stop with procedural cooperation? Why can't we begin, at least among major trading partners, to introduce substantive rules? I think we could all agree that if the rules were the same among major trading partners throughout the world, perhaps among all countries throughout the world, some efficient transactions that are now discouraged or blocked would occur, the efficiency of enforcement would improve, and consumers would be better protected. We've had some success in the substantive area. For example, there is now a single anti-cartel policy adopted by all OECD nations, and also among all countries in the Western Hemisphere.

But adoption of a single policy with respect to hard-core cartels was relatively simple because almost all countries already have an anti-cartel attitude and anti-cartel laws, so it was just a question of writing down what we all were doing already.

Suppose we try to move beyond that. The most interesting area under discussion now would be a common, substantive standard to regulate mergers because an extraordinary merger wave is not just going on in this country, it's going on in Europe and Asia as well. Why can't we have some kind of commonality of approach to mergers? It would be efficient, it would be fairer to the companies, and it would reduce regulatory burdens.

Let me state briefly what the problem is. In the United States, mergers among direct competitors begin to encounter legal problems when the combined market share is about 25 percent and there are high entry barriers. In Europe that occurs when combined market share approaches 50 percent and there are high entry barriers. In Japan, as far as the public record is concerned, there has only been one formal merger challenge in fifty years and that involved a combined market share of over 60 percent, although I am sure under "administrative guidance" other mergers have been blocked in Japan. But that process is not transparent so we don't know. Finally, there are smaller countries that will not challenge any merger that has a primary effect in their own country because their attitude is that their market is so small they not only don't need but they cannot support two, three, or four companies providing the same product.

What are we to do about convergence in a situation like that? Many conclude there is nothing that can be done. Dan and others refuse to stop at that point. What are the possibilities? One is minimum standards, so that at least we could all say anything over 60 percent is unacceptable in all of the countries that subscribe to those standards. The problem with that is it's sort of a race to the bottom. If the United States wants to stick to our standard of beginning to investigate at 25 percent, what does it do to state that, at a minimum, an international rule becomes effective at 60 percent?

One of Dan's most interesting thoughts in the paper, though he goes by it quickly, and I hope Dan will develop it in another paper, addresses the possibility of national variations within a harmonized framework. Maybe you could say the top is 60 percent and the bottom is 25 percent, and countries will adopt whatever suits their cultural and national needs within that range and then explain why it is that they hit 35, 45, or 55 percent. I'm simplifying greatly you understand. But I'm trying to make a point that—at least for the sake of argument—one could begin to converge on a single standard if you began to bring the top down and the bottom up. I don't at this time subscribe to any of these approaches but certainly see the value of discussion and debate.

Another possibility about which I'm enthusiastic is convergence by learning. Treaties are not going to solve the problem here, but what can at least address the problem is a constant exchange of views. This weeklong seminar is an example of that, where people explain what it is that they do and why. And the remarkable thing I've seen in my field is that more and more countries, recognizing the mistakes and the successes of others, begin to bring their own legal regime in line with the regimes of the other countries.

Measurement of market power is a highly technical concept, and yet today we find Europeans examining that question almost exactly the way the United States examines the same question. And that occurs not by treaty, not by contract, and not because the WTO mandated it but because people came around to the view that was the sensible thing to do.

Let me conclude very briefly by saying that it's important with respect to issues relating to convergence, and all of these cooperation efforts, not to overreach, because if we try for too much and fail we will set the whole process back. On the other hand, we ought not to give up because challenges to adoption of a coordinated and converging rule of law are so daunting. We must continue to pursue that goal.

Additional Comments

The merger wave in the United States is remarkable. In the present year it seems likely that two trillion dollars in assets will be swept up in merger activity in the United States, nine or ten times the total a little over a decade ago.

There were over 4,700 filings of mergers of significant size (over $15 million in acquired assets) in each of the past two years; this year the filings appear likely to increase another 15–20 percent.

I do not believe the merger wave itself is anything to lose sleep about. It is probably the consequence of the most dynamic economy we have seen in this country in a long time. Many of these mergers are sensible responses to changing economic conditions in particular sectors of the economy and are likely to be efficient and of benefit to consumers. Many others are neutral from a consumer welfare point of view.

There are, however, some mergers—often of megamerger proportions—among very large firms at the top of their market. It is these large mergers, often in highly concentrated markets, that attract the attention of antitrust enforcement officials.

There is also a question of trend. Even if a particular merger or series of mergers does not immediately threaten competition, antitrust enforcement must take into account not just short-term effects but where the trend appears to be leading. I don't believe we are anywhere near an economywide threat of excessive concentration, but in particular sectors of the economy one must be alert to cumulative anticompetitive effects.

Closing Remarks

Harry T. Edwards

The topic of today's discussion, "Corporate Power, National Sovereignty, and the Rule of Law in a Global Economy," is admittedly broad. It is not surprising, therefore, that no single theme emanates from the panelists' papers. Nonetheless, the panelists today have been illuminating, thought-provoking, and provocative in probing the contours of the rule of law in a global economy.

It is often said that beauty is in the eye of the beholder. The same can be said about assessments of the global economy. Professor Tarullo has reminded us that the basic functions of law in a market economy often are in conflict. Thus, debates continue over the acceptable scope of each function and over the optimal reconciliation of conflicts. In particular, the leaders of our global economy—both government officials and private entrepreneurs—continue to ponder whether and how we should move from the prevailing international regime that stresses limiting the regulatory discretion of national governments. In other words, should international economic law have broader purposes, and, if so, how should these purposes be defined and enforced?

The papers for today's session have tended to focus on international trade organizations, like the World Trade Organization and the World Bank, and the ways in which they facilitate free trade and market growth. Save for the paper by Fali Nariman, however, not much has been said about the impact of corporate power on the rule of law in the global economy. This is somewhat surprising, because there is no reason for us to assume that multinational corporations and organizations such as the WTO always share common goals. And history certainly shows that the means taken by international trade organizations and private corporations to achieve their respective goals are quite different. It is true that there is always the potential that the sovereign power of a nation-state may be used to curb corporate power

within that nation. But we also know that some nations have no incentive to curb corporate power if it will come at the expense of economic growth; some developing nations may lack the power to control large, multinational corporations; and no nation alone has the power to control the acts of a multinational corporation outside its borders. We are therefore left with the question whether international organizations can, or even should, seek to prevent the incursion by multinational corporations on national sovereignty.

This question leads in turn to the ever perplexing issues focused on the relationship between the global economy, democratic institutions, and international standards of basic human rights. More particularly, we must consider to what extent discussions of the global economy must include a dialogue on rights and democracy. We need only think of the perennial debates in the United States over China's inclusion in the WTO to remind ourselves that this question is neither abstract nor rhetorical. Is it correct, as Professor Trebilcock suggests, to elevate the right to engage in consensual market transactions to the same level of importance as the right to education, health care, and basic material well-being? Even if we accept that these rights should be equally valued, are there ways in which they are in tension with each other? When we emphasize the importance of the rule of law in attaining global economic stability and prosperity, do we care what form that rule of law takes? And how do we achieve consensus among national governments on substantive standards and schemes of enforcement with respect to matters that may directly affect important social and political issues within national borders? These questions require more reflection than I can muster from where I am sitting, but the panelists have pushed us to consider these matters.

Finally, some of the discussion today unavoidably calls into question our existing measures of economic growth and development. A strong assumption is made that reducing barriers to international trade is important in encouraging economic development. Most traditional measures of development, however, such as gross national product, do not take into account distributional considerations. If we are to think seriously about a rule of law in a global economy, should we take account of distributional inequities? Or is it enough merely to leave such matters to the political resolutions of each nation-state?

I think that it is fair to conclude this session by posing one of the hardest questions implicit in today's discussion: Can we really divorce international economic issues from national social issues, as some commentators appear to suggest? In other words, if nations are largely unwilling to cede control over social issues to international agencies, and if the global economy invariably will affect the social circumstances of every nation within it, are not international economic issues and national social issues inexorably tied together? It seems to me that the proponents of "divorce" must then accept that national self-interest always will operate as an inherent limitation on the so-called rule of law in the global economy. A contrary view, as we now hear in the current debates over the inclusion of China in the WTO, is that open markets invariably will undermine short-sighted national political regimes and promote social advances across national borders. These are very different positions and neither one is without flaws.

The panel discussion today has been immensely useful in addressing these and other very important questions and in giving us food for thought as we continue to ponder corporate power, national sovereignty, and the rule of law in a global economy. I thank the panelists for their splendid contributions to this most intriguing international symposium on democracy and the rule of law.

Hundreds of thousands of Hutu Rwandan refugees in flight. *Source:* © Mariella Furrer/SABA, 1996.

Session 7

The State and
Human Rights

Editors' Note

In 1215 the Magna Carta of England formally embodied the concept of individual rights against a sovereign based on "the law of the land," but the idea that law is superior to the ruler traces far earlier to China and the Greek city-states several centuries before the Christian era. Yet it was not until 1947 that the international community dedicated itself to a set of principles that would, if implemented, promote human dignity and comprehensively protect individuals and groups against arbitrary discrimination of all kinds. Nevertheless, because of the importance of human rights and because we continue to witness in all parts of the world the most egregious violations of the human body and spirit, both by governments and other entities, we devoted a conference session to human rights and their protection.

The papers address several key issues, all premised on the values of universality and neutrality. Robert Badinter discusses the role of the nation-state in redressing human rights violations through judicial review and the more recent contributions of regional and international tribunals, including the International Criminal Court that soon will be established. Philip Alston concentrates on the lack of accountability of transnational corporations, liberation movements, and the World Bank and International Monetary Fund, none of which is a state entity and none of which is a full partner in the human rights enterprise. And Andras Sajo explores the serious implications for a democratic society of government speech, which can both contribute to or distort the public dialogue in varied circumstances. Ratna Kapur's comment challenges these perspectives by forcefully suggesting that the ideals of universality and neutrality are a heritage of a colonial past and that they reinforce a majoritarian politics and threaten difference and diversity.

The State and Human Rights

Robert Badinter

Traditionally, the role of democratic states is seen as the protection of human and citizens rights, notably through judicial review. In France since the Revolution, this role has been played by Parliament. The rise of constitutionalism only led to the introduction of a unique but imperfect form of judicial review in 1958.

Since the Second World War, democratic states have developed the international protection of human rights through multilateral conventions and control mechanisms to prevent their violation by states. The future of protection of human rights against the worst and most massive violations is the creation of an international criminal court.

1. The State as Protector of Human Rights

France prides itself on its reputation as one of the birthplaces of human rights in Europe. Without wishing to dwell upon the historical causes, it must be stressed that France has long remained fascinated by the primordial importance of the state, its different institutional organization and normative functions. The state is seen as the personification of the sovereign, which explains why it was difficult to conceive of legislation being called into question by a judge.

Thus France, permeated by the philosophy of the Enlightenment, followed the path of "legicentrism" (the so-called cult of legislation and parliament) until the rise of constitutionalism (A). This finally led to the introduction of a unique but imperfect form of judicial review (B).

A. France: From Legicentrism to Constitutionalism

The 1789 Declaration of the Rights of Man and Citizen represents in many ways the most radical departure from the *ancien régime*. It can be regarded as the founding act of a new political society. Ironically, it was in the name of this declaration that legislation became omnipotent (i), long before the same declaration allowed the assertion of constitutionalism (ii).

(i) The 1789 declaration is assuredly a founding act because it no longer places the source of all power in an absolute monarch of divine origin but in the nation. As a consequence of this real reversal of perspective, the law was defined as the expression of the will of the people. This was interpreted as implying that any legislative norm must be indisputable because nobody could object to the will of the people, especially not the courts (called "parliaments" in the ancien régime), which had successfully opposed the king in the past through their right of reproof. This souvenir, along with a misunderstanding of Montesquieu's famous theory of the separation of powers, which describes the judge as a simple "mouth of the law," comforted the revolutionaries to such a point that several texts referred to the sacred nature of the law. Thus, Article 10 of a law voted on August 10, 1790, clearly states that "courts shall not take part directly or indirectly in the exercise of legislative power, neither prevent or suspend the execution of decrees of the Legislative Assembly promulgated by the King, on pain of felony." The 1791 Constitution prescribed—in its Title III, Chapter V, Article 3—that "courts may not interfere in the exercise of legislative power nor suspend the execution of laws." These references participated therefore in the consecration of a "legal" state, which led rapidly to the transfer of national sovereignty into the hands of Parliament.

The link between law and the legitimacy of representatives of the nation promptly became indissoluble to the extent that any attempt, including the most prudent, to submit the law to even the most mediocre review was interpreted by members of Parliament as a violation of their power. French public law reflects this denial of any interference whatsoever with legislative power by courts. The law was thus inaccessible to judicial contradiction, and little by little the dogma of the infallibility of the legislator replaced the old maxim of the ancient law according to which the king may do no wrong.

Before 1958, legicentrism and its corollary, parliamentary omnipotence dominated French constitutional history. Nevertheless, affirmations of constitutionalism were not lacking.

(ii) The 1789 declaration itself limited the law. For example, Article 5 provides that "the law may only forbid acts that are harmful to society," and Article 8 that "The law may establish only those punishments, which are strictly and clearly necessary." These material limits on the law are the direct echo of the preamble of the declaration, according to which ". . . acts of the legislative and the executive powers, when constantly compared with the purpose of all political institutions, are more respected. . . ." However, Article 16 is without doubt the paradigmatic expression of the essence of this text from which all the rest follows: "Any society in which the guarantee of rights is not ensured nor the separation of power determined, has no constitution." These questions of the guarantee of rights and the separation of powers are in fact one and the same. During the debate on the text of the declaration, Rhedon, one of the contributors, made a clear proposal that, although it was not adopted, underlined the unity of the two questions: "it is the distribution wisely combined of the various authorities that ensures the rights of citizens; and such is the object of the Constitution." The legislative power is not exempt from this rule. It remains that, to be effective, such a principle supposes the existence of appropriate means of control. As mentioned above, courts were denied such jurisdiction. Nevertheless, during the nineteenth and twentieth centuries several proposals were made to create a specialized organ in charge of constitutional review.

The first worth noting was the proposal by Sieyes for the creation of a "jury constitutionnaire" in the Constitution of "an III." To be composed of 108 members chosen among the members of previous parliaments,

this jury was to have the "special mission of hearing any complaint concerning the violation of the constitution" (Moniteur, 293). Sieyes anticipated three specific functions for this jury, including judicial review of the acts of the two houses of Parliament and of local assemblies at the request of the opposition within these bodies, a superior court, or even directly by citizens. The drafters rejected the proposal unanimously. This debate, ambitious at the time, showed that judicial review of law was already a subject of concern for the revolutionaries. It should be noted in this respect that the Napoleonic constitutions of 1799 and 1852 established a form of review but by a political body: the conservative Senate. Those two Senates were clearly under the political authority of the emperor and never had sufficient independence for such a sensitive function. They failed because the political situation was unfitted to civil liberties and fundamental rights. Nevertheless, this fed the existing distrust of proponents of legislative supremacy. It was not until the Third Republic that the necessity for a real review was recognized in French doctrine. As a result, a new attempt was made by the Constituent Assembly, which wrote the Constitution of the Fourth Republic. Composed of ten members chosen by the National Assembly, the Council of the Republic (upper house), and the president of the Republic, the Constitutional Committee had only limited powers. It could suggest, at the joint request of the head of state and the Speaker of the two houses, that if the Constitution could not be revised they amend the law to bring it into conformity with the Constitution. In addition, this limited power only applied to provisions concerning the organization of public authorities. As one might expect, this procedure was only used once, and was of little or no significance.

Be that as it may, these unsuccessful attempts underline the fact that the dominant theory of legicentrism was a betrayal of the 1789 declaration. Constitutionalism, on the contrary, respectful of the philosophy of the declaration, focused on the political and legal superiority of the constitution over any other norm. Traditionally, the constitution is defined as the fundamental law as well as the social pact of the nation. But even more important is its contribution to the normative hierarchy. The constitution, at the top of the hierarchy, is no longer an end in itself but a guarantee of the rights of the individual.

B. Originality of the French Model of Judicial Review

This rapid skimming of French constitutional history helps to understand why the creation of the Constitutional Council in 1958 (Constitution of the Fifth Republic) was met with skepticism. Its supporters believed that it could only achieve a limited mission; others that it would obey General de Gaulle just as the conservative Senate had obeyed Napoleon. In fact, the destiny of the Constitutional Council as we can now see, was completely different and totally unforeseen at the beginning of the Fifth Republic. Often presented as an element of rupture with the long tradition of parliamentary sovereignty, it reflects, in reality, the very principle laid down in the 1789 declaration: the guarantee of rights based on the separation of powers. Therefore, French judicial review is special (i), but limited (ii).

(i) Initially conceived as a weapon against deviations of the parliamentary regime, the Constitutional Council's nickname was "the watchdog of the executive." Both its jurisdiction and trigger mechanism were signs of this rationalized regime: besides its jurisdictions over electoral matters (for presidential and general elections) and the organization of referenda, the council had, and still has, the principal mission of reviewing the conformity of bills enacted by Parliament to the Constitution. This review must take place immediately after the vote in Parliament and before promulgation of the law. It was meant to prevent the legislative power from intruding upon executive powers. It is particularly topical that "organic" laws (which implement the Constitution) and the rule of parliamentary procedure are submitted to systematic judicial review. To make sure that members of Parliament respect the limits imposed by the Constitution, the Constitutional Council regulates the activity of the public authorities. Nevertheless, the French model of judicial review has changed profoundly over the last forty years, developing into a unique system.

From a strictly legal point of view, it was the decision that the preamble of the 1958 Constitution forms an integral part of the constitutional text that changed the essence of the Constitutional Council's control, because the preamble refers directly to the 1789 declaration of human rights together with the economic and social rights proclaimed by the 1946 Constitution (Fourth Republic). The first reference to the preamble appeared in a decision of June 19, 1970. But the relevant precedent is the decision of July 16, 1971, in which the council not only relied upon the 1958 preamble but also, as a consequence, the texts of 1789 and 1946 in stating that "among the fundamental principles recognized by the law of the Republic, solemnly reaffirmed by the Preamble of the Constitution, is the principle of freedom of association." In a subsequent decision on December 27, 1973, the council expressly referred to the 1789 declaration. Henceforth, over and above the formal regularity of the law attached, the Constitutional Council also examines the material content of the law to review its conformity with the Constitution and its preamble. Overruling for the first time a law voted by Parliament on the grounds of violation of a constitutional freedom proclaimed in the preamble, the council definitively devoted its jurisdiction to the protection of fundamental liberties. From 1971 on, the council was no longer the docile protector of the executive power.

A second factor had an important influence on this evolution: the extension of the trigger mechanism of the council's jurisdiction. Initially, only the president of the Republic, the prime minister, the president of the National Assembly, and the president of the Senate could solicit the council's advice. This limit was in accordance with the narrow jurisdiction then recognized to the Constitutional Council. In this context judicial review was inaccessible to the political opposition. Unsurprisingly, a constitutional amendment adopted in 1974, authorizing sixty members of the National Assembly or sixty senators to bring a case before the Constitutional Council, contributed to the rapid and irresistible development of the activity of the council. Since then, judicial review has become an important element of the political life of the Fifth Republic: the political opposition, in order to show its disagreement, triggers judicial review more and more often in the name of the protection of fundamental rights. This has permitted the council to assert itself and play a major role in the democratic balance of the regime.

Of course, in our modern parliamentary systems, most laws voted by Parliament are in fact of governmental origin. Thus judicial review of basic legislation is no longer seen as a severe limit on Parliament. It is much more a limitation of the law understood as the product of a complex legislative machinery in which government and public servants have a dominant influence. The objective of judicial review is to guarantee fundamental rights through the application of constitutional norms exclusively interpreted by the Constitutional Council, "mouthpiece of the sovereign people," which adopted the Constitution. This implies strict separation of powers: the organs created by the Constitution (especially the executive and legislative organs) are distinct from the sovereign people, author of the Constitution.

In some ways the French model is closer to the European model, created by Hans Kelsen, than to the American. The European model is now centralized, a single specialized court exercising judicial review, only upon special request, in a separate case. This implies a theoretical control of legislation resulting eventually in the absolute invalidation of the law, which cannot then enter into force. The American model of judicial review, on the other hand, is based on a general jurisdiction of all the courts under the appellate authority of the Supreme Court of the United States and operates *in concreto* after adoption of the law. But the French model is not completely Kelsenian, because the Constitutional Council can only act at the request of political authorities.

No doubt this particularity facilitated the acceptance of review by traditionally hostile French politicians. The council carefully developed its jurisdiction over rights and fundamental liberties, contributing to the pacification of the political debate notably when the Left took power for the first time during periods of so called "cohabitation." Nowadays, council decisions are constantly taken into account, from government preparation of law all through parliamentary hearings. Far from reducing the power of Parliament, the council's case law helps the legislative power to define its own field of competence and offers to the opposition the chance to contest dangerous laws.

Aware of the susceptibility of members of Parliament, the Constitutional Council has taken care to state that it does not, in any case, exercise a power similar to that of Parliament, that is, decide on the political appropriateness of a new law: a bad law is not necessarily unconstitutional. Similarly, the council has developed a review technique by which the law is declared valid under strict conditions of interpretation. This binding interpretation is part of the council's decision, and, therefore, as such the administration and the court must respect it.

(ii) The French model of judicial review is not, however, exempt from criticism. First of all, France does not fully comply with the tenets of the rule of law, which requires effective judicial review. Despite the 1974 constitutional amendment, many laws enacted by Parliament are not submitted to the constitutional scrutiny of the council before their entry into force. This was the case, for example, with the penal code adopted in 1992, although the necessity for such an important law is obvious. The reasons that lead political authorities to request constitutional scrutiny or not are undoubtedly multiple and based on a political analysis of the legislation, with a constant focus on public opinion. When consensus emerges among political parties, constitutional problems are often put aside. This shows the limits of the French system: political questions can freeze judicial review, without consideration always being given to constitutional necessities. Another limit comes from the fact that legislation exposed to scrutiny, having been voted just days before, has not yet developed its full legal effects. The council may consider the law, which may later prove to have unconstitutional effects.

This is why many support the idea of a new constitutional amendment allowing citizens to trigger judicial review. An attempt was made in 1990 with a draft constitutional amendment whose adoption failed in the Senate. Since then, political specialists seem pessimistic about this reform, stating that the political conditions would never be united and therefore that it is useless to continue to promote it. This analysis does not take into account the slow but persistent evolution of French mentalities as regards democratic control of public authorities. No doubt, one day this reform will be adopted. In addition, one has to keep in mind that France is now in a paradoxical situation.

As mentioned above, French courts, whether civil or administrative, don't have jurisdiction as regards constitutional review. They have constantly confirmed this approach. On the other hand, however, the courts overrule domestic legislation in violation of an international treaty ratified by France. Thus, French judges constantly interpret laws in the light of a higher ranking norm, an international treaty, according to Article 55 of the Constitution, which provides that, "treaties and agreements regularly ratified or approved have, from their publication, an authority superior to that of the law." Because France is a party to the European Convention on Human Rights, the court reviewed French law against the fundamental rights protected by the convention. Most of these rights are actually constitutional rights only protected by the Constitutional Council's judicial review. This situation is not satisfactory, as citizens cannot challenge a domestic law before the Constitutional Council on the basis of a violation of fundamental rights recognized in the Constitution, whereas they can challenge the same law before the ordinary courts on the basis of a violation of a treaty that protects the same rights. Once again, the need seems obvious to change the Constitution in order to give citizens the right to challenge laws before the Constitutional Council. This would be a great step forward for the rule of law, as well as a return to the sources of the Republic. The philosopher Alain idealized the Republic in 1910 in writing that universal suffrage alone does not characterize democracy: "what counts is the efficient and continuous control of the governed people over governments . . . Where is democracy if not in this third power that political science has not defined at all, the one I call the Controller?"

This paradox shows that France has progress to make in order to introduce a real judicial review. It also underlines that human rights protection is no longer, at least in Europe, an exclusively state prerogative. Beyond the state, and sometimes against it, human rights are essentially universal.

2. Human Rights Beyond the State

After a long and chaotic struggle, human rights have finally earned their proper place envisaged by the revolutionary reformers. A cornerstone of the state, human rights occupy the summit of the hierarchy of norms and permeate its structure. True to the revolutionary axiom, the state, in a way, "enshrines" human rights. However, the respect for the rule of law that this implies is not an end in itself. A constant requirement, the guarantee of rights here and now, implies permanent revival, an untiring scrutiny of society. Because humans change, their dignity must be preserved perpetually.

The international protection of human rights has burst forth thanks to an acute rise in political consciousness during this century. Was there a change in logic at that time? Was the nature of the protection of human rights altered in some way? It might seem so if one accepts that the state is not only the natural framework for the guarantee of rights but also its impregnable horizon. Alternatively, consider that the state has the monopoly over the destiny of this substance, the "human right," due to the "sacred" mandate of the sovereign. However, the state cannot create human rights because it did not create humanity. By their very essence, human rights are universal; every human is entitled to them, and neither history nor geography can alter them. Over and above any specific formulation set down within a given legal system, ultimately, the contents of these rights cannot depend on states, as well intentioned as the state may be.

On the contrary, what could be more satisfying than the international recognition of universal rights? The universality of human rights thus justifies supplementary protection of rights through a legal and intellectual framework that exceeds the state alone. Moreover, the state being fallible, the international protection of human rights is not only justified but also indispensable. Although the state's primary mission is to guarantee these rights, when it does not completely fulfill its mission, or even threatens fundamental liberties, then succor must be found elsewhere through the application of international norms and, if necessary, by international courts.

If international human rights protection is, theoretically, a simple continuation of national protection, states did not immediately perceive it as such. For too long the terrible maxim attributed to Goebbels has prevailed, "The Reich will do as it will wish with the Jews, the Communists, and our enemies. That is entirely our business. We are the only masters at home." The Nazi regime took the consequences of this reasoning to a paroxysm of horror, proving by negation that the state cannot pretend to be the exclusive guarantor of human rights. Thus, several centuries after the proclamation of the natural and universal rights of man, their "natural" form of protection—that is, international—finally took form after 1945.

The successive steps are well known: the Universal Declaration in 1948, the two covenants in 1966, and the parallel development of humanitarian law through the Geneva Conventions in 1949 and the protocols thereto in 1977. Accompanying this universal progression, specific efforts have led to the adoption of regional conventions taking account of local traditions.

The relationship between the state and human rights has been the subject of a double evolution in favor of international human rights protection: the hierarchy of norms has been enriched by a new level (A), and national courts coexist, henceforth, with other, international, control bodies (B).

A. International Conventions and Internal Norms

Since the end of the Second World War, treatymaking activity with respect to the fundamental human rights has been particularly strong. The Universal Declaration, the fiftieth anniversary of which we celebrated last year, first led to the adoption of the two United Nations Covenants of 1966, transforming the moral exhortations of that most famous of General Assembly resolutions into binding rules of international law. This ensemble, known as the International Bill of Rights, is the foundation of all international human rights protection. Texts agreed to by consensus, they incarnate a fundamental compact of the international community. Subsequent treatymaking activity has essentially consisted either in strengthening the guarantee of specific fundamental liberties, particularly in time of war, or in enumerating the substance of these rights as applied to specific categories of protected persons. Among the treaties included in the first tendency one finds the conventions relating to the prohibition of racial discrimination, apartheid, torture, and the prevention and repression of genocide. The sec-

ond tendency has led to a multitude of treaties covering the protection of refugees, combatants, civilians, workers, children, and minorities.

Similarly, the development of a regional law of human rights has allowed a certain number of like-minded states to offer themselves a higher level of protection. The European example is exemplary. For over fifty years the "old Continent" has shown impressive vitality: along with the European Convention for the Protection of Human Rights and Fundamental Freedoms, signed in 1950, which remains the most comprehensive model for international protection (Cohen, Jonathan 1999), the Council of Europe has also elaborated a European social charter. Within the framework of the European Union, the treaties signed in Maastricht and Amsterdam contain numerous provisions concerning the protection of fundamental rights. Finally, within a wider European context, the Organization for Security and Cooperation in Europe also plays a role in the defense of human rights since the adoption of the Helsinki Final Act in 1975. Traumatized by two major conflicts in the space of half a century, Europe, more than any other region of the world, has understood the inestimable value of the respect of human rights for durable peace.

This international codification work was so dynamic that, counting regional conventions, there are now close to 150 treaties. The credit is largely due to international organizations stimulating effective frameworks for diplomatic negotiations. With the years some conventions have been ratified by the quasi totality of UN member states (Geneva Conventions, New York Convention on the Rights of the Child). With such a profusion of treaties, human rights might appear to run the risk of a conflict of laws. In fact, the substantial convergence between all of these international instruments should be stressed. Moreover, without wishing to enter into details, it should be noted that the basic rule of interpretation of fundamental human rights requires the application of the most favorable norm. Thus universal, regional, general, and specialized rules coexist in relative harmony and, through a liberal interpretation of these instruments, international control organs sometimes draw upon the whole body of rules to ensure greater protection. The European Commission of Human Rights has thus recognized, in *obiter dictum,* that "it may well be useful, in interpreting the provisions of the Convention, to take account of the terms of other international legal instruments which ensure greater protection of fundamental rights than is provided for in the Convention, without ascribing a meaning to the dispositions of the Convention which the High Contracting Parties expressly wished to exclude." (*Gestra v. Italy,* Decision N 21072/92, 16 January 1995.)

The aim is therefore to set minimum standards for all. The individual must be able to have recourse to these standards in order to rectify any deficiency in domestic law. Does this mean that international law replaces domestic law? Nothing is less certain. The majority of international conventions insist that it is, first, the responsibility of states to protect and promote human rights. In democratic states, national constitutions as well as constitutional case law very often meet international provisions on rights and liberties. The question is to determine in each state how the national judge is going to enforce international norms.

It is indeed each judicial system, according to its constitutional provisions, that determines the "reception" of these international norms. Some states demand a transposition of the international norm while others directly incorporate treaties to their legislation at the same level of authority as domestic law or at a higher level (Article 55 of the French Constitution). Whichever system one chooses, the international norm influence is considerable. Little by little, these norms of a particular symbolic nature penetrate internal judicial orders, mostly through constitutional case law. In 1993 the Ninth Conference of European Constitutional Courts met in Paris to analyze the nature of the relationship between national and international protection of human rights. Competitive or complementary? was the question asked, and once each European Court had explained its system and experience the conclusion came as no surprise: it is for constitutional courts to conciliate the contribution of international law and the protection of these rights, and the domestic case law is often similar to that of the international judge. Whether by deliberate effort or through an almost natural concordance of views, they generally take similar positions on the same problems.

Domestic courts are thus, effectively, the "common law courts of first instance" for the application of the international law of human rights. This is all the more so since individuals may rely upon the international norms in question directly before domestic courts. Even so, the self-executing nature of conventional provisions depends as much on the will of state parties, as expressed in the treaty, as on the clarity and precision of its provisions, all subject to interpretation by the domestic courts. Judicial creation then becomes fundamental: the ambit of the international convention in domestic law can vary considerably according to whether direct application is accepted by the domestic judge or not. In France, the case law remains prudent (sometimes excessively), especially since its dual court system leads to a certain amount of variation between the civil law courts and the administrative tribunals. If the European Human Rights Convention is recognized as self-executing, as is the United Nations Covenant on civil and political rights, this is not the case for either the Covenant on Social and Economic Rights or the Convention on the Rights of the Child. The Cour de Cassation (France's highest civil court of appeal) has denied any direct application to the Convention of New York, whereas the Council of State (France's highest administrative court) has identified a certain number of specific provisions conferring rights on children and has recognized their direct effect. As a result, a certain number of claims based on the relevant articles of the convention have thus been heard.

Clearly, far from eclipsing domestic law, the international protection of human rights nourishes a continuous dialogue between the different levels of the hierarchy of norms specific to each legal system. Case law plays a fundamental role here; the accent should be placed on the convergence and correlative nature of domestic and international systems, especially since (and therein resides the real "revolution") national courts no longer have a monopoly on scrutiny in this field.

B. International Control Organs

Indeed, it is written that revolution and human rights would have a long, common history (the term "revolutionary" is not inappropriate to the international law of human rights) as the advent of this new branch of international law has rocked the well-established framework of international society.

The creation and extraordinary development of international mechanisms for the control of state action concerning fundamental rights is the most convincing demonstration of this. As the UN secretary-general pointed out in 1993 during the opening ceremony of the World Conference on Human Rights in Vienna: "At present, it seems less urgent to define new rights than to bring States to adopt existent texts and to apply them effectively." States have thus accepted, by treaty, the traditional expression of state sovereignty, the principle of centralized evaluation of the application of their conventional obligations. The form taken by such control varies considerably according to the convention, but it is possible to distinguish schematically, for our purposes, two major categories: on the one hand, international organs, the operation and competence of which follow an interstate logic (i), and on the other hand, real courts that go beyond the veil of the state to make direct contact with the individual subject of international law, holders' of rights and duties (ii).

(i) The principle extralegal procedures are concentrated, at the universal level, in the activities of the two Human Rights Committees and the UN Commission of Human Rights. The former were created respectively by the international covenants on civil and political rights and on economic and social rights. The Human Rights Commission is none other than a commission of the United Nations Economic and Social Council and thus does not rely upon any specific human rights treaty (apart from the UN charter, of course). In addition to these "general" organs, some international conventions in the penal area also set up committees responsible for following up on the implementation of the convention by state parties. This is the case, in particular, for the convention on torture and the convention on the elimination of all racial discrimination. (It may thus be noted that this sort of control concentrates mainly on civil and political rights to the detriment of economic and social rights.)

The most frequently used tool for the control of the activity of states remains that of periodic reports exchanged between committees and state parties. Composed of experts, the committees examine whether states have adopted the necessary internal legislation and ensure the promotion of the rights concerned. They also have the competence to make any recommendation that may appear necessary.

By virtue of the fundamental principle *Pacta sunt servanda,* such reports should not shock the supporters of state sovereignty unduly: they are simply a centralized form of verification of the application in good faith of international commitments. The novelty resides in the publicity given to such procedures and the possibility for discussion of the national reports in the light of the experience of nongovernmental organizations involved in the protection of human rights. The universality of human rights justifies such transparency, even if only partial. The logic of transparency and control is so strong in the domain of human rights that these nonjudicial mechanisms have gradually developed more rigorous procedures to states, whether it be the nomination by the UN Human Rights Commission of special rapporteurs on the situation of human rights in specific states or through the adoption of additional protocols allowing individual petitions. In the latter case, a panel of experts examines individual claims, and the state must at least bring counter arguments and explain its behavior. The intrusion of the individual onto the international scene, to ask the state to respect his or her rights, destabilizes the classical system of scrutiny by domestic courts. In theory, the state masters these new developments as it is free to refuse to adhere to the procedures in question. But it is becoming harder and harder for a state to claim to respect the rule of law while denying individuals subject to its court access to international commissions and committees. The right of petition or individual claim, although of variable importance depending on the treaty in question, remains therefore the main form of international protection of human rights.

The ideal of effective international protection seems to be within reach once real courts, handing down their decisions after a contradictory procedure opposing individual and state, impose their obligatory interpretation of international human rights.

(ii) The most accomplished example of this process remains the European Court of Human Rights set up within the Council of Europe. Indeed, since 1950 state members must respect the European Convention for the Protection of Human Rights and must submit to its organs any dispute between states or between a state and an individual concerning the interpretation of the convention. Until recently, the European Commission of Human Rights decided on the validity of petitions and attempted to find a friendly settlement or, if necessary, referred the question to the European Court or the Committee of Ministers for final judgment. At the outset, indeed, states could choose an "intergovernmental" judgment rather than the judicial option. In addition, they were not obliged to grant the right of petition to individuals under their jurisdiction. France ratified the convention in 1974 but only accepted the individual right of petition (Article 25) in 1981. Like many states, and even more so by reason of its historical pretensions, up until then France nurtured a certain distrust for any body empowered to dictate the law in place of the state. Twenty-five later years, although the court has condemned France, nobody has come forward to question the legitimacy of the decision as a violation of sovereignty or interference in the internal affairs of the state. The success of this ambitious European model is partly due to its ability to impose its case law progressively while avoiding direct confrontation with states by preserving dialogue with governments and by developing an ensemble of autonomous legal concepts, a sort of European common law. From the beginning, the court and the commission have managed to accompany the evolution of moral values and contemporary judicial concerns through a liberal interpretation of the provisions of the European Convention. There is no lack of examples: censure of states refusing modifications to the legal status for transsexuals in the name of the right to private life, limits on the expulsion of residents without valid papers by reference to the right to family life, condemnation of certain penitentiary treatments inflicted on terrorists of the IRA by British authorities as a violation of the right not to undergo cruel, inhuman, or degrading treatment, banning extradition to the United States where capital prisoners are subjected to the corridor of death syndrome before execution, and violation of the right not to undergo torture by French police for brutality against a suspect.

Membership of the Council of Europe has risen to forty since the collapse of Communism, an ideology that denied the indivisibility of human rights by subordinating civil and political rights to economic and social rights. The major challenge for European protection is now to preserve indispensable coherence or run the risk of instituting a sort of "two speed" protection differentiating the standards applied to old and new members. A reform decided upon in 1998, with the coming into force of Protocol 11 to the convention, attempts to raise this challenge. Henceforth, the commission/court tandem has given way to a single court with compulsory jurisdiction for all state parties, including individual petitions. The new system is also intended to shorten prehearing delays. At the same time, the Council of Europe has developed intense cooperative relations with the new members to ensure smooth integration into the European system of protecting human rights. The task is immense due to the serious difficulties encountered by the legal systems of numerous central and eastern European countries. Moreover, some new members do not seem to have gained the maturity necessary for acceptance of all the consequences of the European system as evidenced by the categorical refusal by Russia to account for its action in Chechnya despite the fact that violations of fundamental liberties can no longer be dismissed as an internal affair.

The way to the future of the protection of human rights against the worst and most massive violations is the creation of an international criminal court.

On 18 July 1998, in Rome, the treaty creating the International Criminal Court (ICC) was adopted after years of preparatory work and decades of jurisprudential activism. The entry into force of the court depends henceforth on reaching the required level of ratification. At the heart of this movement aimed at the establishment of the International Criminal Court is the belief that the protection of fundamental human rights requires international repression of the most serious crimes committed against humanity where competent states fail to do so. The aim is therefore to remedy the deficiencies of states by exercising criminal justice in the name of the international community. Clearly, there is not yet perfect consensus concerning this postulate. Some states deny any such international pretension and have no intention to participate. Perhaps it should be recalled that the ICC has

no jurisdiction to judge states but only individuals suspected of transgressing core rights. Of course, the repression of such crimes is the primary responsibility of states,
and the creation of the ICC does not change this.
Nonetheless, given that the universality of human rights
has been asserted for more than fifty years and that
international protection of human rights has pierced
the veil placed between individuals and international
justice, it is impossible to resign oneself to the impunity
of the perpetrators of war crimes and crimes against
humanity when they are shamefully and illegally protected by a state. This compelling obligation underscores the creation by the UN Security Council of the
ad hoc tribunals for the former Yugoslavia and Rwanda
in 1993 and 1995 after the international crimes committed in these two states.

The state can no longer claim the monopoly over
repression of the most serious violations of human
rights as though this were an absolute principle. The fallibility of the state justifies international repression. In
this respect, the Pinochet case shows that, in the
absence of effective international repression, the refusal
of impunity by a very large section of public opinion
supported by a democratic state leads to resort to other,
more complex, legal means. But those remedies appear
unpredictable in the result unless transparent and really
international.

Rather than turning their backs on these seemingly
irreversible and most desirable developments, democratic states must, with due vigilance, accompany this
new stage in the protection of human rights because
they have dedicated themselves to this end.

Downsizing the State in Human Rights Discourse

Philip Alston

Introduction

The rule that requires editors at the United Nations to always capitalize the word "State" in any UN document goes well beyond symbolism.[1] There is great significance in the fact that no matter how subversive of the legitimacy of a given state a particular analysis might be, every human rights document produced under the auspices of the United Nations requires its author(s) to genuflect in this way before the altar of "State" sovereignty every time the word is mentioned. Apart from recalling the insistence of religious publications that god must always be acknowledged as God, this usage also announces to the world the continuing validity of the assumptions of 1945 when the charter was drafted. It thus sets certain assumptions in stone at a time when they need to be rethought if prevailing realities are to be reflected in the institutional and substantive policy context within which the UN operates and within which international human rights discourse tends to be located. None of this is to suggest that the state is not important, let alone to endorse the more extreme versions of the "state is dead" thesis. It is simply to underline the fact that the world is a much more polycentric place than it was in 1945, and that she who sees the world solely, or even essentially, through the prism of the "State" will be seeing a rather distorted image as we enter the twenty-first century.

In looking at the subject of this panel, "The State and Human Rights," we cannot but be struck by the fact that most analyses of human rights divide the conceptual universe into two parts: the state (or rather the "State") and the rest, which are identified only by reference to the fact that they are not to be equated with the state. Thus civil society actors are described as *nongovernmental* organizations. Terrorist groups or others threatening the state's monopoly of power are delicately referred to as *nonstate* actors. So too are transnational corporations and multinational banks, despite their somewhat more benign influence. International institutions, including those that wield immense influence while disavowing all pretensions to exercise authority per se, such as the International Monetary Fund and the World Bank, are classified as *nonstate* entities.

Apart from its ability to obfuscate almost any debate, this insistence upon defining all actors in terms of what they are not combines both impeccable purism in terms of traditional international legal analysis with an unparalleled capacity to marginalize a significant part of the international human rights regime from the most vital challenges confronting global governance at the dawn of the twenty-first century. In essence, these negative, euphemistic terms stem not from language inadequacies but instead have been intentionally adopted in order to reinforce the assumption that the state is not only the central actor but also the indispensable and pivotal one around which all other entities revolve. Accordingly, for the purposes of international legal discourse—the language of human rights—those other entities can only be identified in terms of their relationship to the state. Anything that is not a state, whether it be me, IBM, the IMF, Shell, Sendero Luminoso, or Amnesty International, is conceptualized as not being a state and thus not having a place at the top table when matters of international law in general, and human rights in particular, are being examined.

The thrust of this paper is that such a unidimensional or monochromatic way of viewing the world is not only misleading but makes it much more difficult to adapt the human rights regime in order to take adequate account of the fundamental changes that have occurred in recent years. The challenge that it lays down is one of reimagining, as the social scientists would put it, the nature of the human rights regime and the relationships among the different actors within it. Lawyers, not being noted for their creativity, might prefer to see the task in terms of reinterpreting existing concepts and procedures rather than reimagining. Hopefully, the outcome will be similar however we label the process.

Putting the Issues into Perspective

The international human rights regime as we know it is only fifty years old. Most nonspecialists would be surprised to learn that sustained and (even partially) effective international efforts to achieve implementation are barely more than twenty years old. While enormous progress has been achieved in that time, the dramatic changes that have taken place over the past decade now pose fundamental challenges to some of the basic assumptions upon which the system has been constructed. As a result, the most pressing tasks in preparing for the twenty-first century are to explore the significance for human rights of the far-reaching developments that have occurred, especially since the watershed year of 1989, and to examine how the international regime might be restructured to enable it to respond effectively to the resulting challenges.

Given the potential breadth of this focus, it is perhaps most instructive to begin by indicating what this paper is not about. In the first place, it does not focus on globalization as such. That topic—as broad, ubiquitous, chameleon-like, and both seductively and irritatingly vague as it is—is the indispensable backdrop against which the present analysis proceeds. Nonetheless, because the issue is addressed by several other papers being submitted to the international dialogue, no attempt at a systematic analysis is made here. Second, the paper is not concerned with the impact of globalization and the phenomena associated with it on

the enjoyment or realization of human rights. That impact is considerable, complex and multifaceted, but it is by no means either an unqualified good or evil.

Third, nor does the paper deal with the new challenges to the content of human rights standards that are being generated by developments in the era of the Internet, cloning, genetic manipulation, or constant twenty-four-hour financial flows and market operations. Those issues range from hate speech and pornography on the Internet to the human genome and a seemingly endless array of other questions arising in the realm of human bioethics to the future of the right to privacy (a very unpromising future if we are to believe *The Economist*!). These and many other issues pose fundamental questions for the development of human rights law and are intimately linked to the challenges of governance in the twenty-first century, but they are well beyond the intended scope of the present paper.

Finally, the focus is not on the issues of ethical or cultural relativism, the clash of civilizations, or the threat from fundamentalism in any of its forms. These catchwords all denote (albeit very inadequately) issues of great import that will assume even greater relevance in the human rights arena in the first part of the next century. This is, of course, not to suggest that the critique of human rights as a quintessentially, uniquely, and irrevocably Western notion is ultimately compelling. Nor does the paper address the related postmodernist critique, sometimes linked to the processes of globalization, that notions of rights cannot be separated from the societies in which they are put forward and that any universalist project for promoting human rights is doomed to fail. As one critic has put it, "the international regime which attempts on a global scale to promote decontextualised human rights is engaging in a near-impossible task."[2] All these issues pose major challenges for the place of a human rights regime within the context of progressive governance for the twenty-first century but are beyond the scope of the present analysis.

So, the reader might reasonably ask, what remains? The focus is essentially on the continuing viability, in the face of globalization and its effects, of a human rights regime that is premised indispensably upon the notion of establishing, and if necessary even imposing, accountability on those entities whose actions impinge significantly upon the enjoyment of human rights. Accountability, as the leitmotif of the whole regime, is greatly weakened if key actors are effectively exempted from its purview. As Kofi Annan stated in his Annual Report presented in September 1999: ". . . the combination of underdevelopment, globalization, and rapid change poses particular challenges to the international human rights regime. . . . [T]he pursuit of development, the engagement with globalization, and the management of change must all yield to human rights imperatives rather than the reverse."[3]

The starting point of this analysis is to reflect upon the extent to which the institutional and other assumptions of the human rights regime are predicated on thinking that is now increasingly anachronistic. In essence, the system as it was designed in 1945, and to a large extent as it has evolved since, is fundamentally state-centric. States alone are the subjects of international law;[4] human rights treaties are negotiated among states and with only limited involvement by other actors; the majority of human rights treaties are adopted on the basis of a consensus among states, thus giving any government at least a potential veto power and certainly the ability to delay the drafting process; human rights obligations attach directly only to states and not to other entities; the international implementation machinery is a creature of states and is dependent upon them legally, politically, and financially; national-level implementation is a function for states to perform; when international bodies monitor compliance, they focus only on governmental compliance; and when sanctions are applied they are imposed upon states and enforced by (or, more commonly, undermined with the acquiescence of) states. Indeed, it has often been said that the international human rights system makes an important contribution to the legitimacy of states both by enabling them to claim the moral high ground and by giving them the opportunity to take on obligations which, in effect, legitimize a more activist or interventionist role for the government within society. Taken to its extreme this critique portrays the human rights enterprise as providing a powerful potential weapon in the suppression of societal freedom rather than being the empowering or liberating force that it is generally assumed to be.

In contrast, the world that the twenty-first century is about to inherit is one in which the overall role of the state

within society is diminishing and is being supplemented and in part replaced by a diverse range of other actors. While some are active at the local level and others at the global level, what they have in common is their bypassing of the centralized apparatus of the state. The latter is no longer the essential intermediary. In this view of current developments the principle of human rights accountability on one hand and globalization on the other might be seen as different trains heading at considerable speed in opposite directions. Globalization (at least as an ideal type) is premised upon flexibility, adaptability, polycentricity, informality, and speedy, tailored, and innovative responses to rapidly changing circumstances. In less positive terms it conjures up adjectives such as opportunistic, ad hoc, uncontrollable, unprincipled, and undemocratic (in the sense that many of its targets have no choice but to conform to its imperatives).[5] The human rights regime (especially the nonideal type portrayed by its critics) is very different. In positive terms it might be characterized as being solid, principled, not easily manipulated, committed to procedural integrity, and careful not to reach beyond its authorized grasp. In more pejorative terms it might be considered to be stolid, excessively gradualist, cautious, rigid, resistant to innovation, and legalistic. In essence then, globalization has a variety of characteristics that are largely alien to the regime of human rights accountability, and the latter is not at all well constructed in order to enable it to adapt, let alone to transform itself, in response to new challenges.

These are, of course, stereotypical images of each and it is not difficult to point to counterexamples. Thus the processes of globalization have been at least diverted if not halted by determined action on the part of civil society, such as the enforced abandonment of efforts to adopt the Multilateral Agreement on Investment within the framework of the OECD, the pressures brought upon the WTO to take greater account of environmental considerations,[6] the concerted campaign against "the worst forms of child labour" within the context of the ILO,[7] and most dramatically in the failure of the WTO Ministerial Meeting in Seattle to be able to launch a new round of trade liberalization negotiations.[8] Similarly, the human rights regime has shown itself on occasion to be innovative and able to adapt. The abrupt change of attitude toward international criminal courts, the eventual (albeit belated) arrival of human rights on the agenda of the Security Council, and the heated debates over the appropriate relationship between human rights violations and military intervention, being examples. More generally, the linkage between territorial jurisdiction and human rights accountability has been greatly expanded to the point where, in certain areas such as torture, hijacking, and hostage taking, a state can be responsible for human rights violations committed anywhere by its agents. But, in general, the stereotypes convey a reasonably accurate image of the competing strengths and weaknesses of the two counterpoints.

Governments are no longer the sole participants in international negotiations over human rights treaties, as was illustrated dramatically (and for some observers, problematically) by the ubiquitous presence of NGO representatives in governmental delegations during the drafting of the Statute of the International Criminal Court, or the role played a decade earlier by the NGO coalition in the drafting of the Convention on the Rights of the Child of 1989. The extension of responsibility from the faceless state to individuals accused of crimes against humanity or other international crimes, was considered as recently as about 1980 to be a dubious concept left over from an overly enthusiastic bout of post–World War II moralizing about war crimes. Indeed, far from ignoring these many examples of adaptability, they are precisely what provides the basis for assuming that continuing adaptability of the international regime is achievable.

Does the Need to Rethink Depend on Either the Death of Sovereignty or the Demise of the State?

Abstract debates over the future of the state and of sovereignty might not yield any clear-cut prescriptions to guide the development of international law and too often seem to amount to little more than clever but futile exercises in shadow boxing. Nonetheless, they are important, primarily because they compel us to analyze more systematically the ways in which changes in the global system are affecting the locus of power and authority in society. Even accepting that reports of the death of the state are greatly exaggerated, the consequences of the relevant developments are highly significant for the human rights regime. They thus demand that those working in the field should seek to come to grips with the need for new approaches.

The prevailing reluctance to do so is partly a result of a sense that the tried and true recipe should not be tampered with, so that an organization like Amnesty International, for all its incomparable achievements, comes to exert a conservatizing influence that favors the status quo and suspects proposed innovations as attempts to undermine the principles that it has fought long and hard to secure. It is partly because the whole regime is perceived to be so firmly rooted within a state-centric framework that it seems potentially suicidal to be playing with those very foundations, because if they come crashing down we will be left with nothing.

The challenge is to combine a reaffirmation of the essentially state-centric architecture of the UN Charter system with a more concerted insistence upon the need for that regime to be systematically adapted rather than to content ourselves with occasional ad hoc measures. Many of the new developments with which we are concerned here call into question the continuing validity of the rationales traditionally proffered in defense of the Westphalian system and demand structural changes.

What shape should such an adaptation take? This paper seeks to provide a preliminary set of suggestions based on an analysis of some of the principal phenomena associated with globalization, including privatization and the shrinking state, deregulation, decentralization, fiscal pressures to conform, the diminishing capacity of the public sector, and the rise of private actors in various spheres. Each of these phenomena has major implications for human rights that do not appear to sit very easily with the assumptions upon which the regime was originally developed.

Defining the Terms of the Debate: Relating Human Rights to Governance

Before 1945, actions could be characterized as abominable, barbaric, or uncivilized, but there were extraordinarily few grounds on the basis of which such behavior could be qualified as violating accepted international standards. It is the great achievement of the past half century that we now have a wide-ranging, relatively detailed, and virtually universally accepted set of norms and thus a terminology on the basis of which states can legitimately be held accountable. It is somewhat ironic, but not especially difficult to explain, that, just at the moment when the normative framework has gained such acceptance and begins to assert its potential to limit the options open to states, Western governments and the international organizations in which they play an especially prominent role have come to place an increasing reliance upon a different concept—governance.

It is thus not surprising, or nearly as platitudinous as it would otherwise seem, that Kofi Annan includes the following comment in his latest annual report:

> In practice, good governance involves promoting the rule of law, tolerance of minority and opposition groups, transparent political processes, an independent judiciary, an impartial police force, a military that is strictly subject to civilian control, a free press and vibrant civil society institutions as well as meaningful elections. Above all, good governance means respect for human rights.[9]

The terms "governance" and "good governance" have come dramatically into vogue in the 1990s. Like any such terms, or more accurately slogans, they have some questionable and some positive contributions to offer our understanding on the issues they touch. Of the former, the only one that warrants a brief mention here is a function more of the way in which the term is used or misused than of its intrinsic value. It is that governance can be defined in very diverse ways and given almost any content that is considered to be important at the time in the eye of the beholder. In other words it is open-ended, and its relationship to human rights concerns is often very uncertain.

But it is the principal strength of the concept that is relevant here. Definitionally, whatever the term might mean, it cannot be synonymous with "government" or even "good government." If it did it would simply be tautologous to insist that governments must practice

governance, or good governments good governance. Its intended scope is thus greater than the traditionally defined sphere of government. It addresses a wider range of activities and seeks to encompass as well those actors whose behavior plays an important role in determining the well-being of states, communities, and individuals. This sense of the term is well captured in the following definition:

> Governance . . . means the framework of rules, institutions, and established practices that set limits and give incentives for behavior of individuals, organizations, and firms.[10]

In a similar vein, Richard Falk has put forward the concept of "humane governance," a formulation that seeks to capitalize on the strengths of the term "governance" while qualifying it with a significantly less open-ended or value-free term than "good."[11] Viewed in this way, a commitment to promote good governance clearly requires a vision that extends beyond both (1) formal rules and (2) an exclusive focus on governments, or the state, as such. It might thus be argued (although I am not aware that it has been) that the concept of human rights is badly placed to serve these purposes and thus needs to be replaced by or subsumed under the broader umbrella of good governance.

Such an argument would rely upon a characterization of human rights as a legalistic concept that depends upon the formulation and application of clear rules defining rights and obligations. The imagery of rights as trumps, borrowed inappropriately from Ronald Dworkin's work, is sometimes used to convey this sense of formalism, rigidity, and relative simplicity. But it is a one-dimensional usage that does not capture the richness of the concept of rights as reflected in international human rights law. That body of law prescribes a normative order whose most formal embodiment is indeed constitutional or legislative and whose most formal instrument is the courts. But the accountability that is the essence of human rights extends far beyond this limited domain to embrace, as the single most widely ratified human rights treaty—the Convention on the Rights of the Child, which has been ratified by every state in the world except Somalia and the

United States—puts it, the obligation to take "all appropriate legislative, administrative, and other measures for the implementation of the rights recognized. . . ."[12] Any suggestion that it is the narrow legalism of human rights that makes governance a preferable term is thus unjustified.

Another possible argument is that the catalog of human rights is insufficient to address all of the issues that are covered by the term governance. In some respects this is justified. Corruption, for example, is not specifically addressed in the human rights texts, although the right to take part in government, the right to equality before the law, and the general principle that human rights should be protected by the rule of law provide a basis upon which to proceed. But in any event this is not the real problem since organizations like the IMF have governance policies but not human rights policies. The principle should be that governance requirements are best invoked in conjunction with reliance upon human rights norms rather than separately.

A final argument in favor of preferring governance to human rights is that the latter concept is applicable only to governments and thus cannot reach the many other actors to whom governance concerns are routinely addressed. This is in fact a potential Achilles heel for the human rights regime. It is taken up in the pages that follow.

In conclusion, governance should be put into a human rights perspective and not vice versa. The same applies to the rule of law and even to democracy as such. Governance is a process, a way of behaving. It is, in theory, value-free, although we have invested it with a number of assumptions for the purposes of the international community. The foundational nature of human rights however makes it the appropriate basis upon which definitions of governance should be evolved rather than the other way around.

Whither Accountability in the Wake of Visions of Progressive Governance?

Progressive governance can reasonably be understood to refer to approaches that seek to adapt or reform governance systems to enable them to better respond to the changing needs of a world caught between the various competing pressures that characterize the situation at the start of the twenty-first century. In addition to globalization, those pressures include the fragmentation or "localization" associated with a resurgence of nationalism, religious revivalism, and growing assertions of ethnic, cultural, and other forms of identity. In complex ways, forms of democratization have sometimes, but by no means consistently, been both a cause and a result of globalization.

There are, in addition, three trends that have particular significance in terms of our concern with the maintenance of principles of human rights accountability. They are privatization, deregulation, and decentralization. A great deal has already been written about the pressures pushing governments toward the first two of these. Objectives sought include the promotion of greater enterprise efficiency, the development of a more service-oriented mentality, the elimination of loss-making assets that drain the capacity of the state to fulfill its core functions, the achievement of the degree of flexibility—in the markets for labor, capital, and production—that is conducive to efficiency, and the provision of the incentive needed to unleash the spirit of enterprise that can energize a free market. It is not necessary to contest the validity of any one of these objectives in order to observe that many of the measures taken in the name of these objectives have the capacity to reduce very significantly the element of accountability that is central to the human rights regime.

Another, not necessarily related, development is the trend toward decentralization, defined as "the process of devolving political, fiscal, and administrative powers to subnational units of government." In order to distinguish it from "deconcentration" in the form of giving greater autonomy to the regional representatives of the central government, the definition assumes that the subnational units in question will be locally elected. At the political level, this strategy is occurring in many places, including, for example, in Great Britain in relation to Scotland and Wales as well as the City of London. The approach adopted to welfare reform in both the United States and Canada involving the decentralization of responsibility and funds from the federal to the state and provincial level is increasingly being replicated, albeit across a broader range of issues, in many developing countries. In India, for example, the recently adopted UN Development Assistance Framework, which lays down the priority goals that international agencies will help to promote through their varied activities, identifies two major priorities. One is the promotion of gender equality and the reduction of sex-based discrimination, and the other is decentralization. While both are admirable goals, they can also, depending on the circumstances and the approach taken, be seen to be incompatible.

In Latin America decentralization has taken place on a major scale over the past fifteen years or so. A recent survey notes that, "since 1983, all but one of the largest countries in the region have seen a transfer of power, resources, and responsibilities to subnational units of government."[13] Because this process requires political reconfigurations involving a shift from appointed to elected governors and mayors, the devolution of responsibilities from central to local government, or the introduction of democratic elections in situations where they did not previously apply, the implications for respect for civil and political rights are obvious, and one would expect a strongly positive impact. These changes have also involved the devolution of major functional responsibilities in sectors such as health, education, sanitation, water supply, and road construction, which in turn have a major potential impact on the enjoyment of economic, social, and cultural human rights.

A major World Bank study published in 1999 suggests that decentralization will continue to be a major growth area in the years ahead and thus one that must be taken fully into account in ensuring the effectiveness of the regime designed to ensure human rights accountability:

The pressures for decentralization are beyond the control of governments. The emergence of modern economies and an urban, literate middle class has created nearly insurmountable pressures for a broader distribution of political power. . . . Rather than attempting to resist them, governments need to accommodate them in a way that maintains political stability while improving public sector performance.[14]

Whether the new urban, literate middle class is likely to press for an equitable distribution of political power,

as opposed to one in which its own narrow interests are better represented, is a question not pursued in the study. It does, however, acknowledge that various problems can be associated with the overall process and lists three in particular. The first is a deterioration in the quality of services offered. The second is the possibility of widening regional disparities at the level of provision of public services, which can be especially problematic in areas such as primary health and primary education. The third set of possible problems arises in relation to macroeconomic policies: "recurring central government deficits, an overexpanded public sector, or the inability to use fiscal policy to adjust to economic shocks."[15] The report rightly identifies accountability as one of the key ingredients in ensuring that decentralization projects are successful. Unsurprisingly, however, the concern is minimal in respect to the first two possible defects of the process, and most of the report is devoted to exploring ways in which macroeconomic accountability can be ensured.

Even within the European Community the principle of subsidiarity (requiring, inter alia, that the Community "shall not go beyond what is necessary to achieve the objectives of the Treaty") that was enshrined in the basic treaty in 1991 at Maastricht has given a significant impetus to decentralization of decision making in certain areas. Central to the argument here, however, it has generally been accompanied by only a limited procedural autonomy being accorded to the member state that is responsible for policy implementation. In other words, a significant element of accountability to ensure compliance with community objectives is ensured through the use of various techniques.

For present purposes the point is not that decentralization is necessarily undesirable in any way. Rather it raises new challenges as to how human rights accountability can best be ensured in the context of a new set of policies and procedures. The problem is potentially acute in circumstances in which the central government, which is the signatory to human rights treaties and the normal interlocutor with the international community in such matters, has less practical control over what is happening and a diminished ability to provide details of current developments. It is even less well placed to ensure that course corrections that might be proposed by international supervisory bodies are given the consideration demanded by the legal framework of applicable international human rights treaties.

In short, new means need to be devised for ensuring that the consequences of privatization, deregulation, and decentralization are not such as to reduce the accountability of governmental or other actors in human rights terms.

Can the Concept of Human Rights Cope Adequately with the Growing Power of Private Actors?

The impact of private actors on the enjoyment of human rights is growing rapidly in a global economy. Privatization, deregulation, and the diminishing regulatory capacities of national governments have all contributed to enhancing the importance of corporations and other private entities in terms of human rights. Although the debate about corporate social responsibility or progressive corporate governance is an old one, it has happily come a long way since the days when Milton Friedman proclaimed that business has "one and only one social responsibility . . . to use its resources and engage in activities designed to increase its profits . . . ." But he added a vital qualification: Maximization of profits and of shareholder value are the golden rules for business, "so long as it stays within the rules of the game, which is to say, engages in open and free competition, without deception or fraud."[16] Standards have changed, and so too has our understanding of the relationship between corporate good conduct and broader conceptions of governance. Corporations can hardly be expected to operate as paragons of virtue, even within the narrow confines of Friedman's strictures, when they are operating in a context which is closed, corrupt, and oppressive (as, for example, in Nigeria, at least until very recently). But consumers and others are increasingly demanding that they should avoid responsibility for, or complicity in, human rights violations.

Ironically, when considering how to approach the issue in an international context, national-level efforts to promote or ensure corporate social responsibility may be a poor guide in various respects and might even be seriously misleading in a number of important ways. Much of the literature talks of social responsibility, corporate good citizenship, and social audits but generally does not talk in terms of human rights. The result is a diverse range of standards varying significantly in scope and focus. They sometimes address issues as wide-ranging as the firm's contribution to employment creation, the amount of revenue it earns per worker, the percentage of its pretax profits that is devoted to philanthropic activities, the active disclosure of information to promote transparency, the commissioning of independent corporate audits of performance in relation to social and other noneconomic goals, and the active engagement in or commitment to movements for social change whether in the environmental, arms control, or human rights areas which are all admirable dimensions of social accountability. On the other hand, in the domestic debates many human rights issues are not addressed at all since it is assumed they are adequately taken care of by domestic regulations by which the corporation is bound.

The point is that many of the national-level debates over corporate responsibility take us significantly beyond what is productively thought of as a human rights agenda. The latter agenda is actually closer to Friedman's model of basic compliance with relevant laws than to these very broad-ranging and potentially open-ended debates over ethics and social responsibility. The principal difference between what might be termed a human rights compliance model and Friedman's model is that the former supplements clearly and directly applicable national legal regulations with international human rights standards that the business has the responsibility, and perhaps also the obligation (but that is to prejudge a complex issue), to avoid violating. It should also eschew complicity with other actors and particularly governments in relation to such violations. There is much to be said, therefore, for focusing on a more limited range of issues in relation to which human rights standards are clearly relevant, and were accountable public authorities rather than corporate officials decide what the standards will be.

Globalization is itself highly conducive to the growing power of transnational corporations (TNCs). In some respects, the essence of the phenomenon is to make business across borders easier in a great many ways, as well as more profitable. Improved mobility, economies of scale, and a greater ability to communicate and manage across long distances have all contributed to an enhancement of the role of TNCs. Many of the principal legal and political initiatives associated with globalization have been designed specifically to improve the capacity for TNCs to do business. Partly as a result, foreign direct investment flows are at record levels. In 1997 they were nearly double what they had been in 1990 and seven times 1980 levels. They are expected to continue growing. Indeed, TNCs have been the principal conduit for globalization. This fact alone would be sufficient to warrant a sustained focus on the relationship between the role of TNCs and efforts to ensure the promotion and protection of human rights.

In addition, several other phenomena closely associated with globalization have further increased the importance of TNCs. Privatization, for example, in the case of certain industries is significantly more likely to create opportunities for TNCs than for local corporations that lack the scale or expertise to bid successfully. The same is often true even for activities such as prison management, some aspects of law enforcement, and even aspects of military security. Deregulation reinforces the same trend. At the same time, pressure on the state to reduce its own expenditures will often lead it to downgrade its efforts to enforce those regulatory arrangements that are left in place. Labor inspection is a simple example in this regard. This combination of factors has led many commentators and groups in civil society to focus on the responsibilities of corporations. In addition, a range of widely publicized instances in which major corporations have been implicated in situations involving either significant violations of human rights or of environmental standards have generated consumer and other pressures upon corporations to demonstrate their responsibility. Shell Oil, Nike, Levi Strauss, and many other firms have responded to strong criticism by adopting codes of behaviors designed to insulate themselves from such criticism and to build an image of good corporate citizenship.

Governments have been supportive of such efforts while at the same time remaining unwilling to take regulatory measures of their own. There has been strong resentment over certain exercises of extraterritorial jurisdic-

tion, including especially some purportedly aimed at upholding human rights. Most notable have been the actions by the U.S. Congress in the Helms-Burton and D'Amato Acts, which seek to punish foreign corporations investing in Cuba, Iran, and other countries considered to be non grata. The result is that the same governments that successfully insisted upon corporate codes of conduct in relation to South Africa at the time of apartheid are not prepared to act in relation to TNCs in general.[17]

There are various reasons for the reticence to use human rights standards, but the most important by far is simply the fact that TNCs, as private or nonstate actors, are not bound by human rights standards as such. Human rights obligations are assumed by governments pursuant to international law (either through treaty ratification or by virtue of the application of principles of customary international law) and are thus not formally or directly opposable to TNCs.

Human Rights Watch, while expressing concern about the lack of human rights accountability of TNCs and the strong reluctance of governments to take an interest in corporate responsibility issues, has nevertheless been encouraged by the trend toward the adoption of voluntary codes of conduct in the footwear, apparel, and other sectors. "While governments are unwilling to insist that corporations not profit from repression, a vibrant and burgeoning NGO movement is leading this campaign." However, existing arrangements for monitoring compliance with human rights standards are ill equipped to respond to these developments. In response to growing corporate awareness and increasing consumer pressure, there has been a significant expansion in the number of voluntary codes of conduct and the like that have been adopted within different business sectors.

These developments have been warmly welcomed by diverse commentators. Some would argue that the fragmentation of authority within the global system has rendered anachronistic the old ideal of a centralized multilateral regulation of TNCs. Others extol the advantages of self-regulation as the only authentic way of ensuring that progressive approaches are entrenched within the corporate mentality. And still others would argue, based particularly on the work of Nicholas Luhmann and Gunther Teubner, that there is an emerging global law that is not located in any one place but instead relies on multiple, often overlapping, norm generators and compliance processes.[18] The lex mercatoria is the classic example of such a set of informal processes. In this view, any attempt at centralization will be ineffectual at best and counterproductive at worst. A further gloss is added by the suggestion by Yves Dezalay and Bryant Garth that the privatization of international commercial justice (primarily through arbitration arrangements designed to obviate the need to rely upon state legal systems) in recent years was driven in large part by the cold war, welfare state interventionism, and "third worldism."[19] On this basis, it can be argued that the more concerted are formal efforts to regulate TNCs, the greater is the likelihood that the target group will devise alternative strategies to circumvent the regulatory attempts. All of these arguments are complex and deserve more careful analysis than they can be given here.

It must suffice for present purposes to argue that while the proliferation of voluntary codes and other initiatives is to be welcomed, such mechanisms are not sufficient in themselves to satisfy the requirement of systematic accountability that are central to the international human rights regime. Such initiatives are very often not based on international human rights standards, their monitoring is uneven, they are mostly overseen by the corporations themselves, and they remain entirely, or at best largely, optional. The same criticism applies to the "global compact of shared values and principles" proposed at Davos in January 1999 by UN Secretary-General Kofi Annan.[20] While this initiative should certainly be developed, it must also begin to explore the possible shape of mechanisms to review the conformity of these various codes with human rights standards and to monitor and report on the private sector monitors.

Ultimately, however, as Human Rights Watch acknowledges, such matters cannot be based on voluntary undertakings.[21] The standards thus set are excessively flexible, and their conformity with international human rights norms is by no means assured. The element of accountability is lacking insofar as firms police their own behavior and the international mechanisms, as well as the representatives of civil society, are often excluded.

Some governmental efforts exist but they are neither comprehensive nor consistent. The European Union (EU) is an example in this regard. In 1977 the Coun-cil of the European Union adopted a code of conduct for businesses operating in South Africa, and in May 1998 it adopted the EU Code of Conduct on Arms Exports. While there are significant differences in the scope and approach of these codes, it is difficult to accept as the last word a recent statement by the European Commission to the effect that existing European Community law makes it impossible to develop a code of conduct to oblige EU-based companies operating in third countries to observe human rights norms. The European Commission should evaluate existing voluntary codes of conduct and prepare a study on the ways in which an official EU code of conduct for corporations could be formulated, promoted, and monitored.

In addition, there is a need to develop more innovative approaches by which existing international arrangements designed to achieve human rights accountability can be adapted to significantly enhance their capacity to monitor violations attributable to corporations but for which state accountability is altogether lacking or inadequate.

International Financial Institutions and the Global Financial Marketplace: Is There Room for a Human Rights Stall?

The issue of the lack of a coherent, detailed, or adequate human rights policy on the part of the International Monetary Fund in particular and the World Bank (albeit to a slightly lesser extent) is an old, complex, and controversial one. It has, however, had new life breathed into it by a series of recent crises ranging from the Asian financial crisis through the question of East Timor and the response to the military coup in Pakistan. Human rights were long argued to be, *ultra vires,* the appropriate mandates of these institutions. Even if that proposition was sustainable in the 1970s and 1980s, it is no longer viable as we enter the twenty-first century. There has been considerable movement over the past two years, and this can easily be traced through the speeches of James Wolfensohn of the World Bank, Michel Camdessus of the IMF, and those of leading economists such as former treasury secretary Lawrence Summers and Joseph Stiglitz of the World Bank.

This is far too large a question to be dealt with in any detail here. The principal point to be made is that a regime of human rights accountability that is worthy of the name can no longer settle for the old orthodoxy according to which neither the IMF nor the World Bank are bound by human rights standards.

The inadequacy of the existing situation may be illustrated by comparing the formal policy position of the IMF with the approaches that it has been taking in recent months in response to particular crises as they have emerged. In essence the IMF's position is still that human rights matters are not within its purview except to the extent that they arise in relation to what it defined, only fairly recently (July 1997), as its governance policy. Rather than seeking to define that elusive concept, the IMF's policy elaboration efforts to date have focused largely on efforts to limit the extent to which its own involvement might be invoked in governance-related matters within the confines of its mandate. Thus, the official position is that:

The IMF is primarily concerned with macroeconomic stability, external viability, and orderly economic growth in member countries. Therefore, the IMF's involvement in governance issues should be limited to economic aspects of governance . . . [including through]: improving the management of public resources through reforms covering public sector institutions (e.g. the treasury, central bank public enterprises, civil service, and the official statistics function), including administrative procedures (e.g. expenditure control, budget management, and revenue collection); and supporting the development and maintenance of a transparent and stable economic and regulatory environment conducive to efficient private sector activities (e.g. price systems, exchange and trade regimes, and banking systems and their related regulations).[22]

The principal criterion determining IMF involvement in a given governance issue is "whether poor governance would have significant current or potential impact on macroeconomic performance in the short and medium term and on the ability of the government credibly to pursue policies aimed at external viability and sustainable growth."[23]

In contrast to such reticence and circumspection, consider the following news items:

World Bank Demands Indonesia Restore Order in East Timor. The World Bank yesterday demanded that Indonesia restore order in East Timor and permit its transition to an independent nation, saying it was "deeply concerned" by the violent situation there, Agence France-Presse reports. . . . [The]Bank said in the statement. "We join with the IMF and our other partners in supporting a rapid response to the deteriorating security situation, in order that initiatives for economic recovery and poverty reduction may proceed in both Indonesia and East Timor." (8 September 1999)[24]

A Comment by William Murray, an IMF Spokesman, September 16, 1999: "The situation in Indonesia is kept under review. For the time being, the IMF has decided not to send any missions to Indonesia. The discussions of the program review which would lead to the disbursement of the next installment of the IMF's financing package, and which were originally scheduled for mid-September, will take place once the right conditions exist."

IMF Managing Director Michel Camdessus said yesterday Pakistan could lose its IMF aid if democracy was not restored after the military coup. . . . Donor countries often suspended their bilateral aid when a coup occurs during the course of an aid program, Reuters says Camdessus noted. . . . "Democracy is in retreat, and when democracy retreats, countries are in danger."[25]

AFP reports that . . . [in] response to questions about the possibility that international aid might be used to finance war by Russian forces in Chechnya and Dagestan, Camdessus replied "If I see that the budget is over-shooting because of an uncontrolled increase of military spending, we shall interrupt our support."[26]

In view of the disconnect between the formal statement of IMF policy and the realities of current practice, it is essential that an effort be made to articulate a more thorough and sophisticated vision of the relationship between the international financial institutions and countries experiencing major human rights problems.

There is a potentially interesting parallel in relation to humanitarian law and international peacekeeping forces. For many years, formalization of the relationship was resisted in line with traditional state-centric conceptions of international law. But in August 1999 the UN Secretary-General promulgated an official bulletin that formally affirmed that "the fundamental principles and rules of international humanitarian law . . . are applicable to United Nations forces."[27] The challenge is to devise an appropriate formulation in relation to the international financial institutions and human rights while avoiding rigidity and politicization.

There are some encouraging precedents. The avalanche of criticism that has descended on the IMF in the past year or two has not only led to a dramatic reversal in its approach to information availability—from being almost entirely closed to one which provides a significant degree of transparency—but has also encouraged it to be more systematic and accountable in relation to its policymaking and policy application procedures. Both the IMF and the World Bank should be directed to produce detailed studies examining the means by which they could give full effect to human rights standards in their activities.

Conclusion

The principal thrust of this paper is that while the normative content of the international human rights regime has long ago transcended the original conceptualization of human rights as a body of norms designed to protect the individual from the predations of the state, the procedural and institutional arrangements designed to give effect to it remain firmly rooted in a mid-twentieth-century mentality that considerably overstates the role played by the state at both the national and international levels and excludes or downplays the role of other actors.

Governments, unsurprisingly, remain reluctant to acknowledge this reality despite the increasingly dramatic impact of globalization and the phenomena associated with it. The ambivalence of most governments is well illustrated by the position taken by the Uruguayan representative at the recent UNCTAD–X Conference in Bangkok in February 2000. He began by noting that the "main problems that we face in the world economy transcend the mandates and competencies of any individual [international] organization." Having discounted the possibility of reconstructing the international system, he called for "a radical change in the manner [in which] we approach international organization," which would involve "leaving aside dogma and facing problems in an integrated and coordinated manner." But after identifying nongovernmental organizations and transnational corporations as the principal new forces that need to be reckoned with, he noted that NGOs "are not accountable" and "often distract governments from facing issues, thus inhibiting international organizations" and concluded that "to incorporate them in the decision-making of intergovernmental organizations would be wrong." TNCs he viewed as "perhaps more dangerous" than NGOs because their "behavior . . . is not subject to our control,"[28] but he offered no prescription for dealing with them. In essence, such an analysis is symptomatic of the current state of affairs.

The challenge then is to move beyond this stalemate by expanding the international community's frame of reference in order to take adequate account of the various roles being played by actors who lie outside the traditional state-centric analysis. This paper points toward a research agenda for the future that will address the various ways in which nonstate actors can (1) be more fully and creatively taken into account within the existing framework of international law and (2) be integrated into a more comprehensive or holistic conception of the international community.

Government Speech
in a Neutral State

Andras Sajo

Introduction

Modern governments participate in the public discourse in a number of ways. Government officials speak; they have to inform and convince the public about future state actions. Still, in the United States, government speech intended to perpetuate power has been held unconstitutional from the founding days. Governments regulate the sphere of communication to shield the public discourse from private monopolists. Activities funded by public money send cultural messages and limit or promote the distribution of certain views. Unless carefully proscribed, such interventions may result in further skewing of the public debate.

Government speech is protected speech like any other speech. However, given the enormous resources at its disposal, unlimited government speech may drive out all other speech. Hence, there is a need to consider the possibilities of its restriction.

Legitimate restrictions to free speech originate from the ideal of the neutral state. The neutrality requirement can be related to a liberal expectation regarding the nature of the state or it may originate from constitutional concerns. Although neutrality in the speech domain has never reached the absolutes of state neutrality in religious matters, certain elements of belief neutrality do exist with regard to speech.

Neutrality considerations are dictated by the requirements of the democratic process, equality, political credibility, and special institutional needs. As these concerns are different, neutrality may have different connotations and therefore does not offer a justifiable standard. The strictest scrutiny of government speech restriction pro-

tects democratic governance against self-perpetuation. In other areas, substantive criteria and institutional and procedural solutions help to avoid governmental indoctrination in the sphere of speech. The most important examples of neutralized spheres are education (higher education in particular), arts (funding), and the press. Institutional immunity from governmental intervention should be accompanied by judicial review of internal speech practices in order to allow a level of neutrality that respects the function of the institution.

This paper contrasts the above normative concerns with the prevailing tendencies toward neutralization of government action in the sphere of speech. In the age of the Internet, government is only one of the many competing centers of power in the communication sphere. Also, modern forms of democracy and corporatism encourage the transfer of decisions to nongovernmental entities. In a decentralized state, politicians try to avoid accountability and delegate decisions to a neutral and professional public bureaucracy.

Neutrality becomes highly suspect when a government undertakes to rectify imperfections in the marketplace of ideas. Some courts, like the U.S. Supreme Court, are basically noninterventionist, allowing considerable cultural shaping by the administration in the spirit of "winner-takes-all." In welfare states like Germany, the government is expected to guard the sphere of public discourse including education and broadcasting. An interventionist attitude is present in transition-to-democracy countries. This approach is particularly dangerous to free speech due to the dominant position of the state in society and in discourse. The emerging solutions depend on the nature of the state, the level of state domination over society, the constitutional stature of speech, and the architecture of the actual discourse space.

Communication Distortion by Government Speech

The impact of government on speech represents two types of problems. First, government communications may have silencing effects or may indoctrinate. Secondly, the state is expected to intervene in public communication where the marketplace of ideas is distorted. The satisfaction of the second expectation may aggravate the first problem.

Government Speech Restricting Other Speech

A large-circulation daily paper took a position against the leader of a state. In interviews and circulars the leader of that state said that newspapers that are lying are conducting a "vicious campaign" against the democratically elected majority and its long overdue reforms. He suggested a tax on lying. Thereafter a tax on large-circulation newspapers was imposed.

This may sound like a typical story from Eastern Europe. In fact, these are the words of Governor Huey Long of Louisiana. The tax was held unconstitutional in 1936.[1] But there is no guarantee that a scheme that redistributes advertisement income to small-circulation papers will not be found constitutional in a different constitutional climate. In Western Europe similar schemes protect the local press in the name of creating and maintaining public forums. Some Eastern European governments, most likely unaware of Governor Huey Long's approach, would like to subsidize only small-circulation, pro-government papers.

Governments not only influence speech, they also speak. Elected government officials and civil servants speak on behalf of the state, or at least their speech is perceived as the voice of the state. Such speech has special authority. Further, certain government decisions, such as subsidies, licenses, and taxes, facilitate or hamper both governmental and private speech.

In the mainstream doctrine, government expression is considered protected speech all over the world. There are good, even compelling reasons for that. In a democracy, elected policymakers are expected to generate support for their actions and convince the public.

Notwithstanding the democratic need for government speech, it is possible or even likely that those who have the opportunity to speak on behalf of government will be biased and that the government's speech will be partisan. Government speech may accommodate the speaker's selfish interests. As a consequence, the government's justified need to speak is abused. As Justice Scalia stated: "[a]ll government displays an enduring tendency to silence, or to facilitate silencing, those voices that it disapproves."[2] Denial of subsidy, free airtime, and authoritative governmental position-taking are the new silencers.

Government speech has special effects on the public discourse. First, it has special authority; it is "official." Any government may have considerable impact on the public discourse and through the discourse on the shaping of social culture. Official language rules and speech regulation are just one judicially recognized, though often contested, aspect of it. Second, when a politician speaks as an oracle of the government she has more opportunities to be heard.[3] Heads of state may legitimately talk on behalf of the community, although their position-taking may have silencing effects. Moreover, legislation speaks by enacting statutes: passing legislative acts is a clear way of expressing preferences, and it has an indirect silencing effect.

Further, when government allocates a certain budget line or other resources under its control to propagate a certain viewpoint or content, it creates additional speech. Viewpoint endorsement through public funding is a double boost. It creates special opportunities for government's preferences to be heard, and, in addition, the legal authorization supplies the subsidized speech with authoritative sanction. While many commentators and justices find it unacceptable to refer to a spending-related speech condition as simply a matter of constitutional spending discretion, the U.S. Supreme Court refused to consider the speech aspects of spending. But even the majority of the Supreme Court recognized the need to set limits on governmental influence on speech (through subsidies).[4] In *Rust v. Sullivan* the Supreme Court realized that its position is getting dangerously close to that of the administration of the day (as voiced by Solicitor General Kenneth Starr), namely that "funding by the Government . . . is invariably sufficient to justify government control over the content of expression."[5] In order to limit these effects of funding, the Supreme Court stated that in public forums and public universities the First Amendment restricts governmental control over subsidized speech. The same applies to government subsidies of the press but not to abortion counselling, that is, confidential physician-client relations that were affected by the funding rules.

There remains a permanent tension between mere allocative spending and tax legislation on one hand and government interference with speech on the other. Government decisions and spending in particular influence the audience and as a result may make ineffective otherwise protected instances of speech. "From the perspective of the audience, the danger lies not in the coercive effect of the benefit on speakers, but in the indoctrinating effect of a monopolized marketplace of ideas."[6]

The impact of government speech on the public discourse architecture is debated. Schauer claims that there is no conclusive evidence that the amplified voice of government will silence other private voices.[7] Tushnet believes that people are intelligent enough to discount government speech.[8] Of course, the capacity to discount varies by political culture. Where it works it often results from the loss of public trust in government and politics.

Both positions imply that there is no need for special regulation regarding government speech. According to this approach all speech is equal—including government speech. Speech is protected for the sake of all, including speakers and listeners. In the liberal tradition the primary concern of free speech law is to protect speakers, not the audience.

Traditional liberal constitutions reflect only the core concern of speech protection, namely, avoiding government-imposed restrictions on free communication or expression.[9] Although proponents of the activist social state emphasize the importance of governmental restraint as negative protection in the speech context, the centrality of speakers' rights is contested, even in liberal democracies. In England it was recently held that

"in addition to freedom of communication there are other rights to be protected, such as freedom from being virtually forced to listen to unsolicited information of a contentious kind, and the danger of the wealthy distorting the democratic process."[10]

If, however, speakers deserve protection only for being instruments of a robust discourse, and if under specific circumstances of communication the overwhelming voice of the government as a speaker endangers robust discourse, traditional liberal free speech theory will be unable to take care of the potential dangers presented by government speech or by regulation and action affecting communication. The protection of the speakers serves the general public, including the audience and other listeners. The function of the speaker would determine the limits of her freedom. Free speech is protected here as the core of communicative freedom, as a constituent element of the public discourse or discussion that is vital to the community of self-governing people.[11] Speech is protected to make public discourse robust. Free speech entails a "systemic freedom for expressive activities."[12] The systemic element here means, among other things, the opportunity to acquire knowledge.[13] With some differences, both France and Germany protect communicative freedom. The protection of communication follows either from the constitutional function of the state as it is understood in Germany, or it is based on a judicial concept of individual rights as acknowledged in France. Although freedom of speech from governmental intervention remains crucial, the whole communicative process is to be protected. This includes the right to be informed, which is an audience-related consideration.[14]

If speech is protected as part of a systemic freedom, then the protection may not be unconditional and perhaps special rules apply to speakers who dominate the communication. Under specific circumstances this might be true of the state, even in the current and future global communication world where the nation-state's control over communication is allegedly diminishing.[15] Moreover, beyond the actual architecture of the public discourse space, one should also look at the role government plays in the life of society. Where there is considerable social dependence on government services government speech and speech-affecting spending will put more pressure on private speech. The more the government is in the position to determine social culture the more likely it is that cultural and educational support will be self-referential. To the extent that the self-referentialism is political it will be highly suspect. But even where cultural self-referentialism is simply support to the existing forms of culture it will be status quo oriented and traditional, which is problematic, although not in the constitutional sense.

In welfare states like Germany many constitutional principles are deducted from the expectations of benevolent state impact on society. At the same time, the influence of government on society is not addressed in the First Amendment of the U.S. Constitution nor in other constitutions.[16] It is not surprising that the different contemporary legal systems have developed special and different techniques and categories to limit government speech. However, in most of the cases this is done in a way outside the sphere of speech (by classifying the activity as being outside the domain of speech (see below).

Irrespective of the restrictive effects of government speech, it is undeniable that government has the means to structure the discourse space. Means at the government's disposal include broadcasting licenses, government spending, and governmental speech. These have the potential to endanger free speech.[17]

Some existing doctrines of free speech offer a shield against such danger. "In the history of free speech, the state has sometimes defended the regulation of speech in the name of liberty. . . . Characteristically, liberals responded that the remedy was more speech, not state regulation."[18] Is this old liberal paradigm of "more speech" still sufficient in an era of private and governmental communication monopolies? Owen Fiss believes that where "the alleged threat to freedom coming from speech is more direct [and] will make it impossible for these disadvantaged groups even to participate in the discussion,"[19] regulation of speech might be appropriate. The protection of fundamental rights may call for government intervention in order to promote public discourse.[20] This strategy assumes that imperfections of the market will make the "more speech" strategy counterproductive.

Governmental Speech Facilitation and Speech Restrictions Resulting from It

Those who advocate an activist, promotional role for the government in social life envision a positive role for the state in public discourse. Social welfare considerations are sometimes elevated to the level of constitutional text in Europe and elsewhere. Many welfare state advocates claim that government has affirmative obligations in shaping the public discourse. Moreover, governments have a responsibility to shape culture, if not a duty to be a *Kulturstaat*. A doctrine of worldwide popularity holds that nineteenth-century constitutional liberalism became a holdout. Constitutionalism used to serve as a shield against governmental abuse of power. Today, however, the most important danger to liberty comes from powerful groups within society. The government is expected to offer protection against such forces.

It is believed that the government should facilitate the protection of liberties and rights, partly by establishing institutions that are capable of promoting rights. Such attitudes are not limited to European Christian conservatives. Shiffrin, for example, argued that government in modern society not only moderates among competing private interests and voices, but its purpose is to promote its view of the "good life."[21] The two approaches may yield similar results. They both mandate certain governmental intervention into public discourse, partly by adding a government voice and partly by creating a level playground through restrictive and promotive regulation. Governments at least should facilitate entry to the market for ideas. In both cases the state goes beyond the role of the umpire. This may be called the *intervention approach*.

The intervention approach has special connotations and consequences in the context of the freedom of expression. On the one hand there is an agreement in constitutional democracies that the freedom of the speaker is the primary object of free speech protection and that freedom of speech should not be restricted for the sake of systemic (institutional) communicative values. In Europe, when it comes to broadcasting, systemic considerations prevail. Although no one is formally silenced by regulations, access to broadcasting is limited. Therefore there is a need for governmental interference to provide fairness and a balance of viewpoints. The German doctrine insists on "equality (fairness) of communicative chances" as a consequence of the constitutional democracy, rule of law, and social state principles.[22] In Austria special statutory provisions determine acceptable levels of market concentration in press and broadcasting. In France the Conseil Constitutionnel developed a constitutional theory of media pluralism resulting in the restriction of media monopolies. The Conseil's concerns were based, among other things, on the "freedom of readers" and the "right of readers to freely choose."[23] In the United States for a long period the public trustee position of broadcasters prevailed, legitimizing certain systemic considerations. Partly related to changes in technology and the increased but not necessarily realized potential for multisource broadcasting architecture, the protection of editorial freedom tends to dominate today, even where government is determining broadcasting.[24]

Following the above considerations, government is allegedly authorized or compelled to intervene into the public discourse because of supposed imbalances and resulting distortions that hamper people's free formation of opinion. The remedy offered to solve this second type of communication mischief runs the risk of aggravating the first problem, that of government speech. Corrective regulatory interventions and spending imply the danger of more government speech and more silencing of voices under the pretext of creating better conditions for handicapped viewpoints. All government intervention entails the danger that under the pretext of restoration of the marketplace of ideas a partisan government viewpoint might emerge. Hence there is a need for government neutrality tempering partisan government speech. Properly speaking, neutrality is not a restriction on government speech but an insistence on the proper role of the state. The neutrality rule is gaining significance where and when the growing power of the government is accompanied by an increased reliance on the benevolent state. However, this is also an era of distrust in private institutions. Such distrust is understandable when the reign of private interests results in oppression and domination over the weaker. Where regulation results in voicing government-dictated view-

points and contents and, in particular, where intervention would increase the likelihood of government's direct control over speech, concerns other than those of the speaker might become decisive. One should also pay attention to the actual power of a government in society and in the communication sphere in general. One should be particularly suspicious in cases where the communication resources of the government and government's power to influence other people's speech and views are preponderant. This prudential consideration is important in the evaluation of the various national solutions.

Self-perpetuation as a Limit on Government Speech

The values considered in structuring government speech in modern democracies and in judicial scrutiny reflect either concerns about unimpeded democracy or expectations of neutrality. Speech protection against governmental restraint contains elements and considerations that originate in constitutional values unrelated to speech. Considerations of democratic government do play a role in election-related speech. Restrictions on speech in elections are accepted even in the United States. These restrictions are constitutional because they are classified as restrictions on electoral activity and not on speech, including government speech.

The protection given to speech in the decision-making process is a function of democratic governance; it is dictated by the need to protect informed decision. On the one hand, democratic accountability requires that public officials explain their past, present, and intended actions. "On the other hand, the legitimacy of the chosen policy rests on the consent, if not consensus, of the governed; excessive or questionable efforts by government to manufacture the consent of the governed calls the legitimacy of its action into question."[25] It follows that there can be no restrictions based on the content of government speech, at least as long as government is not trying to perpetuate or "establish" itself, that is, it is not using its resources to get reelected.

In the election context the intervention of government on behalf of its own (incumbent) candidates goes against principles of representative democracy. Democracy is based on the prohibition against governmental self-perpetuation. Any otherwise authorized expenditure that allows such self-perpetuation through government support is at least suspect.

A somewhat uncertain judicial record points in this direction in most democracies. In the United States the New Jersey Supreme Court found that a school board had an implied authority to issue bonds. Still, it held the expenditure unlawful as the board did not allow the advocacy of anti-issuance positions "and thus imperiled the propriety of the entire expenditure."[26] In another case the court held that despite statutory authority to promote and protect human rights, agencies were prohibited from "advocat[ing] their favored position on any issue. . . . So long as they are an arm of the state government they must maintain a position of neutrality and impartiality."[27] State agencies should not get involved in the democratic process, although the agencies are not enjoined from educating the public.

The limits are not easily drawn. A California statute expressly speaks in advocacy of a certain viewpoint by the Commission of Women's Rights. Here the legislatively mandated official viewpoint was held constitutional, despite that "the imprimatur of government has conferred an advantage upon the commissioners is undeniable. That advantage, however, has not risen to the level of drowning out plaintiffs."[28] There seems to be a more stringent scrutiny in referenda where all advocacy by state bodies seems to frustrate free choice.[29] However, political disputes also exist among various divisions of the state, for instance, a city may advocate a position against the state.

There are surprising similarities in Germany. First, there is strong emphasis on the neutrality of civil servants in political (electoral) matters. Following a long German tradition that civil servants are the servants of the total community (*Gesamtheit*) and not of parties, already the Weimar Constitution (Art. 130 I) insisted that civil servants are obliged to avoid even the appearance that they are politically partisan.[30] This implies certain restrictions of speech rights in civil service. Acceptable restrictions are defined by considerations of loyalty, thus expanding beyond employment relations. Civil service neutrality dictates rules about the use of

office resources. A German civil servant is prohibited to provide any official support to a political candidate. Like in *Burt*,[31] the constitutional ground is to be found in the principle of free elections.[32] The principle imposes a strict obligation of neutrality on all state bodies in their relations to political parties and candidates.[33]

However, in the case of referenda this strict neutrality principle does not apply.[34] As referenda relate to expert matters (*Sachfrage*), Land bodies are entitled to provide an objective presentation helping the public to deliberate so long as they respect the decision-making freedom of the public.[35] On the other hand, the government is expected to provide public information through its agencies and to keep the public informed (*Oeffentlichkeitsarbeit*). Public authorities (including the cabinet) are bound by requirements of neutrality in such activity.[36] Some recent German Land constitutions expressly guarantee to parliamentary opposition some possibilities to equalize the advantages of the majority party in public presence. The government is obliged by the constitution not to be identified with any political party in its official capacity. "In a democracy it is of great importance to protect the formation of political will from state (governmental) influence. This is one of the important elements of the difference between totalitarian states"[37] and free democracies. The neutrality obligation is not limited to the electoral period.

State Neutrality and Neutral Institutions

Neutrality in Government Speech

Beyond the limits on government speech dictated by the integrity of the democratic (electoral) process, less stringent considerations emerge requiring some fairness in government speech. These considerations do not receive full credit in contemporary legal doctrine. Some of these concerns are related to government neutrality, others originate from so-called "spheres of neutrality." Although these considerations are distinct, they often overlap. Certain common patterns prevail in liberal democracies regarding government speech. Excessive government speech becomes suspect in all liberal democracies, notwithstanding culturally determined differences. To the extent modern democracies incorporate liberal values, the liberal concern about the state's attitude toward personal faith and beliefs becomes important or decisive.[38] Unspecified moral considerations and unspecified expectations in public opinion restrain and guide governments in their speech-related activities. The hidden concerns affecting government speech and the discourse space are uncontested but implicit constitutional and moral values and social and legal conventions. Governments are expected to behave impartially; this is a compelling enough interest to trigger some heightened scrutiny of government speech and government action affecting communication.

The importance of state neutrality increases if the public debate depends on government.[39] The actual structure of the communicative sphere is a condition that dictates constitutional choices. In case the press depends on government support, more caution is needed and one should apply much stricter standards to government action.[40]

Restrictions on government speech might be constitutional because these restrictions serve, or are dictated by, the needs of neutralized social spheres. Such neutralization is often very closely related to the needs of communicative activities. The highly valued independence of communicative institutions is poorly and inconsistently protected. The prevailing technique for the protection of the public communicative domain against government is to grant some institutional autonomy[41] to the institution where the public communication takes place. Spheres of neutrality are nonpolitical or nonpartisan realms in which the government is not supposed to interfere or influence public activities. The spheres of neutrality tend to be autonomous realms that were emancipated from the government. Their functions "originally" had been carried out by the state through a public organization. Over time these spheres were emancipated from subordination to government and sometimes became privatized. Other spheres of neutrality are still, in spite of their immunity, perceived as a public or quasi-governmental zone. As long as institutions are speakers, their speech is to be respected by government. Determining

immune institutions or spheres of neutrality is, however, left overwhelmingly to legislation that often follows a logic completely different from that of institutional neutrality.

The theory of state neutrality is underdeveloped in the communicative sphere with alarming consequences. Attempts to ensure government neutrality in government speech did not bring about systemic standards. The importance of the neutrality requirement increases as government permeates the social discourse. The actual power of government depends on the nature of the marketplace of ideas and of the resources available and permissible in a given constitutional arrangement.

Given the neutrality dimension of state activities including government speech, it is necessary to analyze neutral institutions and neutralization. This is followed by a review of the actual impact of neutral operations on government speech restriction. The current protection against governmental intervention into neutral spheres of speech as well as against censorship within neutral spheres of communication is insufficient and contradictory. Therefore, I will discuss the possible requirements of a judicially applicable test upon the assumption that such judicial intervention is feasible, notwithstanding the reluctance of the judiciary to go beyond sporadic intervention.

Constitutional Foundations of State Neutrality

State neutrality is not expressly recognized as a general constitutional principle, although it was a major trait of the self-portrait of the nineteenth-century liberal state. Moreover, in many constitutional systems of liberal stamp, government neutrality is textually institutionalized, at least in one regard, in the context of religion and churches. The nonestablishment provision of the First Amendment of the U.S. Constitution and the separation of church and state in many post-Communist constitutions indicate that the government has to abstain from religious matters. According to an alternative formulation, government should not take sides among the religions. In Posner's formulation the idea of neutrality to religion means that "the government cannot engage in activities that either penalize or subsidize the practice of religion. Judicial scrutiny is high, for whether the government program is sustained or struck down, there is a substantial risk of constitutional error."[42]

It is not by accident that religion was singled out. In a way, separation and the acceptance of the neutral state reflected and institutionalized the failure to structure social homogeneity around salvation. State neutrality in religious matters is the essence of the experience of fratricidal wars of religion. A minimum of social peace and homogeneity quintessential for the existence of the state could be achieved only by neutralizing the government in matters of religious (and, at that time, fundamental) beliefs of the citizenry.

In a secular world, creeds other than religious beliefs might become central (such as ethnic identity). Old arguments regarding toleration are still valid in new contexts, and government should remain neutral for lack of competence. The neutrality of noninterventionism got close to constitutional recognition in laissez-faire economies. "For the Lochner Court, neutrality . . . was a constitutional requirement. The key concepts here are threefold: government inaction, the existing distribution of wealth and entitlements, and the baseline set by the common law."[43] Sunstein claims that the constitutional requirement of neutrality as inaction continues until this day, including such crucial communication-affecting decisions as *Buckley*.[44] Of course, the welfare state undermined this fundamental neutrality of the traditional liberal state.

The abandonment of the moral mission of the state received a new boost with increased social pluralism. Where there are competing concepts of the public good (or none) the state will be forced to take a neutral stand. Both pragmatism and liberal multiculturalism provide justification. Pragmatism is sometimes elevated to virtue in the political culture, as in England where even impartiality toward political regimes or parties is not enough for neutrality if an activity is intended to influence policies of government. Therefore, it was held to be a dictate of broadcasting neutrality to refuse as political the broadcasting of humanitarian advertisements (such as those intended to inform the public about genocide in Rwanda).[45]

The neutrality model is quite attractive for any liberal constitutional setting. Not only because it conforms to underlying personal self-determination values, but also because it helps to avoid situations that would delegitimize or paralyze the state. The neutrality of the state offers opportunities to get rid of imposed identities: in this regard neutrality is liberating. In the postmodern world of complex and uncertain identities, government shares the cultural uncertainty that prevails in postmodern society; it might be reluctant to impose views and solutions on society as it seldom trusts the available solutions. Ignorance dictates nonintervention. Further, even where knowledge plays a central role, it is not understood as something fixed and given but as a process that cannot take place under government-induced censorship. Hence, there is a special justification for creating institutional autonomy for science. Skepticism in the moral sphere likewise dictates that no public authority can dictate models of the good life. Indeed, the state is incapacitated to find out what are the dictates of the good life. Skeptical liberalism suggests that political organizations may follow the dictates of fairness, but the state cannot provide mandatory ideals. For liberal theories of the neutral state based on individual autonomy it is obvious that self-regarding mandatory choices are unacceptable.

Nevertheless, state neutrality as an express tenet of liberal constitutionalism remains limited to religion for the very same reason it was adopted in the domain of religion. In regard to other patterns of behavior, including other forms of expression and beliefs, the fear of a salvation-triggered civil war was less compelling. While religion was historically too divisive to run the risk of state involvement, other personal concerns and beliefs were not held to be central enough to trigger mass social resistance. Moreover, state neutrality contradicted other legitimate state goals and functions such as national homogenization along nonreligious lines. Neutrality may hamper such efforts. Of course, the closer homogenization attempts get to salvation and personal core beliefs, the more compelling neutrality concerns will become.

The parallel practice of homogenization and respect of neutrality results in tension in the speech area. The analogy of religious establishment and free speech clauses was noted in *Buckley v. Valeo,*[46] but the applicability of the nonestablishment clause in the context of government funded elections was rejected. It is constitutionally recognized that beliefs cannot be mandated, but this is seen as unrelated to the right of the government to have and propagate ideological beliefs using public money. Legislatively mandated Flag Days and subsidized flag production are not government imposed beliefs, and in terms of free speech concerns these rules do not represent a problem as long as people are free *not* to observe and to criticize such practices.[47] Here neutrality comes up only as a special application of a speech theory.

There can be no homogenization without singling out values. But the drive to national homogenization is not true for all societies and all times. Germany may believe in it, while the United States seems to vacillate. It is held by the U.S. Supreme Court that only shared values can be legislated, and even in that case no one shall be compelled to share the values that are voiced by government. Further, in the rhetoric of *Barnette,* not even allegedly shared national values can be made compelling in the sense of forcing through sanctions.[48] State neutrality dictates that the choice of a government practice cannot rule out and put an end to the dispute regarding the practice itself.

In the school context the Supreme Court finds itself relatively at ease with the "shared values of a civilized social order."[49] Here shared values can be prescribed. Students can be inculcated. Here the courts find national homogenization more important than neutrality. The mainstream understanding of a democratic society acquiesces to government-induced indoctrination in schools other than universities.[50] The reluctance to protect the speech of students and teachers is understandable as homogeneity is a precondition to a working constitutional system. Legislatively ordered manufacturing of homogeneity in schools was upheld against aliens in *Ambach v. Norwick.*[51] However, a whole series of Supreme Court decisions dealing with education and speech in class sends a completely different message.[52] The concept of shared values is limited to those situations in which the individual is still allowed to find and follow her own concept of the good life, and allows others to do the same. "It is simply untrue that any restriction . . . on the state's ability to shape a homogeneous people in public schools, would 'bar any effort' to inculcate values. . . . Diversity among teachers is a check on government indoctrination distinct from the ability of

groups and individuals outside of the educational system to respond to the government's messages. The former dilutes the government's power to speak, the latter appeals to traditions of pluralism to create countervailing forces in the larger communication networks."[53] Moreover, for lack of judicially cognizable standards, courts feel incompetent to interfere in sublime educational choices. "As a matter of legal doctrine . . . it is virtually impossible in any specific case to draw a line between information and propaganda, or between education and indoctrination."

Where there are no shared values, there is an increased need for values and cultural symbols that integrate local society or the nation-state. With the thinning of the nation-state in pluralist secular societies, those interested in traditional values or in the institutions of the traditional nation-state need to invent shared values and symbols. However, the manufacture of shared values takes place at a time when these values can be and are challenged. The struggle for government-manufactured national cohesion and identity in a critical society produces new conflicts. Flag burning, a protected speech in the United States, and protection of national symbols as well as bans on certain symbols generate tension everywhere. In Germany there is no doubt that certain symbols are to be prohibited and others are to be respected. Germany has no problems with the criminalization of flag burning, and hence, with imposing a certain level of cultural identity (including what is done in the centralized, state-run school system where civil servants and their expert opinions govern).

In life spheres where the centrality of belief plays no role, government neutrality as a kind of "lack of competence" makes less sense. Nevertheless, government neutrality went beyond religion and encompassed at least the economy and perhaps other selected "neutralized" social spheres such as science and universities. In these spheres, neutrality as noninterventionism is often based on the "inherent" nature of government. It is simply against the nature of the state to get into the economy. Laissez-faire economists on the other hand argue on efficiency grounds in favor of state nonintervention. Laissez-faire economists rarely claim that state intervention is immoral, although for nineteenth-century lawyers state inaction was "part of nature." Noninterference into the economy is not based on moral considerations that respect the autonomy of a given activity (except, to a limited extent, private liberties and existing distribution of entitlements). Government withdraws not only from production and business regulation; it transfers its activities to nongovernmental entities due to functional difficulties within the administration.

Even after giving up the night watchman role of the state, neutrality remained a major concern. Wherever the state intervened it tried to do so without undertaking a morally partisan agenda. It followed universalistic, or at least all-national and consequentialist policies. Carl Schmitt recognized with some resignation that life spheres are neutralized one after another, beginning with religion.[54] History is a history of neutralization of the spiritual. Following religion, economy and science were neutralized, although the government's relation to these spheres might correspond to different understandings or patterns of neutrality.

Schmitt regrets that the state gives up its power to rule and dominate (*herrschen*) once it accepts a neutral role. Neutralization is lack of domination. To his mind, however, this is simply the transfer of the crucial sphere of politics from one dimension to another—politics always retains its central position. In politics, only the relationship between friends and enemies matters.

Democratic theories suggest a method different from the friend-enemy opposition. These theories argue that central issues of power shall be decided in the democratic process, within the limits of fundamental rights, with temporary winners who respect the minorities, at least in the sense of allowing them to take their turns next time. Yet, at the heart of democracy the Jacksonian moment of the spoil reigns: the winner takes all. But time and experience have taught that the price of the spoil system is excessive.

Institutional Neutralization of Public Administration

The internal life of modern government has been neutralized in most respects for pragmatic, not moral, reasons. Certain life spheres are more resistant to the political system, although not necessarily for liberal rea-

sons, that is, in the sense of freedom from the state. These reasons include, among others:

- the neutralization of the civil service,
- the cult of expertise where expertise requires independent organizations, and
- decentralization.

Civil service. Civil servants are loyal not to one or another party but to the party in power and to the government as such. Public employees are neutral, therefore the government is neutral. The neutral image of government is built upon the silence of civil servants.[55]

Practical government neutrality is related to the modern understanding of civil service. Although public offices cannot be denied on the basis of political affiliation anymore as was the case in the nineteenth century, the expression of political views in public employment might be restricted.[56] The civil service is increasingly represented as being impartial and nonpartisan, a body following purely legal (neutralized) and professional considerations. "Public service in the United Kingdom is founded on a tradition of a permanent corps of politically neutral officers serving with equal commitment whatever party may be in political control."[57] Conflict of interest rules restricting political roles and advocacy were held as imposing minimum (that is, permissible) impairment to civil servants as long as the preclusion of participation is limited to "only those types of activity which, on account of their visibility, would be likely to link a politically restricted post-holder in the eyes of the public . . . with a particular party political line."[58]

The Supreme Court of Canada is less deferential to the neutralization of civil servants through speech restrictions. In *Osborne v. Canada* (Treasury Board), the court held that by prohibiting public servants from speaking out in favor of a political party or candidate, the law expressly intends to restrict expressive activity and is accordingly inconsistent with s. 2(b) of the Charter.[59]

The image of neutral loyalty of the civil service encompasses loyal execution of instructions coming from political leaders and faithful execution of the laws even if that means the implementation of partisan politics.

A second organizational development that contributes to state neutrality is found in the growth and cult of *independent expert bodies*. In complex societies many traditional governmental functions and spheres of governmental action were transferred to independent organizations that are legitimized in terms of their expertise. Besides the legitimation coming from expertise and independence, these organizations and institutions satisfy the need for mediation between the distant state and society. "As Robert Nisbet and others have urged, the importance of mediating institutions—families, churches, . . . etc.—increases with the increasing scale of government institutions. The government-created mediating institutions may serve similar goals. . . . And such mediating institutions not only serve the purposes of pluralism . . . they may also act as a buffer against the excesses of overreaching government."[60]

However, this tendency also results in avoiding accountability and in minimizing political responsibility, including responsibility for private censorship. The speech of other public entities (such as universities, and scientific institutions) receives institutional protection because they perform special, speech-related activities. The level of protection or special treatment may vary from country to country.[61] From time to time desperate efforts are made to construct these bodies in a way that makes them nonpartisan and increases their neutrality both in terms of impartiality and independence from the government.[62] The more a public body is shielded from partisanship, the more its decisions will look neutral and less subject to political challenge. Decisions of independent agencies that affect speech (including resource allocations) and their statements are not considered to be government speech any more. According to the German doctrine, which expresses the trend the most clearly and authoritatively, the state is required to relate itself in a value-neutral way to science and universities that institutionalize science. Such behavior of the state includes not only the guarantee of scientific (research) freedom but also the provision of the means that enable the work of science.[63] The state institutionalizes the protection of science through proper measures of organization and expenditure. In this process the state is bound by constitutional principles: the organization has to be structured in a way that enables the right to self-management for science and the academic community. The neutrality obligation of the state includes the prohibition against setting up committed universities (*Tendenzuniversitaet*), that is, a university that would satisfy specific social interests in a programmatic way. Likewise, Justice Frankfurter held that a "university ceases to be true to its own nature if it becomes the tool of Church or State."[64]

Decentralization is another factor leading to increased state neutrality. Decentralization is partly unrelated to the abovementioned factors of government neutrality. For the purposes of the present discussion it includes delegation and devolution. Decentralization is dictated by a variety of social needs. In the modern state, government and political power are less centralized. Centralized sovereign power is an image from Rousseau's popular will theory or Carl Schmitt's decisionism. In the modern state there are a number of decision-making centers, and because of decentralization many decisions are made at the local or intermediary level. Hence the state may speak with many voices and therefore, except in a few crucial cases, it is hard to attribute to one or another voice full governmental authority. In many countries, judicial review and lack of finality as a side effect of it, federalism, and multiculturalism add to the trend.

Pluralism is a special form of decentralization. Here a service is rendered by competing, decentralized providers. This situation has specific impacts on the freedom of speech within the neutral institution. The burden of a speech-affecting decision is lessened if the affected parties have the possibility to opt out from the consequences of the decision without substantive burden. A school board or a school library decision censoring books or even proscribing teaching materials will be less onerous if the parents can exit and take the child to another school, or if worse comes to worst, they can move to another state. Even the biased and compelling voice may sound neutral if opting-out from the audience makes it irrelevant.

It is revealing that in areas where governmental speech or governmental partisanship are the most likely, special institutional neutrality emerges as combination of civil service professionalism and decentralization. This tendency is noticeable in the various forms of broadcasting regulation, press subsidies, and in the case of schools, or at least universities (which serve both higher education and science).

It is judicially believed in England that the Radio Authority, an independent expert commission, should be left with a large measure of discretion, because the regulatory authority "is likely to have particular expertise in the field."[65] In Germany, intervention into the marketplace of ideas occurs within the context of the activities of presumedly neutralized bodies. Governmental agencies and political parties may not interfere in broadcasting;[66] public and private broadcasting are supervised by delegates of nongovernmental, socially representative bodies. Land legislation has the power to shape broadcasting by determining the social forces that may participate in the supervisory board. The alleged neutrality helps to satisfy aspirations of non-party-partisan market correction. The mandate to make such corrections was not granted to the winner of the democratic election but to a permanent body of government, that is, civil service, or to nongovernmental agencies "representing" expertise and society.[67] The way bureaucrats outside and inside universities structure higher education will be decisive for the protected speech and culture production in the universities (even if the Constitutional Court intervenes to protect the decisive role of senior professors). The results might be censorial or at least restrictive. The conflicting viewpoints in society are represented and reduced in the majority of the mass media, which are controlled by independent bodies as "ritualistic-symbolic disputes of the big political parties. . . . Deviant positions will be represented, . . . but only for the sake of increasing the amusement."[68] Michel Rosenfeld came to the same conclusion in regard to the (now abandoned) "balance" approach of the United States: "the requirement of 'balance' actually promotes conformity and non-controversy. . . . Any application of a 'reasonableness' standard to determine whether a given issue is controversial almost inevitably will make it impossible for administrators to avoid an inquiry into the content of broadcasting material."[69]

Censorship in Neutral Institutions

The need for institutional neutralization is particularly felt where freedom from government is quintessential for the successful communicative operations of the institution. David Cole, for example, finds that "First Amendment strictures of neutrality and independence apply in these contexts because each of these institutions plays a central role in shaping and contributing to public debate, and because the internal functioning of each institution demands insulation from government content control. A spheres of neutrality approach would require that all public institutions central to a system of free expression operate with a degree of independence from government control."[70] In Cole's view neutrality is needed where "permitting content control poses a substantial risk"[71] of indoctrinating listeners or skewing the public debate. The extent of the danger depends on the relation between the audience and the speaker or regulator and on the distribution of the communication channel or access. The comparative perspective makes it clear that there are additional considerations, such as political credibility and expert function or equal protection, which mandate institutional neutrality. Equality as applied to government intervention into communication also produces neutrality. (In a broader context equal protection of the laws is at the heart of the prohibition of viewpoint discrimination and content-based discrimination.)[72] Of course, if equality is understood as material or substantive, and therefore the state is expected to promote substantive equality, the result will be opposite, namely, equality will dictate governmental (positive) discrimination.

There still might be professional censorship at work in these neutralized decisions, but "preference for this type lies at the heart of the First Amendment."[73] This is the reason for the nearly desperate effort to insulate art funding and its procedures from partisan political considerations by decentralizing decisions to panels of peers.[74] The resistance to neutralization comes from those who attach some kind of spiritual, ethnic, or other mission to democratic spoil; thus, it comes from the wish of *herrschen*. The neutralization or depoliticization of government is a matter of degree and blend. It has a major impact on speech even if it was not meant to neutralize government speech.

Some scholars argue that decisions taken within institutions that affect speech, as well as speech within specific institutions, may or should be subject to a specific set of rules. This is the case in most countries as far as broadcasters' speech rights (editorial rights) are concerned, although it is possible to construe their position as not being that of a speaker.

In principle, decisions of neutralized public institutions should not be governed by partisan politics even where the political branch funding the institution has clear partisan preferences. The decisions should follow professional canons as applied within the specific functional context of the institution.[75] Without legal guarantees, neutral professionalism may backfire.

Neutralization of government through the building of autonomous, professionally motivated institutions and through the delegation of decision making to nongovernmental bodies where the members do not existentially depend on the state is valuable for speech protection. It helps at least to the extent that the arrangement prevents government from shaping the public debate. But there is a price. Neutralization through insulation means that the constitutional protection against censorship may not apply within the institution. While governmental influences diminish, private censorship affecting public discourse may emerge. Unlike in the case of governmental regulation, free speech protection does not protect against restrictions inside private institutions, except if special rules apply. Public discourse might be hampered if school library decisions or speech in school is determined exclusively by dictates of institutional culture and functional considerations. These might become tyrannical if they are not responsive to speakers' interests and if neutralization of the institutions creates a private or nonpublic sphere.

In many countries rules of free speech protection do not apply to the private sphere; in other countries their impact is limited. Institutional neutrality may yield protection from government (political) intervention in decision-affecting speech. Let us take the example of acquisitions in public libraries. A librarian who excludes books denying the Holocaust violates the prohibition of viewpoint discrimination. However, viewpoint discrimination will not be an issue as long as acquisition practices are functionally neutral, that is, as long as the librarian follows a neutral scheme of acquisition dictated by the needs of the readers or other professional concerns. For example, she may prioritize factually uncontested books or books that are required for courses and exams.

Such content-based discrimination might be justified by functional requirements but it shall not be immune to review. Unfortunately, the functional requirements analysis may be of limited help, as the whole idea of expert institutions, and in a broader context governmental decision-making bodies, is based on the assumption that these institutions are the best qualified to know what is needed by their functions. The test used in the United States in the context of free speech of whether "there is an appropriate governmental interest suitably furthered by the differential treatment"[76] is somewhat circular, or at least it leaves undecided what is the proper level of scrutiny regarding appropriateness. In the days of laissez-faire, if we can believe Mill, the harm principle determined what is the appropriate governmental interest for intervention. This relatively clear guidance is lost in a world where all sorts of claims are made on the state. The issue is always what is appropriate—to what extent appropriate is limited by fairness or neutrality. It cannot be limited to being expedient to a goal; the government's goals are also at stake.

Neutrality here means that the discretionary power of a quasi-governmental body is limited when its decisions have a direct impact on the marketplace of ideas. After all, the choices of amplifiers such as librarians or those who provide subsidies to art have a decisive impact on the distribution of ideas and culture-defining images. It is highly problematic and a source of easy abuse if these choices remain within the domain of the discretionary dictates of state reason (*Staatsraison*) or partisanship. Institutional autonomy is valuable only if autonomy will not bar principles of free speech protection, like the U.S. unconstitutional conditions doctrine or the prohibition of viewpoint-based discrimination.[77] (It is a different matter how far courts should and may go in restraining partisanship.) Institutional autonomy is a partial solution to protect private speech from partisan political influences.[78] In addition to internal censorship there is a second cost element: nonaccountability.

As mentioned above, there are institutional developments that result in a degree of neutralization of the government by allocating the decision making to nonpolitical actors (civil service) or to nongovernmental actors. To some extent, such arrangements may result in the loss of protection provided by the free speech provisions of the constitution. After all, private speech in private locations is free to silence other voices. Likewise, proprietary control over private spheres may entail the right to silencing. Employers claim the right to determine the language at the workplace and may claim the right to prohibit the advocacy of certain views at the workplace. Surprisingly, even in the United States, where the Constitution is presumed to affect government behavior only, Congress and the judiciary are ready to take steps to protect speech or intervene into speech in nongovernmental settings, at least where the "space" or institution was created by law or acts in the name of the law. Speech-affecting decisions like library acquisitions by school boards and purely private parental library commissions were subject to judicial review without any thought about the governmental nature of the board.[79] Also, the way Congress established the National Endowment for the Arts made NEA decisions justiciable. The same is true in Germany, for example, in the context of the Library Indexing Committee[80] or the Television Councils.

Institutional neutralization does not satisfy the requirements of state neutrality, as voiced in political philosophy. Certainly, a nongovernmental institutional decision-making environment makes the administration of meritocractic criteria more credible. Courts might be satisfied with the analysis of those structural organizational criteria. In Germany, for example, the Federal Constitutional Court emphasized the importance of such institutional-organizational guarantees, thereby avoiding substantive review of specific decisions. Generally, justices will not engage in the review of the actual criteria application. The "neutral" composition of the decision-making body is deemed to be a sufficient guarantee. A library commission composed of parents is assumed to be the best protector of the children's educational interest, as long as the criteria applied by the parents strictly refer to the needs of the children's moral and cognitive development and do not touch upon the author's political viewpoints or morality. The institutional protection of state neutrality is imperfect from the perspective of free speech as robust discourse. The institutional censorship and the political dependencies of the neutral institutions require therefore some substantive judicial review of the neutrality of speech-affecting decisions and institutional speech.[81]

Schauer claims that although historically "there have been good reasons for the Supreme Court [not to draw] institutional distinctions in the free speech context, the institutional cultural factors should allow for special treatment."[82] This might be a reasonable doctrinal consideration, but it does not answer the question to what extent will a "special treatment" weaken a robust debate.

Here I propose a unified, though sketchy, test that might be used to evaluate both government's and "neutral institution's" impact on speech. Of course, courts in different countries follow their own dogmas, and arguments and tests are bound to the national legal systems. Nevertheless, some common features seem to emerge, and therefore it is not unrealistic to discuss neutrality at a level of abstractness and generality, which, if the test itself is acceptable, can be inserted into the national systems of legal and judicial reasoning. The neutrality test below is developed with reference to certain shortcomings of the U.S. jurisprudence where similar attempts were made by the Supreme Court. These attempts were never systematic and were bound by other preexisting parochial doctrines (for example, public forum).

In order to protect speech (both speakers from censorial silencing and the audience from indoctrination, as well as the public debate from impoverishment), one should look into government speech and government practices (such as funding, spending, licensing) affecting speech and into similar activities within neutralized institutions. A basically unified test shall apply to these two for the simple reason that speech or funding of speech by the state and that of a quasi-governmental or independent body are interchangeable to the extent that speech and decisions might be privatized and nationalized time and again. Of course, governmental authority and direct political influences might diminish with privatization. Indeed, the authoritative effects of the independent bodies are less. Hence there is a justified presumption of some neutrality in the case of independent bodies. But the institutional arrangements do not make additional external supervision futile.

The protection of neutrality through review shall entail both speech and speech-affecting practices (including practices that invigorate the marketplace of ideas) because both speech and speech-influencing have an interrelated impact on public discourse. All this indicates that a high level of generality will be required. The following suggestions are intended to prove the possibility and necessity of scrutiny that guarantees neutrality. National legal systems follow preestablished patterns of scrutiny. Notwithstanding enormous doctrinal differences between the leading constitutional adjudication systems, it seems to me that the structural elements of the neutrality analysis can be absorbed into the prevailing doctrinal cultures.

Neutral standards of Government speech: Meritocracy

In the juridical sense the state will be neutral depending on the definition of neutrality. Neutrality is neither self-explanatory nor self-evident, hence its categories will not automatically yield neutral results.[83] What may seem neutral to some will be considered biased by others. Neutrality is a highly problematic and somewhat vague concept. After all, government neutrality may be satisfied sometimes by impartiality; it may also imply noninterference (laissez-faire); and sometimes it requires equality of chance (for example, among parties in elections).

Neutrality depends on the categories applied; categories that allow government bias and partisanship to prevail will satisfy no expectation of neutrality. The first choice (the first order problem) is a categorical one. Government support of speech (in the form of subsidies or other) has to be categorical in order to remain neutral, although categorization itself is not enough for neutrality. According to Janos Kis,[84] the categorization satisfies the requirements of the neutral state as long as the categories do not discriminate among people, denying their way-of-life choices and, therefore, their equal dignity. There are speech-affecting categories that will per se defy requirements of state neutrality. For example, to give support only to all activities (in the domain of arts, science, health, etc.) that satisfy republican ideas or peasant interests is a violation of neutrality although it may remain within the original categorical division. Further, in order to remain neutral, allocative decisions within the category should look into the intrinsic values of the recipients using equal criteria of desert. This points to meritocracy. Finally, the meritocratic criteria

shall be "substantially related" to the category. If art is the category, the merit condition has to do with art.[85] To the extent a government spending or other authorization (license) goes to categories constitutionally it is seen as an exercise of constitutional expenditure power. However, as soon as it imposes a restriction on speech (even indirectly by favoring some speech to the extent of other communication) it should trigger some kind of heightened scrutiny.[86]

The ideal of and need for neutrality influenced a number of rights-related regulatory government activities. These neutrality concerns affected speech directly and also had a broader intellectual impact. Beginning in 1976, the U.S. Supreme Court became concerned with the neutrality of the criteria applied to minorities' employment.[87] (Earlier, the effects of the criteria were decisive, that is, denial of employment). In the post-1976 decisions, if the employment criteria were neutral (for example, meritocractic or otherwise unrelated to race or any other unconstitutional condition) there was no discrimination. State neutrality emerges as a value taken for granted that, according to Owen Fiss, "might have some sway in the speech area too, where state neutrality is also assumed to be a good. We want the state to be neutral between competing viewpoints, or competing conceptions of the good life."[88]

The idea of neutrality was applied to speech in *Board of Education v. Pico.*[89] The case concerned the decision of a school board to ban certain books from the school's library. Justice Brennan, speaking for a plurality, claimed that "(i)f petitioners intended by removal decision to deny respondents' access to ideas with which petitioners disagreed . . ., then petitioners have exercised their discretion in violation of the Constitution."[90]

Fiss argues that meritocractic (or other noneffect-related) criteria are not satisfactory neither for neutrality nor in terms of consequences. (Meritocracy here means performance or competence-based criteria.) He argues that, on the one hand, when speech-affecting allocative decisions are based on merit there is a content-based choice, because a content-based choice is required to determine the meritocractic criteria. Subsidies to arts are an example of an allocative decision. When high art is preferred to new forms of artistic expression, the choice regarding the scale of values will be a content-based choice. Likewise, there is a substantive value choice when fairy tales, low-circulation papers, or local news content is preferred. It seems that notwithstanding the inevitable substantive choice, certain meritocractic criteria satisfy state neutrality while others are suspect or presumptively value biased. Certain governmental value choices are not precluding or excluding other choices. The substantive choice is undeniably content based or at least subject matter based.[91] It may still satisfy neutrality as long as it is not viewpoint based and serves mischief-remedial goals. The subject choice has to satisfy the following criteria:

(a)   the mischief has to be actual, and
(b)   the choice is not related to political, partisan viewpoints.

Owen Fiss's second objection to meritocractic neutrality is that the "ideal of neutrality in the speech context not only requires that the state refrain from choosing among viewpoints, but also that it not structure public discourse in such a way as to favor one viewpoint over another."[92] With a surprising twist Fiss continues: "The state must act as a high-minded parliamentarian, *making certain that all viewpoints are fully and fairly heard.*"[93]

Although in principle this is far from the right of the government to advocate the good life through speech as it was proposed by Shiffrin, it allows for a similar level of government intervention in speech. Owen Fiss claims that "a seemingly neutral criterion does not insure a neutral impact."[94] David Cole disagrees: "[neutrality] requires that government adopt an agnostic stance toward speech; it demands neutral treatment, not neutral outcomes, [O]utcome neutrality is meaningless in most settings."[95]

This is not to say that the outcome of meritocractic decisions may not be highly problematic for the discourse space. In the regulatory context of broadcasting, neutral criteria of subsidy only help to preserve the status quo. Even worse, such neutral criteria allow for the dominant tendencies of speech to get additional reinforcement. On a meritocractic ground, already successful artists or scholarly papers get funding; it will be the already successful, the existing public bias, that will become dominant. However, the problem is not with

neutrality but with a misreading of meritocracy. It is not a valid objection against government neutrality and allocative government decisions affecting speech that meritocractic criteria disadvantage a minority or a minority viewpoint. If such decisions result in permanent disadvantage of a constitutionally protected minority, or if they disadvantage a minority or a majority in an arbitrary manner, the applied meritocractic criteria are simply wrong. They are wrong either because they are unconstitutional and, therefore, impermissible, or because they do not satisfy the criteria of neutrality and meritocracy.[96] Or, peers may find a recognized artist the best on meritocratic grounds but there is no need to subsidize her (there is no mischief in her case).

No one can deny that it is quite common that imperfect criteria of meritocracy are used. And yet there can be not only bad but also better approximations of government neutrality. If better approximations are applied in a principled fashion, they will help to keep social and moral values within the expectations of neutrality. The ruling out of certain governmental positions that endanger free speech is enough to maintain the credibility of government neutrality. Given the uncertainties of neutrality and the quite justified reluctance of the judiciary to review legislative discretion where the chances of actual compliance are slim, one can realistically assume that neutrality-based judicial review may offer only a limited protection against governmental restrictions of speech through allocative decisions and against biased decisions affecting speech within neutralized institutions. As to neutralized expert institutions, courts will tend to be deferential to legislatively recognized expertise.

Rules of standing further limit judicial review opportunities: in many situations it is difficult for someone whose forum access possibilities were limited by a decision of an independent body to prove injury in fact or substantive interest violation. How could a writer prove that the ban on her book in one or another school library restricted her speech rights? Likewise, in most legal systems library patrons may not have standing (or will lose on other technical grounds) when they complain about the unavailability of a certain book. At this point reference shall be made to the controversial nature of professional and expert neutralization. Transferring speech-affecting decisions and some speech to "independent agencies" diminishes the chances of judicial review[97] as the speech of these bodies is not perceived as political and, consequently, viewpoint biased. Therefore, as quasi-private and expert speech, it is subject to less stringent review or it is held immune to review because immunity is a guarantee against state interference. The judicial protection of speech is further aggravated by the fact that the restrictions on other people's speech resulting from independent agency speech and funding are diffuse, and the impacts on the audience are often indirect and therefore represent difficulties for judicial cognizance.

Neutrality implies the right and opportunity to fair hearing; without being heard impartially, fact-based decisions are impossible. Let us take the example where funding goes to "new forms" of art or to young artists. One might have the impression that such allocative decisions are based on a substantive criterion (funding arts versus funding education versus funding the army). The noncontent-based category applied to sponsorship of the arts here consists of the lack of opportunity for the potential recipient to be heard in the world of art: the artist is young, the artistic technique or even the theme is "recent." First, one shall determine the neutral category of hardship, that is, insufficient access to the public discourse. The application of meritocractic criteria comes only at a second order scrutiny. The best first novels are going to be supported, "best" being established by peer review.

Of course, support to new, unheard expression gets dangerously close to instances where viewpoints that have difficulties of access and therefore are not fully heard receive government support. The difference between unheard individual voices and unsuccessful political views is decisive here. Most political viewpoints (contrary to new artists) had their opportunity—and lost. A second difference is related to the nonpolitical nature of funded or otherwise supported communicative activities. These secondary differences are not always clear. Cultural preferences have a considerable impact on party politics. It follows that in defense of neutrality a rebuttable presumption of partisanship shall apply in case of doubt. Such a presumption would trigger viewpoint discrimination analysis (for example, in the case of contested national symbols).

In light of meritocracy neutrality, the apparently neutral government task of equalizing the chances for all viewpoints to be presented remains highly problematic, even where it is constitutionally mandated, as certain German or Hungarian theories would suggest. According to these theories, the state is required to overrule the decisions of the market (listeners' choice) in order to facilitate the presence of a viewpoint. The standard counterargument is that under this facilitation theory a government that finds that certain extremist viewpoints, such as racist or Nazi views, do not receive a fair measure of public attention due to editorial choices would be required to give government support to these allegedly suppressed views. Moreover, there is no guarantee that mandated correction by the government will not be arbitrary or, even more importantly, that it will be free from partisan political desires and dictates. It is not only a matter of market distortion that certain values are not favored by the public, be those values of artistic nature or those of the good life.

Neutrality as meritocracy is immune to the criticism that can be voiced against rectifying a viewpoint imbalance that is due to lack of public attention. Art with access difficulties will get support but not Nazi art with such difficulties. However, this is not viewpoint discrimination: the peers of Nazi artists—peer review being the institutional guarantee of meritocractic neutrality—simply will not find Nazi propaganda realism to be the "best" according to the inherent criteria of art. The exclusion does not necessarily apply to artists with personal Nazi viewpoints. Of course, in an illiberal democracy with a zealous majority where peers will follow their nonartistic values or where art is also perverted, there is no protection against viewpoint zealots. The ideal of meritocractic control applies only to neutral governments (governments committed to neutrality).

As mentioned above, substantive or subject-based choices are the preconditions to the application of meritocractic criteria. The substantive, first order choice, in regard to which the meritocractic criteria can be applied, often satisfies criteria of neutrality by being professionally functional.

The promotion of novelty in arts funding has to do with the way art "develops." But functionality is not self-evident and professionalism is often just another name for vested biased interests. The problem of state neutrality is that in many regards the state is expected not to be neutral, certainly not in the sense of noninterference. The state is expected to serve and to provide; it has to take action, and democracy legitimates it to take one-sided actions. "One does not, as it were, have to be neutral all the way down."[98] Moreover, the state cannot be neutral in many of its actions. Even its speech is expected to be partisan in support of these actions. State actions include speech or affect speech, hence the need for additional substantive guarantees of state neutrality in speech-affecting regulations and government speech. Where there is a direct relation between government and a protected communicative sphere, state neutrality as impartiality is the standard, at least in regard to the press. This is expressed as a prohibition of viewpoint discrimination (in the United States)[99] or state neutrality obligation[100] in the press subsidy/tax cases.

Speech-enhancing intervention remains the source of abuse or a fig leaf of state interventionism if distortions in the marketplace of ideas cannot be determined along clear and neutral criteria. When unprincipled government intervention intends to create a level playground for speech, the government may get close to promoting its own conception of the good life. The remedial treatment of the marketplace of ideas gets even closer to government interventionism if and when the second order meritocractic criteria are also discredited.

Neutrality might be satisfied with a combined purpose-effects test. As to purpose Larry Alexander states in regard to speech regulation: "the principal focus . . . should be on the government's reasons for regulating."[101] He is concerned with the intent behind the regulation affecting speech. Moreover, in cases of speech regulation one should also look into the actual consequences, although applying a less stringent test should the speech be unrelated to political partisanship. The easy and clear case of an unacceptable consequence of speech or speech support is the one that drives a certain viewpoint out of the marketplace of ideas or one that silences a specific speaker. This consequence analysis differs from the one suggested by Owen Fiss as it looks at actually caused restriction and not at the consequences of the continued operation of the status quo. A combination of purpose

and effect is advocated by Kathleen Sullivan. She suggests "strict review [of] any government benefit condition whose primary purpose or effect is to pressure recipients to alter a choice about exercise of a preferred constitutional liberty in a direction favored by government."[102] The present "purpose and consequences" test that emerged in the context of the substantive basis of the meritocracy test is less stringent than the one suggested by Sullivan in regard to government benefit conditions. However, it is intended for broader use in the sense that it applies to all sorts of speech conditions determined either by government or by government proxies, including independent agencies.

Fiss complained that the shift from effects to policy (allocation) criteria did not satisfy neutrality, as allocation criteria may contribute to discrimination. However, if government action is not intended to promote or advocate a specific value, or opinion against its opposite, the neutrality requirement might be deemed to be satisfied even if accidental consequences enhance a specific viewpoint. The neutrality of governmental intent might be the answer to the subject-matter-based categorization that constituted the first order problem of meritocracy described above (art versus science). In Soviet times political concerns dictated subsidies to folk music rather than to jazz. Of course, as mentioned above, government speech or action that drives out specific speech is still unconstitutional. In regard to specific speech (viewpoints), the effects test applies.

The effects test follows the intermediary test used by the U.S. Supreme Court in *O'Brien*.[103] Here the military applied an administrative requirement that accidentally had an impact on speech. The regulation (as it was seen by the majority of the Supreme Court) did not intend to regulate speech but was dictated by the needs of military administration. The speech impact was held as accidental. This approach provides rather stringent protection to speech where a regulation is directly affecting speech (such as a spending regulation directly affecting speech). *Rust* would be unconstitutional under *O'Brien,* as the gag rule is a condition attached to spending and not an inevitable consequence.[104] Likewise, government speech such as a statement by a public official will meet neutrality requirements as long as it is descriptive, informative, and nonpartisan. If so, the communication is not intended to restrict other people's speech. Information here means factual statements. As fact selection might also be biased, government speech should meet the requirements of fairness and balanced presentation. Given the authoritative nature of government speech, the informational nature should be narrowly construed with the burden of proof on government. The more authoritative and monopolistic a government's statements in a given society, the stricter the information requirement should be.

It has to be admitted that the above standards do not provide protection against elements of metacommunication inherent in neutral communication. Likewise, government action and nonspeech regulation have a metacommunicative element. If the government chooses to fund new art, the value of "novelty" is enhanced and conservatives may feel uncomfortable. In societies where governments are expected to defend social values or intend to be the depositories of truth, such positions will be seen as abandonment and partisan antagonism. The increase in computer science class hours in the national curriculum at the expense of Latin may be interpreted in a similar manner. Novelty is "better"; government sides with innovation. In *O'Brien* the message of the legislation was clear: it "intended" to take the side of the Vietnam War effort. However, the communication is not intended to restrict speech and its effects fall on other speech only by accident. The governmental choice to support computers at the expense of Latin serves functionally a recognized government task (education), hence the category chosen satisfies neutrality.

Choice of national symbols is a particularly problematic and telling area of neutrality. The choice of national symbols, for example, the return to a coat of arms that was used by a previous regime, is not driving out private speech; as a matter of fact, it does not even affect it as long as the protection of a preferred symbol is not extended to the punishment of those who despise the old symbol. And yet, in a given sociopolitical context, such as in the restoration of past national identity in a transition-to-democracy process, the legislator's value choice is a clear example of authoritative government speech. It is probably a violation of neutrality, but certainly not a vice easily cured by legal means. It borders on a state establishment of national identity; it amounts to state advo-

cacy of a historical belief that has structural similarities to the state establishment of a religion.

The state may take an authoritative position in a debate of personal preference (taste) and beliefs simply by stating that one preference is part of the official culture and, therefore, is more valuable. This will have far-reaching consequences in a centralized or nonautonomous educational system. Where the state speaks with legitimate authority (due to its communication monopoly or because of authoritarian tradition), its voice will determine the status of the members of the audience and their views, and in particular it may relegate some people (because of their views) to inferior status.[105] To the extent that the state is constitutionally expected to respect the equal dignity of all, such speech might be unconstitutional. The role of government speech is socially dependent in the sense that societies differ in regard to the status-ascribing power of government speech (and symbolic valuation through spending). Where such status-ascribing power exists, the state is expected to take active positions: if the state fails to condemn racism this is interpreted as tacit support of racism, or complicity. Where the state's power in this regard is limited or constitutionally restricted by neutrality expectations, government's silence cannot be interpreted as support.

Moreover, unless there is a compelling argument (a genuine belief in truth) in support of a position, neutrality requires the state not to take (advocate) that position. The disregard of this precept is objectionable from the perspective of liberal political philosophy and it has, indeed, caused some of the most blatant abuses of power. In ethnocentric societies the government's conservative choice among preferences is based on the assumption that a preference is or is not part of the national tradition. A preference choice is elevated to the rank of truth. In this context ethnocentric preferences are particularly troublesome. The state's ethnocentric choice is based on the assumption that a preference is or is not alien to "our" community. "Alien" means that it will contribute to the loss of "our" identity.[106] The alarming potential of such government speech makes the neutrality requirement even more compelling. In the near future we have to be prepared for continued ethnic politics: government neutrality in speech is a potential intellectual tool to control ethnocentrism.

Where government speech or government's choice of a strongly communicative practice is based on preferences that defy rational consequentialism, neutrality dictates the strictest scrutiny.

Conclusion: Interventionism, Speech, and the State's Place in Society

The very nature of government, as well as our most hidden expectations regarding government, come to light in a most dramatic way in the context of the speech-government relation and, in particular, in the context of government speech. The way one evaluates the government's possibilities and obligations in the context of the marketplace of ideas puts a number of attitudes to test. One's position concerning the relations of the government and the marketplace of ideas compels one to disclose her attitudes toward the free-market economy, toward the proper limits of government, and regarding the kind of speech she likes.

The current majority of the U.S. Supreme Court accepts market outcomes, that is, the actual speech outcomes resulting from the market (especially in *Buckley*[107] and in *Turner*[108]). Most governmental decisions shaping culture are not considered legally relevant interventions into the marketplace of ideas. This is the case with spending rules that contain gag rules in the abortion context and censorship of indecency in the arts funding context; broadcasting licensing and educational decisions are additional illustrations. The noninterventionist justices of the U.S. Supreme Court are not inclined to accept judicial review of the public debate conditions. Distortions of the marketplace of ideas and distortions caused by government action such as spending or school boards' library censorship are beyond review, except if the distortion is based on blatantly impermissible discrimination or narrow partisanship.[109] The same standards may apply if the government is in a privileged position in the marketplace of ideas, including the communications market. In the judicial philosophy of the noninterventionist, politics is just another form of the market. The winners of the political game have all the spending power; influencing of the public

debate and thought is still just spending. This explains the ease that one sees in the characterization and categorization of rules affecting speech as spending. Electoral victories, like the result of any other legitimate investment, allow for the maximization of return without much ado about the First Amendment.[110]

The dominant German approach combines a governmental concern regarding the marketplace of ideas with a reluctant acceptance of a winner-takes-all approach to politics. The allegedly neutral state is seen as having a culture-shaping mandate. In many regards regulation, and regulation affecting speech in particular, are presented as being off-limits to ordinary booty politics. This off-limits approach is partly constitutionalized by shielding certain communicative spheres from party politics and democratic (electoral) control. The electoral process itself is "shielded" through the concept of equality of chances for competing parties. Elections are a game in which the government stands as a neutral entity vis-à-vis the competing parties. The government as state is constitutionally required to provide equality in a material sense in order to promote debate and create a level playground for all (constitutionally admissible) views. Although the German system reduces the possibilities of political winners to impose their views on the marketplace of ideas, or to give discriminatory support, an allegedly neutral reshaping of the marketplace is not only permitted but even encouraged. The civil service is perceived to be entitled to shape the discourse space and even to offer viewpoints to society in the name of their expertise and, moreover, as the voice of a homogeneous governmental position.

Further, while academic freedom is guaranteed and speech at universities is protected, professors are civil servants with ties of political loyalty. Universities remain subject to public management determined by the civil service, with obvious impact on the curriculum (which will have an impact on the professors' speech). Legislation is accepted as a manufacturer of consent, and perhaps not only where there is social consent, although this is promoted by the somewhat consensual parliamentary decision-making process.

Notwithstanding the differences in state interventionism, the processes and the culture of democracy and well-established free-market structures prevent government domination over public discourse. This is not to say that one can take state neutrality for granted in the discourse space of established democracies and does not preclude cases of government bias and partisanship. These numerous and troubling governmental attempts are sometimes quarantined and constrained by legal means, including judicial review.

There are influential forces in every country of the world that argue indoctrination is good and necessary. In transition countries it is often held that patriotic or other indoctrination is legitimate as a remedy to communist indoctrination. The interventionist attitude is, ironically, accompanied and facilitated by a noninterventionist understanding of politics. Elected leaders of Eastern Europe who claim state intervention into the structure of public debate do so in the name of democratic legitimation in terms of "winner-takes-all" politics. In emerging democracies the problems of governmental speech (a biased and partisan interference with the public discourse via governmental measures) are systemic. The governments of the day exercise considerable control over the media, although the degree and manner of the control differ noticeably from country to country. Irrespective of these differences, the governments have decisive control over the manufacturing of social consent. This manufacturing of consent is sometimes impermissibly extended to free elections. In a number of transition-to-democracy countries, governmental shaping of the public debate violates free speech even by noninterventionist standards. Governments make the debate less robust when they claim to promote certain values through government speech and through spending in the name of restoring the balance of viewpoints. The actual impact of governmental restoration of the public discourse balance in the new democracies indicates the dangers of such interventionism elsewhere.

Neutrality and Universality in Human Rights Law

Ratna Kapur

The issues of universality, neutrality, and accountability addressed in the different papers are all primary attributes of a functioning liberal democracy and effective rule of law. Yet none of these features is either static or their meaning uniformly assumed. The meaning and experience of each is mediated, among other things, by gender, sexual status, race, ethnicity, and religion. My comments will focus on how each of these concepts have been and continue to be a zone of contest. They are prefaced by my own location as a postcolonial feminist intellectual, living and working in law in India. From my location, I am acutely aware of the paradox of liberalism and its potential for arbitrariness. While Europe was developing ideas of political freedom, especially in France, Britain, and Holland, it simultaneously pursued and held vast empires where such freedoms were either absent or severely attenuated for the majority of the native inhabitants. Liberalism, and the rights and freedoms that it nurtured, coexisted quite unproblematically with the Empire.[1]

While there was an assumption that certain political practices were indeed universal—such as liberty, equality, and fraternity—these ideals seemed to stumble and falter at the moment of their encounter with the unfamiliar, the "other." Liberalism's response to a world where there were so many different ways in which social and political life were organized was simple—colonialism. These values meet with some of the same difficulties today in their encounters with difference and unfamiliarity in our increasingly transmigratory, transnational world.[2] With these few introductory remarks, let me turn to address some of the specific issues raised by each panelist.

Comments on Professor Robert Badinter's Paper: The State and Human Rights

My comments are focused on Professor Badinter's claim that "human rights are universal, every human is entitled to them, and neither history nor geography can alter them." This claim is based on the belief that there are certain norms or rights that are inviolable and applicable to all societies, regardless of cultural specificity. And these norms and values cannot be abrogated.

But there are a number of countries that regard human rights and human rights instruments as forms of cultural imperialism of the West. Part of this suspicion stems from the history of imperialism and the fact that many countries have been historically subjected to the norms of liberalism and Christianity, imposed upon them through the device of colonialism. Universalism is perceived as a disguise for once again imposing Western norms on different countries and cultures and not respecting difference. It is viewed as a new form of imperialism. Part of the critique of universalism is that it is directed toward eradicating diversity and creating the fantasy of homogeneity in the global community that simply does not reflect the current global reality. This critique is important especially with the increasing mobility of people and the very real cultural tensions that play out as a result of this mobility.

These tensions were vivid in the 1993 case in France involving the expulsion of three girls from their school for wearing the veil.[3] Although the ban was successfully challenged in legal terms, the complex cultural conflicts underlying the controversy were not adequately addressed.

Some members of the immigrant community, and even outsiders, regarded the wearing of the veil as a challenge to French liberal democracy. For others, the veil was a religious symbol for Muslims in much the same way as the wearing of the cross was a religious symbol for many Christians, and as no restrictions were placed on the wearing of a cross in a public space, restrictions on the wearing of the veil could not be justified. And to some the veil represented the continued subordination of women to men being perpetuated by fundamentalists; for others, the veil was essential to the survival of the cultural identity of the immigrant community. Yet the case itself did not address the multidimensional politics surrounding the veil. In France, the wearing of the veil was viewed exclusively as an oppressive symbol, while the banning of it curiously enough was regarded as simply a prerequisite to free choice. The individuals involved did not experience an opposition between culture and human rights, at least not until the authorities imposed the opposition on them.

A broader question that I would like to pose here is Why are issues of culture invariably displaced onto a first world/third world divide? Rarely, for instance, does culture become a point of controversy in the United States, unless of course it is with reference to a minority community. Guns, for example, are not articulated as an aspect of American culture but rather a constitutional right to bear arms, even though for the outsider guns seem as integral to American culture as apple pie and baseball. And gun-related murders of women in the context of domestic violence are never articulated as a cultural issue. In contrast, the discrimination, harms, and death experienced in the developing world or other cultures, by women in particular, are frequently articulated in terms of "death by culture," an argument that has little explanatory value.[4] And human rights casebooks reinforce these stereotypes and assumptions where, invariably, the issues of female genital multilation, sati, dowry murders, and, most recently, honor killings constitute the subject matter of the universality versus cultural relativism chapter. How do these issues get transported into developed world contexts and come to be framed as "cultural"? Why is there little understanding of the thoroughly modern nature of these practices? And why is there so much scholarship and research material available

on these specific issues and not, say, on the number of American women killed by guns in domestic violence situations in the United States?

Comments on Professor Andras Sajo's Paper: Government Speech in a Neutral State

Professor Sajo's paper argues in favor of legitimate speech restrictions in order to perpetuate the liberal ideal of a neutral state. His basic argument is that the neutrality standard should govern the arena of free speech in the same way as it has informed the antiestablishment clause and it's insistence on the separation of religion and state in the United States.

Neutrality and the Wall

I question whether neutrality is an attainable goal or even desirable. The limits of neutrality are apparent when one examines how it has operated in the context of the wall of separation. As an outsider, when I scan the public arena in the United States I find that God seems to occupy a central place in public life—at least in the sense of formal religion. Religion seems to be out of the closet and frequently found in cahoots with the state. There are numerous recent instances that demonstrate this more open relationship between the two. In the fall of 1999, Rudolph Giuliani, responding to Catholic protests against the "Sensation" exhibition, threatened to cut city funding to the Brooklyn Museum of Art for exhibiting a scatalogical portrait of the Virgin Mary;[5] some states are promoting highly controversial school voucher programs whose primary effect seems to be to advance religion;[6] and most intriguingly, at least from the perspective of the outsider, the sin of sex, where the church and state have collaborated to both chastise and absolve President Clinton through nothing less than invoking the edifice of impeachment and breakfast prayer confessions.[7]

These recent controversies aside, what is striking from the point of view of a comparativist, looking at U.S. secularism from the outside is that there appears to be a broad range of widely accepted state-sanctioned religious activities.[8] These include the United States currency, which proudly displays In God We Trust, opening prayers at state assemblies, and state funding of chaplains in the armed forces.[9] More recent contentious examples include the withdrawal of evolution studies from the curriculum of Kansas City public schools. The fact that presidential candidates now also feel obliged to declare their faith credentials to voters leaves the comparativist questioning the impermeability of the "wall" and the ostensibly neutral position on which it is based.

Without going into details, many American critics have argued that the requirement of state nonintervention and neutrality on issues of religion has served to reinforce the power relations of the status quo and thus the dominant position of religious majorities. Indeed the neutral standard has not been unlinked from its majoritarian moorings, and rather than turn the tides of majoritarianism it can play right into it.[10]

My point is that the neutrality standard simply seems to hide more than it reveals. Indeed, it is quite likely that the wall is about to come down in the United States and be replaced by a model of secularism based on the equal treatment of all religions.[11] Ironically, this has been the governing model of secularism in India, where tolerance rather than neutrality characterizes the relationship between religion and the state. It has also been a model that has facilitated the rise of the Hindu Right, a nationalist, religious right-wing party that is currently running the country.[12]

Neutrality and the Right to Free Speech

Let me now consider Professor Sajo's proposal to introduce a neutrality standard in the area of government speech and practice. Speech cannot be treated as something that exists outside of a social context and a dominant ideology. Speech is regulated or deregulated depending on its historical, political, and cultural location. State intervention is contingent on the kind of speech involved and who is speaking and cannot be unlinked from issues of culture, nationalism, and power relations that are operating in and through the right to free speech.

Compare for example the defeat of the hate crimes prevention act with the cases pending on the right to school prayer and other forms of "God talk" being advocated by the religious right in the United States as a part of the right to free speech and expression. These contests are not simply about the protection of free speech. They involve a contest over the role of religion in the public sphere, sexual normativity, and cultural politics.

Today, the Hindu Right has become one of the major and most vicious disseminators of hate speech in India.[13] Yet they have succeeded in relying on the right to free speech to defend their vitriol against minority religious communities, in particular the Muslims, and simultaneously prosecute those who dare to criticize them by invoking the blasphemy laws. When the *fatwa* was issued against Salman Rushdie for writing the *Satanic Verses,* the Hindu Right rushed to his defense, holding themselves out as the defenders of freedom of expression and claiming Rushdie—and themselves—as "a secular voice speaking against the impingement of a monolithic fundamentalism" of Islam. Their support had to be read not merely as an expression of support for the right to free speech but also a way in which to simultaneously attack the Muslim community as fanatical and anti–free speech. When hatred is directed toward a minority, especially a despised minority, whether it is gays in the United States or the Muslim community in India, the speech is defended under the right to free speech and expression. My argument is that the regulation of speech is not and cannot be determined by some neutral position of the state but is influenced by the shaping and shifting of cultural politics, which determines where the line should be drawn between legitimate and illegitimate speech. Nonintervention, or state neutrality, does not in and of itself ensure that the speech has been unlinked from normative understandings of race, religion, class, sexuality, and gender. The same laws governing speech are capable of being used by democratic states in different ways depending on the prevailing ideology and the location of the complainant.

Comments on Professor Philip Alston's Paper: Downsizing the State in Human Rights Discourse

Finally, let me turn to Professor Alston's proposals on how to make transnational corporations (TNCs) and international financial institutions (IFIs) accountable for human rights. I have two concerns. The first regards accountability for harms resulting from the operations of TNCs and development policies of IFIs. The second issue is how to address the fact that these institutions at times serve as vehicles of a particular state's ideology.

The increase in power of TNCs has generated concern over their increased potential to inflict human harms and their lack of accountability for such harms. Perhaps one of the most egregious examples of this potential is the Bhopal gas disaster in India that took place in 1984.[14] Human rights law has demonstrated remarkable flexibility at adapting to new and changing global circumstances. The women's rights movement, for example, was able to subject a whole range of harms occurring in the private sphere to human rights scrutiny and thus successfully challenged the rigid public and private boundaries along which human rights operated. If the family can be made accountable to human rights abuses through creative thinking and adaptation of the human rights regime, then it should not require much more imagination to bring TNCs into the human rights framework. Such a development may be even more readily attainable in the context of TNCs given that many of them already have attributes that give them the character of a state or quasi sovereigns.

The main problem, however, is that corporations have demonstrated little willingness to assist in the promotion of human rights in the contexts in which they operate and at times have actively opposed human rights initiatives. Recently, a U.S. federal judge struck down the Massachusetts selective purchasing legislation targeting corporations doing business with the Burmese junta upon challenge from the National Foreign Trade Council (NFTC), a U.S. corporate lobbying group.[15] This case is one of several challenges that have dealt severe blows to local efforts to rein in corporate complicity with human rights violations. The reality is that corporate lobby groups are very powerful and unlikely to support more binding human rights initiatives.

As regards the second issue, TNCs do serve as conduits for promoting a particular state's ideology. My concern is informed by the history of colonialism and the role of the East India Company in the construction of the British Empire. The company became the primary vehicle for the spread of colonial ideology and carried out pseudo-sovereign functions well before the British state formally established its presence in the region.

I raise this issue to argue that even today the TNC cannot be viewed as an entity that exists outside the interests of the state from which it originates nor the state in which it operates. We might recall here how the major U.S. and European corporations—Ford, Volkswagen, General Motors, and Chase Manhattan Bank—collaborated with Nazi Germany. ITT and others helped overthrow democracy and install the Pinochet dictatorship in Chile with the backing of the U.S. government.[16.] And numerous companies supported apartheid in South Africa. The question for discussion is How can we bring a human rights framework to bear on TNCs that are operating in complicity with a state?

International Financial Institutions

Regarding IFIs, Alston's paper raises two distinct questions for consideration: Should IFIs have a greater role in implementing human rights norms in developing countries (which are the main recipients of funds from these institutions), or should our concerns be limited to evaluating the IFI policies and activities from a human rights standpoint?

If we want to scrutinize the activities of IFIs from a human rights perspective a further concern arises. These institutions can and have supported a large number of projects in the name of human rights, the large dam projects of the 1980s being a prime example. But they subsequently discovered that these projects undermined more rights than they ostensibly safeguarded. In some instances, the bank abandoned the project or withdrew its support, but there was no system in place to render it accountable for the harms already done or liable for supporting harmful development projects. The accountability of IFIs to human rights cannot be achieved without taking into account the overall development policy being pursued by them, which must be sustainable and pro-people.

As for the role of IFIs in pressurizing developing countries to comply with human rights, the fact is that IFIs are linked with powerful states, in particular the

United States. And this relationship has been used at times to exert pressure on a state or country, most often in tandem with economic sanctions. For example, the withholding of bank loans after India and Pakistan tested nuclear devices in May 1998 was justified in the name of international peace and nuclear deterrence. However, such responses only further aggravated tensions in the region and destabilized Pakistan's already fragile economy, which encouraged a flight of capital from the country leading to a declaration of emergency by the prime minister of Pakistan and the suspension of civil rights. The withholding of a World Bank loan to India toward a project to upgrade its power structure, in a country which has interminable electricity and power shortages, hardly contributed toward the nuclear deterrence. If anything, these pressures served to fuel nationalist sentiments and reinforced anti-American positions in both countries. Bringing economic pressure to bear on developing countries through IFIs cannot be an effective means for ensuring or protecting human rights. It is iniquitous partly because it is not a pressure available to developing countries to protest against some of the anti–human rights initiatives taken by developed countries. For example, it was not available to developing countries to protest against the unilateral U.S. missile attacks on Sudan and Afghanistan in 1998.

Nor to protest against the reckless defeat of the Nuclear Test Ban Treaty in the U.S Senate in 1999. Nor could economic pressure be brought to bear against France for detonating eight nuclear devices in the Pacific. Apart from verbal condemnation, sanctions were limited to boycotting French red wine.

Concluding Remarks

My comments are directed toward demonstrating how, at times, universality, neutrality, and accountability are extremely contentious in the context of the United States, as well as in a postcolonial world. In fact, I suggest that these values obscure more than they reveal and that they are recipes for reinforcing a majoritarian politics, raising the specter of neoimperialism. Emphasizing these values does not address the real tension that liberalism has historically had with difference, diversity, and the unfamiliar—the place from where I began my comments. My final question then is, How do we revitalize and retrieve this value of diversity in and through the rule of law in liberal, democratic states and a transcultural world where new orthodoxies are simultaneously emerging and shaming people for their defects and differences and where indeed the mere assertion of the right to be different can entail the very right to exist?[17]

Closing Remarks

John M. Walker Jr.

In recent years, public events have altered the historical assumption that human rights transgressions committed by a country within its borders in violation of norms of international law are exclusively internal affairs. The massacres in Rwanda and the former Yugoslavia have been the subject of prosecution in international war crimes tribunals established to deal with those conflicts. On July 17, 1998, member states of the United Nations met in Rome and adopted a treaty establishing a permanent international criminal court to deal with future violations of international law. To date, ten states have ratified it out of the sixty required for it to become effective.

All of these developments pose the central dilemma of the conflict between the desire of sovereign nations to run their own affairs and the growing belief within the international legal community that when state actors criminally victimize their subjects, in contravention of international law, extra-sovereign action must be taken. The distinguished participants in this panel, entitled "The State and Human Rights," have thought deeply on the basic question of whether and under what circumstances domestic sovereignty should cede to international human rights norms.

Professor Robert Badinter, formerly the minister of justice and president of the Constitutional Council of the French Republic, skillfully analyzes the strengths and weaknesses of human rights enforcement through judicial review in France. Although the 1789 Declaration of the Rights of Man and Citizen established a foundation for human rights enforcement by breaking with the *ancien régime* and returning power to the people, the promise of full human rights enforcement in France remains unfulfilled. Genuine judicial review was not available until the establishment in 1958 of the Constitutional Council, which enjoys exclusive jurisdiction over the review of statutes for conformity with the constitution. However, ordinary citizens may not petition the Constitutional Council even today. On the other hand, ordinary courts are empowered to review statutes for conformity with international treaties, which contain international human rights prescriptions and to which France is a signatory, but Professor Badinter maintains that such protection is inadequate. He believes that a constitutional amendment is needed to permit ordinary citizens to challenge legislative edicts before the Constitutional Council.

Professor Badinter also enthusiastically supports the concept of the universality of international human rights and the establishment of the International Criminal Court. The new court would have jurisdiction over individuals, though not directly over states, who violate certain human rights and who are not adequately prosecuted in domestic courts. Professor Badinter concludes that "the fallibility of the state justifies international [oversight]" and an end to the "monopoly" of the state "over [prosecution] of the most serious violations of human rights."

Professor Philip Alston makes a powerful argument that the current conceptualization of human rights norms will remain incomplete until it abandons its exclusive focus on the state as the actor in question. Professor Alston's claim is that significant human rights transgressions are committed by influential nonstate actors on the international scene who are escaping human rights scrutiny because they are not easily monitored by a state-oriented human rights enforcement system. His examples of such nonstate actors include transnational corporations, nongovernmental organizations, liberation movements, terrorist groups, and financial institutions such as the World Bank and the International Monetary Fund. Professor Alston argues that developments such as privatization, deregulation, and decentralization tend to reduce accountability for the infringement of rights by these entities even as they assume prominence in the governance of people in their daily lives.

The open question for Professor Alston remains: how will fundamental human rights be honored and enforced, particularly when violations are by nonstate actors in a dynamic, changing world environment? There was discussion by the panel that perhaps secondary liability should be placed on individual states that fail to enforce human rights compliance by nongovernmental organizations and other nonstate actors operating within their borders.

Professor Andras Sajo skillfully addresses the enforcement of rights of free expression across the international spectrum. He examines the model of government neutrality in the regulation of speech and enters the debate over the impact of the government's own speech on debate among citizen-speakers. The state is committed on the one hand to protecting and encouraging a robust marketplace of ideas, but on the other hand in carrying out this commitment the government may find it difficult to preserve its neutrality. A further and perhaps even greater tension emerges when the government becomes a speaker in favor of its own policies: its role as an advocate for its policy choices may come into conflict with its commitment to ensuring that all viewpoints are represented in public debate.

Professor Sajo canvasses and critiques the approaches to these tensions within different countries and proposes a meritocratic neutrality paradigm that may be used to ensure government evenhandedness even when it enters the public debate as a participant.

Finally, commentator Professor Ratna Kapur raises important questions about the universalist school of human rights. She argues that the international enforcement of human rights norms can lead to the inappropriate suppression of minority views or cultures. In the face of such suppression, human rights norms can be seen as a new form of cultural imperialism by developed countries over undeveloped ones. She points to the example of a recent French decision that, she argues, inadequately appreciated the cultural importance to Muslim schoolgirls of wearing a Muslim veil in school in France. The court prioritized women's rights over minority religious norms.

Professor Kapur also critiques the neutrality principle for governments, noting that state nonintervention often works to reinforce the predominance of majority values at the expense of minority ones. Here she raises the example of the ruling Hindu party in India that by enforcing a policy of equal treatment of religious groups tacitly bolsters the predominance of the majority Hindu religion.

In sum, the papers by the four distinguished principals on this panel make important contributions to an emerging body of thought in the debate over the development of universal international human rights norms and their enforcement in relation to state sovereignty. In an era of unparalleled interaction among nations and of increasing international involvement in situations of domestic conflict, the questions addressed by the panel will continue to be relevant. The panelists have made significant inroads toward understandings and answers to these questions.

Notes

Foreword

1. Rudolph von Jhering, *Kampf um's Recht* (The Struggle for Law, from the 5th German edition), trans. John J. Lalor (Union, N.J.: Lawbook Exchange, 1997).

Law and the Re-Making of Humanity

1. Friedrich Schiller, *Wallenstein. Ein dramatisches Gedicht*, II: *Wallensteins Tod* (Stuttgart, Philipp Reclam jun.; 1969), Act 5, scene 3,) 113, ". . . in dem Heute wandelt schon das Morgen." St. Augustine (354–430 C.E.) said: ". . . it might be properly said [of the activity of the reality-making human mind], 'there are three times; a present of things past, a present of things present, and a present of things future.'" *Confessions*, book X, trans. E. B. Pusey (London: Dent [Everyman's Library], 1907), 266.

2. Martin Heidegger, *Wegmarken* (Frankfurt am Main: Vittorio Klostermann, 1967), 85. Heidegger's discussion of "the nature of freedom" formed part of a lecture (on the nature of truth) first given in 1930 and included in this volume in a revised version which had first been published in 1943.

3. Samuel Beckett, *Proust* (London: John Calder, 1965), 13. In ancient Greek mythology, Tantalus was condemned by the gods to be perpetually hungry and thirsty while surrounded by food and drink that he could not reach.

4. One might see such proposals as a manifestation of the tendency to banalize evil. See Hannah Arendt, *Eichmann in Jerusalem: a Report on the Banality of Evil* (New York: Viking Press, 1965). See also, Ph. Allott, "Líbranos del mal social," *Revista de Occidente* (October 1999): 19–28.

5. See especially K. R. Popper, *The Open Society and Its Enemies* (London: Routledge & Kegan Paul,1945).

6. Michel Foucault, *The Order of Things: An Archaeology of the Human Sciences* (London: Tavistock Publications, 1970), 387.

7. See especially, Herbert Marcuse, *One Dimensional Man: Studies in the Ideology of Advanced Industrial Society* (London: Routledge & Kegan Paul, 1964). On the psychology of the "fascism" of social structures, see Gilles Deleuze and Felix Guattari, *Anti-Oedipus: Capitalism and Schizophrenia*, trans. Robert Hurley and Helen R. Lane (Minneapolis: University of Minnesota Press, 1983).

8. "Totalitarian movements are mass organizations of atomized, isolated individuals. Compared with all other parties and movements their most conspicuous external characteristic is their demand for total, uncritical, unconditional, and unalterable loyalty of the individual member." Hannah Arendt, *The Origins of Totalitarianism* (London: George Allen & Unwin, 1951/1958), 323. The Internet is yet another social system of psychic dependency, which nevertheless atomizes and isolates the individual internaut.

9. "La biblioteca de Babel" in Jorge Luis Borges's *Ficciones* (Madrid: Alianza Editorial, 1971), 89–100. "The Library of Babel," in Borges's *Labyrinths* (Harmondsworth: Penguin Books, 1970), 78–86, trans. J. E. Irby, 1964.

10. From their beginning the human sciences have been subject to fundamental criticism. They have generated a permanent debate about their method, which is also a debate about their possibility and their effects. "Among the delusions which at different periods have possessed the minds of large masses of the human race, perhaps the most curious—certainly the least creditable—is the modern *soi-disant* science of political economy [an earlier name for what is now known as economics], based on the idea that an advantageous code of social action may be determined irrespectively of the influence of social affection." J. Ruskin, *Unto This Last: Four Essays on the First Principles of Political Economy* (London: George Allen & Sons, 1862/1910), 1. Ruskin likened de-subjectified economics to a study of human physiology restricted to a study of the human skeleton.

11. "What seems to Be, Is, To those to whom / It seems to Be, & is productive of the most dreadful / Consequences to those to whom it seems to Be. . ." William Blake, *Jerusalem* II.36 in *The Complete Writings of William Blake*, ed. G. Keynes (Oxford: Oxford University Press, 1966), 478. Blake was a passionate Romantic critic of the dehumanizing effect of scientific rationalism (as opposed to imagination, feeling, and faith).

12. "[E]in geistiges Objekt." W. Dilthey (1833–1911), "Der Aufbau der geschichtlichen Welt in den Geisteswissen-schaften" in VII *Gesammelte Schriften* (Leipzig: Teubner, 1927), 79–188, at 86. Reprinted in W. Dilthey, *Die Philosophie des Lebens* (Stuttgart: Teubner, 1961), 230–339. He explores the history and philosophy of the mind-sciences (*Geisteswissenschaften*), setting out his own position: the hermeneutic study of "humanity" as "human-social-historical reality" (81, 232).

13. The concept of *challenge and response* was a central feature of Arnold Toynbee's (controversial) hypothesis of the genesis of the historical *civilizations* that he identified. They used "the virtues of adversity" to raise themselves to new levels of organization and sophistication. A J Toynbee, *A Study of History*, 12 vols. (London: Oxford University Press, 1934–61), especially vols. I and II. D. C. Somervell, *Abridgement of Vols. I–VI* (London: Oxford University Press, 1947), especially chaps. V and VI.

14. Blaise Pascal, *Pensées*, trans. A. J. Krailsheimer (London: Penguin, 1966), 154.

15. Immanuel Kant (controversially but cogently) identified space and time as necessary conceptual conditions of possible experience. They make possible the mind's structuring (our knowledge) of physical reality, and so make possible our purposive activity in the physical world. Immanuel Kant, *Critique of Pure Reason*, trans. Norman Kemp Smith (London, 1929), 71 ff.

16. See Immanuel Kant, "Idea for a Universal History with a Cosmopolitan Purpose" and "Perpetual Peace: A Philosophical Sketch," in *Kant's Political Writings*, ed. H. Reiss, trans. H. B. Nisbet (Cambridge: Cambridge University Press, 1970).

17. In one of the many world-changing happenstances of history, the fact that liberal democracy is essentially a law-based social philosophy may be traced to the fact that, in post-medieval England, a society in a state of rapid economic development had need of much society-making legislation (the vertical axis of law) but had a strong Nordic-Germanic

tradition of horizontal law (the common law as the product of dispute-resolution among litigants), a tradition which included conciliar kingship as opposed to the alien idea of absolute monarchy. So it was that the legislator (the king-in-parliament) could be imagined as the horizontal source of ad hoc vertical law, a source which was itself subject to the law (self-government). In this way, nomocratic democracy takes its place within the perennial worldwide traditions of law-based society. See Ph. Allott, "International Societies and the Idea of Constitutionalism," in *The Legitimacy of International Organizations,* ed. V. Heiskanen and J-M Coicaud (Tokyo: UN University Press, forthcoming).

18. [C-L.de Secondat, Baron de] Montesquieu, *Lettres persanes,* letter XCIV (Paris: Librairie Gallimard [Pléiade], 1949), 270. Montesquieu's visiting Persian is describing "public law" in Europe.

19. See generally Ph. Allott, *Eunomia—New Order for a New World* (Oxford: Oxford University Press, 1990). The Greek word *eunomia* (good social order) is associated particularly with the name of Solon (c. 640–588 B.C.E.), a charismatic "law giver" of ancient Athens who laid down what was virtually a new social contract to resolve deepstructural social conflict. It was a new order that did not last (*absit omen!*). He was the author of an elegy entitled *Eunomia,* extolling the virtues of law-based social order.

20. On the reconceiving of international law as the true law of a true international society, see Ph. Allott, "The Concept of International Law," 10 *European Journal of International Law* (1999): 31–50.

21. René Descartes, *Meditations on the First Philosophy,* trans. J. Veitch (London: Dent [Everyman's Library], 1912), 88.

22. "Learn that man infinitely transcends man . . ." Pascal, *Pensées,* 64–5. ". . . nor do I myself comprehend all that I am. Therefore is the mind too strait to contain itself." Augustine, *Confessions,* book X, 212. Book X contains a remarkable psychoanalysis of the human mind.

23. For further discussion of a new idealism, see Ph. Allott, *Eutopia—New Mind for a New Humanity* (forthcoming). The word *eutopia* (good place) is used here in preference to the word *utopia* (no place), another invented word using Greek roots, to emphasize that the nature of the New Enlightenment challenge is to find and to enact new ideals rather than as in Thomas More's *Utopia* (1516) to criticize the actual by reference to an imaginary alternative, which, in More's own pessimistic words (at the end of book II), he wished rather than expected to see realized—echoing, perhaps, Cicero's comment in *De re publica* (II.30.52)

on Plato's ideal republic: *[civitatem] optandam magis quam sperandam.*

24. Samuel Beckett, *Waiting for Godot* (London: Faber and Faber, 1956), 50, 94.

Vindicating the Rule of Law: Balancing Competing Demands for Justice

1. I would like to thank Shirley Woodward for her assistance in the preparation of this article.

2. De l'Espirit des Lois, 1788, Vol. XI, at 3 (quoted in "The Rule of Law in a Dangerous World," The Gauer Distinguished Lecture in Law and Public Policy by the Rt. Hon. Baroness Thatcher, OM, FRS, at 12.)

3. See Ronald J. Rychlak, *Society's Moral Right to Punish: A Further Exploration of the Denunciation Theory of Punishment,* 65 Tul. L. Rev. 299, 301–05 (1990).

4. Emile Durkheim, *The Division of Labor in Society,* trans. George Simpson (Free Press, 1933), 62–63.

5. The 1948 Convention on the Prevention and Punishment of the Crime of Genocide defined genocide as "acts committed with intent to destroy, in whole or in part, a national, ethnic, racial or religious group." Genocide Convention, Dec. 9, 1948, 78 U.N.T.S. 277, 28 I.L.M. 763 (entered into force Jan. 12, 1951) (entered into force with respect to the United States. Nov. 25, 1989). At the time the Genocide Convention was adopted, the Soviet Union opposed extending the definition to include the destruction of political or social groups, as Stalin and his regime had already begun their purges targeted at these very groups. As a result of this relatively narrow definition, the murder of almost 40 percent of the Cambodian population by the Khmer Rouge arguably does not constitute genocide. Nonetheless, the definition has not been altered in subsequent United Nations conventions, and the International Criminal Tribunals for Yugoslavia and Rwanda operate under this 1948 definition. Among scholars, this definition of genocide is the subject of much debate, and the term as commonly used has come to connote mass murder in general. See M. Cherif Bassiouni, *The Normative Framework of International Humanitarian Law: Overlaps, Gaps and Ambiguities,* 8 Transnat'l L. & Contemp. Probs. 199, 212–215 (1998).

6. War crimes are defined in the 1949 Geneva Convention, as well as the Hague Conventions of 1899 and 1907, and include violations of the laws

or customs of war. Such violations include, but are not limited to, murder, ill-treatment or deportation to slave labor, or for any other purpose, of the civilian population of or in occupied territory, murder or ill-treatment of prisoners of war or persons on the seas, killing of hostages, plunder of public or private property, wanton destruction of cities, towns or villages, or devastation not justified by military necessity. See Theodor Meron, *International Criminalization of Internal Atrocities,* 89 Am. J. Int'l L. 554, 555 (1995).

7. Restatement (Third) of Foreign Relations sec. 404 (1987) (defining universal jurisdiction to punish these offenses).

8. See 1 Transitional Justice 55–116, ed. Neil J. Kritz, (1995); Steven R. Ratner, *New Democracies, Old Atrocities: An Inquiry in International Law,* 87 Geo. L. J. 707, 718–20 (1999); Diane F. Orentlicher, *International Criminal Law and the Cambodian Killing Fields,* 3 ILSA J. Int'l & Comp. L. 705 (1997); Theodor Meron, *International Criminalization of Internal Atrocities,* 89 Am. J. Int'l L. 554, 555 (1995); Emily W. Schabacker, *Reconciliation or Justice and Ashes: Amnesty Commissions and the Duty to Punish Human Rights Offenses,* 12 N. Y. Int'l L. Rev. 1 (1999).

9. Ratner, *New Democracies,* 719.

10. Martha Minow, *Between Vengeance and Forgiveness: Facing History After Genocide and Mass Violence* 2 (1998).

11. The Statute of the ICC was adopted in Rome on July 17, 1998. The United States voted against its adoption.

12. See Steven J. Coffey, *Rule of Law and Regional Conflict,* 19 Whittier L. Rev. 257, 258–59 (1997).

13. See generally Orentlicher, *International Criminal Law and the Cambodian Killing Fields,* 705.

14. Restatement (Third) of the Law of Foreign Relations 402, Introductory Note (1987).

15. Kenneth C. Randall, *Universal Jurisdiction Under International Law,* 66 Tex. L. Rev. 785, 793–95 (1988).

16. Ibid., 800–806.

17. See note 5 above.

18. See Gary Sharp Sr., *International Obligations to Search For and Arrest War Criminals: Government Failure in the Former Yugoslavia?,* 7 Duke J. Comp. & Int'l L. 411, 430 (1997); see also Orentlicher, *International Criminal Law and the Cambodian Killing Fields,* 705 (citing Decision on Preliminary Objections, Application of the Convention on the Prevention and Punishment of the Crime of Genocide (*Bosn. & Herz. v. Yugo.*), 1996 I.C.J. (July 11) (in response to Yugoslavia's claim

that the ICJ lacked jurisdiction under the Genocide Convention because the alleged acts of genocide arose in Bosnia, the Court noted that the obligation under the Convention to prevent and punish genocide is not territorially limited).

19. See Randall, *Universal Jurisdiction Under International Law,* 800–806 (citing Convention for the Amelioration of the Condition of the Wounded and Sick in Armed Forces in the Field, Aug. 12, 1949, 6 U.S.T. 3114, TIAS no. 3362, 75 U.N.T.S. 31 [Geneva Convention I]; Convention for the Amelioration of the Condition of Wounded, Sick and Shipwrecked Members of the Armed Forces at Sea, Aug. 12, 1949, 6 U.S.T. 3217, TIAS no. 3363, 75 U.N.T.S. 85 [Geneva Convention II]; Convention Relative to the Treatment of Prisoners of War, Aug. 12, 1949, 6 U.S.T. 3316, TIAS no. 3364, 75 U.N.T.S. 135 [Geneva Convention III]; Convention Relative to the Protection of Civilian Persons in Time of War, Aug. 12, 1949, 6 U.S.T. 3516, TIAS no. 3365, 75 U.N.T.S. 287 [Geneva Convention IV]. The four Geneva Conventions will be referred to collectively as the Geneva Conventions or the Geneva Conventions of 1949).

20. See Randall, *Universal Jurisdiction Under International Law,* 816; Sharp, *International Obligations to Search For and Arrest War Criminals,* 423.

21. Convention Against Torture and Other Cruel, Inhuman or Degrading Treatment or Punishment, adopted Dec. 10, 1984 [Torture Convention], adopted by G.A. Res. 39/46, UN GAOR Supp. (No. 51) at 197, UN Doc. A/Res/39/46 (1985), reprinted in 23 I.L.M. 1027 (1984). This reprint of the Torture Convention is the draft form; minor revisions are indicated in 24 I.L.M. 535 (1985). The United States ratified the treaty in 1994. The offense may derive from crimes against humanity.

22. International Convention Against the Taking of Hostages, Dec. 4, 1979, 18 I.L.M. 1456, adopted by G.A. Res. 34/146, 34 UN GAOR Supp. (No. 39), UN Doc. A/C.6/34/L.23 (1979). The United States is a party.

23. Convention for the Suppression of Unlawful Acts Against the Safety of Civil Aviation, Sept. 23, 1971, 24 U.S.T. 565, TIAS no. 7570, 974 U.N.T.S. 177 (entered into force Jan. 26, 1973) [Montreal Convention], reprinted in 10 I.L.M. 1151 (1971); Convention for the Suppression of Unlawful Seizure of Aircraft, Dec. 16, 1970, 22 U.S.T. 1641, TIAS no. 7192, 860 U.N.T.S. 105 (entered into force Oct. 14, 1971) [Hague Convention], reprinted in 10 I.L.M. 133 (1971). The United States became a party to the Hague Convention on September 14, 1971, and a party to the Montreal Convention on February 28, 1973. A description of the Hague Convention, following the International Civil Aviation Organization's approval of the treaty, is contained in 64 Department of State Bull. 50 (1971).

24. Minow, *Between Vengeance and Forgiveness,* 26.

25. Ibid., at 29.

26. Ibid.

27. Robert H. Jackson, *The Case Against the Nazi War Criminals* 3 (1946). The Nuremberg trials lasted from 1945 to 1949. Nineteen Nazi leaders were convicted of crimes against humanity, among other charges; ten were hanged. See "The Nuremberg Trials," *Washington Post,* October 16, 1999, at 4.

28. Sharp, *International Obligations to Search For and Arrest War Criminals,* 412.

29. Steven R. Ratner and Jason S. Abrams, *Accountability for Human Rights Atrocities in International Law* 166 (1997); see also Sharp, *International Obligations to Search For and Arrest War Criminals,* 439–441.

30. Sharp, *International Obligations to Search For and Arrest War Criminals,* 439–441.

31. Genocide and war crimes are defined in the Genocide and Geneva Conventions, respectively. No treaty has defined the term "crimes against humanity." The definition for crimes against humanity here is provided by the Nuremberg Charter and covers "murder, extermination, enslavement, deportation, and other inhumane acts committed against any civilian population, before or during the war; or persecutions on political, racial or religious grounds in execution of or in connection with any crime within the jurisdiction of the tribunal." See also M. Cherif Bassiouni, *The Normative Framework of International Humanitarian Law: Overlaps, Gaps and Ambiguities,* 8 Transnat'l L. & Contemp. Probs. 199, 205 n.25 (1998).

32. Ratner and Abrams, *Accountability for Human Rights Atrocities in International Law,* 154.

33. Ibid., 174.

34. Ibid.

35. Benjamin B. Ferencz, *International Criminal Courts: The Legacy of Nuremberg,* 10 Pace Int'l L. Rev. 203, 223 (1998).

36. Theodor Meron, *International Criminalization of Internal Atrocities,* 89 Am. J. Int'l L. 554, 557 (1995).

37. Ferencz, *International Criminal Courts,* 225; Ratner and Abrams, *Accountability for Human Rights Atrocities in International Law,* 175.

38. Ibid., 222–23; see also Sharp, *International Obligations to Search For and Arrest War Criminals,* 449–451.

39. See Sharp, *International Obligations to Search For and Arrest War Criminals,* 449–451; see

also Colum Lynch, "Departing War Crimes Tribunal Chief Assails U.N. Inaction," *Washington Post,* Nov. 9, 1999, at A26 (describing difficulty in apprehending and trying indicted war criminals).

40. See Ferencz, *International Criminal Courts,* 224. In a different approach, Spain invoked the concept of universal jurisdiction to seek the extradition of former Chilean head of state Augusto Pinochet to stand trial for alleged crimes committed during his rule from 1973 to 1990. In 1998, British police arrested Pinochet, who was recuperating from back surgery in Britain, on an international arrest warrant issued by a Spanish magistrate, alleging that Pinochet was responsible for acts of torture, hostage taking, and other crimes in Chile. On March 24, 1999, the House of Lords issued its second opinion in the case, holding that Britain's extradition statute requires the extraterritorial conduct to have been a crime under British law at the time the conduct took place. As such, Pinochet could potentially be extradited only for those alleged acts of torture committed after 1988, when Britain ratified the Convention Against Torture and Other Cruel, Inhuman or Degrading Treatment or Punishment. See Curtis A. Bradley and Jack L. Goldsmith, *Pinochet and International Human Rights Litigation,* 97 Mich. L.Rev. 2129, 2130, 2133, 2138 (1999). The same Spanish magistrate, Baltasar Garzon, has also sought the extradition of 98 Argentines, members of the former military junta in Argentina, suspected of involvement in torturing and executing thousands of political dissidents from 1976 to 1983. Argentine President Carlos Menem rejected this effort, however, asserting that foreign courts have no jurisdiction for crimes committed in Argentina. See "Argentine Political Crimes," *The Economist,* November 6, 1999.

41. See Minow, *Between Vengeance and Forgiveness,* 30–31.

42. Ibid.

43. Ibid.

44. See Lloyd L. Weinreb, *Desert, Punishment, and Criminal Responsibility,* 49 Law & Contemp. Probs. 47 (1986).

45. Minow, *Between Vengeance and Forgiveness,* 40.

46. Ibid.

47. *Washington Post,* October 16, 1946, at 1 (reported by Kingsbury Smith, who witnessed the executions as a representative of the combined American press).

48. Stephen Breyer, Associate Justice, United States Supreme Court, Keynote Address, "Crimes Against Humanity," 71 N.Y.U. L. Rev. 1161, 1162 (1996) (quoting from Justice Jackson's Opening Statement at the Nuremberg trials).

49. Minow, *Between Vengeance and Forgiveness,* 49 (quoting Richard H. Minear, "The Individual, the State, and the Tokyo Trials," in *The Tokyo War Crimes Trials* 159, 160, ed. Chihiro Hosoya et al. (Tokyo: Kodansha, 1986)); see also Gary Jonathan Bass, review of *Mass Atrocity, Collective Memory, and the Law,* by Mark Osiel, 97 Mich. L. Rev. 2103, 2104 n.3 (1999).

50. Bass, see note 49, at 2103.

51. Emily W. Schabacker, *Reconciliation or Justice and Ashes: Amnesty Commissions and the Duty to Punish Human Rights Offenses,* 12 N.Y. Int'l L. Rev. 1, 5 nn. 19, 20 (1999).

52. Ibid.

53. Ratner and Abrams, *Accountability for Human Rights Atrocities in International Law,* 193–94.

54. Ibid., 199.

55. Minow, *Between Vengeance and Forgiveness,* 56.

56. Schabacker, *Reconciliation or Justice and Ashes,* 7–8.

57. Ibid., 7–9; Michael P. Scharf, *Swapping Amnesty for Peace: Was There a Duty to Prosecute International Crimes in Haiti?,* 31 Tex. Int'l L. J. 1, 10 (1996).

58. A. James McAdams, ed., *Transitional Justice and the Rule of Law in New Democracies* 270 (1997); Minow, *Between Vengeance and Forgiveness,* 56.

59. McAdams, *Transitional Justice and the Rule of Law in New Democracies,* 277.

60. Ibid.

61. Ibid.

62. Minow, *Between Vengeance and Forgiveness,* 56.

63. Ibid., 59.

64. Ibid.

65. Ibid.

66. Ratner and Abrams, *Accountability for Human Rights Atrocities in International Law,* 193–94.

67. Minow, *Between Vengeance and Forgiveness,* 118.

68. Ibid., 119 (noting William Gladstone's analogous comment that "the cause of the problem in Ireland is that the Irish will never forget and the British will never remember").

69. Ibid., 58.

70. Donna E. Arzt, *Bridge Over Troubled Water: Law and the Emergence of New Democracies,* 22 Syracuse J. Int'l L. & Com. 81, 89 (1996) (reviewing *Transitional Justice* 55–116 (Neil J. Kritz, ed., 1995)).

71. Sandra Day O'Connor, Associate Justice, United States Supreme Court, *The Federalism of Free Nations,* 28 N.Y.U. J. Int'l L. & Pol. 35, n.12 (winter 1995–96) (quoting Immanuel Kant, *The Eternal Peace,* reprinted in *The Philosophy of Kant: Kant's Moral and Political Writings,* ed. Carl J. Friedrich, (1949): 441).

72. In 1971, the United Nations General Assembly passed a resolution calling for the restriction of the number of offenses for which capital punishment may be imposed, with "a view to the desirability of abolishing this punishment in all countries." See Joan Fitzpatrick and Alice Miller, *International Standards on the Death Penalty: Shifting Discourse,* 19 Brooklyn J. of Int'l L. 273 (1993) (citing G.A. Res. 2857 (XXVI), UN GAOR, 26th Sess., Supp. No. 29 at 94, UN Doc. A/8429 (1971)); see also William Schabas, *The Abolition of the Death Penalty in International Law,* 2e, 147–193 (1997).

73. ICCPR, Dec. 19, 1966, 999 U.N.T.S. 171, 6 I.L.M. 368.

74. Ibid.

75. See *Congressional Record,* 138, 8070-8071 (April 2, 1992).

76. UN Doc. ST/LEG/SER.E/13 (1996).

77. UN Doc. ST/LEG/SER.E/13 (1996).

78. 492 U.S. 361, 380 (1989) (plurality opinion).

79. *Trop v. Dulles,* 356 U.S. 86, 101 (1958) (plurality opinion).

80. *Stanford v. Kentucky,* 492 U.S. at 369 n.1

81. *Thompson v. Oklahoma,* 487 U.S. 815, 851–52 (1988) (opinion of O'Connor, S., concurring in the judgment).

82. 6 U.S. (2 Cranch) 64, 118 (1804).

83. 175 U.S. 677, 700 (1900).

84. "The Rule of Law in a Dangerous World," The Gauer Distinguished Lecture in Law and Public Policy by the Rt. Hon. Baroness Thatcher, OM, FRS, at 22 (quote from William Pitt the Elder).

85. Choruses from "The Rock," in T. S. Eliot, *The Complete Poems and Plays 1909–1950,* at 106 (1962).

International Adjudication and U.S. Policy—Past, Present, and Future

1. SS *Wimbledon,* Permanent Court of International Justice, Series A No. 1, at p. 25.

2. 1 Moore, *History and Digest of the International Arbitrations to which the United States Has Been a Party* 29 (1898), at 29.

3. Ibid., 272–73.

4. 1971–2 ICJ Yearbook, at 130.

5. Moore, 495.

6. Dip. Corr. 1865, part 1, p. 565, cited according to 1 Moore, *History and Digest of the International Arbitrations,* 496. See also the statement of Earl Russell, ibid., at 496–7, emphasizing that Britain could not accept the referral of the case to a foreign state but only to arbitration by a special commission.

7. For details see 1 Moore, 504–508.

8. Ibid., at 514. The instructions contain a list of treaties that had been rejected by the legislature before, ibid., at 515. See also ibid., at 555–6, for comparable British domestic difficulties.

9. Ibid., at 546; for the text of the agreement, see ibid., at 547–553; 143 Consolidated Treaty Series (CTS) (ed. Parry) 145 (1871–72). On the ratification by the Senate, see Moore, *History and Digest of the International Arbitrations,* 553–554.

10. Article VI reads: "In deciding the matters submitted to the Arbitrators they shall be governed by the following three rules, which are agreed upon by the High Contracting Parties as rules to be taken as applicable to the case, and by such principles of international law not inconsistent therewith as the Arbitrators shall determine to have been applicable to the case: . . . ."

11. For the conflict arising out of the so-called "indirect claims" of the United States in the *Alabama* case, see 1 Moore, *History and Digest of the International Arbitrations,* 623–47.

12. For the award see 1 Moore, *History and Digest of the International Arbitrations,* 653; 145 CTS 99 (1872-3).

13. Cited according to 1 Moore, *History and Digest of the International Arbitrations,* 559.

14. Ibid., 664.

15. Ibid., 659–661.

16. Ibid., 665–666.

17. See also Art. VI of the *Alabama compromis,* see note 9; Moore, *History and Digest of the International Arbitrations,* 666–678 for a discussion of these rules at the time.

18. *Nottebohm Case (Preliminary Objection),* ICJ Reports 1953, p. 111, at 119: "Since the *Alabama* case, it has been generally recognized, following the earlier precedents, that, in the absence of any agreement to the contrary, an international tribunal has the right to decide as to its own jurisdiction and has

the power to interpret for this purpose the instruments which govern that jurisdiction."

19. Russian Circular of January 11, 1899, in *Texts of the Peace Conferences at the Hague* 3, ed. James Brown Scott (1908).

20. Jörg Manfred Mössner, *Hague Peace Conferences of 1899 and 1907*, II Encyclopedia of Public International Law 671 (1995), at 673.

21. Convention for the Pacific Settlement of International Disputes of 1899 (hereinafter: 1899 Convention), Art. 1 in *Texts of the Peace Conferences*, see note19, at 21; 187 CTS 410; Convention for the Pacific Settlement of International Disputes of 1907 (hereinafter: 1907 Convention), Art. 1, in *Texts of the Peace Conferences*, at 155; 205 CTS 233.

22. Cf. Art. 6 of the 1899 and 1907 Conventions, emphasizing that good offices and mediation never have binding force.

23. 1899 Convention, Art. 14: "The report of the International Commission of Inquiry is limited to a statement of facts, ..." 1907 Convention, Art. 35.

24. 1899 Convention, Art. 18; 1907 Convention, Art. 38 para. 2.

25. Arthur Eyffinger, *The 1899 Hague Peace Conference* 442 (1999).

26. Art. 3 of the 1899 Convention; similarly Art. 3 of the 1907 Convention.

27. *Texts of the Peace Conferences*, see note 19, Art. 1, at 112, 137; 205 CTS 216.

28. Instructions to the American delegates to The Hague Conference, April 18, 1889, 1899 *Foreign Relations of the United States*, p. 511; cited according to 7 *Digest of International Law*, ed. John Bassett Moore (1906): 82.

29. *The Reports to the Hague Conferences of 1899 and 1907*, ed. James Brown Scott (1917): 110.

30. Cited according to Wm. I. Hull, *Obligatory Arbitration and the Hague Conferences*, 2 AJIL 731, 737 (1908).

31. James Brown Scott, *The Work of the Second Hague Peace Conference*, 2 AJIL 1, 26 (1908).

32. Elihu Root, "Letter submitting The Hague Conventions of 1907 for consideration by the Senate," cited according to *Texts of the Peace Conferences*, see note 19, at iii.

33. The U.S. reservation reads: "Nothing contained in this convention shall be so construed as to require the United States of America to depart from its traditional policy of not entering upon, interfering with, or entangling itself in the political questions or internal administration of any foreign State. It is equally understood that nothing contained in the said convention shall be so con-

strued as to imply the relinquishment, by the United States of America, of its traditional attitude toward purely American questions." In Hershey, *Convention for the Peaceful Adjustment of International Differences*, 2 AJIL 29 (1908), at 48; *Texts of the Peace Conferences*, see note 19, at 90; *The Proceedings of the Hague Peace Conferences: The Conference of 1899*, James Brown Scott, ed., (1920): 99–100.

34. Cited after *Editorial Comment: The American Theory of International Arbitration*, 2 AJIL 387 (1908), at 390. For a survey of treaties of arbitration subsequent to the first Hague Peace Conference, see *Editorial Comment: Treaties of Arbitration since the First Hague Conference*, 2 AJIL 823 (1908).

35. Michael Dunne, *The United States and the World Court, 1920–1935* (1988): 13.

36. See especially Dunne, *The United States and the World Court*, 10, 29–46.

37. Letter of the Honorable Elihu Root to Senator Henry Cabot Lodge regarding the Covenant of the League of Nations, 19 June 1919, 13 AJIL 596, 597 (1919).

38. 6 LNTS 390, LNOJ, January/February 1921, at 14; entered into force September 1, 1921.

39. Ibid.

40. *Congressional Record*, 74th Congress, 1st session, at 1145–46; Dunne, *The United States and the World Court*, 1.

41. For a rather subdued comment by Judge Hudson, see Manley O. Hudson, *The United States Senate and the World Court*, 29 AJIL 301, 307 (1935).

42. H.R. 441, 67th Congress, 4th session, *Congressional Record*, 67:4, at 3605. Cited according to Dunne, *The United States and the World Court*, 76.

43. Dunne, *The United States and the World Court*, 32–3.

44. ICJ Yearbook 1984–1985, at 100.

45. *Certain Norwegian Loans*, ICJ Reports 1957, p. 9, at 23–27. Cf. Separate Opinion Lauterpacht, ibid., at 43, 44; Dissenting Opinion Lauterpacht, *Interhandel*, ICJ Reports 1959, at 104–114; Dissenting Opinion Spender, ibid., at 56–7 (considering both the reservation and the declaration as void); Dissenting Opinion Klaestad, ibid., at 77–8 (considering the reservation severable so that the Court can review the domestic character of a measure itself).

46. *Aerial Incident of 27 July 1955*, Observations and Submissions of the Government of the United States of America, ICJ Pleadings 1959, p. 301, at 323.

47. Ibid.

48. *Military and Paramilitary Activities in and against Nicaragua*, Jurisdiction and Admissibility, ICJ Reports 1984, p. 392, at 421–426, para. 67–76; *Military and Paramilitary Activities in and against Nicaragua*, Merits, ICJ Reports 1986, p. 13, at 29–38, para. 37–56.

49. See for example, *Maritime Delimitation and Territorial Questions Between Qatar and Bahrein*, Jurisdiction and Admissibility, ICJ Reports 1995, p. 6.

50. *Nuclear Tests (Australia v. France)*, ICJ Reports 1974, p. 253; *Nuclear Tests (New Zealand v. France)*, ICJ Reports 1974, p. 457.

51. ICJ Reports, *Military and Paramilitary Activities in and against Nicaragua*.

52. C.H.M. Waldock, *Decline of the Optional Clause*, 32 BYBIL 244 (1955–6).

53. See especially *Fisheries Jurisdiction (Spain v. Canada)*, Judgment of 4 December 1998, http://www.icj-cij.org (last visited 1 March 2000); and the powerful dissent of Judge Bedjaoui, ibid.

54. *Land and Maritime Boundary between Cameroon and Nigeria*, Preliminary Objections, ICJ Reports 1998, p. 275; Order of 3 March 1999, ICJ Reports 1999, p. 24.

55. Art. IX of the Genocide Convention reads: "Disputes between the Contracting Parties relating to the interpretation, application or fulfilment of the present Convention, including those relating to the responsibility of a State for genocide or any of the other acts enumerated in article III, shall be submitted to the International Court of Justice at the request of any of the parties to the dispute."

56. Art. 14 para. 1 of the Montreal Convention for the Suppression of Unlawful Acts Against the Safety of Civil Aviation reads: "Any dispute between two or more Contracting States concerning the interpretation or application of this Convention shall, at the request of one of them, be submitted to arbitration. If within six months of the date of the request for arbitration the Parties are unable to agree on the organization of the arbitration, any one of those Parties may refer the dispute to the International Court of Justice by request in conformity with the Statute of the Court."

57. *United States Diplomatic and Consular Staff in Tehran*, ICJ Reports 1980, 3.

58. See extensively Bruno Simma, *From Bilateralism to Community Interest in International Law*, 250 Recueil des Cours 217, 268–283 (1994 VI).

59. See *Questions of Interpretation and Application of the 1971 Montreal Convention Arising from the Aerial Incident at Lockerbie (Libyan Arab Jamahiriya v. United States of America)*, ICJ

Reports 1998, p. 115, at 131–134, paragraphs 45–50.

60. See for example, Gilbert Guillaume, *The Future of the International Judicial Institutions,* 44 ICLQ 849, 853 (1995).

61. *Legality of the Threat or Use of Nuclear Weapons,* Advisory Opinion, ICJ Reports 1996, p. 226, at 266.

62. Most recently, see the opinion concerning the *Difference Relating to Immunity from Legal Process of a Special Rapporteur of the Commission on Human Rights,* reproduced in 38 ILM 873 (1999).

63. Guillaume, *The Future of the International Judicial Institutions,* 851.

64. ICJ Press Communiqué 2000/5, 16 February 2000, http://www.icj-cij.org (last visited 28 February 2000).

65. April 30, 1982, 1833 UNTS 3. As of February 22, 2000, the Convention is in force for 132 states' parties, among them all permanent members of the Security Council except the United States, and the European Union and most of its member States.

66. A.E. Boyle, *Dispute Settlement and the Law of the Sea Convention,* 46 ICLQ 37, 40–1 (1997) referring to the criticism voiced by ICJ Judge Shigeru Oda, *Dispute Settlement Prospects in the Law of the Sea,* 44 ICLQ 863 (1995).

67. Understanding on Rules and Procedures Governing the Settlement of Disputes, April 15, 1994, in *Final Act Embodying the Results of the Uruguay Round of Multilateral Treaty Negotiations,* reproduced in 33 ILM 1144, 1226 (1994).

68. Marcel M.T.A. Brus, *Third Party Dispute Settlement in an Interdependent World,* 31 (1995); J.G. Merrills, *International Dispute Settlement,* 3rd ed. (1998): 218.

69. Rome Statute of the International Criminal Court, July 17, 1998, reproduced in 37 ILM 1002 (1998).

70. Niklas Luhmann, *Die Gesellschaft der Gesellschaft* (1997): 157–171.

71. The article reads:

"The Court of Justice shall have jurisdiction to give preliminary rulings concerning: (a) the interpretation of this Treaty; (b) the validity and interpretation of acts of the institutions of the Community; (c) the interpretation of the statutes of bodies established by an act of the Council, where those statutes so provide.

Where such a question is raised before any court or tribunal of a Member State, that court or tribunal may, if it considers that a decision on the question is necessary to enable it to give judgment, request the Court of Justice to give a ruling thereon.

Where any such question is raised in a case pending before a court or tribunal of a Member State, against whose decision there is no judicial remedy under national law, that court or tribunal shall bring the matter before the Court of Justice."

72. For a contemporary assessment with a number of reform proposals, see Leo Gross, ed., *The Future of the International Court of Justice* (1976).

73. 1976 Digest of the United States Practice in International Law, at 650–651.

74. *Military and Paramilitary Activities in and against Nicaragua,* ICJ Reports 1986, p. 14, at 38, para. 56.

75. Ibid., at 147–8 (operative para. 8).

76. *Ellettronica Sicula S.p.A. (ELSI),* ICJ Reports 1989, p. 15.

77. *Aerial Incident of 3 July 1988,* ICJ Reports 1996, p. 9 (Removal from the list); *Vienna Convention on Consular Relations,* ICJ Reports 1998, p. 426 (Removal from the list).

78. *Legality of Use of Force,* Request for the Indication of Provisional Measures, 38 ILM 1188 (1999).

79. For the first judgment on a preliminary objection by the United States that the Court rejected, see *Questions of Interpretation and Application of the 1971 Montreal Convention Arising from the Aerial Incident at Lockerbie,* ICJ Reports 1998, p. 115.

80. For the first judgment on a preliminary objection by the United States that the Court rejected, see *Oil Platforms,* Preliminary Objection, ICJ Reports 1996, p. 803.

81. For the order on Provisional Measures, see *LaGrand (Germany v. U.S.),* Provisional Measures, ICJ Reports 1999, S. 9.

82. See *Multilateral Treaties Deposited with the Secretary-General, Status as at April 30, 1999,* UN Doc. ST/LEG/SER.E/17 (1999), at 90, 92, 202, 204.

83. *Vienna Convention on Consular Relations (Paraguay v. United States),* Provisional Measures, ICJ Reports 1998, p. 248, at 258 para. 41; *LaGrand (Germany v. United States),* Provisional Measures, ICJ Reports 1999, p. 9, at 16 para. 29.

84. *Breard v. Greene,* 37 ILM 826, 827 (1999); 523 U.S. 371, 375 (1998); 118 S. Ct. 1352, 1354 (1998).

85. *Federal Republic of Germany v. United States,* 119 S. Ct. 1016, at 1017. Justice Souter, joined by Justice Ginsburg, concurring: "I have taken into consideration the position of the Solicitor General on behalf of the United States." See also *Paraguay v. Gilmore,* brief for the United States as amicus curiae, 1997 U.S. Briefs 1390 , at 46–51.

86. See only the contributions to the *Agora: Breard,* 92 AJIL 666 (1998).

87. 19 U.S.C. 3535; 108 Stat. 4809.

88. 19 U.S.C. 2411; 88 Stat. 1978.

89. See Uruguay Round Agreements Act, ibid., Section 102 (a) (2) (B); 19 U.S.C. 3512.

90. US Digest 1976, at 685.

91. Elihu Root, *The Need of Popular Understanding of International Law,* 1 American Journal of International Law 2–3 (1907).

92. John Adams, *Boston Gazette* 1774 No. 7. See also Root, note 37.

Closing Remarks

1. Paul Johnson, "Laying Down the Law," *Wall Street Journal,* March 10, 1999, A22.

2. Sandra Day O'Connor, "Federalism of Free Nations," in *International Law Decisions in National Courts,* ed. Thomas M. Franck and Gregory H. Fox (1996), 18.

3. 20 S. Ct. 459, at 464.

Born Free and Equal in Dignity and Rights

1. We quote from the report of the NGO Physicians for Human Rights: "The Taliban . . . has targeted women for extreme repression and punished them brutally for infractions. To our knowledge, no other regime in the world has methodically and violently forced half of its population into virtual house arrest, prohibiting them on pain of physical punishment from showing their faces, seeking medical care without a male escort, or attending school."

2. As noted by Bina Agarwal, "Rural Women, Poverty and Natural Resources: Sustenance, Sustainability and Struggle for Change," *Economic and Political Weekly,* (October 28, 1989): 46–65: (In India)". . . the ideology of seclusion prescribes that women confine their movements and visibility within circumscribed spaces and restrict interaction with male strangers."

3. Sally Quinn, *Washington Post,* Jan. 19, 1992, C1.

4. *Human Rights Watch Report 1999* concludes that ". . .discriminatory practices, tolerated and even encouraged by states, continued unabated around the globe. Despite commitments made under the convention on the Elimination of All Forms of Discrimination Against Women (CEDAW) and "national platforms for action" to implement the 1995 Forth World Conference on Women Platform for Action adopted in Beijing, many states continued to enforce discriminatory laws and to tolerate discriminatory practices under customary law."

5. The Report of the UN Secretary-General, *1999 World Survey on the Role of Women in Development: Globalization, Gender and Work,* states that: ". . . throughout the developing countries as a whole, the informal sector has been gaining in importance in new employment creation, especially for women."

6. As is the case in Brazil with workers in the manioc flour rudimentary mills and in babaçu coconut processing. In a survival strategy, potentially self-destructive, families withdraw their children from school so that they can contribute to the family budget.

7. The same report quoted in note 5, *1999 World Survey on the Role of Women in Development: Globalization, Gender and Work,* gives the following analysis: "Globalization has had strong gender employment effects. It has led to the steady increase in the female share of paid employment. The increased economic autonomy of women gained through wage employment broadened their life options, strengthened their self-esteem, improved their status within the households and their family's purchasing power. It also had a negative side, as it had significantly altered the pattern of employment such that 'irregular' conditions, which were once associated with women's secondary employment, had become widespread for both sexes. The world of work was now characterized by casual, flexible and temporary employment patterns with the consequent job insecurity and lower enjoyment of basic worker rights." On the occasion the report was presented to the Second Committee (Economic and Financial) of the UN, Mr. Matti Kaariainen, representative of Finland, speaking on behalf of the European Union and eleven East European countries, stated that "many of the negative impacts of liberalization and globalization seemed to have disproportionately affected women. The already large share of women among the world's poorest people was expected to increase in the years to come." Ms. Mariam Aftab, representative of Pakistan said in the same

opportunity that: "The burden placed on women in developing countries, both inside and outside the home, had increased as a result of globalization. . . . much of the job creation resulting from globalization had involved informal, irregular forms of work which were low paying, insecure and with little in the way of training or promotion prospects. Informalization also meant that many of the costs of market volatility and economic recession were borne by the most vulnerable workers, women, since they were less likely to be covered by labor regulations and laws dealing with social and employment security, especially in developing countries."

8. The United States National Administrative Office, in January 1998, found that Mexico's constitution and labor code prohibit discrimination based on sex; pre-employment pregnancy testing did occur in Mexico; there were contradictory interpretations of Mexico's law regarding the illegality of this practice; and while on-the-job, pregnancy-based sex discrimination was clearly illegal under Mexican labor law, greater efforts needed to be made toward awareness programs for women workers. This was the first case heard by the US NAO that dealt explicitly with the right to gender equality in the workforce. [NAO is the body charged with hearing cases of alleged violations of the North American Agreement on Labor Cooperation, commonly referred to as the labor rights side agreement of the North American Free Trade Agreement, (NAFTA)]. (From Human Rights Watch World Report 1999.)

9. According to Human Rights Watch Report 1999: "Bosnian women faced discrimination in the reconstruction period. Micro-credit programs aimed at women provided significantly smaller loan amounts, in some cases only one-third of the amount offered to male entrepreneurs under similar programs."

10. Ibid., see the chapter on "State tolerated Discrimination."

11. No less than the pioneer feminist Betty Friedan declared in an article in *Newsweek* magazine, September 4, 1995: ". . . how, at this time of global economic insecurity, women could even maintain their gains, much less continue to advance. And I've realized that they can't—not as long as they focus on women's issues alone or on women versus men. The problems in our fast changing world require a new paradigm of social policy, transcending all 'identity politics'—women, blacks, gays, the disabled. Pursuing the separate interests of women isn't adequate and is even diversionary. Instead, there has to be some new vision of community. . . . 'Women's issues' are symptoms of problems that affect everyone."

12. This reality is so critical that some countries are trying to adopt stricter legislation in order to ensure that children are not penalized by their parents' divorce. In Argentina, where only three of every ten divorced men regularly pay, the Congress was discussing measures that would "encourage" parents to comply with their alimony duties: after three months without payment, the family judge would report to a centralized database. Not before settling the arrears would the father be allowed to leave the country, renew a driver's license, or receive any loans or credit. (*Clarín,* Friday, March 20, 1998, page 38.)

13. As noted by Hideaki Maruyama, representative of Japan to the 27th meeting of the Second Committee of the UN, Oct. 29, 1999.

14. Laura Butterbaugh, in *An Hour of One's Own,* describes the hassle of a mother's daily life: "A great part of our time is taken up with labor that we don't really even acknowledge as labor. This is because most of this work has been traditionally performed by women and has therefore never been valued, appreciated or even acknowledged as work. Yet this labor accounts for a tremendous number of our waking hours. We spend countless hours each week doing laundry, running errands, neatening up, fixing household items, shopping for food, shopping for clothes and household items, cooking, cleaning, mending, nurturing social ties with others, checking in on family members, caring for sick or elderly people, and, of course, the most time intensive labor of all, raising children."

15. Every day, four women die in the United States as a result of domestic violence, and at least 1,567 are battered, 465 so seriously as to need hospitalization, emergency room care, or a doctor's attention. *Violence against Women: A National Crime Victimization Survey Report,* U.S. Department of Justice, Washington, D.C., January, 1994.

16. Leonie V. Still, of Edith Cowan University prepared for the Human Rights and Equal Opportunity Commission and Westpac a report *The Barriers to the Careers of Women in the Australian Finance Industry.*

17. This expression was coined by Morison, White and Van Velsor (1987) in the book *Breaking the Glass Ceiling,* where they describe the problem as a barrier "so subtle that it is transparent, yet so strong that it prevents women from moving up the corporate hierarchy." According to the authors, the glass ceiling "is not simply a barrier for an individual, based on the person's inability to handle a higher-level job. Rather, the glass ceiling applies to women as a group who are kept from advancing higher because they are women."

18. This survey is the fourth in a series of projects that the *Washington Post,* the Henry J. Kaiser

Family Foundation, and Harvard University are conducting on contemporary issues. (*Washington Post,* Sunday, March 22, 1998, page A1.)

19. We consider that sustainable access to power positions is verified where women in intermediate positions at least double the numbers in the first rank. This critical mass ensures continuance of supply of new "cadres" for first rank positions and enables more women to receive training and information in order to be prepared to assume higher positions. That is not the case in countries where women in ministerial positions double or more the ones in the intermediate level. This situation may reflect only a temporary circumstance, a fad or token gesture by which the administration exonerates itself of any further efforts in order to ensure women permanent conditions of access.

20. As of January 1996, at the ministerial level, 5.9 percent; at the intermediate level, 10.1 percent (Division for the Advancement of Women, DESA—United Nations).

21. And only 6.7 percent at the intermediate level (Division for the Advancement of Women, DESA—United Nations).

22. As of January 1996, at the ministerial level, 8.3 percent; at the intermediate level, 6.6 percent (Division for the Advancement of Women, DESA—United Nations).

23. As of January 1996, at the ministerial level, 2.4 percent; at the intermediate level, 2.6 percent (Division for the Advancement of Women, DESA —United Nations).

24. As of January 1996, at the ministerial level, 2.7 percent; at the intermediate level, 11.9 percent (Division for the Advancement of Women, DESA—United Nations).

25. As of January 1996, 5.6 percent (Division for the Advancement of Women, DESA—United Nations).

26. 1.3 percent of women less than 25 years of age and 7.6 percent of those over 25 (Division for the Advancement of Women, DESA—United Nations).

27. The Feminist Majority Internet newsletter "Womansword," Vol. 2, Issue 2, February 1997, presents the report from Theresa Loar, Senior Coordinator for International Women's Issues, U.S. Department of State (Oct. 1996). The following improvements had been verified: AFRICA: *Botswana:* The government has begun a review process of its national legislation to revise/eliminate laws that discriminate on the basis of sex. Marriage and property laws will be most affected by any revisions. *Cameroon:* The Mothers for Mayor Campaign succeeded in doubling the number of women mayors from 400 to 800 after Bei-

jing. *Egypt:* The government banned female circumcision in government health facilities and by all health care workers affiliated with the health ministry. *Mali:* Adopted a comprehensive four-year plan that will devote $22 million to the betterment of women in areas of education, health, legal rights, the economy, the environment, and institutional support structures. *Namibia:* Passed the Marriage Equality Act, which affords all women legal equality with men. Previously, although single women were considered full adults by law, married women were subject to the legal authority of their husbands. Married women could not even open a bank account, sign a contract, or serve on a board of a company without their husband's permission. This is no longer the case. This is the most significant piece of gender legislation since independence. *South Africa:* The parliament has ratified CEDAW and passed the Commission on Gender Equality Act, which establishes a commission to promote gender equality and advise/make recommendations to parliament on legislation affecting women, and legalized a bill allowing abortion on demand. The president's ruling party has said that this bill reaffirmed the constitutional principles of the right to privacy and personal security. The government has established an Office on the Status of Women, established a provision of free health care for pregnant women and children under six, and adopted a new constitution that includes an equality clause (Section 9.3) that prohibits discrimination on the grounds of gender, sex, pregnancy, marital status, and sexual orientation. The Beijing Platform for Action was used as a reference guide by the South African government while developing their constitution. *Tanzania:* The national legislature passed a bill reserving one-third of parliamentary seats for women. ASIA: *China:* The government has created a five-year plan (1996–2001) to help women escape rural poverty. This plan emphasizes a two-pronged approach of teaching rural women marketable skills so they can become self-reliant and wiping out illiteracy. *India:* A constitutional amendment is currently being considered by the Indian Parliament, which, if passed, would require that one-third of all members of parliament be women. The bill is not likely to be opposed since almost all the political parties support this in their manifestos in recent elections. *Japan:* NGOs and private groups with help from the Japanese government established a "comfort fund" (for women from mainly Korea and the Philippines who were sexually enslaved during World War II) designed to eradicate violence against women, provide medical and welfare assistance to victims, and establish lump sum payments to individual victims. Japanese women's participation in politics has picked up since the Beijing conference. Ten percent of the candidates in the fall 96 elections were

women representing the highest percentage of women on a ballot since receiving the right to vote in 1945, and this is the first time that more than 100 women have run for national office. *Korea:* The legislature passed the Women's Development Act to stipulate basic guidelines for policies supporting women's advancement. The law provides a legal basis for rectifying gender discrimination in such areas as employment, education, social welfare, and human rights. The act further strengthens the mandate of the ministry of political affairs to coordinate and monitor all government policies from a gender perspective. *Mongolia:* The Mongolian government has increased the number of women in Parliament from three to seven after the Beijing conference. *Nepal:* The national legislature is considering legislation to allow women to inherit property; the police has established new crime units to help abused women and children; and a task force of legal experts was formed to amend laws that discriminate against women. *Pakistan:* The Pakistani government set up Beijing follow-up units in each of its four provinces, which include government and nongovernmental officials to address the needs of women on the provincial level. NGOs are working hard at the community level to increase awareness about domestic violence. NGOs are also conducting community-based training to help women become involved in the political process. *The Philippines:* The president approved a 30-year national plan for women, which mandates that all government officials allocate a portion of their annual budget (5 percent) to women-specific and gender-oriented programs; plans to increase the training of rural women and give more access to credit; and imposes more stringent penalties for those who engage in trafficking of women. The legislature is considering reclassifying rape as crime against a person instead of a crime against chastity. The Senate has passed this legislation and it is currently awaiting House approval. A bill to punish offenders of domestic violence is also under consideration. EUROPE: *Bosnia-Herzegovina:* Follow-up by the United States: On July 11, 1996, at the G-7 Summit in Lyon, President Clinton pledged $5 million to aid Muslim women who survived the capture of the town of Srebenicia by Bosnian Serbs in rebuilding their country, opening businesses, and getting back on their feet economically. Follow-up by other countries: During the attack on Srebenicia in the war, most of the survivors fled to Tuzla. On July 11, 1996, women who lost male relatives gathered there for a rally commemorating the fall of the town. The event was sponsored by women from other countries. A representative of the organizers said they had raised over $3 million to finance rehabilitation programs for the survivors. *Denmark:* The government has launched initiatives on equal pay and equal status for men and women.

Poland: The legislature is considering liberalizing its abortion policy. The new bill allows legal abortions to be performed until the twelfth week of pregnancy in difficult personal and economic circumstances. LATIN AND SOUTH AMERICA: *Argentina:* Congress passed a law establishing that women constitute 30 percent of a political party's candidates' list. Argentina's law on reproductive health, rejected for four consecutive years, has now succeeded in receiving partial sanction from congress. Women's groups have still to secure full enactment of this modern legislation designed to protect the health of women and adolescent girls. *Brazil:* Established special police units for domestic violence. Women police officers provide support, protection, and legal advice in cases of abuse. The national congress passed a law that women must constitute 20 percent of a political party's candidate list. The Ministry of Health has committed to reduce women's mortality from cancer by providing free breast and uterus exams through public health systems. The Ministry of Work has committed to undertake a new professional training program to reach 10,000 girls by the end of 1996. *Chile:* As part of a plan to achieve equality for women and girls, the government has committed to: improving the quality of education of women, with special attention to the needs of girls; eliminating hidden curriculum and classroom discrimination; increasing women's participation in the labor force by providing child care and adequate training to give women a greater presence in decision-making positions in public life; and tackling AIDS and adolescent pregnancies. *Colombia:* The congress passed laws addressing domestic violence; protecting women who are heads of the households, which gives preference in housing projects and education to single mothers and requiring both the husband and wife's signature to grant a divorce. *Costa Rica:* Has incorporated training on the proper handling of cases of domestic violence in their basic training course for new police personnel. *Ecuador:* The national congress passed the Law Against Violence Toward Women and the Family. This law protects women in cases of domestic violence and criminalizes spousal abuse for the first time. The law also created family courts and reformed the penal code to include legislation giving the courts the power to separate an abusive spouse from the home. *El Salvador:* The government has created the Salvadoran Institute for the Development of Women. It's board of directors is headed by the first lady and composed of six state ministers, the state attorney, the human rights defense attorney, and two representatives of NGOs. Its objectives are to promote development of women through equal opportunity programs and projects, new legislation, and the reform of legislation and norms that discriminate against women. *Guatemala:* A national university has established scholarships for indigenous women to study political science to help them become involved in the political process, and the same university has established courses in human rights focusing on the effects of the Guatemalan civil war with a particular focus on the human rights of women. *Mexico:* The Mexican government has developed a mechanism to monitor the government's implementation of the Beijing Platform for Action in the areas of health, education, work, social development, and family. *Panama:* The federal government set up a Women's Council, including NGOs and governmental agencies, to implement Beijing, the family code was reformed, laws have been passed categorizing and criminalizing types of domestic violence and concerning victim counseling and training of women in nontraditional areas.

28. For that purpose the International Foundation of Women Judges, the cultural branch of the International Association of Women Judges (IAWJ), with financial support from the Interamerican Development Bank (IDB), developed a series of workshops for judges in five Latin American countries with the objective of raising their awareness on gender issues and women's human rights.

29. Chinese expression made popular after the Beijing World Conference.

Women's Roles and the Promise of American Law

Author's note: The invitation to present this paper prompted me to suggest to the sponsors that the author should be a woman. They responded that most of the speakers at the session would be women. Even so, because no man can know a woman's experience, I want to disclaim any special qualification to pontificate about women's roles.

My thanks to Gillian Lester, Christine Littleton, and Seana Shiffrin for their comments on a draft of this paper.

1. Croly's enthusiasm for solutions employing the national government inclined him toward collectivist or corporatist programs along lines that have been decisively rejected in the United States in the late twentieth century. For a thoughtful critique of Croly from a perspective of social conservatism that I appreciate but do not share, see Michael S. Joyce and William A. Schambra, "A New Citizenship, A New Life," in *The New Promise of American Life,* ed. Chester E. Finn Jr., at 139 (1995).

2. For exceptionally readable short discussions of norms and roles, see Vilhem Aubert, *Elements of Sociology,* (1967), 18–27, 40–51.

3. Although this paper does not discuss special concerns of lesbians about "women's roles," the experience of discrimination may well be distinctive for lesbians in ways bearing some resemblance to the experience of discrimination against women of color. On the tendency for references to "women" implicitly to exclude lesbians, see Cheshire Calhoun, "The Gender Closet: Lesbian Disappearance under the Sign 'Women,'" 21 *Feminist Studies* 7 (1995). Undoubtedly there is a dearth of what Janet Halley calls "doubly intersectional" analysis, but I am not qualified to undertake it in this zone of intersection. See Janet E. Halley, *Introduction to Symposium, Intersections: Sexuality, Cultural Tradition, and the Law,* 8 Yale J. L. & Humanities 93, 103 (1996). Of course sexual orientation is, by itself, a forbidden ground for discrimination under a number of state and local civil rights laws.

4. It also discriminated between the daughters of male and female owners, and between female bartenders and female waiters, who were allowed to take alcoholic drinks from bars to tables.

5. *Goesaert v. Cleary,* 335 U.S. 464, 466–67 (1948). Justice Rutledge's dissenting opinion pointed out the irrationality of a law that allowed a male owner to employ his daughter as a bartender while he worked in a factory across town but would not allow Margaret Goesaert to tend bar with her employer-mother at her side.

6. *Craig v. Boren,* 429 U.S. 190, 210 n.23 (1976).

7. These two changes are in one sense logically connected. Women's constitutional rights to equality typically have been given effect by destroying privileges of men that have constrained women's aspirations. For a general treatment of this theme, see Hendrik Hartog, "The Constitution of Aspiration and 'The Rights That Belong to Us All,'" 74 *J. Am. Hist.* 1013, 1022–25 (1987). On social movements and "status disestablishment," see J. M. Balkin, *The Constitution of Status,* 106 Yale L.J. 2313, 2338–42 (1997).

8. Deborah L. Rhode, *Speaking of Sex: The Denial of Gender Inequality* (1997): 249. As Rhode's subtitle indicates, this book's main subject is the refusal of many Americans to face up to remaining inequalities between women and men—a refusal she calls "the 'no problem' problem."

9. Pamela Warrick, "Legal Sanctuary," *Los Angeles Times,* April 28, 1999, E1, col. 2, at E4.

10. On women's work during World War II and its immediate aftermath, see Alice Kessler-Ross, *Out to Work: A History of Wage-Earning Women in the United States* 273–99 (1982).

11. Ibid., 277.

12. "Women were 29 percent of the work force in 1950, 35 percent in 1965, and 40 percent by

1975—a percentage increase equal to that of the entire sixty years preceding 1950." Ibid., 301.

13. Rose Laub Coser, "Power Lost and Status Gained: A Step in the Direction of Sex Equality," in Kai Erikson and Steven Peter Vallas, eds., *The Nature of Work* 71 (1990).

14. The state legislatures soon followed with similar antidiscrimination laws, some with broader coverage than Title VII's. The Johnson administration imposed similar restrictions on federal government contractors. Exec. Order 11375 (1968).

15. The presence of women in Congress (currently 11 percent, aggregating the Senate and the House) is still important for "women's issues" such as women's health care, day care, and family medical leave. See Cokie and Steve Roberts, "Mothers' Day in Congress," *USA Weekend*, May 9–11, 1997, p. 4. On the role of women members of the House in shaping recent proposals for Social Security reform, see Robert A. Rosenblatt, "Retirement Study Shows Gender Gaps," *Los Angeles Times*, June 10, 1999, A25, col. 1.

16. I discussed this expressive function of law at length in Kenneth L. Karst, *Law's Promise, Law's Expression: Visions of Power in the Politics of Gender, Race, and Religion* (1993).

17. An example is the federal district judge who rejected a woman's Title VII claim saying "she was discriminated against, not because she was a woman, but because she refused to engage in a sexual affair with her supervisor." This decision was reversed on appeal in *Barnes v. Costle*, 501 F.2d 983 (D.C. Cir. 1979), noted in the text immediately following.

18. *Williams v. Saxbe*, 413 F. Supp. 654 (D.D.C. 1976); *Barnes v. Costle*, note 17 above.

19. If I had to make a list of the five most influential works of legal scholarship published during the last four decades, this work would unquestionably be among them. By "influential," I mean influencing not the views of other scholars but the lives of Americans.

20. The Supreme Court decision that firmly establishes the principle is *Meritor Savings Bank, FSB v. Vinson*, 477 U.S. 57 (1986). On the influence of myths about women, men, and sex in the application of *Meritor*, see Judith Olans Brown, Lucy A. Williams, and Phyllis Tropper Baumann, *The Mythogenesis of Gender: Judicial Images of Woman in Paid and Unpaid Labor*, 6 UCLA Women's L.J. 457, 516–29 (1996).

21. Vicki Schultz, *Reconceptualizing Sexual Harassment*, 107 Yale L.J. 1683 (1998). For a contrasting view of the Supreme Court's undertheorized and trivializing views of sexual harassment,

see Katherine M. Franke, *What's Wrong with Sexual Harassment?*, 49 Stan. L. Rev. 691 (1997).

22. See for example, Angela Harris, *Race and Essentialism in Feminist Legal Theory*, 42 Stan. L. Rev. 581 (1990).

23. On the racial segregation of women's work and the double wage penalty paid by black women, see Rhonda M. Williams and Peggie R. Smith, *What Else Do Unions Do? Race and Gender in Local 35*, 18 Rev. of Black Pol. Economy 59 (winter 1990). More generally, see Kimberlé Crenshaw, *Demarginalizing the Intersection of Race and Sex: A Black Feminist Critique of Antidiscrimination Doctrine, Feminist Theory and Antiracist Politics*, 1989 U. Chi. Legal F. 189 ("Demarginalizing"); Kimberlé Williams Crenshaw, *Mapping the Margins: Intersectionality, Identity Politics, and Violence Against Women of Color*, 43 Stan. L. Rev. 1241 (1991).

24. Although a similar statement may be appropriate for employment discrimination against lesbians, the courts have not interpreted Title VII to prohibit sexual orientation discrimination. Some scholars have argued that Title VII should be interpreted broadly to prohibit any harassment that reinforces gender stereotypes. See Schultz, note 21 above, at 1689; I. Bennett Capers, *Sex(ual Orientation) and Title VII*, 91 Colum. L. Rev. 1158 (1991). More narrowly (and predictably), Title VII has been read to forbid same-sex sexual harassment *by* a lesbian harasser. See the discussion in Ruth Colker, *Sexual Orientation: Militarism, Moralism, and Capitalism*, 48 Hast. L.J. 1201, 1217–21 (1997). The Supreme Court brought a different sort of same-sex harassment within the reach of Title VII. *Oncale v. Sundowner Offshore Services, Inc.*, 525 U.S. 75 (1998).

25. I have outlined my own views on the connections between race and culture in an article, *Myths of Identity: Individual and Group Portraits of Race and Sexual Orientation*, 43 UCLA L. Rev. 263, 311–18 (1995).

26. These cases are discussed in Crenshaw, *Demarginalizing*, 141–50.

27. Ibid., 152.

28. The turnaround case was *Jefferies v. Harris County Community Action Ass'n*, 615 F. 2d 1025 (5th Cir. 1980). For comment on *Jefferies* and others following its lead, see Judy Scales-Trent, *Black Women and the Constitution: Finding Our Place, Asserting Our Rights*, 24 Harv. C.R.-C.L. L. Rev. 9 (1989) (also discussing black women as a "discrete" group for purposes of claims under the equal protection clause); Cathy Scarborough, *Conceptualizing Black Women's Employment Experiences*, 98 Yale L.J. 1457 (1989). See also *Lam v. University*

of Hawaii, 40 F. 3d 1551 (9th Cir. 1994). For a critique of post-*Jefferies* decisions and an argument for a more thoroughgoing judicial recognition of "intersectionalities" in Title VII cases, see Kathryn Abrams, *Title VII and the Complex Female Subject*, 92 Mich. L. Rev. 2479 (1994).

29. The complications presented by these choices of strategy are analyzed in depth by Elizabeth M. Iglesias, *Structure of Subordination: Women of Color at the Intersection of Title VII and the NLRA. Not!*, 28 Harv. C.R.-C.L. L. Rev. 394 (1993). The penalty for making the "wrong" choice can be severe, as Anita Hill learned in 1991 when she accused her former boss of sexual harassment. Not the least of the lessons here is the risk of being seen as one who has "betrayed" the minority community. See María L. Ontiveros, *Three Perspectives on Workplace Harassment of Women of Color*, 23 Golden Gate U. L. Rev. 817, 823–24 (1993).

30. See Christopher David Ruiz Cameron, *How the García Cousins Lost Their Accents: Understanding the Language of Title VII Decisions Approving English-Only Rules as the Product of Racial Dualism, Latino Invisibility, and Legal Indeterminacy*, 10 La Raza L.J. 261, 85 Calif. L. Rev. 1347 (joint publication 1998).

31. See generally Clifford Geertz, *The Interpretation of Cultures* (1973); Jerome Bruner, *Acts of Meaning* (1990).

32. On the pervasiveness of gender typing— the encoding of information about society, and even the natural world, in a gender schema—see Sandra Lipsitz Bem, "Gender Schema Theory and Its Implications for Child Development: Raising Gender-aschematic Children in a Gender-schematic Society," 8 Signs 598 (1984). See also J. M. Balkin, *Cultural Software: A Theory of Ideology* (1998): 224–32.

33. Dominance is still the word. On the question of how one can speak of "male power" when the overwhelming majority of men feel anything but powerful, see Christine A. Littleton, *Reconstructing Sexual Equality*, 75 Calif. L. Rev. 1279, 1317–21 and passim (1987). See generally Catharine A. MacKinnon, *Feminism Unmodified: Discourses on Life and Law* 32–45 (1987) (on difference and dominance).

34. MacKinnon, *Feminism Unmodified*, 44.

35. A recent report places women's wages, on average, around 79 percent of men's wages. Lawrence Mishel, Jared Bernstein, and John Schmitt, *The State of Working America 1998–99* 134–35 (1999). In the 1990s the gap decreased mainly because men's real wages were falling; the rise in women's wages was far smaller. Ibid. The disappearance of the gap will not

bring gender equality to the world of work. For an excellent brief analysis of the reasons, see Edward J. McCaffery, *Equality, of the Right Sort,* 6 UCLA Women's L. J. 289 (1996). For a fuller treatment, see Edward J. McCaffery, *Taxing Women* (1997).

36. See Cynthia Fuchs Epstein, "The Cultural Perspective and the Study of Work," in *The Nature of Work,* ed. Kai Erikson and Steven Peter, 88, 91, 93–94 (1990). For some recent examples, see Barbara H. Wooton, "Gender Differences in Occupational Employment," 120 *Monthly Labor Rep.* 15 (April 1997). The notion of "comparable worth" as an index of sex discrimination in pay virtually died in the mid-1980s. For case studies of gendered pay inequities, concluding that such inequities mainly result from organizational factors (such as denial of power positions to women and reinforcement of acculturated views of gender and employment) as opposed to pure market pricing, see Robert L. Nelson and William P. Bridges, *Legalizing Gender Inequality: Courts, Markets, and Unequal Pay for Women in America* (1999).

37. Diane Joyce's struggle in no-woman's-land took her to the Supreme Court, which upheld a county agency's affirmative action program in *Johnson v. Transportation Agency of Santa Clara County,* 480 U.S. 616 (1987). For accounts of the extreme hostility of male workers to Joyce's efforts to work on a road crew and then to serve as a dispatcher, see Rhode, *Speaking of Sex,* 146–47; Susan Faludi, *Backlash: The Undeclared War Against American Women* 388–93 (1991).

38. A famous example in which a federal trial judge was persuaded that women prefer not to do a particular type of work—commission sales, the aptitude for which the company determined by a "vigor" test including views on boxing, wrestling, swearing, hunting, etc.—is the Title VII case of *EEOC v. Sears, Roebuck & Co.,* 628 F. Supp. 1264 (N.D. Ill. 1986). The decision was affirmed on appeal. 839 F.2d 302 (7th Cir. 1988). For a critique, see Joan C. Williams, *Deconstructing Gender,* 87 Mich. L. Rev. 797, 813–21 (1989). For a thorough analysis of the workings of internal company policies at Sears, see Nelson and Bridges, *Legalizing Gender Inequality,* 205–43. The authors note that the litigation itself impeded the parties on both sides from obtaining clear pictures of what was going on in the company. The dilemma in employment discrimination cases, they say, "is how to assess responsibility for patterns of inequality produced in countless small acts, by a changing cast of characters, that incrementally and consistently limit the employment prospects of one group of workers [women] compared with those of another." Ibid., at 242. Similar "patterns of inequality," in the aggregate, add up to the gendered culture that prevails in large portions of the world of work.

39. Gillian Lester, in her article, *Careers and Contingency,* 51 Stan. L. Rev. 73, 113–16 (1998) shows how hard it is to isolate causes of the rise of a contingent work force. For citations to wide-ranging analyses and studies, many of them focused on issues concerning women's choices concerning work, see the notes accompanying the cited passage.

40. Williams, *Deconstructing Gender,* 822–28. See also Joan C. Williams, *Market Work and Family Work in the 21st Century,* 44 Vill. L. Rev. 305 (1999).

41. For an excellent early discussion of culturally embedded attitudes toward women as wielders of weapons, see Wendy Webster Williams, *The Equality Crisis: Some Reflections on Culture, Courts, and Feminism,* 7 Women's Rts. L. Rep. 175 (1982). For other sources, see the notes to Kenneth L. Karst, *The Pursuit of Manhood and the Desegregation of the Armed Forces,* 38 UCLA L. Rev. 499, 523–45 and passim (1991). Since these articles were written, the rules excluding women from combat positions have been eased, and women now serve aboard Navy combat vessels and as combat pilots in the Air Force and Navy.

42. For some sobering details, see Rhode, *Speaking of Sex,* 141–42. One reason why some women fade in the law partnership competition is their sense of responsibilities for children. The typical large firm offers its highest rewards to the person who works "the classic workaholic schedule of an elite American lawyer." Joan C. Williams, *Sameness Feminism and the Work/Family Conflict,* 35 N.Y. Law School Rev. 347, 353 (1990). See the text in the following note.

43. A recent exception to this pattern made front-page news. Lew Platt, the retiring CEO of Hewlett-Packard Co., hand-picked Carleton Florina to be his successor; she had previously been president of the Lucent Technologies group, and now becomes the first woman to head a blue-chip company. Gender, she said, "is not the subject of the story." But surely gender put her on page one. Joseph Menn, "First Woman Named to Lead Blue-Chip Firm," *Los Angeles Times,* July 20, 1999, A1, col. 4.

44. The "wage gap" for black and Latino women professionals and managers has recently widened. For example, "Hispanic women [managers] made roughly 60 percent of what white male managers did [in 1998], while they made nearly 70 percent in 1993." Reed Abelson, "Women Minorities Not Getting to the Top," *New York Times,* July 14, 1999, C4.

45. Elizabeth Hardwick "Domestic Manners," *Daedalus,* vol 107 (1) 1, 10 (1978).

46. The work of Reva Siegel on these issues is indispensable. Reva B. Siegel, *Home as Work: The First Woman's Rights Claims Concerning Wives' Household Labor, 1850–1880,* 103 Yale L.J. 1073 (1994); Reva B. Siegel, *The Modernization of Marital Status Law: Adjudicating Wives' Rights to Earnings, 1860–1930,* 82 Geo. L.J. 2127 (1994) (hereinafter "Modernization"). In the latter article, Siegel shows how judges (who, of course, were men) limited the force of the earnings statutes by giving them restrictive interpretations. On earnings statutes, see also Amy Dru Stanley, "Conjugal Bonds and Wage Labor: Rights of Contract in the Age of Emancipation," 75 *J. Am. Hist.* 471 (1988).

47. George Lakoff, *Women, Fire, and Dangerous Things: What Categories Reveal about the Mind* 80–84 (1987).

48. Cathleen Decker, "Parents Tell of Decisions, Struggles in Child-Rearing," *Los Angeles Times,* June 13, 1999, A1, col. 1. On the origins and effects of such an "ideology of intensive mothering," see Sharon Hays, *The Cultural Contradictions of Mothering* (1996).

49. The classic source here is Arlie Hochschild (with Anne Machung), *The Second Shift: Working Parents and the Revolution at Home* (1989). See also Arlie Hochschild, "The Fractured Family" (review of six books), *The American Prospect* 106 (summer 1991). In an essay that illuminates issues of gender and of race, Devon Carbado has recounted the story of his own working mother as she met the challenge of work and family. Devon W. Carbado, *Motherhood and Work in Cultural Context: One Woman's Patriarchal Bargain,* 21 Harv. Women's L.J. 1 (1998).

50. John P. Robinson and Geoffrey Godbey, *Time for Life: The Surprising Ways Americans Use Their Time* 105, table 3 (1997). I am indebted for this reference to Joan Williams, *Do Women Need Special Treatment? Do Feminists Need Equality?,* 9 J. Contemp. Legal Issues 279, 287 n.39 (1998).

51. See McCaffery, *Equality, of the Right Sort,* 97–99. According to Lewis M. Segal and Daniel G. Sullivan, "The Growth of Temporary Services Work," 11 *J. Econ. Persp.* 117, 121 (spring 1997), in 1993 women constituted 61 percent of the temporary workforce, but the trend had been for this percentage to decline. I am indebted to Gillian Lester for this reference.

52. The inequalities rule many women out of the governmental and employment spheres of the public life of the community by making it "difficult or impossible to be economically self-sufficient through participation in the paid labor market or to be involved in the public sphere of political decision-making." Robin West, *Reconstructing Liberty,* 59 Tenn. L. Rev. 441, 454 (1992).

53. "The story that blames welfare for poverty channels anxiety about economic and social change toward a racialized target." Lucie E. White, *No Exit: Rethinking "Welfare Dependency" from a Different Ground,* 81 Geo. L.J. 1961, 1965 (1993). See generally Jill Quadagno, *The Color of Welfare: How Racism Undermined the War on Poverty* (1994).

54. For a powerful critique of this view as targeting the wrong irresponsibilities, see Linda C. McClain, *"Irresponsible" Reproduction,* 47 Hastings L. J. 339 (1996).

The racial stereotype of promiscuity dates from medieval Europeans' earliest encounters with Africans and was intensified in the era of Jim Crow. See, for example, David Brion Davis, *The Problem of Slavery in the Age of Revolution, 1770–1823* 194 (1975); Winthrop D. Jordan, *White Over Black: American Attitudes Toward the Negro, 1550–1812* 436–37 (1968); George M. Fredrickson, *The Black Image in the White Mind: The Debate on Afro-American Character and Destiny, 1817–1914* 251–55, 275–82 (Wesleyan ed. 1987). On influences in court of a more modern stereotype of promiscuous poor women, see Brown, Williams, and Baumann, *The Mythogenesis of Gender,* 529–37.

55. *Mississippi University for Women v. Hogan,* 458 U.S. 718, 725 (1984) (opinion of the Court by Justice Sandra Day O'Connor).

56. *United States v. Virginia,* 518 U.S. 515 (1996) (opinion of the Court by Justice Ruth Bader Ginsburg).

57. The standard of review today is exacting; official sex discrimination is unconstitutional unless it meets the test of an "exceedingly persuasive justification." *United States v. Virginia,* see note 56 above, 518 U.S. at 531.

58. Even Title VII is inadequate to deal with the glass ceiling in a private company, except when the employer is so unsophisticated as to create evidence of deliberate sex discrimination. In some cases Title VII does extend beyond purposeful discrimination. For example, an employer's weightlifting test for would-be clerical employees would violate Title VII if it were to have the effect of disqualifying a disproportionate number of women, unless the employer could show that weightlifting was a necessary part of the job. The glass ceiling problem typically evades this "effect" principle because there is no identifiable test for leadership positions—no analogy to a weightlifting test—that can be evaluated in court.

59. *Personnel Adm'r of Mass. v. Feeney,* 442 U.S. 256 (1979). The congruence of this principle to the constitutional law governing racial discrimination is dishearteningly close.

60. In the context of the courts' recognition of sexual harassment as employment discrimination,

Catharine MacKinnon said, "Law is not everything in this respect, but it is not nothing, either." See MacKinnon, *Feminism Unmodified,* 116.

61. Robert Max Jackson, *Destined for Equality: The Inevitable Rise of Women's Status* 209 (1998). Mothers of young children are a substantial portion of this workforce: some 65 percent of mothers with children under age six and 74 percent of mothers with children ages six to thirteen. And 55 percent of working women provide half or more of their families' earnings. Children's Defense Fund news release, March 24, 1999, available at http://www.childrens-defense.org/childcare/cc_facts.html.

62. Gerda Lerner, *The Creation of Patriarchy* 213 (1986). On the powerful religious and philosophical traditions, ancient and modern, closely limiting women's reproductive freedom, see Paula Abrams, *The Tradition of Reproduction,* 37 Ariz. L. Rev. 453 (1995).

63. Ibid., 214.

64. See the Declaration of Sentiments issued by the first women's rights convention at Seneca Falls, New York in 1848, in Alice S. Rossi, ed., *The Feminist Papers* 415–18 (1973).

65. See generally Sara Evans, *Personal Politics: The Roots of Women's Liberation in the Civil Rights Movement and the New Left* 212–32 and passim (1979). See also David A. J. Richards, *Women, Gays, and the Constitution: The Grounds for Feminism and Gay Rights in Culture and Law* 224–33 (1998) (on the modern women's movement as a civil rights movement).

66. 381 U.S. 479 (1965).

67. 410 U.S. 113 (1973).

68. See Ruth Bader Ginsburg, *Some Thoughts on Autonomy and Equality in Relation to Roe v. Wade,* 63 N.C. L. Rev. 375 (1985). I argued along these lines in my article, *The Supreme Court, 1976 Term—Foreword: Equal Citizenship Under the Fourteenth Amendment,* 97 Harv. L. Rev. 1, 57–59 (1977), and pursued the point in the context of the *Casey* decision, see note 77 below, in Karst, *Law's Promise, Law's Expression,* 195–202. For a full elaboration of this equality theme, soundly underpinned by analysis of the development of antiabortion laws in nineteenth century America, see Reva Siegel, *Reasoning from the Body: A Historical Perspective on Abortion Regulation and Questions of Equal Protection,* 44 Stan. L. Rev. 261 (1992) (including a compilation of citations to recent writings on abortion regulation as an issue of sex equality, at 263 n.5). See also Erin Daly, *Reconsidering Abortion Law: Liberty, Equality, and the New Rhetoric of Planned Parenthood v. Casey,* 45 Am. U. L. Rev. 77 (1995).

69. Michael Walzer, *Spheres of Justice: A Defense of Pluralism and Equality* 240 (1983).

70. John Hart Ely, *The Wages of Crying Wolf: A Comment on Roe v. Wade,* 82 Yale L.J. 920, 935 (1973).

71. *Reed v. Reed,* 404 U.S. 71 (1971). Shortly after the *Roe* decision, the Court came within one vote of holding that sex was a "suspect" legislative classification, requiring "strict" judicial scrutiny of asserted justifications. *Frontiero v. Richardson,* 411 U.S. 677 (1973). Three years later, in *Craig v. Boren,* see note 6 above, the Court adopted an "intermediate" principle, requiring "important" justification for sex discrimination. More recently, the Court has reshaped that principle to require "an exceedingly persuasive justification" for sex discrimination—a virtual equivalent of strict scrutiny. *United States v. Virginia,* 518 U.S. 515 (1996).

72. 410 U.S. at 223.

73. Justice Blackmun, in *Roe v. Wade,* 410 U.S. at 116.

74. On this point I agree with the views in Gerald N. Rosenberg, *The Hollow Hope: Can Courts Bring About Social Change?* 175–201, 247–70 (1991). Rosenberg properly credits the Supreme Court with one crucial contribution to maintaining an effective right of choice: protecting birth control clinics against hostile governmental action. Ibid., at 195–201.

75. See Karst, *Law's Promise, Law's Expression,* 50–57 and passim.

76. The most ominous decisions, in the view of abortion rights advocates, were *Webster v. Reproductive Health Services,* 492 U.S. 490 (1989), and *Rust v. Sullivan,* 500 U.S. 173 (1991).

77. 505 U.S. 833 (1992). The commentary on *Casey* is voluminous. For a sensitive analysis, emphasizing the *Casey* plurality's determination to preserve women's right of reproductive choice but to allow the states a wide latitude to express official opposition to abortion, see Robert J. Goldstein, *Reading Casey: Structuring the Woman's Decisionmaking Process,* 4 Wm. & Mary Bill of Rights J. 3 (1996). In the view of David Garrow, author of a major study of *Roe v. Wade,* see note 67 above, "*Casey* was without any doubt a tremendous prochoice victory. . . ." David J. Garrow, *Abortion Before and After* Roe v. Wade: *An Historical Perspective,* 62 Albany L. Rev. 833, 845 (1999).

78. The authors of the joint opinion concluded that, on the record before the Court, Pennsylvania's twenty-four-hour waiting period had not been shown to impose an "undue burden" on the right of choice.

79. Indeed, as the dissenters pointed out, the plurality opinion of Justices O'Connor, Kennedy, and Souter did not follow *Roe* closely. For example, the

"undue burden" test, see note 78 above, replaced a very different doctrinal structure in the *Roe* opinion.

80. It is commonly understood that Justice Kennedy drafted the joint opinion's discussion of due process liberty, Justice Souter drafted the discussion of precedent, and Justice O'Connor drafted the discussion of the "undue burden" test as applied to the husband-notice rule and the other parts of the Pennsylvania law before the Court.

81. 505 U.S. at 898.

82. 505 U.S. at 852.

83. 505 U.S. at 860, 856.

84. Renato Rosaldo, *Culture and Truth: The Remaking of Social Analysis* 105 (1989).

85. See Elizabeth M. Schneider, *The Dialectic of Rights and Politics: Perspectives from the Women's Movement,* 61 N.Y.U. L. Rev. 598, 623–34 (1986); on abortion, see ibid. at 634–42.

86. Balkin, *The Constitution of Status,* 2340, 2342.

87. State funding is available in a number of states, including California and New York.

88. Rhode, *Speaking of Sex,* 204.

89. Faludi, *Backlash,* 427.

90. Barbara Omolade, "Hearts of Darkness," in Ann Snitow, Christine Stansell, and Sharon Thompson, *Powers of Desire: The Politics of Sexuality* 350, 363 (1983).

91. I refer to the irony of intense race-consciousness in the imposition of burdens, followed by a policy of race-blindness in official responses to the resulting disadvantages. The irony was noted in the text at note 25 above.

92. Peggy Cooper Davis, *Neglected Stories and the Lawfulness of Roe v. Wade,* 28 Harv. C.R.-C.L. L. Rev. (1993). See also Richards, *Women, Gays, and the Constitution,* 244–52 (human rights in "intimate life" founded on the Constitution's rejection of slavery). On the black-white "sexual economy" in the South before the Civil War, see Adrienne D. Davis, *The Private Law of Race and Sex: An Antebellum Perspective,* 51 Stan. L. Rev. 221 (1999).

93. See Rosalind Pollack Petchesky's preface to the second edition of her book, *Abortion and Woman's Choice: The State, Sexuality, and Reproductive Freedom* xviii–xxi (1990 ed.), and accompanying endnotes at xxx–xxxi. For her earlier general discussions of race and class divisions concerning abortion, see ibid. at 148–55, 230–32.

94. For a brief survey, see Dorothy E. Roberts, *The Future of Reproductive Choice for Poor Women*

and Women of Color, 12 Women's Rts. L. Rep. 59 (1990). Dorothy E. Roberts, *Killing the Black Body* (1997) is a comprehensive treatment, including the subjects of earlier articles: Dorothy E. Roberts, *Punishing Drug Addicts Who Have Babies: Women of Color, Equality, and the Right of Privacy,* 104 Harv. L. Rev. 1419 (1991); Dorothy E. Roberts, *Rust v. Sullivan and the Control of Knowledge,* 61 Geo. Wash. L. Rev. 587 (1993); Dorothy E. Roberts, *Crime, Race, and Reproduction,* 67 Tul. L. Rev. 1945 (1993); Dorothy E. Roberts, *The Genetic Tie,* 62 U. Chi. L. Rev. 209 (1995). On the attitudes of California officials toward the overblown "crack babies" question, see Laura E. Gómez, *Misconceiving Mothers: Legislators, Prosecutors, and the Politics of Prenatal Drug Exposure* (1997). See also Lynn M. Paltrow, *Pregnant Drug Users, Fetal Persons, and the Threat to Roe v. Wade,* 62 Albany L. Rev. 999 (1999); Lisa C. Ikemoto, *The Code of Perfect Pregnancy: At the Intersection of the Ideology of Motherhood, the Practice of Defaulting to Science, and the Interventionist Mindset of Law,* 53 Ohio St. L.J. 1205 (1992).

95. Battering is undoubtedly "a problem of epidemic proportions." Neil S. Jacobson and John M. Gottman, *When Men Batter Women: New Insights into Ending Abusive Relationships* 267 (1998). There are strong inhibitions against women's reporting of domestic violence; indeed, the inhibitions—most prominently fear and denial—are often built into the patterns of violence. Even so, the lowest estimates of the extent of battering run to about 12 percent of all marriages, with estimates reaching as high as 50 percent. And "battering," for these statistical purposes, means repeated hitting or beating. See Christine A. Littleton, *Women's Experiences and the Problem of Transition: Perspectives on Male Battering of Women,* 1989 U. Chi. Legal F. 23, 28 and accompanying notes; Martha R. Mahoney, *Legal Images of Battered Women: Redefining the Issue of Separation,* 90 Mich. L. Rev. 1, 10–11 (1991). Women writers have for some time remarked on group sex differences in reactions to such figures: disbelief by many men, acceptance by many women. A similar group disparity in the related field of forced sex is noted by Edward O. Laumann, John H. Gagnon, Robert T. Michael, and Stuart Michaels, *The Social Organization of Sexuality* 333–39 (1994), who report that 22 percent of women say they have been forced to engage in sex at some time after age thirteen. The forced-sex aspect of the same study is also reported in Robert T. Michael, John H. Gagnon, Edward O. Laumann, and Gina Kolata, *Sex in America* 219–29 (1994). Reporting that only 3 percent of men say they have forced a woman sexually, these scholars suggest that men as a group do not understand how coercive their behavior is to women. Ibid. at 227–29. Isn't it time, in the year 2000, to

listen to the women? For the Laumann and Michael references I am indebted to Martha Nussbaum's thoughtful essay on sexual violence in her book, *Sex and Social Justice* 136–44 (1999).

96. Two Canadian studies reported that 30 percent and 50 percent, respectively, of women assault victims were pregnant, and another survey of pregnant women reported that 7 percent had been assaulted, mostly by blows to the abdomen. Some miscarriages result from these attacks. An excellent short treatment of the subject is Ann Duffy, "The Feminist Challenge: Knowing and Ending the Violence," in Nancy Mandel, ed., *Feminist Issues: Race, Class, and Sexuality* 132 (study reports at 151 n.6) (1998).

97. Reva B. Siegel, *"The Rule of Love" Wife Beating as Prerogative and Privacy,* 105 Yale L.J. 2117 (1996).

98. See, for example, Elizabeth M Schneider, *The Violence of Privacy,* 23 Conn. L. Rev. 973 (1991). On judges and prosecutors who "see domestic violence as a family matter," see Jacobson and Gottman, *When Men Batter Women,* 273 and passim. On "must arrest" laws as a remedy for police unresponsiveness, see Deborah Epstein, *Redefining the State's Response to Domestic Violence: Past Victories and Future Challenges,* Geo. J. of Gender and the Law 127, 132–37 (Inaugural issue, summer 1999); Linda G. Mills, *Killing Her Softly: Intimate Abuse and the Violence of State Intervention,* 113 Harv. L. Rev. 550 (1999).

99. G. Chezia Carraway, *Violence Against Women of Color,* 43 Stan. L. Rev. 1301, 1303 (1991).

100. For references, see Schneider, *The Violence of Privacy,* 981 n.37. On race and the conceptualization of rape, see Crenshaw, *Mapping the Margins,* 1266–71.

101. Joel Williamson, *The Crucible of Race: Black-White Relations in the American South Since Emancipation* 111–39 (1984) (images of the "black beast rapist").

102. Linda L. Ammons, *Mules, Madonnas, Babies, Bath Water, Racial Imagery and Stereotypes: The African-American Woman and the Battered Woman Syndrome,* 1995 Wis. L. Rev. 1003, 1018–22.

103. Ibid. 1023; Jenny Rivera, *Domestic Violence Against Latinas by Latino Males: An Analysis of Race, National Origin, and Gender Differentials,* 14 B.C. Third World L.J. 231, 249 (1994).

104. See Crenshaw, *Mapping the Margins,* 1248–49.

105. A systematic refusal of police to enforce the criminal law of battery against husbands who

beat their wives would, in theory, be a constitutional violation, but detection of such a practice is difficult. See Siegel, *The Modernization of Marital Status Law,* 2191–94.

106. Pub. L. No. 103–322, 108 Stat. 1941, codified in 42 U.S.C. sec 13981.

107. The Act does not apply to "random acts of violence unrelated to gender or for acts that cannot be demonstrated, by a preponderance of the evidence, to be motivated by gender." This limitation, as Professor Siegel compellingly shows, is designed by its sponsors to promote the same kind of "domestic harmony" or "privacy" interests as did the earlier generations of judges who shielded "the marital relationship" from unseemly inquiries into wife beating. Siegel, *The Modernization of Marital Status Law,* 2196–2206.

108. *Brzonkala v. Virginia Polytechnic Institute and State University,* 169 F.3d 820 (4th Cir. 1999). The court of appeals held (by a 7–4 vote) that Congress lacks power to enact the law; the proponents argue that Congress's powers to regulate interstate commerce and to enforce the equal protection guarantee of the Fourteenth Amendment are sufficient to support the law. As a formal matter, my comments in the text are more relevant to the latter power than to the former, but it is entirely possible that the culture of women's roles may influence a swing vote in a case for which a doctrinal formula can be found to explain a decision either way. While this book was nearing publication, the Supreme Court affirmed the court of appeals, holding the law unconstitutional. *United States v. Morrison,* 519 U.S. 598 (2000).

109. I examined this subject in detail in a 1993 book. See Karst, *Law's Promise, Law's Expression.*

110. Family Issues Voting Index, National Christian Action Coalition, a report card on legislators quoted in Erling Jorstad, *The Politics of Moralism: The New Christian Right in American Life* 63 (1981). This passage is eerily reminiscent of Justice Joseph Bradley's concurring opinion a century earlier, when the Supreme Court upheld an Illinois law limiting the practice of law to men:

> The paramount destiny and mission of woman are to fulfill the noble and benign offices of wife and mother. This is the law of the Creator.

Bradwell v. Illinois, 83 U.S. 130, 141 (1873). Before the end of 1873 the Illinois legislature made women eligible to practice law. Chief Justice Samuel P. Chase was the lone dissenter, and he did not write an opinion. For a suggestion of an "acculturation" explanation for this dissent—Chase's closeness to his daughter, who had lived as public a life as a women could live in her day—see Richard L. Aynes, *Bradwell v. Illinois: Chief Justice Chase's Dissent and the "Sphere of Women's Work",* 59 La. L. Rev. 521 (1999).

111. Quoted in Karst, *Law's Promise, Law's Expression,* 39.

112. I have set out my own views on this debate in my article, *Boundaries and Reasons: Freedom of Expression and the Subordination of Groups,* 1990 U. Ill. L. Rev. 95, 131–47 and passim.

113. Kristin Luker, *Abortion and the Politics of Motherhood* (1984). For a somewhat different perspective, see Faye Ginsburg, *Contested Lives: The Abortion Debate in an American Community* (1989).

114. See Peter Skerry, "The Class Conflict Over Abortion," 52 *Pub. Interest* 69 (1978) (approval of abortion choice positively correlated with income and educational level).

115. Petchesky, *Abortion and Woman's Choice,* 208.

116. Kristin Luker, "Dubious Conceptions: The Controversy Over Teen Pregnancy," *The American Prospect,* spring 1991, p. 73, at 79.

117. Ibid., 81.

118. See Petchesky, *Abortion and Woman's Choice,* 209.

119. See Jackson, *Destined for Equality.*

120. "Changes in access to divorce, women's sexuality, and cultural images of gender will not play a central role in this study. They are important indicators of women's status, but they are derivative rather than formative." Ibid. at 6.

121. Ibid., 247–54 and passim.

122. For suggestions why this must be so, see Percy Cohen, *Modern Social Theory* 174–206 (1968). Clifford Geertz expresses a skepticism that I share:

> Human beings, gifted with language and living in history, are, for better or worse, possessed of intentions, visions, memories, hopes, and moods, as well as of passions and judgments, and these have more than a little to do with what they do and why they do it. An attempt to understand their social and cultural life in terms of forces, mechanisms, and drives alone, objectivized variables set in systems of closed causality, seems unlikely of success.

Clifford Geertz, *After the Fact: Two Countries, Four Decades, One Anthropologist* 127 (1995).

123. "To know the politics of women's situation is to know women's personal lives." Catharine A. MacKinnon, "Feminism, Marxism, Method, and the State: An Agenda for Theory," in *Feminist Theory: A Critique of Ideology* 1, 21 (1982).

124. Oliver Wendell Holmes [Jr.,] *Collected Legal Papers* 305 (1952).

125. Guyora Binder and Robert Weisberg, *Cultural Criticism of Law,* 49 Stan. L. Rev. 1149, 1192 (1997).

126. "Just Let Her Fly," *Discover Magazine,* April 1999, p. 18.

127. On the benefits to men from a reconstruction of gender, see Nancy Levit, *Feminism for Men: Legal Ideology and the Construction of Maleness,* 43 UCLA L. Rev. 1037 (1996).

Redefining Muslim Women's Roles in the Next Century

1. This is not to suggest the absence of a women's movement or of women's participation in public life in certain Muslim countries in earlier centuries. The movement today is distinguished by its broad base spanning most, if not all, Muslim countries.

2. Law No. 1 of the Year 2000, organizing certain litigation measures and procedures relating to matters of personal status (henceforth, "Law 2000"). Egypt has separate codes for non-Muslims based on their religious laws. This is a continuation of the *melli* system used by the Ottoman Empire.

3. Seif Nasr, *Majlis al-Sha'b Yabda' Ghadan Munaqashat Qanun al-Ahwal al-Shakhsiyah* (Parliament Commences Discussion Tomorrow of the Personal Status Law), Al-Ahram, Jan. 15, 2000, at 1.

4. See note 9 below and related text; see also Ahmad al-Batriq, et al., *Majlis al-Sha'b Yuwafiq 'ala Qanun al-Ahwal al-Shakhsiyah* (Parliament Approves Personal Status Law), Al-Ahram, Jan. 27, 2000, at www.ahram.org.eg/Arab/Ahram/2000/1/27/INV1.HTM (visited May 12, 2000) (noting that "hot debates" and exchange of accusations surrounded the approval of the law).

5. See, for example, Abdallah Hilal, *Hawl al-Qanun al-Masluq li al-Ahwal al-Shakhsiyah* (On the Rushed Law of Personal Status), Al-Sha'b, Jan. 28, 2000, at 4 (arguing that this law is only one manifestation of the Egyptian government's submission to the power of the United States and attempts at globalization); see also the Statement of the Azhari Scholars, published in Al-Sha'b, Jan. 25, 2000, at 2 (warning that by changing Islamic law, there will be no peace or safety); Abd al-Salam Ibrahim Ghaidhan, *Fakhamat Ra'is al-Jumhuriyah: La Tuwaqi' 'Ala al-Qanun al-Mashbuh* (Mr. President: Do Not Sign This Suspicious Law), Al-Sha'b, Jan. 25, 2000, at 2 (noting that not even colonialists dared separate personal status law from religion); Majdi Ahmad Hussein, *Al-Sayyed Ra'is Majlis al-Sha'b: Itha Kunta Takh.sha allah fala Tasluq al-Qanun* (Head of the Parliament: If You Fear God, Do Not Rush the Law),

Al-Sha'b, Jan. 11, 2000, at 3 (arguing that globalization and westernization are behind the law).

6. Law 2000, Bk. 3, Ch.1, Art. 20.

7. See *Khurshid Bibi v. Muhammad Amin,* PLD
1967 SC 79. In fact, the opinion in this case entitled the wife to *Khul'* if she satisfied the conscience
of the Court that it will otherwise mean forcing her
into a hateful union in which she is unable to live in
compliance with her religious obligations. See ibid.
at 99, 121. Law 2000, Bk. 3, Ch.1, Art. 20 uses
similar language. This is not surprising, given that
scholars in each case relied on a Prophetic incident
that legitimated this form of divorce. See *Khurshid
Bibi v. Muhammad Amin,* at 122–23.

8. *Mashyakhat al-Azhar* [the governing body of
al-Azhar] and *Majma' al-Buhuth al-Islamiyyah* [the
Academy of Islamic Research] both examined and
approved the proposed changes. Among the major
scholars providing thoughtful support for this law was
Muhammad Salim El-Awa. See Muhammad Salim
El-Awa, *Mashru' al-Ahwal ash-Shakhsiyyah* [Draft Personal Status Law], Al-Ahram, (visited Jan. 17, 2000)
http://www.ahram.org.eg/Arab/Ahram/2000/1/17/O
PIN3.HTM.

9. See Kamal Habib, *Akthar Min Thalathin 'Ali-
man Azhariyan Minhum A'dha' bimajma' al-Buhuth
al-Islamiyah Yarfudun Mashru' Qanun al-Ahwal al-
Shakhsiyah* [More Than Thirty Azhari Scholars
Among Them Members of the Islamic Research
Council Reject the Draft Personal Status Law], Al-
Sha'b, Jan. 18, 2000, at 1 (reporting that thirty-one
Azhari scholars, including members of the Islamic
Research Council, issued a press release demanding
that discussion of the law be delayed, and that views
of additional religious scholars be solicited, to ensure
that the law is not incompatible with the Islamic
shari'ah. The scholars also compared the law with an
earlier one that was later repealed).

10. The Parliament as a whole began considering the law on January 16. It was passed on Jan.
26, 2000. President Mubarak signed it into law on
Jan. 29, 2000.

11. Law 44 was passed in 1979.

12. See Jane Friedman, "As Islamic Fundamentalism Rises in Egypt, Government Feels Heat,"
Christian Science Monitor, June 14, 1985, at 9; see
also, Sarah Gauch, "Opening Door to the Present
Stirs Uproar," *Chicago Tribune,* Aug. 6, 1995, at 1.
Many women's organizations and religious leaders
were involved in the consultations and discussions
leading up to the formulation of this law, though
perhaps for not the same length of time and with a
smaller group of supporters than those involved in
the recent revisions. Since the seventies, it appears
that more individuals have recognized the need for
change. See Jehan Sadat, *A Woman of Egypt* 356–57

(1987). See also Majdi Ahmad Hussein, supra note
5, at 3, referring to the period of the earlier failed
revisions as the "Jihani era."

13. See Habib, supra note 9, at 1.

14. See Subhi Mahmassani, *Al-Awda' al-
Tashri'yah fi al-Duwal al-'Arabiyah* [Legal Systems
in the Arab States] 438–442 (Dar al-'Ilm li al-
Malayin: Beirut 1965); see also Muhammad
Hashim Kamali, *Principles of Islamic Jurisprudence*
283–295 (1991).

15. Western legal thought influenced the
Ottoman legal system. Subsequently, colonialist
rule augmented and accelerated the influence of
the Western legal traditions in Muslim countries.
See, for example, Mahmassani, supra note 14, at
510–13; Keith Hodkinson, *Muslim Family Law: A
Source Book* 11–13 (1984); see also, *Mannaa' al-
Qattan, Tarikh al-Tashri' al-Islami* 399–402 (Maktabat al-Ma'arif: Riyadh 1996).

16. See, for example, Azizah al-Hibri, "Islamic
Law and Muslim Women in America," in *One
Nation Under God?* 134–35 (1999); Marnia
Lazreg, *The Eloquence of Silence: Algerian Women
in Question,* 59–61 (1994).

17. See Amnesty International, "Egyptian
Human Rights Defender Faces Years of Imprisonment," Afr. News Serv., Feb. 16, 2000, available in
LEXIS-NEXIS Library, Newspaper Stories Combined Papers File (reporting that initial charges
against an Egyptian human rights activist were
"accepting funds from a foreign country with the aim
of carrying out acts that would harm Egypt," and
"disseminating false information abroad that would
harm the country's national interest"); MENA news
agency, "President's Aid Says NGOs Should Not Be
Used as Pretext to Interfere," BBC Worldwide Monitoring, Feb. 6, 2000, available in LEXIS-NEXIS
Library, Newspaper Stories Combined Papers File
(reporting that President Mubarak's aid said that
"these organizations should be national rather than a
Trojan Horse or a facade for activities of foreign organizations"); see also Muddassir Rizvi, "Media-Pakistan: Editor Muzzled by paper Under Government
Pressure," Inter Press Serv., June 21, 1999, available
in LEXIS-NEXIS Library, Newspaper Stories Combined Papers File (reporting a crackdown on NGOs
that are being accused of having a "western agenda"
and misusing funds, targeting major women organizations, such as Shirkat Gah and Aurat Foundation).

18. See, for example "A Hundred Years of Fortitude," *The Economist,* Nov. 27, 1999, available in
LEXIS-NEXIS Library, Newspaper Stories Combined
Papers File (reporting that the parliament voted down
the ruler's decree that would have granted women
political rights, and that members of parliament voted
it down in part because they were annoyed with the
government for trying to rule by decree).

19. See, for example, Fahmi Houidi, *Rabihat al-
Dimocratiyah wa Khasir al-Islamiyun* [Democracy Won
and the Islamists Lost], (visited May 16, 2000)
http://www.alhewar.com/images/Fahmi%20Houidi.jpg

20. This number was provided to me by the president of a university in the area when I visited his
campus. It was later confirmed by female officials.

21. Azizah al-Hibri, "Marriage Laws in Muslim
Countries, Family Law and Gender Bias," 4 *International Review of Comparative Public Policies*
231–238 (1992); Law 2000, Bk. 3, Ch.1, Art. 20,
relating to *khul'.*

22. See Azizah Y. al-Hibri, *Islam, Law and Custom,* 12 Am. U. J. Int'l L. & Pol'y 1, 25–34 (1997)
(discussing this claim at length).

23. See, for example, Abu Ja'far al-Tabari, 4
Jami' al-Bayan fi Tafsir al-Qur'an [The Comprehensive Clarifications of Qur'anic Interpretation]
34 (Dar al-Kutub al-'Ilmiyah: Beirut, reprint
1992) (9th century); see also Abu Bakr bin Abdallah (known as Ibn 'Arabi), 1 Ahkam al-Qur'an
[Qur'anic Rulings] 188–89, 416 (Dar al-Ma'rifah:
Beirut, reprint 1987) (12th century).

24. See, for example, Nasser al-Din al-Baydawi,
Tafsir (Dar al-Fikr: n.p., reprint 1982) (19th century) (explaining that male superiority is reflected
in the fact that males have been selected over
women for prophethood, being imams and *walis,*
and in such matters as laws of witnessing and
inheritance); see also Abu Bakr bin Abdallah, supra
note 23, at 416 (noting that males are superior in,
among other things, mind, rationality, and piety);
Muhammad Rashid Ridha, 5 Tafsir al-Qur'an al-
Hakim 67 (Dar al-Ma'rifah: Beirut, reprint 1973)
(stating that males are superior in physical strength
and power, causing differences in responsibilities).

25. See notes 37–43 below and related text.

26. See Ibn Hisham, *Al-Sirah al-Nabawiyyah*
[The Prophetic Biography] 187–88 (Dar al-Fikr:
Amman, reprint n.d.) (9th century).

27. Ibid., at 187 n.2, 189–90.

28. Ibid., at 240; see also Abd al-Halim Abu
Shuqqah, 1 Tahrir al-Mar'ah fi 'Asr al-Risalah [Lib-
eration of Women in Early Islam] 191 (Dar al-
Qalam: Kuwait 1990).

29. See Abbas Mahmoud al-Aqqad, Fatimah
al-Zahra passim, esp. 45–52 (Dar al-Kitab al-
'Arabi: Beirut 1967); Muhammad Baqir Sadr for
passages from and commentary on Fatimah's
speech, Fadak [name of property Fatimah was to
inherit], passim., esp. 87–88, 92–110 (Dar al-
Ma'arif li al-Matbu'at: Beirut 1990).

30. See 3 Al-Tabari, *Tarikh al-Umam wa al-
Muluk* [The History of Nations and Kings]

339–40 (Dar al-Kutub al-'Ilmiyyah: Beirut, reprint 1988) (9th century) (describing how Zainab called Yazid an oppressive ruler); 8 Ibn Kathir, *Al-Bidayah wa al-Nihayah* [The Beginning and the End] 195–96 (Maktabat al-Ma'arif: Beirut, reprint 1974) (14th century).

31. See Abu Shuqqah, supra note 28, at 231.

32. See Sa'id Fayez al-Dakhil, *Mawsu'at Fiqh 'A'ishah Um al-Mu'mineen* [The Encyclopedia of the Jurisprudence of 'A'ishah, the Mother of the Believers] passim (Dar al-Nafa'is: Beirut 1993).

33. See Saif al-Assadi, *Al-Fitnah wa Waq'at al-Jamal* 144–172 (Turmoil and the Battle of the Camel) (Dar al-Nafa'is: Beirut 1993) (8th century).

34. See Abu al-Hussein bin Muslim, 6 *Sahih Muslim bi Sharh al-Nawawi* [The True Statements of the Prophet with Exegesis by al-Nawawi] 190–95 (containing a whole chapter on warrior women); see also Abu Shuqqah, supra note 28, at 171–73, 175–76, 118–22, 126–27; Umar Kah.halah, 2 *A'lam al-Nisa'* [Famous Women] 43 (Mu'assasat al-Risalah: Beirut 1977); Ibrahim al-Wazir, *'Ala Masharif al-Qarn al-Khamis 'Ashar al-Hijri* [At the Cusp of the 15th century Hejirah] 62–65, 71 (Dar al-Shuruq: Cairo 1989); Muhammad Sa'id Mubayad, *Mawsu'at Hayat al-Sahabiyat* [Encyclopedia of Female Companions' Biographies] passim (Maktabat al-Ghazali: Damascus 1990).

35. See Sa'di Hussein Ali Jabr, *Fiqh al-Imam Abi Thawr* [The Jurisprudence of Imam Abi Thawr] 225 (Dar al-Furqan: Beirut 1983).

36. See, for example, 1 Kah.halah, supra note 34, at 27–28, 86, 179–80, 253–54; see also 2 Kah.halah, supra note 34, at 47–56, 65–66, 68–70, 71–72, 75–77, 91–99, 105–107, 166–72, 202–24.

37. See, for example, Family Law No. 84-11 (1984) (the Algerian Code), Bk. 1, Tit. 1, Ch.4, Art, 38; see also, Personal Status Code, Provisional Law No. 61 (1976) [The Jordanian Code], Ch. 9, Art. 69; Royal Decree No. 343.57.1 (1957), as amended by Royal Decree No. 347.93.1 (1993) [The Moroccan Code], Bk. 1, Ch. 6, Art. 35. See also Azizah al-Hibri, supra note 22, at 12; Ahmad al-Khamlishi, 1 *Al-Ta'liq 'Ala Qanun al-Ahwal al-Shakhsiyyah* [Commentary on Personal Status Code] 227–40. (Maktabat al-Ma'arif: Rabat 1987).

38. See, for example, Hussein's critique of the travel provision of the law as against *Shari'ah,* supra note 5, at 3.

39. Ibid.

40. Sa'id Fayez al-Dakhil, supra note 32, at 542–46.

41. Ibid.

42. See supra note 37, and infra note 43.

43. See supra note 37; see also Law No. 51 (1984) Regarding Personal Status [Kuwaiti Code] Part 1, Bk. 1, Tit. 3, Art. 89; Law No. 25 (1920) in respect of Maintenance and Some Questions of Personal Status, as amended, [Egyptian Code] Bk. 1, Ch. 1, Art. 1. See also Jordanian Code, Ch. 9, Art. 68 (a woman who works outside the home without her husband's permission is not entitled to maintenance); Syrian Code, Decree No. 59 (1953) Regarding Personal Status Law, amended by Law No. 34 (1975) Bk. 4, Ch. 3, Art. 73 (stating that the woman who works outside the house, despite her husband's prohibition, is not entitled to maintenance).

44. See Law 2000, Bk. 2, Ch. 1, Art. 9, section 3.

45. See, for example, Abu Shuqqah, supra note 28 (providing many instances in early Islam where women had more rights than later jurists accorded them); Taha Jabir al-Alwani *The Testimony of Women in Islamic Law,* 13 American Journal of Islamic Social Sciences 173-96 (1996) (explaining witnessing laws in a less patriarchal fashion); Muhammad Mahdi Shams al-Din, *Ahliat al-Mar'ah li Tawalli al-Sultah* [The Eligibility of Women to Assume Power], (Al-Mu'assasah al-Duwaliyah li al-Dirasaat wa al-Nashr: Beirut 1995) (arguing that women are eligible).

46. See, for example, Subhi Mahmassani, *Falsafat al-Tashri' fi al-Islam* [The Philosophy of Legislation in Islam] 201 (Dar al-'Ilm li al-Malayin: Beirut 1975); 2 Wihbah al-Zuhaili, *Usul al-Fiqh al-Islami* [The Foundations of Islamic Jurisprudence] 835–37, 1116–18 (1986); see also Azizah al-Hibri, *Islamic and American Constitutional Law: Borrowing Possibilities Or a History of Borrowing,* 1 Univ. of Penn. J. Const. L. 492, 509 (1999); Azizah al-Hibri, *Islamic Constitutionalism and the Concept of Democracy,* 24 Case W. Res. J. Int'l L. 1, 8 (1992).

47. Comments made at "Women in International Law: A Closer Look at the Arab and Muslim World," Panel Forum at the U.S. Supreme Court, Sept. 28, 1999.

48. Personal Status Code Decree, dated 13 August, 1956, as amended 1993 [The Tunisian Code], Bk. 1, Art. 18, 23 (as amended, 1993).

49. See al-Zuhaili, supra note 46, at 600–716; Muhammad Shalabi, *Usual al-Fiqh al-Islami* [Foundations of Islamic Jurisprudence] 200–266 (Al-Dar al-Jami'yah: Beirut, n.d.).

50. See, for example, Qur'an, 3:190–91, 2:242, 6:98–9; see also, Seyyed Hossien Nasr, *An Introduction to Islamic Cosmological Doctrines* 6–7 (1964).

51. See al-Hibri, supra note 46, at 8–9. See, e.g., 2 al-Zuhaili, supra note 46, at 752–827; al-Shalabi, supra note 49, at 294–324; Subhi Mahmassani, supra note 14, at 480.

52. See, for example, 2 al-Zuhaili, supra note 46, at 828–837; al-Shalabi, supra note 49, at 325–348; Mahmassani, supra note 14, at 428–39; Mahmassani, *Muqaddimah fi Ihya' 'Ulum al-Shari'ah* [Introduction to Reviving Shari'ah Sciences] 66–70, 72–77 (Dar al-'Ilm li al-Malayin: Beirut 1962); Abd al-Hamid Mutawalli, *Al-Islam wa Mabadi' Nitham al-Hukm* [Islam and the Principles of Governance] 71–72 (Mansha'at al-Ma'arif: Alexandria 1976); see also al-Hibri, *Islamic Constitutionalism,* supra note 46, at 8.

53. See 2 al-Zuhaili, supra note 46, at 831–32; al-Shalabi, supra note 49, at 332, 338.

54. See, for example, Mahmassani, supra note 14, at 478; al-Zuhaili, supra note 46, at 1116–18.

55. Muhammad Abu Zahrah, *Muhadarat fi 'Aqd al-Zawaj wa Atharuh* 15 (Dar al-Fikr al-'Arabi: Cairo n.d.).

56. See, for example, Egyptian Code, Law 78 for the Year 1931, Bk. 4, Chap. 1, Art. 280; Executive Order Promulgating Law 2000, Art. 3.

57. See Muhammad Abu Zahrah, *Al-Shafi'I* 145–46 (1948); al-Hibri, supra note 46, at 509.

58. There were many reasons for this development. Major among them is decline of democracy and colonialism. See, for example, Hussein Zein, *Al-Islam wa al-Fikr al-Siyasi al-Mu'asser* [Islam and Contemporary Political Thought] 45–48 (Dar al-Fikr al-Hadith: Beirut 1997); see also Azizah al-Hibri, *Legal Reform: Reviving Human Rights in the Muslim World,* 20 Harv. Int'l L.J. 50–51 (1998); al-Hibri, supra note 46, at 6–7.

59. See supra note 58.

60. Among the women are Amina al-Nusair, a professor with extensive knowledge of Islamic jurisprudence, and Muna Zulfaqar, a practicing attorney and women's rights activist.

61. See, for example, Amal al-Sibki, *Al-Harakah al-Nisa'iyyah fi Masr* [The Egyptian Women's Movement] (Matabi' al-Hay'ah al-Misriyah li al-Kitab: n.p. 1986); see also, Margot Badran, *Feminists, Islam, and Nation* 14–16, 223–26 (1995); Afaf Marsot, "The Revolutionary Gentlewomen of Egypt," in *Women in the Muslim World* 261–276 (Lois Beck and Nikki Keddie eds., 1978); Thomas Philipp, "Feminism and Nationalist Politics in Egypt," in *Women in the Muslim World* 277–294 (Lois Beck and Nikki Keddie eds., 1978).

62. Abu Hamid Al-Ghazali, *Ihya' 'Ulum al-Din* [Reviving Religious Sciences] 15 (Matba'at

Mustafa al-Babi al-Halabi: Cairo, reprint 1939) (12th century); 2 Abu Shuqqah, supra note 28, at 41; 1 Muhammad Ibn Majah, Sunan 80–83 (Dar al-Kutub al-'ilmiyyah: Beirut, reprint n.d.) (9th century); see also, al-Hibri, supra note 37, at 36.

63. Witness the example of Afghanistan under the Taliban government.

64. Qur'an, 4:1, 6:98, 7:189.

65. Qur'an, 30:21

66. See, for example, Qur'an, 9:71, 24:12, 48:25, 33:35.

67. Qur'an, 9:71.

68. Qur'an, 4: 34.

69. See, for example, Badr al-Din al-Zarkashi, 2 *Al-Burhan fi 'Ulum al-Qur'an* [Proof in Qur'anic Sciences] 175–6 (Dar al-Jil: Beirut 1988) (stating that the best method for interpreting the Qur'an is by having parts of it explain the other parts); Ridha, supra note 24, at 22 (noting that Qur'anic verses interpret each other).

70. See supra notes 34, 36.

71. A major contemporary female *sufi* figure with a large male following is Fatimah al-Yashru-tiyyah of Damascus. See also Margaret Smith, *Rabi'a The Mystic*, passim, esp. 1–3 (1974)

72. See supra note 58.

73. Two specific verses are fundamental, Qur'an 2:256 (there is no compulsion in religion), and Qur'an 17:70 (God gave humans dignity).

74. The Prophet was given *bay'ah* (a form of election) to the leadership position in Madinah. See al-Hibri, supra note 46, at 511–516.

75. Ibid., at 510–516.

76. See al-Wazir, supra note 34, at 63–67; see also Ruth Roded, *Women in Islamic Biographical Collections* 15–44 (1994); Hassan Khalid, *Mujtama' Al-Madinah* [The Society of Madinah] 214–15, 219 (Dar al-Nahdah al- 'Arabiyah: Beirut 1886); Muhammad bin Sa'd, *Al-Tabaqat al-Kubra* [The Great Categories] 131 (Dar al-Tahrir: Cairo 1970).

77. Qur'an, 60:12 (mentioning the *bay'ah* of women to the Prophet); see also 1 Abu Shuqqah, supra note 28, at 125–26, 230–31; al-Wazir, supra note 34, at 63–67; see also, al-Hibri, supra note 22, at 39.

78. 1 Abu Shuqqah, supra note 28, at 171–73; see also Roded, supra note 76, at 19–30.

79. 1 Abu Shuqqah, supra note 28, at 175–76, al-Wazir, supra note 34, at 71–72; see also supra note 34.

80. Qur'an, Chap. 58; see Abu Shuqqah, supra note 28, at 103 (explaining this incident).

81. Bangladesh and Pakistan have both had women in high governmental positions, such as that of prime minister.

82. In the case of Benazir Bhutto, former prime minister of Pakistan, she succeeded her executed father. In the case of Khalida Zia, former prime minister of Bangladesh, she succeeded her assassinated husband.

83. See Shams al-Din, supra note 45; see also Jabr, supra note 35, at 224–25.

84. See Kah.halah, supra note 34, at 61 (1977); Ali Ibrahim Hassan, *Nisa' Lahunna fi al-Tarikh al-Islami Nasib* [Women Who have a Share in Islamic History], passim, esp. 59–61, 78–100 (Maktabat al-Nahdhah al-Masriyah: Cairo 1950); Roded, supra note 76, passim.

85. Qur'an, 27: 23-33

86. Supra note 67 and related text.

87. See supra note 23; see also Wazarat al-Awqaf wa al-Shu'un al-Islamiyah, 34 *Al-Mawsu'ah al-Fiqhiyah* [The Encyclopedia of Fiqh] 77–8 (Dar al-Sufwah: Kuwait 1995); Abd al-Wahab al-Shis-hani, *Huquq al-Insan wa Hurriyatuhu al-Siyasiyah* [The Rights of a Human Being and His Political Rights] 691 (Matabi' al-Jam'iyah al-Islamiyah al-Malakiyah: Saudi Arabia 1980) (describing the view that the *qiwamah* verse justifies excluding women from higher education).

88. For a thorough translation and discussion of this verse, see al-Hibri, supra note 22. Also helpful is Maysam al-Faruqi, "Women's Self Identity in the Qur'an and Islamic Law," in *Windows of Faith* 82–97 (Gisela Webb ed., 2000)

89. Al-Hibri, supra note 22, at 30–32.

90. See supra notes 34, 79.

91. See, for example, Muhammad Abu Zahrah, *Al-Wilayah 'ala al-Nafs* 127 (Dar al-Ra'ed al-'Arabi 1970), Mahmassani, supra note 14, at 495.

92. See supra note 91.

93. See, for example, Muhammad al-Dusuqi, *Al-Usra fi al-Tashri' al-Islami* [The Family in Islamic Legislation] 155–56 (Dar al-Thaqafah: Doha 1995), Abu Zahrah, supra note 55, at 269; Mahmassani, supra note 14, at 496–97.

94. See, for example, 34 Wazarat al-Awqaf, supra note 87, at 77–8; al-Shishani, supra note 87, at 691.

95. See supra note 24.

96. Ibid.

97. See, for example, Taha Jabir al-Alwani, *The Ethics of Disagreement in Islam*, passim (1996); Mahmassani, supra note 52, at 30, 35–55.

98. Muslim, supra note 34, at 19, 21, 24, 26, 27; see also Abu al-Barakat al-Dardir, 1 *Al-Sharh*

al-Saghir [The Little Exegesis] 739 (Dar al-Ma'arif: Cairo, reprint n.d.) (19th century); 2 al-Dardir, at 765, 3 al-Dardir at 728.

99. Quoted in Mahmassani, supra note 52, at 30.

100. Ibid.

101. There are two major arguments supporting the need for a *wali*. The first revolves around protecting the woman, the second revolves around protecting her family, but both arguments are based on the same assumption, namely, that the woman is weak-minded and emotional. The first argument states that women are emotional and weak-minded, thus they may be ensnared by designing men unworthy of them. The second states that an emotional woman may marry beneath her station, thus sullying the name of the family. So the family has a vested interest in the matter. See, for example, Abd al-Karim Shahbun, 1 *Sharh Mudawwanat al-Ahwal al-Shakhsiyah al-Maghribiyah* [Exegesis of Moroccan Personal Status Law], 91(Maktabat al-Ma'arif: Rabat 1987?), 4 Abdul Rahman Al-Jaziri, *Kitab al-Fiqh 'ala al-Mathahib al-Arba'ah* 49 (Dar Ihya' 'Ulum al-Din: Beirut 1969); Muhammad Abu Zahrah, *Al-Wilayah 'ala al-Nafs* 125–26 (Dar al-Ra'ed al-'Arabi 1970).

102. Ahmad Ghandour, *Al-Ahwal al-Shakhsiyah fi al-Tashri' al-Islami* 126 (Jami'at al-Kuwait Press: Kuwait 1972), Muhammad Zakariyah al-Bardisi, *Al-Ahkam al-Islamiyah fi al-Ahwal al-Shakhsiyah* 199 (Dar al-Nahdah al-'Arabiah: Egypt 1965); Abu Zahrah, supra note 101, at 122–23 (Dar al-Ra'ed al-'Arabi 1970)

103. See Abu Zahrah, supra 101, at 127–29. See also Ghandour, supra note 102 at 126; al-Jaziri, supra note 101, at 46; al-Bardisi, supra note 102, at 199.

104. See Abu Zahrah, supra note 101, at 129–30. See also al-Jaziri, supra note 101, at 51, 56, al-Bardisi, supra note 102, at 192; 1 Muhammad al-Dijwi, *Al-Ahwal al-Shakhsiyah li al-Masryin al-Muslimin*, 48, 539–53, esp. 544–45 (Dar al-Nashr li al-Jami'at al-Masriyah: Cairo 1969) .

105. See Abu Zahrah, supra note 55, at 163–67; see also al-Jaziri, supra note 101, at 54–58; al-Bardisi, supra note 102, at 217–19.

106. See al-Bardisi, supra note 102, at 217 (noting that the Prophet ordered that the Ethiopian former slave Bilal be permitted to marry a woman from an Arab tribe). See also Abu Zahrah, supra note 55, at 167; al-Jaziri, supra note 101, at 58.

107. See El-Awa, *On the Political System of the Islamic State* 111 (1980); Muhammad Hamidullah, *Majmu'at al-Watha'iq al-Siyasiyah* [Collection of Poltical Documents] 362, 364, 367 (Dar al-Nafa'is: Beirut 1987). See also supra note 106.

108.See al-Hibri's discussion of this concept, supra note 22, at 9. See also, Mahmassani, supra note 14, at 179–80; al-Khamlishi, *Wijhat Nathar* [A Point of View], 36 (Dar Nashr al-Ma'rifah 1988).

Conceptualizing Women's Rights

1. As Ronald Dworkin suggested, equal treatment does not guarantee treatment as an equal (*De Funis v. Sweatt*, in Cohen, Nagel, and Scanlon, *Equality and Preferential Treatment*, pp. 63, 68).

2. *Affirming Affirmative Actions*, NYRB 22-10-98 and *Affirmative Action Doomed?* NYRB 5-11-98.

3. If he disappears or cannot pay a court-ordered living allowance, she will be able to draw from a special state bank to keep her family afloat.

4. Among the critics are Katherine Franke (Stanford Law Review, April 1997) and Vicki Schulz (The Yale Law Journal, January 1998).

5. *Baskerville v. Culligan Int'l Co.*, 50 F.3d 428,430 (7th Cir. 1995).

6. Stanford Law Review, April 1997, p. 696.

7. Richard Sennett, *The Corrosion of Character: The Personal Consequences of Work in the New Capitalism* (New York: W. W. Norton, 1998).

8. S. Sassen, *Migranten, Siedler, Fluechtlinger. Von der Massenauswanderung zur Festung Europa*, (Frankfurt am Main, 1996).

9. *Newsweek*, 4 September 1995.

10. Discussion of this issue in D. L. Rhode, *Justice and Gender* (Harvard Univ. Press, 1989) 306 ff.

Ethnic Strife and Democracy

Adam, Heribert, 1999, "The Presence of the Past: South Africa's Truth Commission as a Model?" Abdulkader Tayob and Wolframm Weisse, eds., *Religion and Politics in South Africa*, Muenster: Waxmann, 139–58.

Adam, Heribert and Kogila Moodley, 1993, *The Opening of the Apartheid Mind*, Berkeley: University of California Press.

Adorno, Th. W. et al., 1950, *The Authoritarian Personality*, New York: Harper.

Agnew, Vijay, 1996, *Resisting Women from Asia, Africa, and the Caribbean and the Women's Movement in Canada*, Toronto.

Bannerji, Himani, 1996, *Thinking Through: Essays on Feminism, Marxism and Anti-Racism*, Toronto.

Banting, Keith, 1999, "Social Citizenship and the Multicultural Welfare State," in Allen Cairns et al., 108–136.

Barrett, Stanley R. 1987, *Is God a Racist? The Right Wing in Canada*, Toronto: University of Toronto Press.

Bibby, Reginald, 1990, *Mosaic Madness*, Toronto: Stoddart.

Bissoondath, Neil, 1994, *Selling Illusions. The Cult of Multiculturalism in Canada*, Toronto: Penguin.

Cairns, Allen et al., ed., 1999, *Citizenship, Diversity, and Pluralism: Canadian and Comparative Perspectives*, Montreal and Kingston: McGill-Queens University Press.

Cohen, Philip, 1992, "Hidden Narratives in Theories of Racism," in *Race, Culture, and Difference*, edited by J. Donald and Ali Rattansi, London: Sage, 62–103.

Enzensberger, Hans Magnus, 1994, *Civil War*, London: Granta Books.

Fredrickson, George, 1999, "Mosaics and Melting Pots," *Dissent*, summer 1999, 36–42.

Gilroy, Paul, 1992, "The End of Anti-Racism," in *Race, Culture, and Difference*, ed. J. Donald and Ali Rattansi, London: Sage, 49–61.

Gourevitch, Philip, 1998, *We Wish to Inform You that Tomorrow We Will Be Killed with Our Families*, New York: Farrar, Straus and Giroux.

Henry, Frances, Carol Tator, Winston Mattis, and Tim Rees, ed. *The Colour of Democracy: Racism in Canadian Society*, Toronto: Harcourt Brace.

Hobsbawn, E., 1990, *Nations and Nationalism Since 1780*, Cambridge: Cambridge University Press.

Horowitz, Donald, 1985, *Ethnic Groups in Conflict*, Berkeley: University of California Press.

Ignatieff, Michael, 1996, *Blood and Belonging*, London: Vintage.

Kakar, Sudhir, 1996, *The Colors of Violence*, Chicago: University of Chicago Press.

Kuper, Leo, 1981, *Genocide*, New York: Penguin.

Koonz, Claudia, 1987, *Mothers in the Fatherland*, New York: St. Martins Press.

Li, P. S., ed., 1990, *Race and Ethnic Relations in Canada*, Toronto: Oxford University Press.

Lijphart, Arend, 1977, *Democracy in Plural Societies*, New Haven: Yale University Press.

Merkl, Peter H., and Leonard Weinberg eds., 1993, *Encounters with the Contemporary Radical Right*, Boulder.: Westview Press.

Moodley, Kogila, 1999, "Antiracist Education through Political Literacy: The Case of Canada," in *Critical Multiculturalism*, ed. Stephen May, London: Falmer Press, 138–152.

Moodley Kogila, ed., 1992, *Beyond Multicultural Education*, Calgary: Detselig.

Palmer, F., ed., 1986, *Anti-Racism: An Assault on Education and Value*, London: Sherwood Press.

van den Berghe, Pierre L., 1987, *The Ethnic Phenomenon*, New York: Praeger.

Ward, P. W., 1990, *White Canada Forever: Popular Attitudes and Public Policy Towards Orientals in B. C.*, Montreal: McGill-Queens University Press.

Weinfeld, Morton, "Social Identity in the 1990s," in *Clash of Identities*, ed. James Littleton, Toronto: Prentice Hall/CBC.

Zack, Naomi, 1993, *Race and Mixed Race*, Philadelphia: Temple University Press.

Democracy and the State in Multiethnic Societies in Conflict: Perspectives from Sri Lanka

1. For an elaboration of this point, see Uyangoda, Jayadeva, 1999, "A Political Culture of Conflict," in *Creating Peace in Sri Lanka: Civil War and Reconciliation*, ed. Robert Rotberg (Washington, D.C.: Brookings Institution Press), 157–168.

2. For Sri Lanka's postcolonial constitutional history, Jennings, Ivor, 1953, *The Constitution of Ceylon,* Oxford University Press; Wilson, 1980, *The Gaulist System in Asia, Constitution of Sri Lanka 1978,* London: MacMillan; A. J. Coomaraswamy, Radhika, 1984, *Sri Lanka: The Crisis of the Anglo-American Constitutional Traditions in a Developing Society,* Delhi; Cooray, LJM, 1984, *Constitutional Government in Sri Lanka, 1796–1977,* Colombo: Lake House.

3. The breakdown in Sinhala-Tamil ethnic relations and the emergence of postcolonial ethnonationalist movements in Sri Lanka have been well documented in a number of studies. For example, Wriggins, Howard (19..), *Ceylon: Dilemmas of a New Nation;* Kearney, R. N., 1967, *Communalism and the Language in the Politics of Ceylon,* Durham: Duke University Press; Jupp, James, 1978, *Sri Lanka: A Third World Democracy,* London: Frank Cass; Roberts, Michael, 1978, "Ethnic Conflict in Sri Lanka and Sinhalese Perspectives, Barriers to Accommodation," in *Modern Asian Studies,* No. 12, 353–76; de Silva, K. M., 1986, *Managing Ethnic Tensions in Multi-Ethnic Societies,* University Press of America; Tambiah, S.J., 1986, *Sri Lanka: Ethnic Fratricide and the Dismantling of Democracy,* Chicago: University of Chicago Press.

4. I use the term "fantasy" here not in its political-pejorative sense but as a metaphor to describe Sinhalese and Tamil nationist imaginations. In using this metaphor, I also have in the back of my mind the horrendous fact that both nationalist projects have succeeded in sending thousands of young men and women to death. Death in custody, in battlefield, under most sadistic torture, and in suicide, almost as a voluntary exercise preferred by young men and women to seek the ultimate meaning in life in the negation of individual life.

5. Horowitz, Donald, 1985, *Ethnic Groups in Conflict.*

6. Rawls, John, 1971, *A Theory of Justice,* Cambridge: Harvard University Press. Rawls revisits his ideas in 1993, *Political Liberalism,* New York: Columbia University Press.

7. I thank Justice Albe Sachs of South Africa's Constitutional Commission for the formulation "new constitution as peace treaty." Justice Sachs introduced this idea at a conference in Colombo in January 2000.

Minority Rights in Multiethnic and Multiracial States

1. See in this connection the differing perspectives in the essays assembled in the excellent collections David Wippman, ed., *International Law and Ethnic Conflict* (Ithaca: Cornell University Press, 1998) and Catherine Brolmann, Rene Lefeber, and Marjoleine Zieck, ed., *Peoples and Minorities in International Law* (Dordrecht: Maritinus Nijhoff Publishers, 1993).

2. On the Spanish experience with constructing a multiethnic democracy, see Christopher Abel and Nissa Torrents, ed., *Spain: Conditional Democracy* (New York: St. Martin's Press, 1984); Andrea Bonime-Blanc, *Spain's Transition to Democracy: The Politics of Constitution-making* (Boulder: Westview Press, 1987); Victor Perez-Diaz, *The Return of Civil Society: The Emergence of Democratic Spain* (Cambridge: Harvard University Press, 1993).

3. James Brook, "On Ethnic Battlefield, the French Retake a Bridge," *New York Times,* February 23, 2000, A4.

4. A valuable recent assessment of this problem can be found in Henri J. Barkey and Graham E. Fuller, *Turkey's Kurdish Question* (Lanham, Md.: Rowman and Littlefield Publishers, 1998).

5. Kemal Kirisci and Gareth M. Winrow, *The Kurdish Question and Turkey: An Example of a Trans-State Ethnic Conflict* (London: Frank Cass, 1997).

6. Leyla Boulton, "Kurds' arrest dents Turkey's EU hopes," *Financial Times,* February 21, 2000.

7. "Turkey's top judge eyes presidency," *Agence France Presse,* April 25, 2000, available in LEXIS-NEXIS Library, ALLWLD File. See also Stephen Kinzer, "Turkey's Highest-Ranking Judge is Likely to Be Next President," *New York Times,* April 26, 2000, A7.

8. For background on ethnic and racial differences and resulting conflicts in the Sudan, see the insightful analysis in Francis M. Deng, *War of Visions: Conflicts of Identities in the Sudan* (Washington, D.C.: Brookings Institution Press, 1995).

9. I am indebted to my colleague Professor Ann Lesch for alerting me to this recent correspondence and to Stephen Wondu for helping me to obtain the text of John Garang's letter. On the issues raised at the important Abuja conference, one of the failed attempts to bring about a peace settlement and end the civil war, see Ann Lesch and Stephen Wondu, *The Battle for Peace in the Sudan: An Analysis of the Abuja Conference, 1992–1993* (Lanham, Md.: University Press of America, 2000).

10. See, for example, Norimitsu Onishi, "New Strife Tests Nigeria's Fragile Democracy," *New York Times,* March 15, 2000, A1, and Norimitsu Onishi, "Deep Political and Religious Rifts Disrupt the Harmony of Nigerian Towns," *New York Times,* March 26, 2000, p. 22.

Democracy, Legitimacy, and the Rule of Law: Linkages

1. Fareed Zakaria, "The Rise of Liberal Democracy," 76 *Foreign Affairs,* No. 6, 22, 22–23.

2. Martin Kilson and Mitchell Cohen, "Introduction to Africa Today: Crisis and Change," *Dissent* (summer 1992): 293, 295.

3. David Gonzales, "A Killing Shocks Jamaicans," *New York Times,* Oct. 18, 1999, A3.

4. Donatella della Porta and Alberto Vannucci, "The 'Perverse Effects' of Political Corruption," 45 *Political Studies* 516, (1997): 537.

5. See, for example, Robert A. Dahl, *Democracy and Its Critics* (1989); James L. Hyland, *Democratic Theory: the Philosophical Foundations* (1995); Carlos Santiago Nino, *The Constitution of Deliberative Democracy* (1996), 67–106.

6. *New York Times,* Sept. 5, 1999, at 16.

7. Ibid.

8. Maureen Dowd, "Liberties," *New York Times,* Oct. 17, 1999, sec. 4, at 17.

9. Frank Rich, "Send in More Clowns," *New York Times,* Oct. 23, 1999, at A17.

10. *New York Times,* Oct. 6, 1999, at A22.

11. Tim Weiner, "A Congressman's Lament," *New York Times,* Oct. 4, 1999, at A14.

12. *New York Times,* Oct. 6, 1999, at B10.

13. Thomas M. Franck, *The Power of Legitimacy Among Nations* (1990), 152–53.

14. Jean Hampton, "Democracy and the Rule of Law," in *The Rule of Law* 13, ed. Ian Shapiro, Nomos 34 (1994).

15. Albert O. Hirschman, *A Propensity to Self-Subversion* (1995), 54–55.

16. William N. Eskridge Jr. and John Ferejohn, "Politics, Interpretation, and the Rule of Law," in *The Rule of Law,* ed. Ian Shapiro (1994), 265, 289.

17. 5 U.S. (1 Cranch) 137, 176, 2 L. Ed. 60 (1803). See Herbert Wechsler, *Toward Neutral Principle of Constitutional Law,* 73 Harv. L. Rev. 1 (1959).

18. Report to the UN Security Council on the Current Situation in Africa, A/52/871–5/1998/318 (April 13, 1998).

19. James C. N. Paul, "The Need for International Law," in *The Governance of Internal Security*

Forces in Sub-Saharan Africa 226 (Third World Legal Studies—1996–97) (1999).

20. Speech to the Woodrow Wilson International Center, Washington, D.C., quoted in Zakaria, supra note 1, at 34.

21. Robert Filmer, *The Anarchy of a Limited or Mixed Monarchy* (1648), 20, quoted in Jean Hampton, "Democracy and the Rule of Law," in *The Rule of Law,* ed. Ian Shapiro (1994), 13, 21 (*Nomos* 36).

22. See James Paul and Clarence Dias, *Incorporating Rights Into Human Development* (1999).

23. Introduction to the Secretary-General's Annual Report to the General Assembly, Press Release, SG/SM/7136, GA/9596, 20 September 1999.

24. *New York Times,* International, Oct. 24, 1999, at 15.

25. Dec. 16, 1966, 999 UNTS 171, reprinted in 6 ILM 368 (1967). Entered into force March 23, 1976.

26. Treaty Ser. No. 36, OAS Off. Rec. OEA/Ser.A/16.

27. March 20, 1952, 213 UNTS 262. Entered into force May 18, 1954.

28. The descriptive literature on this subject is vast. Cf. Thomas M. Franck, *Fairness in International Law and Institutions* (1995), 83–139; Hugo Caminos, *The Role of the Organization of American States in the Promotion and Protection of Democratic Governance,* 273 Recueil des Cours 117–236 (1999).

29. See Douglas Lee Donoho, *Evolution or Expediency: The United Nations Response to the Disruption of Democracy,* 29 Cornell Int'l L.J. 329 (1996). The use of force was authorized by S.C. Res. 940 (1994).

30. Ellen L. Lutz, *Strengthening Core Values in the Americas: Regional Commitment to Democracy and the Protection of Human Rights,* 19 Hous. J. Int'l L. 643, 649–50 (1997).

Our "Virtous Trilogy"

1. This became enacted as law in November 2000.

Beyond Punishment: Justice in the Wake of Massive Crimes in Argentina

1. *Nunca Más: Informe de la Comisión Nacional sobre la Desaparición de Personas* [hereinafter *Nunca Más*] (Buenos Aires: Eudeba, 1984), 54; and *Fallos de la Corte Suprema de Justicia de la Nación,* Tomo 309, Vols. 1 and 2 (Buenos Aires: Supreme Court, 1988), 15 and following.

2. Luis Moreno Ocampo, *Cuando el poder perdío el juicio* (Buenos Aires: Editorial Planeta, 1996), 85.

3. Ibid., 83.

4. Ibid., 55.

5. Ibid., 163 and following.

6. Ibid., 104.

7. Ibid., chap. 5.

8. Ibid., 102.

9. Ibid., chap. 5.

10. Ibid., 120.

11. Ibid., 113.

12. Ibid., 195 and following.

13. Alicia S. García, *La Doctrina de la Seguridad Nacional* (Buenos Aires: Centro Editor de América Latina, 1991).

14. Marguerite Feitlowitz, *A Lexicon of Terror: Argentina and the Legacies of Torture* (New York: Oxford University Press, 1998), 21.

15. Moreno Ocampo, 157–158.

16. The change in world politics made Argentine generals, in their crusade against so-called Marxism, allies of the former Soviet Union against the United States. While killing youngsters in their anti-Communist frenzy, they hated the U.S. president, broke Carter's embargo against Moscow, and decorated Soviet generals who praised Lenin while visiting army headquarters in Buenos Aires.

17. Moreno Ocampo, 181 and following.

18. Ibid., 218 and following.

19. Ibid., 227.

20. Ibid., 228.

21. *La Nación,* 18 November 1980.

22. Moreno Ocampo, 231 and following.

23. Ibid., 236.

24. Ibid., 10.

25. La Ley de Pacificación Nacional, no. 23.040 [National Congress] (29 December 1983). This act nullified the Amnesty Law.

26. Telephone interview with Luis Yanis, president of Eudeba Publishing (October 1998).

27. As a popular Brazilian saying states, "Everything to my friends, to my enemies the law."

28. Moreno Ocampo, 249 and following.

29. Records of the trials [National Congress] (1987) p. 10

30. *Fallos de la Corte Suprema de Justicia de la Nación,* Tomo 309, Vols. 1 and 2, 5 and following.

31. C. H. Acutidna, I. Gonzáalez Bombal, E. Jelin, O. Landi, L.A. Quevedo, C. Smulovitz, A. Vacchieri, and A. Przeworksi, *Juicios, castigos y memorias: derechos humanos y la justicia en la poltica Argentina* (Buenos Aires: Ediciones Nueva Visacion, 1995), 60.

32. Moreno Ocampo, 258.

33. See Mark Ossiel, *Mass Atrocity, Collective Memory, and the Law* (New Brunswick: Transaction Publishers, 1997).

34. Carlos Niño, *Radical Evil on Trial* (New Haven: Yale University Press, 1996).

Remembrance, Accountability, and Magnanimity

1. Unpublished essay, 1998.

2. George Santayana, *The Life of Reason,* volume 1, *Reason in Common Sense* (New York: Charles Scribner's Sons, 1905), 284.

3. Kathleen Smith, *Remembering Stalin's Victims: Popular Memory and the End of the USSR* (Cornell: Cornell University Press, 1996).

4. Timothy Garton Ash, *The File: A Personal History* (New York: Random House, 1997).

5. Bruce Ackerman, *We the People: Transformations,* Volume 2 (Cambridge: Harvard University Press, 1998).

6. Ibid.

7. Carlos Santiago Nino, *Radical Evil on Trial* (New Haven: Yale University Press, 1966) Introduction, vii.

8. Ibid., vii.

9. Ibid., 137.

10. Hannah Arendt, *The Human Condition: A Study of the Central Conditions Facing Modern Man* (Garden City, New York: Doubleday Anchor Books, 1959) 212–213.

11. Ibid.

Environmental Law and Liberty

1. For an overview of the property rights movement and the political and legal debate that it has engendered, see John D. Echeverria, *The Political of Property Rights,* 50 Okla. L. Rev. 351 (1997).

2. See Richard Stewart, *Paradoxes of Liberty, Integrity, and Fraternity: The Collective Nature of Environmental Quality and Judicial Review of Administrative Action,* 7 Envir. L. 463 (1977).

3. The classic exposition of this conception of the rule of see is Ernst Freund, *Administrative Powers Over Persons and Property* (1928).

4. For a discussion of the often complex relation between standards of tort liability and industrialization in the United States in the nineteenth century, see Gregory, *Trespass, to Negligence, to Absolute Liability,* 37 Va. L. Rev. 359 (1951); M. Horowitz, *The Transformation of American Law, 1780–1860,* 99–101; G. Schwartz, *Tort Law and the Economy in Nineteenth Century America: A Reinterpretation,* 90 Yale L. J. 1717 (1981).

5. 113 Pa. 126, 149 (1986).

6. 51 N.Y. 483, 484–485 (1973).

7. 117 Misc. 2d 960, 966, 459 N.Y.S. 2d 971 (N.Y. Sup. Ct. 1983).

8. 56 Wis. 2d 7, 17, 23, 201 N. W. 2d 761, 768, 771 (1971).

9. See P. Menell, "The Limitations of Legal Institutions for Addressing Environmental Risks," 5 *J. Econ. Perspectives* 93 (1991).

10. See Timothy O. Riordan and James Cameron, ed., *Interpreting the Precautionary Principle* (1994).

11. For an exposition of the thesis that the competing values at stake in environmental law can be resolved through institutional processes of pragmatic adjustment, see Daniel A. Farber, *Eco-Pragmatism* (1999).

12. See E. Weinrib, *Causation and Wrongdoing,* 63 Chi-Kent L. Rev. 407 (1987). See generally H. Hart and A. Honoré, *Causation in the Law* 2d ed. (1985).

13. Clean Air Act, Section 108(a)(I)(A), 42 U.S.C. 7408(a)(1)(A). The scope of the Administrator's regulatory discretion is underscored by the quite broad statutory definition of "welfare" in Section 302(h) of the Act, 42 U.S.C. § 7602(h):

(h) All language referring to effects on welfare includes, but is not limited to, effects on soils, water, crops, vegetation, manmade materials, animals, wildlife, weather, visibility, and climate, damage to and deterioration of property, and hazards to transportation, as well as effects on economic values and on personal comfort and well-being, whether caused by transformation, conversion, or combination with other air pollutants.

14. The federal Superfund statute, the Comprehensive Environmental Response, Compensation and Liability Act, 42 U.S.C. § 9601–9625, imposes liability for the costs of cleaning up a hazardous waste site on a broad range of actors, including on any person who generated a hazardous waste (which is so broadly defined as to include a ballpoint pen) that was deposited at the site at any point in the past. The government need not show that the generator deposited or was responsible for depositing the wastes at the site or that its wastes contributed to the environmental threat necessitating the cleanup. Moreover, a single generator may be held liable for 100 percent of the cleanup costs, even though the site was mismanaged by the site operator, contains wastes contributed by many other generators, and its contribution is small.

15. See William J. Baumol, *The Theory of Environmental Policy* 2d ed. (1988) (setting forth the economic approach to environmental policy).

16. See R. Stewart, *Regulation in a Liberal State, The Role of Non-Commodity Values,* 92 Yale L. J. 1537 (1983).

17. See E. Weinrib, *Corrective Justice,* 44 Iowa L. Rev. 403 (1992).

18. See Michael B. Gerrard, editor, *The Law of Environmental Justice: Theories and Procedures to Address Disproportionate Risks* (1999); V. Been, *What's Fairness Got to Do with It? Environmental Justice and the Siting of Locally Undesirable Land Uses,* 78 Cornell L. Rev. 1001 (1993).

19. For an overview of the debate over whether environmental controls on land use represent regulatory "taking" of property for which government must pay compensation, see Robert Meetz, *The Takings Issue: Constitutional Limits on Land Use Control and Environmental Regulation* (1998); Robert Meltz, Dwight H. Merriman, and Richard M. Frank, *The Takings Issue: Constitutional Limits on Land Use Control and Environmental Regulation* (1999).

20. See A. Kiss, "An Introductory Note on a Human Right to the Environment," in *Environmental Change and International Law: New Challenges and Dimensions,* 199 (1992), ed. Edith B. Weiss.

21. See R. Stewart, *Madison's Nightmare,* 57 U. Chi. L. Rev. 335 (1990).

22. For an overview of U.S. environmental law, see Richard B. Stewart, "Environmental Law," in *Fundamentals of American Law,* 481 (1996), ed. Alan B. Morrison. A detailed account is provided in William H. Rodgers Jr., *Environmental Law* 2d ed. (1994).

23. J. Clarence Davies, *Regulating Pollution, Does the U.S. System Work?* (1997).

24. See R. Stewart, Environmental Quality as a National Good in a Federal State, 1997 University of Chicago Legal Forum 1999.

25. James Landis, *The Administrative Process,* 123 (1938).

26. See 42 U.S.C. § 202–250.

27. 42 U.S.C. § 1344(a).

28. See Thomas Schoenbrod, *Power Without Responsibility: How the Congress Abuses the People Through Delegation* (1993).

29. See Nancie G. Marzulla and Roger J. Marzulla, *Property Rights: Understanding Government Takings and Environmental Regulation* (1997).

30. See B. Ackerman and W. Hassler, *Clean Coal/Dirty Air: Or How the Clean Air Act Became a Multibillion-Dollar Bail-Out for the High Sulfur Coal Industry and What Should Be Done About It* (1981).

31. Stewart, *Madison's Nightmare.*

32. See B. Ackerman and R. Stewart, *Reforming Environmental Law: The Democratic Case For Market Incentives,* 13 Colum. J. Envir. L. 171 (1988).

33. See Thames E. Caballaro, *Project XL: Making It Legal, Making it Work,* 17 Stanford Envir. L. J. 399 (1998). Dennis Hirsch, *Bell and AI's XL-ent Adventure, An Analysis of EPA's Legal Authority to Implement the Clinton Administration's Project XL,* 1998 Univ. Ill. L. Rev. 129.

34. See Richard Epstein, *Takings: Private Property and the Power of Eminent Domain* (1985); Bernard H. Siegan, *Property and Freedom* (1997).

35. See works referenced at note 19 above (discussing relevant Supreme Court decisions and the environmental regulatory takings debate).

36. See Marzulla and Marzulla, 163–177 (summarizing legislative proposals).

37. Margaret J. Radin, *Reinterpreting Property* (1993).

38. See Garrett Hardin, "The Tragedy of the Commons," 162 *Science* 1243 (1968); Ronald Coase, "The Problems of Social Cost," 3 *Journal of Law & Economics* (1960); Peter Menell and Richard B. Stewart, *Environmental Law and Policy,* 44–67 (1994).

39. See Terry Anderson and Donald R. Leal, *Free Market Environmentalism* (1991); Terry Anderson and Donald R. Leal, *Enviro-Capitalists* (1997).

40. See Peter Menell, *Institutional Fantasylands: From Scientific Management to Free Market Environmentalism,* 15 Harv. Jl. *Law & Public Policy* 489 (1992).

41. See Richard B. Stewart, *The Reformation of American Administrative Law,* 88 Harv. L. Rev. 1669 (1976).

42. Menell and Stewart, *Environmental Law and Policy,* 777–897.

43. Stephen G. Breyer, Richard B. Stewart, Cass Sunstein, and Matthew Spitzer, *Administrative Law and Regulatory Policy,* 4th ed. 102–123 (1999).

44. See Richard Pildes and Cass Sunstein, *Reinventing the Regulatory State,* 62 U. Chi. L. Rev. 1 (1995); Richard D. Morgenstern, editor, *Economic Analysis at EPA Assessing Regulatory Impact* (1997).

45. See B. Graham and Jonathan B. Wiener, *Risk-Risk Tradeoffs* (1995); Cass R. Sunstein, *Health-Health Tradeoffs,* 63 U. Chi. L. Rev. 1533 (1996).

46. See Stephen G. Breyer, *Breaking the Vicious Circle: Toward Effective Risk Regulation* (1993).

47. See Robert W. Hahn, *Regulatory Reform: Assessing the Government's Numbers,* AEI Brookings Joint Center for Regulatory Reform, Working Paper 99-106, 1999. See also Robert W. Hahn and Robert E. Litan, *Improving Regulatory Accountability* (1997).

48. 175 F.3d 1027 (D.C. Cir. 1999).

49. 145 F.3d 1399, 330 U.S. App. D.C. 329 (D.C. Cir. 1998).

50. *Babbitt v. Sweet Home Chapter of Communities for a Great Oregon,* 515 U.S. 687, 115 S. Ct. 2407 (1995).

51. For an overview that examines in greater detail and documents the characteristics of and experience with economic incentives for environmental protection discussed in the remainder of this section, see Richard B. Stewart, "Economic Incentives for Environmental Protection: Opportunities and Obstacles" in *Environmental Law, the Economy, and Sustainable Development: Europe, the United States, and the Global Regime,* Richard Revesz, Philippe Sands, and Richard Stewart (2000).

52. See references at note 33 above.

53. See Stewart, note 51, (reviewing experience with economic incentive systems for environmental protection).

54. See Jonathan Bart Wiener, *Global Environmental Regulation: Instrument Choice in Legal Context,* 108 Yale L. J. 622 (1999).

55. Ackerman and Stewart, *Reforming Environmental Law.*

Building Bridges for People and Repaying Debts to Nature

1. UNEP, ECNC, *The Pan-European Biological Diversity Strategy,* (Strasbourg: Council of Europe, 1996), 50.

2. Graham Bennett, ed., *Conserving Europe's Natural Heritage: Towards a European Ecological Network* (London, Dordrecht, Boston, 1994), 334.

Property Rights, Environmental Regulations, and the Legal Culture of Postrevolutionary Mexico

1. An example of what a cultural approach to law can achieve is the work of Paul Kahn (1999).

2. As Michael Mann has shown, some authors have gone too far in proclaiming, for example, the demise of the nation-state (Mann, 1997).

3. French jurist Leon Duguit, 1912, (writing at the beginning of the century within Comtian positivism) is quoted as the main theoretical source for this doctrine.

4. Few people would dare give Pancho Villa or Emiliano Zapata the treatment Lenin and Mao are getting after *The End of History.*

5. See Córdova, 1973.

6. See Ignatieff, 1999.

7. Previous legislation on town planning was weak and did not receive any public attention.

8. See Azuela, 1999.

9. Jurists like Ignacio Burgoa used to maintain that only the federal government, because it is the only power that represents the nation, was entitled to impose restrictions on private property, a legal thesis that clearly mirrored the nationalist postrevolutionary ideology.

10. In 1983 an amendment to the law allowed citizens to demand the suspension of a development that violated the land use established by plans and that affected their quality of life.

11. *Ley General del Equilibrio Ecológico y la Protección al Ambiente.*

12. They include national parks, biosphere reserves, sanctuaries, marine parks, and other categories.

13. See *Procuraduría Federal de Protección al Ambiente,* 1998.

14. We use the term "juridification" in the sense of mainstream sociology of law (such as Teubner).

15. Two examples are the statutes on the liability of civil servants (*Ley de Responsabilidades de Funcionarios Públicos,* 1983) and on legal procedures conducted by state agencies (*Ley Federal de Procedimiento Administrativo,* in force since 1995).

16. The case of Metalclad will be a landmark in this respect.

17. NAFTA is the first commercial treaty with a parallel agreement on environmental protection.

18. In this respect, Mexico has been recognized for its accomplishments in the area of enforcement. See Commission for Environmental Cooperation, 1998.

19. The first scholar to recognize the importance of civil society in modern political thought in Mexico was Carlos Pereyra (1979).

20. In fact, the most currently active nationwide environmental organizations are those created in the second half of the eighties.

21. The reform to Article 27 in 1992 that ended land distribution was one of the most debated initiatives of President Carlos Salinas and one that marked a clear departure from postrevolutionary land law.

22. See Article 26 of the Constitution.

23. It must be stressed that this is mainly a cultural phenomenon; if we look closely at legal texts it is possible for local authorities to regulate *ejido* lands. But the belief that they cannot is more powerful.

24. See the Austin Memorandum in Revista Interamericana de Planificación, November (?) 1995.

25. For an analysis of corporatism as a dominant feauter of Mexican political system, see Schmitter (1984).

26. The stabilization of rural property is underscored by *Procede,* or *Programa de Certificación de Derechos Ejidales,* a government program directed to issue and register titles of *ejidos* and *ejidatarios* over their lands. They include both individual titles to arable parcels and plots in the village as well as collective titles to common use lands.

27. New Institutionalism is also becoming relevant for other disciplines like sociology (Britton and Nee, 1998).

28. Most notably, the new agrarian legislation that ended land distribution.

29. Duguit and other pioneers of twentieth-century doctrines about property may have had a pragmatic preoccupation. That is certainly the case for the Benthamite tradition. But social sciences today have many more resources, which allows for a better understanding of the dynamics of property relations.

30. For a discussion on the possibility of "translating" the economic analysis of law into

Roman-Germanic legal systems, see Cossío-Díaz, 1997.

31. The preeminence of the conceptual apparatus of the common-law tradition can be observed in other circles. For example, in the international debate about regularization of land tenure in the context of rapid urbanization, a debate that one would expect to see dominated by cultural pluralism, common-law categories are used like a lingua franca.

32. For the use of the concept of narcissism in the analysis of nationalism, see Ignatieff, 1999.

33. Centro Operacional para la Vivienda y el Poblamiento.

34. In order to fulfill this right, specific procedures were created for the first time in the 1996 reforms of the environmental legislation.

35. Mexico is the leading silver producer in the world.

36. In modern social theory, Habermas's idea of "life-world" is just a way of recovering the integrity of human experience. See Habermas, 1981.

37. At most, new ideas such as those in the law and economics movement can help to discuss the most efficient way to obtain the desired results, but this is not incompatible with the doctrine.

38. Debates about ADR systems of conflict resolution are the obvious example.

Environmental Governance and the Uses of Science

1. National Science Foundation, ed. P. B. Thompson, *Workshop on Science, Technology, and Democracy: Research on Issues of Governance and Change.* (Washington, D.C., 1994): 36.

2. Garrett Hardin, "The Tragedy of the Commons," *Science* 162 (1968): 1243–1248.

3. Garrett Hardin, "Living on a Lifeboat," *Bioscience* 24 (1974): 561–568.

4. Center for Strategic and International Studies, *The Environmental Protection System in Transition: Toward a More Desirable Future* (Washington, D.C.: CSIS Press, 1998): . 97.

5. American Industrial Health Council, (Washington, D.C., 1998). Available online at: http://www.riskworld.com/Nreports/1998/STAKEHOLD/HTML/nr98aa01.htm

6. "EPA Emphasis on Stakeholder Process Exasperates Risk Experts," Risk Policy Report Volume 6, Number 10: (October 16, 1998): 6–7.

7. D. T. Case, and J. B. Ritter, "Disconnects Between Science and the Law," *Chemical and Engineering News* 78 (7) (2000): 49–60.

8. R. Costanza, "Visions of Alternative (Unpredictable) Futures and Their Use in Policy Analysis," *Conservation Ecology* 4(1) (2000): 5.

Trophy Art Law as an Illustration of the Current Status of Separation of Powers and Legislative Process in Russia

1. James H. Billington, *The Icon and the Axe: An Interpretive History of Russian Culture* (New York: Alfred A. Knopf, 1966). George F. Kennan, *Memoirs, 1925–1950* (Boston-Toronto: Little, Brown, and Co., 1967), 528–9. And if contradictions are not just an isolated phenomenon but an "essence of Russia," attempts to eradicate them (to "civilize" Russia) are not possible without fundamental changes of Russia and, as a rule, doomed to fail from the start. The problem, therefore, is not how to "cure" Russia of her contradictions but how to use them for Russia's development.

2. See *The Russian Civilization and Sobornost* (Moscow: The Russian Sobornost Fund, 1994), 30. Cited in: Nikolay Zlobin, "Will Russia Be Crushed by Its History?" 159 *World Affairs* 2 (fall 1996). Richard Pipes, *Russia Under the Old Regime* (London: Weidenfeld and Nicolson, 1974. Series: History of Civilization).

3. Harold J. Berman, *Justice in the USSR,* 2d ed. (1963), 5.

4. "Russia does not differ essentially from Europe but Russia is not yet essentially one with Europe," wrote Thomas Garrigue Masaryk, Czech historian and first president of the Czecho-Slovak Republic, in his remarkable study of Russian history (Thomas G. Masaryk, *The Spirit of Russia* Volume 1 (London: Allen and Unwin, New York: Macmillan, 1919), 6).

5. "Anyone imagining the course of Russian pre-modern history to have been particularly barbarous or bloodstained should remember the near-absence, in comparison with Western lands, of witch-hunting, crusading, institutionalized capital punishment (abolished under Elizabeth in the mid-eighteenth century). The brutal episodes in

the reigns of Ivan the Terrible and Peter the Great were traumatic because uncharacteristic" (Robin Milner-Gulland, *The Russians* (Malden, Mass.: Blackwell Publishers, 1997), 228).

6. The First Russian Republic ended with the violent dissolution of the first democratically elected Russian parliament and suspension of the Constitutional Court of Russia in September–October 1993; the Second Republic was initiated by an adoption of the new Constitution in December 1993.

7. The only other law that can probably belong to the same category is the Law on Freedom of Conscience and Religious Associations.

8. Mark Boguslavsky, "Legal Aspects of the Russian Position in Regards to the Return of Cultural Property," in *The Spoils of War: World War II and Its Aftermath: The Loss, Reappearance, and Recovery of Cultural Property,* ed. Elizabeth Simpson, (New York: Abrams in association with the Bard Graduate Center for Studies in the Decorative Arts, 1997), 186–190.

9. See, for instance: Elissa S. Myerowitz, "Protecting Cultural Property During a Time of War: Why Russia Should Return Nazi-Looted Art," 20 *Fordham International Law Journal,* (June 1997); S. Shawn Stephens, "The Hermitage and Pushkin Exhibits: An Analysis of the Ownership Rights to Cultural Properties Removed from Occupied Germany," 18 *Houston Journal of International Law* (fall 1995); Steven Costello, "Must Russia Return the Artwork Stolen from Germany during World War II?" 4 *ILSA Journal of International & Comparative Law* (fall 1997); Sylvia L. Depta, "Twice Saved or Twice Stolen? The Trophy Art Tug-of-War Between Russia and Germany," 10 *Temple International and Comparative Law Journal* (fall 1996); Amy L. Click, "German Pillage and Russian Revenge, Stolen Degas, Fifty Years Later—Who's Art Is It Anyway?" 5 *Tulsa Journal of Comparative & International Law* Tulsa Journal (fall 1997); Alexander Blankenagel, "Eyes Wide Shut: Displaced Cultural Objects in Russian Law and Adjudication," 8 *East European Constitutional Review* 4 (fall 1999).

10. See Central and East European Law Initiative, American Bar Association (ABA CEELI), *Analysis of the Constitution of the Russian Federation* (New York, 1995), 38. An American scholar correctly concludes that the presidential provisions of the Russian Constitution contain "all the brittleness of the U.S. Constitution but lack its balanced division of powers." (Edward W. Walker, "Politics of Blame and Presidential Powers in Russia's New Constitution," *East European Constitutional Review,* fall 1993/winter 1994, at 116.) Another observer argues that the Russian Constitution is "plagued by contradictions that undermine the separation of powers in the new Russian government, and the aggrandized position of the president in the Constitution is all but frankly anti-

democratic." (Jeffrey Waggoner, "Valor at the Russian Constitutional Court: Adjudicating the Russian Constitutions in the Civil-Law Tradition," 8 *Indiana International & Comparative Law Review* 1997, at 193.)

11. ABA CEELI, *Analysis of the Constitution of the Russian Federation*, at 40.

12. In September 1993, "with a stroke of the pen, Yeltsin had wiped out Russia's embryonic and uneasy separation of powers. Mao had bested Montesquieu," concluded an unbiased American scholar (Robert Sharlet, "Russian Constitutional Crisis: Law and Politics Under Yeltsin," 9 *Post-Soviet Politics*, no. 4, October–December 1993, 327). "It was a highly risky decision, since it was plainly illegal," wrote *The Guardian* (Jonathan Steele, see note 66). "Rarely in history there has been a coup prepared so ineptly and so openly. Yeltsin violated the constitution so flagrantly that there could be no talk of his having 'made a mistake' or 'exceeding his powers,'" commented a deputy of the Moscow City Council (Boris Kagarlitsky, *Square Wheels: How Russian Democracy Got Derailed* (New York: Monthly Review Press, 1994), 197).

13. *Justice Delayed: The Russian Constitutional Court and Human Rights* (New York: Lawyers Committee for Human Rights, 1995), 6.

14. Although the original decree "On the Gradual Constitutional Reform in the Russian Federation" contained a provision saying that representative bodies in the Russian regions continued functioning (Article 8), it was a deceptive maneuver aimed at guaranteeing neutrality of the regional legislatures in President Yeltsin's conflict with the Russian Supreme Soviet. As a result of issuance of Decree No. 1723 of October 22, and Decree No. 1760 of October 26, the regional legislatures were dissolved too.

15. Yeltsin's attempt to block any public discussion of the draft was characterized by British scholars as "hardly a sound precedent of democratic practice" (see Stephen White and Ronald J. Hill, "Russia, Former Soviet Union, and Eastern Europe," in *The Referendum Experience in Europe*, ed. Michael Gallagher and Pie Vincenzo Uleri (London: Macmillan, 1996), 163. For more on the interregnum period of September–December 1993 in Russia, see Tanya Smith, "The Violation of Basic Rights in the Russian Federation," *East European Constitutional Review* (summer/fall 1994).

16. See *A Modern Day Czar? Presidential Power and Human Rights in the Russian Federation* (New York: Lawyers Committee for Human Rights, 1995), iii; Stephen Holmes, "Superpresidentialism and its Problems," *East European Constitutional Review*, fall 1993/winter 1994, 123; John Kohan, "What Would Lenin Say?" *Time*, December 20,

1993, 44. The "superpresidentialism" of the new Russian Constitution was quite a logical step in the Russian reforms: "If you are determined to impose capitalism by any means, to pour the medicine down people's throats against their will, you can't achieve your objective with genuine consent. So you opt for some kind of iron fist, for a czar, even if you choose to call him—as did *Izvestia's* Washington correspondent, unaware of the contradiction—a 'democratic dictator.'" (Daniel Singer, "Putsch in Moscow," *The Nation*, October 25, 1993, 449).

17. Robert Sharlet, "Citizen and State under Gorbachev and Yeltsin," in *Developments in Russian and Post-Soviet Politics*, ed. White, Pravda, and Gitelman (1994), 109, 128.

18. In an alarming conclusion of another objective American scholar, Yeltsin "demonstrates how attempts to copy the American system are likely to end up in dictatorship, as they have so often in Latin America." (Robert V. Daniels, "Yeltsin's No Jefferson. More Like Pinochet," *New York Times*, October 2, 1993, 23).

19. See Amy J. Weisman, "Separation of Powers in Post Communist Government: A Constitutional Case Study of the Russian Federation," 10 *The American University Journal of International Law & Policy* (summer 1995), 1394.

20. Ibid., 1397.

21. The process of lawmaking in the Federal Assembly is determined by Article 105 of the Russian Constitution. Federal laws are adopted by a majority vote of the total number of state Duma deputies (Article 105.1.) These laws are submitted to the Federation Council within five days of their passage in the Duma (Article 105.3.) If a majority of the total number of deputies of the Federation Council vote for the law, or if the Council fails to consider the legislation within 14 days, it will be deemed adopted (Article 105.4.) If the Federation Council rejects the legislation, both houses may convene a reconciliatory commission to settle their differences and then resubmit the legislation for consideration by the Duma (Article 105.4.) If the Federation Council again rejects the bill, the Duma may still enact the legislation if two-thirds of its membership vote in favor of it (Article 105.5.).

22. Elections of the last appointed governor, in Karachaevo-Cherkessia, happened only in 1999.

23. By 1998, Germany has reportedly provided the USSR and Russia with over 100 billion deutsche mark credits (ITAR-TASS, July 20, 1998). Since the disintegration of the USSR, over 50 billion deutsche marks in aid have been given to Russia.

24. Jan Cleave, "Russia: Parliament Rejects Yeltsin's Veto of Trophy Art Law," *Radio Free Europe/Radio Liberty*, May 16, 1997.

25. The poll involved 1,500 urban and rural residents. Backers of the law included both people with a scarce educational background and with higher education. (ITAR-TASS, June 16, 1997)

26. See, for instance, "Nationalists and Communists contend that the art is merely compensation for the enormous losses of Russian cultural treasures." ("An Amber Light on Wartime Loot," *New York Times*, July 19, 1997, editorial); "The negotiations between Russia and Germany have stalled with Russian nationalists seizing upon the issue with particular fervor. . . . As early as 1993, however, the Russian position began to harden and nationalist voices became louder." (Stephan Wilske, "International Law and Spoils of War: To the Victor the Right of Spoils? The Claims for Repatriation of Art Removed from Germany by the Soviet Army During or as a Result of World War II," 3 *UCLA Journal of International Law and Foreign Affairs* (spring/summer 1998), at 226, 280); "The 308–15 vote could help Russia to hang on to priceless cultural treasures. . . . The ballot reflected an upsurge of nationalist feeling throughout Russia." (Chrystina Freeland, "Looted German Art: Duma Snubs Yeltsin," *Financial Times*, April 5, 1997); "The trophy art has become a key part of a power struggle between Russia's nationalist Parliament, which has attempted to nationalize the art treasures, and President Boris Yeltsin." (Victoria A. Birov, "Prize or Plunder?: The Pillage of Works of Art and the International Law of War," 30 *New York University School of Law Journal of International Law and Politics* (fall 1997/winter 1998) at 213).

27. *Great Patriotic War of the Soviet Union 1941–1945: A General Outline* (Moscow: Progress Publishers, 1974), 434.

28. See Mikhail Shvidkoi, "Russian Cultural Losses During World War II," *The Spoils of War: World War II and Its Aftermath: The Loss, Reappearance, and Recovery of Cultural Property*, 67–71.

29. Lynn H. Nicholas, *The Rape of Europa: The Fate of Europe's Treasures in the Third Reich and the Second World War* (New York: Alfred A. Knopf, 1994), 193–4. Indeed, what else could be expected from Nazi invaders whose attitude to the Soviet people was expressed by Heinrich Himmler (in his speech of July 13, 1941, just three weeks after the beginning of German aggression against the USSR) in the following terms: "A population of 180 million, a mixture of races, whose very names are unpronounceable, and whose physique is such that one can shoot them down without pity and compassion . . . welded by the Jews into one religion, one ideology . . ." (R. Breitman, *Architect of Genocide: Himmler and the Final Solution* (New York: Knopf, 1991), 177).

30. Nicholas, *The Rape of Europe*, 200. That's how an American military correspondent Marcus Hindus

described destruction by Nazis of Peterhof, Peter the Great's lavish palace on the Gulf of Finland: "I had neither seen nor heard anything like it in France after the World War. Only windblown tall reeds rising out of deep snow give one a feeling of some life within nature itself. . . all Peterhof is gone. It isn't even a ghost town like Kiev, Kharkov, Poltava, Orel or Kursk. . . it is a desert strewn with wreckages from which, perhaps, has been blown away some of the most exquisite and most joyful art man has created." (*New York Herald Tribune,* February 17, 1944. Cited in Nicholas, *The Rape of Europa,* 200–201). Overall, 34,000 precious objects were taken from Peterhof to Germany (Shvidkoi, *The Spoils of War,* 69).

31. For comparison, in Great Britain its loss of citizens during World War II was equal to 375,000 (or 0.9% of the British population); in the United States, 405,000 (or 0.3% of the U.S. population); even in Japan the human toll, including victims of atomic bombings of Hiroshima and Nagasaki, was equal to 2.6 million (or 3.4 % of its population). (*Great Patriotic War of the Soviet Union,* 434).

32. Ellen Barry, "Total War to Trophy War: Berlin's Lost Art," *Moscow Times,* November 16, 1994.

33. In the 1990s, the most significant of those cultural objects were exposed in a series of "stunning exhibitions," as they were called by Western press (Richard Beeston, "Yeltsin Shrugs off Duma to Give Kohl Looted Work of Art," *The Times,* April 16, 1997) at Moscow's Pushkin Museum of Fine Arts and the Hermitage in St. Petersburg.

34. The archive of the Weimar Republic Foreign Minister Walther Rathenau, who in April 1922 signed the treaty establishing diplomatic relations with the USSR.

35. RFE/RL Newsline, Vol. 1, No. 12, Part I, April 16, 1997.

36. In the first case, a lawyer from Bremen tried to sell a fragment of the Amber Room mosaic for $2.5 million. A second object turned up when a reader in Berlin recognized in a news picture a cabinet she had bought in the 1970s in East Germany. Both of those "discoveries" indicate that the Amber Room could survive and is still located somewhere in Germany.

37. "An Amber Light on Wartime Loot," *New York Times,* July 19, 1997.

38. See, for instance, Dmitry Zaks, "President Hits Back At Court," *Moscow Times,* April 8, 1998.

39. In an apparent attempt to stress his special relations with Germany, President-elect Putin welcomed the return to St. Petersburg of the remains of the Amber Room and thanked "our German friends" for the return home of "one of our national sacred objects." According to Putin, that exchange was an indication that "people in Russia understand, value, and treasure Russian-German relations" (Interfax, April 29, 2000).

The Globalization of World Trade and Corporate Power

1. An organization that performed its main operations, either manufacturing or the provision of services, in at least two countries.

2. One of the several recommendations of the Group of Eminent Persons was that a commission on multinational corporations should be established under the Economic and Social Council "composed of individuals with a profound understanding of the issues and problems involved."

3. A typical integrated circuit label now reads: "made in one or more of the following countries, Korea, Hong Kong, Malaysia, Singapore, Taiwan, Philippines; the exact country of origin is unknown."

4. See El Hadji Guisse, Working Document on the Impact of Activities of Transnational Corporations on the Realization of Economic Social and Cultural Rights, E/CN4/Sub.2/1998/6, 10 June 1998, 2, prepared for the UN Commission on Human Rights: "The Realization of Economic Social and Cultural Rights: The Question of Transnational Corporations."

5. Sarah Anderson and John Cavanagh, "Top 200—The Rise of Global Corporate Power" (Institute of Policy Studies, Washington, D.C.).

6. In 1995 negotiations were launched within the Organization for Economic Cooperation and Development (OECD) for the conclusion of a multilateral agreement on investment (MAI). Although negotiated by the European Community and the twenty-nine OECD member countries, the MAI would also be open to accession by non-OECD members. The current draft (the MAI negotiated text as of 24 April 1998) provides substantive protections as to general standards of treatment, currency transfers, protection against expropriations, and so on. But since the MAI negotiations were launched, the initiative has come under criticism from a number of well-known nongovernmental organizations (NGOs). The MAI raises the specter of local laws regarding the environment, health, and labor being challenged by investors in investor-to-state proceedings under the MAI; the mechanism is also criticized for not being transparent. (See the article of Antonio R. Parra, Legal Advisor, ICSID (International Centre for Settlement of Investment Disputes), on "The Limits of Party Autonomy in Arbitration Proceedings under the ICSID Convention," published in the ICC Court of Arbitration Bulletin, Vol.10/No. 1, Spring 1999, 27–37, at 37.

7. See UNCTAD Division on Transnational Corporations and Investment, *International Investment Instruments: A Compendium,* vol.1 *Multinational Instruments* (1996), xvii.

8. See R. Dolzer and M. Stevens, *Bilateral Investment Treaties (1995).*

9. ICSID, the International Centre for Settlement of Investment Disputes, is a public international organization established by a multilateral treaty, the 1965 Convention on the Settlement of Investment Disputes between States and Nationals of other States, commonly called the ICSID (or Washington) Convention. As of April 1998, 129 countries have signed and ratified the ICSID Convention to become contracting states. Pursuant to the provisions of the ICSID Convention, the Centre provides facilities for the conciliation and arbitration of investment disputes between contracting states and nationals of other contracting states, which the parties to the disputes consent in writing to submit to ICSID. In 1978 the administrative council of the Centre, which is ICSID's governing body and comprises one representative of each contracting state, approved a set of so-called Additional Facility Rules under which the ICSID Secretariat is authorized to administer certain types of proceedings between states and nationals of other states that fall outside the scope of the convention. These include among others conciliation and arbitration proceedings for the resolution of investment disputes where either the state party or the home state of the foreign national is not an ICSID contracting state.

10. Reported in the ICCA Yearbook Vol. 17 (1992), 106–152.

11. For example, the more recent award of February 1997 passed by the Arbitral Tribunal appointed by the ICSID in the case of *American Manufacturing and Trading Inc. v. Republic of Zaire,* Case CIRDI-ARD 1993/1, which is along the same lines as the decision in the Sri Lanka case.

12. See Jan Paulsson, *Arbitration Without Privity,* 10 ICSID Rev. F1LJ 232 (1995)1.

13. See the article "TNCs and the Social Issues in the Developing World" by Paddy O'Reilly and Sophia Tickell (who work for the Oxfam International Network), 273–287, in the recent publication of Kluwer Law International 1999 *Human Rights Standards and the Responsibility of Transnational Corporations,* edited by Prof. Michael K. Addo of the School of Law, University of Exeter. The book contains the papers presented at a conference held in September 1998 at the University

of Exeter on the broad theme of human rights in international business.

14. Round Two—Text of Principles for Global Corporate Responsibility (EECR, ICCR, TCCR), 1998.

15. A large number of NGOs have become active in drafting or advising on ethical business standards in relation to transnational corporations. Amnesty International has produced a leaflet called "Human Rights Guidelines for Companies." Human Rights Watch, OXFAM, and others are also assisting transnational corporations in drafting and implementing ethical business standards.

16. See *International Investment Instruments: A Compendium,* vol.1 *Multinational Instruments,* published in 1996 by the UNCTAD Division on Transnational Corporations and Investment: xxiii.

17. See Bryar Apleyard, "Globaloney or Visionary?" *London Times Sunday,* October 21, 1999.

18. The International Monetary Fund's 1998 Annual Meeting, held in Washington, D.C., during the first week of October, 1998, provided a forum for the IMF and its member countries to address this issue. The meeting reviewed a wide range of initiatives for strengthening the "architecture" of the international monetary system. The preventive features of the IMF's initiative have been to forestall future balance of payments crises before they emerge basically in three areas: (i) strengthening fund surveillance, (ii) strengthening the financial systems of member countries, and (iii) promoting transparency and accountability. See the article "The International Monetary Law and Strengthening the Architecture of the International Monetary System," by Ross B. Leckow, Senior Counsel of the IMF in the *International Law Journal of the Georgetown University Law Center* (1999) Vol. 30 (Supplement), 117–130, and see the Report of the Managing Director IMF to the Interim Committee on Strengthening the Architecture of the International System (October 1, 1998).

19. The most scarring indictment in recent times of an unjust international economic order is contained in the book *When Corporations Rule the World,* by David C. Korten (published by the Kumarian Press 1995). In it the author spells out the reality and consequences of a corporate-dominated globalization process and how it is undermining democracy. It argues for an agenda of regaining "citizen-sovereignty" as the starting point on "the long road back to democracy."

20. Suggested by Daniel K. Tarullo in his paper *Corporate Power, National Sovereignty, and the Rule of Law.*

21. Expressions used in the *UN Human Development Report 1994.*

22. *UN Human Development Report 1999,* 5.

23. So described by the president of the International Court of Justice in his foreword to a book (published by Kluwer) in 1996 commemorating the fiftieth anniversary of the ICJ.

24. See *Cambridge Law Journal,* March 1999: "International Law in a Changing International System." Through its UK business group, Amnesty International has been canvassing for human rights standards in the business fields. This has been recently reiterated by the High Commissioner for Human Rights, Mrs. Mary Robinson, in her address to the Economic Council: "The Business Case for Human Rights" 1998.

25. As of June 30, 1999, 141 states had ratified this covenant.

26. See paragraph 18 of the Maastricht Guidelines on Violations of Economic, Social, and Cultural Rights, adopted in Maastricht, January 1997.

27. See Mathew Craven, *International Covenant on Economic, Social, and Cultural Rights: A Perspective on its Development* (Oxford, Clarendon Press, 1995), 113: "The Committee is thus clear that the realm of State responsibility extends not only to the acts of agents of the States but also those of third parties over whom the State has or should have control." The same attitude is reflected in the Inter-American Human Rights Commission's opinion in a complaint about injuries to indigenous peoples and their environment in the Amazon rain forest as a result of oil exploration by transnational corporations. The report is quoted in Martin Geer's article in Vol. 38 (1998) *Virginia Journal of International Law,* 331: "Foreigners in their own land—cultural lands and transnational corporations— emergent international rights and wrongs."

28. This is the thesis of Professor Anne-Marie Slaughter of the Harvard Law School in her article "The Real New World Order," in *Foreign Affairs* September/October 1997. The author believes that disaggregating the state into its functional components permits the disaggregation (perhaps some dilution) of sovereignty as well—making it possible to create a network of institutions engaged in a transnational common enterprise even while these institutions continue to represent distinct national interests.

29. This is the theme of a recently published treatise: *Constitutionalising Globalization: The Post Modern Revival of Confederal Arrangements,* by Daniel Elazar, (Rowman & Littlefield, 1998).

30. In the first referendum a slim majority voted no. After negotiations with other EC countries, Denmark was granted an option of making certain reservations pursuant to the so-called Edinburgh Agreement. In 1993 the Maastricht Treaty, including the Edinburgh Agreement, obtained the requisite majority in Danish Parliament but the government nevertheless decided for political reasons to hold a new ref-

erendum on the Maastricht Treaty. In the said referendum the majority of voters said yes. The Danish government subsequently ratified the treaty and enacted it as Danish law Act No. 281 of April 28,1993.

31. In a comment on the decision of Supreme Court of Denmark reproduced in the *American Journal of International Law* January 1999, Vol. 93, 209–214. Prof. Sten Harck and Henrick Palmer Olsen of the University of Copenhagen have suggested that the lowering of expectations among members of the European Union would be helpful "to fashion a common strategy for dealing with the adjudication of claims that legal Acts issued by the Community are ultra virus." Until then the European Community will be seen as a regional organization whose authority and power would depend in the end on its members' states and national courts.

32. UNDP, *Human Development Report 1999* (Oxford University Press), 2.

International Economic Law and Democratic Accountability

1. The fact that legal sovereignty remains intact is not to say that all is well. When multinational corporations bribe foreign officials or otherwise pervert host government processes, they seriously undermine the accountability of a host government to its citizens.

Post–Seattle Reflections: A Qualified Defense of the WTO and an Unqualified Defense of the International Rule of Law

1. "Global Monoculture," *New York Times,* November 15, 1999; "Globalization v. Nature," *New York Times,* November 22, 1999; and "Invisible Government," *New York Times,* November 29, 1999.

2. Amartya Sen, *Development as Freedom* (New York: Alfred Knopf, 1999).

3. Francis Fukuyama, *The End of History and The Last Man* (New York: Free Press, 1991).

4. See Glenn Gottselig, *Canada and Culture: Can Current Cultural Policies be Sustained in the Global Trade Regime?* (LL.M. thesis, University of Toronto Faculty of Law, 1999); Trevor Knight, *The Dual Nature of Cultural Products: An Analysis of the World Trade Organization's Decisions Regarding Canadian Periodicals,* (1999) 57 University of Toronto Faculty of Law Review 165.

5. Sen, *Development as Freedom,* chap. 10.

6. See William Kline, *Trade and Economic Distribution* (Washington, .D.C.: Institute for International Economics, 1997); Dani Rodrik, "Sense and Nonsense in the Globalization Debate," summer 1997 *Foreign Policy* 19; Rodrik, *Has Globalization Gone Too Far?* (Washington, D.C.: Institute for International Economics, 1997); Philippe Aghion, "Inequality and Economic Growth," in Philippe Aghion and Jeffrey Williamson, *Growth, Inequality and Globalization: Theory, History, and Policy* (Cambridge University Press, 1998).

7. See Russell Roberts, *The Choice: A Fable of Free Trade and Protectionism* (N.J.: Prentice Hall, 1994), 16.

8. Paul Krugman, "Competitiveness: A Dangerous Obsession," in *Pop Internationalism* (Cambridge: MIT Press, April 1997), chap. 1.

9. See Rodrik, "Sense and Nonsense in the Globalization Debate."

10. See Paul Brenton, Henry Scott, and Peter Sinclair, *International Trade* (Oxford University Press, 1997), 86 and following.

11. See Michael Trebilcock and Robert Howse, *The Regulation of International Trade* 2d ed. (London and New York: Routledge, 1999), chap. 14.

12. John Whalley, "The North-South Debate and the Terms of Trade: An Applied Equilibrium Approach," (1984) 66 *Rev. of Economics and Statistics* 224.

13. Gary Hufbauer and Jeffrey Schott, *NAFTA: An Assessment* (Washington, D.C.: Institute for International Economics, 1993), 12, 13.

14. See also Michael Todaro, *Economic Development,* 6th ed., (Addison-Wesley, 1996), 40, 41.

15. See Dani Rodrik, *The New Global Economy and Developing Countries: Making Openness Work* (Washington, D.C.: Overseas Development Council, 1999); Michael Trebilcock, "What Makes Poor Countries Poor? The Role of Institutional Capital in Economic Development" in *The Law and Economics of Development,* ed. Buscaglia and Cooter, (JAI Press, 1997).

16. Aghion and Williamson, *Growth, Inequality and Globalization.*

17. See David Dollar and Aart Kraay, "Growth is Good for the Poor" (working paper, World Bank, March 2000).

18. See, for example, Noam Chomsky, *Profits Over People: Neoliberalism and Global Order* (New York: Seven Stories Press, 1999).

19. See Dani Rodrik, *Has Globalization Gone Too Far?;* Robert Reich, *The Work of Nations* (New York: Vintage, 1991), chap. 25 (Who Is 'Us'?).

20. See "Survey of the World Economy," *The Economist,* September 20, 1997; Michael Trebilcock and Ron Daniels, "Journeys Across the Institutional Divides: Reinterpreting the Reinventing Government Movement," (working paper, University of Toronto Faculty of Law, March 15, 2000).

21. See David Vogel, *Trading Up: Consumer and Environmental Regulation in a Global Economy* (Cambridge: Harvard University Press, 1995).

22. Julie Soloway, "Institutional Capacity to Constrain Suboptimal Welfare Outcomes From Trade-Restricting Environmental, Health and Safety Regulation Under NAFTA" (SJD thesis, University of Toronto Faculty of Law, 1999).

23. These cases are discussed in Trebilcock and Howse, *The Regulation of International Trade,* chaps. 6 and 15.

24. See Robert Howse and Michael Trebilcock, "The Fair Trade-Free Trade Debate: Trade, Labour, and the Environment," (1996) 16 *International Review of Law and Economics* 61.

25. Trebilcock and Howse, *The Regulation of International Trade,* 256; *The Economist,* December 12, 1992, 7.

26. See Douglass North and Robert Thomas, *The Rise of the Western World,* (Cambridge University Press, 1973) for an account of how the growth of trading routes and networks undermined the medieval manorial system.

27. See Trebilcock and Howse, *The Regulation of International Trade,* chap. 3.

28. For a nuanced and balanced assessment of critiques of the WTO as undemocratic, see Robert Howse, *The Legitimacy of the World Trade Organization,* University of Michigan L. Rev. (forthcoming).

29. See "Sins of the Secular Missionaries," *The Economist,* January 29, 2000.

The World Bank's Role in a Global Economy

1. Articles of Agreement of the International Bank for Reconstruction and Development (IBRD Articles), Article I.

2. IBRD Articles, Article IV, Section 10.

3. Agreement Establishing the European Bank for Reconstruction and Development (EBRD Agreement), Article I.

4. EBRD Agreement, Preamble.

5. "Authorized Purposes of Loans Made or Guaranteed by the Bank," Memorandum of the Vice President and General Counsel, May 10, 1988, in I. F. I. Shihata, *Collection of Legal Opinions of the General Counsel of the World Bank* (forthcoming).

6. "Prohibition of Political Activities in the Bank's Work," Legal opinion by the Senior Vice President and General Counsel, July 12, 1995, in I. F. I. Shihata, *Collection of Legal Opinions of the General Counsel of the World Bank.*

7. "Prohibition of Political Activities Under the IBRD Articles of Agreement and Its Relevance to the Work of the Executive Directors," Opinion of the Vice President and General Counsel, December 21, 1987, in I. F. I. Shihata, *Collection of Legal Opinions of the General Counsel of the World Bank.*

8. "Prohibition of Political Activities in the Bank's Work," supra note 6.

9. James D. Wolfensohn, "Development Choices in a Changing World" (RAF Penrose Memorial Lecture, American Philosophical Society, Philadelphia, November 11, 1999).

10. James D. Wolfensohn, "Comprehensive Development Framework," (January 21, 1999).

Downsizing the State in Human Rights Discourse

1. Interestingly, the only UN document in which it is not capitalized is the UN Charter itself. That document pays linguistic homage to "Members" rather than states per se.

2. Chris Brown, "Universal Human Rights: A Critique," 1 *International Journal of Human Rights* (1997): 41, 59 ("Proponents of universal human rights are, in effect, proposing the delegitimation of all kinds of political regimes except those that fall within the broad category of 'liberal democracy.' Although such a delegitimation might be regarded as desirable, it is by no means clear that a majority of societies worldwide are actually capable of becoming liberal societies, at least in the medium run, and it is equally unclear on what moral authority those who require them to take this step can rely.") See also Martti Koskenniemi, "The Effect of Rights on Political Culture," in *The EU and Human Rights,* ed. P. Alston, M. Bustelo, and J. Heenan, (1999): 99.

3. United Nations, *Report of the Secretary-General on the Work of the Organization*, A154/1, 1999, paragraph 275.

4. While international lawyers have long debated the circumstances under which other actors might also be characterized as subjects, the bottom line is that while various actors have been accorded some form of international legal personality for specified purposes, this hardly justifies the conclusion that international law treats them as subjects and thus on a par with states. See generally P. Malanczuk, *Akehurst's Modern Introduction to International Law* 7th ed., (1997): chap. 6.

5. Thomas Friedman is perhaps the best known exponent of this view. In his view, efforts by Western European nations to defend the welfare state as they know it are doomed. "The inevitable adjustment will be enormously painful, but they will be forced to do it in order to maintain anything like their current standards of living." *The Lexus and the Olive Tree* (1999). For a strong European rejection of such "inevitablism," see Ignacio Ramonet, "A New Totalitarianism," in "Dueling Globalisms: A Debate Between Thomas L. Friedman and Ignacio Ramonet," *Foreign Policy* (fall 1999): 110, 116.

6. The most recent testimony to the strength of these pressures is the publication by the WTO of a major report: Hikan Nordstrom and Scott Vaughan, *Trade and Environment*, WTO Special Studies 4, October 1999.

7. ILO Convention No. 182, Convention Concerning the Prohibition and Immediate Action for the Elimination of the Worst Forms of Child Labour, adopted on 17 June 1999.

8. Commenting on the outcome of the meeting, *The Economist* characterized "the battle of Seattle" as "only the latest and most visible in a string of recent NGO victories." It concluded that "citizens' groups are increasingly powerful at the corporate, national, and international level." "The Non-governmental Order," *The Economist*, 18 Dec. 1999.

9. United Nations, *Report of the Secretary-General on the Work of the Organization*, A/54/1, 1999, paragraph 53.

10. United Nations Development Programme, *Human Development Report 1999*, 34.

11. Richard Falk, *On Human Governance: Towards a New Global Politics* (1995), 212.

12. General Assembly Resolution 44/25 (1989), Annex, Article 4.

13. Shahid Saved Burki, Guillermo E. Perry, William R. Dillinger, *Beyond the Center: Decentralizing the State* (Washington D.C.: World Bank, 1999), 1.

14. Ibid., 34.

15. Ibid.

16. Friedman, M. *Capitalism and Freedom* (1962), 133.

17. Holland, M., *The European Community and South Africa: European Political Cooperation Under Strain* (1988).

18. Teubner, Gunther, "Global Bukowina: Legal Pluralism in the World Society," in *Global Law Without a State*, ed. Teubner (1997).

19. Dezalay, Yves, and Bryant Garth, *Dealing in Virtue: International Commercial Arbitration and the Construction of a Transnational Legal Order* (1996).

20. UN Press Release SG/SM/6881, 1 Feb. 1999.

21. Human Rights Watch World Report 1998, xvii.

22. IMF, *The Role of the IMF in Governance Issues: Guidance Note* (Approved by the Executive Board, 25 July 1997) at paragraph 5. See also paragraph 15: "[C]onditionality, in the form of prior actions, performance criteria, benchmarks, and conditions for completion of a review, should be attached to policy measures, including those relating to economic aspects of governance that are required to meet the objectives of a program. This would include policy measures that may have important implications for improving governance but are covered by the IMF's conditionality primarily because of their direct macroeconomic impact (e.g. the elimination of tax exemptions or recovery of non-performing loans)."

23. IMF, *The Role of the IMF in Governance Issues: Guidance Note* (Approved by the Executive Board, 25 July 1997) at paragraph 9.

24. World Bank, "Development News," Dec. 8, 1999, 1.

25. Ibid., Oct. 13, 1999, p. 5.

26. Ibid., p. 6.

27. UN Doc. ST/SGB/1999/13 (6 Aug. 1999).

28. Carlos Perez del Castillo, UN Press Release TAD/1915, 17 Feb. 2000, 2.

Government Speech in a Neutral State

1. *Grosjean v. American Press Co.*, 297 U.S. 233 (1936). A state statute imposing license tax for privilege of engaging in business upon all publishers of newspapers having weekly circulation of more than 20,000 copies was held unconstitutional because such disguised schemes were traditionally censorial.

2. *Arkansas Writers' Project v. Ragland*, 481 U.S. 221, 235 (1987).

3. I find no difficulty with the public subsidy of the speech of people's representatives. (If one accepts the German constitutional theory on the constitutional function of political parties the subsidy may be used by party politicians, too.) As long as a politician cannot legitimately use the first plural ("us"), people will have no difficulty in understanding the speech as private, that is, being without public authority. Public money is used here to improve the communication between the constituency and its elected representatives. There are convincing grounds for facilitating such communication under democratic theory, even if it may work as an unfair disadvantage to the critics of the speaker.

4. *Rust v. Sullivan*, 500 U.S. 173 (1991).

5. Ibid., 199.

6. David Cole, *Beyond Unconstitutional Conditions: Charting Spheres of Neutrality in Government-Funded Speech*, 67 NYU L. Rev. 675, 680 (1992). In the context of standing, Justice Stevens (joined by Justice Blackmun) stated: "When a subsidy makes a given activity more or less expensive, injury can be fairly traced to the subsidy for purposes of standing analysis because of the resulting increase or decrease in the ability to engage in the activity." *Allen v. Wright*, 468 U.S. 737, 786 (1984) (dissenting opinion).

7. Frederick Schauer, *Principles, Institutions, and the First Amendment*, 112 Harv. L. Rev. 84 (1997).

8. Mark Tushnet, *Talking to Each Other: Reflections on Yudof's "When Government Speaks,"* Wisconsin L. Rev. 129 (1984). See also *Alabama Libertarian Party v. City of Birmingham*, 694 F. Supp. 814, 820 (1988).

9. "As a matter of constitutional tradition, in the absence of evidence to the contrary, we presume that governmental regulation of the content of speech is more likely to interfere with the free exchange of ideas than to encourage it." *Reno v. ACLU*, 521 U.S. 844, 117 S.Ct. 2329, 2351 (1997) (Stevens, J.).

10. *R v. Radio Authority*, ex parte Bull and another [1995] 4 All ER 481, QB (Kennedy L. J.).

11. *Buckley v. Valeo*, 424 U.S. 1, 93 (1976).

12. Laurence Tribe, *American Constitutional Law* 2nd ed. (Mineola: Foundation Press, 1991), 944.

13. *Meyer v. Nebraska*, 262 U.S. 390 (1923).

14. The German Constitution expressly grants a limited right of access to information. German Constitution, Art. 5 (1).

15. I think that Stanley Hoffman's twenty-year-old recognition of the "limited but real powers" of the nation-state will be valid in the foreseeable future. See Stanley Hoffman, "Reflections on the Nation-State in Western Europe Today," 21 *Journal of Common Market Studies* 1–2, 21 (1983).

16. Provisions prohibiting government control of the media are the exception.

17. Cole, *Beyond Unconstitutional Conditions,* 680.

18. Owen Fiss, *The Irony of Free Speech* (Cambridge: Harvard University Press, 1996), 15–16.

19. Ibid., 16.

20. Without textual support in the U.S. Constitution a similar position is stated by Owen Fiss:

"The call for state intervention is based on the theory that the activity to be regulated is inherently a violation of the First Amendment (a claim that would require, as a purely technical matter, a showing of state action) but only on the theory that fostering full and open debate—making certain that the public hears all that it should—is a permissible end for the state . . . The state is merely exercising its police power to further a worthy public end. . . . In this case, the end happens to be a conception of democracy which requires that the speech of the powerful not drown out or impair the speech of the less powerful." Fiss, *Irony,* 17.

21. Steven H. Shiffrin, *Government Speech,* 27 U.C.L.A. L. Rev. 565, 566 (1980).

22. *Kommentar zum Grundgesetz fuer die Bundesrepublik Deutschland,* 2d ed., Vol.1 (Neuwied: Luchterland, 1989), 430 (Hoffmann-Riem).

23. 84-181 DC (Entreprises de Presse). This was held by Pierre Avril and Jean Gicquel "as the confirmation of the interventionist concept of legislation." Quoted in Louis Favoreu-Loïc Philip, *Les grandes décisions du Conseil constitutionnel.* 7th ed. (Paris: Sirey, 1993), 601.

24. *Arkansas Educational Television Commission v. Forbes,* 523 U.S. 666 (1998).

25. *Burt v. Blumenauer,* 299 Or. 55, 66 (Or., Apr. 23, 1985). In this case public employees were held financially liable for using public money to promote a water fluoridation campaign when an antifluoridation measure was on the ballot.

26. *Citizens to Protect Public Funds v. Board of Education,* 13 N.J. 172, 181 (N.J. Sup. Ct. 1953).

27. *Stern v. Kramarsky,* 375 N.Y.S.2d 235, 239 (N.Y.Sup.Ct.1975)

28. *Miller v. California Com'n on Status of Women,* 151 Cal. App.3d. 693, 702 (1984).

29. However, in *Carter v. City of Las Cruces,* 121 N.M. 580 (1996), cert. denied, 121 N.M. 644 (1996) the spending of city funds to advertise a bond issuance was not held illegal.

30. Cf. Theodor Maunz, Günter Dürig, *Grundgesetz-Kommentar.* (Mumunchen: Beck, 1993), Art 5. Abs 1, 2 Rz. 112. (Herzog). See also below, civil service neutrality.

31. *Burt v. Blumenauer,* 299 Or. 55 (Or., Apr. 23, 1985).

32. German Constitution, Art. 38 (1).

Article 21 of the German Constitution deals with the constitutional role of political parties in the expression of popular will. Under this article it is understood that it follows from the constitutional function of the parties that there is need for equality of chances for the parties including equal access to media. *Kommentar zum Grundgesetz,* Vol. 1, 1530 (Preuss).

33. BVerfGE 104, 323, 326. The prohibition extends to an advertisement signed by local mayors in favor of the reelection to the Land Council of the person representing the district where the mayors were holding elected office. BVerfGE 8 C 5.96. The action of the elected officials goes beyond the exercise of their civic rights. However, a public position taken by civil servants favoring the reelection of their mayor was not held as an undue influence of the election process if it was made in reaction to factual allegations regarding the activities of the city management. VGH Mannheim, Beschl. V. 30. 1. 1997. NVwZ-RR 1198. Heft 2. 126.

34. See *Miller v. California Com'n on Status of Women,* 151 Cal. App. ed. 693, 702 (1984)

35. BremStGH, Urt. v. 29. 7. 1996. JuS 1997. 7. 652.

36. LVerfG Sachsen-Anhalt, Urteil v. 22.2.1996. The governmental department of Sachsen-Anhalt responsible for informing the public published a pamphlet on the yearly budget in which the title of one of the chapters suggested that the family subsidies were related to the politics of one of the majority parties.

37. LVerfG Sachsen-Anhalt, Ibid. JZ 1996 724. The Constitutional Court held, in conformity with U.S. doctrine originally expressed by the Founding Fathers, that neutrality prohibits the government of the day from perpetuating its power through the use of state power. (BVerfGE 44, 125, 142). Political advertising by government is the clear limit to public information.

38. Waldron points out that liberal neutrality is only a recent attempt to express what the liber-

als "have always held about the attitude the state should take to the personal faith and beliefs of its citizens." Jeremy Waldron, *Liberal Rights* (Cambridge: Cambridge University Press, 1993), 143.

In the text above, state neutrality goes beyond personal faith influencing state action. This is not intended to suggest that it is not the government's attitude to personal faith that stands at the heart of the issue. To a varying extent the latter is the model for state neutrality.

39. Dependency is described in terms of public communication monopolies or dependency of the press on government subsidies where there are only a few voices that are dependent on the state in terms of license or subsidy.

40. This dependency is not limited to the welfare state. "Subsidies can come to be experienced like entitlements because they have become so integrated into the fabric of everyday life." Robert Post, *Subsidized Speech,* 106 Yale L. J. 151, 179 (1996). Traditionally, freedom of expression is protected against government incursion. The restriction of an entitlement that enables speech may amount to speech restriction.

41. The strategy of the U.S. Supreme Court is to single out certain institutions that are deemed to have their own speech. The Supreme Court has no constitutional theory for the status of these neutral institutions. Sometimes the courts try to satisfy requirements of neutrality and promotion of speech relying on a theory of public forum. Under U.S. doctrine, government expression may create a public forum that shall be accessible to all speakers, partly to remedy speech by more speech. The state shall be neutral in regulating (providing) access to the forum. But government speech in itself does not turn a forum into a public one with public access rights. In the United States, government's involvement in speech promotion (access rights) is most often discussed by the Supreme Court in terms of "public forum." The advocates of governmentally created public forum for public discussion argue that such public space is needed to improve the chances of robust dialogue. It is hard to deny that allocation decisions concerning rules of operation in a restricted access forum (broadcasting) do have an impact on the nature and structure of the public discourse. The Supreme Court recently applied its doctrine of public forum in a way that allows increasing restrictions of the neutral sphere.

42. Richard A. Epstein, *Unconstitutional Conditions, State Power, and the Limits of Consent,* 102 Harvard L. Rev. 4, 83 (1987). Epstein notes that the "test is more stringent than in the speech area, where only restrictions that burden private speech are suspect, while those that subsidize it are not." Ibid., 84. Epstein does not discuss the

possible consequences of an error in the speech subsidy context.

43. Cass R. Sunstein, *Lochner's Legacy,* 87 Colum. L. Rev. 873, 874 (1987).

44. *Buckley v. Valeo,* 424 U.S. 1, 93 (1976).

45. *R. v. Radio Authority,* ex parte Bull and another [1995] 4 All ER 481, 503 QB (McCullough J.).

46. *Buckley v. Valeo* 424 U.S.1, 92–93, note 127 (1976).

47. Tribe, *American Constitutional Law,* 807.

48. *West Virginia Board of Education v. Barnette,* 319 U.S. 624 (1943).

49. *Bethel School District v. Fraser,* 478 U.S. 675, 683 (1986).

50. In many countries it is acceptable to fund private, and mainly religious, indoctrination from public resources. Hence two concepts of state neutrality emerge. The strong version argues that public money cannot be used for any indoctrination. The weak version of neutrality is satisfied if funding does not depend on promoting indoctrination by government, that is, the distribution of funds is not conditioned upon the support of the government's viewpoints.

51. 441 U.S. 68 (1979)

52. For an overview see Martin H. Redish and Daryl I. Kessler, *Government Subsidies and Free Expression,* 80 Minnesota L. Rev. 543, 582 (1996).

53. Mark G. Yudof, *When Government Speaks: Politics, Law, and Government Expression in America* (Berkeley: University of California Press, 1983), 223–24.

54. The reconstruction of Schmitt's theory is based on Carl Schmitt, "Das Zeitalter der Neutralisierungen und Entpolitisierungen," 79–96, in Carl Schmitt, *Der Begriff des Politischen* (Berlin: Duncker-Humblot, 1996) (1934).

55. Party affiliation of employees cannot be a concern in their continuing employment; in exchange they cannot have opinions, at least not at their workplace. For them the neutrality of government results in silence and nonpartisan speech. Through the denial of speech protection to civil servants, government and its organizations may emerge as "neutral," nonparty-partisan speakers.

56. *McAuliffe v. City of New Bedford,* 55 Mass. 216 (Mass. Sup. Ct. 1892) (per Holmes, J.).

57. Report of the Widdecombe Committee (1986), par. 6.180. On quote in the *Case of Ahmed and Others v. The United Kingdom,* ECHR, (65/1997/849/1056), par. 9.

58. *Case of Ahmed and Others v. The United Kingdom,* ECHR, (65/1997/849/1056), par. 63.

59. [1991] 2 S.C.R. 69

60. Yudof, *When Government Speaks,* 107.

61. Schauer claims that U.S. "[u]niversities have generally been unsuccessful in gaining special rights under the rubric of academic freedom." The case he cites is hardly a matter of special speech protection: the fact that peer review is made accessible to interested parties does not seem to undermine free speech. What the University of Pennsylvania claimed—a decline in the quality of instruction and scholarship—is only indirectly related to academic freedom as freedom of the university. Schauer, *Principles,* 84–85. In *Rust v. Sullivan* the Supreme Court held that a university "is a traditional sphere of free expression so fundamental to the functioning of our society that the Government's ability to control speech within that sphere by means of conditions attached to the expenditure. Government funds is restricted by the vagueness and overbreadth doctrines of the First Amendment." 500 US 173, 111 S.Ct. 1759, 1776 (1991).

62. Sometimes the review of a regulation affecting speech is limited to the analysis of the composition and situation of the independent body that makes allocative decisions.

The German legal theory of state-supported art is that here the government has broad discretionary powers due to the openness of art. Arbitrariness is the limit. There is even more freedom of choice when it comes to acquisition and subsidies to art. Here the state is free to limit its discretionary powers through the establishment of expert bodies. *Kommentar zum Grundgesetz,* Vol. 1, 607. (Ladeur).

63. BVerfGE 35, 114. See also *Kommentar zum Grundgesetz,* Vol. 1, 559. (Denninger).

64. *Sweezy v. New Hampshire,* 354 U.S. 234 at 262 (1957) (Frankfurter, J., concurring).

65. *R. v. Radio Authority* [1995] 4 All ER 481, QB (Kennedy LJ.).

66. In Germany there are a few important direct restrictions on government regarding speech, primarily due to the Nazi abuse of the government's broadcasting monopoly for government propaganda.

67. One should add that this not a centralized Prussian bureaucracy anymore; it is subject to political-democratic and judicial control. Although one shall keep in mind that the judiciary has no mandate, desire, or standards to review the bureaucracy's decisions shaping the public discourse or the activities of nongovernmental public bodies that bring corporative elements into the complex situation.

68. *Kommentar zum Grundgesetz,* Vol. 1, 420. (Hoffmann-Riem)

69. Michel Rosenfeld, *The Jurisprudence of Fairness: Freedom through Regulation in the Marketplace of Ideas,* 1976 Fordham L. Rev. 877, 912 (1976).

70. Cole, *Beyond Unconstitutional Conditions,* 682.

71. Ibid., 732.

72. See *Police Department of Chicago v. Mosley,* 408 U.S. 92 (1972). "The equal protection claim . . . is closely intertwined with First Amendment interests." Ibid., 95. These requirements are generally intended to scrutinize governmental speech regulation and not government speech or government action.

73. Schauer, *Principles,* 114, note 143.

74. In Hungary a national cultural fund was established with a similar structure. The cultural government found the panel decisions unacceptable and contrary to the government's cultural policy, which advocated a return to traditional Christian and national values. The fund's allocation mechanism was changed, bringing half of the fund into the discretionary power of the minister of National Heritage.

75. However, for (as he then was) Justice Rehnquist, "ideas no more accessible or no less suppressed if the school board merely ratifies the opinion of some other group [of experts] rather than following its own opinion." *Board of Education v. Pico,* 457 U.S. 853, 909 (1982).

76. *Police Department of Chicago v. Mosley,* 408 U.S. 92, 95 (1972).

77. Schauer, *Principles,* 115, refers to the fact that as librarians are state employees, the external influence in the acquisition process raises First Amendment problems.

78. Ironically, the autonomy of universities (a sphere of free speech carved out from government intervention) resulted in speech restriction resembling civil servants' loss of speech rights which was offered in exchange for job security. Universities have the right to deny jobs on the basis of viewpoint discrimination. A historian sympathetic to Nazi warfare cannot be surprised at being denied tenure. In France scholars denying the Holocaust were subject to disciplinary procedures and the dissertation of a revisionist historian employed as a researcher was rejected. Roger Errera, "In Defence of Civility: Racial Incitement and Group Libel in French Law," 154, in *Striking a Balance: Hate Speech, Freedom of Expression and Non-Discrimination,* ed. S. Coliver (London: Article 19, 1992).

79. *Board of Education v. Pico,* 457 U.S. 853 (1982).

80. Mutzenbacher Case, BVerfGE 87, 130.

81. Mark G. Yudof, *When Governments Speak: Toward a Theory of Government Expression and the First Amendment,* 57 Tex. L. Rev. 863, 912–917 (1979) argued that neutrality is not a feasible requirement in funding and it is not for the courts to exercise review of speech-affecting spending. Cole, *Beyond Unconstitutional Conditions* 714, note 155, finds Yudof's position insufficient as "the fact that selective government speech is sanctioned by the legislature provides no guarantee that it will not skew the intellectual marketplace or indoctrinate the citizenry."

82. Schauer, *Principles,* 86.

83. "[N]eutrality itself is far from a straightforward concept. Certainly the recent debate has shown that it is not particularly amenable to uncontroversial logical analysis." Waldron, *Liberal Rights,* 145.

84. Janos Kis, *Az állam semlegessége [The neutrality of the state] (Budapest: Atlantisz, 1997).*

85. [T]he government's selection is constitutional as long as it is based on criteria "substantially related" to the prescribed goals and purposes of the program pursuant to which the category of speech is funded. Redish and Kessler, *Government Subsidies,* 572.

86. "[A]llocation of the benefit would normally be subject to deferential review, while imposition of a burden on the constitutional right would normally be strictly scrutinized." Kathleen M. Sullivan, *Unconstitutional Conditions,* 102 Harv. L. Rev. 1415, 1422 (1995). Fiss claims that abstention from subsidization of art and other forms of expression might constitute prior restraint and, therefore, are not matters of constitutional spending power exercise. Owen Fiss, *State Activism and State Censorship,* 100 Yale L.J. 2087, 2104–2105 (1991).

87. *Washington v. Davis,* 426 U.S. 229 (1976).

88. Owen Fiss, *State Activism and State Censorship,"* 100 Yale L.J. 2087, 2100 (1991).

89. *Board of Education v. Pico,* 457 U.S. 853 (1992).

90. *Board of Education v. Pico,* 457 U.S. 853, 871 (1982). The dissenting justices found the "disagreement with ideas" criterion vague or one that will result in constant judicial determination. In the view of the dissenters, only cases of clear and present danger and extreme cases of total racial or partisan bias would justify judicial intervention in what otherwise would be an educationally legitimate exercise of discretion.

91. For a limit on subject-based choice, see below.

92. Fiss, *State Activism,* 2100.

93. Ibid., (emphasis added).

94. Ibid.

95. Cole, *Beyond Unconstitutional Conditions,* 713.

96. Fiss argues that decisions affecting speech should be reviewed by courts on the grounds of their effects on the public debate. Obviously this will not find sympathy among those who are afraid of replacing political decisions with that of the judiciary. An additional objection is that there is no applicable judicial standard regarding the impact of regulation on the public discourse. Is the public debate more robust if there are more abstract hyper-realist artists; is it better off if there is more broadcasting of folk songs? Even if there is more discussion of serious issues (like health care), instead of gossiping about the personal integrity of politicians or emotional life of ETs, I would say that there is improvement but there is no legitimacy to paternalistically impose our elite views on the public discourse with the support of state intervention.

97. The nondelegation doctrine would offer some grounds for review, except that the doctrine is in disrepute everywhere.

98. Waldron, *Liberal Rights,* 147.

99. *Grosjean v. American Press Co.,* 297 U.S. 233 (1936).

100. In the context of special mail delivery rates, see BverfGE 80 124, 132. Herzog claims that the state's neutrality obligation, which is implicit in the free speech protection clauses of the German Constitution, prohibits differentiation according to newspaper content. Maunz-Dürig, Abs I.II Art 5. Rdnrn. 144a.

101. Larry Alexander, "Free Speech and Speaker's Intent," 12 *Const. Comm.* 21, 22 (1995).

102. Sullivan, *Unconstitutional Conditions,* 1499–1500.

103. *U.S. v. O'Brien,* 391 U.S. 367 (1968).

104. *Rust v. Sullivan,* 500 U.S. 173 (1991).

105. Kis, *Az állam semlegessége,* 92.

106. Ibid., 415, note 28.

107. *Buckley v. Valeo,* 424 U.S. 1, 93 (1976).

108. *Turner Broadcasting System, Inc. v. FCC,* 512 U.S. 622 (1994).

109. Justice Brennan in *Board of Education v. Pico,* 457 U.S. 853, 870 (1982), quoted by Justice Rehnquist: "cheerfully conceding" it, dissenting opinion. Id. 907.

110. Critics would separate market and speech. They argue that appreciating the marvels of capitalism as an economic system does not entail that the First Amendment or the political domain in general should be dominated by the norms of the economy. The decisions of government are not proprietary decisions; they shall serve to preserve democracy that dictates "bringing before the public viewpoints and options that otherwise might be slighted or ignored." Fiss, *State Activism,* 2106. For a reconciliation of republican self-government with liberalism (marketplace of ideas and individual liberty) see Cass Sunstein, *Beyond the Republican Revival,* 97 Yale L. J. 1539, 1541 (1988).

Neutrality and Universality in Human Rights Law

1. Uday Singh Mehta, *Liberalism and Empire* (1999).

2. See Tayyab Mahmud, *Migration, Identity, and the Colonial Encounter,* 76:3 Oregon L. R. (fall 1997) 633.

3. Joseph H. Carens and Melissa S. Williams, "Muslim Minorities in Liberal Democracies: The Politics of Misrecognition," in *Secularism and Its Critics,* ed. Rajeev Bhargava (1998). See also Miriam Feldblum, "Paradoxes of Ethnic Politics: The Case of Franco-Maghrebis in France," 16:1 *Ethnic and Racial Studies* 52; Norma Claire Moruzzi, "A Problem with Head Scarves: Contemporary Complexities of Political and Social Identity," 22:4 *Political Theory* 653–72.

4. Uma Narayan, "Cross-Cultural Connections, Border-Crossings, and 'Death by Culture,'" in *Dislocating Cultures* (1997) 85. See generally Inderpal Grewal, "Women's Rights as Human Rights: Feminist Practices, Global Feminism, and Human Rights Regimes in Transnationality," 3:3 *Citizenship Studies* (1999) 337.

5. Reference to Rudolph Giuliani's opposition to the staging of "Sensation: Young British Artists from the Saatchi Collection" that opened at the Brooklyn Museum of Art on October 2, 1999. The mayor of New York attacked the exhibit as "desecrating somebody else's religion," referring specifically to the work of 1998 Turner Prize winner Chris Ofili's painting of a black Madonna enhanced with elephant droppings. The museum has filed a lawsuit in a federal court against the mayor, accusing him of violating the First Amendment for threatening to withdraw funding to the museum if the "offending" works were not removed.

6. A challenge has been brought against the Ohio Pilot Scholarship Program on the grounds that it violates the establishment of the First Amendment of the U.S. Constitution. The program was enacted to address an educational crisis in the public schools

in Cleveland in the wake of a U.S. District Court–ordered takeover by the state of the administration of the Cleveland city school district. The project includes a scholarship program to enable students to attend "alternative schools" (the voucher program). The private schools who want to participate in the program must register with the state superintendent. Those students eligible are chosen by lot and receive a fixed amount of the tuition charged by the alternative school of their choice up to the amount of $2,500. A large majority of the schools participating in the program are sectarian as are most of the students receiving the scholarship. The challenge concerned the fact that many of the schools had a pervasive religious orientation. See the order of Judge Solomon Oliver Jr. dated August 24, 1999 in Case No: 1:99 CV 1740 and Case No. 1:99 CV 1818 pending in the United States District Court, Northern District of Ohio, Eastern Division, in *Doris Simmon-Haris, et al., v. Dr. Susan Tave Zelman, Superintendent of Public Instruction, State of Ohio, et al.,* and *Sue Gatton v. Dr. Susan Tave Zelman, Superintendent of Public Instruction, State of Ohio.*

7. See Ratna Kapur, *The Fundamentalist Face of Secularism and Women's Rights in India* (forthcoming, Cleveland State Law Rev., 2000). See also "The Two Faces of Secularism and Women's Rights in India," in *Religion and Fundamentalism,* ed. Courtney Howland (1999).

8. Although the idea of a wall of separation goes back to the words of Jefferson, it was only given judicial expression as a basic principle of constitutional law by the United States Supreme Court in the 1940s. In *Everson v. Board of Education of Ewing Township* 330 US 1 (1947), Justice Black writing for the majority emphasized the requirement of strict government neutrality on issues of religion.

9. See generally, Brenda Cossman and Ratna Kapur, *Secularism's Law Sigh? Hindutva and the (Mis)-Rule of Law* (1999).

10. Ibid. See also Ratna Kapur, "Secularism: A Comparative Perspective," in *Comparative Constitutional Law,* ed. Mark Tushnet and Vicki Jackson, (forthcoming, 2000).

11. A challenge is currently pending in the United States Supreme Court on the temporary restraining order given by the United States District Court of Southern Texas on September 3, 1999, against the saying of school prayer at high school football games in the case of *Marian Ward v. Sante Fe Independent School District.*

12. Supra note 4. See also Ratna Kapur and Brenda Cossman, *Subversive Sites: Feminist Engagements with Law in India* (1996), chap. 4.

13. Ratna Kapur, "The Profanity of Prudery:

The Moral Face of Obscenity Law in India," *Women's Cultural Review* (Oxford University Press, 1997). Ratna Kapur, "Who Draws the Line? Contemporary Issues of Speech and Censorship in India," *Economic and Political Weekly,* WS15–30 (April 20–27, 1996).

14. See Ratna Kapur, *From Human Rights to Human Tragedy: Accountability of Multinational Corporations for International Human Rights Violations* 10:1 Boston College Third World L. J., 1–42 (winter 1990).

15. Supra note 7.

16. See Gregory Palast, "Goodbye Allende. Hello Pinochet," *London Observer,* Sunday November 8, 1998. See also Bradford C. Snell, *American Ground Transport: A Proposal for Restructuring the Automobile, Truck, Bus, and Rail Industries,* a report presented to the Committee of the Judiciary, Subcommittee on Antitrust and Monopoly, United States Senate, February 26, 1974, (Washington D.C.: Government Printing Office, 1974) 16–24.

17. For some ideas see Gary A. Olson and Lynn Worsham, "Staging the Politics of Difference: Homi Bhabha's Critical Literacy," in *Race, Rhetoric, and the Postcolonial,* ed. Gary A. Olson and Lynn Worsham (1999).

Bibliography

A. J. Coomaraswamy, Radhika. *Sri Lanka: The Crisis of the Anglo-American Constitutional Traditions in a Developing Society.* Delhi: Cooray, 1984.

Abel, Christopher, and Nissa Torrents, ed. *Spain: Conditional Democracy.* New York: St. Martin's Press, 1984.

Abelson, Reed. "Women Minorities Not Getting to the Top." *New York Times.* July 14, 1999.

Abrams, Kathryn. *Title VII and the Complex Female Subject.* 92 Mich. L. Rev. 1994.

Abrams, Paula. *The Tradition of Reproduction.* 37 Ariz. L. Rev. 1995.

Abu Zahrah, Muhammad. *Al-Wilayah 'ala al-Nafs.* Dar al-Ra'ed al-'Arabi, 1970.

Ackerman, Bruce. *We the People: Transformations.* Volume 2. Cambridge: Harvard University Press, 1998.

Ackerman, Bruce A., and William T. Hassler. *Clean Coal/Dirty Air: Or How the Clean Air Act Became a Multibillion-Dollar Bail-out for the High-Sulfur Coal Producers and What Should Be Done About It.* New Haven: Yale University Press, 1981.

Acutidna, C. H., I. González Bombal, E. Jelin, O. Landi, L.A. Quevedo, C. Smulovitz, A. Vacchieri, and A. Przeworksi. *Juicios, castigos y memorias: derechos humanos y la justicia en la política Argentina.* Buenos Aires: Ediciones Nueva Visíon, 1995.

Adam, Heribert. "The Presence of the Past: South Africa's Truth Commission as a Model?" in *Religion and Politics in South Africa.* Ed. Abdulkader Tayob and Wolframm Weisse. Muenster: Waxmann, 1999.

Adam, Heribert, and Kogila Moodley. *The Opening of the Apartheid Mind.* Berkeley: University of California Press, 1993.

Adam, Heribert, Van Zyl Slabbert, and Kogila Moodley. *Comrades in Business: Post Liberation Politics in South Africa.* Utrecht: International Publishers, 1999.

Adams, John. 7 *Boston Gazette.* 1774.

Adorno, Theodor W. et al. *The Authoritarian Personality.* New York: Harper, 1950.

Aerial Incident of 27 July 1955. Observations and Submissions of the Government of the United States of America, ICJ Pleadings. 1959.

Aerial Incident of 3 July 1988. ICJ Reports. 1996.

Affirmative Action Doomed?. NYRB. November 5, 1998.

Affirming Affirmative Actions. NYRB. October 22, 1998.

Agarwal, Bina. "Rural Women, Poverty and Natural Resources: Sustenance, Sustainability and Struggle for Change." *Economic and Political Weekly.* October 28, 1989.

Aghion, Philippe. "Inequality and Economic Growth," in *Growth, Inequality and Globalization: Theory, History, and Policy.* Philippe Aghion and Jeffrey Williamson. Cambridge University Press, 1998.

Agnew, Vijay. *Resisting Women from Asia, Africa, and the Caribbean and the Women's Movement in Canada.* Toronto, 1996.

Agora: Breard. 92 AJIL. 1998.

Alexander, Larry. "Free Speech and Speaker's Intent." 12 *Const. Comm.* (1995): 21, 22.

Allott, Philip. "The Concept of International Law." 10 *European Journal of International Law.* 1999.

———. *Eunomia—New Order for a New World.* Oxford: Oxford University Press, 1990.

———. *Eutopia—New Mind for a New Humanity.* Forthcoming.

———. "International Societies and the Idea of Constitutionalism," in *The Legitimacy of International Organizations.* Ed. V. Heiskanen and J-M Coicaud. Tokyo: UN University Press, forthcoming.

———. "Libranos del mal social." *Revista de Occidente.* October 1999.

al-Alwani, Taha Jabir. *The Ethics of Disagreement in Islam.* 1996.

———. "The Testimony of Women in Islamic Law." *The American Journal of Islamic Social Sciences.* 1996.

Ammons, Linda L. *Mules, Madonnas, Babies, Bath Water, Racial Imagery and Stereotypes: The African-American Woman and the Battered Woman Syndrome.* 1995 Wis. L. Rev.

Amnesty International. "Egyptian Human Rights Defender Faces Years of Imprisonment." Afr. News Serv. Feb. 16, 2000.

Anderson, Terry, and Donald R. Leal. *Free Market Environmentalism.* 1991.

al-Aqqad, Abbas Mahmoud. Fatimah al-Zahra'. Dar al-Kitab al-'Arabi: Beirut 1967.

Arendt, Hannah. *Eichmann in Jerusalem: A Report on the Banality of Evil.* New York: Viking Press, 1965.

———. *The Human Condition: A Study of the Central Conditions Facing Modern Man.* Garden City, New York: Doubleday Anchor Books, 1959.

———. *The Origins of Totalitarianism.* London: Allen & Unwin, 1951/1958.

"Argentine Political Crimes." *The Economist.* November 6, 1999.

Arzt, Donna E. *Bridge Over Troubled Water: Law and the Emergence of New Democracies.* 22 Syracuse J. Int'l L. & Com. 1996.

Ash, Timothy Garton. *The File: A Personal History.* New York: Random House, 1997.

al-Assadi, Saif. *Al-Fitnah wa Waq'at al-Jamal* [Turmoil and the Battle of the Camel]. Dar al-Nafa'is: Beirut, 1993.

Aubert, Vilhem. *Elements of Sociology.* 1967.

Augustine. *Confessions,* book X. Trans. E. B. Pusey. London: Dent (Everyman's Library), 1907.

el-Awa, Muhammad Salim. *Mashru' al-Ahwal ash-Shakhsiyyah* (Draft Personal Status Law). Al-Ahram.

al-Awqaf wa al-Shu'un al-Islamiyah, Wazarat. 34 *Al-Mawsu'ah al-Fiqhiyah* [The Encyclopedia of Fiqh]. Dar al-Sufwah: Kuwait, 1995.

Aynes, Richard L. *Bradwell v. Illinois: Chief Justice Chase's Dissent and the "Sphere of Women's Work."* 59 La. L. Rev. 1999.

Azuela, Antonio. *La Ciudad, la Propiedad Privada y el Derecho.* México: El Colegio de México. 1999.

———. "Ciudadanía y gestión urbana en los poblados rurales de Los Tuxtlas," in *Estudios Sociológicos* Vol. XIII, núm. 39, septiembre–diciembre. 1995.

———. "Pluralismo jurídico y cambio institucional: La regulación de los usos del suelo en la Ciudad de México (1976–1993)," in *Participación y democracia en la Ciudad de México.* Ed. Lucía Alvarez. México: Centro de Investigaciones Interdisciplinarias en Ciencias y Humanidades, 1997.

Bakr bin Abdallah, Abu. 1 Ahkam al-Qur'an [Qur'anic Rulings]. Dar al-Ma'rifah: Beirut, reprint 1987.

Balkin, J. M. "The Constitution of Status," 106 *Yale L.J.* 1997.

———. *Cultural Software: A Theory of Ideology.* 1998.

Bannerji, Himani. *Thinking Through: Essays on Feminism, Marxism and Anti-Racism.* Toronto, 1996.

Banting, Keith. "Social Citizenship and the Multicultural Welfare State," in Allen Cairns et al., 1999.

al-Bardisi, Muhammad Zakariyah. *Al-Ahkam al-Islamiyah fi al-Ahwal al-Shakhsiyah.* Dar al-Nahdah al-'Arabiah: Egypt, 1965.

Barkey, Henri J., and Graham E. Fuller. *Turkey's Kurdish Question.* Lanham, Md.: Rowman & Littlefield, 1998.

Barrett, Stanley R. *Is God a Racist? The Right Wing in Canada.* Toronto: University of Toronto Press, 1987

Bass, Gary Jonathan. Review of *Mass Atrocity, Collective Memory, and the Law,* by Mark Osiel. 97 Mich. L. Rev. 1999.

Bassiouni, M. Cherif. *The Normative Framework of International Humanitarian Law: Overlaps, Gaps, and Ambiguities.* 8 Transnat'l L. & Contemp. Probs. 1998.

al-Batriq, Ahmad, et al. *Majlis al-Sha'b Yuwafiq 'ala Qanun al-Ahwal al-Shakhsiyah* (Parliament Approves Personal Status Law). Al-Ahram. Jan. 27, 2000.

Baumol, William J. *The Theory of Environmental Policy.* 2d ed. 1998.

al-Baydawi, Nasser al-Din. *Tafsir.* Dar al-Fikr: n.p., reprint 1982.

Beckett, Samuel. *Proust.* London: John Calder, 1965.

———. *Waiting for Godot.* London: Faber and Faber, 1956.

Becvar, J., and M. Kokine, eds. *Role of Economic Instruments in Integrating Environmental Policy with Sectoral Policies.* UN: New York and Geneva, 1998.

Bem, Sandra Lipsitz. "Gender Schema Theory and Its Implications for Child Development: Raising Gender-aschematic Children in a Gender-schematic Society." 8 *Signs* 598 (1984).

Bennett, Graham, ed., *Conserving Europe's Natural Heritage: Towards a European Ecological Network.* London, Dordrecht, Boston. 1994.

Berger, Suzanne, and Dore, Ronald, eds. *National Diversity and Global Capitalism.* Ithaca: Cornell University Press, 1996.

Berman, Haroid J. *Justice in the USSR.* 2d ed. 1963.

Bibby, Reginald. *Mosaic Madness.* Toronto: Stoddart, 1990.

Billington. James H. *The Icon and the Axe: An Interpretive History of Russian Culture.* New York: Knopf, 1966.

Binder, Guyora, and Robert Weisberg. *Cultural Criticism of Law.* 49 Stan. L. Rev. 1997.

Birov, Victoria A. "Prize or Plunder?: The Pillage of Works of Art and the International Law of War." 30 *New York University School of Law Journal of International Law and Politics.* Fall 1997–winter 1998.

Bissoondath, Neil. *Selling Illusions. The Cult of Multiculturalism in Canada.* Toronto: Penguin, 1994.

Blake, William. *The Complete Writings of William Blake.* Ed. G. Keynes. Oxford: Oxford University Press, 1966.

Blankenagel, Alexander. "Eyes Wide Shut: Displaced Cultural Objects in Russian Law and Adjudication." 8 *East European Constitutional Review.* Fall 1999.

Boguslavsky, Mark. "Legal Aspects of the Russian Position in Regards to the Return of Cultural Property," in *The Spoils of War: World War II and Its Aftermath: The Loss, Reappearance, and Recovery of Cultural Property.* Ed. Elizabeth Simpson. New York: Abrams, 1997.

Bonime-Blanc, Andrea. *Spain's Transition to Democracy: The Politics of Constitution-making.* Boulder: Westview Press, 1987.

Borges, Jorge Luis. *Ficciones.* Madrid: Alianza Editorial, 1971.

———. *Labyrinths.* Penguin Books, 1970.

Boulton, Leyla. "Kurds' arrest dents Turkey's EU hopes." *Financial Times.* February 21, 2000.

Boyle, A. E. *Dispute Settlement and the Law of the Sea Convention.* 46 International and Comparative Law Quarterly. 1997.

Bradley, Curtis A., and Jack L. Goldsmith. *Pinochet and International Human Rights Litigation.* 97 Mich. L. Rev. 1999.

Breitman, R. *Architect of Genocide: Himmler and the Final Solution.* New York: Knopf, 1991.

Brenton, Paul, Henry Scott, and Peter Sinclair. *International Trade.* Oxford University Press, 1997.

Britton, Mary C. I., and Victor Nee. *The New Institutionalism in Sociology.* New York: Russell Sage Foundation, 1998.

Brolmann, Catherine, Rene Lefeber, and Marjoleine Zieck, ed. *Peoples and Minorities in International Law.* Dordrecht: Maritinus Nijhoff Publishers, 1993.

Brook, James. "On Ethnic Battlefield, the French Retake a Bridge." *New York Times.* February 23, 2000.

Brown, Chris. "Universal Human Rights: A Critique." 1 *International Journal of Human Rights.* 1997.

Brown, Judith Olans, Lucy A. Williams, and Phyllis Tropper Baumann. *The Mythogenesis of Gender: Judicial Images of Woman in Paid and Unpaid Labor.* 6 UCLA Women's L. J. 1996.

Bruner, Jerome. *Acts of Meaning.* 1990.

Brus, Marcel M. T. A. *Third Party Dispute Settlement in an Interdependent World.* 1995.

Bryan, Lowell, and Farrell, Diana. *Market Unbound.* New York: Wiley, 1996.

Butler, William. *Russian Law.* Oxford: Oxford University Press, 1999.

Butterbaugh, Laura. *An Hour of One's Own.*

Cairns, Allen, et al. ed. *Citizenship, Diversity, and Pluralism: Canadian and Comparative Perspectives.* Montreal and Kingston: McGill–Queens University Press, 1999.

Calhoun, Cheshire. "The Gender Closet: Lesbian Disappearance under the Sign 'Women.'" *Feminist Studies.* 1995.

Caminos, Hugo. *The Role of the Organization of American States in the Promotion and Protection of Democratic Governance.* 1999.

Capers, I. Bennett. *Sex(ual Orientation) and Title VII.* 91 Colum. L. Rev. 1991.

Carbado, Devon W. *Motherhood and Work in Cultural Context: One Woman's Patriarchal Bargain.* 21 Harv. Women's L. J. 1998.

Cardinal, Harold. *The Unjust Society.* Vancouver, B.C.: Douglas and McIntyre and Seattle: University of Washington Press, 1999.

Connor, Walker. Ethnonationalism: *The Quest for Understanding.* Princeton: Princeton University Press, 1994.

Carens, Joseph H., and Melissa S. Williams, "Muslim Minorities in Liberal Democracies: The Politics of Misrecognition," in *Secularism and Its Critics.* Ed. Rajeev Bhargava (1998).

Carraway, G. Chezia. *Violence Against Women of Color.* 43 Stan. L. Rev. 1991.

Case, D. T., and J. B. Ritter. "Disconnects Between Science and the Law." *Chemical and Engineering News* 78 (7) (2000).

Center for Strategic and International Studies. *The Environmental Protection System in Transition: Toward a More Desirable Future.* Washington, D.C.: CSIS Press, 1998.

Central and East European Law Initiative, American Bar Association. *Analysis of the Constitution of the Russian Federation.* New York, 1995.

Certain Norwegian Loans. ICJ Reports. 1957.

Charney, J. I. *Is International Law Threatened by Multiple International Tribunals?* 217 Recueil des Cours. 1998.

Chomsky, Noam. *Profits Over People: Neoliberalism and Global Order.* New York: Seven Stories Press, 1999.

Cicero. *De re publica.*

Click, Amy L. "German Pillage and Russian Revenge, Stolen Degas, Fifty Years Later—Who's Art Is It Anyway?" 5 *Tulsa Journal of Comparative & International Law.* Fall 1997.

Coffey, Steven J. *Rule of Law and Regional Conflict,* 19 Whittier L. Rev. 1997.

Cohen, Percy. *Modern Social Theory.* 1968.

Cohen, Philip. "Hidden Narratives in Theories of Racism," in *Race, Culture, and Difference.* Ed. J. Donald and Ali Rattansi. London: Sage, 1992.

Cole, David. *Beyond Unconstitutional Conditions: Charting Spheres of Neutrality in Government-Funded Speech.* 67 NYU L. Rev. (1992): 675, 680.

Colker, Ruth. *Sexual Orientation: Militarism, Moralism, and Capitalism.* 48 Hast. L. J. 1997.

Collier, John, and Vaughan Lowe. *The Settlement of Disputes in International Law.* 1999.

Commission for Environmental Cooperation. *North American Environmental Law and Policy.* Montreal, 1998.

Congressional Record. H.R. 441, 67th Congress, 4th session, 67:4.

Congressional Record. 74th session, 1st session, 1145–46.

Cooper, Robert. *The Post-Modern State and the World Order.* London: Demos, 1996.

Córdova, Arnaldo. *La Ideología de la Revolución Mexicana.* México: Era. 1973

Coser, Rose Laub. "Power Lost and Status Gained: A Step in the Direction of Sex Equality," in *The Nature of Work.* Ed. Kai Erikson and Steven Peter Vallas. 1990.

Cossío-Díaz, José Ramón. *Derecho y Análisis Económico.* México: Fondo de Cultura Económica—Instituto Tecnológico Autónomo de México. 1997.

Cossman, Brenda, and Ratna Kapur. *Secularism's Law Sigh? Hindutva and the (Mis)Rule of Law.* 1999.

Costanza, R. "Visions of Alternative (Unpredictable) Futures and Their Use in Policy Analysis." *Conservation Ecology* 4(1) (2000).

Costello, Steven. "Must Russia Return the Artwork Stolen from Germany during World War II?" 4 *ILSA Journal of International & Comparative Law.* Fall 1997.

Crenshaw, Kimberlé. *Demarginalizing the Intersection of Race and Sex: A Black Feminist Critique of Antidiscrimination Doctrine, Feminist Theory and Antiracist Politics.* U. Chi. Legal F. 1989.

———. *Mapping the Margins: Intersectionality, Identity Politics, and Violence Against Women of Color,* 43 Stan. L. Rev. 1991.

Dahl, Robert A. *Democracy and Its Critics.* 1989

al-Dakhil, Sa'id Fayez. *Mawsu'at Fiqh 'A'ishah Um al-Mu'mineen* [The Encyclopedia of the Jurisprudence of 'A'ishah, the Mother of the Believers]. Dar al-Nafa'is: Beirut, 1993.

Daly, Erin. *Reconsidering Abortion Law: Liberty, Equality, and the New Rhetoric of Planned Parenthood v. Casey.* 45 Am. U. L. Rev. 1995.

Daniels, Robert V. *Russia's Transformation: Snapshot of a Crumbling System.* Lanham, Md.: Rowman & Littlefield, 1998.

al-Dardir, Abu al-Barakat. 1 *Al-Sharh al-Saghir* [The Little Exegesis]. Dar al-Ma'arif: Cairo, reprint n.d.

Davis, Adrienne D. *The Private Law of Race and Sex: An Antebellum Perspective.* 51 Stan. L. Rev. 1999.

Davis, David Brion. *The Problem of Slavery in the Age of Revolution, 1770–1823.* 1975.

Davis, Peggy Cooper. *Neglected Stories and the Lawfulness of Roe v. Wade.* 28 Harv. C.R.-C.L. L. Rev. 1993.

De Funis v. Sweatt, in *Equality and Preferential Treatment.* Cohen, Nagel, and Scanlon.

de Silva, K. M. *Managing Ethnic Tensions in Multiethnic Societies.* University Press of America, 1986.

Decker, Cathleen. "Parents Tell of Decisions, Struggles in Child-Rearing," *Los Angeles Times.* June 13, 1999.

Deleuze, Gilles, and Felix Guattari. *Anti-Oedipus: Capitalism and Schizophrenia.* Trans. Robert Hurley and Helen R. Lane. Minneapolis: University of Minnesota Press, 1983.

della Porta, Donatella, and Alberto Vannucci. "The 'Perverse Effects' of Political Corruption." 45 *Political Studies.* (1997).

Deng, Francis M. *War of Visions: Conflicts of Identities in the Sudan.* Washington, D.C.: Brookings Institution Press, 1995.

Depta, Sylvia L. "Twice Saved or Twice Stolen? The Trophy Art Tug-of-War Between Russia and Germany." 10 *Temple International and Comparative Law Journal.* Fall 1996.

Descartes, René. *Meditations on the First Philosophy.* Trans. J. Veitch. London: Dent [Everyman's Library], 1912.

Dezalay, Yves, and Bryant Garth. *Dealing in Virtue: International Commercial Arbitration and the Construction of a Transnational Legal Order.* 1996.

al-Dijwi, Muhammad. *Al-Ahwal al-Shakhsiyah li al-Masryin al-Muslimin.* Dar al-Nashr li al-Jami'at al-Masriyah: Cairo, 1969.

Dilthey, W. *Die Philosophie des Lebens.* Stuttgart: B.G. Teubner, 1961.

al-Din, Muhammad Mahdi Shams. *Ahliat al-Mar'ah li Tawalli al-Sultah* [The Eligibility of Women to Assume Power]. Al-Mu'assasah al-Duwaliyah li al-Dirasaat wa al-Nashr: Beirut, 1995.

Dispute Settlement Prospects in the Law of the Sea. 44 ICLQ. 1995.

Dollar, David, and Aart Kraay. "Growth Is Good for the Poor." Working paper, World Bank, March 2000.

Donoho, Douglas Lee. *Evolution or Expediency: The United Nations Response to the Disruption of Democracy.* 29 Cornell Int'l L. J. (1996)

Dowd, Maureen. "Liberties." *New York Times.* Oct. 17, 1999.

Duffy, Ann. "The Feminist Challenge: Knowing and Ending the Violence," in *Feminist Issues: Race, Class, and Sexuality.* Ed. Nancy Mandel. 1998.

Duguit, Leon. *Las Transformaciones generales del derecho privado desde el Código Napoleón.* Madrid: Librería de Francisco Beltrán. 1912

Dunne, Michael. *The United States and the World Court, 1920–1935.* 1988.

Durkheim, Emile. *The Division of Labor in Society.* Trans. George Simpson. Free Press, 1933.

al-Dusuqi, Muhammad. *Al-Usra fi al-Tashri' al-Islami* [The Family in Islamic Legislation]. Dar al-Thaqafah: Doha, 1995.

Editorial Comment: The American Theory of International Arbitration. 2 AJIL. 1908.

Editorial Comment: Treaties of Arbitration since the First Hague Conference. 2 AJIL. 1908.

El-Awa. *On the Political System of the Islamic State.* 1980.

Eliot, T. S. *The Complete Poems and Plays 1909–1950.* 1962.

Ellettronica Sicula S.p.A. (ELSI). ICJ Reports. 1989.

Ely, John Hart. *The Wages of Crying Wolf: A Comment on Roe v. Wade.* 82 Yale L. J. 1973.

Entrikin, J. Nicholas. "Political Community, Identity and Cosmopolitan Place," in *International Sociology.* Vol. 14, Number 3. 1999.

Enzensberger, Hans Magnus. *Civil War.* London: Granta Books, 1994.

"EPA Emphasis on Stakeholder Process Exasperates Risk Experts." Risk Policy Report Volume 6, Number 10. October 16, 1998.

Epstein, Cynthia Fuchs. "The Cultural Perspective and the Study of Work," in *The Nature of Work.* Ed. Kai Erikson and Steven Peter. 1990.

Epstein, Deborah. *Redefining the State's Response to Domestic Violence: Past Victories and Future Challenges.* Geo. J. of Gender and the Law. Summer 1999.

Epstein, Richard A. *Unconstitutional Conditions, State Power, and the Limits of Consent.* 102 Harvard L. Rev. (1987): 4, 83.

Errera, Roger. "In Defence of Civility: Racial Incitement and Group Libel in French Law," in *Striking a Balance: Hate Speech, Freedom of Expression and Non-Discrimination.* Ed. S. Coliver. London: Article 19, 1992.

Eskridge Jr., William N., and John Ferejohn. "Politics, Interpretation, and the Rule of Law," in *The Rule of Law.* Ed. Ian Shapiro. 1994.

Evans, Sara. *Personal Politics: The Roots of Women's Liberation in the Civil Rights Movement and the New Left.* 1979.

Eyffinger, Arthur. *The 1899 Hague Peace Conference.* 1999.

Falk, Richard. *On Human Governance: Towards a New Global Politics.* 1995.

Fallos de la Corte Suprema de Justicia de la Nación, Tomo 309. Vols. 1 and 2. Buenos Aires: Supreme Court, 1988.

Faludi, Susan. *Backlash: The Undeclared War Against American Women.* 1991.

al-Faruqi, Maysam. "Women's Self Identity in the Qur'an and Islamic Law," in *Windows of Faith.* Ed. Gisela Webb. 2000.

Favoreu-Loïc Philip, Louis. *Les grandes décisions du Conseil constitutionnel.* 7th ed. Paris: Sirey, 1993.

Feinerman, James V., and Koichiro Fujikura. "Japan: Consensus-Based Compliance," in *Engaging Countries: Strengthening Compliance with International Environmental Accords.* Ed. Edith Brown Weiss and Harold K. Jacobson. Cambridge: MIT Press, 1998.

Feldblum, Miriam. "Paradoxes of Ethnic Politics: The Case of Franco-Maghrebis in France," 16:1 *Ethnic and Racial Studies* 52

Ferencz, Benjamin B. *International Criminal Courts: The Legacy of Nuremberg.* 10 Pace Int'l L. Rev. 1998.

Filmer, Robert. *The Anarchy of a Limited or Mixed Monarchy.* 1648.

Fiss, Owen. *The Irony of Free Speech.* Cambridge: Harvard University Press, 1996.

————. *State Activism and State Censorship.* 100 Yale L. J. (1991): 2087, 2104–2105.

Fitzpatrick, Joan, and Alice Miller. *International Standards on the Death Penalty: Shifting Discourse.* 19 Brooklyn J. of Int'l L. 1993.

Flemming, Denna Frank. *The United States and the World Court 1920–1966.* 1968.

Foucault, Michel. *The Order of Things: An Archaeology of the Human Sciences.* London: Tavistock Publications, 1970.

Franck, Thomas M. *Fairness in International Law and Institutions.* 1995.

————. *The Power of Legitimacy Among Nations.* 1990.

Franke, Katherine M. *What's Wrong With Sexual Harassment?* 49 Stan. L. Rev. 1997.

Fredrickson, George. "Mosaics and Melting Pots," *Dissent.* Summer 1999.

Fredrickson, George M. *The Black Image in the White Mind: The Debate on Afro-American Character and Destiny, 1817–1914.* 1987.

Friedan, Betty. *Newsweek.* September 4, 1995.

Friedman, Jane. "As Islamic Fundamentalism Rises in Egypt, Government Feels Heat." *Christian Science Monitor.* June 14, 1985.

Friedman, M. *Capitalism and Freedom.* 1962.

Friedman. Thomas. *The Lexus and the Olive Tree.* 1999.

Fukuyama, Francis. *The End of History and The Last Man.* New York: Free Press, 1991.

Garrow, David J. *Abortion Before and After Roe v. Wade: An Historical Perspective.* 62 Albany L. Rev. 1999.

Gauch, Sarah. "Opening Door to the Present Stirs Uproar." *Chicago Tribune.* Aug. 6, 1995.

Geertz, Clifford. *After the Fact: Two Countries, Four Decades, One Anthropologist.* 1995.

————. *The Interpretation of Cultures.* 1973

Ghai, Y. "Rights, Social Justice, and Globalization in East Asia," in *The East Asian Challenge for Human Rights.* Ed. J. Bauer and D. Bell. Cambridge: Cambridge University Press, 1999.

Ghandour, Ahmad. *Al-Ahwal al-Shakhsiyah fi al-Tashri' al-Islami.* Jami'at al-Kuwait Press: Kuwait, 1972.

al-Ghazali, Abu Hamid. *Ihya' 'Ulum al-Din* [Reviving Religious Sciences]. Matba'at Mustafa al-Babi al-Halabi: Cairo, reprint 1939.

Gilroy, Paul. "The End of Anti-Racism," in *Race, Culture, and Difference.* Ed. J. Donald and Ali Rattansi. London: Sage, 1992.

Ginsburg, Faye. *Contested Lives: The Abortion Debate in an American Community.* 1989.

Ginsburg, Ruth Bader. *Some Thoughts on Autonomy and Equality in Relation to Roe v. Wade.* 63 N.C. L. Rev. 1985.

"Global Monoculture." *New York Times.* November 15, 1999.

"Globalization v. Nature." *New York Times.* November 22, 1999.

Goldstein, Robert J. *Reading Casey: Structuring the Woman's Decisionmaking Process.* 4 Wm. & Mary Bill of Rights J. 1996.

Gómez, Laura E. *Misconceiving Mothers: Legislators, Prosecutors, and the Politics of Prenatal Drug Exposure.* 1997.

Gottselig, Glenn. *Canada and Culture: Can Current Cultural Policies Be Sustained in the Global Trade Regime?* LL.M. thesis, University of Toronto Faculty of Law, 1999.

Gonzales, David. "A Killing Shocks Jamaicans." *New York Times.* Oct. 18, 1999.

Gourevitch, Philip. *We Wish to Inform You that Tomorrow We Will Be Killed with Our Families.* New York: Farrar, Straus and Giroux, 1998.

Great Patriotic War of the Soviet Union 1941–1945: A General Outline. Moscow: Progress Publishers, 1974.

Greig, D. W. *Nicaragua and the United States: Confrontation over the Jurisdiction of the International Court.* 62 British Year Book of International Law. 1991.

Grewal, Inderpal. "Women's Rights as Human Rights: Feminist Practices, Global Feminism, and Human Rights Regimes in Transnationality," 3:3 *Citizenship Studies.* 1999.

Gross, Leo, ed. *The Future of the International Court of Justice.* 1976.

Guillaume, Gilbert. *The Future of the International Judicial Institutions.* 44 International and Comparative Law Quarterly. 1995.

Habermas, Jurgen. *The Theory of Communicative Action.* Boston: Beacon Press, 1981.

Habib, Kamal. *Akthar Min Thalathin 'Aliman Azhariyan Minhum A'dha' bimajma' al-Buhuth al-Islamiyah Yarfudun Mashru' Qanun al-Ahwal al-Shakhsiyah* (More Than Thirty Azhari Scholars Among Them Members of the Islamic Research Council Reject the Draft Personal Status Law). Al-Sha'b. Jan. 18, 2000.

al-Halim Abu Shuqqah, Abd. 1 *Tahrir al-Mar'ah fi 'Asr al-Risalah* [Liberation of Women in Early Islam]. Dar al-Qalam: Kuwait 1990.

Halley, Janet E. *Introduction to Symposium, Intersections: Sexuality, Cultural Tradition, and the Law.* 8 Yale J. L. & Humanities. 1996.

Hamidullah, Muhammad. *Majmu'at al-Watha'iq al-Siyasiyah* [Collection of Political Documents]. Dar al-Nafa'is: Beirut, 1987.

Hampton, Jean. "Democracy and the Rule of Law," in *The Rule of Law.* Ed. Ian Shapiro. 1994.

Hardin, Garrett. "Living on a Lifeboat." *Bioscience* 24 (1974).

———. "The Tragedy of the Commons." *Science* 162 (1968).

Hardwick, Elizabeth. "Domestic Manners." *Daedalus.* Vol 107. 1978.

Harris, Angela. *Race and Essentialism in Feminist Legal Theory.* 42 Stan. L. Rev. 1990.

Hartog, Hendrik. "The Constitution of Aspiration and 'The Rights That Belong to Us All,'" 74 *J. Am. Hist.* 1987.

Hassan, Ali Ibrahim. *Nisa' Lahunna fi al-Tarikh al-Islami Nasib* [Women Who Have a Share in Islamic History]. Maktabat al-Nahdhah al-Masriyah: Cairo, 1950.

Hays, Sharon. *The Cultural Contradictions of Mothering.* 1996.

Heidegger, Martin. *Wegmarken.* Frankfurt am Main: Vittorio Klostermann, 1967.

Held, David. *Democracy and the Global Order: From the Modern State to Cosmopolitan Governance.* Cambridge: Polity Press, 1995.

Held, D., et al., ed. *Global Transformations: Politics, Economics, and Culture.* Palo Alto: Stanford University Press, 1999.

Henry, Frances, Carol Tator, Winston Mattis, and Tim Rees, eds. *The Colour of Democracy: Racism in Canadian Society.* Toronto: Harcourt Brace.

Hershey. *Convention for the Peaceful Adjustment of International Differences.* 2 AJIL. 1908.

al-Hibri, Azizah Y. *Islam, Law and Custom,* 12 Am. U. J. Int'l L. & Pol'y. 1997.

———. *Islamic and American Constitutional Law: Borrowing Possibilities Or a History of Borrowing.* 1 Univ. of Penn. J. Const. L. 1999.

———. *Islamic Constitutionalism and the Concept of Democracy.* 24 Case W. Res. J. Int'l L. 1992.

———. "Islamic Law and Muslim Women in America," in *One Nation Under God?* 1999.

———. *Legal Reform: Reviving Human Rights in the Muslim World.* 20 Harv. Int'l L.J. 1998.

———. "Marriage Laws in Muslim Countries, Family Law and Gender Bias." 4 *International Review of Comparative Public Policies.* 1992.

Hilal, Abdallah. *Hawl al-Qanun al-Masluq li al-Ahwal al-Shakhsiyah* (On the Rushed Law of Personal Status). Al-Sha'b. Jan. 28, 2000.

Hirschman, Albert O. *A Propensity to Self-Subversion.* 1995.

Hisham, Ibn. *Al-Sirah al-Nabawiyyah* [The Prophetic Biography]. Dar al-Fikr: Amman, reprint n.d.

Hobsbawn, E. *Nations and Nationalism Since 1780.* Cambridge: Cambridge University Press, 1990.

Hochschild, Arlie. "The Fractured Family." *The American Prospect.* Summer 1991.

Hochschild, Arlie, and Anne Machung. *The Second Shift: Working Parents and the Revolution at Home.* 1989.

Hodkinson, Keith. *Muslim Family Law: A Source Book.* 1984.

Hoffman, Stanley. "Reflections on the Nation-State in Western Europe Today," 21 *Journal of Common Market Studies* (1983): 1–2, 21.

Holland, M. *The European Community and South Africa: European Political Cooperation Under Strain.* 1988.

Holmes, [Jr.] Oliver Wendell. *Collected Legal Papers.* 1952.

Holmes, Stephen. "Superpresidentialism and Its Problems." *East European Constitutional Review.* Fall 1993–winter 1994.

Horowitz, Donald. *Ethnic Groups in Conflict.* Berkeley: University of California Press, 1985.

Howland, Courtney, ed. "The Two Faces of Secularism and Women's Rights in India," in *Religion and Fundamentalism.* 1999.

Howse, Robert. *The Legitimacy of the World Trade Organization,* University of Michigan L. Rev. (forthcoming).

Howse, Robert, and Michael Trebilcock. "The Fair Trade-Free Trade Debate: Trade, Labour, and the Environment," (1996) 16 *International Review of Law and Economics* 61.

Hudson, Manley O. *The United States Senate and the World Court.* 29 AJIL. 1935.

Hufbauer Gary, and Jeffrey Schott. *NAFTA: An Assessment.* Washington, D.C.: Institute for International Economics, 1993.

Hull, Wm. I. *Obligatory Arbitration and the Hague Conferences.* 2 AJIL. 1908.

"A Hundred Years of Fortitude," *The Economist.* Nov. 27, 1999.

al-Hussein bin Muslim, Abu. 6 *Sahih Muslim bi Sharh al-Nawawi* [The True Statements of the Prophet with Exegesis by al-Nawawi].

Hussein, Majdi Ahmad. *Al-Sayyed Ra'is Majlis al-Sha'b: Itha Kunta Takh.sha allah fala Tasluq al-Qanun* (Head of the Parliament: If You Fear

God, Do Not Rush the Law). Al-Sha'b. Jan. 11, 2000.

Hyland, James L. *Democratic Theory: the Philosophical Foundations.* 1995.

ICJ Yearbook 1984–1985.

Iglesias, Elizabeth M. *Structure of Subordination: Women of Color at the Intersection of Title VII and the NLRA. Not!.* 28 Harv. C.R.-C.L. L. Rev. 1993.

Ignatieff, Michael. *Blood and Belonging: Journeys into New Nationalism.* London: Vintage, 1994.

———. "Nationalism and the Narcissism of Minor Differences," in *Theorizing Nationalism.* Ed. Ronald Beiner. New York: State University of New York Press, 1999.

———. *Warrior's Honour.* Toronto: Penguin Books, 1998.

Ikemoto, Lisa C. *The Code of Perfect Pregnancy: At the Intersection of the Ideology of Motherhood, the Practice of Defaulting to Science, and the Interventionist Mindset of Law.* 53 Ohio St. L. J. 1992.

IMF. *The Role of the IMF in Governance Issues: Guidance Note.* Approved by the Executive Board, 25 July 1997.

"Invisible Government." *New York Times.* November 29, 1999.

IUCN, UNEP and WWF. *Caring for the Earth: A Strategy for Sustainable Living.* Gland, 1991.

IUCN, UNEP and WWF. *World Conservation Strategy: Living Resource Conservation for Sustainable Development.* Gland, Nairobi, Washington, 1980.

Jabr, Sa'di Hussein Ali. *Fiqh al-Imam Abi Thawr* [The Jurisprudence of Imam Abi Thawr]. Dar al-Furqan: Beirut, 1983.

Jackson, Robert H. *The Case Against the Nazi War Criminals.* 1946.

Jackson, Robert Max. *Destined for Equality: The Inevitable Rise of Women's Status.* 1998.

Jacobson, Neil S., and John M. Gottman. *When Men Batter Women: New Insights into Ending Abusive Relationships.* 1998.

Al-Jaziri, Abdul Rahman. *Kitab al-Fiqh 'ala al-Mathahib al-Arba'ah.* Dar Ihya' 'Ulum al-Din: Beirut, 1969.

Jennings, Ivor. *The Constitution of Ceylon.* Oxford University Press, 1953.

Johnson, Paul. "Laying Down the Law." *Wall Street Journal.* March 10, 1999.

Jordan, Winthrop D. *White Over Black: American Attitudes Toward the Negro, 1550–1812.* 1968.

Jorstad, Erling. *The Politics of Moralism: The New Christian Right in American Life.* 1981.

Joyce, Michael S., and William A. Schambra. "A New Citizenship, A New Life," in *The New Promise of American Life.* Ed. Chester E. Finn Jr. 1995.

Jupp, James. *Sri Lanka: A Third World Democracy.* London: Frank Cass, 1978.

"Just Let Her Fly." *Discover Magazine.* April 1999.

Justice Delayed: The Russian Constitutional Court and Human Rights. New York: Lawyers Committee for Human Rights, 1995.

Kagarlitsky, Boris. *Square Wheels: How Russian Democracy Got Derailed.* New York: Monthly Review Press, 1994.

Kah.halah, Umar. 2 *A'lam al-Nisa'* [Famous Women]. Mu'assasat al-Risalah: Beirut, 1977.

Kahn, Paul. *The Cultural Study of Law: Reconstructing Legal Scholarship.* Chicago: University of Chicago Press, 1999.

Kakar, Sudhir. *The Colors of Violence.* Chicago: University of Chicago Press, 1996.

Kamali, Muhammad Hashim. *Principles of Islamic Jurisprudence.* 1991.

Kant, Immanuel. *Critique of Pure Reason.* Trans. Norman Kemp Smith. London, 1929.

———. "Idea for a Universal History with a Cosmopolitan Purpose" and "Perpetual Peace: A Philosophical Sketch," in *Kant's Political Writings.* Ed. H. Reiss, trans. H. B. Nisbet. Cambridge: Cambridge University Press, 1970.

———. *The Philosophy of Kant: Kant's Moral and Political Writings.* Ed. Carl J. Friedrich. 1949.

Kapur, Ratna. *From Human Rights to Human Tragedy: Accountability of Multinational Corporations for International Human Rights Violations.* 10:1 Boston College Third World L. J. Winter 1990.

———. *The Fundamentalist Face of Secularism and Women's Rights in India.* Cleveland State Law Rev. forthcoming, 2000.

———. "The Profanity of Prudery: The Moral Face of Obscenity Law in India," *Women's Cultural Review.* Oxford University Press, 1997.

———. "Secularism: A Comparative Perspective," in *Comparative Constitutional Law.* Ed. Mark Tushnet and Vicki Jackson. forthcoming, 2000.

———. "Who Draws the Line? Contemporary Issues of Speech and Censorship in India," *Economic and Political Weekly.* WS15–30 April 20–27, 1996.

Kapur, Ratna, and Brenda Cossman. *Subversive Sites: Feminist Engagements with Law in India.* 1996.

al-Karim Shahbun, Abd. 1 *Sharh Mudawwanat al-Ahwal al-Shakhsiyah al-Maghribiyah* [Exegesis of Moroccan Personal Status Law]. Maktabat al-Ma'arif: Rabat, 1987?.

Karst, Kenneth L. *Boundaries and Reasons: Freedom of Expression and the Subordination of Groups.* U. Ill. L. Rev. 1990.

———. *Law's Promise, Law's Expression: Visions of Power in the Politics of Gender, Race, and Religion.* 1993.

———. *Myths of Identity: Individual and Group Portraits of Race and Sexual Orientation.* 43 UCLA L. Rev. 1995.

———. *The Pursuit of Manhood and the Desegregation of the Armed Forces.* 38 UCLA L. Rev. 1991.

———. *The Supreme Court, 1976 Term—Foreword: Equal Citizenship Under the Fourteenth Amendment.* 97 Harv. L. Rev. 1977.

Kathir, Ibn. *Al-Bidayah wa al-Nihayah* [The Beginning and the End]. Maktabat al-Ma'arif: Beirut, reprint 1974.

Kearney, R. N. *Communalism and the Language in the Politics of Ceylon.* Durham: Duke University Press, 1967.

Kennan, George F. *Memoirs, 1925–1950.* Boston: Little, Brown, 1967.

Kessler-Ross, Alice. *Out to Work: A History of Wage-Earning Women in the United States.* 1982.

Khalid, Hassan. *Mujtama' Al-Madinah* [The Society of Madinah]. Dar al-Nahdah al- 'Arabiyah: Beirut, 1886.

al-Khamlishi. *Wijhat Nathar* [A Point of View]. Dar Nashr al-Ma'rifah. 1988.

al-Khamlishi, Ahmad. 1 *Al-Ta'liq 'Ala Qanun al-Ahwal al-Shakhsiyyah* [Commentary on Personal Status Code]. Maktabat al-Ma'arif: Rabat, 1987.

Kilson, Martin, and Mitchell Cohen. "Introduction to Africa Today: Crisis and Change." *Dissent.* Summer 1992.

Kinzer, Stephen. "Turkey's Highest-Ranking Judge is Likely to Be Next President." *New York Times.* April 26, 2000.

Kirisci, Kemal, and Gareth M. Winrow. *The Kurdish Question and Turkey: An Example of a Trans-State Ethnic Conflict.* London: Frank Cass, 1997.

Kis, Janos. *Az állam semlegessége.* (The neutrality of the state). Budapest: Atlantisz, 1997.

Kline, William. *Trade and Economic Distribution.* Washington, D.C.: Institute for International Economics, 1997.

Knight, Trevor. *The Dual Nature of Cultural Products: An Analysis of the World Trade Organization's Decisions Regarding Canadian Periodicals.* (1999) 57 University of Toronto Faculty of Law Review 165.

Kohan, John. "What Would Lenin Say?" *Time.* December 20, 1993.

Kommentar zum Grundgesetz fuer die Bundesrepublik Deutschland. 2d ed. Vol.1. Neuwied: Luchterland, 1989.

Koonz, Claudia. *Mothers in the Fatherland.* New York: St. Martins Press, 1987.

Koskenniemi, Martti. "The Effect of Rights on Political Culture," in *The EU and Human Rights.* Ed. P. Alston, M. Bustelo, and J. Heenan. 1999.

Krasner, Stephen. *Sovereignty: Organized Hypocrisy.* Princeton: Princeton University Press, 1999.

Krugman, Paul. "Competitiveness: A Dangerous Obsession," in *Pop Internationalism.* Cambridge: MIT Press, April 1997.

Kuper, Leo. *Genocide.* New York: Penguin, 1981.

Kymlicka, Will. *Multicultural Citizenship: A Liberal Theory of Minority Rights,* 1995.

LaGrand (Germany v. U.S.). Provisional Measures, ICJ Reports.

Land and Maritime Boundary between Cameroon and Nigeria. Preliminary Objections, ICJ Reports. 1998.

Laumann, Edward O., John H. Gagnon, Robert T. Michael, and Stuart Michaels. *The Social Organization of Sexuality.* 1994.

Lawson, Frederick. *The Rational Strength of English Law.* London: Steven and Sons Limited, 1951.

Lazreg, Marnia. *The Eloquence of Silence: Algerian Women in Question.* 1994.

Legality of the Threat or Use of Nuclear Weapons. Advisory Opinion, ICJ Reports. 1996.

Legality of Use of Force, Request for the Indication of Provisional Measures. 38 ILM. 1999.

Lerner, Gerda. *The Creation of Patriarchy.* 1986.

Lesch, Ann, and Stephen Wondu. *The Battle for Peace in the Sudan: An Analysis of the Abuja Conference, 1992–1993.* Lanham, Md.: University Press of America, 2000.

Lester, Gillian. *Careers and Contingency.* 51 Stan. L. Rev. 1998.

Letter of the Honorable Elihu Root to Senator Henry Cabot Lodge regarding the Covenant of the League of Nations, 19 June 1919. 13 AJIL. 1919.

Levit, Nancy. *Feminism for Men: Legal Ideology and the Construction of Maleness.* 43 UCLA L. Rev. 1996.

Li, P. S., ed. *Race and Ethnic Relations in Canada.* Toronto: Oxford University Press, 1990.

Lien, Molly Warner. "Red Star Trek: Seeking a Role for Constitutional Law in Soviet Disunion," 30 *Stanford Journal of International Law.* (1994).

Lijphart, Arend. *Democracy in Plural Societies.* New Haven: Yale University Press, 1977.

Littleton, Christine A. *Reconstructing Sexual Equality.* 75 Calif. L. Rev. 1987.

———. *Women's Experiences and the Problem of Transition: Perspectives on Male Battering of Women.* 1989 U. Chi. Legal F.

LJM. *Constitutional Government in Sri Lanka, 1796–1977.* Colombo: Lake House, 1984.

Lowe, Vaughan, and Malgosia Fitzmaurice, ed. *Fifty Years of the International Court of Justice: Essays in Honour of Sir Robert Jennings.* 1996.

Luhmann, Niklas. *Die Gesellschaft der Gesellschaft.* 1997.

Luker, Kristin. *Abortion and the Politics of Motherhood.* 1984.

———. "Dubious Conceptions: The Controversy Over Teen Pregnancy." *The American Prospect.* Spring 1991.

Lutz, Ellen L. *Strengthening Core Values in the Americas: Regional Commitment to Democracy and the Protection of Human Rights.* 19 Hous. J. Int'l L. (1997): 643, 649–50.

MacKinnon, Catharine A. "Feminism, Marxism, Method, and the State: An Agenda for Theory," in *Feminist Theory: A Critique of Ideology.* 1982.

———. *Feminism Unmodified: Discourses on Life and Law.* 1987.

Mahmassani, Subhi. *Al-Awda' al-Tashri'yah fi al-Duwal al-'Arabiyah* (Legal Systems in the Arab States). Dar al-'Ilm li al-Malayin: Beirut 1965.

Mahmassani, Subhi. *Falsafat al-Tashri' fi al-Islam* [The Philosophy of Legislation in Islam]. Dar al-'Ilm li al-Malayin: Beirut, 1975.

Mahmud, Tayyab. *Migration, Identity, and the Colonial Encounter,* 76:3 Oregon L. R. (Fall 1997):633.

Mahoney, Martha R. *Legal Images of Battered Women: Redefining the Issue of Separation.* 90 Mich. L. Rev. 1991.

Malanczuk, P. *Akehurst's Modern Introduction to International Law* 7th ed. 1997.

Mann, Michael. "Has Globalization Ended the Rise and Rise of the Nation-State?" in *Review of International Political Economy* 4 (autumn): 472–976. 1997.

Marcuse, Herbert. *One Dimensional Man: Studies in the Ideology of Advanced Industrial Society.* London: Routledge & Kegan Paul, 1964.

Maritime Delimitiation and Territorial Questions Between Qatar and Bahrein. Jurisdiction and Admissibility, ICJ Reports. 1995.

Marsot, Afaf. "The Revolutionary Gentlewomen of Egypt," in *Women in the Muslim World.* Ed. Lois Beck and Nikki Keddie. 1978.

Masaryk, Thomas G. *The Spirit of Russia.* Volume 1. London: George Allen and Unwin, New York: Macmillan, 1919.

Maunz, Theodor. Günter Dürig, *Grundgesetz-Kommentar.* München: Beck, 1993.

McAdams, A. James, ed. *Transitional Justice and the Rule of Law in New Democracies.* 1997.

McCaffery, Edward J. *Equality, of the Right Sort.* 6 UCLA Women's L. J. 1996.

———. *Taxing Women.* 1997.

McClain, Linda C. *"Irresponsible" Reproduction.* 47 Hastings L. J. 1996.

Meltz, Robert, Dwight H. Merriman, and Richard M. Frank. *The Takings Issue: Constitutional Limits on Land Use Control and Environmental Regulation.* 1999.

MENA News Agency. "President's Aid Says NGOs Should Not Be Used as Pretext to Interfere." BBC Worldwide Monitoring. Feb. 6, 2000.

Menn, Joseph. "First Woman Named to Lead Blue-Chip Firm." *Los Angles Times.* July 20, 1999.

Merkl, Peter H., and Leonard Weinberg eds. *Encounters with the Contemporary Radical Right.* Boulder: Westview Press, 1993.

Meron, Theodor. *International Criminalization of Internal Atrocities.* 89 Am. J. Int'l L. 1995.

Merrills, J. G. *International Dispute Settlement.* 3rd ed. 1998.

———. *The Optional Clause Revisited.* 64 British Year Book of International Law. 1993.

Michael, Robert T., John H. Gagnon, Edward O. Laumann, and Gina Kolata. *Sex in America.* 1994.

Military and Paramilitary Activities in and against Nicaragua. Jurisdiction and Admissibility, ICJ Reports. 1984.

Military and Paramilitary Activities in and against Nicaragua. Merits, ICJ Reports. 1986.

Military and Paramilitary Activities in and against Nicaragua. ICJ Reports. 1986.

Miller, David. *On Nationality.* Oxford: Clarendon Press, 1995.

Mills, Linda G. *Killing Her Softly: Intimate Abuse and the Violence of State Intervention.* 113 Harv. L. Rev. 1999.

Milner-Gulland, Robin. *The Russians.* Malden, Mass.: Blackwell Publishers, 1997.

Minear, Richard H. "The Individual, the State, and the Tokyo Trials," in *The Tokyo War Crimes Trials.* Ed. Chihiro Hosoya et al. Tokyo: Kodansha, 1986.

Minow, Martha. *Between Vengence and Forgiveness: Facing History After Genocide and Mass Violence.* 1998.

Mishel, Lawrence, Jared Bernstein, and John Schmitt. *The State of Working America 1998–99.* 1999.

Mittelman, J. *The Globalization Syndrome: Transformation and Resistance.* Princeton: Princeton University Press, 2000.

Modern Day Czar? Presidential Power and Human Rights in the Russian Federation, A. New York: Lawyers Committee for Human Rights, 1995.

Montesquieu, [C-L.de Secondat, Baron de]. *Lettres persanes,* letter XCIV. Paris: Librairie Gallimard [Pléiade], 1949.

Moodley, Kogila. "Antiracist Education Through Political Literacy: The Case of Canada," in *Critical Multiculturalism.* Ed. Stephen May. London: Falmer Press, 1999.

Moodley, Kogila, ed. *Beyond Multicultural Education.* Calgary: Detselig, 1992.

Moore John Bassett. *History and Digest of the International Arbitrations to which the United States Has Been a Party.* 1898.

Moore, John Bassett, ed. *Digest of International Law.* 1906.

More, Thomas. *Utopia.*

Moreno Ocampo, Luis. *Cuando el poder perdío el juicio.* Buenos Aires: Editorial Planeta, 1996.

Morison, White, and Van Velsor. *Breaking the Glass Ceiling.* 1987.

Mortimer, Edward. *Faith and Power: the Politics of Islam.* New York, Vintage Books, 1982.

Moruzzi, Norma Claire. "A Problem with Head Scarves: Contemporary Complexities of Political and Social Identity," 22:4 *Political Theory* 653–72.

Mössner, Jörg Manfred. *Hague Peace Conferences of 1899 and 1907,* II. Encyclopedia of Public International Law. 1995.

Movchan, Ya. I., and Yu. R. Shelyag-Sosonko, ed. *National Report of Ukraine on Conservation of Biological Diversity.* Kyiv: MEP/Prospect Ltd., 1997.

Mubayad, Muhammad Sa'id. *Mawsu'at Hayat al-Sahabiyat* [Encyclopedia of Female Companions' Biographies]. Maktabat al-Ghazali: Damascus, 1990.

Muller, A. S., D. Raič, and J. M. Thuránszky, ed. *The International Court of Justice: Its Future Role after Fifty Years.* 1997.

Multilateral Treaties Deposited with the Secretary-General, Status as at April 30, 1999, UN Doc. ST/LEG/SER.E/17. 1999.

Myerowitz, Elissa S. "Protecting Cultural Property During a Time of War: Why Russia Should Return Nazi-Looted Art." 20 *Fordham International Law Journal.* June 1997.

Narayan, Uma. "Cross-Cultural Connections, Border-Crossings, and 'Death by Culture,'" in *Dislocating Cultures.* 1997.

Nasr, Seif. *Majlis al-Sha'b Yabda' Ghadan Munaqashat Qanun al-Ahwal al-Shakhsiyah* (Parliament Commences Discussion Tomorrow of the Personal Status Law). Al-Ahram. Jan. 15, 2000.

Nasr, Seyyed Hossien. *An Introduction to Islamic Cosmological Doctrines.* 1964.

National Science Foundation, P. B. Thompson, ed. *Workshop on Science, Technology, and Democracy: Research on Issues of Governance and Change.* Washington, D.C., 1994.

Neier, Aryeh. *War Crimes: Brutality, Genocide, Terror, and the Struggle for Justice.* New York: Times books, 1998.

Nelson Robert L., and William P. Bridges. *Legalizing Gender Inequality: Courts, Markets, and Unequal Pay for Women in America.* 1999.

Nicholas, Lynn H. *The Rape of Europa: The Fate of Europe's Treasures in the Third Reich and the Second World War.* New York: Alfred A. Knopf, 1994.

1976 Digest of the United States Practice in International Law.

Niño, Carlos. *Radical Evil on Trial.* New Haven: Yale University Press, 1996.

Nordstrom, Hikan, and Scott Vaughan. *Trade and Environment.* WTO Special Studies 4, October 1999.

North, Douglass, and Robert Thomas. *The Rise of the Western World.* Cambridge University Press, 1973.

Nuclear Tests (Australia v. France). ICJ Reports. 1974.

Nuclear Tests (New Zealand v. France). ICJ Reports. 1974.

Nunca Más: Informe de la Comisión Nacional sobre la Desaparición de Personas. Buenos Aires: Eudeba, 1984.

Nussbaum, Martha. *Sex and Social Justice.* 1999.

O'Connor, Sandra Day. "Federalism of Free Nations," in *International Law Decisions in National Courts.* Ed. Thomas M. Franck and Gregory H. Fox. 1996.

Oil Platforms. Preliminary Objection, ICJ Reports. 1996.

Olson, Gary A. and Lynn Worsham. "Staging the Politics of Difference: Homi Bhabha's Critical Literacy," in *Race, Rhetoric, and the Postcolonial.* Ed. Gary A. Olson and Lynn Worsham. 1999.

Omolade, Barbara "Hearts of Darkness," in Ann Snitow, Christine Stanstell, and Sharon Thompson. *Powers of Desire: The Politics of Sexuality.* 1983.

Onishi, Norimitsu. "Deep Political and Religious Rifts Disrupt the Harmony of Nigerian Towns." *New York Times.* March 26, 2000.

———. "New Strife Tests Nigeria's Fragile Democracy." *New York Times.* March 15, 2000.

Ontiveros, María L. *Three Perspectives on Workplace Harassment of Women of Color.* 23 Golden Gate U. L. Rev. 1993.

Orentlicher, Diane F. *International Criminal Law and the Cambodian Killing Fields.* 3 ILSA J. Int'l & Comp. L. 1997.

Ossiel, Mark. *Mass Atrocity, Collective Memory, and the Law.* New Brunswick: Transaction Publishers, 1997.

Ostrom, Elinor. *Governing the Commons: The Evolution of Institutions for Collective Action.* Cambridge: Cambridge University Press, 1990.

Palast, Gregory. "Goodbye Allende. Hello Pinochet." *London Observer.* November 8, 1998.

Palmer, F., ed. *Anti-Racism: An Assault on Education and Value.* London: Sherwood Press, 1986.

Paltrow, Lynn M. *Pregnant Drug Users, Fetal Persons, and the Threat to* Roe v. Wade. 62 Albany L. Rev. 1999.

Panel forum at the U.S. Supreme Court. "Women in International Law: A Closer Look at the Arab and Muslim World." Sept. 28, 1999.

Pascal, Blaise. *Pensées.* Trans. A J. Krailsheimer. London: Penguin Books, 1966.

Paul, James C. N. "The Need for International Law," in *The Governance of Internal Security Forces in Sub-Saharan Africa.* Third World Legal Studies—1996–1997, 1999.

Paul, James, and Clarence Dias. *Incorporating Rights Into Human Development.* 1999.

Pereyra, Carlos. "Estado y sociedad," en *México Hoy.* Ed. Pablo González Casanova and Enrique Florescano. México: Siglo Veintiuno, 1979.

Perez-Diaz, Victor. *The Return of Civil Society: The Emergence of Democratic Spain.* Cambridge: Harvard University Press, 1993.

Petchesky, Rosalind Pollack. *Abortion and Woman's Choice: The State, Sexuality, and Reproductive Freedom.* 1990.

Petro, Nicolai N. *The Rebirth of Russian Democracy: An Interpretation of Political Culture.* Cambridge: Harvard University Press, 1995.

Philipp, Thomas. "Feminism and Nationalist Politics in Egypt," in *Women in the Muslim World.* Ed. Lois Beck and Nikki Keddie. 1978.

Picciotto, S., and R. Mayne, ed. *Regulating International Business: Beyond Liberalization.* New York: St. Martin's Press, 2000.

Pildes, Richard, and Cass Sunstein. *Reinventing the Regulatory State.* 62 U. Chi. L. Rev. 1 (1995).

Pipes, Richard. *Russia Under the Old Regime.* London: Weidenfeld and Nicolson, 1974.

Polanyi, Karl. *The Great Transformation: The Political and Economic Origins of Our Time.* Boston: Beacon Press, 1944.

Popper, K. R. *The Open Society and Its Enemies.* London: Routledge & Kegan Paul, 1945.

Post, Robert. *Subsidized Speech.* 106 Yale L. J. (1996): 151, 179.

Procuraduría Federal de Protección al Ambiente. *Informe Trianual de Actividades: 1995–1977.* México. 1998.

Quadagno, Jill. *The Color of Welfare: How Racism Undermined the War on Poverty.* 1994.

Questions of Interpretation and Application of the 1971 Montreal Convention Arising from the

Aerial Incident at Lockerbie (Libyan Arab Jamahiriya v. United States of America). ICJ Reports. 1998.

Ramonet, Ignacio "A New Totalitarianism," in "Dueling Globalisms: A Debate Between Thomas L. Friedman and Ignacio Ramonet." *Foreign Policy.* Fall 1999.

Randall, Kenneth C. *Universal Jurisdiction Under International Law.* 66 Tex. L. Rev. 1988.

Ratner, Steven R. *New Democracies, Old Atrocities: An Inquiry in International Law.* 87 Geo. L. J. 1999.

Ratner, Steven R., and Jason S. Abrams. *Accountability for Human Rights Atrocities in International Law.* 1997.

Rawls, John. *Political Liberalism.* New York: Columbia University Press, 1993.

———. *A Theory of Justice.* Cambridge: Harvard University Press, 1971.

Redish, Martin H., and Daryl I. Kessler, *Government Subsidies and Free Expression.* 80 Minnesota L. Rev. (1996): 543, 582.

Reich, Robert. *The Work of Nations.* New York: Vintage, 1991.

Reinicke, Wolfgang. *Global Public Policy: Governing Without Government?* Washington, D.C.: Brookings, 1998.

Report of the UN Secretary-General. *1999 World Survey on the Role of Women in Development: Globalization, Gender and Work.*

Rhode, Deborah L. *Justice and Gender.* Harvard Univ. Press. 1989.

———. *Speaking of Sex: The Denial of Gender Inequality.* 1997

Rich, Frank. "Send in More Clowns." *New York Times.* Oct. 23, 1999.

Richards, David A. J. *Women, Gays, and the Constitution: The Grounds for Feminism and Gay Rights in Culture and Law.* 1998.

Ridha, Muhammad Rashid. 5 *Tafsir al-Qur'an al-Hakim.* Dar al-Ma'rifah: Beirut, reprint 1973.

Rivera, Jenny. *Domestic Violence Against Latinas by Latino Males: An Analysis of Race, National Origin, and Gender Differentials.* 14 B.C. Third World L. J. 1994.

Rizvi, Muddassir. "Media-Pakistan: Editor Muzzled by Paper Under Government Pressure." Inter Press Serv. June 21, 1999.

Roberts, Cokie, and Steve Roberts. "Mothers' Day in Congress." *USA Weekend.* May 9–11, 1997.

Roberts, Dorothy E. *Crime, Race, and Reproduction.* 67 Tul. L. Rev.

———. *The Future of Reproductive Choice for Poor Women and Women of Color.* 12 Women's Rts. L. Rep. 1990.

———. *The Genetic Tie.* 62 U. Chi. L. Rev. 1995.

———. *Killing the Black Body.* 1997.

———. *Punishing Drug Addicts Who Have Babies: Women of Color, Equality, and the Right of Privacy.* 104 Harv. L. Rev. 1991.

———. *Rust v. Sullivan and the Control of Knowledge.* 61 Geo. Wash. L. Rev. 1993.

Roberts, Michael. "Ethnic Conflict in Sri Lanka and Sinhalese Perspectives, Barriers to Accommodation," in *Modern Asian Studies.* No. 12, 1978.

Roberts, Russell. *The Choice: A Fable of Free Trade and Protectionism.* Upper Saddle River, New Jersey: Prentice Hall, 1994.

Robinson, John P., and Geoffrey Godbey. *Time for Life: The Surprising Ways Americans Use Their Time.* 1997.

Roded, Ruth. *Women in Islamic Biographical Collections.* 1994.

Rodrik, Dani. *Has Globalization Gone Too Far?* Washington, D.C.: Institute for International Economics, 1997.

Rodrik, Dani. "Sense and Nonsense in the Globalization Debate." *Foreign Policy* 19. Summer 1997.

———. *The New Global Economy and Developing Countries: Making Openness Work.* Washington, D.C.: Overseas Development Council, 1999

Rome Statute of the International Criminal Court, July 17, 1998. Reproduced in 37 ILM. 1998.

Root, Elihu. *The Need of Popular Understanding of International Law.* 1 American Journal of International Law. 1907.

Rosaldo, Renato. *Culture and Truth: The Remaking of Social Analysis.* 1989.

Rosenberg, Gerald N. *The Hollow Hope? Can Courts Bring About Social Change?* 1991.

Rosenblatt, Robert A. "Retirement Study Shows Gender Gaps." *Los Angeles Times.* June 10, 1999.

Rosenfeld, Michel . *The Jurisprudence of Fairness: Freedom through Regulation in the Marketplace of Ideas.* 1976 Fordham L. Rev. (1976): 877, 912.

Rossi, Alice S., ed. *The Feminist Papers.* 1973.

Ruggie, J. G. "International Regimes, Transactions, and Change: Embedded Liberalism in the Postwar Economic Order." *International Organization* 36 (1982).

Ruiz Cameron, Christopher David. *How the García Cousins Lost Their Accents: Understanding the Language of Title VII Decisions Approving English-Only Rules as the Product of Racial Dualism, Latino Invisibility, and Legal Indeterminacy.* 10 La Raza L.J. 261, 85 Calif. L. Rev. 1998.

Ruskin, J. *Unto This Last: Four Essays on the First Principles of Political Economy.* London: George Allen, 1862/1910.

Rychlak, Ronald J. *Society's Moral Right to Punish: A Further Exploration of the Denunciation Theory of Punishment.* 65 Tul. L. Rev. 1990.

Sa'd, Muhammad bin. *Al-Tabaqat al-Kubra* [The Great Categories]. Dar al-Tahrir: Cairo, 1970.

Sadat, Jehan. *A Woman of Egypt.* 1987.

al-Salam Ibrahim Ghaidhan, Abd. *Fakhamat Ra'is al-Jumhuriyah: La Tuwaqi' 'Ala al-Qanun al-Mashbuh* (Mr. President: Do Not Sign This Suspicious Law). Al-Sha'b. Jan. 25, 2000.

Sands, Philippe, ed. *Manual on International Courts and Tribunals.* 1999.

Santayana, George. *The Life of Reason.* Volume 1, *Reason in Common Sense.* New York: Scribner's, 1905.

Santiago Nino, Carlos. *The Constitution of Deliberative Democracy.* 1996.

———. *Radical Evil on Trial.* New Haven: Yale University Press, 1996.

Sassen, S. *Migranten, Siedler, Fluechtlinger. Von der Massenauswanderung zur Festung Europa.* Frankfurt am Main, 1996.

Saved Burki, Shahid, Guillermo E. Perry, and William R. Dillinger. *Beyond the Center: Decentralizing the State.* Washington D.C.: World Bank, 1999.

Scales-Trent, Judy. *Black Women and the Constitution: Finding Our Place, Asserting Our Rights.* 24 Harv. C.R.-C.L. L. Rev. 1989.

Scarborough, Cathy. *Conceptualizing Black Women's Employment Experiences.* 98 Yale L. J. 1989.

Schabacker, Emily W. *Reconciliation or Justice and Ashes: Amnesty Commissions and the Duty to Punish Human Rights Offenses.* 12 N. Y. Int'l L. Rev. 1999.

Schabas, William. *The Abolition of the Death Penalty in International Law.* 2d ed. 1997.

Scharf, Michael P. *Swapping Amnesty for Peace: Was There a Duty to Prosecute International Crimes in Haiti?* 31 Tex. Int'l L. J. 1996.

Schauer, Frederick. *Principles, Institutions, and the First Amendment.* 112 Harv. L. Rev. (1997): 84

Schiller, Friedrich. *Wallenstein. Ein dramatisches Gedicht. II: Wallensteins Tod.* Stuttgart, Philipp Reclam jun.; 1969.

Schmitt, Carl. "Das Zeitalter der Neutralisierungen und Entpolitisierungen," in Carl Schmitt. *Der Begriff des Politischen.* Berlin: Duncker-Humblot, 1996.

Schmitter, Phillippe. "Continuamos en el siglo del corporativismo?" *El Buscon* (3) Mexico. 1984.

Schneider, Elizabeth M. *The Dialectic of Rights and Politics: Perspectives from the Women's Movement.* 61 N.Y.U. L. Rev. 1986.

———. *The Violence of Privacy.* 23 Conn. L. Rev. 1991.

Schultz, Vicki. *Reconceptualizing Sexual Harassment.* 107 Yale L. J. 1998.

Scott, James Brown. *The Work of the Second Hague Peace Conference.* 2 American Journal of International Law. 1908.

Scott, James Brown, ed. *The Proceedings of the Hague Peace Conferences: The Conference of 1899.* 1920.

———. *The Reports to the Hague Conferences of 1899 and 1907.* 1917.

———. *Texts of the Peace Conferences at The Hague.* 1908.

Segal, Lewis M., and Daniel G. Sullivan. "The Growth of Temporary Services Work," 11 *J. Econ. Persp.* Spring 1997.

Sen, Amartya. *Development as Freedom.* New York: Knopf, 1999.

Sennett, Richard. *The Corrosion of Character: The Personal Consequences of Work in the New Capitalism.* New York: W. W. Norton, 1998.

Shalabi, Muhammad. *Usual al-Fiqh al-Islami* [Foundations of Islamic Jurisprudence]. Al-Dar al-Jami'yah: Beirut, n.d.

Sharlet, Robert. "Citizen and State Under Gorbachev and Yeltsin," in *Developments in Russian and Post-Soviet Politics.* Ed. White, Pravda, and Gitelman. 1994.

———. "Russian Constitutional Crisis: Law and Politics Under Yeltsin." 9 *Post-Soviet Politics.* No. 4, October–December 1993.

———. "Transitional Constitutionalism: Politics and Law in the Second Russian Republic," 14 *Wisconsin International Law Journal* 3 (1996).

Sharp, Gary Sr. *International Obligations to Search For and Arrest War Criminals: Government Failure in the Former Yugoslavia?* 7 Duke J. Comp. & Int'l L. 1997.

Shelyag-Sosonko, Yu. R., V. S. Krysachenko, and Ya. I. Movchan. *Methodology of Geobotany.* Kyiv: Nauk. dumka, 1991.

Shiffrin, Steven H. *Government Speech,* 27 U.C.L.A. L. Rev. (1980): 565, 566.

Shihata, I. F. I. *Collection of Legal Opinions of the General Counsel of the World Bank.* Forthcoming.

Shvidkoi, Mikhail. "Russian Cultural Losses During World War II," *The Spoils of War: World War II and Its Aftermath: The Loss, Reappearance, and Recovery of Cultural Property.*

al-Sibki, Amal. *Al-Harakah al-Nisa'iyyah fi Masr* [The Egyptian Women's Movement]. Matabi' al-Hay'ah al-Misriyah li al-Kitab: n.p. 1986.

Siegel, Reva B. *Home as Work: The First Woman's Rights Claims Concerning Wives' Household Labor, 1850–1880.* 103 Yale L. J. 1994.

———. *The Modernization of Marital Status Law: Adjudicating Wives' Rights to Earnings, 1860–1930.* 82 Geo. L. J. 1994.

———. *Reasoning from the Body: A Historical Perspective on Abortion Regulation and Questions of Equal Protection.* 44 Stan. L. Rev. 1992.

———. *"The Rule of Love": Wife Beating as Prerogative and Privacy.* 105 Yale L. J. 1996.

Simma, Bruno. *From Bilateralism to Community Interest in International Law.* 250 Recueil des Cours. 1994.

Simpson, Elizabeth, ed. *The Spoils of War: World War II and Its Aftermath: The Loss, Reappearance, and Recovery of Cultural Property.* New York: Abrams, 1997.

Singer, Daniel. "Putsch in Moscow." *The Nation.* October 25, 1993.

Singh Mehta, Uday. *Liberalism and Empire.* 1999.

"Sins of the Secular Missionaries." *The Economist.* January 29, 2000.

Skerry, Peter. "The Class Conflict Over Abortion." 52 *Pub. Interest.* 1978.

Smith, Kathleen. *Remembering Stalin's Victims: Popular Memory and the End of the USSR.* Ithaca: Cornell University Press, 1996.

Smith, Margaret. *Rabi'a The Mystic.* 1974.

Smith, Tanya. "The Violation of Basic Rights in the Russian Federation." *East European Constitutional Review.* Summer–fall 1994.

Snell, Bradford C. *American Ground Transport: A Proposal for Restructuring the Automobile, Truck, Bus, and Rail Industries.* A report presented to the Committee of the Judiciary, Subcommittee on Antitrust and Monopoly, United States Senate, February 26, 1974. Washington D.C.: U.S. Government Printing Office, 1974.

Soloway, Julie. "Institutional Capacity to Constrain Suboptimal Welfare Outcomes From Trade-Restricting Environmental, Health and Safety Regulation Under NAFTA." SJD thesis, University of Toronto Faculty of Law, 1999.

Somervell, D. C. *Abridgement of Vols. I–VI.* London: Oxford University Press, 1947.

Stanley, Amy Dru. "Conjugal Bonds and Wage Labor: Rights of Contract in the Age of Emancipation," 75 *J. Am. Hist.* 1988.

Stephens, S. Shawn. "The Hermitage and Pushkin Exhibits: An Analysis of the Ownership Rights to Cultural Properties Removed from Occupied Germany." 18 *Houston Journal of International Law.* Fall 1995.

Stewart, Richard B. "Environmental Law," in *Fundamentals of American Law.* Ed. Alan B. Morrison. 1996.

Stewart, Richard B. *Madison's Nightmare.* 57 U. Chi. L. Rev. 335 (1990).

Strange, Susan. *The Retreat of the State: The Diffusion of Power in the World Economy.* Cambridge: Cambridge University Press, 1996.

Sullivan, Kathleen M. *Unconstitutional Conditions.* 102 Harv. L. Rev. (1995): 1415, 1422.

Sunstein, Cass R. *Beyond the Republican Revival.* 97 Yale L. J. (1988): 1539, 1541.

———. *Lochner's Legacy.* 87 Colum. L. Rev. (1987): 873, 874.

"Survey of the World Economy." *The Economist.* September 20, 1997

Symposium Issue: The Proliferation of International Tribunals: Piecing Together the Puzzle. 31 New York University Journal of International Law and Politics. No. 4, 1999.

al-Tabari, Abu Ja'far. 4 *Jami' al-Bayan fi Tafsir al-Qur'an* [The Comprehensive Clarifications of Qur'anic Interpretation] Dar al-Kutub al-'Ilmiyah: Beirut, reprint 1992.

———. *Tarikh al-Umam wa al-Muluk* [The History of Nations and Kings]. Dar al-Kutub al-'Ilmiyyah: Beirut, reprint 1988.

Tambiah, S. J. *Sri Lanka: Ethnic Fratricide and the Dismantling of Democracy.* Chicago: University of Chicago Press, 1986.

Teubner, Gunther, "Global Bukowina: Legal Pluralism in the World Society," in *Global Law Without a State.* Ed. Teubner. 1997.

"The Non-governmental Order." *The Economist.* 18 Dec. 1999.

The Russian Civilization and Sobornost. Moscow: The Russian Sobornost Fund, 1994. Cited in Zlobin, Nikolay. "Will Russia Be Crushed by Its History?" 159 *World Affairs.* Fall 1996.

Thomas, C., and A. Taylor, ed. *Global Trade and Global Social Issues.* New York: Routledge, 1999.

Todaro, Michael. *Economic Development* 6th ed. Addison-Wesley, 1996.

Toynbee, A. J. *A Study of History.* London: Oxford University Press, 12 vols., 1934–61.

Trebilcock, Michael. "What Makes Poor Countries Poor? The Role of Institutional Capital in Economic Development" in *The Law and Economics of Development.* Ed. Buscaglia and Cooter. JAI Press, 1997.

Trebilcock, Michael, and Robert Howse. *The Regulation of International Trade* 2d ed. London and New York: Routledge, 1999.

Trebilcock, Michael, and Ron Daniels. "Journeys Across the Institutional Divides: Reinterpreting the Reinventing Government Movement." Working paper, University of Toronto Faculty of Law, March 15, 2000.

Tribe, Laurence. *American Constitutional Law.* 2nd ed. Mineola: Foundation Press, 1991.

Tushnet, Mark *Talking to Each Other: Reflections on Yudof's "When Government Speaks".* Wisconsin L. Rev. (1984): 129.

U.S. Department of Justice. *Violence Against Women: A National Crime Victimization Survey Report.* Washington, D.C. January, 1994.

"Understanding on Rules and Procedures Governing the Settlement of Disputes, April 15, 1994," in *Final Act Embodying the Results of the Uruguay Round of Multilateral Treaty Negotiations,* reproduced in 33 ILM. 1994.

UNEP, ECNC. *The Pan-European Biological Diversity Strategy.* Strasbourg: Council of Europe, 1996.

United Nations. *Human Rights Watch Report 1999.*

United Nations. *Report of the Secretary-General on the Work of the Organization.* A154/1, 1999

United Nations Development Programme. *Human Development Report 1999.*

United States Diplomatic and Consular Staff in Tehran. ICJ Reports. 1980.

Utting, P. *Business Responsibility for Sustainable Development.* Geneva: UN Research Institute for Social Development, 2000.

Uyangoda, Jayadeva. "A Political Culture of Conflict," in *Creating Peace in Sri Lanka: Civil War and Reconciliation.* Ed. Robert Rotberg. Washington, D.C.: Brookings Institution Press, 1999.

"Valuing the Global Environment." Washington, D.C.: GEF, 1998.

van den Berghe, Pierre L. *The Ethnic Phenomenon.* New York: Praeger Publishers, 1987.

Vicutidna, Francisco Orrego, and Chistopher Pinto. *The Peaceful Settlement of Disputes: Prospects for the Twenty-First Century.* Preliminary report prepared for the 1999 Centennial Commemoration of the First Peace Conference. 1999.

Vienna Convention on Consular Relations (Paraguay v. United States). Provisional Measures, ICJ Reports. 1998.

Vienna Convention on Consular Relations. ICJ Reports. 1998.

Vogel, David. *Trading Up: Consumer and Environmental Regulation in a Global Economy.* Cambridge.: Harvard University Press, 1995.

von Jhering, Rudolph. *Kampf um's Recht* (The Struggle for Law, from the 5th German edition). Trans. John J. Lalor. Union, N.J.: Lawbook Exchange, 1997.

Waggoner, Jeffrey. "Valor at the Russian Constitutional Court: Adjudicating the Russian Constitutions in the Civil-Law Tradition." 8 *Indiana International & Comparative Law Review.* 1997.

al-Wahab al-Shishani, Abd. *Huquq al-Insan wa Hurriyatuhu al-Siyasiyah* [The Rights of a Human Being and His Political Rights]. Matabi' al-Jam'iyah al-Islamiyah al-Malakiyah: Saudi Arabia, 1980.

Waldock, C. H. M. *Decline of the Optional Clause.* 32 British Year Book of International Law. 1955–56.

Waldron, Jeremy. *Liberal Rights.* Cambridge: Cambridge University Press, 1993.

Walker, Edward W. "Politics of Blame and Presidential Powers in Russia's New Constitution." *East European Constitutional Review.* Fall 1993–winter 1994.

Walzer, Michael. *Spheres of Justice: A Defense of Pluralism and Equality.* 1983.

Wandeweerd, V., ed. *Global Environment Outlook.* New York, Oxford: Oxford University Press, 1997.

Ward, P. W. *White Canada Forever: Popular Attitudes and Public Policy Towards Orientals in B. C.* Montreal: McGill-Queens University Press, 1990.

Warrick, Pamela. "Legal Sanctuary." *Los Angeles Times*. April 28, 1999.

al-Wazir, Ibrahim. *'Ala Masharif al-Qarn al-Khamis 'Ashar al-Hijri* [At the Cusp of the 15th century Hejirah]. Dar al-Shuruq: Cairo, 1989.

Wechsler, Herbert. *Toward Neutral Principle of Constitutional Law*. 73 Harv. L. Rev. (1959).

Weinfeld, Morton, "Social Identity in the 1990s," in *Clash of Identities*. Ed. James Littleton. Toronto: Prentice Hall/CBC.

Weinreb, Lloyd L. *Desert, Punishment, and Criminal Responsibility*. 49 Law & Contemp. Probs. 1986.

Weisman, Amy J. " Separation of Powers in Post-Communist Government: A Constitutional Case Study of the Russian Federation." 10 *American University Journal of International Law & Policy*. Summer 1995.

Weiss, Linda. *The Myth of the Powerless State*. Ithaca: Cornell University Press, 1998.

Welch, Claude E. and Virginia A. Levy (eds). *Asian Perspectives on Human Rights*. Boulder: Westview, 1990.

West, Robin. *Reconstructing Liberty*. 59 Tenn. L. Rev. 1992.

Whalley, John. "The North-South Debate and the Terms of Trade: An Applied Equilibrium Approach," (1984) 66 *Rev. of Economics and Statistics* 224.

White, Lucie E. *No Exit: Rethinking "Welfare Dependency" from a Different Ground*. 81 Geo. L. J. 1993.

White, Stephen, and Ronald J. Hill. "Russia, For-

mer Soviet Union, and Eastern Europe," in *The Referendum Experience in Europe*. Ed. Michael Gallagher and Pie Vincenzo Uleri. London: Macmillan, 1996.

Williams, Joan C. *Deconstructing Gender*. 87 Mich. L. Rev. 1989.

———. *Do Women Need Special Treatment? Do Feminists Need Equality?*. 9 J. Contemp. Legal Issues. 1998.

———. *Market Work and Family Work in the 21st Century*. 44 Vill. L. Rev. 1999.

———. *Sameness Feminism and the Work/Family Conflict*. 35 N.Y. Law School Rev. 1990.

Williams, Wendy Webster. *The Equality Crisis: Some Reflections on Culture, Courts, and Feminism*. 7 Women's Rts. L. Rep. 1982.

Williams. Rhonda M., and Peggie R. Smith. *What Else Do Unions Do?: Race and Gender in Local 35*. 18 Rev. of Black Pol. Economy. Winter, 1990.

Williamson, Joel. *The Crucible of Race: Black-White Relations in the American South Since Emancipation*. 1984.

Wilske, Stephan. "International Law and Spoils of War: To the Victor the Right of Spoils? The Claims for Repatriation of Art Removed from Germany by the Soviet Army During or as a Result of World War II," 3 *UCLA Journal of International Law and Foreign Affairs*. Spring–summer 1998.

Wilson. *The Gaulist System in Asia, Constitution of Sri Lanka 1978*. London: Macmillan, 1980.

Wippman, David, ed. *International Law and Eth-

nic Conflict*. Ithaca: Cornell University Press, 1998.

Wooton, Barbara H. "Gender Differences in Occupational Employment." 120 *Monthly Labor Rep*. April 1997.

Wriggins, Howard. *Ceylon: Dilemmas of a New Nation*.

Yergin, Daniel, and Stanislaw, Joseph. *Commanding Heights: The Battle Between Government and the Marketplace that is Remaking the Modern World*. New York: Simon & Schuster, 1998.

Yudof, Mark G. *When Government Speaks: Politics, Law, and Government Expression in America*. Berkeley: University of California Press, 1983.

———. *When Governments Speak: Toward a Theory of Government Expression and the First Amendment*. 57 Tex. L. Rev. (1979): 863, 912–917.

Zack, Naomi. *Race and Mixed Race*. Philadelphia: Temple University Press, 1993.

Zakaria, Fareed. "The Rise of Liberal Democracy." *Foreign Affairs*, No. 6.

al-Zarkashi, Badr al-Din. 2 *Al-Burhan fi 'Ulum al-Qur'an* [Proof in Qur'anic Sciences]. Dar al-Jil: Beirut, 1988.

Zein, Hussein. *Al-Islam wa al-Fikr al-Siyasi al-Mu'asser* [Islam and Contemporary Political Thought]. Dar al-Fikr al-Hadith: Beirut, 1997.

al-Zuhaili, Wihbah. *Usul al-Fiqh al-Islami* [The Foundations of Islamic Jurisprudence]. 1986.

List of Contributors

EDITORS

Norman Dorsen is the Frederick and Grace A. Stokes Professor of Law and faculty chair of the Global Law School Program at New York University School of Law. He wrote briefs in such leading cases as *Gideon v. Wainwright,* the Pentagon papers case, *Roe v. Wade,* and the Nixon tapes case. He served as president of the American Civil Liberties Union from 1976 to 1991. He was chairman of the Lawyers Committee for Human Rights for four years and is founding president of the U.S. Association of Constitutional Law. Dorsen has written scores of articles and written or edited nine books, including *Human Rights in Northern Ireland, Political and Civil Rights: The ACLU Report on Civil Liberties Today,* and *The Rights of Americans: What They Are, What They Should Be.*

Prosser Gifford is the director of Scholarly Programs at the Library of Congress. He has served as an editor of volumes on African history, United States foreign policy, and, most recently, *Creating French Culture: Treasures from the Bibliothèque nationale de France.*
Contributors

CONTRIBUTORS

Philip Allott is a reader in international public law and a fellow of Trinity College, University of Cambridge. He was formerly a legal counselor in the British Foreign and Commonwealth Office. Allott served at one time as the legal adviser to the British Military Government in Berlin. He was the legal counselor in the British Permanent Representation to the European Communities, Brussels, at the time of British accession to membership of the European Community. He is the author of *Eunomia—New Order for a New World,* a general social and legal theory of international society for the new millennium.

Philip Alston is professor of international law at the European University Institute in Florence, Italy, and codirector of the Academy of European Law. Alston is editor of the *European Journal of International Law.*

Shlomo Avineri is professor of political science at Hebrew University of Jerusalem. His publications include *The Social and Political Thought of Karl Marx, Karl Marx on Colonialism and Modernization, Israel and the Palestinians, Marx' Socialism, Hegel's Theory of the Modern State, Varieties of Marxism,* and *The Making of Modern Zionism.*

Antonio Azuela is attorney general for environmental protection in the federal government of Mexico. He is the author of *La Ciudad, la Propiedad Privada y el Derecho* (The City, Private Property and the Law).

Robert Badinter is a senator in the Parliament of France; he is also on the global law faculty, New York University School of Law. His influence on the French Constitutional Council is the subject of a book, *Sur le Conseil constitutionnel: la doctrine Badinter et la démocratie.* He is the author or coauthor of numerous books, including *Liberté, libertés: réflexions du comité pour une charte des libertés* and *Antisémitsme ordinaire: vichy et les avocats juifs.*

James H. Billington has been the Librarian of Congress since September 1987. He is the author of *Mikhailovsky and Russian Populism, The Icon and the Axe,*

Fire in the Minds of Men, and *Russia Transformed: Breakthrough to Hope, August 1991.* He is also the author of *The Face of Russia,* a companion book to the television series, *The Face of Russia,* which he wrote and narrated for Public Broadcasting Service in 1998. He is on the board of the Center for Theological Inquiry and a member of the American Philosophical Society and the American Academy of Arts and Letters.

Alexander Boraine is vice chairperson of South Africa's Truth and Reconciliation Commission established to investigate the nature, causes, and extent of gross violations of human rights committed since 1960. He was elected to Parliament, a position he held from 1974 until his resignation in 1986. He is the coeditor of *South Africa and the World Economy in the 1990s, Dealing with the Past,* and *The Healing of a Nation.* He is director of the Project on Transnational Justice at the New York University School of Law.

Stephen G. Breyer is an associate justice of the U.S. Supreme Court. His publications include *Administrative Law and Regulatory Policy: Problems, Text, and Cases* and *Breaking the Vicious Circle: Toward Effective Risk Regulation.*

Eva Cantarella is a classicist and professor of Roman law at the University of Milan. Her interests include examining ancient law from a law and society perspective and relating it to modern legal issues. Among her many books is *Pandora's Daughters: The Role and Status of Women in Greek and Roman Antiquity.*

Alexander N. Domrin is a senior research fellow at the Institute of Legislation and Comparative Law, a research and legislation-drafting division of the Russian federal government. He is the author or coauthor of more than sixty publications, including *The Constitutional Mechanism of a State of Emergency, Essays in the Constitutional Law of Foreign Countries* and *The Law of Presidential Power in Russia and the USA.*

Sidney Draggan is senior science and science policy advisor to the assistant administrator for research and development at the U.S. Environmental Protection Agency. He is on the editorial advisory board of the *International Journal of Environmental Studies.* Draggan has edited four volumes on long-term federal environmental research and development activities, requested by the President's Council on Environmental Quality.

Harry T. Edwards was appointed to the U.S. Court of Appeals in 1980 and became chief judge in 1994. He has coauthored four books and published scores of law review articles on labor law, higher education law, federal courts, legal education, professionalism, and judicial administration.

Jean Bethke Elshtain is the Laura Spelman Rockefeller Professor of Social and Political Ethics in the Divinity School at the University of Chicago. She has written eleven books, edited five, and produced more than 200 scholarly articles. The most recent of her books, *The King is Dead: Sovereignty at Century's End,* concerns international relations.

Thomas Franck is the Murray and Ida Becker Professor of Law at New York University School of Law. His books include *Resignation in Protest: Political and Ethical Choices Between Loyalty to Team and Loyalty to Conscience in American Public Life, Nation Against Nation: What Happened to the U.N. Dream and What the U.S. Can Do About It, Political Questions Judicial Answers, Does the Rule of Law Apply to Foreign Affairs?,* and *Fairness in International Law and Institutions.*

Koichiro Fujikura is on the faculty of law and policy, Tezukayama University, Nara, Japan. His publications include *Environmental Law in Japan, A Comparative View of Legal Culture in Japan and the United States,* and *The Role of Law and Lawyers in Japan and the United States.*

Daniel Fung is senior counsel of the Hong Kong Bar, specializing in commercial, corporate, and public law.

Ruth Bader Ginsburg is an associate justice of the U.S. Supreme Court. She is the coauthor of *Text, Cases, and Materials on Sex-Based Discrimination.*

Dieter Grimm was a justice of Germany's Federal Constitutional Court from 1987 to 1999.

Inder Kumar Gujral served as prime minister of India from 1997 to 1998.

Orrin G. Hatch is the U.S. senator from Utah. He is the author of *Equal Rights Amendment: Myths and Realities* and *Higher Laws: Understanding the Doctrines of Christ.*

Azizah Y. al-Hibri is professor of law at the T. C. Williams School of Law, University of Richmond. She is the founding editor of *Hypatia: a Journal of Feminist Philosophy* and founder and current president of Karamah: Muslim Women Lawyers for Human Rights. Her publications include chapters on "Islamic Jurisprudence and

Critical Race Feminism" in *Global Critical Race Feminism* and "An Introduction to Muslim Women's Rights" in *Windows of Faith* and an essay "Is Western Patriarchal Feminism Good for Third World/Minority Women?" in *Is Multiculturalism Bad for Women?*.

Rosalyn Higgins was the first woman elected as a judge of the International Court of Justice. Her most recent publication is an edited compilation, *Terrorism and International Law*.

Stephen Holmes is professor of law at New York University School of Law. He is the editor in chief of the *East European Constitutional Review*. Among other books, he published (with Cass Sunstein) *The Cost of Rights: Why Liberty Depends on Taxes*.

Ratna Kapur is a director of the Centre for Feminist Legal Research in New Delhi, India. She is the Joseph C. Hostetler-Baker and Hosteteler Professor of Law Endowed Chair at Cleveland-Marshall College of Law. She has published extensively on issues of secularism, freedom of expression, equality, and women's rights, including an edited collection entitled *Feminist Terrains in Legal Domains: Interdisciplinary Essays on Women and Law*, as well as coauthoring *Subversive Sites: Feminist Engagements with Law* and *Secularism's Last Sigh?: Hinduvata and the (Mis)Rule of Law*.

Kenneth L. Karst is the David G. Price and Dallas P. Price Professor of Law at the University of California, Los Angeles. His books include *Belonging to America: Equal Citizenship and the Constitution* and *Law's Promise, Law's Expression: Vision of Power in the Politics of Gender, Race, and Religion*.

Stanley N. Katz is a lecturer with the rank of professor at the Woodrow Wilson School of Public and International Affairs, Princeton University. His publications include *Colonial America: Essays in Politics and Social Development, Philanthropy in the World's Traditions*, and *Constitutionalism in East Central Europe: Some Negative Lessons from the American Experience*.

Yuri Kostenko was, in 1989, one of the founders of Rukh, the popular movement for independence in Ukraine. He has been a member of the Verkhovna Rada (Parliament) for three consecutive terms since 1990. Kostenko has published more than thirty-five academic papers.

Ann Elizabeth Mayer is associate professor of legal studies in the department of legal studies at the Whar-

ton School of the University of Pennsylvania. She has published extensively in law reviews and scholarly journals concerned with comparative and international law and the contemporary Middle East and North Africa. Her book *Islam and Human Rights: Tradition and Politics* is in its third edition.

Rubens Medina is the Law Librarian, Library of Congress. He is project director of the Global Legal Information Network (GLIN), a multinational cooperative legal information system currently centered in the Law Library, Library of Congress.

Nadezhda Mihailova was a member of the Parliamentary Foreign Policy Commission and of the Bulgarian delegation to the Council of Europe. She was appointed deputy chairperson of the Union of Democratic Forces in 1995 and reelected in 1997. In 1997 she was appointed minister of foreign affairs in Ivan Kostov's cabinet.

Kogila Moodley is professor of sociology in the department of educational studies, University of British Columbia, Vancouver, where she was the first holder of the David Lam Chair of Multicultural Studies. She is the coauthor of *Comrades in Business: Post-Liberation Politics in South Africa* and *Opening of the Apartheid Mind: Options for the New South Africa*.

Luis Moreno Ocampo is in private practice in Buenos Aires, where he specializes in corruption-control programs for large organizations. His publications include *In Self Defense, How to Avoid Corruption* and *When Power Lost the Trial: How to Explain the Dictatorship to Our Children*.

Fali Sam Nariman is a member of the Indian Parliament (Rajya Sabha). He is also senior advocate of the Supreme Court of India and has practiced law for forty-seven years. In 1991 the president of India awarded him the Padma Bhushan, India's second-highest civil honor, in recognition of his distinguished service in the field of jurisprudence.

Ellen Gracie Northfleet is the first woman to become a member of the Supreme Court of Brazil. She also serves as professor of constitutional law at the University of Vale do Rio dos Sinos.

Sandra Day O'Connor is an associate justice of the U.S. Supreme Court.

Hisashi Owada serves as president of the Japan Institute of International Affairs, advisor to Japan's minister of foreign affairs, and senior advisor to the president of the World Bank. His recent articles include "Japan's Constitutional Power to Participate in Peacekeeping" and "The International Law Commission and the Process of Law-formation".

Robert Pitofsky is chairman of the U.S. Federal Trade Commission. His publications include legal casebooks on both trade regulation and antitrust law.

William H. Rehnquist is chief justice of the United States. His books include *The Supreme Court, All the Laws but One: Civil Liberties in Wartime,* and *Grand Inquests: The Historic Impeachments of Justice Samuel Chase and President Andrew Johnson.*

Andras Sajo is professor, legal studies department, and chair of comparative constitutional programs at the Central European University, Budapest, Hungary. He also is a visiting professor with the Global Law School Program, New York University School of Law. His most recent book is *Limiting Government: An Introduction to Constitutionalism.*

John E. Sexton is dean and Warren E. Burger Professor of Law at New York University School of Law. He is the author of *Redefining the Supreme Court's Role: A Theory of Managing the Federal Court System, A Non-Lawyer's Guide to the Constitution,* and *Modern Federal Jury Instructions—Civil.* He has also written numerous book chapters, articles, and Supreme Court briefs.

Bruno Simma is professor of international law and European Community law and director of the Institute of International Law at the University of Munich. He is currently visiting professor at the University of Michigan Law School. Simma is cofounder and coeditor of the *European Journal of International Law.* His many publications include two edited compilations, *The Charter of the United Nations: A Commentary* and *International Protection of the Environment, Second Series: Treaties and Related Documents.*

Anne-Marie Slaughter is the J. Sinclair Armstrong Professor of International, Foreign, and Comparative Law and director of graduate and international legal studies at Harvard Law School. Her publications include "International Law and International Relations Theory: A New Generation of Interdisciplinary Scholarship," with Andrew Tulumello and Stepan Wood, 92 *American Journal of International Law* 367 (1998); "Toward a Theory of Effective Supranational Adjudication," with Laurence

Helfer, 107 *Yale Law Journal* 273 (1997); and "International Law in a World of Liberal States," 6 *European Journal of International Law* 503 (1995).

Richard Stewart is the Emily Kempin Professor of Law at New York University School of Law. In collaboration with Richard Revesz and Philippe Sands, he is developing an Environmental Law Center at NYU to focus on government and the environment. Among his current projects are assisting in the efforts of the United Nations to combat global warming by developing an international market for credits for carbon dioxide emissions reductions and advising China's National People's Congress on its revisions of environmental laws. His publications include *Natural Resources Damages: A Legal, Economic and Policy Analysis* and *Markets Versus Environment?.*

Daniel K. Tarullo teaches international economic regulation, international law, and banking law at Georgetown University Law Center. His publications include the *World Economic Update.*

Michael John Trebilcock is professor of law and economics and director of the Law and Economics Program at the University of Toronto Law School. He is the author or coauthor of seven books, including, *International Trade Regulation* and *The Making of the Mosaic: History of Canadian Immigration Policy.*

Ko-Yung Tung is vice president and general counsel of the World Bank. He serves as vice-chairman of the board of governors of the East-West Center and cochairs the Advisory Committee of Human Rights Watch/Asia.

Jayadeva Uyangoda is a senior lecturer in political science at the University of Colombo; director, Center for Policy Research and Analysis, University of Colombo; and director, Center for Policy Alternatives, Colombo. He coedited *Essays in Constitutional Reform* and *Matters of Violence: Reflections on Social and Political Violence in Sri Lanka.* He is working on a book to be titled *Sri Lanka: Modernity, Social Change, and Claims of Justice.*

Nur Vergin is professor of political science at the Public Administration Department, Istanbul University. She is the author of *Industrialization and Social Change in Rural Areas, Political Sociology,* and *Witnessing Turkey.*

John M. Walker Jr. has been a judge of the U.S. Court of Appeals since 1989.

Index